Organizations, Civil Society, and the Roots of Development

National Bureau of
Economic Research
Conference Report

Organizations, Civil Society, and the Roots of Development

Edited by **Naomi R. Lamoreaux and John Joseph Wallis**

The University of Chicago Press

Chicago and London

The University of Chicago Press, Chicago 60637
The University of Chicago Press, Ltd., London
© 2017 by the National Bureau of Economic Research
Published 2017
Printed in the United States of America

26 25 24 23 22 21 20 19 18 17   1 2 3 4 5

ISBN-13: 978-0-226-42636-5 (cloth)
ISBN-13: 978-0-226-42653-2 (e-book)
DOI: 10.7208/chicago/9780226426532.001.0001

Library of Congress Cataloging-in-Publication Data

Names: Lamoreaux, Naomi R., editor. | Wallis, John Joseph, editor.
Title: Organizations, civil society, and the roots of development / edited
    by Naomi R. Lamoreaux and John Joseph Wallis.
Other titles: National Bureau of Economic Research conference report.
Description: Chicago ; London : The University of Chicago Press,
    2017. | Series: National bureau of economic research conference
    report | Includes bibliographic references and index. | Papers
    developed over the course of three conferences held at NBER and
    Yale University between 2013 and 2014.
Identifiers: LCCN 2017012526 | ISBN 9780226426365 (cloth : alk.
    paper) | ISBN 9780226426532 (e-book)
Subjects: LCSH: Civil society—Economic aspects—Europe—
    History—Congresses. | Civil society—Economic aspects—United
    States—History—Congresses. | Freedom of association—Europe—
    History—Congresses. | Freedom of association—United States—
    History—Congresses. | Economic development—Political aspects—
    Europe—History—Congresses. | Economic development—Political
    aspects—United States—History—Congresses. | History,
    Modern—19th century—Congresses. | History, Modern—18th
    century—Congresses.
Classification: LCC JC337 .O74 2017 | DDC 369.094/09034—dc23
LC record available at https://lccn.loc.gov/2017012526

♾ This paper meets the requirements of ANSI/NISO Z39.48-1992
(Permanence of Paper).

Relation of the Directors to the
Work and Publications of the
National Bureau of Economic Research

1. The object of the NBER is to ascertain and present to the economics profession, and to the public more generally, important economic facts and their interpretation in a scientific manner without policy recommendations. The Board of Directors is charged with the responsibility of ensuring that the work of the NBER is carried on in strict conformity with this object.

2. The President shall establish an internal review process to ensure that book manuscripts proposed for publication DO NOT contain policy recommendations. This shall apply both to the proceedings of conferences and to manuscripts by a single author or by one or more co-authors but shall not apply to authors of comments at NBER conferences who are not NBER affiliates.

3. No book manuscript reporting research shall be published by the NBER until the President has sent to each member of the Board a notice that a manuscript is recommended for publication and that in the President's opinion it is suitable for publication in accordance with the above principles of the NBER. Such notification will include a table of contents and an abstract or summary of the manuscript's content, a list of contributors if applicable, and a response form for use by Directors who desire a copy of the manuscript for review. Each manuscript shall contain a summary drawing attention to the nature and treatment of the problem studied and the main conclusions reached.

4. No volume shall be published until forty-five days have elapsed from the above notification of intention to publish it. During this period a copy shall be sent to any Director requesting it, and if any Director objects to publication on the grounds that the manuscript contains policy recommendations, the objection will be presented to the author(s) or editor(s). In case of dispute, all members of the Board shall be notified, and the President shall appoint an ad hoc committee of the Board to decide the matter; thirty days additional shall be granted for this purpose.

5. The President shall present annually to the Board a report describing the internal manuscript review process, any objections made by Directors before publication or by anyone after publication, any disputes about such matters, and how they were handled.

6. Publications of the NBER issued for informational purposes concerning the work of the Bureau, or issued to inform the public of the activities at the Bureau, including but not limited to the NBER Digest and Reporter, shall be consistent with the object stated in paragraph 1. They shall contain a specific disclaimer noting that they have not passed through the review procedures required in this resolution. The Executive Committee of the Board is charged with the review of all such publications from time to time.

7. NBER working papers and manuscripts distributed on the Bureau's web site are not deemed to be publications for the purpose of this resolution, but they shall be consistent with the object stated in paragraph 1. Working papers shall contain a specific disclaimer noting that they have not passed through the review procedures required in this resolution. The NBER's web site shall contain a similar disclaimer. The President shall establish an internal review process to ensure that the working papers and the web site do not contain policy recommendations, and shall report annually to the Board on this process and any concerns raised in connection with it.

8. Unless otherwise determined by the Board or exempted by the terms of paragraphs 6 and 7, a copy of this resolution shall be printed in each NBER publication as described in paragraph 2 above.

Contents

Acknowledgments   ix

Introduction   1
Naomi R. Lamoreaux and John Joseph Wallis

1.   **The East Indian Monopoly and the Transition from Limited Access in England, 1600–1813**   23
Dan Bogart

2.   **Adam Smith's Theory of Violence and the Political Economics of Development**   51
Barry R. Weingast

3.   **Pluralism without Privilege?** *Corps Intermédiaires,* **Civil Society, and the Art of Association**   83
Jacob T. Levy

4.   **Banks, Politics, and Political Parties: From Partisan Banking to Open Access in Early Massachusetts**   109
Qian Lu and John Joseph Wallis

5.   **Corporation Law and the Shift toward Open Access in the Antebellum United States**   147
Eric Hilt

6.   **Organizational Poisedness and the Transformation of Civic Order in Nineteenth-Century New York City**   179
Victoria Johnson and Walter W. Powell

7.   **Voluntary Associations, Corporate Rights, and the**
        State: Legal Constraints on the Development of
        American Civil Society, 1750–1900   231
        Ruth H. Bloch and Naomi R. Lamoreaux

8.   **The Right to Associate and the Rights of**
        Associations: Civil-Society Organizations in
        Prussia, 1794–1908   291
        Richard Brooks and Timothy W. Guinnane

9.   **Opening Access, Ending the Violence Trap:**
        Labor, Business, Government, and the
        National Labor Relations Act   331
        Margaret Levi, Tania Melo, Barry R. Weingast,
        and Frances Zlotnick

        Contributors   367
        Author Index   369
        Subject Index   375

Acknowledgments

We owe a tremendous debt of gratitude to James Poterba and Claudia Goldin for their unflagging support for this project and to the staff at the National Bureau of Economic Research, particularly Helena Fitz-Patrick, for her editorial assistance, and Carl Beck, for organizing the first and third conferences. We are also grateful to the Program in Economic History at Yale University for supporting the second conference and to Lindsay Young for taking charge of the organization. A number of scholars who do not appear in this volume participated in one or more of the three conferences. We are grateful to Avinash Dixit, Neil Fligstein, Robert Gibbons, Avner Greif, Richard Grossman, Jonathan Levy, Robert Margo, William Novak, Orlando Patterson, Emma Rothschild, Raffaella Sadun, and Ezra Zuckerman Sivan for their stimulating comments and their help in shaping the volume and the essays that make it up. Finally, we would like to thank the editors at the University of Chicago Press and the two anonymous referees who reviewed the volume for publication.

Introduction

Naomi R. Lamoreaux and John Joseph Wallis

All societies have organizations. However, the numbers, types, and effectiveness of these organizations vary considerably from one place to the next. During the nineteenth century, a small number of countries began to experience sustained economic growth and a movement toward more open governments that guaranteed their citizens a greater measure of civil and political rights. At the same time, these countries also began to develop rich civil societies, and the quantity and variety of their economic, social, political, religious, and educational organizations increased dramatically. In countries that underwent this transformation, organizations gained more autonomy from the state and could form and dissolve freely to suit the purposes of their membership. Equally important, organizations in these countries could depend on the state to enforce their internal rules and external contractual relationships with other associations or individuals. As a result, organizations in these more open societies tended to be more effective than organizations in other places.

Although the economic and political changes of the nineteenth century have been intensely studied, both together and separately, the importance of this accompanying organizational transformation has been relatively neglected. Most scholars have simply assumed that the growth of organizations was a by-product of economic development—an endogenous consequence of increasing incomes and rising investments in physical and

Naomi R. Lamoreaux is the Stanley B. Resor Professor of Economics and History at Yale University and a research associate of the National Bureau of Economic Research. John Joseph Wallis is professor of economics at the University of Maryland and a research associate of the National Bureau of Economic Research.

For acknowledgments, sources of research support, and disclosure of the authors' material financial relationships, if any, please see http://www.nber.org/chapters/c13503.ack.

human capital. Others have acknowledged that civil-society organizations were important for the development of stable democratic polities, but have said little about why the number of organizations increased so markedly in the nineteenth century. The chapters in this volume remedy the lack of attention to these issues by collectively examining the circumstances under which societies began first passively to allow and then actively to encourage their citizens to form organizations for a wide range of purposes. The chapters also examine the implications of this growth in organizations for how these societies functioned.

In 2012 we brought together a group of people at the National Bureau of Economic Research (NBER) who shared an interest in organizations as well as in understanding the process by which societies grow and develop. After our initial meeting, many participants proposed to write papers that, though they came out of their own independent research agendas, addressed questions we had posed about the importance of civil-society organizations for economic and political development. Members of the group met a second time at Yale University in 2013 to discuss initial drafts of the chapters that appear in this volume. New versions were then presented at a third conference at the NBER in October 2014, and they have been revised since in light of the comments received there.

The core problem that we asked participants in these conferences to consider was how societies have made the transition from a "limited access" to an "open access" social order, to use the vocabulary that Douglass North, John Wallis, and Barry Weingast (hereafter NWW) developed for their book *Violence and Social Orders* (2009). Throughout human history, NWW argue, most societies have been (and still are) limited access social orders in the sense that the elites that dominate them strictly control who can form organizations and for what purposes. They exert this control because organizations are vital sources of rents that can be used to reward supporters and strengthen their rule, and more importantly to structure relationships between powerful organizations in ways that reduce the likelihood of violence and civil war. To the extent that organizational rents are valuable, of course, they can be an impetus for elites to rebel in order to increase their share, but in most times and places such revolts have accomplished little more than the replacement of one limited access social order with another. In the nineteenth century, however, a small number of countries experienced a more radical transformation. Governing elites not only stopped repressing organizations formed by other groups in their societies, but very consciously, very deliberately made the legal tools needed to form more effective organizations readily available to a much larger share of the population. North, Wallis, and Weingast hypothesized that this transformation ushered in a new equilibrium in which the widespread ability to form organizations created the competitive conditions necessary to sustain both economic growth and democratic politics.

We did not set out to produce a book about how hard it was for societies to open access to organizations, but that was what our collective scholarly inquiry yielded. As the chapters in this volume show, the most important thinkers of the eighteenth and early nineteenth centuries had only the dimmest glimmerings of the transformation that was to come and were as worried about the destabilizing implications of a broad-based civil society as they were intrigued by its promise. The United States led the shift toward open access, but in a much more halting and incomplete way than contemporaries like Alexis de Tocqueville recognized. In the economic realm, powerful elites continued for more than a half century after independence to use the allocation of organizational rents (especially in the banking sector) as a tool of coalition building, opening up access by enacting general incorporation laws only when it became clear that competitive politics was making it possible and perhaps necessary to disentangle and separate control of economic organizations from control of the government. Although American governments stopped repressing most (though not all) types of voluntary associations in the aftermath of the Revolution, for many decades they still restricted access to the corporate form (important for organizational effectiveness), allowing only associations that served conventional religious, educational, and charitable purposes to incorporate. In France, Germany, and elsewhere on the European continent, governments actively repressed all noneconomic organizations that did not have the explicit approval of the state. Business people could freely form partnerships of various types, but in most places they needed government approval to form corporations. By the 1870s governments in France and Germany had passed general incorporation laws for most types of businesses, but other organizations still required state permission to exist.

As even this brief summary suffices to indicate, there was no clear one-to-one correspondence between the level of economic development or the type of government in place and the achievement of open access. In some places general incorporation led industrialization; in other places it lagged industrialization. In some places democratic governments repressed associational life; in other places they tolerated it or even reveled in it. Open access was never complete in the sense that some types of associations were always subject to restrictions by the state and some types of people were always at a disadvantage in forming organizations, but as barriers to forming most types of organizations fell and as legal devices like the corporate form became generally available, the dynamics of societies changed in ways that fostered economic growth and democratic politics.

We develop this argument in greater detail later in this introduction when we explicate the contributions of the individual essays and the general findings that can be drawn from them about the relationship between civil society and economic and political development. First, however, we lay out the basic theory of limited access social orders that provided the impetus for this collective scholarly endeavor. We begin with a discussion of how organizations produce rents.

Organizations and Rents

Organizations are bundles of relationships. They coordinate human behavior and in the process they create rents that increase the well-being of their members, consequently enabling them to hold their organizations together. The first step in articulating a theory of what organizations do, therefore, is to be clear about what we mean by the term "rent." The simplest definition of an economic rent is a return above opportunity cost. If a worker is willing to work for $10 an hour (the value of the best alternative use of his time) and receives a wage of $15 an hour, the rent for an hour's work is $5. A consumer who is willing to buy a pair of shoes for $15 but pays only $10 receives a rent of $5. A producer who is willing to sell shoes for $5 but sells a pair for $10 receives a rent of $5. These examples all involve standard economic activities such as production and consumption that can easily be valued in monetary terms, but the concept of rent applies to human choices more generally. Two individuals who like each other enjoy a rent from their relationship. The rent is the subjective value they place on their relationship compared to alternative relationships they might have with other people. The rents that organizations create are very often nonmonetary. They involve value that is created by forming individuals into groups.

Rents are always relative in their magnitudes. Suppose, as above, that a consumer values shoes at $15 a pair and can buy them from a particular producer for $10. The rent the consumer receives from buying the shoes is $5, but if he can buy an identical pair of shoes from another seller for $11, then the rent he receives from buying from the first seller in particular is only $1. Rents are also multidimensional, and the magnitude of the rent on different dimensions often moves in opposite directions when circumstances change. Extending the shoe example, if the number of sellers increases, the rent the consumer gets from buying shoes may increase, even if the price does not change, because he may enjoy increased variety or increased ease of purchasing. At the same time, the rent he gets from buying from any specific seller is likely to decrease.

Rents are important because they create incentives to perform actions (make choices), and the probability that arrangements between people will continue in the face of uncertain and changing circumstances is directly related to the size of the rents associated with the action. If a consumer agrees to buy shoes from a producer for $10, that agreement is more likely to continue if the consumer receives $5 in rents from buying each pair of shoes than if he receives a rent of only $1. The extent to which the producer believes she can count on the consumer's continued business thus depends on her perception of the rents the latter receives. More generally, parties are more likely to make investments in relationships that continue through time when each perceives that the other obtains rents from the relationship.

Organizations create rents in two basic ways. The first is characteristic of all relationships that persist over time. When two individuals come to know each other and expect to interact in the future, they have a relationship. Relationships create rents when the alternative to which they are compared is the prospect of dealing with strangers whom one expects never to meet again.[1] These rents come both from our increased knowledge of the other person and from the expectation that our interaction will continue. These elements enable us credibly to coordinate our behavior.

The value of coordination is the second source of the rents that organizations create.[2] For many activities, people who work in teams are more productive than people who work individually. If the organization is a firm that produces goods, the gains can be measured in terms of physical output. But again, the gains from coordination are not limited to standard economic activities. Churches are organizations that coordinate behavior in ways that enhance the value of the community and the religious experience. Individual churchgoers receive rents from their participation in the church's activities, and it is those rents and the personal knowledge of each other that results from participation that enable churchgoers to coordinate.

Organizations, then, provide a framework for relationships that are more valuable to individuals than one-shot interactions with strangers. The value of relationships makes it possible for people to coordinate their actions, and that coordination in turn generates rents in the form of higher output or benefits than could be obtained by a comparable group of uncoordinated (unorganized) individuals.

What Holds Organizations Together?

Understanding how organizations work has been a major preoccupation of the social sciences.[3] Drawing together several different lines of inquiry in economics, sociology, and business, Robert Gibbons (1998, 1999, 2003) has argued that organizations can be thought of as interlaced bundles of relationships and contracts. Although some organizations can be understood as self-enforcing sets of relationships sustained by repeated interactions and the existence of rents, most rely on some form of contractual enforcement

1. When we get to know a person we may learn that we do not want to interact with him or her, but even that negative information produces a rent in comparison to dealing with a person whom we do not know.

2. Organizations are not the only way in which people coordinate. In markets the price mechanism coordinates individual decisions.

3. Economics, political science, sociology, and business management all have long traditions of theoretical, empirical, and historical studies of organizations. In economics, see, for example, the new institutional economics, beginning with Ronald Coase's insights about the firm (1937) and continuing on through Oliver Williamson (1975, 1985) and Sanford Grossman and Oliver Hart (1985); in business, see March (1962), Cyert and March (1963), March and Simon (1958); in sociology, see Weber (1968), Blau and Scott (1962), Padgett and Powell (2012), Scott (2014), and DiMaggio and Powell (1991), as well as the papers assembled in Powell and DiMaggio (1991).

using third parties. A robust theory of organizations should encompass both relationships and contracts, rather than relying on one or other as the "organizing" principle.

A useful starting point for a theory of organizations is the folk-theorem intuition that two individuals can maintain a relationship over time if both individuals receive a rent from the relationship. The players in the folk theorem receive rents from their specific relationship, so their individual identity and the nature of their partnership matter. The existence of the rent is what makes their relationship incentive compatible. The folk theorem partnership is what we call an *adherent* organization, an organization where both or all members have an interest in cooperating at every point in time. Adherent organizations are inherently self-sustaining or self-enforcing; they do not require the intervention of anyone outside of the organization. Mancur Olson's famous *Logic of Collective Action* (1965) essentially relies on the existence of rents enjoyed by members of the organized group, which he calls selective incentives, to explain voluntary associations. Members only cooperate if the rents are positive and, critically, if the rents can only be attained within the organization.

As in the shoe examples above, the higher the rents the more predictable is the behavior of the members of the organization. That is, partners can sustain a higher degree of cooperation when they receive higher rents on an ongoing basis from the relationship. Members who are pushed to the margin are not reliable partners: if a member receives total benefits that are just equal to the total costs of membership, then rents are zero and that member is indifferent to cooperating. Any small change in circumstances may lead him or her to defect. Organizations want to ensure as much as possible that all members earn positive rents so that their behavior is predictable.

If the members of an adherent organization look forward into the future and anticipate that rents may not be sufficient to ensure the cooperation of every member at every point in time, then they will expect defection and cooperation may unravel. There are, however, ways for the members to protect against defection. For example, they may insist on hostages as insurance against the possibility that rents will become zero or negative at some point. The threat that hostages will be killed imposes large penalties on defection, making possible incentive compatible and time-consistent arrangements for the organization. The various folk theorems lay out how such punishments for deviators (noncooperators) might be credibly imposed (Benoit and Krishna 1985; Fudenberg and Maskin 1986).[4]

The folk-theorem logic can explain the existence of organizations. How-

---

4. A historical example comes from the slave trade, where British merchants insisted that their African counterparts place relatives on slave ships in exchange for credit to use in acquiring slaves. If the African merchants failed to live up to their bargain, their relatives could be sold into slavery (see Lovejoy and Richardson 1999).

ever, organizations that depend only on the coordinated interests of their members without recourse to external enforcement are likely to remain small. Ensuring cooperation is expensive, particularly when cooperation is attained through the continual ex ante transfer of real economic assets or costly threats to destroy economic assets. *Contractual* organizations—that is, those that can appeal to an external agency, a third party, to enforce the terms of their internal agreements—can be much more effective. In principle, anything that an adherent organization can do a contractual organization can do, but many things that contractual organizations can do are impossible to accomplish with purely adherent organizations (North, Wallis, and Weingast 2009).

It is difficult to overstate the importance of contractual organizations. Those of us who live in societies with open access to organizational tools may have trouble appreciating just how many of the organizations we consider "voluntary" are contractual, not adherent, organizations. One of the authors was commissioner of a soccer league for six- to nine-year-olds organized by a Boys and Girls Club. The club, as a matter of course, obtained liability insurance for the commissioner. Even though participation was completely voluntary, it was well understood that an aggrieved or upset parent had the ability to sue the club, the coach, and the commissioner if their child was harmed through inappropriate behavior. In other words, the larger society provided this voluntary association with a set of extremely sophisticated and powerful organizational tools to structure and enforce its internal arrangements. Virtually all organizations in modern societies are contractual in this sense, no matter how informal they appear to be. They all swim in a sea of organizational tools so pervasively present that participants often do not even notice their existence.

Third Parties and Governments

We typically think of governments as providing the third-party enforcement that enables contractual organizations to flourish. But, of course, governments with the capacity to enforce rules and contracts in the larger society did not always exist. Nor were they, either in theory or in fact, necessary for contractual organizations to emerge. Just as individuals can create adherent organizations that are held together by the value of the relationships involved, organizations can form adherent organizations of organizations. Moreover, the value that holds these organizations of organizations together can be precisely their ability to serve as third-party enforcers for each other.

North, Wallis, and Weingast develop this insight about organizations and third-party enforcement to explain how societies organize to limit violence. Think of two individuals, each a member of a different group. We will call them A and B. The groups to which they belong are, to begin with, egalitarian in the sense that no individual is capable of coercing the other members and economic outcomes are relatively equal. Suppose, however, that if A and B can cooperate and form a coalition, they can overawe the other members of their respective groups.[5] They accordingly promise not to fight each other, to recognize each other's rights to the land, labor, and capital in their respective groups, and to come to each other's aid in the case of a conflict with other members of their groups. Because of this agreement to form a coalition, each partner is able to gain control over his group's resources. The land, labor, and capital each now controls are more productive under conditions of peace than of violence. If violence breaks out between the coalition partners, the rents each gets from his own domain will go down. Both partners therefore recognize that there is a range of circumstances in which each can credibly believe that the other will honor the agreement. In other words, the rents each partner receives from his respective group serve as a mechanism for limiting violence among the coalition partners. North, Wallis, and Weingast call this outcome the "logic of the natural state."

The coalition is not a government. It is an adherent organization, and it is the rents from the relationship between the coalition members that provide the incentives for the partners to continue to cooperate. These rents also provide the means for the vertical relationships between A, B, and their clients to become contractual organizations because A and B can serve as third-party enforcers for each other's organizations. The adherent relationship between A and B makes it credible for A to serve as a third-party enforcer for B and his organization, and B to serve as a third-party enforcer for A and his organization. In other words, there is a reciprocal effect whereby the vertical arrangements depend on the horizontal arrangements and vice versa. The agreement between the coalition partners enables each of them to better structure their client organizations because they can call on each other for external support. At the same time, the additional rents that A and B derive from the greater sophistication of their client organizations make their ongoing cooperation all the more valuable.

In NWW's analysis, the coalition partners do not need to possess any special physical characteristics. If the partners can cooperate, then they can overawe the other members of their respective groups. Their strength comes from their organization, not their personal attributes. Of course, this model with just two coalition partners is a very simple and abstract representation of relationships in the actual world, but it focuses our attention on the fact that elites do not have influence in the coalition because they are powerful as individuals; they are powerful because they are integrated into the coalition.

---

5. The idea that a coalition of just two members will be able to overawe either of the two groups is unrealistic. But beginning with a coalition of just two members is easier to describe and visualize. Burkett, Steckel, and Wallis (2015) develop a formal model of coalitions and violence.

Unlike a Hobbesian world, where the most powerful competitor emerges as the sovereign, in this analysis the ability to create and enforce rules—that is, the terms of the agreement among the coalition partners—is based on the relationship between A and B. The *kinds* of rules that A and B can enforce derive from their organizational relationship. They are "identity" rules in the sense that they are specific to the two coalition partners. Identity rules are rules whose form and enforcement depend on the social identity of the people to whom they apply. The rules stipulate the privileges that A and B each enjoy. They also identify two organizations, A's organization and B's organization, whose members have different social identities from those of A and B, but also from one another. By contrast, impersonal rules are rules whose form and enforcement apply equally to everyone. The identity rules that apply to A and B will depend on the nature of their relationship, and the rules that apply within A's organization and within B's organization will be specific to those organizations.

We can scale up the logic of the relationship between A and B and imagine a society with more coalition members, each of whom leads organizations that are, in turn, clusters of coalitions. The power and privileges of the leaders still depend on the dynamics of their interactions with each other, as do those of the members of the subcoalitions. Some organizations and individuals are more powerful than others, but their power rests on the horizontal agreements that sustain their organizations and the relationships among them. In this kind of society, where there are multiple organizations with the capacity for violence, sustaining these relationships requires more sophisticated coordination mechanisms. To improve stability, therefore, organizations emerge whose purpose is to signify publicly the agreements that structure relationships among the coalition partners. These organizations are what we call governments (Wallis 2015). Governments may be organizations with a superior capacity for violence (Tilly 1990), but more importantly they are organizations that coordinate the organizations that make up the coalitions.

Limited versus Open-Access Social Orders

In a natural state, the rules that governments signify are identity rules. Their content depends on the relationships among the various members of the coalition. They cannot be enforced against partners who do not wish to follow them. That is, whether they are enforceable depends on the value of the rents created by the relationship, which in turn depends on the value of the organizations that this relationship makes it possible to create. Because organizational rents can be dissipated by competition, the ability to form organizations must be strictly limited. The privilege to form organizations, as well as to gain access to the third-party enforcement that enhances the organizations' effectiveness, is a privilege conferred to a greater or lesser degree on coalition members depending on what they bring to the relationship. The resulting barriers to entry fetter economic activity, and people cannot easily form associations to achieve socially desired goals.

Open-access societies are fundamentally different. An open-access society still consists of organizations, and of organizations of organizations; and horizontal relationships still create value for members. But the rules that the government publicly signifies are now impersonal in the sense that they apply in a visibly unbiased manner to a large part of society, if not absolutely everyone, and horizontal identity no longer matters for how the rules are enforced or whether an individual can form an organization. Once citizens gain both the ability to form organizations and access to the third-party enforcement that enables their organizations to be larger and more effective, society is transformed. The economy becomes more competitive and dynamic, and citizens can join together to accomplish a multitude of social ends that previously were beyond their reach.

The central question of this volume is how societies make the transition to open access. North, Wallis, and Weingast postulated that as natural states grew in complexity, they would develop more formal organizational structures that would facilitate this change. They called these structures "doorstep" conditions and highlighted three developments that they considered particularly important. The first, rule of law for elites, is a condition where elites agree to abide by a set of rules and methods of enforcement. The rules at stake are still identity rules. They do not treat all elites equally, but nonetheless they are still credibly enforced. The ability to create and enforce stable identity rules facilitates economic growth in natural states. Conversely, failure to enforce them according to the agreement can lead to social disorder and the loss of valuable rents. Many developing countries are incapable of creating and sustaining credible rule of law, even for elites.

The second doorstep condition is the creation of perpetually lived organizations. Perpetually lived organizations do not have an infinite life. Their defining characteristic is that their existence is independent of the lives and identity of their members. The organization lives on as an organization even if its membership changes. Perpetually lived organizations are important because identity rules only have the possibility of becoming impersonal rules when there are organizations that can credibly ensure that commitments made in the present are honored in the future.

The third doorstep condition is consolidated control of the military. As we have seen, the central problem that the logic of the natural state addresses in functional terms is limiting violence. Before powerful organizations can credibly treat each other the same, they must believe that the organization with the capacity to suppress intraelite violence is under the control of a collective agreement.

Taken together, the doorstep conditions allow elites to believe that the rules they have agreed upon can be enforced, that the rules will continue to be enforced if the members of the enforcing organization change, and that enforcement will not depend upon the current configuration of coercive power among elite organizations. The doorstep conditions are necessary but not sufficient conditions for a transition to open access, and there is no implication that a transition will automatically follow when a society achieves them. In a natural state powerful individuals are always embedded in political coalitions dependent on the rents generated by limited access and by special privileges more generally. It is extremely difficult to induce them, willingly or not, to give up their privileges. Nonetheless, a small number of western societies managed at least to begin this shift toward open access during the first half of the nineteenth century. How? The chapters in this volume explore this history in order to better understand the dynamics of this fundamental transformation.

The Chapters

The first three chapters in the volume focus on the period before the transition from limited to open access. The pioneering western countries were advanced, mature natural states by the end of the eighteenth century. They were still governed by identity rules, but their institutions had evolved to the point where elites could conceivably find it advantageous to move toward a system of impersonal rules. The chapters show how difficult it was even to conceptualize the change, let alone effectuate it.

Dan Bogart uses the case of the British East India Company to study the emergence of doorstep conditions in Britain over the course of the seventeenth and eighteenth centuries. The company was originally chartered in 1600 by Queen Elizabeth, who granted it a monopoly over trade with all parts of the world between the Cape of Good Hope and the Straits of Magellan. Despite its royal charter, for the next century and a half the company had to struggle for its existence against continuous attempts by the various monarchs and Parliament to take away its charter, profit from encouraging competing ventures, extract bonus payments and loans, and otherwise expropriate its returns. Scholars often focus on the Glorious Revolution as a key turning point in the economic and political development of Great Britain, and in an important sense it was. However, as Bogart shows, the implications of the new political settlement for "monied" companies, like the East India Company, emerged only gradually and in a highly contingent way. In the years immediately following the Glorious Revolution, the company experienced the same threats to its existence and resources as it had before, but by the middle of the eighteenth century the achievement of political stability and the growing fiscal strength of the government had put a stop to this tampering. Indeed, after midcentury the company only faced such exigencies when the term of its charter formally expired, a sign of a new respect for the rule of law among elites. What happened when the charter expired, however, continued to depend on personal relationships—on the strength of its members' connections with the governing coalition. When those connections were powerful, as they were when the charter was up for renewal in 1780, the exactions on the company could be relatively modest. When they were feebler, however, the negotiations could be more difficult. The new elections held in the wake of Prime Minister Lord Perceval's assassination in 1812 did not go well for the company's supporters. Thus the company was in a weakened position when its charter came up for renewal in 1813, and it was stripped of its monopoly on trade with India. The loss of this monopoly was a step in the direction of open access, but it was a step that occurred within the logic of the natural state and did not point the way toward more general change.

Barry R. Weingast's analysis of Adam Smith's writings provides another vantage point on the emergence of doorstep conditions in Europe. Looking back over European history from the perspective of the late eighteenth century, Smith explained in Book III of *The Wealth of Nations* how countries like Britain and France managed to escape the conflict that had kept them in poverty for centuries after the fall of the Roman Empire. As Weingast shows, Smith understood that economic development depended on making people secure in their property against the violence of the local lords. The key breakthrough, in Smith's (and Weingast's) view, was the formation of mutually beneficial (rent generating) alliances between the various European monarchs and the towns within their domains in opposition to the lords. When the kings granted towns rights of self-governance, trading, and defense in exchange for taxes and military service, they created conditions conducive to the growth of long-distance trade and the commercialization of agriculture. Translating Smith's account into the language of NWW, Weingast shows how the pacts between kings and towns also facilitated the achievement of the doorstep conditions by constituting towns as perpetually lived organizations, fostering the rule of law within them, and consolidating the control of violence.

Writing on the eve of the transition to open access, Smith could not see the change coming. He was famously critical of chartered monopolies like the East India Company and believed, as Jacob T. Levy shows, that the religious pluralism that would follow from disestablishment of the Church of England would be a positive development. More generally, however, the pluralism that Smith thought would preserve liberty was a pluralism based in the ancient privileges granted to towns, provinces, and even the nobility. In this way, Levy shows, Smith fit squarely in a line of thinkers stretching from Montesquieu to Tocqueville who saw the traditional *corps intermédiaires* as the main bulwark against tyranny. As Levy puts it, these writers embraced "an oppositional pluralism that drew its strength from privilege." Because the groups that constituted the *corps* had their own power bases and could rally support against infringements on their longstanding rights, they could check monarchical power before it became despotic. The pluralism that these writers embraced was fundamentally different from the pluralism of the open-access state. The rights and privileges of the *corps* were not open to all; rather, they were identified with particular families and groups. It was that specificity that gave them their legitimacy and hence their power. In the views of Montesquieu and the other writers Levy discusses, impersonal rules were a technique for clipping the power of the *corps*, and as such, were means of despotism rather than a doorstep condition for further progress.

As Levy's chapter demonstrates, the great thinkers of the eighteenth century did not, indeed could not, envision what an open-access society would be like. When they wrote about how privileged organizations ensured social order, they were articulating the logic of the natural state, which was all they had ever known. Nor could the societies they inhabited be said to be progressing gradually in the direction of open access. As Weingast points out, citing Cox, North, and Weingast (2014), the natural state is an equilibrium that when perturbed tends to reestablish itself. Thus the transition to an open-access order cannot occur through a series of small, incremental steps. The achievement of the doorstep conditions does mean, however, that under the right circumstances it would be possible for elites to reconfigure relationships among themselves in a transformative way.

The remaining six chapters focus on the implementation of open access in specific historical settings. They show how difficult it was to effectuate the transformation and how limited the scope of the achievement was in the nineteenth century. At the same time, they document the importance of the change for economic and political development and for society's ability to accomplish important goals. The first of this set of chapters, by Qian Lu and John Joseph Wallis, describes the highly contingent way in which banking moved toward open access in Massachusetts during the early nineteenth century. Banks were important rent-generating organizations that the coalitions in control of the various state governments in the decades following the American Revolution used to solidify their political positions. As a result, charters went almost exclusively to members of the faction that controlled the government. Because those who controlled a bank had preferred access to credit in this capital-scarce economy, whenever a rival political faction came to power, the first thing it did was charter new banks for its supporters. In Massachusetts, the Federalists had almost a complete monopoly on banking, and so when the Republicans took control of both houses of the legislature and the governorship in 1811, they immediately chartered new banks to serve the Republican elite. More importantly, most of the charters of the existing Federalist banks were set to expire in 1812 and the Republican legislature threatened not to renew them. Before they could carry out their threat, however, they had to win another election. The Republicans lost control of the lower house and the governor's mansion in 1812, and the Federalists got their banks rechartered. Things could then have reverted to the status quo ante, but in the context of the increasingly competitive electoral politics of the period surrounding the War of 1812, the incident seems to have given elites in both parties pause. As Lu and Wallis acknowledge, it is difficult to know exactly what went on behind the scenes, but in the years that followed it seems that the parties agreed, at least implicitly, to take banking off the table and allow the legislature to grant all viable applications for bank charters. The number of banks in the state soared, and the tremendous growth that ensued in the amount bank capital and bank money per capita helped fuel economic development.

The move toward open access in banking in Massachusetts is a good example of how, once the doorstep conditions were met, the political equilibrium could suddenly shift if circumstances were right. Massachusetts politicians lived in a world where there was rule of law and agreements were enforceable despite changes in the identity of the enforcer (the Federalists' bank charters could not be revoked until their terms actually expired). They also lived in a world where members of a political faction did not fear violence if they lost an election. When the Federalists and Republications began to charter each other's banks regardless of who was in power, they were in effect further reducing the stakes of controlling the government and ensuring that their private enterprises could flourish regardless of voters' shifting preferences. Although this resolution might seem to be obviously beneficial ex post, it was not easy for politicians to perceive its advantages ex ante, and there was nothing inevitable about the outcome in Massachusetts. Indeed, New York went through a similar episode of political competition around the same time, but instead Martin Van Buren's faction of the Republican Party, dubbed the Albany Regency, ruthlessly used control of bank charters to reward supporters and punish opponents. When the machine finally lost power after the Panic of 1837, the opposition (by then called the Whig Party) took steps to insure that the Regency would never again be able to use bank charters for political purposes, passing New York's famous free banking law in 1838. Banking then thrived in New York as well, though New Yorkers were not able to close the gap with Massachusetts until after the Civil War (Bodenhorn 2006; Hilt 2017). A number of states followed New York's example, but others were never able to move on their own toward open access in banking before it was imposed on them by the federal government as a way of financing the Civil War (Lamoreaux and Wallis 2015).

One lesson that leaps out from the chapters in this volume is that a shift to open access in one sector of the economy or society did not automatically trigger a shift in other sectors, much less an across-the-board movement in that direction. In the case of the United States, not only was there considerable heterogeneity across states in the timing of the move toward open access, but within states the shift in one sector, say banking, often occurred at a very different time than the shift in another sector, say, manufacturing. Before the passage of general incorporation laws, corporations could only be organized with the special permission of the state legislature. Charters for manufacturing ventures granted shareholders limited liability, as well as giving the enterprise the benefits of legal personhood. Charters were thus favors that could be used to reward political supporters and denied to members of the opposition, even if they were not as valuable as bank charters.

In his chapter, "Corporation Law and the Shift toward Open Access in the Antebellum United States," Eric Hilt provides the most complete time series to date of general incorporation laws for manufacturing passed by the various US states before 1860. New York was the pioneer in this case. It passed the first general incorporation statute for manufacturing in 1811, nearly three decades before the passage of its free banking law. New York's early act did not, however, start a trend toward open access. Indeed, its statute was imitated by only three states, all of whom subsequently repealed the legislation. Three other states passed acts in the 1830s, but the big wave of adoptions started in the late 1840s and accelerated during the 1850s. By the Civil War most states and organized territories (twenty-seven out of thirty-two) had passed general incorporation laws for manufacturing.

Even then, however, there were striking differences in the content of the various states' statutes. Corporations had been an important technique of elite control, and many opponents of the old regime worried that open access would not solve that problem but rather would provide members of the elite with the tools they needed to perpetuate their dominance. For example, critics of corporations worried that the standard features of the form, such as limited liability, would give businesspeople with superior access to capital advantages that would enable them to run roughshod over competitors. They also worried that rich shareholders would seize control of otherwise innocuous corporations for this very purpose. Not surprisingly, therefore, many states imposed strict limits on what corporations could do, how big they could grow, how long they could last, and what forms their internal governance could take. Not all, however. Iowa's 1847 statute imposed no restrictions whatsoever on corporations' size or internal governance, though the durations of their charters were limited to twenty years. There were not many people in Iowa in this period, and the liberal general incorporation law might have been a bid to attract settlement. But geography was not fate. Nearby Wisconsin took a very different tack and passed a remarkably restrictive general incorporation act that imposed a voting rule of one vote per shareholder. The southern states were generally outliers in another way. Although the statutes themselves contained relatively few restrictions, they gave the governor or another official the authority to insist on modifications to charters or even to refuse to approve corporate filings. More research is needed on the implementation of these statutes before it is possible to say for certain whether the South was moving toward open access. What is abundantly clear, however, is that the internal politics of the states mattered for both the timing and content of these general incorporation statutes.

Most of the chapters in the volume discuss the rules and policies that affected citizens' ability to form organizations. Stepping back to view the consequences of opening up access to organizational tools, Victoria Johnson and Walter W. Powell compare two different efforts to create botanical gardens in New York City. The first effort in the early 1800s failed; the second in the 1890s was a resounding success. Johnson and Powell frame the two efforts as a controlled comparison that allows them to isolate the importance of the shift toward open access. The basic circumstances in the two cases were essentially the same. Both efforts were spearheaded by leaders with the requisite human capital and connections to powerful political and social elites, in both cases there were existing European models of successful gardens to imitate, and in both cases there was scientific validation for the importance of the gardens as a source of knowledge and benefit to the larger population.

That the second botanical garden succeeded where the first failed owed largely to what Johnson and Powell term the greater "poisedness" of American society in the 1890s than at the start of the century. As they define it, poisedness "refers to circumstances that are rich with potential, in which relations and trends at one level are available to be coupled with innovations at a different one," creating "a self-sustaining pool for these innovations" with "cascading effects." Translated into the terms we have laid out above, New York society had greater poisedness in the 1890s than in the first decade of the nineteenth century because it offered entrepreneurs a much richer set of organizational tools with which to work.

Organizations, as we have argued, can readily serve as third parties for one another. It follows, therefore, that as the environment of organizations deepens and becomes more varied, the kinds of intraorganizational outcomes that can be supported increase exponentially. Johnson and Powell identify the relative paucity of private and public organizations capable of supporting a botanical garden in 1800 and contrast that situation with the depth of organizations available for this purpose in 1890. Part of the richer environment was the proliferation of organizations of all sorts made possible from an opening of access, part was the greater wealth produced by growth and multiplication of financial and business firms discussed by Lu and Wallis and by Hilt, and part was the result of the interaction of those elements.

Thus far we have said very little about organizations outside the business sphere. Here it is useful to adopt the distinction that Richard Brooks and Timothy W. Guinnane develop for their chapter between the right *to* associate and the rights *of* associations—that is, between the right of people to come together and form relationships and the right of organizations to access the tools (e.g., the corporate form) that enable their organizations to be larger and more effective (contractual rather than adherent). As Ruth H. Bloch and Naomi R. Lamoreaux note in "Voluntary Associations, Corporate Rights, and the State: Legal Constraints on the Development of

American Civil Society, 1750–1900," Americans could (with a few glaring exceptions) freely form any organizations they wished. However, states strictly controlled which types of associations could organize as corporations. The right to adopt the corporate form mattered because incorporation enabled associations to accumulate financial resources and hold property in the name of their organizations, as well as to enforce their rules and agreements. Although in the late eighteenth century, states began to pass general incorporation laws that allowed first limited types of voluntary associations (churches, schools, libraries) and then increasingly other kinds of "nonprofit" groups to adopt the corporate form, for the most part they systematically withheld such valuable associational rights from groups that challenged the social order in some fundamental way—for example, by opposing the institution of slavery, advocating political rights for women, or even seeking a better deal for labor. Bloch and Lamoreaux argue that the view of nineteenth-century American society that many scholars have taken from their reading of Tocqueville requires significant modification. Although Americans could form almost any kind of association they wished, they depended on government approval for the tools they needed to make those organizations more effective.

The role of the state was even more apparent in Tocqueville's France and elsewhere on the European continent, where governments actively repressed most civil-society organizations. In Prussia, as Brooks and Guinnane show, citizens organized many new types of associations beginning in the late eighteenth century, but these organizations were in an important sense extralegal and were often actively repressed. Although the legal rules varied over time, for all practical purposes Prussians lacked the right to associate for much of the nineteenth century. Fredrick the Great's 1794 Law Code ostensibly granted citizens the right to associate for socially beneficial purposes, but it also allowed the government to restrict this right in order to maintain order, which it soon did. Prussia's 1850 constitution granted citizens the right to meet together without seeking prior permission from the authorities, so long as the meetings were held indoors and the participants were not armed, but the government subsequently enacted legislation that undermined these constitutional guarantees. For example, if public affairs were to be discussed at a meeting, the police needed to be informed in advance and had the right to send observers. These regulations would not be repealed until the creation of the Weimar Republic after World War I. Lest this history of repression seem like a peculiarly German phenomenon, Brooks and Guinnane show that French practice was remarkably similar. Beginning in 1791 with the passage of *loi Le Chapelier* and continuing until the enactment of a new law on associations in 1901, French law severely restricted citizens' ability to form organizations or even to meet without the explicit approval of the state.

In both Germany and France, the rules governing business organizations were much more lenient than the rules governing civil-society organizations more generally. Although in the early nineteenth century businesses in France and Germany, like elsewhere, could only become corporations with the special permission of the state, they could get most of the benefits of the corporate form without charters. By a simple registration process they could freely organize limited partnerships in which all but one of the partners had limited liability. Moreover, they could make the shares of the limited partners tradable (Guinnane et al. 2007). Full general incorporation came to France in 1867 and Germany in 1870 at a time when governments in both countries were still actively interfering with citizens' right to associate. Corporate charters were particularly valuable in this context because they conveyed not just standard organizational tools, but also government approval of the organization's right to exist. As Brooks and Guinnane document, fears of harassment by government officials led leaders of the cooperative movement in Germany to push (successfully) for what was in effect a general incorporation law. Thus cooperatives thrived in Germany at a time when it was difficult even to form other kinds of organizations.

Behind the repression of associational life that Brooks and Guinnane document for Germany and France, and also the restrictions on the availability of the corporate form that Bloch and Lamoreaux detail for the United States, was a fear of social unrest. Once elites relinquished the tight control of the organizational rents that they had previous used to bolster their social and economic dominance, they had to find new ways of maintaining order. The problem was easier to solve in places like the United States where (especially after the Civil War) the stakes involved in who had control of the government were no longer very high, but even in the United States there was still concern that some types of organizations could be sources of disorder. As Bloch and Lamoreaux show, the range of organizations that elites perceived as threatening grew smaller over time, and access to organizational tools consequently became more open. But some types of oppositional groups retained their disfavored status deep into the twentieth century, in part because the threat that they would use violence to pursue their aims was very real. Margaret Levi, Tania Melo, Barry R. Weingast, and Frances Zlotnick examine the case of labor unions and show that these organizations only gained organizational legitimacy when institutions were created that enabled both unions and businesses credibly to commit to engage in good faith bargaining and not resort to violence. Building the necessary institutions required changes in the distribution of political power that only finally occurred during the Great Depression of the 1930s. It also required considerable learning about how to structure the rules so as not to run afoul of the courts. The end result, the Wagner Act of 1935, granted workers the right to organize, but it still circumscribed that right in a number of ways in order to maintain labor peace. Even so, there was nothing inevitable about the solution or even that that the parties involved would arrive at a solution. To the present day, of course, there are groups in the United States that are denied access to organizational tools or even actively repressed because they threaten (or are perceived to threaten) the social order.

The Difficulty of the Transition to Open Access

At the heart of this volume is the idea that the ability to establish and enforce impersonal rules for forming organizations—that is, open access—is the key to modern economic and political development. The chapters collectively explore the history of the transition to open access in the first societies to undergo it. They document how slow, difficult, and contingent the change was. They also show that no one, not even the greatest thinkers of the late eighteenth and early nineteenth centuries, grasped the importance of what was happening—that is, understood how opening up the ability to organizations of all kinds could spark sustained economic growth and enhance the workings of democratic politics.

One might naively think that, once the transition occurred in these pioneering countries, elites elsewhere would observe the economic and political benefits that open access brought and consequently be more likely to support a similar shift in their own domains. Both the theory and empirical work in this volume suggest otherwise, however. Regardless of the magnitude of the benefits to be derived from the transition, if change threatens the existence and stability of the social hierarchy, it is unlikely to happen. The key to the development process thus goes back to the connection between organizations and rents we laid out above. Most countries in the world today are still natural states, where identity rules create rents that are specific to individual organizations. If opening access eliminates the rents that sustain relationships between powerful organizations, the result could well be an increase in social instability. Moreover, elites at the top of these societies must always question whether they will benefit from the change. Only in countries where, as in the pioneering cases, the doorstep conditions have already been met does the answer have a chance at being positive. But, even there, the transition is likely to be as fraught for countries today as it was for the pioneers of the early nineteenth century.

References

Benoit, Jean-Pierre, and Vijay Krishna. 1985. "Finitely Repeated Games." *Econometrica* 53 (4): 905–22.

Blau, Peter M., and W. Richard Scott. 1962. *Formal Organizations: A Comparative Approach.* San Francisco: Chandler Publishing Company.

Bodenhorn, Howard. 2006. "Bank Chartering and Political Corruption in Antebellum New York: Free Banking as Reform." In *Corruption and Reform: Lessons from*

America's Economic History, edited by Edward L. Glaeser and Claudia Goldin, 231–57. Chicago: University of Chicago Press.

Burkett, Justin, Richard H. Steckel, and John Wallis. 2015. "Stones, Bones, Cities, and States: A New Approach to the Neolithic Revolution." Unpublished manuscript. http://econweb.umd.edu/~davis/eventpapers/BurkettStones.pdf.

Coase, Ronald H. 1937. "The Nature of the Firm." *Economica* 4 (16): 386–405.

Cox, Gary W., Douglass C. North, and Barry R. Weingast. 2014. "The Violence Trap: A Political-Economic Approach to the Problems of Development." Working Paper, Hoover Institution, Stanford University.

Cyert, Richard, and James G. March. 1963. *A Behavioral Theory of the Firm*. Englewood Cliffs, NJ: Prentice-Hall.

DiMaggio, Paul J., and Walter W. Powell. 1991. "Introduction." In *The New Institutionalism in Organizational Analysis*, edited by Walter W. Powell and Paul J. DiMaggio, 1–40. Chicago: University of Chicago Press.

Fudenberg, Drew, and Eric Maskin. 1986. "The Folk Theorem in Repeated Games with Discounting or with Incomplete Information." *Econometrica* 54 (3): 533–54.

Gibbons, Robert. 1998. "Game Theory and Garbage Cans: An Introduction to the Economics of Internal Organization." In *Debating Rationality: Nonrational Aspects of Organizational Decision Making*, edited by Jennifer J. Halpern and Robert N. Stern, 36–52. Ithaca, NY: Cornell University Press.

———. 1999. "Taking Coase Seriously." *Administrative Science Quarterly* 44 (1): 145–57.

———. 2003. "Team Theory, Garbage Cans and Real Organizations: Some History and Prospects of Economic Research on Decision-Making in Organizations." *Industrial and Corporate Change* 12 (4): 753–87.

Grossman, Sanford J., and Oliver D. Hart. 1986. "The Costs and Benefits of Ownership: A Theory of Vertical and Lateral Integration." *Journal of Political Economy* 94 (4): 691–719.

Guinnane, Timothy W., Ron Harris, Naomi R. Lamoreaux, and Jean-Laurent Rosenthal. 2007. "Putting the Corporation in its Place." *Enterprise and Society* 8 (3): 687–729.

Hilt, Eric. 2017. "Early American Corporations and the State." In *Corporations and American Democracy*, edited by Naomi R. Lamoreaux and William J. Novak, 37–73. Cambridge, MA: Harvard University Press.

Lamoreaux, Naomi, and John Joseph Wallis. 2015. "States not Nation: The Sources of Political and Economic Development in the Early United States." Johns Hopkins Institute for Applied Economics, Global Health, and the Study of Business Enterprise, American Capitalism Working Papers, AC/No.1/March 2016.

Lovejoy, Paul E., and David Richardson. 1999. "Trust, Pawnship, and Atlantic History: The Institutional Foundations of the Old Calabar Slave Trade." *American Historical Review* 104 (2): 333–55.

March, James. 1962. "The Business Firm as a Political Coalition." *Journal of Politics* 24 (4): 662–78.

March, James G., and Herbert A. Simon. 1958. *Organizations*. New York: John Wiley & Sons.

North, Douglass C., John Joseph Wallis, and Barry R. Weingast. 2009. *Violence and Social Orders: A Conceptual Framework for Interpreting Recorded Human History*. New York: Cambridge University Press.

Olson, Mancur, Jr. 1965. *Logic of Collective Action: Public Goods and the Theory of Groups*. Cambridge, MA: Harvard University Press.

Padgett, John F., and Walter W. Powell. 2012. *The Emergence of Organizations and Markets*. Princeton, NJ: Princeton University Press.

Powell, Walter W., and Paul J. DiMaggio, eds. 1991. *The New Institutionalism in Organizational Analysis*. Chicago: University of Chicago Press.

Scott, W. Richard. 2014. *Institutions and Organizations: Ideas, Interests, and Identities*, 4th ed. Los Angeles: Sage.

Tilly, Charles. 1990. *Coercion, Capital, and European States: 990–1992*. Cambridge, MA: B. Blackwell.

Wallis, John Joseph. 2015. "Conceptualizing Government." Unpublished manuscript.

Weber, Max. 1968. *Economy and Society: An Outline of Interpretive Sociology*, edited by Guenther Roth and Claus Wittich. Berkeley: University of California Press.

Williamson, Oliver. 1975. *Markets and Hierarchies, Analysis and Antitrust Implications: A Study in the Economics of Internal Organization*. New York: Free Press.

———. 1985. *The Economic Institutions of Capitalism: Firms, Markets, Relationship Contracting*. New York: Free Press.

1

The East Indian Monopoly and the Transition from Limited Access in England, 1600–1813

Dan Bogart

History shows that many important markets are limited by laws and customs enforced by political and religious authorities. Examples are bans on trade, prohibitions on migration, and grants of monopoly. The result in all cases is that favored individuals and firms earn "rents," or an excess payment over and above the amount expected in open markets. Introductory economics suggests that limiting markets generally reduces social welfare and hampers development by lowering incentives for innovation.

The importance of limited markets has led to much theorizing and analysis. North, Wallis, and Weingast (2009) is an important recent work tackling this issue. They argue that most societies in human history can be described as "limited-access orders," where the ruling coalition limits entry to markets and the political system. The resulting rents give elites in the ruling coalition an economic incentive to support the regime rather than undermine it through violence or other means. Some limited-access orders can be fragile, such that commitments to elites are fluid and unstable. Shocks can easily lead to violence and the creation of a new coalition. There are alternative systems called "open-access orders." In these societies, governing coalitions do not limit entry to markets and the political system. Instead, social stability is sustained through political and economic competition. Open-access orders are also capable of sustained development above and beyond what

Dan Bogart is associate professor of economics at the University of California, Irvine.

I would like to thank conference and seminar participants at Yale University and Colby College. I would also like to thank Richard Grossman, Stergios Skaperdas, John Wallis, Naomi Lamoreaux, Barry Weingast, Sandra Bogart, and Jean-Laurent Rosenthal for valuable comments on earlier drafts. I would like to thank Kara Dimitruk for valuable research assistance and comments. All errors are my own. For acknowledgments, sources of research support, and disclosure of the author's material financial relationships, if any, please see http://www.nber.org/chapters/c13506.ack.

is possible in limited access. The interesting question then is why don't all societies transition from limited- to open-access orders?

Providing a satisfactory answer to this question is extremely difficult. The approach taken by North, Wallis, and Weingast (2009) is to use history to illuminate the transition. They propose three doorstep conditions in the transition from limited to open access: the rule of law for elites (doorstep 1), the existence of perpetually lived organizations (doorstep 2), and consolidated political control of the military (doorstep 3). Rule of law for elites is achieved when law is applied equally to all elites and is enforced without bias. In such settings, elite-owned assets and organizations are protected from predation even when the ruling coalition changes. Perpetually lived organizations are those whose existence does not require the sanction of the governing coalition. Companies formed under general incorporation law are good examples of perpetually lived organizations, but there are many other examples in the public and religious spheres.

This chapter studies the English East India Company, with the aim of understanding how the doorstep conditions were met in England. The English Company is notable in the broader literature because it paved the way for Britain's colonization of India starting in the mid-eighteenth century.[1] But for more than a century prior, it was a privileged company with a monopoly over all trade between England and Asia. The East India monopoly is an excellent example of limited access. The Company gave the monarch added tax revenues through special customs duties and a share of the prizes from captured ships. It also provided defense against other European nations in Asia. In return, the Company got the right to earn profits from its monopoly privileges. This partnership was made explicit by the original charter in 1600 and those that followed.

The English Company's monopoly lasted several centuries, but it was far from secure, especially before the early eighteenth century. The government (at first the monarchy and then parliament) authorized groups known as interlopers to trade in East Indian markets, which violated the terms and spirit of the Company's monopoly. The government also forced the Company to lend money and demanded extra payments. As I argue below, political instability and fiscal incapacity were the root causes of the insecurity. The Company usually had political connections to the government to strengthen its privileges, but these were less effective or counterproductive when politics became unstable, as often happened in the seventeenth century. The government was also desperate for loans and taxes, usually in times of war, and thus it could not commit to allow the Company to earn profits in accordance with its charter and agreement.

---

1. There are several important historical works on the East India Company. A few include Philips (1961), Chaudhuri (1965, 1978), Desai (1984), Bowen (2005), Robins (2006), Webster (2009), and Stern (2011).

Remarkably, the East Indian monopoly became more secure by the mid-eighteenth century. Previously, the Company's trading privileges were renegotiated according to the dictates of politics and finance. But after 1744, the monopoly was renegotiated only when the terms of the previous charter expired. Thus an important step was taken toward the rule of law for elites. The achievement of political stability under the early Hanoverian monarchs (1715–1760) and the greater capability of Britain's fiscal system were some of the key factors behind this step.

Despite these developments Britain had not yet reached the second doorstep condition, in which most organizations operate without sanction from the governing coalition. From 1781 to 1813, the monarch and parliament continued to renew the Company's trading privileges for terms of ten or twenty years despite pressures to end them. Key reasons were the Company's strong political connections and its value in defending India against the French. British governments were also keen to preserve the monopoly because the Company earned vast new revenues following the Battle of Plassey and its takeover of tax collection rights in Bengal in the 1760s.

A huge step toward open access was taken in the 1813 charter act. In this act, the Company lost its monopoly over trade with India. From that point forward, private traders could enter the Indian market with few restrictions. The opening of Indian market access was due to several factors. First, manufacturers in the north of England, whose economic interests went against the Company's monopoly, became more influential by 1813. Lord Liverpool's "Liberal Tory" government believed it was necessary to accommodate the growing manufacturing interest and end the monopoly. Second, a random event played a related role. In May of 1812 the Prime Minister Perceval was assassinated. In the election that followed the Company's connections to the governing party in the Commons were much weaker than in previous years, and it could not defend itself against opponents. The timing was bad for the Company because its charter was up for renegotiation in the winter of 1813. Third, the fiscal value of the Indian monopoly diminished as the customs revenues from Indian trade fell in the early 1800s. Notably customs revenues in the lucrative Chinese tea trade rose sharply in the early 1800s, and partly for this reason the Chinese monopoly was kept intact until 1833.

This chapter contributes to a broader understanding of the transition from limited to open-access orders.[2] It also contributes to the literature on the evolution of markets and British institutions.[3] The history of the Company suggests there was no moment when the rule of law for elites and open

2. See North et al. (2012) and Franke and Quintyn (2014) for some examples.
3. A sample of papers in this literature include North and Weingast (1989), Clark (1996), O'Brien (2001), Acemoglu, Johnson, and Robinson (2005), Pincus (2009), Cox (2011, 2012), Zahedieh (2010), Sussman and Yafeh (2006), Mokyr (2009), Stasavage (2003), Broz and Grossman (2004), Quinn (2001), Wells and Wills (2000), Klerman and Mahoney (2005), Griffiths, Hunt, and O'Brien (1991), and Carruthers (1999).

markets emerged in Britain. In particular there was no dramatic shift to open access following constitutional reforms, like the Glorious Revolution. The gradual building of political stability and fiscal capacity by the mid-eighteenth century were the key processes leading to the rule of law. The growth of northern manufacturing interests in the late eighteenth century was also significant in bringing the monopoly to the end. The last finding raises more general questions about the relationship between the transition to open access and economic growth. It is not clear which caused the other. The conclusion returns to these broader themes.

1.1   The Origins of Monopoly in the East Indian Trade

The East India Company was founded in 1600 through a charter granted by Queen Elizabeth. Management was in the hands of a governor and a board of directors. Shareholders with a minimum number of shares elected the governor and directors. The Company was given a monopoly over all trade and traffic from the Cape of Good Hope to the Straits of Magellan—an area encompassing much of the world's population (Scott 1912, 92).

The East Indian trade was not unique in being organized around monopoly. Jha (2005) identifies twenty-eight chartered companies in foreign trade from 1555 to 1640. Most of these companies were granted a monopoly over trade with a particular region, like the East Indies. Monopoly was common because it offered the monarchy added tax revenues, a source of loans in times of emergency, and assistance in governing at home and abroad.[4] In the East Indian context, there is an argument that monopoly was also selected because of the efficiency benefits to directors and employees due to the violent trading environment in Asia, and the challenges of corporate governance in an age with poor communication.[5] The social welfare implications of the monopoly are not obvious, but for our purposes this is not the main issue. The monopoly was mainly selected because it suited the needs of the monarch.

It is important to note that the legal foundation for the East Indian monopoly was weak. The original charter from Queen Elizabeth allowed any privileges to be voided by the monarch with two years notice and with little justification (Scott 1912, 92). Therefore, is not surprising that the Company's first directors tended to be closely connected to the monarch, and were part of the governing coalition. The Company's first governor, Thomas Smythe, was connected to Queen Elizabeth because his father had improved

---

4. See Johnson and Koyama (2014) and Quinn (2008) for examples of sovereign borrowing from privileges companies in early modern Europe.

5. See Chaudhuri (1978), Carlos and Nicholas (1988, 1996), and Hejeebu (2005) for a discussion of the monopoly and efficiency.

Elizabethan customs collection.[6] Smythe strengthened his connections to the Queen in his early life. He was appointed as a trade commissioner to negotiate with the Dutch in 1596 and 1598. In the 1590s he became purveyor for the troops in Ireland. Smythe remained the Company's governor over the next two decades. He retained connections to the monarchy after James I came to the throne. Smythe was made joint receiver of the Duchy of Cornwall in 1604 and receiver for Dorset and Somerset. In that same year he was appointed special ambassador to the Tsar of Russia. See North, Wallis, Weingast (2009) for a discussion of the natural state.

1.2   The East Indian Monopoly under the Stuarts

At the start of the King James I reign in 1603, the Company's monopoly appeared secure. But it quickly became apparent that the Stuart monarchs would not honor the terms of the charter. King James I, and later King Charles I, regularly authorized "interloper" traders to enter the East Indian market. This section details these events and argues that the Stuart's actions were linked with their need for revenues and to reallocate rents to an evolving coalition of supporters.

The first group of interloper traders was headed by Sir Edward Michelborne. In 1604, Michelborne obtained a license from King James I "to discover the countries of Cathay, China, Japan, Corea [Korea], and Cambaya [Cambodia], and to trade there." The license claimed to supersede all previous grants and allowed Michelborne to trade in the East India Company's territory.[7] Michelborne had strong political connections to King James I through the patronage of Thomas Sackville, the first Baron of Buckhurst. Sackville was one of James I's closest advisors, serving as Lord Treasurer beginning in 1603, just one year before Michelborne was granted the license to trade in Asia.[8] After receiving the license Michelborne sailed two ships to Asia, but he was ultimately not successful and returned to England in 1606.[9]

The next interlopers were headed by Richard Penkevell. In 1607, they were given a grant to discover the northern passage to China, Cathay, and other parts of the East Indies (Scott 1912, 100). Less is known about Penkevell

---

6. Basil Morgan, "Smythe, Sir Thomas (c. 1558–1625)," *Oxford Dictionary of National Biography*, Oxford University Press, 2004; online ed., Jan. 2008 (http://www.oxforddnb.com/view /article/25908, accessed Sept. 25, 2013).

7. D. J. B. Trim, "Michelborne, Sir Edward (c. 1562–1609)," *Oxford Dictionary of National Biography*, Oxford University Press, 2004; online ed., Jan. 2008 (http://www.oxforddnb.com /view/article/18650, accessed Sept. 25, 2013).

8. Rivkah Zim, "Sackville, Thomas, first Baron Buckhurst and first Earl of Dorset (c. 1536–1608)," *Oxford Dictionary of National Biography*, Oxford University Press, 2004; online ed., Oct. 2009 (http://www.oxforddnb.com/view/article/24450, accessed Sept. 25, 2013).

9. D. J. B. Trim, "Michelborne, Sir Edward (c. 1562–1609)," *Oxford Dictionary of National Biography*.

except that he was a member of Parliament in the late sixteenth century.[10] After Penkevell, the Company reaffirmed its legal position by getting a new charter from King James I in 1609. In the charter, James I stated that the whole trade in Asia was conferred upon the Company forever, except if the king or his heirs deemed that the Company was not profitable to the monarchy or to the realm.

James I honored the letter of the charter, but not the spirit. In 1617 the king granted a charter to a new interloper group under the name of the Scottish East India Company (Scott 1912, 104). The Scottish Company was headed by Sir James Cunningham, a member of the Scottish Privy Council. The Scottish Company was authorized to trade in the East Indies, the Levant, Greenland, and Muscovy. It appears that James I exploited that he was also the King of Scotland and chose to charter the rival company under the Scottish royal seal, not the English seal. The Scottish East India Company posed a significant threat to the East India Company and the Levant Company, another chartered company operating at the time. The two bought the license from the Scottish East India Company and paid a "valuable consideration" to its leaders and promoters (Bruce 1810, 193–94).

The 1620s marked the beginning of a prolonged period in which the monarchy tried to extract revenues from the East India Company. Scott's (1912, 125–26) analysis of the Company's early dividends shows that the trade had proven profitable. At the same time, tax revenues were stagnating, making the Company an attractive target for royal extraction. In 1620 James I ordered the Company to pay £20,000 to himself and the Duke of Buckingham for captured prizes from Portuguese ships (Chaudhuri 1965, 31). A few years later, in 1624, James I offered to become an adventurer and to send out ships under the royal standard. The Company refused the offer on the grounds that "the whole undertaking would revert to the Crown, since there could be no partnership with the King." In 1628 there was another scheme to admit King Charles I as an adventurer for one-fifth of the stock and profits in return for taking the Company under royal protection. The Company refused once again (Scott 1912, 108–12).

Charles I's failed attempt to gain ownership in the Company provided an opportunity for the interlopers. In 1635 a new syndicate obtained a license from Charles I for a trading voyage to Goa, Malabar, China, and Japan, an activity considered to be within the bounds of the Company's monopoly (Scott 1912, 112). One of the main promoters of the syndicate, Endymion Porter, had been in the service of Edward Villiers, the royal favorite of King James I in the 1620s. Porter's connections to the monarchy continued under Charles I, serving as the "Groom of the King's Bedchamber." Another promoter, William Courteen was a wealthy merchant who made loans to

---

10. See Irene Cassidy, "PENKEVELL, Richard" The House of Commons, online ed. (http://www.historyofparliamentonline.org/volume/1558–1603/member/penkevell-richard-1616).

Charles I through Villiers.[11] Charles I eventually became an adventurer in what became known as the Courteen Association. The king was credited with stock worth £10,000, and his secretary of state, Windebank, was also credited with £1,000. The East India Company protested that the license to the Courteen Association violated their charter. Charles I responded that no hindrance or damage was intended to the Company's trade as the ships being prepared by Courteen were for a voyage of discovery. The king also stated that the East India Company neglected to make discoveries and plantations in the East, and thus had no legal basis to protest.[12] The Courteen Association received further support from Charles I in 1637 when the king authorized the partners to send out ships and goods to the East for five years "without impeachment or denial of the East India Company or others" (Scott 1912, 113–14). The Courteen Association was generally unsuccessful in its trading ventures, but in the process the Association caused much financial damage to the Company.

The Company experienced further extractions in 1636 and 1641. In 1636, Charles I increased the customs duties on pepper by 70 percent. The result was that the customs duties derived from the Company's trade were yielding around £30,000 per year by the early 1640s (Foster 1904, 1929, xxviii). At this same time, the political conflicts between Charles I and Parliament were increasing. This made the king's fiscal situation dire. In this context, the king forced the Company to hand over its stock of pepper, which was valued at £63,283. The so-called pepper loan of 1641 was to be repaid in four installments and was secured by the farmers of the customs. The Company had recovered around £21,000 by the late 1640s, but at this point Charles I was executed and the monarchy was abolished. The remainder of the pepper loan was lost for the moment, and was only partly recovered in the 1660s.[13]

1.3   The East Indian Monopoly under the Commonwealth and Restoration

The pepper loan of 1641 set a precedent in which the Company made loans to the government in exchange for promises to respect their monopoly privileges. However, the loans were not sufficient to secure the monopoly because of the instability created by the English Civil War. Parliamentary forces ultimately prevailed in the war, and in the late 1640s a new governing coalition came into being under the Commonwealth government. Executive

11. Ronald G. Asch, "Porter, Endymion (1587–1649)," *Oxford Dictionary of National Biography*, Oxford University Press, 2004; online ed., Jan. 2008 (http://www.oxforddnb.com/view /article/22562, accessed Sept. 26, 2013).

12. John C. Appleby, "Courten, Sir William (c. 1568–1636)," *Oxford Dictionary of National Biography*, Oxford University Press, 2004; online ed., Jan. 2008 (http://www.oxforddnb.com /view/article/6445, accessed Sept. 26, 2013).

13. According to Foster (1904, 463) £10,500 more was recovered in the early 1660s from the former farmers of the customs, leaving £31,500 unpaid.

powers were now held by the Council of State, which was appointed by leaders of the Rump Parliament. The Council immediately faced pressures to undermine the Company's monopoly. In 1649 a group of interlopers known as the "Assada Adventurers" applied for a voyage to Asia. The Adventurers offered a loan of £4,000 to the Council to advance their cause. In the same year, the Company also appealed to the Council of State to protect its interests and offered a loan of £6,000. The Council of State recommended a merger of the two companies, which was enacted in 1650 and became known as the "United Joint Stock" (Scott 1912, 120).

The United Joint Stock financed a series of voyages in the early 1650s but it was not a success, in part, due to continual entry by interlopers. In 1651 an appeal to suppress interlopers was made to Oliver Cromwell, whose authority in the Council of State was increasing. Cromwell gave a disinterested reply in writing stating that "he has much public business and that he neither could nor would attend to private matters" (Scott 1912, 121). Once Cromwell rose to the position of Lord Protector of the Commonwealth in December 1653, the Company again tried to seek his assistance. In 1655 the Company lent £50,000 to the Council of State, and two years later, in 1657, the Company received a new charter. It created a permanent joint stock company, eliminating the financing of individual voyages by investors.

The establishment of the new United East India Company moved forward in 1657, but it was not a great success. Subscriptions for capital amounted to just over £739,000, but the directors limited their calls on investors to £369,000 (Scott 1912, 121). The death of Oliver Cromwell is perhaps one reason. Richard Cromwell, Oliver's son, succeeded as Lord Protector. Richard Cromwell followed in the footsteps of previous English monarchs by undermining the charter. In 1658 Richard granted a license to an independent trader named Rolt. Little is known about Rolt's voyage except that the Company directed its officers in India to seize any articles and dispose of them on their own account (Bruce 1810, 537). In the end, Richard Cromwell was unable to build a ruling coalition in the protectorate and was forced to step down. A new Council of State was formed, and like previous governments it turned to the East India Company for a loan. The Council demanded £30,000, but the company negotiated the loan to a smaller amount of £15,000 (Scott 1912, 130). To put these figures into perspective, the total tax revenues of the Commonwealth government were £1.2 million in 1659 (Dincecco 2011).

The restoration of the monarchy in 1660 represented another change in political power, but it was more lasting than the Commonwealth and Protectorate. The immediate effect on the Company was a series of losses. The Company's loans to the Council of State in 1655 and 1659 were canceled (Foster 1929, vi–vii, xxxii). Its recent charter from Cromwell was also nullified. In the wake of these events, the Company set out to renew its charter by appealing to King Charles II. As a sign of loyalty the Company gave the new king a plate estimated to be worth £3,000, and his brother James, Duke of York, received cash worth £1,000. These "gifts" were followed by a new charter in 1662 and a loan of £10,000 to Charles II (Scott 1912, 131).

More loans followed in Charles II's reign. The Company lent the King £120,000 in 1666 and 1667 and £150,000 in 1676 and 1678. These loans were linked with the Second Anglo Dutch War (1665–67) and Third Anglo Dutch War (1672–74), which tightened the king's finances. The loans were also linked to a suit against the Company for the king's share of prize money from seized ships. The king had sold his rights to the Duke of Monmouth, who then pursued the Company in court for a failure to pay. Following the loan of 1676, the king issued a warrant that all such suits against the Company before 1676 must be withdrawn.[14] The loans of the mid-1670s were also linked with an attack against the Company by a coalition of interlopers, the Levant Company, and the woolen cloth industry. Together these three groups submitted petitions and wrote pamphlets arguing that the Company's trade was not profitable to the realm. The king effectively ended this attack in 1676 by granting the East India Company a new charter confirming its trading privileges (Scott 1912, 178).

Over the course of the 1670s, the East India Company earned large profits and its share price rose from around £80 in 1672 to £365 in 1681 (Scott 1912, 139). In part because of the Company's financial success, a new group of interlopers emerged to challenge its monopoly. The interlopers raised £1,000,000 and submitted a proposal to Charles II for a new joint stock company. They were refused and the Company was granted a new charter. Two factors were important in the interlopers' failure. First, the Company gave Charles II a gift of 10,000 guineas (around £10,000) and promised to offer a similar gift every New Year's Day for the rest of his reign. Second, the Company's governor, Josiah Child, was a strong political supporter of Charles II.[15] Child's support for the king became a controversial issue in the Company. Some of the directors, like Thomas Papillion, were favorable to the Whigs, an emerging political party at this time. The rivalry between Child and Papillion was so severe that Papillion's group sold their shares and left the Company.

1.4 The East Indian Monopoly in the Aftermath of the Glorious Revolution

The Glorious Revolution of 1688–89 is thought to be a watershed moment in the evolution of Britain's institutions because it gave Parliament greater political authority and increased the security of property rights (North and Weingast 1989). While there may be some truth to this view, in the case of

14. Ottewill, *Calendar of Court Minutes*, 1674–76, p. xxvii–xviii, 1677–79, p. 134.
15. Richard Grassby, "Child, Sir Josiah, first baronet (*bap.* 1631, *d.* 1699)," *Oxford Dictionary of National Biography*, Oxford University Press, 2004; online ed., Jan. 2008 (http://www.oxforddnb.com/view/article/5290, accessed Sept. 27, 2013).

the East India Company, the Glorious Revolution looks similar to earlier regime changes in which interlopers were emboldened by a weakening in the Company's political connections. What was different is that interlopers came to be allied with a powerful political party, the Whigs. Also, in the short term, the Glorious Revolution greatly increased the king's need for loans because it led to an expensive war with France.

The opponents of the Company, including Thomas Papillion, were strongly represented in the Convention Parliament of 1688.[16] In 1690, Papillion led an interloper syndicate and raised £180,000 as a campaign fund to influence Parliament. The Company responded by requesting an act of Parliament ratifying their previous charters, but no action was taken (Scott 1912, 150–52). In 1692 the Papillion Syndicate petitioned King William asking him to dissolve the Company and to incorporate a new one. William encouraged the two groups to come to an accommodation. The Company offered stock to half of the members of the syndicate. The other half appealed to the Privy Council for regulations that would change voting rights and effectively allow them to take control from the governor, Josiah Child. They also proposed that in twenty-one years the holdings of the Company should be wound up and a completely new subscription of capital should then be made. It is revealing that the Company responded to these proposals by likening its monopoly to landed property and appealing to the rule of law. An anonymous author, clearly working in the interest of the Company, argued that restricting voting rights of shareholders in the Company is "against the laws and customs of England."[17]

The Company successfully defended itself against the Papillion Syndicate in 1692. A year later it also got a new charter from King William. The charter enlarged the Company's capital and imposed voting regulations, but it did not allow for the removal of Josiah Child. For the moment, it appeared the Company survived the aftermath of the Glorious Revolution. It even took legal actions against interlopers in the following legislative session. However, it appears that the Company was too bold. Numerous petitions were submitted to the House of Commons complaining of attacks on interlopers. The Commons then resolved that "all subjects of England have equal right to trade in the East Indies, unless prohibited by act of parliament." The validity of the Company's royal charter was now in doubt. The Commons also began investigating accusations of bribery by Company officials in the

---

16. Perry Gauci, "Papillon, Thomas (1623–1702)," *Oxford Dictionary of National Biography*, Oxford University Press, 2004; online ed., Jan. 2008 (http://www.oxforddnb.com/view/article /21247, accessed Sept. 27, 2013).

17. The author goes on to argue that "the Company by the true rules of policy ought never to alter nor any man be forced to sell its stock, any more than he can be forced to buy a stock that has none; or any gentlemen that has an over-growth estate in land in any country can be forced to sell part to make way for some purchasers that pretend they will buy land in that country." Quoted in Scott (1912, 155).

spring of 1695. It was alleged that the Company spent upward of £200,000 to influence the king and MPs (Scott 1912, 157–60).

The Company's fortunes turned for the worse in 1697 when King William needed new loans to finance the Nine Years' War against France. The Company offered a loan of £500,000 at 4 percent interest. This was a substantial offer considering the total funded debt of the government was £3.4 million in 1697 (Mitchell 1988, 600). However, an interloper syndicate went much further and offered a loan of £2 million at 8 percent interest along with the condition that it would get exclusive trading rights to Asia. The interlopers were emboldened by their strong connections to the Whigs, who had recently come into favor with King William. For example, Samuel Shepheard, one of the largest interloper investors, had a strong connection to the Whig leader Charles Montagu, who served as the Chancellor of the Exchequer.[18] The end result was that the king and Parliament accepted the offer of the rival syndicate. An act in 1697 (9 William III, c. 44) authorized the formation of the "New" East India Company. It got exclusive rights to the East Indian trade with the proviso that the "Old" East India Company could trade until September 29, 1701 (Scott 1912, 165–68).

Despite its recent failure, the Old East India Company was not finished. It began a successful campaign to reestablish its monopoly through a merger with the New Company. A deal to merge Old and New Companies was brokered in 1701 and signed just after Queen Anne took the throne. The deal would lead to the re-creation of monopoly in a single East Indian Company.

Reflecting on this whole episode, it is clear that political instability was one of the important factors. In the 1690s the Whigs and Tories were engaged in a fierce partisan struggle for control over the House of Commons and King William's government.[19] From 1690 to 1695 the Tories had a slight majority in the Commons and in the ministry, but their relationship with King William weakened. After the election of 1695 the Whigs had a majority in the Commons and by 1696 they had a majority in the ministry as well. The Whigs aggressively pushed their policies and purged the Tories whenever possible. The tables turned in 1700 as the Whigs lost influence and several of their leaders were impeached. The Tories were able to take advantage and regain a slight majority in the Commons and the ministry in 1701. The Whigs regained some influence late in December 1701 just before King William died early in 1702.

The shifts in political power mattered for the East India trade because the Company was connected to the Tories and its opponents were linked with the Whigs (Horwitz 1978). An analysis of the actions of MPs and their party affiliation shows the difference in political connections. The actions

---

18. Watson and Gauci (2002).

19. See Cruickshanks, Handley, and Hayton (2002) and Horwitz (1997) for a more general discussion of parties.

Table 1.1   MPs acting for or against the Company and their party affiliation

Session	No. favoring EIC	No. against EIC	No. favoring EIC, Tory	No. against EIC, Tory
A. 1690–95 Parliament				
1690–91	5	2	3	1
1691–92	23	40	13	8
1692–93	13	16	9	5
1693–94	6	7	3	2
1694–95	4	19	2	4
Total	51	84	30	20
Share Tory			0.588	0.238
T-stat for difference in shares				4.176
$P(T < = t)$ two-tail				0
B. 1695–98, 98–1700 Parliaments				
1695–96	1	6	1	2
1696–97	1	1	0	0
1697–98	12	10	2	8
1698–99	9	7	1	5
1699–00	8	2	3	1
Total	31	26	7	16
Share Whig			0.226	0.615
T-stat for difference in shares				–3.15
$P(T < = t)$ two-tail				0.003
C. 1701 Parliament				
1701	10	3	10	0
Share Tory			1	0

Sources: See text.
Notes: See text.

of MPs relating to the East India Company are found in the biographies of every MP edited by Cruickshanks, Handley, and Hayton (2002) in the *History of Parliament* series.[20] A keyword search identified whether an MP spoke or told on a bill or made a motion favorable or unfavorable to the Company. For example there was a motion in 1693 to address King William, asking him to dissolve the East India Company. Some MPs spoke in favor of this motion and others spoke against. To organize the data, I created an indicator variable for each legislative session equal to 1 if an MP acted in the Company's favor at least once and another indicator if the MP acted against the Company (EIC) at least once in a session. I also use new data identifying whether each MP in the 1690–95, 1695–98, 1698–1700, and 1701 parliaments were affiliated with the majority party, either Tory or Whig (Bogart 2016). The results are shown in table 1.1. In the 1690–95 and 1701

20. See http://www.historyofparliamentonline.org/research/members.

Table 1.2   Tax revenues, expenditures, and deficits in the reign of King William

Year	Tax revenues in £	Expenditures in £	Ratio deficit to tax revenue
1692	4,111	4,255	0.035
1693	3,783	5,576	0.474
1694	4,004	5,602	0.399
1695	4,134	6,220	0.505
1696	4,823	7,998	0.658
1697	3,298	7,915	1.4
1698	4,578	4,127	−0.099
1699	5,164	4,691	−0.092
1700	4,344	3,201	−0.263
1701	3,769	3,442	−0.087

Source: Mitchell (1988, 575–78).

parliaments, MPs acting in favor of the Company were more likely to be with the majority Tories than the MPs who spoke against the Company. By the same token, the MPs who acted in favor in the parliaments from 1695 to 1700 were less likely to be with the majority Whigs compared to those who spoke against the Company.

In the context of the 1690s, changes in the party in power could end the Company's trading privileges. The Company was under attack throughout the 1690–95 Parliament, but it was able to defend itself with the help of the Tories, who were in the majority. However, once power shifted to the Whigs from 1695 to 1700, the Company was unable to defend its privileges against its opponents who were now better connected. The Whig leader Montagu argued strongly in favor of the New Company, which eventually gained the exclusive right to trade. Also telling is the fact that the Old Company was able to force a merger with the New Company in 1701 when the Tories regained political power. The timing again suggests that shifts in political power contributed to successful attacks on trading privileges, including those of the New Company.

Fiscal instability was another important factor in the events following the Glorious Revolution. The Nine Years' War against France brought new levels of government expenditure. To meet its fiscal needs, the government raised taxes and borrowing. It also established the Bank of England in 1694. However, by 1697 expenditures were greatly outstripping revenues. Table 1.2 shows figures for English government revenues, expenditures, and deficits in William's reign. The deficit was building from 1693 and reached new heights in 1697. Recall that it was in 1697 that King William made it known that he expected a loan from the East India Company. As discussed earlier, the Old Company's loan offer (£500,000) was one-fourth the offer by its rival (£2,000,000). Had the government's fiscal deficit been smaller, then perhaps the Old Company's modest offer would have been accepted and its privileges would have remained intact.

1.5   The East Indian Monopoly from the Merger to the Battle of Plassey

The United East India Company was formed in 1709 from the merger of the Old and New East India Companies. Just before the merger was to be completed, Queen Anne demanded an interest-free loan of £1,200,000 from the United Company. Like King William before, Anne's government was facing a fiscal crisis due to its involvement in the War of Spanish Succession. The United Company consented to the loan and in return it got confirmation of its monopoly over all trade between Britain and the East Indies. The monopoly was to last for a minimum of eighteen years, at which point the government had the option to repay its £3.2 million in debts to the Company and repeal the trading privilege with three years' notice.

After 1709 the Company would get its monopoly extended again in 1712, 1730, and 1744 by acts of Parliament. The act in 1712 was a relatively minor event, but it extended the guarantee for the Company's monopoly over East Indian trade until at least 1733 when the government had the option to open the trade with three years' notice and upon repayment of its debts to the Company. In 1730 merchants from London, Bristol, and Liverpool submitted a petition to the House of Commons proposing a new company that would control the whole trade and grant licenses to traders for a fee. In return, the merchant group offered to redeem the government's debt to the Company at a lower interest rate. They proposed to make five payments totaling £3,200,000 between 1730 and 1735. The petition for a rival company failed in the Commons by a vote of 223 to 138 (Sutherland 1962, 29). In the same session, the Company got an act of Parliament extending its monopoly trading rights to at least 1769. In return the Company had to make a £200,000 payment to King George II and they had to accept a lower interest rate on the £3.2 million debt owed to them by the government.[21]

The events of 1730 reveal much about the Company's evolving status in the governing coalition. After the Hanoverian succession of 1715, the Company became more connected to the Whig party, which held a majority in the Commons for many decades in the early to mid-eighteenth century. According to Sutherland (1962, 23), connecting to the Whig leadership, especially the first Prime Minister Robert Walpole, was a deliberate strategy by the Company to secure its privileges. One indication of the Whig connection is provided by the political affiliation of the Company's current or former directors who held seats in the House of Commons.[22] In the 1722 to 1727 Parliament, the Company had eight or nine directors in the Commons and 67 percent of them can be classified as Whigs. The overall percentage of

---

21. House of Commons, *Public Income and Expenditure* (532), and Desai (1984, 122).
22. The directors are identified using a keyword search for directors or governors in the East India Company found in the History of Parliament, http://www.historyofparliamentonline .org/. See Cruickshanks, Handley, and Hayton (2002) and Sedgwick (1970) for the printed version of biographies.

Whigs in the 1722 to 1727 Parliament is 56 percent, and thus the Company directors were more likely to be Whig than the average MP.[23] The Company's connections to the majority party weakened, however, in the next parliament. Its representation in the Commons contracted to between five and eight directors in the 1727 to 1734 Parliament, and only 28 percent are classified as Whigs when nearly 50 percent of MPs in the Commons were Whigs. Thus the Company's connections to the majority Whigs were weakest at the moment it was attacked by interlopers in 1730.

Moreover, the interlopers of 1730 were supported by several Tory MPs and a new coalition, called the Opposition Whigs (Sutherland 1962, 29). The Opposition Whigs defected from the majority Whigs because they thought Robert Walpole was too corrupt. The close connection between Walpole and the so-called monied companies, like the East India Company, was a prime example. Walpole was aware of the antimonopoly sentiment, and the threat that it posed to his party's rule. On this basis, it is likely that Walpole's support for the East India Company was tenuous in 1730. Perhaps for this reason, the Company made efforts to move closer to the majority Whigs in the years that followed. In the 1734 to 1741 Parliament the Company had seven to eight directors in the Commons, and on average 75 percent were affiliated with the Whigs. In the 1741 to 1747 Parliament the Company had between four and seven directors, and 83 percent were affiliated with the Whigs.

Political connections helped to protect the Company's monopoly, but they could not prevent extractions, especially in times of fiscal crisis. In 1744 the Company was forced to lend £1,000,000 to King George II at 3 percent interest. It was reminiscent of earlier loans made by the Company in the reigns of Charles II, William, and Anne. In this case, Britain had been at war with Spain between 1739 and 1742 and then became involved in a broader European conflict, the War of the Austrian Succession, which lasted until 1748. The war was the most expensive that Britain had fought to that date, and the government's budget deficit rose by £9 million between 1740 and 1744 (Mitchell 1988, 575–78). The Company's £1 million loan helped to finance just over 10 percent of the deficit.

In return for the loan in 1744, the Company got an extension of their monopoly trading privileges until at least 1780.[24] Importantly, this commitment was upheld as there was no legislation changing the Company's trading privileges until 1781. In that year another charter act guaranteed the Company's monopoly until at least 1791, and it too was honored. In 1793 another charter act guaranteed the Company's monopoly until at least 1813. Thus by the mid-eighteenth century the Company's trading privileges came to be renegotiated in accordance with the law as defined by the provisions of

---

23. For details on the party affiliation of MPs, see Bogart (2016).
24. See House of Commons, *Public Income and Expenditure* (532).

the charter acts. The change is remarkable considering the Company's early history where its rights were renegotiated according to politics and finance. In this context, Britain had reached one of the first doorstep conditions, rule of law for elite organizations.

The relative security that the Company enjoyed was related to the evolution of Britain's politics. By the 1750s party strife had largely disappeared. The Whig party had held a majority in the Commons for over thirty-five years. Their long-time adversaries, the Tories, continued to challenge Whig policies, but according to Colley (1985) most remained loyal to the Hanoverian regime and did not seek to destabilize the political system. The Opposition Whigs lost influence by the late 1740s and many chose to join the majority Whigs by the 1750s. The transition from party strife under William and Anne to the stability of Hanoverian politics in the mid-eighteenth century has been described by historians as one of the most "striking changes in English history." According to Sutherland (1962, 18), stability was due to the "good sense and absence of rancor of the English landed and commercial classes" and to the skill and determination of Robert Walpole in consolidating and manipulating political power.

Greater fiscal capacity was the other long-term factor at work. Figures show that government tax revenue per capita increased by over 60 percent between 1690 and 1750. This was achieved through tax innovations, bureaucratic innovations, and political compromise (O'Brien and Hunt 1993; Cox 2011). The growth of tax revenues helped build fiscal capacity, but it was not sufficient to pay for Britain's wars. Public borrowing was necessary. The East India Company was forced to lend to the government in each of the wars up to 1750, but not during the Seven Years' War from 1756 to 1763. What changed? Arguably, one key development was the emergence of the Three Percent Consol, which was a redeemable, perpetual 3 percent annuity. As Neal (1993, 117) explains, there were several precedents to the Three Percent Consol from the 1720s. They allowed the Exchequer, Army, and Navy to issue bills in times of emergency and the bills could then be retired from the proceeds of selling new issues of perpetual annuities. Following the consol, the government had less need to seek emergency loans from the East India Company. Instead, it could rely on conventional borrowing backed by tax levies.

1.6   Survival of the East Indian Monopoly in the Late Eighteenth Century

The Company's trading monopoly survived the late eighteenth century. However, the monopoly could have ended earlier as the Company's charter expired in 1781 and 1791. This section examines why the monopoly was renewed several times. In this period, it is important to point out that the environment was quite different because the Company gained significant territorial possessions in India for the first time. Robert Clive, originally a company official and later a commander in the British Army, led a war against the Nawabs of Bengal in 1757. The end result was that the Company gained political control over Bengal, including its tax revenues by 1765. The new territorial revenues were vast and led to corruption and abuse by Company officials. Thereafter discussions of the Company's trading monopoly became intertwined with discussions of its territory in India.[25]

The added profits from Indian territories were immediately seen by the government as a new source of tax revenue. In 1767 and 1769 the Company was compelled to pay £400,000 annually to the government subject to conditions on the payment of dividends (Sutherland 1962). The Company made these payments for several years but then it ran into financial difficulties in 1773. The causes of financial distress were mainly due to the cost of war in India, but also partly to the new taxes levied by government. The end result was that the Company needed an emergency loan from the government, which they received in the amount of £1.4 million. The Company also got extended privileges over the tea trade in North America, which led to the famous Boston Tea Party. The crisis for the Company proved to be short lived, and it was able to repay the loan in 1777.

Financial transfers were again an issue in the negotiations over the renewal of the charter in 1781. Prime Minister Lord North proposed that the Company lend £2 million to the government in order to renew its monopoly for another term of years (Sutherland 1962, 340). The loan was deemed necessary in part because the government was facing a deficit problem due to the cost of the American Revolution. The Company did not react favorably to the proposal. Negotiations continued and in 1779 Lord North declared that the Company would need to lend £1.4 million to renew its monopoly. After being rebuffed, North threatened that he would terminate its charter following its expiration. In 1781 North's government dropped demands that the Company make a large loan. Instead it required the Company make a one-time payment of £400,000 and it required that all dividends beyond 8 percent had to be split three-fourths to the government and one-fourth to shareholders. The agreement was approved by the king and Parliament in the 1781 charter act (Sutherland 1962).

The Company did not pay all of the £400,000 owed to the government. Moreover, the Company's payment of customs duties went in arrears throughout the 1780s (House of Commons 1869, 553–34). There are at least two reasons why the government did not get more from the Company in the 1780s. First, the Company played a vital role in defending India against the French. Britain's rival sought to capture the territorial revenues of India, and their strong naval presence made the threat credible. The Company and

---

25. See Bowen (2005) and Stern (2011) for an analysis of the transition to territorial rule. Note also that there were two important acts in 1773 and 1784 that increased government control over the company in India.

the government coordinated military strategies, and it was agreed that the former would pay for the army in Asia (Bowen 2005, 46). Thus the government could not seriously challenge the Company at such a delicate moment for national defense.

Second, the Company came to be a bigger force in Parliament. The Company had more than 60 MPs in the Commons representing its interests by the 1780s (Philips 1961). It could pressure its MPs to support the opposition party if the Company's interests were sufficiently threatened. It is notable that the opposition in 1781, the Rockingham Whigs, rallied to support the Company when Lord North's government made its strongest threats. The Company's defense against government leader Charles James Fox provides another illustration. In 1783 Fox proposed a bill that would increase government control over the Company. Directors and shareholders formed a coalition with the king and defeated the bill in the House of Lords. The failure of Fox's India bill helped to bring down the governing coalition and paved the way for a new government led by William Pitt (Philips 1961, 24–25).

By the time of the negotiations over the charter renewal in 1792, the political environment evolved in a direction that was more troubling for the Company. For the first time, Liverpool merchants and Manchester manufacturers were particularly active in lobbying to open the export trade from Britain (Philips 1961, 75). Manchester's aim was to lower the cost of exporting cotton textiles to India. Liverpool had similar aims, but it also wanted exports to be shipped from its port rather than London, which was the hub of the Company's activity.

The lead negotiator for the government in 1792, Henry Dundas, was open to free trade in exports. But Dundas strongly favored the continuance of the Company's monopoly on imports because it was the best way to remit the Indian territorial surplus to England (Philips 1961, 73). To reach a compromise, Dundas proposed that the Company would retain its overall monopoly for another twenty years, but the Company would guarantee at least 3,000 tons a year for the export of British manufactured goods. This was not a large volume in comparison to the total, but it provided something to the Liverpool and Manchester interests. In the end, the 1793 Charter Act largely maintained the Company's monopoly. It did require the Company to repay its accumulated debts to the government to the amount of £500,000 per year, but only after making 10 percent dividend payments to its stockholders. Notably these debts went largely unpaid.[26]

The Company's relative success in the negotiations of 1792 is again related to their importance to national defense. War with France looked increasingly likely after its revolution, and the government needed the assistance of the Company to defend India. Another key factor was the Company's strength in Parliament and its connections with the government. Table 1.3 shows the

26. See House of Commons, *Public Income and Expenditure* (534).

Table 1.3   **The Company influence in Parliament**

Date (1)	EIC MPs (2)	EIC share of all MPs (3)	Govt. (4)	EIC MPs share with govt. (5)	EIC MPs share with opp. (6)	All MPs, share with govt. (7)	All MPs, share with opp. (8)
May 1784	57	0.1	Pitt	0.63	0.25	0.56	0.39
Aug. 1790	69	0.12	Pitt	0.51	0.36		
May 1796	69	0.12	Pitt	0.48	0.38		
Aug. 1802	93	0.14	Addington	0.4	0.32		
Apr. 1805	101	0.15	Pitt	0.37	0.34		
Dec. 1806	83	0.13	Grenville-Fox	0.4	0.22	0.47	0.14
June 1807	84	0.13	Portland	0.5	0.38	0.33	0.33
Apr. 1812	89	0.14	Perceval	0.57	0.38		
June 1813	87	0.13	Liverpool	0.28	0.31		
Aug. 1818	62	0.09	Liverpool	0.66	0.21	0.43	0.27

Sources: Company MPs are taken from Philips (1961, 307–35). The share of all MPs with the government coalition and opposition is taken from Evans (2014, 486).

Notes: Before 1801 the number of MPs was 558 and after 1801 the number is 658. Number of EIC MPs and government affiliation is taken from Philips (1961, 307–25). A selection of parliaments from Philips is analyzed. The list with some notes follows: May 1784 is after 1784 election and shortly before the Pitt India Act. Aug. 1790 is after 1790 election. May 1796 is just before 1796 election. Aug. 1802 is just after the general election of 1802. Apr. 1805 is after the change in ministry to Pitt. Dec. 1806 is just after 1806 general election. June 1807 is just after 1807 general election. June 1813 is after the 1812 election and at the same time as the Charter Act of 1813. Aug. 1818 is after the general election of 1818.

number of MPs representing the Company in the House of Commons, and their share of all MPs starting in 1784. Also reported is the government leader, the share of EIC MPs connected to the governing coalition, and the share of EIC MPs connected to the opposition. The data come from Philips (1961) and are drawn from parliamentary lists and Company records. To compare with the overall size of the governing coalition and opposition, columns (7) and (8) report the share of all MPs with each. According to Phillips' data, Company MPs were numerous and they were more connected to the governing coalition than the opposition. At the 1790 Parliament, when the charter was renewed, thirty-five or 51 percent of Company MPs sided with Pitt's government and twenty-five or 36 percent of its MPs sided with the opposition. These figures suggest that if the Company persuaded its thirty-five government MPs to withdraw support due to unfavorable negotiations, it could have significantly affected Pitt's ability to govern.

1.7   The Beginning of the End for the Company's Monopoly, 1813

The Charter Act of 1813 is one of the most significant events because it resulted in the Company losing its monopoly trading privileges to India. What changed? While there are many potential explanations for the opening of trade in 1813, several stand out. First, ideology on free trade evolved, especially the views of government officials. The philosophy of Liberal Toryism was born in this period, which among other things, articulated the economic benefits of free trade (Webster 2009). In 1811 Lord Melville, an important regulator of the Company, wrote a notable memo on free trade with India and the efficiency of competition:

> If the Company carry on their trade more expensively and with less activity and industry than private individuals, it is unjust to the country, as well as the inhabitants of British India, that the exclusive monopoly should be continued; and in such a state of things, the trade is more likely to be advantages to the country, and beneficial to the individuals in their hands, than in those of the Company: but if the latter shall conduct it with skill and enterprise, and with due and unremitting attention to economy, the extent of their capital, and the superior facilities which they must continue to possess, of providing their investment in India at the cheapest rate, will undoubtedly afford them the means of successful rivalship with all other competitors.[27]

Melville's views on opening the trade to India were shared by other government officials. Most notably, the views were shared by Lord Buckinghamshire, who was the lead negotiator for the government on the renewal of the charter in 1812 (Philips 1961, 184–86).

The government's position on opening the trade was also influenced by politics. Trading and manufacturing interests lobbied extensively to liberalize the trade in the charter renegotiation. Led by Liverpool and Manchester, 130 petitions were sent to Parliament arguing for the opening of trade in 1813 (Philips 1961, 184). Their campaign was better coordinated and more united than in 1791 (Webster 2009, 58). The government ultimately sided with the provincial manufacturing and trading interests and worked in Parliament to end the Company's monopoly with India. One reason is that the provincial manufacturing economy had grown significantly from 1791 to 1813, probably more than the London economy on which the Company's trade depended. Thus the government had to give more weight to provincial interests when making policy, otherwise they risked undermining the most dynamic part of the economy. Webster (2009, 59) also argues that rampant inflation in 1812 was raising concerns about riots in cities. As manufacturing was increasingly concentrated in cities, the government felt it could placate towns by opening trade.

A chance event also played a role in the Company losing its monopoly. The Company had a large number of MPs representing its interests in Parliament through the early 1800s. As shown in table 1.3, its MPs were also more likely to be connected to the government than the opposition. Most

---

27. Letter from Lord Melville to Chairman and Deputy of the East India Company, 1812, in *Papers Respecting the Negotiation with His Majesty's Ministers for a Renewal of the East-India Company's Exclusive Privileges* (80).

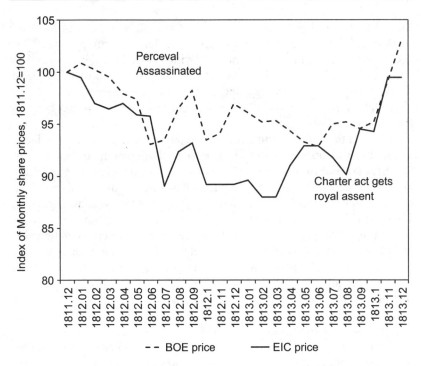

Fig. 1.1   Share prices of East India Company and Bank of England following assassination of Prime Minister Perceval

Sources: See text.
Notes: See text.

notably, the Company was highly connected to Prime Minister Perceval's government in April 1812 just prior to the charter renewal. But its connections changed dramatically after Perceval was assassinated on May 12, 1812. Lord Liverpool was named as the new prime minister in June, but he was unable to form a government. An election was held in October 1812, which led to a new governing coalition in the Commons. In the new parliament, which opened in November 1812, the Company had 87 MPs, but only 28 percent were affiliated with the government and 31 percent were affiliated with the opposition. This was much smaller than in April 1812. The Company's weak numbers seem to have hurt their cause when the trading provisions of the 1813 charter bill were being debated in the Commons. In a revealing statement, a director in the Company said, "I had no idea we stood on such weak ground . . . from that moment I felt myself humbled."[28]

The effects of Perceval's assignation can be seen in the Company's share price. Figure 1.1 shows an index of the Company's monthly price (EIC) from

28. Quoted in Philips (1961, 190).

the beginning of 1812 to the end of 1813. It also plots an index of the Bank of England share (BOE) price over the same dates for comparison.[29] The decline in the Company's share price following Perceval's assignation and the new election in October 1812 is evident. Relative to the Bank of England, the Company's stock declines by nearly 6.4 percent between the end of May 1812 and the end of March 1813 when the debate over the charter began in Parliament.

The evolution of government and company finances was a final factor in the move to open trade in 1813. East Indian customs duties were an important source of funding to the government for much of the Company's history. Table 1.4 shows the Company's customs revenues at decadal frequency from 1710 to 1810. The decadal figures are two-year averages (e.g., 1769 and 1770) to smooth some of the annual variation. Panel A in table 1.4 also reports Company customs for tea, all government customs revenues, and all government tax revenues for comparison. Company customs grow over time, as do all customs revenues and government tax revenues. There was an especially large increase in government revenues after the introduction of income taxes in the early 1800s. In panel B, the shares of Company customs revenues are shown. They rise as a share of all government customs and all government revenues up to 1770. Afterward, the Company customs decline as a share of both, especially between 1799 and 1810. Thus increasing government revenues meant that Company customs revenues were less important by 1813.

The rationale for taxing a monopoly East India Company made less sense in the post-1800 environment of greater fiscal capacity, but as noted earlier, the monopoly was only ended in the Indian trade in 1813. The monopoly in the China trade continued until 1833. One reason is that the Chinese trade was dominated by tea imports, and as table 1.4 shows, the customs revenue share from tea becomes substantial between 1799 and 1810. Customs from non-tea, which mainly came from Indian trade, fell sharply. Thus, in 1813 the monopoly was only eliminated in the trade whose fiscal importance declined. The government of 1813 still prized collecting tax revenues from monopolists in a thriving overseas trade.

1.8 Conclusion

Many markets in history are limited by laws and customs enforced by governing authorities. One prominent theory argues that the transition out of limited access requires a series of steps like rule of law for elites and the creation of perpetually lived organizations, or in other words, open markets. This chapter studies how these steps were taken in Britain in the case of the East Indian market. The Company had a legal monopoly over all trade

29. The stock price data come from Neal (1996).

Table 1.4   Company customs revenues and government tax revenues in pounds.

Year	EIC customs, all	EIC customs, tea	All govt. customs	All govt. revenues
		A.		
1710	253,544		1,223,542	5,213,518
1720	384,431		1,559,358	6,138,752
1730	407,853		1,562,552	6,172,649
1740	401,994		1,427,494	5,994,973
1750	no data		1,562,332	7,282,000
1760	528,637		2,152,422	9,400,926
1770	833,814		2,790,119	11,179,604
1780	619,438		2,896,433	12,901,965
1790	1,041,996	330,503	3,739,985	17,759,693
1799	1,443,811	579,685	5,898,699	29,364,292
1810	3,110,547	2,975,471	1,2010,816	66,830,560

	Share EIC customs in all customs	Share EIC in all govt. revenues	Share of EIC tea customs in all govt. revenues	Share of EIC non-tea customs in all govt. revenues
		B.		
1710	0.207	0.049		
1720	0.247	0.063		
1730	0.261	0.066		
1740	0.282	0.067		
1750				
1760	0.246	0.056		
1770	0.299	0.075		
1780	0.214	0.048		
1790	0.279	0.059	0.019	0.040
1799	0.245	0.049	0.020	0.029
1810	0.259	0.047	0.045	0.002

Sources: Chaudhuri (1978, 438), Bowen (2005), and Mitchell (1988).
Notes: From 1760, the EIC customs includes all customs including those coming from the company, private trade, and tea duties as distinguished in Bowen (2005).

between Britain and the East Indies, but its trading privileges were far from secure. The monarchy and Parliament authorized interlopers to enter the Company's market and it forced the Company to lend in order to retain its monopoly. The root causes behind these actions were the political instability and fiscal incapacity of British institutions in the seventeenth and early eighteenth centuries. The Company was part of the governing coalition, but its political connections diminished when the government changed. Credibility was also weakened by the fiscal system that evolved slowly to meet the costs of warfare.

A secure East Indian monopoly only emerged in the mid-eighteenth century when political stability and fiscal capacity increased. The Company's trading privileges were renegotiated only after the terms of the charter expired, and not according to the dictates of politics and finance. Thus after 1750 Britain was moving toward one of the doorstep conditions: rule of law for elites. However, the liberalization of the market had to wait several more decades. Monopoly remained stable because of the Company's strong political connections and also because the fiscal system had not yet reached full capacity. Further development of the fiscal system during the Napoleonic Wars, the growing influence of provincial manufacturing interests opposed to the Company's monopoly, and a negative shock to the Company's connections following an assassination brought the monopoly to an end in 1813.

The case of the East India Company described here has parallels in other markets. The Bank of England transitioned from a privileged monopoly to a central bank. Britain also liberalized access to the corporate form through general incorporation laws. In its wake, many banks and manufacturing companies were incorporated. Thus there was a broader movement toward open access throughout Britain from the mid-eighteenth century to the early nineteenth century. The consequences for economic development in Britain were substantial, yet as this case shows the process of development helped to undermine limited access. Growth of non-Indian taxes and the beginnings of the Industrial Revolution in Manchester and Liverpool played a role in bringing an end to the monopoly. The connection between economic development and the transition to open access needs to be further explored in Britain and other important historical cases.

References

Acemoglu, Daron, Simon Johnson, and James Robinson. 2005. "The Rise of Europe: Atlantic Trade, Institutional Change, and Economic Growth." *American Economic Review* 95:546–79.

Bogart, Dan. 2016. "Political Party Representation and Electoral Politics in England and Wales, 1690–1747." *Social Science History* 40 (2): 271–303.

Bowen, Huw V. 2005. *The Business of Empire: The East India Company and Imperial Britain, 1756–1833.* Cambridge: Cambridge University Press.

Broz, Lawrence, and Richard Grossman. 2004. "Paying for Privilege: The Political Economy of Bank of England Charters, 1694–1843." *Explorations in Economic History* 41:48–72.

Bruce, John. 1810. *Annals of the Honorable East India Company.* London: Black, Parry, and Kingsbury.

Carlos, Ann M., and Stephen Nicholas. 1988. "'Giants of an Earlier Capitalism': The Chartered Trading Companies as Modern Multinationals." *Business History Review* 62 (3): 398–419.

———. 1996. "Theory and History: Seventeenth-Century Joint-Stock Chartered Trading Companies." *Journal of Economic History* 56 (4): 916–24.

Carruthers, Bruce G. 1999. *City of Capital: Politics and Markets in the English Financial Revolution.* New York: Princeton University Press.

Charters Granted to the East-India Company From 1601, Also The Treaties and

Grants, Made with, or obtained from, the Princes and Powers in India, From the Year 1756 to 1772. (London, 1773).

Chaudhuri, K. N. 1965. *The English East India Company: The Study of an Early Joint Stock Company 1600–1640.* London: Kelley.

———. 1978. *The Trading World of Asia and the English East India Company 1660–1760.* Cambridge: Cambridge University Press.

Clark, Greg. 1996. "The Political Foundations of Modern Economic Growth: England, 1540–1800." *Journal of Interdisciplinary History* 26:563–88.

Colley, Linda. 1995. *In Defiance of Oligarchy: The Tory Party 1714–60.* Cambridge: Cambridge University Press.

Cox, Gary. 2011. "War, Moral Hazard and Ministerial Responsibility: England after the Glorious Revolution." *Journal of Economic History* 71:133–61.

———. "Was the Glorious Revolution a Constitutional Watershed?" *Journal of Economic History* 72:567–600.

Cruickshanks, Eveline, Stuart Handley, and D. W. Hayton. 2002. *The House of Commons 1690–1715.* Cambridge: Cambridge University Press.

Desai, Tripta. 1984. *The East India Company: A Brief Survey from 1599 to 1857.* New Delhi: Kanak Publications.

Dincecco, Mark. 2011. *Political Transformations and Public Finances: Europe, 1650–1913.* Cambridge: Cambridge University Press.

Evans, Eric J. 2014. *The Forging of the Modern State: Early Industrial Britain, 1783–1870.* London: Routledge.

Foster, William. 1904. "Charles I and the East India Company." *English Historical Review* 19:456–63.

———. 1929. "Introduction." In *A Calendar of the Court Minutes etc. of the East India Company*, edited by Ethel Bruce Sainsbury. Oxford: Oxford University Press.

Franke, Sophia Gollwitzer, and Marc Quintyn. 2014. "Doorsteps Toward Political and Economic Openness: Testing the North-Wallis-Weingast Transition Framework." *Emerging Markets Finance and Trade* 50:212–36.

Griffiths, Trevor, Philip Hunt, and Patrick O'Brien. 1991. "Political Components of the Industrial Revolution: Parliament and the English Cotton Textile Industry, 1660–1774." *Economic History Review* 44:395–423.

Hejeebu, Santhi. 2005. "Contract Enforcement in the English East India Company." *Journal of Economic History* 65 (2): 496–523.

Horwitz, Henry. 1978. "The East India Trade, the Politicians, and the Constitution: 1689–1702." *Journal of British Studies* 17:1–18.

———. 1997. *Parliament, Policy, and the Politics in the Reign of William III.* Manchester: Manchester University Press.

House of Commons. 1869. *Public Income and Expenditure*, part II. London: Her Majesty's Press.

Jha, Saumitra. 2005. "Financial Innovations and Political Development: Evidence from Revolutionary England." Working Paper, Graduate School of Business, Stanford University.

Johnson, Noel D., and Mark Koyama. 2014. "Tax Farming and the Origins of State Capacity in England and France." *Explorations in Economic History* 51:1–20.

Klerman, D., and P. G. Mahoney. 2005. "The Value of Judicial Independence: Evidence from Eighteenth Century England." *American Law and Economics Review* 7:1–27.

Matthew, Henry, Colin Gray, Brian Harrison, and R. James Long, eds. 2004. *The Oxford Dictionary of National Biography.* Oxford: Oxford University Press.

Mitchell, B. R. 1988. *British Historical Statistics.* Cambridge: Cambridge University Press.

Mokyr, Joel. 2009. *The Enlightened Economy: An Economic History of Britain.* New Haven, CT: Yale University Press.

Neal, Larry. 1993. *The Rise of Financial Capitalism: International Capital Markets in the Age of Reason.* Cambridge: Cambridge University Press.

———. 1996. "Course of the Exchange, London, 1698–1823 and Amsterdamsche Beurs, Amsterdam, 1723–1794. ICPSR01008-v1." Ann Arbor, MI: Inter-University Consortium for Political and Social Research [distributor], 1996-01-03. http://doi.org/10.3886/ICPSR01008.v1.

North, D. C., J. J. Wallis, S. B. Webb, and B. R. Weingast, eds. 2012. *In the Shadow of Violence: Politics, Economics, and the Problems of Development.* Cambridge: Cambridge University Press.

North, D. C., J. Wallis, and B. Weingast. 2009. *Violence and Social Orders: A Conceptual Framework for Interpreting Recorded Human History.* Cambridge: Cambridge University Press.

North, D. C., and B. Weingast. 1989. "Constitutions and Commitment: The Evolution of Institutions Governing Public Choice in Seventeenth-Century England." *Journal of Economic History* 49:803–32.

O'Brien, Patrick. 2001. "Fiscal Exceptionalism: Great Britain and Its European Rivals: From Civil War to Triumph at Trafalgar and Waterloo." Working Paper no. 65/01, Department of Economic History, London School of Economics.

O'Brien, Patrick, and Philip Hunt. 1993. "The Rise of the Fiscal State in England, 1485–1815." *Historical Research* 66:129–76.

Ottewill, W. T. 1929. "Introduction." In *A Calendar of the Court Minutes etc. of the East India Company,* 1674–76, 1677–79, edited by Ethel Bruce Sainsbury. Oxford: Oxford University Press.

Papers Respecting the Negotiation with His Majesty's Ministers for a Renewal of the East India Company's Exclusive Privileges. (London, 1813).

Philips, C. H. 1961. *The East India Company 1784–1834.* New York: Barnes and Noble.

Pincus, Steven. 2009. *1688: The First Modern Revolution.* New Haven, CT: Yale University Press.

Quinn, Stephen. 2001. "The Glorious Revolution's Effect on English Private Finance: A Micro-History, 1680–1705." *Journal of Economic History* 61:593–615.

———. 2008. "Securitization of Sovereign Debt: Corporations as a Sovereign Debt Restructuring Mechanism in Britain, 1694–1750." Available at SSRN: https://ssrn.com/abstract=991941.

Robins, Nick. 2006. *The Corporation that Changed the World.* London: Pluto.

Scott, W. R. 1912. *The Constitution and Finance of English, Scottish, and Irish. Joint-Stock Companies to 1720,* vol. II. Cambridge: Cambridge University Press.

Sedgwick R. 1970. *The House of Commons 1715–1754.* Oxford: Oxford University Press.

Stasavage, David. 2003. *Public Debt and the Birth of the Democratic State: France and Great Britain, 1688–1789.* Cambridge: Cambridge University Press.

Stern, Philip J. 2011. *The Company-State: Corporate Sovereignty and the Early Modern Foundations of the British Empire in India.* Oxford: Oxford University Press.

Sussman, N., and Y. Yafeh. 2006. "Institutional Reforms, Financial Development and Sovereign Debt: Britain 1690–1790." *Journal of Economic History* 66:906–35.

Sutherland, Lucy. 1962. *The East India Company in Eighteenth Century Politics.* Oxford: Oxford University Press.

Watson, Paula, and Perry Gauci. 2002. "Shepheard, Samuel I (c. 1648–1719), of St. Magnus the Martyr, and Bishopsgate Street, London," In *The History of Parlia-*

ment: the House of Commons 1690–1715, edited by E. Cruickshanks, S. Handley, and D. W. Hayton. Cambridge: Cambridge University Press.

Webster, Tony. 2009. *The Twilight of the East India Company: The Evolution of Anglo-Asian Commerce and Politics, 1790–1860*. Suffolk, UK: Boydell & Brewer.

Wells, J., and D. Wills. 2000. "Revolution, Restoration, and Debt Repudiation: The Jacobite Threat to England's Institutions and Economic Growth." *Journal of Economic History* 60:418–41.

Zahedieh, Nuala. 2010. "Regulation, Rent-Seeking, and the Glorious Revolution in the English Atlantic Economy." *Economic History Review* 63:865–90.

Adam Smith's Theory of Violence and the Political Economics of Development

Barry R. Weingast

2.1 Introduction

What accounts for the differing levels of opulence across countries? Why do so many countries fail to achieve high standards of living? In short, what accounts for the differences in the "wealth of nations"? Smith poses this issue as a puzzle in both Book III of *The Wealth of Nations* and in his *Lectures on Jurisprudence* (*LJ*):[1] "Given the important effects of the division of labour, what an immediate tendency it has to improve the arts, it appears somewhat surprizing that every nation should continue so long in a poor and indigent state" (*LJ*(B), 521). With persistently high levels of poverty throughout the world (Collier 2007), these questions are as relevant today as they were in Smith's time. So too, I argue, are Smith's answers.

Smith's approach is complex and multifaceted, and has yet to be fully understood. On the economic side, his answer is well known and includes the division of labor, capital accumulation, and the absence laws and regulations that encumber competition and markets, such as mercantilism and barriers to free trade.[2]

Yet Smith did not confine himself to economic issues when addressing the problem of development, instead turning also to politics. In *The Wealth of*

Barry R. Weingast is a senior fellow of the Hoover Institution and the Ward C. Krebs Family Professor in the Department of Political Science at Stanford University.

The author gratefully acknowledges Anthony Endres, Timothy Guinnane, Glory Liu, Naomi Lamoreaux, Margaret Levi, Emma Rothschild, and John Wallis for helpful comments. For acknowledgments, sources of research support, and disclosure of the author's material financial relationships, if any, please see http://www.nber.org/chapters/c13509.ack.

1. Abbreviations for Smith's works are given at the end of the text, just before the references.
2. See, for example, Aspromourgos (2009), Eltis (1975), Hollander (1973), Myint (1977), O'Brien ([1975] 2004), and Rothschild and Sen (2006).

Nations, Smith discusses two interrelated institutions as impeding medieval European development: feudalism in Book III and the Catholic Church in Book V. I study the first in this chapter and provide an interpretation of the second from the same perspective in Weingast (2017). Smith's discussion of the transformation of feudalism and the growth of the commercial society hinges on politics, political exchange, and violence.[3]

As I shall demonstrate, violence is central to Smith's approach to development, especially the failure to develop. Just as modern scholars of development systematically underappreciate problems of violence (see North, Wallis, and Weingast 2009), scholars studying Adam Smith have systematically ignored or underappreciated the importance of violence in his theories of economics, politics, and development. Smith does not provide a systematic, abstract theory about the role of violence. Smith instead embeds his analysis of the political economics of development of Western Europe in a narrative, so the underlying theory is easy to miss.[4] Nonetheless, we can extract a theory of Smith's political economics of development from his many discussions of this topic, especially, his analyses of European history from the fall of Rome through the rise of the commercial society.[5] Smith's analysis represents what economists and political scientists call applied theory—or, in this case, an "analytic narrative" (Bates et al. 1998)—explaining the evolution of Western Europe from the fall of Rome to Smith's time.

Violence is a principal impediment to economic growth in Smith's approach. Moreover, violence arises in multiple ways; it can occur within a society as different lords, factions, religions, or regions fight one another, from hostile neighbors. It also occurs when the government plunders its citizenry. Smith's answer to the puzzle of the "slow progress of opulence" or the lack of economic development involves violence, especially in the form of government plunder: "The causes of ['slow progress of opulence'] may be considered under these two heads, first, natural impediments [such as geography], and secondly, the oppression of civil government" (*LJ*(B), 521).

Smith explains the unfortunate effects of incentives fostered by violence and the "oppression of the civil government": "In those unfortunate countries, indeed, where men are continually afraid of the violence of their superiors, they frequently bury and conceal a great part of their stock [i.e., capi-

---

3. Skinner (1975, 168), in his famous characterization of Smith's argument about development, concludes that "the motivation behind many of the most important changes was in fact political rather than simply economic."

4. Most economists studying the history of economic thought dismiss *WN*, Book III, one of the main sources of Smith's theory of political development in *The Wealth of Nations*. See, for example, Blaug (1978), Brue and Grant (2007), and Robbins (1998). Although Schumpeter (1954, 187) observed that "This third Book did not attract the attention it seems to merit," he devotes only two other sentences to this topic. Skinner (1975, 1996) is an obvious exception.

5. Smith presents sustained historical analyses in *WN*, Book III, in Book V on the medieval church, and in both *LJ*(A) and *LJ*(B).

tal], in order to have it always at hand to carry with them to some place of safety, in case of their being threatened with any of those disasters to which they consider themselves as at all times exposed" (*WN* II.i.30–31, 284–85).

The purpose of this chapter is to develop Smith's answer to the questions asked at the outset about the differences in the wealth of nations. His analysis can be summarized as follows. The invasions of the Roman Empire ultimately forced it to collapse, and with it, the Roman system of property rights, division of labor, and exchange. Smith characterizes the consequences of the invasions and the violent environment that followed, "The rapine and violence which the barbarians exercised against the antient inhabitants, interrupted the commerce between the towns and the country. The towns were deserted, and the country was left uncultivated, and the western provinces of Europe, which had enjoyed a considerable degree of opulence under the Roman empire, sunk into the lowest state of poverty and barbarism" (*WN* III.ii.1, 381–82).

Eventually, the feudal form of governance arose.[6] In this system, land represented the means to power, wealth, and security. Violence, as Smith emphasizes, was a constant presence. The most powerful lords typically obtained the largest and best land, allowing them to support many retainers and large armies. The lords constantly fought each other and the king. All organizations in the feudal era were closely connected to the state and supported the ability of the king and lords to project force.

The feudal society can be characterized by the "violence trap" (Cox, North, and Weingast 2017),[7] which works as follows. Economic growth requires both capital accumulation and economic integration that accompany an increasing division of labor; moreover, economic integration raises the costs of fighting. But violence threatens the value of the investments necessary for economic integration, especially integration across regions or factions that might fight each other. Smith again and again explains that, given the risk of violence, rational investors will not invest in economic integration:

> In the infancey of society, as has been often observed, government must be weak and feeble, and it is long before it's authority can protect the industry of individuals from the rapacity of their neighbours. When people find themselves every moment in danger of being robbed of all they possess, they have no motive to be industrious. There could be little accumulation of stock, because the indolent, which would be the greatest number, would

---

6. Smith argues that allodial arrangements arose following the fall of Rome. Eventually the feudal system replaced the allodial one. My analysis begins at this point, once the feudal system has been established (*WN* III).

7. Poverty traps are common in economics as explanations of the persistence of poverty and the lack of economic development (Azariadis and Stachurski [2005] provide a recent survey).

live upon the industrious, and spend whatever they produced. Nothing can be more an obstacle to the progress of opulence. (*LJ*(B), 522)

Given these incentives, the violence trap is self-sustaining and difficult to escape; most incremental changes—a modest increase in investment or economic integration—are insufficient to escape the trap.[8] Set in the context of Smith's arguments about violence, Smith's logic reflects the violence trap. Hence the feudal equilibrium of violence and low growth was stable.

How did Western Europe escape the violence trap? According to Smith, the rise of towns represented the essential step in the political-economic development of Europe. In the midst of the feudal equilibrium, the king and town (small groups of traders) engaged in a political exchange, forming a coalition against their common enemy, the local lords. The king granted the towns rights of self-governance, control over a wide array of local organizations, trading, and defense in exchange for taxes and military service. The new system represented a nonincremental change that simultaneously produced liberty, commerce, and security, allowing the town to escape the violence trap and a positive feedback system with increasing returns.[9]

As the towns grew, they extended their reach into the countryside, transforming self-sufficient agriculture into communities with specialists producing food and raw materials for the towns and, often, long-distance trade. A necessary component of the towns' escape from the violence trap is that the towns gained military superiority relative to the local lords. This superiority allowed them to protect property rights, trade, amass wealth, and grow opulent while defending themselves against the arbitrary exactions and rapacious violence of the local lords—and also the king.

To explain the towns' escape from the violence of the feudal basic natural state, we need two different but complementary arguments, one at the microinstitutional level involving organizations, one at the macroinstitutional level involving political exchange, and the (small "c") constitution. Addressing changes at both the micro and macro level is necessary to understand the rise of and economic growth of towns.

This chapter proceeds as follows: In the second section, I present elements of Smith's theories of the political economics of development. Section 2.3 presents Smith's theory of the feudal equilibrium, explaining why feudalism was stable even though it prevented growth. Section 2.4 provides a deeper understanding of violence and its implications for Smith's work. Sections

---

8. Smith understood the logic of poverty traps. For example, he argued that: "This is one great cause of the slow progress of opulence in every country; till some stock be produced there can be no division of labour, and before a division of labour take place there can be very little accumulation of stock" (*LJ*(B) 287, 522).

9. "Increasing Returns and Economic Progress"—the title of Young's (1928) well-known paper—have long been a part of the literature on Smith. See also the "virtuous circle" of Macfarlane (2000) and Rothschild and Sen (2006, 334–37).

2.5 and 2.6 explain his theory of the towns' escape from that equilibrium. My conclusions follow.

2.2   Elements of Smith's Theory of the Political Economics of Development

In Book III of *The Wealth of Nations*, and in parallel sections of his *Lectures on Jurisprudence*, Adam Smith provides a theory of the political economics of development of Western Europe. The theory is easy to miss because Smith embeds his approach in a historical narrative. A small but important group of Smith scholars examine Book III carefully, helping to extract Smith's theoretical argument. In this section, I draw on these works to explore several general theoretical propositions about the political economics of development proposed by Smith in his historical jurisprudence focusing on Western Europe.[10]

In reporting on Smith's understanding of development in Western Europe, I take the history as Smith conceived it, not as we think of these events today. Indeed, the importance of Smith's history is not its fidelity with actual fact, but how Smith uses it to devise a theoretical explanation for the events of this era.

2.2.1   Violence

Adam Smith understood violence to be a first-order problem hindering development; any solution to the development problem, therefore, had to involve limiting violence. Smith studies several types of violence, including predation by the government, plunder by neighbors, and invasions by distant foes. These sources of violence reduce the incentives for industry, saving, investment, and specialization. To develop, a society must therefore mitigate these sources of violence.

2.2.2   The Feudal Equilibrium

Smith shows why the violence of the feudal era created a stable political-economic equilibrium of very low growth. The high level of violence forced a particular form of economic, political, and social organization with the ability to protect local communities and to project force when the occasion arose. The rules of the game were designed to further the decentralized military organization of local government. As argued in section 2.4, property rights in land, the most valuable asset in medieval times, were designed to promote security and other military goals, not economic efficiency.

---

10. See, for example, Skinner (1975), Winch (1978, ch. 4), Moss (1979), Haakonssen (1981, 165–71), Henderson (2006, chs. 7–8), Aspromourgos (2009, ch. 5), Hont (2009, 2015), and Kennedy (2010, chs. 5, 8, and 9).

The institutions of feudalism, including property rights, had economic consequences. Because of the risk of violence and plunder, people rationally avoided hard work, initiative, savings, and investment. "[T]he occupiers of land in the country were exposed to every sort of violence. But men in this defenceless state naturally content themselves with their necessary subsistence; because to acquire more might only tempt the injustice of their oppressors" (*WN* III.iii.12, 405).[11] As we will see, Smith's views of the feudal equilibrium were a form of a violence trap of no growth (Cox, North, and Weingast 2017). The constant risk of violence deterred investment and hence economic growth. Given the omnipresent security concerns, incremental steps at reform were inadequate to alter this setting.

2.2.3   Political Exchange and the Escape from the Violence Trap

Smith explains that the escape from the violence trap was nonincremental. King and town made an alliance against their common enemies, the local lords. The political exchange accompanying the alliance redefined rights and political authority; this exchange therefore encompassed an explicit revision of the constitution governing the towns. The alliance made the king more powerful—through revenue and military service from the towns—and the towns gained a nonincremental increase in control over their own destiny.

Smith suggests three necessary conditions for the growth of towns following the political exchange with the king. These features of town organization reflect the creation of market infrastructure that constitute "the economic role of political institutions" (Weingast 1995). The first required that the town became capable of providing for its security. Given the plunder of the great landholders, the towns' survival required that they gain a local advantage in fighting. Without this advantage, the towns could not have fended off plunder. Commerce was also necessary, for it provided the gains from exchange and hence the engine of town growth. With growth came the means for financing the towns' public goods and market infrastructure such as order, security, and justice, including strong property rights. Liberty—in the form of strong property rights, a system of justice, and the absence of predation—was also necessary; liberty provided economic actors, for example, with the incentives to save, invest, and take initiative.

The new arrangements were not solely a reconfiguration of existing feudal organization. They represented both a nonincremental change in the nature of organizations and of the tools available for the towns' organizations. Towns created the organizations of a working government, including court systems, guilds, governing bodies, military organizations, and various business organizations.

---

11. Further, a "person who can acquire no property, can have no other interest but to eat as much, and to labour as little as possible" (*WN* III.ii.9, 387–88).

2.3 The Feudal Equilibrium, or the "Lowest State of Poverty and Barbarism"

Smith argued that violence was the principal impediment to both economic growth and the escape from poverty.[12] Smith applied his approach to the history of the West from prehistoric times to his own (*LJ*). Along the way, he discusses the impediments to greater opulence.

I begin with Smith's observations about the consequences of the fall of Rome. For several centuries prior to the invasions, the Roman Empire sustained sufficient security to foster a substantial division of labor, specialization and exchange, and hence opulence. The various invasions destroyed this stability, with disastrous economic effects.

Having displaced the Romans, the invaders settled down. Property in this world was more than an economic asset. As the principal means of supporting warriors, property also represented power. Those who held higher quality and larger tracts of land commanded larger armies.

No one, Smith says, could keep the peace. Kings were insufficiently powerful to enforce their authority, law, and order throughout their domain. The result was violence and disorder. The great lords "were always at war with each other and often with the king, their whole power depended on the service of their retainers and tenants" (*LJ*(A) iv.126–27, 249).

At the microinstitutional level, this setting had implications for local political-economic organization. Because kings could not keep the peace within their realm, they were forced of necessity to concede local political control to the lords (*LJ*(A) iv.119, 246). The great landlords ruled their territory, serving as executive, legislature, and judge; they also led their tenants in war.[13] This setting did not encourage markets or economic growth.

Smith characterized the feudal world as violent and predatory, with little overall growth. Most people lived at subsistence, with minimal degrees of trade, division of labor, and specialization and exchange. Centered around the manor, the local agrarian economy was largely self-sufficient and based on custom with little monetary exchange. The local lord captured most of the local surplus, converting it into security through local military organization (North and Thomas 1973) and by dividing the surplus among retainers in exchange for various service obligations, especially military obligations.

---

12. This section draws on work of: Aspromourgos (2009, ch. 5), Bell (1992), Haakonssen (1981, 165–71), Henderson (2006, chs. 7–8), Hollander (1979), Hont ([1989] 2005), Kennedy (2010, chs. 5, 8, and 9), Winch (1978, ch. 4), and especially Skinner's (1975) classic treatment.

13. "In those disorderly times, every great landlord was a sort of petty prince. His tenants were his subjects. He was their judge, and in some respects their legislator in peace, and their leader in war. He made war according to his own discretion, frequently against his neighbours, and sometimes against his sovereign" (*WN* III.ii.3, 383).

Investment, in Smith's view, was generally fruitless because of violence and predation. Indeed, to invest, improve, and better one's condition was to become a target of plunder. Violence and plunder meant that people focused on subsistence "because to acquire more might only tempt the injustice of their oppressors" (*WN* III.iii.12, 405). Those working the land could not acquire property. They had little incentive to work hard, indeed to work at all beyond their own maintenance (*WN* III.ii.9, 387–88).

More generally, Smith argues that to be independent individuals and groups needed to be powerful—that is, to possess their own violence potential to protect themselves from the violence of others. If they did not possess power, they were forced to ally with a powerful group for mere survival (*WN* III.iii.8, 401).

Access to organizations in this world was limited. In a primitive subsistence economy, economic and military organizations were parallel. The church was also an organization of organizations, but Smith separates his discussion of the church from his discussion of feudalism and the growth of towns.[14] As just noted, government was not well articulated, but centered on the local lords, who ran the local polity as their personal property.

More generally, the economic organization under the lords paralleled the military hierarchy. The great lords commanded considerable land. They granted rights to work the land to their vassals and their dependents. Members of the hierarchy who were also part of the military organization oversaw the local economic production on the land gained from the king. As Smith observes, these men were specialists in violence, not professional managers of agriculture estates and production.

2.3.1   Economic Effects of the Feudal Equilibrium

At the macroinstitutional level, violence and predation had clear economic effects. The violence associated with the invasions and the fall of the Roman Empire produced a downward economic spiral as exchange—the basis for the division of labor and hence of opulence—became risky and vulnerable. Trade and communication fell precipitously. Speaking of the great lords, Smith says: "Their lawless and freebooting manner of life also destroyed all the commerce and industry of the former inhabitants, who were obliged to leave the cities and seek possessions and protection in the lands of the several lords" (*LJ*(A) iv.124, 248). Put simply, plunder inhibited political-economic development.[15]

---

14. For example, in *The Wealth of Nations*, Smith discusses feudalism and the rise of towns in Book III and the church in Book V.

15. "In a rude state of society there are no great mercantile or manufacturing capitals. The individuals who hoard whatever money they can save, and who conceal their hoard, do so from a distrust of the justice of government, from a fear that if it was known that they had a hoard, and where that hoard was to be found, they would quickly be plundered" (*WN* V.iii.9, 911).

2.4   A Deeper Understanding of Violence and Its Implications for Smith's Arguments

Violence is a strategy by which some groups obtain resources through plundering the efforts of others (Hirschleifer 1994; Dixit 2004).[16] In what follows, I draw on the conceptual framework in North, Wallis, and Weingast (2009), as extended by Cox, North, and Weingast (2017). As Cox, North, and Weingast show, intrastate violence is remarkably high in today's developing world. Violent takeover of leadership, for example, occurs once every seven years for the median developing country in the poorest half of the distribution of countries by income. From Smith's discussion, the feudal world was, if anything, more violent.

2.4.1   The Logic of Violence

The framework holds that developing states, past and present, must devise a means of mitigating the manifestation of violence, even if they cannot rid themselves of multiple and independent sources of violence. How they do so affects their ability to develop. As with all developing countries, past and present, the feudal organization was a natural state. The two central features of natural states are that there exists multiple individuals and groups with violence potential, and that these states limit violence by inducing individuals and groups with violence potential to cooperate rather than fight. The principal mechanism is rent creation. Natural states create and limit access to privileges, state services, and organizations; to create and support these rents, they limit competition in seemingly endless ways.

Natural states use these rents to induce cooperation. They distribute the rents to powerful individuals and groups with violence potential. Because violence typically lowers rents, rents targeted to those with violence potential makes the latter better off than fighting. North, Wallis, and Weingast (2009) call these societies natural states because they have been by far the dominant way of organizing states throughout history, and this observation remains so today.

A simple bargaining model of the natural state helps elucidate the natural state logic (see Cox, North, and Weingast 2017). Suppose two groups with violence potential compete for control of the state and its potential for producing surplus. The two groups face a choice; they may either fight or

---

16. Students of development fail to systematically incorporate violence in their approaches (as North, Wallis, and Weingast [2009] emphasize). For example, almost all models of the political development of the state assume that the state is a unified actor with monopoly control on violence (Barzel 2002; Bates 2001; Levi 1988; North 1981, ch. 5; Olson 1993; Tilly 1992). This reads the solution to the problem of multiple sources of intrastate violence back into history long before the problem was solved. These models therefore cannot explain the emergence of the modern, developed state with a monopoly on violence since they assume the result from the outset. To understand this aspect of development we must start elsewhere.

bargain to an agreement. The two groups may differ in their military capacities, so the probability that each wins a fight may differ. Finally, fighting is costly, so each pays a price to exercise violence. The bargaining approach implies that each group can assess their expected value of fighting.

To maintain peace and cooperation among the powerful, the *no-fight conditions* must hold: that is, the rents each receives from the natural state must exceed the expected value of fighting. If the no-fight conditions hold for both groups, then both are better off cooperating. Under these conditions, the natural state is a stable equilibrium, at least in the short term. In contrast, if the no-fight condition fails for either group, then this group is better off resorting to violence, so peace and cooperation is not an equilibrium in the natural state. The no-fight conditions also imply that more powerful groups—those with larger expected values of fighting—must, in turn, receive more privileges and rents to make cooperation the preferred choice over fighting.

This bargaining framework has a dynamic element. As North (2005) observed, the world is constantly changing, even nonergodic. All states experience episodic shocks, such as changes in relative prices, changes in military technology, or the appearance of a hostile and threatening neighboring regime. In natural states, these shocks often alter the relative power of groups with violence potential.

Sufficiently large shocks in a natural state's environment alter the distribution of relative power so that the no-fight conditions no longer hold. These shocks break down the old bargaining agreement so that the parties must bargain to reallocate benefits or risk violence. Absent any change in the allocation of benefits, at least one group now prefers to fight.

What happens next depends on information and incentives. If the effects of the shock on power are common knowledge, then it is possible for the two parties to reach a new bargaining agreement to prevent violence by transferring some rents and privileges from one player to the other. To succeed, the renegotiation must reestablish the no-fight conditions given the new circumstances.

Yet peaceful adjustment is not always possible. A problem arises when the common knowledge assumption about the effects of a shock fails. In this case, three major problems hinder renegotiation: low economic costs of violence, commitment problems, and asymmetric information. For example, given uncertainty about the implications of a shock, asymmetric information may lead one party to believe itself far more powerful after a shock than the second party believes the first to be. If so then the minimum bargain the first is willing to accept can be higher than the maximum the other is willing to grant. As Fearon (1995) demonstrates in his classic paper on war, fighting is inevitable under these circumstances (see also Powell 1999; Muthoo 1999).

Implications of the Framework for Political-Economic Development

The main value of the bargaining framework is that it helps us to understand the role of violence in Smith's approach to the failure of opulence. Put simply, a violence trap prevents nearly all natural states from developing, feudalism in particular. The need to solve the problem of distributed violence potential leads natural states to policies creating rents and limiting access to organizations. These policies are necessary to establish the no-fight conditions. They also prevent development. An important route to both development and nonviolence is greater economic integration, which raises the costs of intrastate violence. But in the face of distributive violence potential, investments in greater economic integration are risky; their value falls precipitously in the event of violence.

Herein lies the violence trap. Economic integration is necessary to raise the costs of violence, but people will not make investments in economic integration because the threat of violence makes the investments too risky. These states are caught in a low-growth, low-investment, nondevelopment equilibrium. The great difficulty for development is moving from the violence trap to economic integration and development.

2.4.2   The Feudal Equilibrium as a Violence Trap

We can understand why violence is an impediment to growth and development. The form of property rights, the degree of open access to organizations, and, generally, the political manipulation of markets reflect the degree of violence in a society. Societies secure from violence threats are capable of producing property rights in which economic agents have incentives to invest in physical, financial, and human capital. An expanding division of labor and economic integration follows. In contrast, societies that face an everyday threat of violence must organize themselves differently. In very violent societies, leaders and landholders must of necessity be a warrior class, not economic managers. To support military organization, Smith explains, property rights in land must differ considerably from those that maximize the value of production. Rights develop that foster the ability of the lord to project force.

The bargaining model discussed in the previous subsection applies to the feudal setting. Regularly changing circumstances, asymmetric information, and the absence of credible commitments plagued the possibility of agreements to maintain peace. In modern terms, the feudal society represented an equilibrium in the sense that, though the fortunes of individual lords changed over time, the basic structure of the political and economic arrangements remained stable.

At the microinstitutional level, military competition drove the economic, political, and social organizational structure. The constant threat to security meant that lords who failed to capture most of the surplus and use it to maintain their violence potential became vulnerable. The feudal organization thus had features of an arms race. All the lords would be better off if they could, somehow, agree not to fight and to invest instead. But this bargain was vulnerable to defection. A single lord who continued to extract maximum rents for military purposes had a military advantage over other lords who did not. Further, because the king was insufficiently powerful, he could not easily subdue a large coalition of the lords. Their bargain-distributing political power reflected this fact; hence, the king was forced to allow the lords political control over their domains.

The militarized environment had implications for the macroinstitutional level; this environment afforded few gains from specialization and exchange, and it also limited the possible organizations. The main agricultural products, such as grain, could not be carried profitably far over land. The absence of a state that could provide order and security (*WN* III.iv.9, 418) meant great risks to specialization and exchange as transporting items risked being stolen in the attempt.

Virtually all secular organizations had to be associated with the local lord, or else they were destroyed or captured with their assets expropriated. As described by Smith, the feudal equilibrium reflects the logic of the natural state. Outside of the church, organizations existed largely to the extent they strengthened the violence capacity of the local lords.[17] The feudal hierarchy illustrates this, with its comingling of the organization of military force, the system of vassalage, the nature of rights in land (discussed in the next subsection), and the form of labor organization (which Smith considers a form of slavery). All these organizational elements reflected the feudal logic of violence. As we have seen, this environment of political opportunism and predation provided poor incentives for saving and investment. Violence prevented the accumulation of stock, without which the economy could not grow.

The bargaining approach discussed in the previous subsection suggests that the rents and privileges were distributed according to the no-fight conditions and adjusted as shocks and changing circumstances required. When bargaining failed to make adjustments according to the no-fight conditions, violence occurred. Agreements between lords and the king, among lords, or between lords and their retainers were constantly broken or adjusted unilaterally. Increases in inclusion could occur only if it reflected new sources of violence potential.

In North, Wallis, and Weingast's (2009) terms, regular violence meant the absence of perpetuity and impersonality. Perpetual institutions stand in the way of natural state adjustments to changing circumstances, and impersonality implied violations to the no-fight conditions. The natural state

---

17. I discuss Smith's argument about the church's coexistence with the secular lords in Weingast (2017).

bargaining setting requires regular adjustment of the rules and privileges to changing circumstances. The failure of perpetuity and impersonality, in turn, meant the absence of the rule of law in natural states (Weingast 2010). Needless to say, this world was poor, violent, and undeveloped.

2.4.3   Property Rights in Land

At the microinstitutional level, land represented power in the feudal society. The form of property rights and the organizations supported by the feudal system was central to the feudal society's survival.[18] The form of rights privileged security needs over efficiency. In Smith's argument, the rights in land are endogenous to the larger feudal environment. He explains why modern, private property rights in land could not be sustained. Moreover, the form of property directly affected—and limited—the types of organizations that could be sustained.

Modern, developed open-access orders have a complex system of legal infrastructure that facilitates exchange and efficient allocation of land based on a strong system of property rights. Some of the characteristics of this legal infrastructure include: (a) strong protections from expropriation and plunder by the state and by others; (b) a system of titling, ownership rules, and a judiciary to enforce them; (c) the right to devise property by will among heirs; (d) rights of free alienation of land with an absence of encumbrances on selling the land and to whom the land may be sold; and (e) a legal system that enforces contacts, including the exchange of land (see, e.g., Posner 2006; Barzel 1997; Alston et al. 2016). Each of these characteristics facilitates the exchange of land from lower- to higher-valued users; in particular, to individuals who would improve the land.

The feudal system of property rights in land involved none of these characteristics. The problem of violence and the need to support military organizations to maintain security forced wholesale deviations from the set of characteristics just outlined. Lords regularly fought one another, and the winners often forced the losers to transfer portions of their land; condition (a) therefore failed. The absence of a government and a judicial system implies that conditions (b) and (c) failed.

Security required that a wide range of restrictions be imposed on the right of property holders to alienate their property or to devise property by will. In particular, *primogeniture* arose, preventing the division of the land among several sons; so too did *entails*, which prevented a landowner from dividing his property and alienating some of the pieces. The feudal system of land rights dramatically restricted the transfer of land from low-valued users to higher-valued users, and, also, of markets to engineer movement toward the optimal organization of parcels and generally more efficient production.

---

18. The discussion of Smith's views of property rights in land draws on Aspromourgos (2009, ch. 5) and Henderson (2006, ch. 8).

Smith explains why this system was stable. The logic involves violence, especially the failure of conditions (c) and (d).[19] In economies where land is largely a means of subsistence, characteristics of land law can reflect characteristics (a)–(e) noted above. In contrast, "when land was considered as the means, not of subsistence merely, but of power and protection, it was thought better that it should descend undivided. . . . The security of a landed estate, therefore, the protection which its owner could afford to those who dwelt on it, depended upon its greatness. To divide it was to ruin it, and to expose every part of it to be oppressed and swallowed up by the incursions of its neighbours" (*WN* III.ii.3, 382–83). Smith's central insight is the conclusion in the last sentence: to divide the land was to ruin it as a means of security.

The relationship between lord and retainer, organizations, and power all centered around land. The feudal society bundled rights to land with service obligations to the lord as part of the organization of the feudal hierarchy. Individuals did not own the land in the modern sense of clear title with an absence of the ability of the government or other individuals to force the property holder to give up the land. Instead, the organization of economic production paralleled the military organization.

Many of the most inimical features of feudalism's rights in land can be explained by their role in supporting violence potential. These constraints on property improved local security even though they harmed the local economy by restricting land from moving to higher-valued uses. Adam Smith argued that the emergence, role, and stability of primogeniture, entails, and wardship all improved a lord's ability to project force and maintain local security.[20]

Primogeniture prevented lords from dividing their property among many heirs, requiring instead that all of a lord's property go to his firstborn son. In the violent feudal society, primogeniture enhanced security. One larger parcel had clear advantages, in Smith's account, to the same land divided up into many smaller parcels. Because each locality had to provide for its own security, small properties were not secure. They "could not defend [themselves] and must be entirely dependent on the assistance of some of the neighbouring great men . . . [A]s the only security in the other case was from the strength of the possessor, small property could be in no security" (*LJ* i.130–31, 55). Smith then draws the main implication: "If therefore an estate which when united could easily defend itself against all its neighbours should be divided in the same manner as moveables were, that is, equally

---

19. The example of the deviation of rights in land from those best suited to markets to those best suited for feudalism illustrates Smith's contention that Europe did not take the natural path to opulence, but deviated from that path considerably (*WN* III.i.8–9, 380).

20. Ober and Weingast (forthcoming) show that ancient Sparta failed to employ this form of property rights. Over a series of generations, Sparta lost the ability to defend itself.

betwixt all the brothers, it would be in no state of equality with those to whom it was before far superior" (*LJ* i.131, 55).

The same logic applies to entails. If primogeniture preserved a lord's estate at time of death, entails preserved the estate during the lord's life. Entails "preserve[d] a certain lineal succession, of which the law of primogeniture first gave the idea, and to hinder any part of the original estate from being carried out of the proposed line either by gift, or devise, or alienation; either by the folly, or by the misfortune of any of its successive owners" (*WN* III. ii.5, 384).

Wardship, the practice whereby the king or lord appointed another the right to use the land of an estate while an heir remained a minor, provides a variant on this logic. Though hated by the landed elite, wardship represented a solution to an important security problem. Recall that vassals of a lord held land by virtue of an exchange to supply military and other services. A problem arose when an heir as ward could not meet the feudal obligations associated with his land. Wards could not provide the required leadership of the estate's military organization and, consequently, failed to provide the obligated service to the lord. Given the constant threat of violence, no lord could afford to have property in his domain that failed to contribute to his power and security. Wardship as a form of organization allowed the lord to assign rights to run the property to another person for the duration of the wardship in order to finance violence potential and meet the military service obligations to the lord that accompanied the ward's property.

To summarize, the feudal world was violent, stable, and undeveloped. We characterize this world as a "violence trap"; or, in somewhat different terms, a "vicious circle of poverty" (Macfarlane 2000, 98) and the failure to become a "virtuous circle" (Rothschild and Sen 2006, 336).

2.5 From Feudalism to the Commercial Economy

The transformation of Western Europe out of feudalism began with the chartering of towns, creating a significant, nonmarginal constitutional and organizational change affecting a small but important subset of the feudal society. These changes had unintended consequences, helping specific parts of Western Europe—notably the towns and the territory surrounding them—to escape the violence trap. Small-time traders during the feudal era, typically in "servile, or very nearly servile" relations to local lords, paid the lords for the right to trade (*WN* III.iii.2, 397–98).[21] These traders, often liv-

---

21. Smith says in *LJ*(A) (iv.142–43, 255–56) that the burghers: "were at first slaves or villains who belonged to a certain lord or master to whom they paid a summ of money for the liberty of trading. They lived in small towns or villages for the convenience of trading, but in but very small numbers."

ing together in tiny towns, worked under remarkably unfavorable conditions of violence and predation. Potentially significant gains existed from specialization and exchange in long-distance trade. But the feudal system's threat of violence and plunder prevented these gains from being realized. The "wealth which [the traders] did manage to accumulate under such unfavorable conditions was subject to the arbitrary exactions of both the king and those lords on whose territories they might happen to be based on through which they might pass" (Skinner 1975, 162, citing *WN* III.iii.2, 397–98).

To take advantage of profitable opportunities in long-distance trade, the towns and traders needed various investments (port facilities, ships), a range of new organizations (judicial, firms, labor, markets, military), and nonmarginal increases in security. Increased security, in turn, allowed the towns to govern themselves, producing islands of perpetuity, impersonality, and order for elites. Towns that failed to produce order were at a disadvantage relative to their competitors, hence less likely to survive. The more secure political environment fostered investment, specialization and exchange, and economic expansion. It also fostered organizational innovation. Rothschild and Sen (2006, 334–37) capture this logic: "The progress of opulence can be seen as a virtuous circle, in which legal and political improvement leads to economic improvement, and economic improvement, in turn leads to further improvement in political and legal institutions."

I explore Smith's logic of the towns' escape from the violence trap in four stages; I evaluate Smith's logic in the following section.

2.5.1   Political Exchange between King and Town

Smith's explanation for the escape from feudalism involves three distinct groups: the king, the lords, and the traders. Under feudalism, as we have seen, the king and lords were constantly fighting, and each plundered the towns. Political uncertainty and the constant threat of predation from the lords hindered the towns' ability to capture the gains from long-distance trade.

The political exchange between town and king created a coalition against a common enemy. Importantly, this political exchange allowed the towns to initiate the transformation out of the no-growth feudal equilibrium and to capture the benefits of specialization, exchange, and long-distance trade.

Smith makes four points about this political exchange, which I disaggregate and number:

1. In order to understand [the kings' grant of independence to the towns], it must be remembered, that in those days the sovereign of perhaps no country in Europe, was able to protect, through the whole extent of his dominions, the weaker part of his subjects from the oppression of the great lords.
2. The inhabitants of cities and burghs, considered as single individuals, had no power to defend themselves: but by entering into a league of

mutual defence with their neighbours, they were capable of making no contemptible resistance.

3. The lords despised the burghers. . . . The wealth of the burghers never failed to provoke their envy and indignation, and [the lords] plundered them upon every occasion without mercy or remorse. The burghers naturally hated and feared the lords. The king hated and feared them too; but though perhaps he might despise, he had no reason either to hate or fear the burghers.

4. Mutual interest, therefore, disposed [the burghers] to support the king, and the king to support them against the lords. They were the enemies of his enemies, and it was his interest to render them as secure and independent of those enemies as he could. By granting them magistrates of their own, the privilege of making bye-laws for their own government, that of building walls for their own defence, and that of reducing all their inhabitants under a sort of military discipline, he gave them all the means of security and independency of the barons which it was in his power to bestow. Without the establishment of some regular government of this kind, without some authority to compel their inhabitants to act according to some certain plan or system, no voluntary league of mutual defence could either have afforded them any permanent security, or have enabled them to give the king any considerable support. (*WN* III.iii.8, 401–2)

Let's unpack this passage into Smith's four points. First, Smith describes the initial conditions involved a natural state logic based on violence potential. Autocratic lords oppressed merchants within their domain. Second, Smith suggests how new possibilities arose for the defense of towns against the lords. Third, Smith discusses the interests of the three parties, king, lord, and town, explaining that mutual self-interest drove the king and town together in alliance against their common enemies, the local lords. And finally, Smith explains the basis for political exchange between king and town in which the king granted the town political freedom in exchange for fixed taxes and military support.

The feudal environment afforded the possibility for generating substantial gains for the town through long-distance trade, greater specialization and division of labor, and exchange. These opportunities provided the king and the towns with strong incentives to engineer a political exchange: The king granted the town political freedom, self-governance, and independence in exchange for financial and military support against the barons (*WN* III. iii.3, 399). This freedom allowed the town to provide its own rules, property rights, governance, justice, the rule of law, and security. All of these activities required organizations, and the town itself can be thought of as an organization of the organizations, as I discuss in the next section. The right to build walls and military organizations allowed towns to protect themselves against the local lords, but also the king.

In exchange, the towns lent the king military support and paid the king taxes, which were to be fixed for all time, lowering the king's ability to expropriate the gains of investment through ex post rises in taxes. According to Smith, the tax agreement became perpetual and impersonal (*WN* III.iii.4, 400).

2.5.2   Towns Escape the Violence Trap

The advantage of the political exchange to members of the town is obvious: they obtained greater security, protection for their investments, and growth of their economy. The king gained a security alliance with the towns and larger resources up front with which to deal with the local lords.

These agreements led to the first real emergence of liberty in late medieval Europe. "Order and good government, and along with them the liberty and security of individuals, were, in this manner, established in cities at a time when the occupiers of land in the country were exposed to every sort of violence" (*WN* III.iii.12, 405). Smith next explains his insights, ideas now central to modern political economics of development. When men capture the fruits of their efforts, they exert themselves to "better their condition" and to "acquire not only the necessaries, but the conveniencies and elegancies of life." In contrast, in the feudal environment, people had little incentive to work hard. Those living near towns who managed to accumulate a small amount sought protection of the towns as sanctuaries (*WN* III.iii.12, 405).[22]

Another aspect of the political exchange helped the towns protect their interests. As the towns grew richer and more powerful, the king granted the burghers political representation in "the general assembly of the states of the kingdom," in part to counterbalance the great lords. The towns' charters, backed by their growing economic and military power, meant that the king could impose no additional taxes (beyond those specified by charter) without the towns' consent (*WN* III.iii.11, 404).

2.5.3   The Towns Incrementally Extend Their Reach into the Countryside

Smith titled chapter IV of Book III, "How the Commerce of the Towns Contributed to the Improvement of the Country" (*WN* III.iv, 411). As the towns grew, he explains, they had incentives to expand their reach—bringing military security, the security of property rights, and markets—into the surrounding countryside.

Smith argued that the towns' military advantage over the local lords fostered the extension of the towns' reach. The towns more easily coordinated men, weapons, and supplies, and they could assemble their forces more quickly than the local lords. "The militia of the cities seems, in those times,

---

22. Smith notes the result with some irony, "the sovereigns of all the different countries of Europe . . . have . . . voluntarily erected a sort of independent republics in the heart of their own dominions" (*WN* III.iii.7, 401).

not to have been inferior to that of the country, and as they could be more readily assembled upon any sudden occasion, they frequently had the advantage in their disputes with the neighbouring lords" (*WN* III.iii.10, 403).

Over time, the towns became far richer than the local lords, improving the towns' military advantage and providing an expanding area secure from predation. These changes, in turn, transformed local agriculture surrounding the towns. Property rights and security fostered growing specialization and exchange, helping to transform self-sufficient farmers into market specialists. Agricultural products and raw materials went to the towns for local consumption and production, and, often, for long-distance trade, while the products of the towns moved to the countryside. Allen (2009, 106) explains the reciprocal and positive-feedback relationship; the growth of cities fostered the growth of local agriculture production, and, at the same time, a more productive agriculture led to greater urbanization.

2.5.4   The Growing Reach of the Towns Transformed Economic and Social Relations, Undermining Feudalism

Subduing the nearby lords had far-reaching though unintended consequences as the lords became integrated into the towns' commercial and security umbrella. The towns' military superiority solved the security problem for nearby lords within the towns' security umbrella. This umbrella, in turn, diminished the local lords' need for military organization and defense against their neighbors. In the new security environment, the lords reorganized their local polities, dismantling the organization of society around the projection of military force. Retainers, once a necessary part of security, became an expensive burden with little benefit, so the lords demilitarized and let go of their retainers (*WN* III.iv.10, 418).

The nonincremental changes in local security, Smith argues, had further unintended consequences in the countryside surrounding the towns: "commerce and manufactures gradually introduced order and good government, and with them, the liberty and security of individuals, among the inhabitants of the country, who had before lived almost in a continual state of war with their neighbours, and of servile dependency upon their superiors. This, though it has been the least observed, is by far the most important of all their effects" (*WN* III.iv.4, 412).[23] As the towns expanded their security and legal umbrella, a "regular government was established in the country as well

---

23. Further, "A revolution of the greatest importance to the publick happiness, was in this manner brought about by two different orders of people, who had not the least intention to serve the publick. To gratify the most childish vanity was the sole motive of the great proprietors. The merchants and artificers, much less ridiculous, acted merely from a view to their own interest, and in pursuit of their own pedlar principle of turning a penny wherever a penny was to be got. Neither of them had either knowledge or foresight of that great revolution which the folly of the one, and the industry of the other, was gradually bringing about" (*WN* III. iv.17–18, 422).

as in the city, nobody having sufficient power to disturb its operations in the one, any more than in the other" (*WN* III.iv.14, 421).

The security umbrella fostered a revolution in the organization of the countryside surrounding the towns. The lords, seeking to increase their consumption, had incentives to grant—and tenants had incentives to pay for—longer leases, which encouraged investment, specialization, and exchange (*WN* III.iv.1–2, 410; III.iv.13, 421). The lords leased out their lands and lived off the rents combined with the profits from the portion of their estates that they managed directly. In the absence of expensive military obligations, local lords became consumers. In taking advantage of the growing opportunities provided by the towns' commercial economy, the lords found luxury items especially alluring. Smith derisively explains how the lords gave up their political power for trinkets and baubles (*WN* III.iv.15, 421).

Smith's central pillars of economic growth—the division of labor and capital accumulation—appear throughout this process. The towns transformed self-sufficient farmers into specialists in complex and growing markets (*WN* III.iv.13, 420–21). Greater division of labor made these farmers better off. Improvements in property rights, such as better rules on devising property upon death, slowly emerged and fostered a more efficient allocation of land. At the same time, prosperous burghers moved into the countryside, bringing with them their ambitions and their culture of investment, specialization, and exchange (*WN* III.iv.3, 410).

The consequences were revolutionary. "[W]hat all the violence of the feudal institutions could never have effected, the silent and insensible operation of foreign commerce and manufactures gradually brought about. These gradually furnished the great proprietors with something for which they could exchange the whole surplus produce of their lands, and which they could consume themselves without sharing it either with tenants or retainers" (*WN* III.iv.10, 418). Over time, as long-distance trade grew, the town became richer, it produced more manufactured goods, and many carried local agricultural surplus to foreign destinations. As this process occurred across large parts of Europe, overall trade expanded; and with this expansion of the market, so too the division of labor. The commercial trading economy grew richer. Feudalism disappeared in these areas.

2.6   Interpreting the Transformation of the Towns

To explain the towns' escape from the violence of the feudal basic natural state, I draw on the two different but complementary arguments of the microinstitutional level involving organizations, and the macroinstitutional level involving political exchange and the (small c) constitution. Addressing changes at both levels is necessary to understand the rise and economic growth of towns.

2.6.1   Microinstitutional Analysis

The microinstitutional level involves the organizational revolution following the towns' provision of liberty, exploiting commercial opportunities, and enhancing security. Building commercial towns capable of providing liberty, maintaining security, and supporting long-distance trade required an organizational revolution—the growth of the civil society—with dozens if not hundreds of new types of organizations. Moreover, the sets of organizations must also fit together in the sense that they complement one another rather than get in each other's way or, worse, plunder and fight one another. Organizations direct and coordinate the efforts of people to produce the outcomes we characterize as liberty, wealth, and security. We have too little theory that explains how separate but complementary public organizations work together to create the market infrastructure necessary for a functioning society capable of long-term economic growth.

Although economic theory does a good job of modeling the interaction of economic organizations in modern markets in states characterized by the rule of law and other market infrastructure, we lack the extensions of this theory to include political and social organizations, especially those organizations that provide market infrastructure, a civil society helping to maintain the town organization (North, Wallis, and Weingast [2009, ch. 4], provides an initial attempt for open-access orders).

The Medieval Town as an Organization of Organizations

Town organization, in contrast to feudal organization, exhibits much greater specialization. At the highest level, the town's corporate charter formed the town as an organization vested with various rights, including the right to self-governance and to provide security. All other town organizations flow from this charter, making the town an organization of organizations. Many of these organizations were independent of the state, although sanctioned by the official system, which restricted access to organizations to specific classes of people for specific purposes.

Consider the basis for implementing each of the three revolutions associated with the towns: liberty, commerce, and security.

Liberty. Liberty is a term that has fallen into disuse in economics. In the mid- to late twentieth century, many of the great economists used it; notably, James M. Buchanan and Friedrich Hayek. Smith also used this term (see Aspromourgos 2009, 223–38; Forbes 1975; see also Lieberman 2006; Rothschild and Sen 2006, 334–37) in a way that parallels issues raised in the modern literatures on economic development and economic history, for example, by Douglass North (1990); namely, liberty as freedom from predation, expropriation, and arbitrary action by the state, therefore allowing secure property rights and contract enforcement.[24]

The town's right to self-government was vested in its charter. Town government was more highly differentiated than that in the surrounding countryside. Each of its functions was embodied in organizations, including a form of governing body, an executive, and a judiciary.

If commerce represents the development of markets in Smith's approach, liberty and security provided the legal and military infrastructure necessary to sustain markets. As sections 2.4 and 2.5 demonstrate, Smith argued that markets require the legal infrastructure of justice, secure property rights, and protection from predation. Commerce and economic growth also depend on a military advantage by which the commercial society could defend itself in a world of hostile groups, both internal and external.

Although Smith does not explain how, the system of liberty provided for perpetuity and impersonality (at least for the elite), two critical ingredients in the rule of law and the doorstep conditions that represent important elements of the political economics of development (Weingast 2010). Liberty also provided merchants with the incentives to specialize, to engage in long-distance trade, and to accumulate capital. The towns experienced economic growth in two related senses. The economy grew through division of labor and capital accumulation, but also through extension into the surrounding countryside.

Commerce. Although Smith does not discuss this aspect of town organization, central to the towns' economic and political success were the guild organizations and merchant firms. These organizations created and coordinated much of the towns' economic activities and many of the political functions. In addition, the trading towns created the exchanges represented in long-distance trade. All of this had to be organized efficiently so that the towns could compete successfully on the international market and with neighboring towns, which were often close substitutes.

The infamous apprenticeship system represented another set of organizations at once creating barriers to entry, ensuring the education of an apprentice into the skills of the trade or craft, and organizing the entry of potentially talented individuals into the business. Smith famously criticized this system (e.g., *WN* I.x.c.1–17, 135–40). The system of guild restrictions and the apprenticeship system remind us that the towns were far from modern open-access orders.

Security. Each town also had a carefully crafted set of military organization necessary to provide security for the town and the surrounding countryside, especially as the town's umbrella expanded over time. Survival required that

---

24. His definition of liberty is, of course, not the sole one.

the town possess a military organization superior to that of the lords in the surrounding countryside.

In addition to these sets of organizations, towns made use—indeed, often required—a wide range of other organizations. Some provided public goods, such as schools and hospitals. Other organizations involved various products and services sought after by citizens, such as clothing, shoes, linens, ale houses, inns, and food establishments. Finally, the church was generally represented through organizations, notably the local parish. Over time, as the towns grew larger, other church organizations established a presence in the towns, such as the mendicant order.[25]

2.6.2 Macroinstitutional Analysis: Political Exchange and the Constitution

The macroinstitutional or constitutional level involves the forces that foster the movement from basic natural state of feudalism to that of the towns on the doorstep. The political exchange between king and towns created a new constitutional order for the towns—the corporate form of organization—essential to the towns' success. In particular, I explain the macrolevel forces underlying the towns' escape from the violence trap (Cox, North, and Weingast 2017).

In this subsection, I interpret Smith's account of the feudal equilibrium and initiation of the transformation to the commercial economy. In North, Wallis, and Weingast's (2009) terms, the feudal equilibrium was a natural state with low levels of the division of labor and hence quite poor. Many localities experiencing considerable violence were fragile natural states, while the more stable ones were basic natural states. All secular organizations were directly associated with the dual military-economic hierarchy.

Arbitrary use of authority by the lords, known in modern terms as executive moral hazard, was a major problem during feudalism, and at many levels;[26] for example, the local lord was at once the local executive, lawmaker, and judge with all the problems of governance that such an arrangement implies. As we have seen, predation was an omnipresent problem; fighting and violence characterized this world. In Adam Smith's view, the feudal world provided minimal incentives for investment, specialization, and exchange. Most people lived at subsistence.

Liberty, commerce, and security brought the towns from fragile and basic natural states to a state on the doorstep. They engineered perpetuity, both of the state and of organizations. The result was rule of law (at least for the elite), the growth of the commercial economy, and control of the military.

---

25. On the institutions and organizations of the medieval church, see Ekelund, Hébert, and Tollison (2006). In Weingast (2017), I explain Smith's approach to how the church contributed to the stability of the no-growth feudal equilibrium. See also Hont (2009, 164).

26. Besley and Persson (2011) provide an extended study of the relationship of executive moral hazard and economic performance.

2.6.3   The Emergence of Towns

The towns also engineered political development, creating new governance structures that differed radically from those of the feudal system. I define political development as involving the increases in state capacity that provides the market infrastructure necessary for the economic development of markets. This state capacity must therefore include the ability to protect property, to enforce contracts, and to provide security without the threat of predation (Besley and Persson 2009). As we have seen, the growth of towns involved all these features. Perpetuity, impersonality, and inclusion in governance all appeared to varying degrees. These changes resulted in justice, secure property rights, and mechanisms for contract enforcement within the towns. Economic and political development proceeded in tandem, fostering investments, specialization and exchange, economic integration, and the growing reach of markets and the price mechanism (*WN* III.iv).

The towns' economic and political development arose simultaneously as part of a single process; neither antedated nor caused the other. Smith appreciated the "reciprocal relationship between commerce and liberty," and much of *The Wealth of Nations* examines how economic liberty fostered "the growth and diffusion of commercial prosperity," especially Books I, II, and IV (Winch 1978, 70). Nonetheless, as Winch argues, the literature has neglected Smith's arguments about the reverse relationship, namely how commerce helped promote liberty and property rights (Winch 1978, 70).[27]

The political exchange between king and towns granted the towns the ability to make nonincremental changes that, in turn, allowed the towns to enter the positive feedback loop leading to a new and better equilibrium than feudalism. The political exchange altered the condition of the towns sufficiently that they became more powerful than the local lords. A central feature of the towns' economy was economic integration. The specialists in long-distance trade depended on the towns' military organization for security and the towns' economy for many raw materials and food. Local specialists in food and raw products depended on the towns' demand for their products. Put in Smith's terms, economic integration at once expanded the "extent of the market," creating greater division of labor and fostering investment, all features of economic growth.[28]

In terms of the violence trap, economic integration raised the economic costs of violence. High costs of violence lowered the value of violence,

---

27. Skinner, an exception, explains that the arrangements Smith "had themselves been developed and protected in an attempt to solve a political problem" generated from the economic desire to foster trade (Skinner 1975, 164). Many of Smith's contemporaries connected commerce and liberty, including Montesquieu ([1748] 1989), Hume (1985a, 1985b), Cantillon ([1755] 1959), and Bonnot ([1776] 2008). Hirschman (1977) reviews this literature.

28. Smith clearly understood the nature of economic integration. For example, he explains the surprising level of economic integration in the modern commercial economy through his analysis of all the inputs necessary to produce a woolen coat (*WN* I.i.11, 22–24). See Kennedy (2010, ch. 6, especially table 6.1) for an extensive discussion.

hence giving disputing parties the incentives to solve their problems non-violently. Moreover, the towns had strong incentives to expand markets. As they extended their reach into the countryside, the towns sought to earn profits from long-distance trade and from encouraging local marketization that transformed local, highly inefficient, and self-sufficient agriculture into market specialists. The towns typically did not use their military might to become another type of local lord who extracted from the local economy. Instead, the towns used their economic and military power to create markets and political freedom (for the elite, at least).

The opportunities for expanding commerce made possible a new form of political exchange, producing new political institutions governing the towns. These political institutions, in turn, fostered the townsmen's ability to exploit new economic opportunities provided by trade. Here, too, political and economic development is inextricably intertwined, reflecting Winch's "reciprocal relationship."

The nonincremental change—reflecting simultaneous changes in perpetuity, impersonality, inclusion, and in investment, specialization and exchange, and military organization—allowed the towns to escape the violence trap and enter the positive feedback loop. Once the towns were organized and generated sufficient security, they extended their reach into the countryside, increasing the size of the market and the division of labor. Expanding long-distance trade increased the towns' wealth. All these changes led the towns to extend yet again the reach of a larger security umbrella, with greater expansion of its reach into the countryside, further deepening the division of labor, and so on through the positive feedback loop. The result, as Winch argues, is that the "Commercial society is not merely one in which more people are engaged in producing capital goods . . . it is one in which more people are drawn into the wider circle of commercial relationships. It is the situation arrived at once the division of labor has been thoroughly established, and men can supply only part of their needs from their own produce. It is the form of society in which 'every man . . . lives by exchanging, or becomes in some measure, a merchant'" (Winch 1978, 80; quoting *WN* I.iv.1, 37).

Another factor contributed to perpetuity; namely, towns expanded inclusion beyond a narrow elite in comparison with the feudal world, although it did not come close to achieving open access. For one, the towns absorbed many from the countryside in their market system, allowing the towns and markets to draw on a larger talent pool. The very specialized apprenticeship system organized by the guilds did the same thing for the most specialized production and merchant activities.

2.7 Conclusions

Adam Smith's *Wealth of Nations* is, among many other things, a study in why so many countries remain poor and why a few have become "opulent" or rich. Smith addressed this question in many different ways in his rambling work. Although many scholars focus on just one of these discussions, Smith's discussions make it hard to say any one of his answers is the definitive explanation. In Book I, he explains how the division of labor produces opulence. In Book II, he emphasizes the importance of savings and capital accumulation. Book IV emphasizes the central importance of appropriate public policies, explaining, for example, why mercantilism hinders a state's progress toward opulence in comparison to free trade. Each of these arguments resonates with modern economics. Further, each presumes a context of a state with high state capacity; namely, a serviceable judiciary, property rights, and liberty—Smith's "peace, easy taxes, and a tolerable administration of justice" (as reported by Stewart [1793] 1982, 322).

The force of this chapter is that Smith provides a fourth component explaining why so many countries fail to become opulent, one that differs in kind from the other three. In Book III of *The Wealth of Nations*, Smith discusses the necessary political foundations of markets and how, absent these foundations, countries cannot grow. He presents this argument, not in the abstract as he does with, say, the division of labor, but in a historical narrative about feudalism and the rise of towns. Smith embeds in the narrative a theory that drives the logic of the development of a commercial society out of the natural state of feudalism.

In this chapter, I interpret Smith's argument as a form of violence trap. Indeed, the no-growth feudal equilibrium was based on the violence trap. The prevalence of violence meant that property rights were insecure, as, therefore, were savings, investment, and innovation. In this world, most people lived at subsistence level. No one, neither king nor great lord, was capable of providing order.

The towns arose through political exchange between king and towns that granted them the right to a corporative form of self-governance. This exchange allowed the towns to make nonincremental changes, fostering their escape from the violence trap through a threefold revolution that simultaneously created liberty (including justice and the security of property rights), commerce, and hence economic growth, and security from the menacing outside world. All three were necessary for the towns' escape. The towns grew through long-distance trade, specialization and exchange, capital accumulation, and expansion into the local countryside where they helped transform the local economy from poor, self-sufficient agriculture into specialists in food and inputs into manufacturing shipped to the town and often entering long-distance trade.

The central elements of Smith's argument of the escape from the violence trap are as follows: The incorporation of towns in the context of political exchange with the king allowed them to enter the positive feedback loop of economic growth. The political exchange granted the towns the ability to enhance state capacity through nonincremental changes in security and investment in economic activities. The towns' more effective military organization subdued the local lords, expanding both long-distance trade and trade with the local countryside. As the towns extended their security umbrella, the local countryside experienced a nonincremental increase in the security of property rights, with incentives for investment, hard work, and exchange. The towns also transformed what Smith called "unproductive labor" (labor facing predation that had no incentive to work hard or invest) into productive labor. At the same time, as the local lords came under the towns' jurisdiction, they no longer needed their expensive retainers for defense. As they demilitarized, the lords became consumers, expanding the demand for the traders' goods and services. The demand for luxury goods by the lords also facilitated this process.

Towns also represented an explosion of new organizations—the corporate form, as mentioned, the overall government, specific units within the government, such as the executive, the judiciary, and a town council. Merchants organized their guilds and their firms, and the towns' military organization provided defense. The church also had its organizational reach into the towns. As noted above, the town became an organization of organizations. In Levy's (chapter 3, this volume) terms, towns can be seen as organizations at once in vertical competition with the local lords and an oppositional, if generally cooperative one, with the king. As with Levy's analysis of the privileges of the *corps intermédiaires*, towns gained privileges, but ones that helped them sustain a better or more opulent social and economic outcome.

The explanation provided of the escape from violence satisfies the three conditions mentioned at the outside for a theory of the initiation of political economics of development: a microlevel analysis of the organizations providing the heavy lifting of ensuring the various parts of the movement to the doorstep conditions occurred; a macrolevel analysis of the political exchange and constitution necessary to make the escape work; and an analysis showing why the new arrangements were stable; that is, an equilibrium, so that the towns were not a temporary aberration that would fall back into the old, feudal equilibrium.

Adam Smith's discussion of the transformation of feudalism to the commercial society fits well with aspects of the emerging literature on the political economics of development, and it adds ideas relatively lacking. Economic and political development are not separate tasks in Smith's view, but inextricably intertwined as a single process (see such diverse scholars as Acemoglu and Robinson [2006, 2012]; Bates [2001]; Besley and Persson [2009, 2011]; Tilly [1992]). Attempts to reform one without reform of the other generally fail. Smith's view of the rise of towns and the commercial society out of feudalism demonstrates that the escape from the poverty and violence required simultaneous changes in the economy, polity, and in security. When the three elements coexist, growing opulence is the result. Similarly, when any of the three elements is missing, growing opulence fails.

Finally, the central importance of violence in Smith's approach is relatively lacking in the literature (North, Wallis, and Weingast 2009).[29] Reflecting the trade-off between security and efficiency, societies facing existential threats take actions to defend themselves, and these actions—as Smith argues—force substantial deviations from political institutions and policies that generate opulence or long-term economic growth. Put simply, Smith argued that feudal Europe failed to develop due to violence and oppression.

Abbreviations

The works of Adam Smith. All references to the Glasgow edition, as reprinted by the Liberty Fund.

LJ   Smith, Adam. 1762–63; [1767] 1981. *Lectures on Jurisprudence*, edited by R. L. Meek., D. D. Raphael, and P. G. Stein. Indianapolis: Liberty Fund. The lecture notes are comprised of two parts:

LJ(A)   The first set of lecture notes, corresponding to the 1762–63 term;

LJ(B)   The second set of lecture notes, dated 1767 though thought to correspond to the 1763–64 term.

WN   Smith, Adam. [1776] 1981. *An Inquiry into the Nature and Causes of The Wealth of Nations*, edited by R. H. Campbell, A. S. Skinner, and W. B. Todd. Indianapolis: Liberty Fund.

References

Acemoglu, Daron, and James A. Robinson. 2006. "Economic Backwardness in Political Perspective." *American Political Science Review* 100:115–31.
———. 2011. *Why Nations Fail*. New York: Crown Business.
Allen, Robert C. 2009. *The British Industrial Revolution in Global Perspective*. Cambridge: Cambridge University Press.
Alston, Lee J., Bernardo Mueller, Marcus Melo, and Carlos Pereira. 2016. *Beliefs, Leadership and Critical Transitions; Brazil, 1964–2012*. Princeton, NJ: Princeton University Press.
Aspromourgos, Tony. 2009. *The Science of Wealth: Adam Smith and the Framing of Political Economy*. London: Routledge.
Azariadis, Costas, and John Stachurski. 2005. "Poverty Traps." In *Handbook of Economic Growth*, vol. 1A, edited by Philippe Aghion and Steven N. Durlauf. Amsterdam: Elsevier.
Barzel, Yoram. 1997. *Economic Analysis of Property Rights*. Cambridge: Cambridge University Press.

29. Exceptions exist to the dominant view that ignores violence, notably, Collier (2007), Cox, North, and Weingast (2017), Dixit (2004), and Hirschleifer (1994). Other exceptions involve rationalist explanations for interstate war (Fearon 1995; Powell 1999; Wittman 2009) and a large literature on the relationship between interstate conflict and development outside of economy (e.g., Acemoglu and Robinson 2012; Bates 2001; Besley and Persson 2009, 2011; Tilly 1992).

————. 2002. *The Theory of the State*. Cambridge: Cambridge University Press.

Bates, Robert H. 2001. *Prosperity & Violence: The Political Economy of Development*. New York: W. W. Norton.

Bates, Robert H., Avner Greif, Margaret Levi, Jean-Laurent Rosenthal, and Barry R. Weingast. 1998. *Analytic Narratives*. Princeton, NJ: Princeton University Press.

Bell, Joe A. 1992. "Adam Smith's Theory of Economic Development: 'Of the Natural Progress of Opulence.'" *Journal of Economics and Finance* 16 (1): 137–45.

Besley, Timothy, and Torsten Persson. 2009. "The Origins of State Capacity: Property Rights, Taxation, and Politics." *American Economic Review* 99 (4): 1218–44.

————. 2011. *Pillars of Prosperity*. Princeton, NJ: Princeton University Press.

Blaug, Mark. 1978. *Economic Theory in Retrospect*, 3rd ed. Cambridge: Cambridge University Press.

Bonnot, Étienne, Abbé de Condillac. (1776) 2008. *Commerce and Government Considered in Their Mutual Relationship*. Indianapolis: Liberty Fund.

Brue, Stanley L., and Randy R. Grant. 2007. *The Evolution of Economic Thought*, 7th ed. Mason, OH: Thomson South-Western.

Cantillon, Richard. (1755) 1959. *An Essay on the Nature of Commerce in General*. London: Frank Cass and Co., Ltd.

Collier, Paul. 2007. *The Bottom Billion: Why the Poorest Countries Are Failing and What Can Be Done About It*. Oxford: Oxford University Press.

Cox, Gary W., Douglass C. North, and Barry R. Weingast. 2017. "The Violence Trap: A Political-Economic Approach to the Problems of Development." Unpublished manuscript.

Dixit, Avinash K. 2004. *Lawlessness: Alternative Modes of Governance*. Princeton, NJ: Princeton University Press.

Ekelund, Robert B., Jr., Robert F. Hébert, and Robert D. Tollison. 2006. *The Marketplace of Christianity*. Cambridge, MA: MIT Press.

Eltis, W. A. 1975. "Adam Smith's Theory of Economic Growth." In *Essays on Adam Smith*, edited by Andrew S. Skinner and Thomas Wilson. Oxford: Clarendon Press.

Fearon, James D. 1995. "Rationalist Explanations for War." *International Organization* (Summer) 49: 379–414.

Forbes, Duncan. 1975. *Hume's Philosophical Politics*. Cambridge: Cambridge University Press.

Haakonssen, Knud. 1981. *The Science of a Legislator: The Natural Jurisprudence of David Hume and Adam Smith*. Cambridge: Cambridge University Press.

Henderson, Willie. 2006. *Evaluating Adam Smith: Creating the Wealth of Nations*. London: Routledge.

Hirschleifer, Jack. 1994. "The Dark Side of the Force." *Economic Inquiry* 32:1–10.

Hirschman, Albert O. 1977. *Passions and the Interests: Political Arguments for Capitalism before Its Triumph*. Princeton, NJ: Princeton University Press.

Hollander, Samuel. 1973. *The Economics of Adam Smith*. Toronto: University of Toronto Press.

————. 1979. "Historical Dimension of *The Wealth of Nations*." In *Adam Smith and Modern Political Economy: Bicentennial Essays on The Wealth of Nations*, edited by Gerald P. O'Driscoll, Jr. Ames: Iowa State University Press.

Hont, Istvan. (1989) 2005. "Adam Smith and the Political Economy of the 'Unnatural and Retrograde' Order." In *The Jealousy of Trade*. Cambridge, MA: Harvard University Press.

————. 2009. "Adam Smith's History of Law and Government as Political Theory." In *Political Judgement: Essays for John Dunn*, edited by R. Bourke and R. Geuss. Cambridge: Cambridge University Press.

————. 2015. *Politics in Commercial Society: Jean Jacques Rousseau and Adam Smith*. Edited by Béla Kapossy and Michael Sonenscher. Cambridge, MA: Harvard University Press.

Hume, David. (1752) 1985a. "Of Commerce." Essay I, Part II. In *Essays: Moral, Political, and Literary*, edited by Eugene Miller. Indianapolis: Liberty Fund.

————. (1752) 1985b. "Of Refinement in the Arts." Essay II, Part II. In *Essays: Moral, Political, and Literary*, edited by Eugene Miller. Indianapolis: Liberty Fund.

Kennedy, Gavin. 2010. *Adam Smith*, 2nd ed. Houndmills, UK: Palgrave Macmillan.

Levi, Margaret. 1988. *Of Rule and Revenue*. Berkeley: University of California Press.

Lieberman, David. 2006. "Adam Smith on Justice, Rights, and Law." In *The Cambridge Companion to Adam Smith*, edited by Knud Haakonssen. Cambridge: Cambridge University Press.

Macfarlane, Alan. 2000. *The Riddle of the Modern World: Of Liberty, Wealth and Equality*. London: Palgrave.

Montesquieu, Charles de. (1748) 1989. *The Spirit of the Laws*. Translated and edited by Anne M. Cohler, Basia Carolyn Miller, and Harold Samuel Stone. New York: Cambridge University Press.

Moss, Laurence S. 1979. "Power and Value Relationships in *The Wealth of Nations*." In *Adam Smith and Modern Political Economy: Bicentennial Essays on the Wealth of Nations*, edited by Gerald P. O'Driscoll. Ames: Iowa State University Press.

Muthoo, Abhinay. 1999. *Bargaining Theory with Applications*. Cambridge: Cambridge University Press.

Myint, Hla. 1977. "Adam Smith's Theory of International Trade in the Perspective of Economic Development." *Economica* 44 (175): 231–48.

North, Douglass C. 1981. *Structure and Change in Economic History*. New York: Norton.

————. 1990. *Institutions, Institutional Change, and Economic Performance*. Cambridge: Cambridge University Press.

————. 2005. *Understanding the Process of Economic Change*. Princeton, NJ: Princeton University Press.

North, Douglass C., and Robert Paul Thomas. 1973. *The Rise of the Western World: A New Economic History*. Cambridge: Cambridge University Press.

North, Douglass C., John Joseph Wallis, and Barry R. Weingast. 2009. *Violence and Social Orders: A Conceptual Framework for Interpreting Recorded Human History*. New York: Cambridge University Press.

Ober, Josiah, and Barry R. Weingast. Forthcoming. "The Sparta Game: Violence, Proportionality, Austerity, Collapse." In *How to Do Things with History*, edited by Paul Millett. Oxford: Oxford University Press.

O'Brien, D. P. (1975) 2004. "The Smithian Growth Process." *The Classical Economists Revisited*. Princeton, NJ: Princeton University Press.

Olson, Mancur. 1993. "Democracy, Dictatorship, and Development." *American Political Science Review* 87 (3): 567–75.

Posner, Richard. 2006. *Economic Analysis of Law*. 7th ed. Austin, TX: Wolters Kluwer/Aspen Publishers.

Powell, Robert. 1999. *In the Shadow of Power: States and Strategies in International Politics*. Princeton, NJ: Princeton University Press.

Robbins, Lionel. 1998. *A History of Economic Thought: The LSE Lectures*, edited by Steven G. Medema and Warren J. Samuels. Princeton, NJ: Princeton University Press.

Rothschild, Emma, and Amartya Sen. 2006. "Adam Smith's Economics." In *The*

Cambridge Companion to Adam Smith, edited by Knud Haakonssen. Cambridge: Cambridge University Press.

Schumpeter, Joseph A. 1954. *History of Economic Analysis*. New York: Oxford University Press.

Skinner, Andrew S. 1975. "Adam Smith: An Economic Interpretation of History." In *Essays on Adam Smith*, edited by Andrew S. Skinner and Thomas Wilson, pp. 155–78. Oxford: Clarendon Press.

———. 1996. *A System of Social Science: Papers relating to Adam Smith*. New York: Oxford University Press.

Stewart, Dugald. (1793) 1982. "Account of the Life and Writings of Adam Smith, LL.D." From the Transactions of the Royal Society of Edinburgh (edited by I. S. Ross). In *Adam Smith: Essays on Philosophical Subjects*, edited by W. P. D. Wightman and J. C. Bryce. Indianapolis: Liberty Classics.

Tilly, Charles. 1992. *Coercion, Capital, and European States, AD 990–1992*, rev. ed. Cambridge, MA: Blackwell.

Weingast, Barry R. 1995. "The Economic Role of Political Institutions: Market-Preserving Federalism and Economic Development." *Journal of Law, Economics, and Organization* 11 (Spring 1995): 1–31.

———. 2010. "Why Developing Countries Prove So Resistant to the Rule of Law." In *Global Perspectives on the Rule of Law*, edited by James J. Heckman, Robert L. Nelson, and Lee Cabatingan. New York: Routledge.

———. 2017. "Adam Smith's Industrial Organization of Religion: Explaining the Medieval Church's Monopoly and Its Breakdown in the Reformation." Working Paper, Hoover Institution, Stanford University.

Winch, Donald. 1978. *Adam Smith's Politics: An Essay in Historiographic Revision*. New York: Cambridge University Press.

Wittman, Donald. 2009. "Bargaining in the Shadow of War: When Is a Peaceful Resolution Most Likely?" *American Journal of Political Science* 53 (3): 588–602.

Young, Allyn A. 1928. "Increasing Returns and Economic Progress." *Economic Journal* 38 (152): 527–42.

Pluralism without Privilege?
Corps Intermédiaires, Civil Society, and the Art of Association

Jacob T. Levy

3.1 Competition, Integration, Opposition

The decades of the mid-eighteenth through the mid-nineteenth centuries span the emergence of fully liberal political and social theory, and an early version of liberal practice, in France, the United Kingdom, and the United States. In political theory, elitist Whig and civic republican ideas about virtue—skeptical of commerce, political parties, and religious division— gave way in fits and starts to ideas that were both more egalitarian and more pluralistic. Commercial markets, competitive electoral democracy, and religious liberty came to occupy pride of place in theories about free social orders.[1]

Political practice did not start in the same place—in the early eighteenth century civic republicanism and country Whig ideology were languages of criticism, not apologies for the status quo. But the theoretical transformation came to converge in meaningful part with changes in practice. Sometimes theory probably led practice, as in the development of religious liberty. Sometimes practice probably led theory, as theorists noticed new features

Jacob T. Levy is the Tomlinson Professor of Political Theory at McGill University.

Thanks to Emma Rothschild, John Wallis, Naomi Lamoreaux, Paul Dragos Aligica, Deborah Boucoyannis, David McIvor, Abraham Singer, and audiences at the 2015 Annual Meeting of the Association for Political Theory and at Texas A&M University and the King's College London Department of Political Economy for comments and suggestions. Kelsey Brady provided valuable research assistance, supported by the Arts Research Internship Award at McGill University. This research was supported by an Insight Grant from the Social Sciences and Humanities Research Council of Canada. For acknowledgments, sources of research support, and disclosure of the author's material financial relationships, if any, please see http://www.nber.org/chapters/c13510.ack.

1. See Wood (1969), Pocock (1975), and Kalyvas and Katznelson (2008). I discuss this transformation further in Levy (2006).

of an emerging social order, and came to understand what might be attractive about them. Often, they reinforced one another. The *doux commerce* theorists observed economic changes that were already under way, but their theoretical redescriptions of them supported legal and political changes that could support or even accelerate them.

This liberalization in part consisted of substantive policy changes: increased religious liberty and freedom of the press, for example. And it in part consisted of major changes in the politics that generates and maintains policies. Sometimes these reinforced each other in a virtuous spiral. North, Wallis, and Weingast have argued that this happened with the democratization of organizational tools that had previously been open only to members of the elite: the shift from specially chartered monopolistic corporations to general incorporation laws, and from parliamentary oligopolistic party competition to modern parties competing in wide-suffrage elections.[2] These new "open-access" orders found a secure foundation for generalized associational and commercial liberty by overcoming the system that confined politics to intraelite rent-seeking competitions.

The liberal political and social theorists who lived through the era had serious doubts that the new democratized politics could successfully support the new liberalized policies. In this chapter I hope to make their argument accessible, first in a generalized way and then through a reading of four key thinkers. They looked forward to the possibility of a pluralism without privilege, but had doubts about its sustainability. They offered some reasons to prefer pluralism *with* privilege to the absence of both. They worried that centralization, democratic or otherwise, might be the preeminent fact of modern state consolidation, and that purely voluntary, equal, associational pluralism might not be powerful enough to check it. The kinds of pluralism grounded in *ancien régime* privilege and status, in entrenched jurisdictional pluralism within the constitutional order, or in pre-political cultural and customary ties might be needed to motivate the oppositional political action that could protect pluralism and freedom.

I begin with three simplified ways of thinking, deliberately stylized and abstract, about the relationships among intermediate bodies and between them and the larger society. These do not necessarily describe different types of groups or different legal regimes governing group life; the same groups might interact with each other or with the larger society in any or all of them. They do, however, draw our analytical attention to different features of pluralistic social orders.

First, and perhaps most typical of open-access orders, groups and associations might be thought of as *competitive* with one another, analogously to the competitive character of incorporated firms in an open market under laws of general incorporation. The associations that exist, and their rela-

---

2. North, Wallis, and Weingast (2009).

tive success, represent the choices made by members who have the right to form, join, and exit groups relatively easily. Universities and private schools compete for students and teachers; religious denominations under conditions of religious freedom compete for adherents; municipalities compete for residents and capital through Tiebout sorting and as the kind of agents in a polycentric order analyzed by Elinor and Vincent Ostrom;[3] and political parties compete for votes and members. Different activist groups devoted to the same issue, or different recreational or fraternal clubs of the same type, might compete with each other as well. Competitive groups are similar enough, with members who are similar enough, to be meaningfully rivalrous; a church is not competitive with a municipality or a bowling league. When we think of groups as competitive, we emphasize not only their similarity but also their horizontal relation: cities compete with cities, not with provinces or with neighborhoods. Competitive associational life, of course, relies in part on the kind of "exit" described by Albert Hirschman, but that feature is easily overstated; exit might happen only at the margins and yet exert important disciplining effects on groups that are otherwise characterized by a great deal of loyalty and voice.[4] Voters do not desert their political parties as easily as consumers do a product brand, and residents are not quick to move out of their cities, but in both cases the possibility creates a competitive dynamic nonetheless.

This competitive understanding of intermediate groups is congenial to the analysis of the open-access order found in North, Wallis, and Weingast. It also figures prominently in Ernest Gellner's account of civil society, an order populated by "modular man" who can leave one group and join another without essential change in his identity or status.[5] Gellner influentially argued that civil society so conceived, not democratization or capitalism, was the key to the breakthroughs of western modernity. The social world of many fluid, overlapping, and competing horizontal organizations offered a superior, freer, model than the purposive unity of whole polities, or than centralized command-based absolutism, or than segmentary and tribalistic social orders. This liberal pluralism, he thought, had allowed the emergence of democratic market societies in the first place, and was the key to establishing them or reestablishing them in the post–Cold War world.

Second, group life might be thought of as an *integrative* phenomenon. In the service of common and overarching ends, there is value in local participation and the sense of personal agency that comes from being part of a subgroup, and so smaller groups can be a way of drawing their members into overarching ones. Here the analytical emphasis is vertical, not hori-

3. See, for example, Ostrom (1990), Ostrom, Tiebout, and Warren (1961), Tiebout (1956), and compare Weingast (1995).
4. Hirschman (1970).
5. Gellner (1994).

zontal, and relations among groups and the same kind at the same level is comparatively unimportant. A variety of groups at the same horizontal level are often, in integrative models, drawn together into the larger whole. But their plurality is not in itself the point; they are only the local, visible, accessible aspect of a larger whole. Each parish might have its own school and its own poor relief as the instantiation of communal projects of education and charity. Each town in an administratively decentralized unitary state might have its own local officials who implement the centrally decided policies. In belonging to the local group, members also belong to the larger one, and take part in its activities.

Integrative group life, in which groups interact as parts and wholes, cooperatively rather than competitively, is perhaps most widely known in social theory through the doctrine of subsidiarity in Catholic social thought.[6] Subsidiarity emphasizes the importance of local decisions and actions, of local group life, within the context of an organically integrated whole community, whether the church as such or social life more generally. In a different intellectual tradition, the corporations that mediate citizenship in Hegel's *Philosophy of Right* are organized by industry and profession, with no mention of or apparent value in having (say) competing corporations of lawyers. Members belong to a corporation or estate and, through that, to the state.

The "deep diversity" advocated by Charles Taylor[7]—at once perhaps the leading living Catholic political philosopher and the leading living Hegelian political philosopher—treats smaller units as ways of belonging to the larger. These need not all represent the *same* way of belonging. Quebec, in Taylor's vision, represents a different mode of belonging to Canada, a substantively different type of membership in the federation, from the other provinces. But that does not mean that the other provinces lacking that distinctiveness should be abolished, only that they do not mediate membership in Canada in the same thick way that Quebec does. In any case, the question for everyone is "how do we belong to Canada?," that is, how do our intermediate groups mediate our membership in the larger whole?

If competitive associations can be compared to competitive firms, the political economy analogue of integrative associational life is corporatism, as in the postwar economic model in some European countries wherein encompassing organizations representing labor and capital negotiated nationwide agreements with the help of a government concerned with the whole economic system.[8] In corporatism as in subsidiarity, organizations are actually nested. But the integrative way of looking at group life does not require this. The so-called neo-Tocquevillian studies of associational life associated with Robert Putnam also emphasize belonging to associations

---

6. Golemboski (2015).
7. Most famously in Taylor (1992). See also "Shared and Divergent Values," in Taylor (1993).
8. Schmitter (1974).

as a way of belonging to a larger social whole, united by bonds of trust and building social capital for the benefit of the whole community.[9]

Third, we might think of group life as *oppositional*. If the competitive model emphasizes horizontal rivalry, and the integrative model emphasizes harmonious vertical nonrivalry, the oppositional model emphasizes vertical rivalry: our local or particular or intermediate group offers the possibility of dissent, difference, or resistance.[10] The church provides its members with social norms that meaningfully differ from those of the wider society, and the organizational resources with which to defend their religious liberty against state intrusion. Any type of adversarial federalist theory—the intercession theories of the Kentucky and Virginia Resolutions, the rivalry for loyalties between states and center envisioned in *Federalist* numbers 45–46, the Hapsburg-inspired multinational federalism defended in Lord Acton's *On Nationality*—uses these lenses, emphasizing not that (e.g.) Quebec is *how I belong* to Canada, but rather that it is *how I sometimes do not*, that it is the place where I can stand when I wish to say *no* to Canada.[11] Dissenting churches under religious establishment obviously lend themselves to this kind of analysis, but orthodox or established churches can too, when they have enough institutional weight to counterbalance decisions made by political elites and state actors. An oppositional stance is relative to another group or set of groups. The medieval walled city might be oppositional relative to the local lord but integrative with political order of the kingdom as a whole; the walled university or the church giving sanctuary might be oppositional relative to the city.

With these three models in mind, it would be easy to think of the emergence of liberalism, of civil society in the contemporary sense, and of open-access orders as being a matter of the replacement of integrative and oppositional styles of group relations with a competitive model. I hope to show that matters were, and remain, more complicated than that. I will draw on theorists who lived through the transition to early open-access societies to suggest that the competitive mode of group relations might not be self-sufficient. The open-access order may remain dependent on institutional inheritances and forms from what North, Wallis, and Weingast term the

---

9. See, especially, Putnam (2000).

10. This typology obviously omits one category: horizontal nonrivalry. This suggests cartelism in political economy, or rigid segmented communalism in group life such as the millet system in the Ottoman Empire, or perhaps some kinds of confederalism in government structures. It is the "segmented society" discussed by Gellner as a contrast to civil society. I mention it here for completeness. It does not, however, play much part in the debates surrounding the emergence of the liberal order, save perhaps in some early discussions of American federalism, and I do not discuss it further.

11. In Levy (2007), I discussed some of these cases in the context of offering an oppositional understanding of federalism, distinct from both competitive federalism and subsidiarity, though I did not use the competitive/integrative/oppositional typology or draw the connections to questions of associational life and civil society. See Lord Acton, "On Nationality," in Fears (1988).

"mature natural state," "characterized by durable institutional structures for the state and the ability to support elite organizations outside the immediate framework of the state,"[12] in order to undergird, in particular, pluralism of the oppositional type.

The general argument that appears over the course of most of a century has two main parts. First is the claim that (at least in the postmedieval era) there is a general tendency for states to become more centralized, and a corresponding temptation on the part of those who wield state power to impose uniformity across the territory they govern. This, so it is argued, makes pluralism of all kinds vulnerable. Second is the idea that only some kinds of group life are generative of an oppositional politics that can keep that tendency in check. These are, especially, those that have a strong extrapolitical motivational claim on their members, from aristocratic honor to religious commitment to provincial or linguistic-national loyalty. The recurring worry is that even such motivations will not *suffice* to support the needed oppositional work, if group members do not have the added motivation and added political resources that come from institutionalized status or privileges.

3.2 Montesquieu, *Corps*, and Uniformity

Montesquieu's 1748 *The Spirit of the Laws* famously identified *corps intermédiaires* as the crucial constitutional pillars of a moderate monarchy.[13] Montesquieu treated the self-government of cities, provinces, guilds, and the church as a part of the defense of limitations on centralized state power, the kinds of limits that were sorely needed in the era of would-be absolutist kings. The argument depended in part on the quasi-public or public character of the *corps*: their privileges made up part of the constitutional order. And it depended in part on their base in extralegal social facts not susceptible to direct royal intervention, such as the nobility's attachment to their honor and the independent belief system that animates the church. Montesquieu's was an oppositional pluralism that drew its strength from privilege; drawing on their respective social bases of support and appealing to law, the *corps* could limit monarchies and prevent them from degenerating into despotism.[14]

Montesquieu distinguished moderate monarchies and immoderate despotisms on the basis of the former's respect for the *corps*. "Intermediate,

---

12. North, Wallis, and Weingast (2009, 47). They add "at the limit, a mature natural state is able to create and sustain perpetually lived organizations, but that is not a common feature of mature natural states." Common or not, the perpetually lived organizations with independent legal personality, the *corps* with corporate form, were very much a feature of the mature natural states that we find in early modern, pre-Revolutionary Europe. Since the theorists I discuss here take the possibility of the *corps* for granted, I will not discuss the alternative of mature natural states that lack them. See also North, Wallis, and Weingast (2009, 158–69).

13. Montesquieu ([1748] 1989).

14. Sections 3.2–3.4 draw on Levy (2015).

subordinate, and dependent powers constitute the nature of monarchical government, that is, of the government in which one alone governs by fundamental laws."[15] The "lords, clergy, nobility, and towns" maintain a monarchy in its proper conceptual form. The most "natural" intermediate power is the nobility as a class, so much so that "nobility is the essence of a monarchy, whose fundamental maxim is: *no monarch, no nobility; no nobility, no monarch*; rather, one has a despot." Even the church, which he sharply criticizes for intolerance and persecution, has a crucial role to play, and he suggests that ecclesiastical autonomy should be respected and legally firmly established. It provides the final check against despotism when a monarchy has otherwise abolished all of its old laws. This is, importantly, a defense of the nobility in a monarchy, not of nobles as such. The aristocracy in a monarchy defends the laws; aristocratic government without a monarch to overawe the nobles tends toward arbitrariness and corruption. Their privileges are "odious in themselves"—a view that will persist throughout the theorists discussed below—but instrumentally useful in aligning their honor with the defense of the constitution.[16]

The continued freedom of the *corps* was a visible sign of a monarchy's continued adherence to lawful limits, but it was not only that. Montesquieu held that monarchies could only *remain* moderate and lawful regimes over time because of the continued existence of the *corps*. As their liberties and privileges diminished, the monarchy would slip farther and farther toward despotism. This was because only the *corps* could have both the motivation and the power to successfully check the urge of monarchs to absolutism. Without them, there is no one who can refuse the king, particularly not in the name of law. Of special importance are those intermediate bodies he calls the "depositories of the laws" as they will have a special connection with the retention and enforcement of legality and liberties: in France, the aristocratic courts known as *parlements*, which even in their weakened eighteenth-century state "do much good."[17]

Montesquieu admired the British constitution, the subject of extended discussions in II.11 and III.19. But his enthusiasm for England's system was limited precisely by the decline of England's *corps* since the Civil War. "If you abolish the prerogatives of the lords, clergy, nobility, and towns in a monarchy, you will soon have a popular state or else a despotic state [. . .] In order to favor liberty, the English have removed all the intermediate powers that formed their monarchy. They are quite right to preserve that liberty," he drily concludes; "if they were to lose it, they would be one of the most enslaved peoples on earth" because of their abolition of intermediate powers.[18]

---

15. Montesquieu ([1748] 1989, II.4, 17).
16. Montesquieu ([1748] 1989, II.11.6, 161).
17. Montesquieu (2012, 192).
18. Montesquieu ([1748] 1989, II.4, 18–19).

The conviction that the *corps*, including those staffed by hereditary nobility, are crucial to the maintenance of a lawful and balanced monarchy helps to explain Montesquieu's apparently odd identification of *honor* as the animating principle of a monarchy. Aristocratic honor, after all, does not derive directly or solely from the monarch, but rather from a sense of the dignity and respect that is due as a matter of family standing and personal merit. For aristocrats who are drawn to court, that is, Versailles, the monarch has an outsized influence on their status and standing. But those driven by honor could not be the kinds of subservient flatterers demanded by despots. They could not help but stand up for the dignity of their own offices and authority. Indeed, they could not even be counted on to obey direct royal commands: aristocratic officers had been known to disobey orders that we would think of as war crimes but that they construed as dishonorable. However poorly justified a person's view of his own honor might be, it remained *his*, not only outside the direct control of the monarch but sometimes a psychological source of the willingness to resist him.[19] If the *corps* were needed to affirm and enforce legal limits on royal power and prevent despotism, honor or some other extralegal motivation was needed to animate the *corps*, and to keep their members dedicated to their defense. This is why, notwithstanding the "ignorance natural to the nobility, its laxity, and its scorn for civil government,"[20] it is the *sine qua non* of lawful and moderate monarchy.

Montesquieu critiqued the turn to absolutism and centralization under Louis XIV, albeit always with a slight, politic opacity. The recurring comparisons and contrasts between monarchies and despotisms often come just to the edge of saying that Bourbon France had crossed, or risked crossing, the line between them. The *corps* had been steadily undermined in "a great European state" over the preceding centuries. "In certain European monarchies," the autonomous provinces that govern themselves well and thus thrive are constantly threatened with the loss of "the very government that produces the good," to better allow them to "pay even more."[21] This strategy of killing the golden goose is another sign of despotism; "when the savages of Louisiana want fruit, they cut down the tree and gather the fruit. There you have despotic government."[22]

Montesquieu added to his political and constitutional critique of despotic uniformity an understanding of a social world autonomous of, and not created by, political rule. Geography and climate, historical and cultural change, economic forces, and religion all constrained in various ways what rulers

---

19. For discussions of honor as a source of strength for political resistance, though in a more democratic spirit, see Krause (2002) and Appiah (2010).

20. Montesquieu ([1748] 1989, II.4, 19).

21. Montesquieu ([1748] 1989, II.13.12, 221). For an account of Montesquieu's defense of provincial autonomy that amounts to a kind of federalist constitutionalism for monarchies, see Ward (2009).

22. Montesquieu ([1748] 1989, I.5.13, 59).

could do—and in different ways in different places. He advises legislators and rulers to notice the particularities of their societies and govern accordingly, rather than in accordance with abstract plans. Like his followers for the rest of the eighteenth century—social theorists studying manners and mores, classical economists elaborating an economic world that transcended political boundaries and operated according to its own discoverable rules—Montesquieu sought to describe *societies* rather than simply polities, and societies that shaped and constrained the polities set over them.[23]

Near the end of *The Spirit of the Laws*, in the midst of an extended constitutional history of France, we find a surprising chapter on the idea of uniformity of laws, against which Montesquieu warns the would-be legislator:

"There are certain ideas of uniformity, which sometimes strike great geniuses (for they even affected Charlemagne), but infallibly make an impression on little souls. They discover therein a kind of perfection, which they recognize because it is impossible for them not to see it; the same authorized weights, the same measures in trade, the same laws in the state, the same religion in all its parts. But is this always right and without exception? Is the evil of changing constantly less than that of suffering? And does not a greatness of genius consist rather in distinguishing between those cases in which uniformity is requisite, and those in which there is a necessity for differences? In China the Chinese are governed by the Chinese ceremonial and the Tartars by theirs; and yet there is no nation in the world that aims so much at tranquility. If the people observe the laws, what signifies it whether these laws are the same?"[24]

Near the beginning of the book Montesquieu had said that when a ruler "makes himself more absolute, his first thought is to simplify the laws."[25] Then, it had appeared as something like a deliberate strategy, as the simplified state would be simpler to rule. But at the end of the book it appears rather as an unjustified taste or a psychological affliction of those who hold power or make laws. Shortly before the remarks on uniformity, he wrote that "it seems to me that I have written this work only to prove [. . .] that the spirit of moderation should be that of the legislator; the political good, like the moral good, is always found between two limits."[26] But the spirit of moderation was not normally or naturally that of the legislator.

While Montesquieu's multistranded defense of pluralism and the privileges of the *corps* were highly influential through the eighteenth century, two rivals to it were as well. One, the civic republican suspicion of factions, was associated with Rousseau, Mably, and Sièyes as well as with important strands in the American and French Revolutions. The elevation of extrale-

---

23. This is the sense in which Durkheim saw Montesquieu as one of the founders of sociology, set apart from political philosophy. See also Taylor (1990).
24. Montesquieu ([1748] 1989, VI.29.18, 617).
25. Montesquieu ([1748] 1989, I.6.2, 75).
26. Montesquieu ([1748] 1989, VI.29.1, 602).

gal social pluralism into a public constitutional fact became identified with both intolerable privilege and illegitimate disunity. The other, a rationalistic individualism, looked forward to the use of modernized state power to check or abolish the *corps*, not backward toward imagined pasts of uncorrupted unity. It is in principle distinguishable from the civic republican view, most prominently by its greater enthusiasm for commerce but also by its greater tolerance for associational pluralism provided that privilege was stripped away. The gradual shift from a civic republican suspicion of all factions in politics to a pluralist view that competitive factions (and, later, parties) might be attractive and necessary features of republican politics is well known. And there is, I suspect, something to be said for the idea that this shift corresponds with (and contributes to) that from regulated intra-oligarchic contestation to the early open-access orders of the nineteenth century.

In the remainder of this essay, however, I follow an intellectual path from Montesquieu onward. Montesquieu and his successors wanted no part of the civic republican obsession with unity, but the pluralism they espoused was never only that of freely created associations peacefully competing. Although Smith, Constant, and Tocqueville did value competitive associational life, they also followed Montesquieu in his attention to oppositional pluralism—and they offered reason to think that oppositional pluralism might require deeper social roots than open access and individual consent could provide.

3.3   The Man of System and the Religious Marketplace

One of the first powerful analyses of associations as competitors appears in *The Wealth of Nations*' treatment of religious groups.[27] It is, of course, not a coincidence that this analysis is offered by Adam Smith, in the course of a work that shows the beneficial consequences of competitive behavior in a range of domains and that is remembered as the key intellectual defense of free economic competition against oligarchic mercantile monopolies. His treatment in Book V of vibrant competition among churches for members, however, is surprisingly dissimilar to his examinations of marketplace behavior in Books I and II. His is not a model of parishioners casually shopping from one church to another at arm's length, but of believers being provided with community, structure, and meaning by sects that might counteract the anonymity and alienation of modern urban life.

The discussion is framed in part as a reply to David Hume's wry defense of an established church, an argument in favor of indolent salaried priests as against the tendency of a free religious marketplace to favor passionate religious enthusiasm and the sects that march a population toward religious civil war. Smith *agrees* with Hume that energetic and excessively rigorous

27. Smith (ed. Campbell, Skinner, and Todd [1776] 1981, 788–814).

churches will have a competitive advantage over their distant, lazy, bureaucratic counterparts. (Not to put too fine a point on it: they both saw the rise of Methodism at the expense of traditional Anglicanism as recalling the earlier rise of Puritanism, and as examples of a general truth about religious competition.) He importantly disagrees about the political conclusion, arguing that in the absence of establishment, religious competition tends to multiply sects and to create diffuse contestation, not the concentrated type that can lead to civil war. Indeed, he blames the established bureaucratic churches, not their passionate opponents, for civil wars; it is the establishment that makes use of state power and elevates disagreement into organized violence. The critique of established churches resembles that of mercantilist monopolies: the privileged and powerful make illegitimate use of the state and entrench their own advantages. But his model of competitive behavior among the sects does not much resemble that of his understanding of marketplace behavior. Indeed, the anonymous and arm's-length character of market and city life partly creates the need that passionate sects fulfill: a need for intense community based on strong emotional connection and mutual knowledge. Whereas commerce is generally a mild and moderating force in Smith's thought, moderation is precisely what *does not* result from religious competition. Competition does not turn religious life into something calm and rational, deliberately chosen and deliberately exited from. Rather, it changes the institutional setting for our expression of deep commitments, and can thereby serve valuable social functions (relief from anonymity, mitigation of social and moral decay in the city) rather than creating political dangers.

And this attention to the deep attachments we hold to our identities and memberships sometimes pushed Smith from a competitive to an oppositional understanding of pluralism, as in his indictment of the "man of system" in the final edition of *The Theory of Moral Sentiments*, published during the early stages of the French Revolution.[28] Its best-known lines have sometimes been read as if they were criticisms of centralized economic planning and treated as a kind of adjunct to *The Wealth of Nations*.

"The man of system, on the contrary, is apt to be very wise in his own conceit [. . .] He seems to imagine that he can arrange the different members of a great society with as much ease as the hand arranges the different pieces upon a chess-board. He does not consider that the pieces upon the chess-board have no other principle of motion besides that which the hand impresses upon them; but that, in the great chess-board of human society, every single piece has a principle of motion of its own, altogether different from that which the legislature might chuse to impress upon it."

In fact, the passage concerns constitutional reform, privilege, and politics, not economics at all. Smith's man of system bears a closer resemblance to

---

28. Smith (ed. Campbell and Skinner [1790] 1981, 233–34).

Montesquieu's legislator of uniformity than to the modern would-be economic planner. In his desire to abolish privilege, the man of system proposes "to new-model the constitution, and to alter, in some of its most essential parts, that system of government under which the subjects of a great empire have enjoyed, perhaps, peace, security, and even glory, during the course of several centuries together." In seeking to implement the far-reaching reforms that appear in his mind as uniform, symmetrical, and beautiful, the man of system holds special fury for those elements of society that might have the constitutional power to obstruct them. "The great object of their reformation, therefore, is to remove those obstructions; to reduce the authority of the nobility; to take away the privileges of cities and provinces, and to render both the greatest individuals and the greatest orders of the state, as incapable of opposing their commands, as the weakest and most insignificant."

By contrast, "the man whose public spirit is prompted altogether by humanity and benevolence, will respect the established powers and privileges even of individuals, and still more those of the great orders and societies, into which the state is divided. Though he should consider some of them as in some measure abusive, he will content himself with moderating, what he often cannot annihilate without great violence."

In other words, while Smith sees that the differential privileges of the "orders and societies," the nobles, provinces, and cities, are often abusive ("odious in themselves," as Montesquieu put it), he also thinks that they serve as a valuable political and constitutional counterweight to centralized and rationalizing power. The wise reformer would seek to mitigate the abuses but *not* to abolish the special constitutional standing.

While the *monopolistic* privileges of an established church or of the mercantile companies normally tend to augment unitary central power, the constitutional privileges of a *plurality* of cities, provinces, or nobles can be quite different. Just as Montesquieu had seen, their various bases of independent social power mean that they are in a good position to oppose abuses on the part of the state itself, whether committed by "imperial and royal" centralizers or by the leaders of revolutionary factions.

Smith's discussion of the man of system includes the idea of competitive political parties of a sort—and party competition is the problem, not the solution. Moderate reform is less likely to appeal to the passionate partisan base than is wholesale abolition; even party leaders who know better may be radicalized by the competitive dynamic. And the bodies he names as moderating forces, the "orders and societies," could not be created by associational free competition: provinces are not clubs, and nobles are not a party. They are limited in number, privileged, and rest on or engender very particularistic commitments on the part of their members.

In Smith we thus see a crucial *range* of treatments of pluralism, which includes not only the kind of competitive behavior among firms that we most associate with competition in open-access orders, but also the passionate and particularistic competition among churches, and an oppositional status of privileged pluralistic orders. His appreciation for the value of something very like open access in the spheres of the market and religion coexisted with a not-entirely-grudging tolerance for the constitutional institutions of the mature natural state.

3.4 Constant's Pluralism

Benjamin Constant was the first major political theorist to call his thought "liberal" and to identify with liberalism as a party position. While we might think of Adam Smith as the most important exponent of a theory of open-access markets, and James Madison as the crucial figure in developing an account of factional political competition through electoral politics, Constant is the first theorist of the emerging liberal order as a whole: freedom of religion, speech, and the press; due process of law and equality before the law; competitive and responsible representative democracy; free markets and free trade; and the elevation of individual private liberty to a privileged moral position. He famously opposed Rousseau's democratic holism and celebrated modern individuality. He could see the possibility of competitive pluralism without privilege, and he welcomed it. But he shared many of Montesquieu's and Smith's worries, as well.

Much of Constant's writing on associational pluralism embraced competitive models, and defended group life as an aspect of individual freedom in the private sphere; and his instincts were always opposed to group privilege. Like Smith, indeed in very similar terms, he wrote sharply against guilds and exclusive corporations and in support of market liberalization.[29] In religion he supported the proliferation of sects and denominations as a positive good, and as in any case inevitable wherever persons cared about religious questions enough to think about them, rather than mindlessly following empty rituals. Schism and proliferation tended—through competition—to improve the moral purity of all sects, as the Reformation improved a previously corrupt Catholicism; and it also conduced to civil peace.[30] His religious sensibility was a romantic Protestant individualism.[31] He was instinctively unsympathetic to Catholicism and skeptical of all sacerdotal corporations: organized churches, a privileged priesthood, and monastic orders. The religion to which he was so concerned to preserve free access was a religion of individual spirituality that develops the soul and the mind.

Yet he recognized that for many people their religious sentiments came to be tied up in external "forms," and that this was a reason for freedom of religious practice with respect to those forms—a freedom that had been

---

29. Constant ([1822–24] 2015, 143–50); Constant ([1810] 2003, 229–51).
30. Constant ([1810] 2003, 129–46).
31. Rosenblatt (2008).

violated under the Revolution. However little he liked them, he supported the liberty to form and live in associations such as monasteries. Provided that freedom of exit was protected, life within them was an option legitimately open to free persons. "There are two ways of suppressing monasteries; you may open their doors; or you may drive out their occupants. If you adopt the first solution, you do something good without causing any harm; you break chains without violating refuges. If you adopt the second, you upset calculations based upon public faith; you insult old age, which you drag languishing and unarmed into an unknown world; you violate an incontestable right of all individuals in the social state, the right to choose their own way of life, to hold their property in common, to gather in order to profess the same doctrine, to enjoy the same leisure, to savour the same rest."[32]

These religious cases were of central importance to Constant, and they offer reason to think that he might have viewed group life competitively: break the chains, let the sects proliferate, open the doors, let believers choose. Certainly he opposed the integrative style of thinking of the Catholic Church as providing believers with their way of belonging *to France*. And often he emphasized that the pluralism of group life was tightly connected to the ordinary private liberty of living as one chooses, including in customary ways. In his most enduring work of political theory, "The Liberty of the Ancients Compared with That of the Moderns," he held to the view that "the changes brought by the centuries require from the authorities greater respect for customs, for affections, for the independence of individuals."[33] Habits and affections are a crucial part of a free person's happiness and, therefore, of his or her interests. In social life, particularly but not only in religion, the liberty of the moderns was closely tied to pluralism. Free people, not joined together by ancient republican devotion to the public, would not be socially homogenous.

But, like Smith, Constant drew on the oppositional style found in Montesquieu when it came to pluralism in the constitutional order.[34] In the wake of a generation of Jacobin and Bonapartist centralization, Constant pointed to Montesquieu's insight about the perils of the spirit of uniformity. He argued both against the spirit of system that accompanies and initiates governors' desire to rationalize, and in active defense of the sentiments that attach

---

32. "On innovation, reform, and the uniformity and stability of institutions"; chapter 1 of the material added to the fourth edition of *Conquest and Usurpation*; Constant ([1819] 1988, 153).

33. Constant, "Liberty of the Ancients Compared with that of the Moderns" ([1819] 1988, 324).

34. More so than Smith, Constant drew directly on Montesquieu throughout his writings. "What a keen and profound eye!" he wrote in his diary. "All that he said, even in the smallest things, proves true every day." Constant, "Journaux Intimes," Jan. 28 ([1804] 1957). As Jeremy Jennings puts it, the argument for "the preservation of local independence as a means of restricting the power of despotic, central government" that Constant established as a central theme of French liberalism "was an updated supplement to Montesquieu's defence of the rights of the provincial nobility" (Jennings 2011, 164).

people to their local traditions and rules. The desire to create order and rationality in society need not be destructive in itself; but it is too-easily joined with coercive force, as governors imagine that a uniform society will be more easily governed. "The spirit of system was first entranced by symmetry. The love of power soon discovered what immense advantages symmetry could procure for it."[35] A kind of philosophical aesthetic motivated benevolent legislators in the first instance; but the desire for uniformity led to the destruction of the *corps* and nonstate institutions, enhancing the relative power of the center and creating a dynamic that outraced that initial public-spirited impulse. With Montesquieu and against such uniformity-craving *philosophes* as Voltaire, he wrote sympathetically about the provincial variety of laws in the old regime.[36] The plurality of public jurisdictions and legal traditions attached people's natural sentiments of familiarity and home to the constitutional order. Rationalization from the center broke that tie.

Constant indicts the tendencies toward uniformity of centralized and metropolitan legislatures. The members of the latter tend to acquire an *esprit de corps*, identifying with each other and with the capital. So they "lose sight of the usages, needs, and way of life of their constituents. They lend themselves to general ideas of leveling, symmetry, uniformity, mass changes, and universal recasting, bringing upset, disorder, and confusion to distant regions. It is this disposition we must combat, because it is on particular memories, habits, and regional laws that the happiness and peace of a province rest. National assemblies are scornful and careless with these things."[37] The better course is to allow the cities and provinces to keep their natural hold on our affections. "The interests and memories that arise from local customs contain a germ of resistance that authority is reluctant to tolerate and that it is anxious to eradicate. It can deal more easily with individuals; it rolls its heavy body effortlessly over them as if they were sand."[38] That "germ of resistance" seems to me the crucial idea that runs throughout Constant's writings on pluralism and constitutionalism: the oppositional relationship between the various customary local jurisdictions and groupings on one hand, and the central state on the other.

During his years of exile from Napoleonic France, Constant worked on (but never finished) a book on the possibility of republican government in a large state, a possibility Montesquieu famously denied and one that Constant was at pains to establish. This work, dedicated to refuting one of the best-known of Montesquieu's arguments, is nonetheless steeped in Montesquieu's intellectual style and ideas. Constant understood that Mon-

35. Constant, "On Uniformity," in *The Spirit of Conquest and Usurpation and Their Relation to European Civilization* ([1814] 1988, 74).
36. Constant, *Conquest and Usurpation* ([1814] 1988, 154).
37. Constant, Book XV ch. 4, "Application of This Principle to the Composition of Representative Assemblies" ([1810] 2003, 328).
38. *SCU*, 74.

tesquieu's skepticism was not aimed at the idea of *freedom* in a large state but at the idea of freedom in a *republic*. He thought that Montesquieu had looked at the virtuous, anticommercial, unfree republics of antiquity and attributed those features to *republics*, when they were better attributed to the ancient era as such.[39]

This was Constant's position throughout his life: that freedom was possible in a large and extended republic, and that much that Montesquieu attributed to the spirit of a nation or of its laws is in fact attributable to the spirit of the age. Constant's political agenda never included the recreation of the ancient constitution of Montesquieu's time. But he sympathized with Montesquieu's defense of that constitution and tried to draw appropriate lessons from it; he did not view it as a defense of local tyranny and arbitrariness. On the central claim that intermediate bodies, a hereditary class, and corporations were essential for freedom, Montesquieu had been right to see them as the bulwarks of freedom against the king of his era. Their irrationality and inegalitarianism did not condemn them out of hand; uniformity under a tyrannical law was, for Constant as for Montesquieu, no virtue. The task for republican and post-Revolutionary thought was, in part, to find ways to recapture the pluralistic benefits without the abusive privilege.

Constant criticized the idea of hereditary rights of rule and the existence of a hereditary principle in a constitution. But his understanding of Montesquieu's defense of such things was that under an "abusive" government, "heredity can be useful; where rights have disappeared, privileges offer asylum and defense. In spite of its inconveniences, heredity is better than the absence of any neutral power. The hereditary interest . . . creates a sort of neutrality.[40] In order to dispose of heredity, it is necessary to have an excellent constitution. Montesquieu knew this; under the pressure of despotism there is a terrible leveling equality."[41] The supposed neutrality of the aristocratic class was closely linked with their judicial role in the House of Lords and the *parlements*. Generating a neutral power that could take the place of the hereditary class was a long-term preoccupation of Constant's constitutional thought.

Constant agreed that a monarchy depended on an aristocracy in order to protect freedom; he differed from Montesquieu in insisting that the reverse was also true (a monarch might check the local tyranny of lords) and in maintaining that this provided an argument against monarchy altogether. He thought that the benefits of the ancient constitution's division of pow-

39. This was, of course, the direction Constant's own arguments would lead him years later in "The Liberty of the Ancients Compared with that of the Moderns."

40. The supposed neutrality of the aristocratic class was closely linked with their judicial role in the House of Lords and the *parlements*. Generating a neutral power that could take the place of the hereditary class was a long-term preoccupation of Constant's constitutional thought.

41. Constant ([1810] 1991, 118).

ers and classes could be simulated in an extended and federal republic; but he certainly agreed with Montesquieu that there had been such benefits. In the defenses of provincial and *parlementaire* rights and privileges, the *ancien régime* French conducted debates and engaged in struggles in which "everyone's heads were filled with the principles of liberty."[42]

When Constant advised Bonaparte on the creation of a new constitution during the Hundred Days, he argued (against Bonaparte's inclinations) in favor of a new hereditary aristocracy. The emperor did not wish to be challenged, and in any event had no suitable candidates—the traditional aristocrats were his enemies. Constant, however, called a hereditary aristocracy "indispensable" for a constitutional monarchy. He would certainly have rather had a republic with no hereditary distinctions; but after the republic fell, there was a need for an aristocracy to moderate the imperial monarchy. He hoped to prevent the reemergence of feudal privileges, but to create a hereditary house parallel to the House of Lords.

In the *Memoirs sur les Cent-Jours*, there is a passage that begins much the same way, reporting the same arguments of Bonaparte against an aristocracy. But now Constant says that his longstanding doubts about a monarchy without an aristocracy had likely arisen because he, like Montesquieu, was "seduced" by the example of the British constitution. Here Constant himself criticizes the creation of a new, imperial, aristocracy—but not on rationalist or egalitarian grounds. Instead, he maintains that "nothing is created by artifice" in politics. "The creative force in politics, like the vital force in the physical world, cannot be supplemented by any act of will or by any act of law";[43] rather, the spirit of the age and of a people would in some important way shape political developments and institutions. This is a Montesquieuian critique of one of Montesquieu's doctrines, and returned Constant to one of the themes of *SCU*—Bonaparte's status as a usurper, the inability to create new bloodlines and institutions and traditions from scratch that would have the same legitimacy as those that had come before. It moreover recalls the comment that it would be irrational to deliberately *create* the diversity in local laws, weights, measures, and so on that Constant defended in his chapter on uniformity.

In other words, Constant was torn between two Montesquieuian impulses. He perceived the need for an intermediate and independent body of aristocrats to balance the Emperor; but such a body would be a deliberate and artificial creation, out of keeping with the spirit of the nation and of the age. In his later writings and political work under the Restoration it seems to me that we can see the same dynamic. The social background, the spirit of the society in which Constant lived, was one that had been shaped by

---

42. Constant ([1810] 1991, 208).
43. Destutt de Tracy, *The Commentary*, 317.

the Revolution and what followed it. Counter-revolution no more appealed to him in the 1820s than it had in the 1790s[44]—and in both decades one of his arguments against counterrevolution was that it would be at odds with changes in social character that had taken place. He argued that reforms should not outpace social change and that customs should be allowed to evolve freely without being coercively rushed by the state, but also, and for the same reasons, that political reactions should not attempt to undo social change that has already taken place.

Constant never *supported* the particular group privileges of the ancient constitution. He was keenly aware of the costs to individual freedom of state-sanctioned group privileges. Constant's pluralism had to differ from Montesquieu's, however much he admired his predecessor; the post-revolutionary world he inhabited differed too greatly from the *ancien régime*. But he was far from certain about whether a society made up only of individuals and voluntary associations could keep centralization at bay. In his more optimistic moments he hoped that revitalized federalism or local self-government overlaid on a population with substantial provincial and local sentiment could provide the "germ of resistance" with a political vehicle without formal group-differentiated privileges, and that a literate and enlightened population with the franchise could check despotism. But sometimes, even late in his life when his hostility to contemporaneous Restoration nobles was at its height, he looked back to the institutions Montesquieu defended and the energy that privilege provided to resistance, and wondered.

> Formerly, in all European countries there were institutions associated with many abuses but which, by giving certain classes privileges to defend and rights to exercise, kept up activity among these classes and thus preserved them from discouragement and apathy. To this cause must be attributed the energy of character existing up to the sixteenth century, an energy of which we no longer find any trace by the time of the revolution which shook thrones and reforged souls. These institutions had been everywhere destroyed, or changed so much that they had lost almost all their influence. . . . [D]efective institutions which nevertheless invest some powerful classes with certain privileges they are permanently interested in defending possess many disadvantages, yet they also possess the advantage of not letting the whole nation be degraded and bastardized. The beginning of Louis XIV's reign was disturbed by the Fronde, in truth a childish war, but one which was the remnant of a spirit of resistance accustomed to action, and still acting almost without purpose. Despotism greatly increased around the end of that reign.[45]

In this he anticipated questions that would be of central concern to his successor as the intellectual leader of French liberalism, Alexis de Tocqueville.

---

44. Constant, "Des Réactions Politiques" (1797) in Louandre (1874).
45. Constant ([1822–24] 2015, 45, 51).

3.5   Tocqueville: Is the Art of Association Enough?

One might think that it is in Tocqueville above all that we would find an appreciation of a pluralism that arises out of freely formed voluntary associations. He was, after all, the theorist of the "art of associating," the one who saw and appreciated the Americans' ability and eagerness to be "freely and constantly forming associations" both in political life and in the pursuit of their various social ends. Even his understanding of the structure of American government was associational; he was less struck by federalism and the extent of state authority than he was by self-government in townships—a level of political organization he explicitly referred to as an "association."

He witnessed phenomena in American society that one might think solved the problem of pluralism without privilege: a social sphere of free and open associational creation, entry, and exit. As Tocqueville understood it, the associational world he found among the Americans differed from *ancien régime* pluralism among the *corps* not only by its equality but also by its fluidity. The *corps* were longstanding; Americans had mastered the art of associating *anew*, creating new associations easily, almost casually, for reasons great or small.

Tocqueville identified one root of this art in the American inheritance from English dissenting Protestantism, but perhaps overlooked others in the new American models of economy and law. Eighteenth- and early nineteenth-century uses of the phrase "civil society" referred mainly to the development of what was also called *commercial society*, and also to the modern unified legal system that underlay commercial society. Civil society replaced the world of privilege—including trading companies with monopolistic privilege, churches with ecclesiastical jurisdictional privilege, and nobles with status privilege—with a unified free and equal legal system. This system encompassed importantly laws governing commercial exchange, such that Hegel identified "civil society" with the open market and Marx dismissed it as *bourgeois* civil society. It was just such an open-access legal regime—associated with the move toward a democratized law of commercial incorporation—that allowed for the associational world Tocqueville saw, the associational world to which we most often reserve the phrase "civil society" today.

Yet, as with Smith and Constant, matters are not so simple, and Tocqueville cannot simply be read as celebrating an order of competitive associational life. The animating concern of Tocqueville's two greatest works is that the conjoined historical movements toward equality and centralization will leave despotism impossible to resist and freedom impossible to defend. He was clear in *Democracy in America* that his concerns were either European or universal, not narrowly American (though the American canonization of Tocqueville is prone to overlook this). In the penultimate chapter of volume 1, he refers to both the mores that once kept government limited, and to the institutions that did so such as the prerogatives of the nobility, of the authority of sovereign courts, of the rights of corporations, or of provincial privileges, all things which softened the blows of authority and maintained a spirit of resistance in the nation . . . political institutions which, though often opposed to the freedom of individuals, nevertheless served to keep the love of liberty alive in men's souls with obviously valuable results. . . . When towns and provinces form so many different nations within the common motherland, each of them has a particularist spirit opposed to the general spirit of servitude; but now that all parts of a single empire have lost their franchises, usages, prejudices, and even their memories and names and have grown accustomed to obey the same laws, it is no longer more difficult to oppress them all together than to do this to each separately.[46]

Here we see not only a *précis* for his study of the French old regime decades later, we also find by implication the animating questions of *Democracy in America* itself. Have the Anglo-Americans so far avoided this descent into servility? If so, how, and what can be learned from them about how to maintain liberty in a democratic age? In old regime France he saw the gradual erosion of intermediate bodies by a centralizing and homogenizing power that became almost irresistible as it aligned with the world-historical force of democratization. In the France of his own day he saw what he took to be the direction of the modern world: democratic equality and statist centralization reinforcing each other and grinding down freedom, distinctiveness, and accomplishment. In contemporaneous America he saw a democratic society that was resisting these trends, in part thanks to local government and to voluntary associations. But in the American future he saw the possibility of "soft despotism" of homogeneous mediocrity and centralized bureaucratic paternalism. While American associations (including the township) allowed for collective action in an egalitarian age when the individual actor was impotent, they were still small and powerless relative to the bureaucratic state or the democratic majority behind it.

While both *Democracy in America* and *The Old Regime and the Revolution* offer famously complex and multicausal accounts, group life and decentralized government figure prominently in each. The Americans benefited from their institutions of local self-government and from their mania for forming voluntary associations. And the French old regime, by the time of the Revolution, was ready to collapse into a democracy that eventually yielded Bonaparte's despotism in large part because the Bourbon kings had centralized the state so dramatically, undermining urban liberty, provincial liberty, and the privileges of the *corps* so effectively.

Tocqueville described medieval Europe as being everywhere much the same, with provincial liberties and urban self-government coexisting with feudal privileges and assemblies of the Estates. But—and this is the central

---

46. Tocqueville ([1835/1840] 1969, 312–313).

thesis of *Old Regime*—that shared order was eroded and replaced by a centralized state gradually over the course of early modernity, not suddenly by the Revolution. By the eighteenth century, "the ancient constitution of Europe" was "half-ruined everywhere"[47] and no longer able to check absolutist monarchs. At the highest level of abstraction, Tocqueville attributes this to the increasing equality of condition over the later Middle Ages and early modernity, a change in historical stage from feudal inequality to democratic equality. "The nobles were already beaten down and the people had not yet risen; the former were too low and the latter not high enough to hinder the movements of power."[48] Germanic customary law had been supplanted by Roman civil law, a "law of servitude," opportunistically deployed across the continent by monarchs set on establishing their "absolute power" "on the ruins of the old liberties of Europe."[49] Tocqueville offers a history of royal suppression of provincial liberties, of urban self-government, and of guild and *corps* privileges, as well as of the deliberate Bourbon undermining of the social role of the nobility.

The decayed institutions of the eighteenth century created a paradoxical situation for the old regime. On the one hand, they were unloved, indeed, often detested. A nobility that no longer had any useful purpose in the countryside retained feudal privileges and immunity from taxation, and the wealthy urban classes naturally resented them for it. Moreover, they served to divide people against each other. While all were becoming more alike in social fact, they remained sharply legally and politically differentiated, and mutual antagonism resulted. But such freedoms as remained, such limits on royal absolutism as still existed, were thanks to these unloved institutions. They "preserved the spirit of independence among a great number of subjects, and inclined them to stiffen their necks against abuses of authority."[50]

And so Tocqueville emphasized the role of the prerevolutionary *corps intermédiaires*, at the same time that he described the inevitability of their decline. Like Montesquieu and Constant before him, he acknowledged their privileges and prerogatives to have been often "odious in themselves," and he thought that they became progressively more intolerable as French society became leveled and homogenized. The *esprit de corps* found in the nobility, the clergy, the lawyers, and each city's bourgeoisie, their commitment to the group's privileges and rights of self-rule, provided them with both the motive and the means to resist royal despotism.

About the *parlements* in particular, Tocqueville thought much as Constant had; their role in government "was a great evil which limited a greater one." Tocqueville wrote admiringly about the *parlementaires'* resolve dur-

---

47. Tocqueville ([1856] 1998, 103).
48. Tocqueville ([1856] 1998, 259).
49. Tocqueville ([1856] 1998, 258).
50. Tocqueville ([1856] 1998, 172).

ing the dissolution of the *Parlement* of Paris in 1771. All of them accepted their loss of status "without a single one of them personally surrendering to the royal will," inspiring other judges and lawyers to stand with them and refuse to cooperate with this suspension of legality. However socially unjust their position was, the *parlementaires* proved themselves to be courageous and committed defenders of liberty and the rule of law: "I know of nothing greater in the history of free nations than what happened on this occasion."[51]

3.6   The Open-Access Order and Civil Society

North, Wallis, and Weingast analyze the "doorstep conditions" for the transition from limited-access to open-access orders in terms of impersonality and equality. This means, among other things, that elite privileges and power politics be transformed into common, impersonal rights for members of the elite, subject to the rule of law; and that among these elite rights is the right to create perpetually lived impersonal corporate organizations. Crossing the threshold consists in part in extending the right to those legal and organizational resources to nonelites. Privilege and personality give way to equal-access pluralism.

In Tocqueville's analysis of the behavior of the *parlementaires* and their supporters, we can see that even within the doorstep stage, there might be tensions among these desiderata. The *parlements* defended the rule of law among elites in *ancien régime* France, they did so from a position of personal aristocratic privilege, and their status-oriented, personalistic willingness to defend their status provided crucial motivation for them to act in defense of the rule of law. Members of the *corps* of the *parlementaire* nobility and members of the lawyers' guild were willing to act oppositionally, standing against the crown in defense of their status and prerogatives. And on the other side of the Revolutionary transition, in the midst of France's step across the threshold into an open-access order, Tocqueville worried that without this motivational energy, opposition would be lacking. This, it seems to me, is the kind of thought that runs through these pluralist liberals across the transition from the mature natural state to the early open-access order.

In order to bridge the gap between the mid-nineteenth century and contemporary social theory, I suggest that we return to Ernest Gellner's model of civil society mentioned earlier. We might fairly read Gellner's post-1989 writings on liberal democracy as, in part, a celebration of open-access orders.[52] While he did not anticipate the North, Wallis, and Weingast arguments in full, he shares their emphasis on the character of associational and organizational life, the impersonality of the state, and access to political resources including military power. And he sees this order as crucially

---

51. Tocqueville ([1856] 1998, 178).
52. See, especially, Gellner (1994).

individualistic—not in the sense that in civil society we lack associations, but in the sense that these are *merely* associations, nothing thicker or deeper.

"Modular man," Gellner wrote of his ideal-typical inhabitant of civil society, "is capable of combining into effective associations and institutions, *without* these being total, multi-stranded, underwritten by ritual and made stable through being linked to a whole inside set of relationships, all of these being tied in with each other and so immobilized. He can combine into specific-purpose, *ad-hoc*, limited associations, without binding himself by some blood ritual."[53]

Gellner insists that the organizational triumph of the modern state over its medieval predecessors was one precondition for the emergence of a truly civil society, one in which associations may be formed, and exited, at will. This eliminates the potency of group ties to shape access to political and military power because the nation-state has trumped all substate competitors. Gellner's unified account depicts a social world of equal liberal agents creating new voluntary associations as easily, and with the same rules, as they create economic firms or political parties. This is an idealization of the open-access order—a strange word to use for a thinker so chastened as Gellner, but I mean it both in the sense that it is a Weberian ideal type and in the sense that it was, by Gellner's own moral lights, normatively ambitiously better than really existing open-access orders.

But it is important to note that Gellner's image of civil society fit neatly with his functionalist account of the emergence of nationalism; indeed, he insisted that "modular man is a nationalist."[54] Workers in an industrial economy shed guild identities and inherited employment, and need a modular education that will allow them to perform a variety of jobs in a variety of industrial workplaces. This in turn requires a nationally homogenous language in which workers can become literate, so that they might move around the country in response to labor needs and work alongside those whose ancestral dialects might have been incomprehensible to them. In other words, so that individual persons might be able to equally access the labor opportunities in a modern economy, premodern, ethnocultural, regional, and linguistic differences must be overcome. The affinities between the industrial firms in this story and the associations in his depictions of civil society are not a coincidence.

While Gellner thought it a kind of virtue that modular man is a nationalist, these nation-building projects of modern states were just the kind of centralizing pursuits of uniformity that so worried the eighteenth- and nineteenth-century pluralist liberals.[55] The increasingly unitary nation-

---

53. Gellner (1994, 99).
54. Gellner (1994, 103) and Gellner (1983).
55. While he lies beyond the scope of this essay, I would add Lord Acton to the theorists I have discussed here. See chapter 9 in Levy (2015).

state, they feared, provided a very uncertain political home for liberal freedom, including the associational freedoms of civil society. Faced with what they took to be an underlying tendency for modern states (and, increasingly, nation-states) to become uniform and centralized, these theorists hoped that pluralism could be recovered without privilege. They regarded the republican terror of faction and disunity as pathological, and appreciated Montesquieu's diagnosis of centralization's evils, but saw that the *corps* could not and should not survive in a democratic age. But the kinds of pluralism they both sought to legitimize rested more than is often appreciated on *ancien régime* foundations. The more liberal freedom of association, religious freedom, and local government they hoped could replace the *corps* still depended on extralegal social pluralism for its energy. The horizontal competition of firms and associations, with persons joining and leaving them at will, lacks a mechanism for the vertical constitutional constraint of centralizing states. And the abolition of privilege, the democratization and opening of organizational life, the shift from nobles defending their honor or lawyers standing on their guild rights to "modular man" putting on and taking off associational identities, may make that oppositional energy hard to come by.

References

Appiah, Anthony. 2010. *The Honor Code*. New York: W. W. Norton.
Constant, Benjamin. (1804) 1957. "Journaux Intimes." In *Oeuvres*, edited by Alfred Roulin. Paris: Gallimard.
———. (1810) 1991. *Fragments d'un Ouvrage Abandonné Sur la Possibilité d'une Constitution Républicaine Dans un Grand Pays*, edited by Henri Grange. Paris: Aubier.
———. (1810) 2003. *Principles of Politics Applicable to All Governments*, translated by Dennis O'Keefe. Indianapolis: Liberty Fund.
———. (1819) 1988. "Liberty of the Ancients Compared with that of the Moderns." In *The Political Writings of Benjamin Constant*, edited by Biancamaria Fontana, 324. Cambridge: Cambridge University Press.
———. (1822–24) 2015. *Commentary on Filangieri's Work*, translated and edited by Alan S. Kahan. Indianapolis: Liberty Fund.
Destutt de Tracy, Antoine Claude. (1811) 1969. *A Commentary and Review of Montesquieu's Spirit of the Laws*, translated by Thomas Jefferson. New York: Burt Franklin.
Fears, J. Rufus, ed. 1988. *Selected Writings of Lord Acton*, vol. I. Indianapolis: Liberty Fund.
Gellner, Ernest. 1983. *Nations and Nationalism*. Ithaca, NY: Cornell University Press.
———. 1994. *Conditions of Liberty: Civil Society and Its Rivals*. New York: Penguin.
Golemboski, David. 2015. "Federalism and the Catholic Principle of Subsidiarity." *Publius* 45 (4): 495–525.
Hirschman, Albert. 1970. *Exit, Voice, and Loyalty*. Cambridge, MA: Harvard University Press.

Jennings, Jeremy. 2011. *Revolution and the Republic: A History of Political Thought in France since the Eighteenth Century*. Oxford: Oxford University Press.

Kalyvas, Andreas, and Ira Katznelson. 2008. *Liberal Beginnings: Making a Republic for the Moderns*. Cambridge: Cambridge University Press.

Krause, Sharon. 2002. *Liberalism with Honor*. Cambridge, MA: Harvard University Press.

Levy, Jacob T. 2006. "Beyond Publius: Montesquieu, Liberal Republicanism, and the Small-Republic Theses." *History of Political Thought* 27 (1): 50–90.

———. 2007. "Federalism, Liberalism, and the Separation of Loyalties." *American Political Science Review* 101 (3): 459–77.

———. 2015. *Rationalism, Pluralism, and Freedom*. Oxford: Oxford University Press.

Louandre, Charles, ed. 1874. *Oeuvres Politiques de Benjamin Constant*. Paris: Charpentier et Cie.

Montesquieu, Baron de. (1748) 1989. *The Spirit of the Laws*, edited by Anne M. Cohler, Basia Carolyn Miller, and Harold S. Stone. New York: Cambridge University Press.

———. 2012. *My Thoughts*, translated by Henry C. Clark. Indianapolis: Liberty Fund.

North, Douglass, John Wallis, and Barry Weingast. 2009. *Violence and Social Orders*. Cambridge: Cambridge University Press.

Ostrom, Elinor. 1990. *Governing the Commons: The Evolution of Institutions for Collective Action*. Cambridge: Cambridge University Press.

Ostrom, Vincent, Charles M. Tiebout, and Robert Warren. 1961. "The Organization of Government in Metropolitan Areas: A Theoretical Inquiry." *American Political Science Review* 55 (5): 831–42.

Pocock, J. G. A. 1975. *The Machiavellian Moment*. Princeton, NJ: Princeton University Press.

Putnam, Robert D. 2000. *Bowling Alone: The Collapse and Revival of American Community*. New York: Simon and Schuster.

Rosenblatt, Helena. 2008. *Liberal Values: Benjamin Constant and the Politics of Religion*. Cambridge: Cambridge University Press.

Schmitter, Philippe C. 1974. "Still the Century of Corporatism?" *Review of Politics* 26 (1): 85–131.

Smith, Adam. (1776) 1981. *An Inquiry into the Nature and Causes of the Wealth of Nations*, edited by R. H. Campbell, A. S. Skinner, and W. B. Todd. Indianapolis: Liberty Fund.

———. (1790) 1981. *Theory of Moral Sentiments*, edited by R. H. Campbell and A. S. Skinner. Indianapolis: Liberty Classics.

Taylor, Charles. 1990. "Modes of Civil Society." *Public Culture* 3 (1): 95–118.

———. 1992. *Multiculturalism and the Politics of Recognition: An Essay by Charles Taylor*. Princeton, NJ: Princeton University Press.

———. 1993. *Reconciling the Solitudes: Essays on Canadian Federalism and Nationalism*. Montreal, QC: McGill-Queen's University Press.

Tiebout, Charles M. 1956. "A Pure Theory of Local Expenditures." *Journal of Political Economy* 64 (5): 416–24.

Tocqueville, Alexis de. (1835/1840) 1969. *Democracy in America*, edited by J. P. Mayer. New York: Harper & Row.

Tocqueville, Alexis de. (1856) 1998. *The Old Regime and the Revolution*, vol. 1, edited by François Furet and Françoise Mélonio, translated by Alan S. Kahan. Chicago: University of Chicago Press.

Ward, Lee. 2009. "Montesquieu on Federalism and Anglo-Gothic Constitutionalism." *Publius: The Journal of Federalism* 37 (4): 551–77.

Weingast, Barry. 1995. "The Economic Role of Political Institutions: Market-Preserving Federalism and Economic Development." *Journal of Law, Economics, and Organization* 11:1–31.

Wood, Gordon S. 1969. *The Creation of the American Republic, 1776–1787*. Chapel Hill: University of North Carolina Press.

Banks, Politics, and Political Parties
From Partisan Banking to Open Access in Early Massachusetts

Qian Lu and John Joseph Wallis

4.1 Introduction

The United States was the first nation to allow open access to the corporate form to its citizens. The state of Massachusetts was not only one of the first states to provide its members with legally sanctioned tools to create organizations and enable open access but, on a per capita basis, had many more banks and other corporations than other states as early as the 1820s. Early nineteenth-century Massachusetts is a natural place to look for the social processes that enabled societies to create large numbers of independent organizations. By looking closely at banking in the early nineteenth century, we are able to address several central questions raised in this volume in a specific historical setting. We are able to show that banking was dominated by a group of economic and political elites. Moreover, that a faction within those elites, the Federalists, were for thirty years able to successfully limit access to bank charters to themselves and deny them to their opponents, the Democratic-Republicans, even though the opposition elites were powerful individuals themselves. Bank charters were necessary for commercial note-issuing banks to operate and the Democratic-Republican elites were effec-

Qian Lu is an assistant professor at the Central University of Finance and Economics. John Joseph Wallis is professor of economics at the University of Maryland and a research associate of the National Bureau of Economic Research.

We thank Howard Bodenhorn, Eric Hilt, Ethan Kaplan, Naomi Lamoreaux, Peter Murrell, William Novak, James Snyder, Richard Sylla, Robert Wright, and seminar participants at the University of Maryland and the 2013 Cliometric Society meeting for their comments and suggestions on an earlier related paper. Qian Lu thanks Yiqing Xu and the staffs at the Massachusetts State Library and Massachusetts State Archives. Special thanks to Alix Quan of Massachusetts State Library for providing valuable data. For acknowledgments, sources of research support, and disclosure of the authors' material financial relationships, if any, please see http://www.nber.org/chapters/c13507.ack.

tively shut out of banking until 1812. Then we show that a crisis occurred because of limited access. In 1812, the Democratic-Republicans gained control of the state government and threatened to eliminate twenty-two of the twenty-three existing banks, as well as chartering two new Democratic-Republican banks. In the aftermath of the crisis, both factions realized that political competition in a democratic setting threatened valuable economic organizations, and Massachusetts moved to take the granting of bank charters out of the political process. By the 1820s Massachusetts had de facto open access in banking and more banks and more bank capital per capita than any state in the Union.

A large literature describes what happened in Massachusetts, as well as explanations for why it happened. The title of Pauline Maier's (1993) article "The Revolutionary Origins of the American Corporation" gives the flavor of answers: political events in the revolution created the conditions under which democracy emerged and the movement toward modern corporations and open access to those corporate forms almost inevitably followed. The Handlin's classic *Commonwealth: A Study of the Role of Government in the American Economy, 1774–1861* has much the same tone and analysis. The state found itself confronted with political demands for corporate charters from a wide variety of citizens that it simply could not deny.[1] The Handlins' and Maier's explanation that Americans adopted open access for organizations because of the political and economic dynamics set in motion by the movements toward democracy in the colonial experience and the revolution is certainly correct. Something definitely happened to political and economic institutions in Massachusetts that led to open organizational access. The difficulty is accepting at face value the assertion that the forces set in motion during the revolution were the ones that mattered. For thirty years, the Massachusetts Federalists prided themselves on their democratic republic and, nonetheless, systematically denied their political opponents the ability to form banks.

The Handlins, Maier, and many others focus on the emergence of an inclusive political democracy, contested but nonetheless ultimately triumphant.[2] Intraelite conflict does not play a central role in this history. The histories subsume intraelite conflict into intraparty competition in the new American

1. "The public purpose which justified extension of government powers to a bank, to a bridge, and to a factory soon comprehended a wide and ever widening circle of enterprises. The Commonwealth's concern with the entire productive system, its solicitude for the welfare of many diverse activities, all interdependent and all adding to the strength of Massachusetts, quickly put the corporate form to the use of many new ventures. The political balance deflated any notion of keeping the device exclusive; the expansive thinking, the excited spirits of the young state, brooked no casual denial. Charters in steadily mounting volume clothed with living tissues the skeletal hopes for an economy to serve the common interest" (Handlin and Handlin 1969, 106).

2. For recent general histories see Wilentz (2005) and Howe (2007). Inclusive political systems are a key element in Acemoglu and Robinson's (2012) concept of modern development.

democracies (national and state), which can lead us to miss an important set of institutional changes that made inclusive democracy feasible. What political parties would become was an open question in 1800. Would political parties systematically manipulate economic privileges to benefit and tie together their members? The Federalist Party in Massachusetts certainly did before 1812. If most societies fail to develop politically and economically because they cannot solve the problem of intraelite conflicts, including conflicts about the formation of organizations like political parties and banks, then we would like to know how the United States managed to solve the problem. An American history that passes over the intense conflicts between elites in the early nineteenth century hamstrings our ability to understand what happened in Massachusetts, as well as why it happened. If intraelite conflict in Massachusetts produced a political crisis that was resolved by allowing all elites to form organizations, in effect moving from limited to open access to organizational tools, then learning that history should help us understand some of the dynamics involved in opening access.[3]

To be clear, we are not arguing that a competitive electoral democracy was not an important element of what happened in Massachusetts: it was. We are arguing that a competitive electoral democracy was neither self-implementing nor did it produce open access. For the first thirty years, democracy produced a limited-access oligarchic banking system. Banking offers a particularly rich area to explore the dynamics of elite competition because of the close connection between politics and banking. We are able to connect the presidents and directors of banks in Massachusetts with state legislators; they were literally the same people. Before 1812, over 70 percent of the bankers we can identify were a state legislator at some point in their lives; moreover, most of them were Federalists. Individuals who were both a state legislator and a president or director of a bank are taken as the "elites." While the connection between political parties and banking weakened after 1813, the close connection between politics and banking continued. From 1813 to 1860, between 40 and 50 percent of all bank presidents and bank directors also served in the state legislature at some point in time. Unlike the earlier period, however, no political party dominated banking the way the Federalists had before 1811 and no groups complained about systematic exclusion from bank chartering. Banking remained an elite occupation throughout the entire period, but it ceased to be an occupation only available to politically connected elites as evidenced by their party affiliations. Control of bank entry ceased to be a mode of intraelite competition. Open access does not mean elimination of elites, it means that elites stop manipulating the economy to produce economic rents that enable them to coordinate coalitions.

3. For a wider discussion of limited and open access in the early nineteenth-century United States, see Wallis (2005, 2006) and North, Wallis, and Weingast (2009).

We begin by describing the sources of data that enable us to identify elites. Then we recount the history of banking in Massachusetts in some detail, particularly the events in 1811, 1812, and after that produced a political crisis and then the movement to open access. After considering whether Massachusetts bankers remained elites after access opened, some specific explanations for why open access was sustained are considered, in light of the experience of other states. We conclude with connections between Massachusetts and the larger set of issues considered in the volume.

4.2   Historical Sources on Elites, Factions, and Banks

The history of banking in Massachusetts is rich and complicated. This section provides the bare bones historical background, first on politics and then on banking, that we need to track the history. The history of banking policy in Massachusetts falls into four periods. In the first, from statehood until 1811, banking was dominated by the Federalist Party. Of the twenty-three banks that were chartered, all but a handful were connected directly with the Federalist Party. At one point, 80 percent of the bankers that we can identify, either bank presidents or directors, were state legislators at some point in their lives. This was a well-integrated political and economic elite. The second period was the brief interlude between 1811 and 1815. In 1811 and 1812, Democratic-Republican Elbridge Gerry, of gerrymandering fame, was governor and, in his second term, the Democratic-Republicans controlled a majority in the House and Senate for the only time between 1790 and 1830. In that narrow window the Democratic-Republicans chartered two new Democratic-Republican banks and threatened to close all but one of the existing Federalist banks. The third period from 1815 to 1829 saw continued political competition between the two parties, but a gradual opening of access to banking. This culminated in a general regulatory act for banks in 1829. The act required that all bank charters be identical, and that any new privilege granted to one bank must apply to all banks. The last period from 1830 to 1860 was a period of open access, without strong party ties to bank entry.

From the early 1780s on, Massachusetts had an elected government comprised of a governor, a Senate, and a House. Annual elections for all three were held in May, with terms that ran until the next election (so, for example, the legislature elected in the spring of 1811 held sessions in both 1811 and 1812, and the governor served in both years as well).[4] Towns had the opportunity to send representatives or not, so the number of legislators

---

4. The 1820 Constitutional Convention proposed an amendment that would have moved the beginning of the political year to the first Wednesday in January, but it was rejected by the voters. Ten years later, the voters ratified Amendment X of the constitution making January the start of the political year. After 1832, the legislative sessions start in early January and end in late March or April.

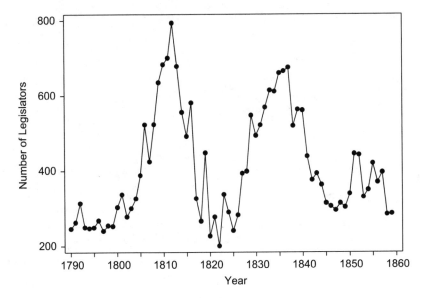

Fig. 4.1   Number of legislators, 1790–1859
Source: Massachusetts Legislators' Biographies, Massachusetts State Library.

fluctuated, sometimes wildly. Figure 4.1 gives the number of legislators by legislative year.

In the early years of the nineteenth century, from 1792 to 1824, the first national party regime was dominated by Federalists and Democratic-Republicans. The second national party regime, from 1829 to 1859, included National Republicans, Whigs, Democrats, Americans, Know Nothings, and other parties. In the first national party system, two parties dominated for roughly thirty years. In the second party system, multiple parties competed with each other, both over time and at any point in time.

The difference in the two party regimes can be seen in the fortunes of parties in the Massachusetts's legislature in figures 4.2–4.5. We take the overall party composition of each legislature from Dubin (2007).[5] Figure 4.2 gives the party composition of the Senate for the first period, 1797 to 1824, and figure 4.3 gives the party composition of the Senate for the second period. Figures 4.4 and 4.5 show the party composition of the House for the two periods as well. We take the party identification of individual legislators from the Massachusetts *Legislative Biographies*. There are no party IDs before 1797, which is when Dubin's data start.

While Federalists dominated the Senate in the earliest years, the Democratic-Republicans were able to compete effectively from roughly 1805 on and controlled a majority in six legislatures from 1808 to 1824. The

5. Dubin's data on party affiliations in Massachusetts begin in 1797.

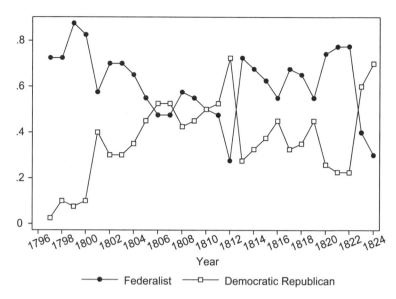

Fig. 4.2   Senate composition, 1797–1824

Source: Dubin (2007).

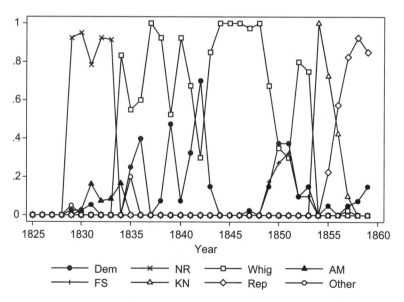

Fig. 4.3   Senate composition, 1825–1859

Source: Dubin (2007).

Note: Dem = Democrat, NR = National Republican, AM = Anti-Mason, FS = Free Soil, KN = Know-Nothing, and Rep = Republican.

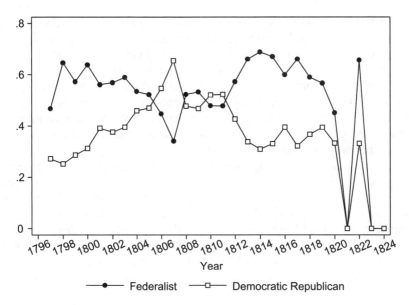

Fig. 4.4   House composition, 1797–1824
Source: Dubin (2007).

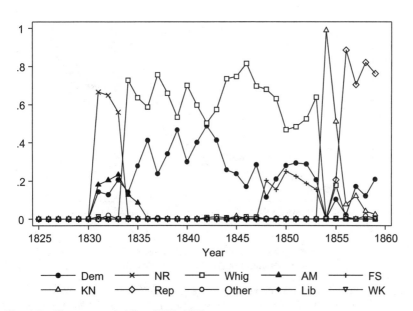

Fig. 4.5   House composition, 1825–1859
Source: Dubin (2007).

House follows roughly the same pattern as the Senate. Federalists dominated the early in the period, but Democratic-Republicans were competitive after 1805, controlling the majority in four sessions. In the second party system, a kaleidoscope of parties contended for control of the Massachusetts Senate and House (figures 4.3 and 4.5). The National Republicans and then the Whigs usually controlled a majority of Senate seats, but in a much more competitive political regime. National Republican, Whig, and then Republican domination of the House is also apparent, again in the context of extensive party competition and entry.

Massachusetts was an innovator in banking as well. Throughout the early nineteenth century, the state had more banks and more bank capital per capita than any other state (Wallis, Sylla, and Legler 1994). The number of banks in operation each year is given in figure 4.6. We take data on banks, bank presidents, and bank directors from the *Massachusetts Registers*. Our count of banks closely tracks the count of banks in operation of Warren Weber, except for the period between 1837 and 1848 when the *Register* does not provide any information on banks outside of Boston. The number of new banks entering the sample each year is shown in figure 4.7. Our sample matches closely the data on bank charters collected by Richard Sylla and Robert Wright, shown in the figure.

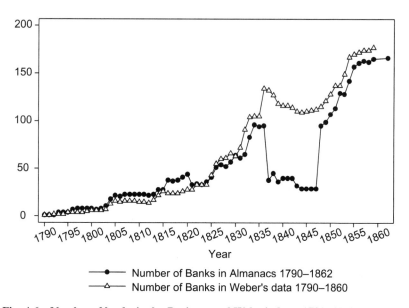

Fig. 4.6   Number of banks in the *Registers* and Weber's data, 1790–1862

Sources: Number of banks in the *Registers* comes from *Massachusetts Registers* (1790–1862), Massachusetts State Library. Number of banks in Weber's data comes from Weber "Census of State Banks" (2015).

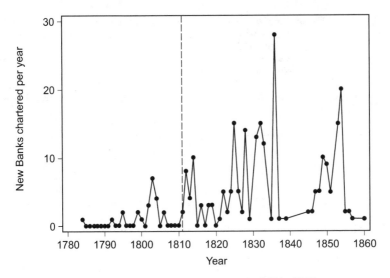

Fig. 4.7   Number of new charters, excluding renewals (1780–1860)
Source: Sylla and Wright (2015).

Tabular data on banks and bankers in presented in tables 4.1, 4.2, and 4.3. In most years, bank directors are only available for banks in Boston. No data was collected on banks outside of Boston, the "country" banks, between 1837 and 1848, as shown in figure 4.6. After 1852, the *Registers* list all the bank directors for all banks in the state. We were able to match individual bankers from the *Registers* to the complete biographies of Massachusetts state legislators. We always have complete data on bank presidents and directors for the Boston banks. In most years we have the names of the bank presidents of banks outside of Boston, except between 1837 and 1848, where we have no data outside of Boston. After 1852, we have a complete sample of all presidents and directors. Although the sample is not ideal, we can compare results from different periods to see if the patterns in one sample are reflected in the others.

Table 4.1 shows the number of bankers in the *Registers* for roughly decade intervals. The numbers are banker years, since a banker can appear in more than one year. The total number of banker years are in column (1), the number of those bankers who were a legislator at some point in their lives in column (2), and the number of bankers who were legislators whose party ID was reported in the legislative biographies in column (3). The share of bankers who were or who were not a legislator at some point in their lives is given in columns (4) and (5), and the share of banker years in each interval for whom we have a party ID in column (6). Party ID matters, since we are using parties to sort the bankers into the competing elite coalitions. The

Table 4.1   The number of bankers in the *Massachusetts Registers* total, the number of bankers who had been or would be legislators, and the number of bankers who were legislators with a party ID

Period	Number of bankers (1)	Number of bankers who were legislators (2)	Number of bankers who were legislators w/party ID (3)	Share of bankers who were not legislators (4)	Share of bankers who were legislators (5)	Share of legislators w/party ID (6)
1790–1799	307	233	98	0.24	0.76	0.42
1800–1809	545	391	272	0.28	0.72	0.70
1800–1812	771	562	399	0.27	0.73	0.71
1810–1819	954	664	503	0.30	0.70	0.76
1820–1825	842	475	395	0.44	0.56	0.83
1825–1839	5,036	2,302	1,883	0.54	0.46	0.82
1840–1859	12,599	5,585	5,032	0.56	0.44	0.90
Total	21,054	10,212	8,582			

Source: Data taken from the Massachusetts State Library *Legislative Biographies*, and *Massachusetts Registers*.

Notes: For each time period the total number of banker years is counted, column (1), an individual banker may be included in more than one year. Then bankers who had been or would be legislators are counted, column (2). Then bankers who were legislators and were given a party ID in the *Legislative Biographies* were counted, column (3). Column (4) = ([1]–[2])/(1), column (5) = (2)/(1), and column (6) = (3)/(2).

signal feature of the table is that over 70 percent of all banker years were for individuals who were also legislators at some point in their lives before 1819 (column [5]). After 1820 that share falls steadily to 44 percent in the 1850s. The dramatic increase in the number of bankers in the last row of the table reflects a growth in banking and in the fact that the *Registers* reported all of the bank directors of all the banks after 1852. The full population of bankers after 1852 has the same proportion of bankers who were also legislators than the preceding decades: the under count of country banks does not appear to bias the estimated relationship between bankers and legislators.

The *Registers* provide information on bankers each year, and since some bankers appear in multiple years, the data in table 4.1 give heavier weight to bankers who served longer terms. Table 4.2 includes each banker only once, the year that they first appear in the *Registers* and enter the banker sample. We call this the "new" banker sample. The table lists the number of bankers who entered the sample in each time period, column (1), and whether they were only a banker, column (2), or had been or became a state legislator, column (3), and the shares of those measures in columns (4) and (5). The same time pattern appears in table 4.2 and in table 4.1, but is less marked. Bankers who were also legislators tended to be bankers for a longer period, and thus have a greater weight in table 4.1, column (5), than they do in table 4.2, column (5).

Table 4.2			Number of new bankers in sample, and number of new bankers who are also legislators		
	All (1)	Banker only (2)	Banker & legislator (3)	Banker only (%) (4)	Banker/legislator (%) (5)
1790–1799	74	25	49	0.34	0.66
1800–1809	81	32	49	0.40	0.60
1800–1812	105	40	65	0.38	0.62
1800–1815	142	54	88	0.38	0.62
1810–1815	61	22	39	0.36	0.64
1815–1819	95	47	48	0.49	0.51
1815–1825	309	171	138	0.55	0.45
1820–1825	214	124	90	0.58	0.42
1820–1829	396	221	175	0.56	0.44
1830–1839	482	286	196	0.59	0.41
1840–1849	176	110	66	0.63	0.38
1850–1859	1,346	749	597	0.56	0.44

Note: All bankers, column (1), are all the individual bankers reported in the *Massachusetts Registers*. In contrast to table 4.1, each banker is only counted once in table 4.2. Bankers only, column (2), are never legislators. Bankers and legislators, column (3), either had been or would become a legislator.

Table 4.3 groups the bankers into three longer chronological periods roughly corresponding to the four periods we discuss below, gives the numbers and share of bankers who were legislators, and for the bankers who were legislators and were identified with a party in the legislative biographies and which parties the bankers belonged to.

Because the sample of bankers reported in the *Registers* varies over time, we organize the data in several ways. We have a complete count of banks, bank presidents, and bank directors for Boston banks throughout the entire period. The number of Boston bankers is shown in figure 4.8. Sometimes we focus on all the banks in the *Registers* even though we usually only have the names of bank presidents for those banks, and are missing many of them from 1837 to 1848. After 1853 the *Registers* began reporting bank presidents and directors for all the banks in the state. The number of all bankers in the state that appear in the *Registers* for the entire period is given in figure 4.9. The large movements in the figure are caused by changes in the banks reported by the *Registers*. The conclusions we draw from the two samples are the same, but it is often easier to see the continuity in the Boston bank sample. The third way to organize the data is by banks rather than by bankers.

The data and sources are described in more detail in the data appendix available from the authors.

Table 4.3 All new bankers, by legislator or not, and by party or not

	1790–1815 (1)	1816–1824 (2)	1825–1859 (3)	As share of all bankers 1790–1815 (4)	1816–1824 (5)	1825–1859 (6)	As share of all banker/legislators 1790–1815 (7)	1816–1824 (8)	1825–1859 (9)
Bankers	217	218	2,285						
Not legislators	80	121	1,310	0.37	0.56	0.57			
Legislators	137	97	975	0.63	0.44	0.43	1.00	1.00	1.00
With party ID	87	80	857	0.40	0.37	0.38	0.64	0.82	0.88
Parties:									
Federalist	54	49		0.25	0.22		0.39	0.51	
Democratic-Republican	29	17		0.13	0.08		0.21	0.18	
Other	4	14		0.02	0.06		0.03	0.14	
Whig			316			0.14			0.32
Republican			169			0.07			0.17
Democrat			159			0.07			0.16
Nat/Republican			80			0.04			0.08
Federalist			59			0.03			0.06
Know Nothing			25			0.01			0.03
Other			49			0.02			0.05
No party	50	17	118	0.23	0.08	0.05	0.36	0.18	0.12

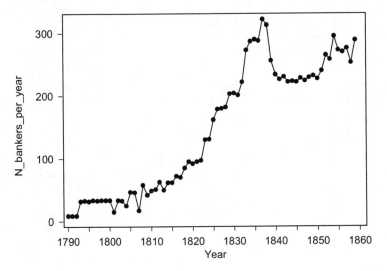

Fig. 4.8   **Number of Boston bank directors and presidents in the *Registers*, 1790–1859**

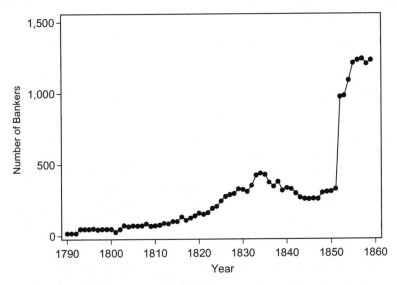

Fig. 4.9   Number of bank directors and presidents in the *Registers*, 1790–1859

4.3   The History

4.3.1   Politics, Parties, and Banks from 1784 to 1811

Massachusetts chartered its first bank in 1784, the Massachusetts Bank. It gave out four more charters before 1799, when the state changed the rules for private banks, prohibiting bank note issue by unchartered private banks.

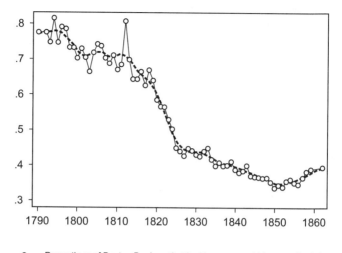

**Fig. 4.10   Proportions of Boston bank directors and presidents who had been or
would become legislators, and local polynomial smooth plot (1790–1859)**
Source: Massachusetts Registers (1790–1859), and *Massachusetts Legislators Biographies*
(1780–2003). Both are from Massachusetts State Library.

What followed was an increase in chartering in 1801, 1802, and 1803, as
shown in figure 4.7. By 1810, twenty-three banks had been chartered and
were in operation.

The Federalist Party controlled Massachusetts politics in the 1790s and
1800s and it showed in the party composition of bankers. Figures 4.10, 4.11,
4.12, and 4.13 use Boston bankers, for which we have all the bank presidents
and directors, from 1790 to 1827 (figures 4.10 and 4.11 cover 1790 to 1859).
Figure 4.10 shows the share of all bankers in a given year that either had been
a legislator already or would at some point in their lives become a legislator.
At its peak, the share was 80 percent, and before 1811 fell below 70 percent
in only one year. Figure 4.11 divides the bankers into those who became a
legislator before they became a banker, and those who became a banker first
and legislator later in life. There was only one bank in Massachusetts in 1790,
and half of its board of directors had already been a state legislator. All of
them were Federalist legislators.

In 1799 the state required all note-issuing banks to have charters, producing a marked increase in charters in 1801, 1802, and 1803. As the new banks
acquired charters, many of their directors had not been legislators, but they
quickly became legislators. Figure 4.11 gives the proportion of all bankers
who had been a legislator before they became a banker, or would become a
legislator after they became a banker. The proportion of bankers who had
been a legislator falls from 1790 to 1805 as the new banks come on line, and

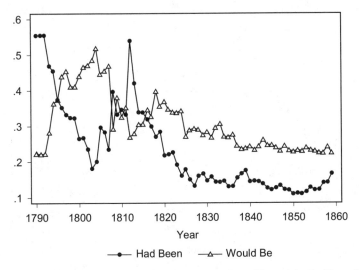

Fig. 4.11   Proportions of Boston bank directors and presidents who had been legislators, and proportions of Boston bank directors and presidents who would be legislators (1790–1859)

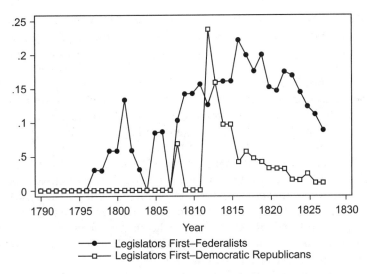

Fig. 4.12   Proportions of Boston bankers that had been Federalist or Republican legislators before they became bank directors and presidents, 1790–1827

the share of bankers who would become legislators rises to 50 percent of all bankers in 1805. The new bankers all ended up in the Federalist Party. Figure 4.12 tracks the proportion of new Boston bankers who were legislators by party (so the existing bankers and legislators in 1790 are not counted). All of the bankers who had been legislators were Federalists until 1808

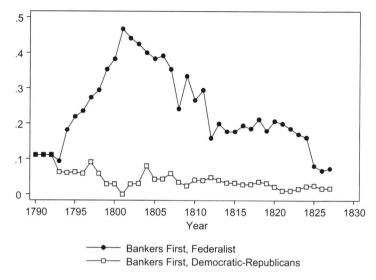

Fig. 4.13   **Proportions of Boston bankers who became Federalist or Republican legislators after they became bankers, 1790–1827**

(and 1812 when the State Bank was formed with all Democratic-Republican directors). As the number of new bankers increased, they quickly moved into the Federalist ranks in the state legislature, as shown in figure 4.13, which tracks the number of bankers who became legislators after they enter the banker sample.

There is a clear association between bankers and Federalist state legislators and the Federalist Party in the years before 1810. Beginning in 1790, over 20 percent of the bankers who were not legislators when they became bankers eventually would become a legislator, a share that grew through time. Remember that we do not have party IDs for legislators before 1797. In figure 4.12, of the bankers before 1810, only one had already been a Democratic-Republican legislator (out of roughly fifty bankers), while a significant number had already been Federalist legislators. Even more striking, figure 4.13 shows that bankers who were not legislators when they became bankers were much more likely to become Federalist legislators than Democratic-Republican legislators.

Of the sixty-eight bankers in the statewide sample in 1810, including the banks outside of Boston, forty-seven, or 70 percent, had been (33 percent) or would become (37 percent) legislators. Of those forty-seven bankers, four had no party affiliation, thirty-eight were Federalists (81 percent), and five were Democratic-Republicans (11 percent). By 1810 banking in Massachusetts was not quite a Federalist monopoly, but it was close. Of the twenty-three banks in our sample in 1810, only three banks can be identified as Democratic-Republican banks because they have presidents who were

Democratic-Republican legislators. Two other Democratic-Republican legislators were directors in banks dominated by Federalists. Perhaps even more telling, of the twenty-three banks only four did not have a state legislator as president or a director in 1810. Even this is an underestimate, however, since we do not have directors for most country banks. While representation in the House and Senate was roughly 60 percent Federalist and 40 percent Democratic-Republican over these years, the Federalist banks outnumbered the Democratic-Republican banks by roughly a 5-to-1 ratio.

Democratic-Republicans complained bitterly about the Federalists' exclusive control of banking. "Monopolies of all kinds are odious in all countries; but they are more so in a free country like ours; they are here directly opposed to the genius and spirit both of the people and their government. And there can be no monopoly more invidious, than to give exclusive privileges by the acts of government to a few very rich men for improving their money in Banks, and to refuse the same privilege to the active merchants, and to the widows and orphans."[6] Banks were "engines of oppression," enabling Federalists to exploit enterprising merchants and shopkeepers. Federalists monopolized "all the exclusive privileges . . . until the voice of private citizens is lost in the overbearing influence of privileged companies."[7] As long as "combined court parties grant banks and other privileged corporations to favored companies, equal rights cannot exist."[8] The purpose of chartering banks was to give exclusive privileges to federal friends and "every incorporation for wealth and profit is a bulwark to aristocracy."[9] As most bank charters would expire in 1812, "incorporations should not be renewed unless the proprietors of banks consent that every officer of their banks be appointed by the State Government."[10] In 1803, after the legislature refused a petition for a "Town and Country Bank," Democratic-Republicans blamed Federalists and painted them as the champions of bank monopoly, opposed to "every measure calculated to promote the interest of the middling class of citizens."[11] "Will a director of the Boston Bank, or a man, whose 'projects' gripe every monied institution within the town, be advocates for such salutary measures as our situation calls for?" "Let the charters be free for all, if they are granted to any."[12] Before 1811, Federalist elites dominated politics, controlled banks, and excluded the Democratic-Republicans from banking. Democratic-Republicans demanded reforms to allow them access to banking. They seized the chance in 1811.

6. *Columbian Centinel*, Feb. 16, 1803. Quoted in Lake (1932, 32).
7. *Eastern Argus*, Apr. 2, 1807. Quoted in Goodman (1964, 176).
8. *Eastern Argus*, Dec. 13, 1805, Feb. 22, 1805, and Dec. 6, 1805; *Salem Register*, Mar. 30, 1807, and Apr. 2, 1807. Quoted in Goodman (1964, 176).
9. *Eastern Argus*, Nov. 15, 1805. Quoted in Robinson (1916, 103).
10. *Eastern Argus*, Dec. 13. 1805. Quoted in Robinson (1916, 104).
11. *Republican Gazette*, Apr. 27, 1803. Quoted in Goodman (1964, 172).
12. *Boston Democrat*, May 1804. Quoted in Goodman (1964, 173).

4.3.2   The Massachusetts Bank War, 1811–1815

What stands out in many of the figures, most clearly in figure 4.12, is the year 1812. Although Massachusetts had elected Democratic-Republican majorities to the Senate and House before, it was only in the election of 1811 that the Democratic-Republicans held both houses and the governorship. Eldbridge Gerry was elected governor in both 1810 and 1811 and vice president of the United States in November 1812. He died in office in 1814.[13] In his first term as governor, he sought to conciliate the two parties and work out a compromise with Federalists over banking and a number of other issues. He restrained radical Democratic-Republicans who hoped to remove Federalists from office. While Democratic-Republicans held power in the House, the Senate was equally divided. The Federalist leader Harrison Gray Otis was the Senate president and blocked every Democratic-Republican reform. Since they were not threatened, Federalists also adopted a moderate tone.[14]

In 1811, however, Gerry abandoned his conciliatory policy. The admission of Louisiana to the Union had already aroused animosities against President Madison among Federalists, and when Congress approved Madison's Non-Intercourse Act to cease commerce with Britain in March, Boston Federalists organized a mass meeting and protested against the law, denouncing it as tyrannical and oppressive. They threatened to call for measures "short of force," and to elect officers who would "oppose by peaceable, but firm measures, the execution of the laws, which if persisted in must and will be resisted."[15] Gerry denounced the Boston mass meeting, claiming it advocated revolution. He was convinced that if Federalists returned to power, they would nullify the Non-Intercourse Act or resist its enforcement. The result would be: "our constitutions are nullities, our constituted authorities are usurpers, and we are reduced to a state of nature."[16] In his second inaugural address in June 1811, Gerry publically accused Federalists who "excite the spirit of the insurrection and rebellion to destroy our internal peace and tranquility."[17]

In the elections of 1811, Democratic-Republicans captured both houses of the state legislature. The Democratic-Republican legislature helped Gerry implement a series of reforms to capture patronage in the state, to remove Federalists from the office, and to occupy Federalist-controlled organiza-

---

13. Billias (1976).

14. On Gerry and the issues in 1811, see Formisano (1983, 74–75), Billias (1976, 314–22), James T. Austin ([1828] 2009, 333–42, 346–47), Seaburg and Paterson (1971, 228), Goodman (1968, 154–81), and Morison (1929).

15. "Governor's Speech to the Representatives' Chamber, June 7," *Massachusetts Acts and Resolves* (1812, 184).

16. Ibid., 184.

17. Ibid., 185.

tions.[18] One of the most famous changes was the "gerrymander." In February 1812, Democratic-Republicans passed a bill to divide the state into senatorial districts along partisan lines. This change redistricted the state to make the Democratic-Republican votes count as much as possible and the Federalist ones as little as possible. This practice was not new nor was Gerry an active supporter of the plan, but has long since been associated with Gerry's name.[19]

The legislature of 1811–12 changed the banking policy of the state. It chartered two new banks: the State Bank and the Merchant's Bank of Salem. The State Bank was a very large bank, with three times the capital of any existing bank. All twelve directors and the bank president had been or would be state legislators: eleven were Democratic-Republicans. The sharp jump in the number of Democratic-Republican bankers who had been legislators in figure 4.12 for 1812 was the result of placing Democratic-Republicans legislators on the bank's board of directors.

The State Bank was also intended to be a reform bank. One-third of the $3 million capital was subscribed by the state government, with an option to subscribe an additional $1 million. The bank was to pay the state a tax equal to one-half of 1 percent of its paid-in capital each year. The reform ideas behind both state ownership of stock and the capital tax was that the bank, rather than being a source of private privilege to its owners, would be a source of revenue for the state government.[20]

The other aspect of the Democratic-Republican bank offensive resulted from the unusual fact that the charters of all but one of the existing banks in Massachusetts expired in 1812.[21] In the 1811–1812 legislative session, the Democratic-Republicans refused to renew the charters of any of the existing banks. It was, literally, an existential crisis for the Federalist bankers. Without their charters they would not be able to issue bank notes, a basic function of their banks. The Federalists regained the governorship and the House in the elections of 1812, but the Democratic-Republicans retained control of the Senate as a result of the "Gerrymander." In the fall of 1812 (the 1812–13 legislative session), the charters of the existing Federalist banks were renewed. Significantly, all of the renewals contained the reform provisions included in the State Bank charter, including the bank capital tax.

The political dynamics unleashed by the events of 1811 and 1812 show clearly the intraelite nature of competition over banking. Before 1811, Salem already had two Federalist banks—the Salem Bank and the Essex Bank. Unable to get loans from either bank, a number of Salem's most prominent Democratic-Republicans, led by the Crowninshield family, decided to start

18. For Republican reforms in other sectors, see Goodman (1964).
19. Griffith (1907, 17–21), Austin ([1828] 2009, 322), and Dean (1892, 374–83).
20. The charter of the State Bank can be found in Massachusetts (1812, 501), June 26, 1811, "An act to incorporate the President, Directors, and Company of the State Bank."
21. The original charter of the Massachusetts Bank had no termination date.

a new Democratic-Republican bank. Their petitions for bank charters, however, were rejected by the Federalist legislature for many years. It was not until 1811 that they finally secured a charter, as the minister William Bentley described in his diary, "To give weight to the Republican Interest in Massachusetts, the last Legislature placed several banks into the hands of their friends, and among others, one in Salem, which was completely organized this day, under the name of Merchant's Bank."[22]

The first two presidents of the Merchant's Bank are good examples of the kind of Democratic-Republican elites who were denied access to banking. Benjamin Crowninshield, the first president, left the bank in 1814 to become Secretary of the Navy under Madison. He had served in the state legislature eight times, three in the Senate and five in the House; he would be a national congressman for four terms from 1823 to 1831, and candidate for governor in 1818 and 1819. The man who replaced him, Joseph Story, was president of the bank for the next twenty years. He had been appointed Associate Justice of the Supreme Court of the United States in November 1811, and sat on the Supreme Court for thirty-three years. Men like Crowninshield were powerful elites. Democratic-Republicans did not want for bank charters because they lacked powerful elites. It was the political dynamics of intraelite competition in the early Massachusetts democracy that denied them charters.

The reaction of the Federalists to the Merchants Bank mirrored the charges the Democratic-Republicans levied against the Federalists. Even before it opened on September 10, 1811, the Federalist *Salem Gazette* gave grave censure of the "new bank":

> It requires but little foresight to predict the influence which the institution will, and which the legislature intended it should have on the political circumstances of our Commonwealth, and particularly its elections. Viewing it in this light, it cannot be considered as an institution for the common benefit of our citizens, but on the contrary for the purpose of unblushing political corruption. Federalists will be excluded entirely from accommodation, as they were from the privilege of subscribing for shares, and Democrats only enjoy its benefits. We hesitate not to assert, that (until the Spring elections are over, at least) *any Democrat* (or "friend of the government" as the committee call them) who can bring good proofs of his attachment to the cause, *will be furnished with what money he wishes from this Bank, while federalists, let them be never so competent, will be sedulously refused a discount, except perhaps a few*, who will be held up as a mask to cover their gross, corrupt partially. Let every candid man consider this course of conduct, lay his hand on his heart, and say if he can call it by any other name than BRIBERY.[23]

The State Bank was a much more ambitious project. Throughout its early history, Democratic-Republicans directed the State Bank. Eleven of its first

---

22. Dennis (1908, 7).
23. *Salem Gazette*, Sept. 10, 1811 (emphasis added).

twelve bank directors had been Democratic-Republican legislators. The first president was William Gray, a leader of the Democratic-Republican Party, the lieutenant governor of the state, as well as a rich merchant ship operator. In the circular of the bank, July 1811, the bank committee said, "the establishment of the present institution should be so conducted that its benefits shall be diffused as extensively as possible among the friends of the government throughout this Commonwealth."[24]

The State Bank drew even more criticism from the Federalists than the Merchant's Bank. The *Columbian Centinel* of July 1811 called the State Bank "the mammoth bank," and denounced it as a "party bank." In the *Boston Gazette* of August 22, 1811, "A Massachusetts Yeoman" addressed a letter to William Gray, "it was beyond all precedent, and wicked in the extreme, to grant a set of men, who have always been borrowers, the whole control of the circulating medium of the State." In the *Centinel*, August 31, 1811, "A Constitutional Republican" said, "1st, That the grant of a charter to the State Bank is a violation of the Constitution; 2d, that those who gave it countenance and voted for it have acted corruptly." The *Worcester Spy* said it was "a bill to secure to Mr. Gray and his political associates, for twenty years, a stupendous monopoly of all the banking privileges of the Commonwealth, or at least of the metropolis. The community would suffer incalculable injury from the uncontrolled speculations of a bank without a rival, and the total loss of confidence in the stability of corporations dependent upon the will of the legislature."

The *Salem Gazette* denounced the bank: "The State Bank is managed as a powerful engine of bribery and corrupt influence. . . . The constitutions and the principles of republican government are derided and contemned . . . It is unblushingly avowed that the new bank is intended as a machine to *create* Democrats and *destroy* Federalists. In this State there has been so much clamor by this very party against banks, bank directors, and exclusive privileges, that consistency required them to discountenance all. It appears that in each county an electioneering committee has been appointed, who through the influence of the new bank are to act as almoners of democratic bribes and commissioners of official corruption."[25]

Such was the state of interelite conflict in Massachusetts in 1811 and 1812.

4.3.3   Moving toward Open Access, 1815–1829

The Democratic-Republican legislature seized the chance in 1811 to implement a series of reforms. However, Madison's unpopular foreign policy cost them subsequent state elections. In 1812, Federalists won back a majority in the House, as well as the governorship, and rechartered the existing banks in 1812. Significantly, all the new charters included a provision specifying

---

24. Stetson (1893, 13).
25. This and the preceding quotes are from Stetson (1893).

a bank capital tax and allowing the state to make investments in the banks, just as in the State Bank charter.[26]

In 1813, when the Federalists again controlled the state, they denounced the State Bank: "A monied institution was created, founded on the determination to abolish those already existing, and its capital was apportioned to counties and towns, upon a digested scheme of premiums for political corruption."[27] Under the Federalists, Massachusetts began chartering more banks after 1812. According to the report of the Joint Committee on Banks in 1820, for several years the liberal policy had granted bank charters in "almost all cases of apparent utility, leaving it to the actual wants of the community, and to the true perception of interest among its members, to fix the limits of capital, which would thus be employed."[28] The rate of bank formation was high in 1811, 1812, and 1813, when both Democratic-Republicans and Federalists became presidents and directors (figure 4.12). The rate of bank formation slowed during the active part of the war in 1814 and 1815, and the economic recession in 1818. The explosion of banking occurred in the 1820s, as figures 4.6 and 4.7 show. By 1830 Massachusetts had only 4.7 percent of the nation's population, but 20 percent of the nation's banks and 18.5 percent of the nation's banking capital (Wallis, Sylla, and Legler 1994). In his research on free banking of different states, Sylla claimed, "After 1820, Massachusetts had essentially free banking in the general sense of that term, and the state remained a leader in terms of numbers of incorporated banks and capital invested in banking enterprises for several decades" (Sylla 1985, 111).

This was the same period in which the proportion of bankers who had been or would become legislators declined sharply, from roughly two-thirds of all bankers to around 45 percent of all bankers. Unfortunately, the increase in the number of banks occurs just at the time that party identification became problematic. For much of the 1820s, many state legislators were not identified with parties in the *Legislative Biographies*. Figure 4.14 gives the share of all legislators identified in each year with a party. The sharp drop in the late 1820s reflects that disarray of the parties at the national level. Unfortunately, we cannot track the party association of the bankers who became legislators in this important decade.

Nonetheless, there was a distinct break in the connection between bankers and legislators after 1815. Table 4.2 breaks down new bankers entering in five-year intervals in the middle panel of the table. Between 1810 and 1815, sixty-one bankers entered and 64 percent of them had been or would become state legislators. In the next five-year period, 1815 to 1819, ninety-five bankers entered and 51 percent had been or would become state legislators. Between 1820 and 1825, 214 bankers entered and only 42 percent had

26. Handlin and Handlin (1969, 129) and Dodd (1954, 210).
27. Dodd (1954, 209).
28. *Columbian Centinel*, June 17, 1820.

Fig. 4.14   Share of all legislators (not just bankers) who have a party ID in the *Legislative Biographies*

been or would become state legislators. In the decade of the 1820s, when party identification was weakest, so too the association between bankers and state legislators became permanently weakened.

The 1820s also produced a significant and permanent change in the banking policies of the state. The earliest indications were the rechartering of the existing Federalist banks in 1812, which included the same provisions as the State Bank charter. When new banks were chartered after 1813, their charters contained the provision "That the rules, restrictions, limitations, reservations and provisions, which are provided in and by the third section of an Act, entitled, 'An Act to incorporate the President, Directors, and Company of the State Bank,' shall be binding on the bank hereby established."[29] Rather than reverse the "reform" provisions of the State Bank charter, the Federalists embraced them.

This was clearly a shift in policy by the Federalists. Whether the move toward adopting the same charter provisions for all banks played an important role in Federalist thinking is not clear. Unlike the banks chartered up to the State Bank, which sometimes included special provisions and often included implicit geographic monopolies, all the banks chartered after 1812 contained the same provisions. That part of the agreement was codified when new bank charters formally became standardized on February 29, 1829, with the passage of the general regulatory act: "An Act to Regulate Banks and Banking." The act required "That from and after the passing of

29. This is the language used in the charter of the Worcester Bank. Massachusetts, 1821, chapter 26, "An Act to incorporate the President, Directors, and Company of the Worcester Bank," p. 422.

this Act, every Bank which shall receive a Charter, from or by the authority of this Commonwealth, and every Bank whose Capital shall be increased, or whose Charter shall be extended, shall be governed by the following rules, and subjected to all the duties, limitations, restrictions, liabilities and provisions, contained in this Act."[30] The act reconfirmed the bank capital tax and the ability of the state to invest in any bank, as well as borrow from it. The clincher was section 31: "*Be it further enacted*, That if, during the continuance of any Bank Charter, granted or renewed under the provisions of this Act, any new or greater privileges shall be granted to any other bank now in operation, or which may hereafter be created, each and every Bank in operation at the time shall be entitled to the same" (161). The general regulatory act not only guaranteed that all existing bank charters would have the same provisions, but any new provisions introduced in the future would retroactively apply to all existing banks. Massachusetts had adopted an "impersonal" rule for the creation and governance of banks: it was a rule that treated all banks the same.

Massachusetts did not adopt a general incorporation act for banking until the 1850s, but essentially allowed de facto open entry after 1820. Significantly, the complaints by one party that the other party was restricting access to bank charters effectively stopped. As the Handlins noted, the compromise reached in 1812 seems to have signaled the end of banking competition. "The settlement of 1812 had substantially stabilized the banking system, withdrawing it from the grasping hands of a favored few. For a time thereafter, the question of currency was academic only."[31] When the general incorporation act was passed in 1854, only four banks requested charters under the general act.

4.3.4   Politics, Parties, and Banks in the Second Party Regime, 1830–1860

National party politics in the United States fragmented in the 1820s. In three of the four national elections between 1824 and 1836, three or more candidates received electoral votes in the presidential elections. Figures 4.3 and 4.5 show the mix of parties that competed for dominance in Massachusetts between 1830 and 1860. The dominant parties in succeeding elections were National Republicans, Whigs, and Republicans, with a brief period in which the Democrats challenged, and a second brief ascendancy of the Know Nothing Party. The sequence of parties was not one continuous coalition that simply changed its name over time. The National Republicans, Whigs, and Republicans were reconfigurations of existing political alignments.[32] The lack of party IDs for legislators before 1797 and in 1820s

---

30. Massachusetts, 1831, Chapter XCVI, "An Act to regulate Banks and Banking," Section 1, pp. 145.

31. Handlin and Handlin (1969, 175).

32. The idea that the Whigs were a simple continuation of the Federalist party has a long history, but it appears to be wrong. Holt summarizes the idea: "Even historians routinely echoed

(figure 4.14) and the growing number of political parties makes it difficult to draw a neat comparison between the period after 1830 and the period before 1815. We do not have any party IDs for legislators before 1797, and as we saw earlier, many of the early bankers had been legislators before they became bankers. In table 4.3, of the 217 individual bankers in the *Registers* between 1790 and 1815, 137 were also legislators, but we only have party IDs for 87 of those. Most of the missing IDs are for legislators who served in the 1790s and not later (if they served after 1797 we would be more likely to link them with a party). There were forty-nine legislator/bankers who appeared in the *Registers* between 1790 and 1799.

As shown in the lower panel of table 4.3, legislators with Federalist Party IDs accounted for 25 percent of all bankers between 1790 and 1815 and 39 percent of all bankers who were legislators. The portion that was connected to the Federalists would surely be significantly higher if we had party IDs for legislators before 1797.

We can compare the pre-1815 banker-legislators to the post-1830 banker-legislators by making an extreme assumption: take the Federalist, National Republican, Whig, and Republican legislators as a continuation of the "dominant party" for the entire period between 1825 and 1859. This is a problematic assumption, since combining the four parties gives an overestimate of the number of people in the dominant party. But it biases the results against our hypothesis that party connections played a smaller role in bank chartering after 1830. The combined party legislators account for 28 percent of the bankers after 1825. This is significantly less than the 40 percent of all banker/legislators who were Federalists in the pre-1811 period (which is biased downward by the missing party IDs before 1797). Entry into banking before 1811 was limited by the need for political party connections, after 1830 much less so.

After 1830, Massachusetts appears to have essentially open entry into banking. As we discuss in the sections that follow, banking remained a privileged occupation. Bankers were still likely to be state legislators and they were wealthy, even when compared to other wealthy people, but the partisan aspects of banking competition so prevalent between 1790 and 1811 had all but disappeared.

4.4   Resolving Possible Complications with the Data

Information on bankers and state legislators changed through time. Did changes in the sample of bankers produce the results we have just described? We need to dig deeper into the connection between banks, bankers, and leg-

---

Democratic propaganda and described Whigs as ex-Federalists. Experts now know better. Massive research in the past forty years has shown that the Whig Party evolved not from the Federalists but from divisions within the Jeffersonian party" (Holt 1999, 2). Holt cites Benson (1961) and McCormick (1966) as examples of a literature "too vast to list here."

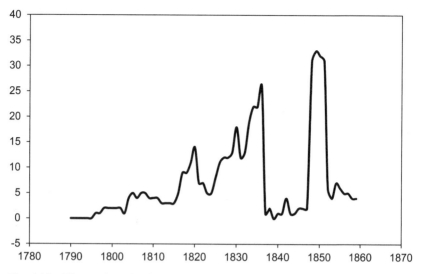

Fig. 4.15   The number of banks with no legislators as president or a director, all banks (whether they have directors or not), 1790–1859

islatures. There are two major problems: the fact that the *Registers* usually only report the name of the bank president for country banks and the lack of most country bank data from 1837 to 1848. Since the *Registers* usually report only the name of the bank president for the country banks, we have only one banker associated with those banks. The fact that the president is not a legislator does not mean that the bank is not associated with the legislature through a director.

Figure 4.15 shows the number of all banks that had no legislators in each year. Figure 4.16 excludes banks without directors reported in the *Registers*, that is, the banks where only the president's name was listed. The picture is much different. Only one bank, the Bangor Bank in 1819 and 1820, reported the names of directors and had no directors who had been or would become legislators among its president or directors. No bank in our sample before the late 1840s that reported directors failed to have a legislator on the board, other than the Bangor Bank.[33]

33. This criterion is narrow. To include a legislator in the board of bank directors may not mean it is an elite organization. For example, it may be that out of its ten directors, nine are ordinary people but they need one famous person on the board to make the banks more influential, build more social connections, or give people more confidence. Besides, if banks were mostly used as a tool for rich people to be able to channel funds to their family business, as claimed by Lamoreaux, it cannot be a bank serving the ordinary people. These banks were commercial banks, not savings institutions or saving banks. Its purpose is not to serve the ordinary people to save their money and get a good investment opportunity. It is not surprising that they were connected to some legislator. One interesting question is, after the saving banks became more important after the Civil War, whether or not they were elite organizations. It is beyond what we study in this chapter.

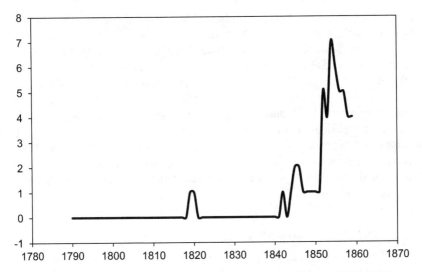

Fig. 4.16   Number of banks with directors who have no legislators, 1790–1859
(This sample excludes banks with only presidents in the *Registers*.)

We cannot follow the share of all banks that have a legislator as a director because the *Registers* do not report bank directors for most of the country banks, and there is missing data on most of the country banks between 1837 and 1848. Beginning in 1852, however, the *Registers* did begin reporting bank directors for all banks, Boston and country, and the number of bankers we can identify jumps from around 350 to almost 1,000, as shown in figure 4.9. One might expect that the addition of over 600 directors of country banks would reduce the share of bankers that had been or would become legislators, and increase the share of banks with no legislators on their boards. But table 4.2 shows that is not the case. Indeed, after 1852 the share of all bankers who had been legislators begins to rise. The country banks were just as likely to have a state legislator on their boards as the Boston banks. In 1859, when we have information on over 150 banks, including all their directors, there are only four banks without a legislator on their boards of directors or their president.

While the association of bankers with political parties weakened, their association with state government did not. When we are very careful to compare apples to apples, using parts of the samples that are consistent and comparable over time, what we find is the same conclusions that we get from the Boston banks with a continuous series on bank presidents and directors for the entire period. In the early years there was a close association between bank officers and state legislators. Before 1811 over 70 percent of the bankers were also state legislators, and most of them were Federalists. After 1820 the percentage of bankers who were also state legislators fell to around 40 percent. It was a significant decline from the pre-1811 period, but still a substantial number. Nonetheless, the association of bankers with the dominant political party weakened considerably. An underestimate of the number of bankers associated with the Federalist Party before 1811 is 40 percent. An overestimate of the number of bankers associated with the series of majority parts after 1825 is 28 percent, and the 28 percent include legislators from four different political coalitions with overlapping, but by no means identical, membership.

Bankers were still elites, still associated with powerful political positions, but no longer was the granting of a bank charter strongly associated with a political coalition. Open access appears to have arrived, but what about the wealth of bankers?

4.5 The Wealth of Bankers

Did bankers suffer a relative decline in wealth as access opened? As we will see later, there is some evidence that the rate of return on bank capital in Massachusetts was lower than it was in other states. We were able to link the names of Boston bankers to the Boston property tax assessments to get a measure of their wealth. In 1826, the City of Boston published a "List of Persons, Co-Partnerships, and Corporations who were taxed . . ."[34] The list was a sample of the wealthiest taxpayers, not of all taxpayers. There are a number of technical issues about the property tax data, but the bottom line with respect to the relative wealth of bankers to all other wealthy taxpayers is clear and robust to a series of adjustments (Lu 2014). From 1829 to 1859, there were an average of 3,845 persons, partnerships, and corporations listed (ranging from a low of 1,836 in 1830 to a high of 5,883 in 1848).[35] We identified all the bankers in the sample whose names we could match, then drew several random samples of nonbankers from the tax lists to compare them to. Our largest random sample includes an average of 1,617 individuals (excluding partnerships and corporations), or a 42 percent sample on average (only in 1833 and 1839 does the sample size fall below 20 percent).

34. The title varied somewhat from year to year, as did the minimum amount of tax paid to qualify a person, copartnership, or corporation from inclusion in the list. The lists of wealthy taxpayers in the city of Boston—from List of Persons, Copartnerships, and Corporations, Taxed in the City of Boston—document a person's or an organization's real and personal holdings and taxes paid between 1829 and 1859 (1831, 1834, 1854, 1855, and 1856 are missing). Only wealthy taxpayers with wealth above certain thresholds are included in the tax lists. From 1829 to 1848, the list includes wealth for individuals taxed $25 and upward (since the tax rate was roughly 0.8 percent of wealth, the property cut-off was approximately $3,125); from 1849 to 1853, the list includes individuals whose personal property was $6,000 and upward, and from 1857 to 1859, $10,000 and upward.

35. We begin with the 1829 tax lists, as the first few years of the list exhibit too much variation in names and assessments to warrant our confidence.

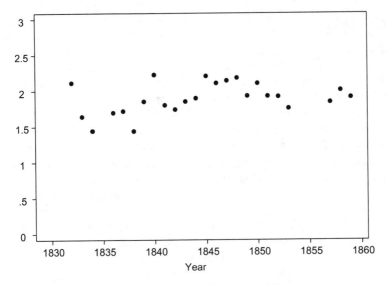

Fig. 4.17   The ratio of average wealth of bankers to wealthy taxpayers

The *Registers* identify an average of 244 bankers in Boston (from a low of 200 in 1829 to a high of 281 in 1859), of which we identify an average of 102, or 42 percent (with identification share below 20 percent only in 1833, 1837, and 1839).

Figure 4.17 shows the wealth of Boston bankers relative to the other wealthy individuals included in the tax lists. There is no trend in the relative wealth of Boston bankers relative to the rest of the wealthy population; it stayed steady at around 150 percent. The wealth of bankers does not appear to have declined relative to other wealthy groups. Steckel and Moehling (2001) match the Massachusetts Census records to property tax lists for the entire population and show that wealth distributions became increasingly unequal between 1820 and 1860. Given the stable relative wealth of bankers to wealthiest taxpayers, we expect that bankers grew wealthier relative to all taxpayers between 1830 and 1860. The wealth data gives us the same picture as the banker-legislator data: banking remained a largely elite preserve from 1820 to 1860.[36]

36. Our results from the Boston tax lists paint a different picture of the relative wealth of bankers in Boston than Lamoreaux and Glaisek (1991), which show that in Rhode Island, new bankers were less wealthy than old bankers. In part, this is the result of different samples. We do not have all the bankers in Boston, just the richest ones. Lamoreaux and Glaisek compare two cross sections of bankers in 1830 and 1845. Hilt and Valentine (2012) analyze stockholding and wealth in New York City from 1791 to 1826 and show that stock ownership was becoming more diversely held by less wealthy households.

4.6   How and Why?

Massachusetts banking provides a clear case of limited access before 1812, opening access afterward, and full access by the 1850s. Why were the reforms in Massachusetts sustained? Why didn't the dynamics of elite competition in an electoral democracy produce more attempts to manipulate access to organizations to create and cement a new political coalition? The Democratic-Republican move to eliminate the Federalist banks might have repeated itself over and over again if control of the government brought with it the ability to dismantle the economic organizations of opposing factions. The answer involves more than banking; institutional changes occurred that changed the dynamic relationship between elites and parties in general, as well as in the operation of the legislature. But, we can see the new patterns in the institutions governing banking policy. It wasn't as though bankers were still not well represented in the state legislature, roughly 40 percent of all the bankers we can identify were state legislators at some point in their lives. Bankers were clearly in a position to pursue their best interests. Why did that turn out to be open-access banking?

Somewhat surprisingly, the arrangements grew out of the charter of the State Bank in 1812. Surprising, because the State Bank was part of an attempt by the Democratic-Republicans to turn the tables on the Federalists and take control of banking. The Democratic-Republicans put the State Bank model forward as a reform bank, but it was also an attempt to shift the economic privileges that the Federalists had enjoyed to the Democratic-Republicans by chartering a very large Democratic-Republican bank closely tied to state finances, and denying the Federalists their banks. The power grab failed the next year, when the Federalists recovered enough influence to recharter their banks. The reforms, however, had lasting effects.

Although all the details of the State Bank charter matter, perhaps none was more important than the requirement that all future bank charters contain the same provisions. The tax on bank capital, for example, was a reform proposal intended to return some of the profits of the bank to the state and the state's taxpayers. "*Provided however*, That the same tax, payable in manner aforesaid, shall be required by the Legislature of all banks that shall be hereafter incorporated within this Commonwealth, from and after the said first Monday of October: *And provided further*, That nothing herein contained shall be construed to impair the right of the Legislature to lay a tax or excise upon any bank already incorporated, under the authority of the Commonwealth, whenever they may think proper to do so."[37] The capital tax applied to all banks. The provision could have been reversed by the Federalists when they came back into power, but it was not. The capital

---

37. Massachusetts, 1811, Chapter LXXXIV, "An Act to Incorporate the President, Directors, and Company of the State Bank," p. 507.

tax provision was included in all the bank charter renewals in 1812 and thereafter.

Rather than reverse the reform provisions of the State Bank charter, the Federalists embraced them. It is significant that the legislature moved first to treat all banks the same, but still retain the ability to grant or deny charters. Legislators were not immediately willing to give up the privilege of deciding who would get a charter. But the legislative dynamics surrounding banking changed when the legislature effectively tied its hand when it came to manipulating the privileges granted in bank charters. Gradually the legislature stopped limiting entry. In 1851, when a formal general incorporation act was passed, only four new banks were created. There was no pent up demand for bank charters in 1851.

A contributing factor was the unanticipated importance of the tax on bank capital. As Wallis, Sylla, and Legler show, by the decade of 1825–1834, the bank capital tax provided over 60 percent of all Massachusetts state revenues. They developed a "fiscal interest" argument to explain why states that taxed bank capital, like Massachusetts, had a fiscal incentive to create more banks and more bank capital. States that taxed bank capital had many more banks and bank capital than states that owned stock in banks or charged high charter fees. States that owned bank stock, like New York, wanted to maximize bank profits and so limited the number of banks in competition with each other. States that earned substantial revenues from bank charter fees, like Pennsylvania, wanted to limit the number of banks to maximize the entry fees the state could extract. Their analysis was comparative across states and not as detailed as here, but it brings out an important implication of the bank capital tax. Everyone in the Commonwealth, all political interests, even ones without a direct interest in banking or in a bank in a specific town, would find it in their interests to support the chartering of new banks to the extent that it raised revenues for the state that could be expended on other favored projects. The bank capital tax supplied a common interest to Massachusetts elites and nonelites to support more banks, particularly given the significance of the tax to the state treasury.

The Democratic-Republicans intended to create a large state bank that would dominate Massachusetts banking. The state took a significant position in the bank, investing $1,000,000 in the bank's initial capital. They set up a state bank that would compete with private banks. But it soon became apparent that the tax on bank capital was returning substantially more to the state than dividends on bank stock (Wallis, Sylla, and Legler 1994). The state sold off its bank stock and began chartering banks in large numbers.

Naomi Lamoreaux (1994) stressed another important feature of the growing number of small, elite banks in her study of New England banking in the early nineteenth century, *Insider Lending*. Many banks in Massachusetts were established to facilitate the business of local elite manufacturing and commercial interests. The banks were dominated by elite families, but offered the opportunity through stock ownership for nonelites to share in some of the returns of banking. The large number of small banks meant that most banks did not make above normal profits; there was enough competition to prevent that. Warren Weber's work documents that the dividends paid by Massachusetts banks declined after 1812.[38] These small banks were not intended to raise long-term capital investment funds to their owners, they were commercial banks whose benefits consisted primarily in the ability to access commercial credit on favorable terms at low transaction costs.[39] The close connection between banking and manufacturing may help explain why lower dividends on bank stock did not seem to have lowered the relative wealth of Boston bankers.

The pattern of insider lending lay behind the promoters of the Merchants Bank in Salem's complaint that they needed "a new bank in Salem because all the other banks belonged to a different party and refused to lend their money to political opponents" (Dennis 1908, 7). Insider lending was also a feature of land banks in the South (Wallis 2008; Schweikart 1987; Sparks 1932; Worley 1950). This pattern of many small banks closely allied with local economic and political elites was not the pattern in New York or Pennsylvania. Those states chartered a few large banks from which the state extracted revenues (in Pennsylvania) or political organizations extracted financing for political machines (New York).[40] These banks, by necessity, had more outsider lending. What happened in Massachusetts was not that banks stopped lending to insiders, instead, all the important insiders got their own bank. This is consistent with movement toward impersonal rules for banks as well. Every elite group who wanted a bank and was able to exert a minimum level of political influence got a bank, but all the banks would be the same.

As the Handlins noted, the compromise reached in 1812 seems to have signaled the end of banking competition. "The settlement of 1812 had substantially stabilized the banking system, withdrawing it from the grasping hands of a favored few. For a time thereafter, the question of currency was academic only."[41] And "the critical decisions in 1812 had already implicitly circumscribed the capacity to exercise that power [withholding bank charters]" (Handlin and Handlin 1969, 163). Yet, their history of 1812 (113–122) contains no discussion of what those critical decisions were. More or less by chance, the charter of the State Bank in 1812 contained a provision requir-

38. http://www.minneapolisfed.org/research/economists/wewproj.cfm#discounts.
39. As Hildreth (1840, 151–52) notes: "Many of the Massachusetts and Rhode Island banks are constituted and managed much upon this principle. The stock is chiefly held by business men, who hold it, not for the sake of the dividends, which in these States are always moderate, but on account of the business facilities they derive from their concern in the bank."
40. See Wallis, Sylla, and Legler (1994) for the numbers and the history. Schwartz (1987) discusses Pennsylvania, and there is a large literature on New York (Bodenhorn 2006).
41. Handlin and Handlin (1969, 175).

ing that all future charters follow the State Bank charter and levying a tax on bank capital. These were not longstanding demands of bank reformers, but a short-term strategy to get control of banking on the part of the Democratic-Republicans. Both provisions could have been reversed by subsequent legislatures, but they were not. Federalists might have been startled when the state legislature refused to renew the charters of any Federalist banks, and Democratic-Republicans could certainly see what might happen if the Federalists returned the favor in kind when they were in power. What ensued probably began as a temporary arrangement to allow either party to charter a bank under the State Bank charter rubric. The critical decisions of 1812 and the decade that followed was to take bank chartering out of the legislative process altogether.

4.7   Lessons and Conclusions

When we started this chapter, we were very much of the mind that Richard Sylla's conclusion about banking in Massachusetts after 1820 was essentially correct: "Massachusetts had essentially free banking in the sense that entry into banking was open or free, and the state remained a leader in terms of numbers of incorporated banks and capital invested in banking enterprises for several decades" (Sylla 1985). Figures 4.6, 4.7, and 4.12 seemed to clearly confirm the idea that something important happened in 1811 and 1812, events that took a decade or so to work themselves out. The decline of bank presidents and directors who were legislators seemed to offer concrete evidence that an elite coalition of bankers, legislators, and party under the Federalist Party system had given way to open access.

As appealing as that conclusion was and how well it sets with the dominant strain in American history that banking, like other parts of the American economy, opened up to everyone as democracy became more inclusive, the evidence we found did not support that sweeping conclusion. The substantial evidence for a large change in the relationship between banks, legislatures, and parties that occurred in Massachusetts in the 1810s and 1820s seems beyond dispute. The 1820s changes have their roots in the crisis of 1811 and 1812, before the War of 1812 broke out. But as long as we maintain the working definition of elite banks as those banks with a president or director who served as a legislator, we find that almost all the banks up to 1850 were elite banks (keeping in mind the caveat about country banks for which the *Registers* only report the name of the bank president).

Institutional development in Massachusetts followed a path in which the first step toward open access was homogenizing the elite privileges that came with a banking charter. Those privileges were essentially open to all individuals with the economic wherewithal to start a bank or the social standing to be elected to the legislature. By 1829, Massachusetts had moved to impersonal rules for forming and operating a bank. Those rules provided sophisticated and powerful tools to banking organizations. The tools were not just listed in the charters, they were embedded in the economic, political, and legal systems that gave shape and substance to the organizations created by the charters. Nonelites banks (by our measure) did not begin to appear until the 1850s, and they did not spring up en masse even after the free banking law in 1851 had removed any obstacles to bank chartering. Massachusetts moved to open access banking in the 1820s, but it was access that only elites took advantage of.

It would require much more detailed investigation into petitions for bank charters for the entire antebellum period to see if nonelite petitions were denied with higher or lower frequency over time and whether nonelite petitions were common. We have not attempted that very large empirical project, but the narrative evidence suggests that bank charters were readily available after the 1820s. We have shown how the complex relationship between bankers, legislators, and parties in Massachusetts changed to enable public support for private organizations in banking that evolved in a critical time in American history.

Does this history hold more general lessons for the process of development? The central question for this volume is how societies come to provide organizational tools to large blocs of their citizens. That has to be a process that begins with the interests of elites who, in most societies, fail to provide organizational tools to anyone but themselves and the rising elites who demand recognition. What happened in the United States, as exemplified by Massachusetts bankers, was a change in the internal dynamic of intraelite competition. The change produced a set of institutional changes that created a set of impersonal rules for elites. At that point the politics of banking moved from creating special privileges through unique provisions in charters (geographic monopolies, for example) to a system where all elites enjoyed the same organizational tools. Entry was open, but in practice all of the banks continued to maintain a connection with the government in the form of bank officers who were closely connected to the state legislature. Impersonal rules and relative open elite entry produced a large number of relatively small banks. The banks were profitable, but did not enjoy substantial rents from limited entry. Instead, banks were useful in combination with the growing manufacturing and commercial sectors (Lamoreaux 1994). Under those conditions, extending banking privileges to nonelites no longer threatened existing arrangements tying political and economic elites together. When a formal general incorporation act for banks was passed in 1851, there was no rush of banks to take advantage of it. Access to banking was already effectively open to everyone who wanted a bank.

The primary lesson to learn from Massachusetts is that even in a society with a long democratic tradition, with cultural norms that stress the importance of equality and charity, that it is difficult for a society to consciously and deliberately eliminate elite organizational privileges. Support for, and limits on, organizations is a key element in those privileges. Until we understand the dynamics of how elites decide to move to impersonal rules for elites that can genuinely create and sustain open access for elites, we are unlikely to understand how to do it for the larger population.

References

Acemoglu, Daron, and James A. Robinson. 2012. *Why Nations Fail.* New York: Crown Business.

Austin, James. [1828] 2009. *The Life of Elbridge Gerry: With Contemporary Letters to the Close of the American Revolution*, vol. 1. Carlisle, MA: Applewood Books.

Benson, Lee. 1961. *The Concept of Jacksonian Democracy: New York as a Test Case.* Princeton, NJ: Princeton University Press.

Billias, George Athan. 1976. *Elbridge Gerry, Founding Father and Republican Statesman.* New York: McGraw-Hill.

Bodenhorn, Howard. 2006. "Bank Chartering and Political Corruption in Antebellum New York: Free Banking as Reform." In *Corruption and Reform: Lessons from America's Economic History*, edited by Edward L. Glaeser and Claudia Goldin, 231–57. Chicago: University of Chicago Press.

Dean, John W. 1892. "The Gerrymander." *New England Historical and Genealogical Register* 46 (1): 374–83.

Dennis, Albert Woodbury. 1908. *The Merchants National Bank of Salem, Massachusetts: An Historical Sketch.* Hackensack, NJ: Salem Press.

Dodd, Edwin Merrick. 1954. *American Business Corporations until 1860, with Special Reference to Massachusetts.* Cambridge, MA: Harvard University Press.

Dubin, Michael J. 2007. *Party Affiliations in the State Legislatures: A Year by Year Summary, 1796–2006.* Jefferson, NC: McFarland & Company.

Formisano, Ronald P. 1983. *The Transformation of Political Culture: Massachusetts Parties, 1790s–1840s.* New York: Oxford University Press.

Goodman, Paul. 1964. *The Democratic-Republicans of Massachusetts: Politics in a Young Republic.* Greenwood Press.

———. 1968. "Social Status of Party Leadership: The House of Representatives, 1797–1804." *William and Mary Quarterly* 25 (3): 465–74.

Griffith, Elmer Cummings. 1907. *The Rise and Development of the Gerrymander.* Glenview, IL: Scott, Foresman and Company.

Handlin, Oscar, and Mary Flug Handlin. 1969. *Commonwealth: A Study of the Role of Government in the American Economy: Massachusetts, 1774–1861.* Cambridge, MA: Belknap Press of Harvard University Press.

Hildreth, Richard. 1840. *Banking, Banking, and Paper Currencies.* Boston: Whipple & Damrell.

Hilt, Eric, and Jaqueline Valentine. 2012. "Democratic Dividends: Stock Holding, Wealth, and Politics in New York, 1791–1926." *Journal of Economic History* 72 (2): 332–63.

Holt, Michael F. 1999. *The Rise and Fall of the American Whig Party.* New York: Oxford University Press.

Howe, Daniel Walker. 2007. *What Hath God Wrought: The Transformation of America, 1815–1848.* New York: Oxford University Press.

Lake, Wilfred Stanley. 1932. "The History of Banking Regulations in Massachusetts 1784–1860." PhD diss., Harvard University.

Lamoreaux, Naomi R. 1994. *Insider Lending: Banks, Personal Connections, and Economic Development in Industrial New England.* Cambridge: Cambridge University Press.

Lamoreaux, Naomi R., and Christopher Glaisek. 1991. "Vehicles of Privilege or Mobility? Banks in Providence, Rhode Island, during the Age of Jackson." *Business History Review* 65 (Autumn): 502–27.

Lu, Qian. 2014. "From Partisan Banking to Open Access: A Study on the Emergence of Free Banking in Early Nineteenth Century Massachusetts." PhD diss., University of Maryland.

Maier, Pauline. 1993. "The Revolutionary Origins of the American Corporation." *William and Mary Quarterly* 50 (Jan.): 51–84.

Massachusetts. 1812. *Laws of the Commonwealth of Massachusetts passed at the Several Sessions of the General Court Holden in Boston beginning May 31, 1809 and ending on the 29th of February, 1812.* Boston: Adams, Rhoades, and Co. Usually cited as *Massachusetts Acts and Resolves, 1812.*

———. 1831. *Laws of the Commonwealth of Massachusetts passed at the Several Sessions of the General Court, Beginning May 1828 and Ending March 1831, vol. XI.* Boston: Dutton and Wentworth. Usually cited as *Massachusetts Acts and Resolves, 1812.*

McCormick, Richard P. 1966. *The Second American Party System: Party Formation in the Jacksonian Era.* Chapel Hill: University of North Carolina Press.

Morison, Samuel Eliot. 1929. "Elbridge Gerry, Gentleman-Democrat." *New England Quarterly* 2 (1): 6–33.

North, Douglass C., John Joseph Wallis, and Barry R. Weingast. 2009. *Violence and Social Orders: A Conceptual Framework for Interpreting Recorded Human History.* New York: Cambridge University Press.

Robinson, William Alexander. 1916. *Jeffersonian Democracy in New England*, vol. 3. New Haven, CT: Yale University Press.

Seaburg, Carl, and Stanley Paterson. 1971. *Merchant Prince of Boston: Colonel TH Perkins, 1764–1854.* Cambridge, MA: Harvard University Press.

Schwartz, Anna. 1987. "The Beginning of Competitive Banking in Philadelphia, 1782–1809." In *Money in Historical Perspective*, NBER Monograph, 3–22. Chicago: University of Chicago Press.

Schweikart, Larry. 1987. *Banking in the American South from the Age of Jackson to Reconstruction.* Baton Rouge: Louisiana State University Press.

Sparks, Earl Sylvester. 1932. *History and Theory of Agricultural Credit in the United States.* New York: Thomas Crowell.

Steckel, Richard H. and Carolyn M. Moehling. 2001. "Rising Inequality: Trends in the Distribution of Wealth in Industrializing New England." *Journal of Economic History* 61 (1): 160–83.

Stetson, Amos W. 1893. *Eighty Years: An Historical Sketch of the State Bank, 1811–1865; The State National Bank, 1865–1891.* Boston: Private Distribution.

Sylla, Richard. 1985. "Early American Banking: The Significance of the Corporate Form." *Business and Economic History* 14:105–23.

Sylla, Richard, and Robert E. Wright. 2015. "US Corporate Development 1790–1860." Philadelphia: McNeil Center for Early American Studies. http://repository.upenn.edu.

Wallis, John Joseph. 2005. "Constitutions, Corporations, and Corruption: American States and Constitutional Change, 1842 to 1852." *Journal of Economic History* 65 (Mar.): 211–56.

————. 2006. "The Concept of Systematic Corruption in American History." In *Corruption and Reform: Lessons from America's Economic History*, edited by Edward L. Glaeser and Claudia Goldin, 23–62. Chicago: University of Chicago Press.

————. 2008. "Answering Mary Shirley's Question or: What Can the World Bank Learn from American History?" In *Political Institutions and Financial Development*, edited by Stephen Haber, Douglass North, and Barry Weingast, 92–124. Redwood City, CA: Stanford University Press.

Wallis, John Joseph, Richard E. Sylla, and John B. Legler. 1994. "The Interaction of Taxation and Regulation in Nineteenth-Century U.S. Banking." In *The Regulated Economy: A Historical Approach to Political Economy*, edited by Claudia Goldin and Gary D. Libecap, 121–44. Chicago: University of Chicago Press.

Weber, Warren E. 2015. Census of Early State Banks in the United States. https://www.webereconomics.com/data-archive.

Wilentz, Sean. 2005. *The Rise of American Democracy*. New York: Norton and Company.

Worley, Ted. R. 1950. "Control of the Real Estate Bank of the State of Arkansas, 1836–1855." *Mississippi Valley Historical Review* 37 (3): 403–26.

5

Corporation Law and the Shift toward Open Access in the Antebellum United States

Eric Hilt

5.1 Introduction

Over the course of the nineteenth century, business corporations became increasingly common elements of the American economy, and their proliferation transformed economic life. Among the most important legal innovations that facilitated this expansion in the use of the corporate form was the enactment of general incorporation statutes by the states. Prior to the adoption of a general statute, a business could only incorporate if the state passed a special law granting it a corporate charter.[1] This regime of special charters created problems, both practical and political: petitioning the legislature could be slow or prohibitively costly for some entrepreneurs, and legislative discretion over access to incorporation led to serious problems of corruption.[2] Many states responded to these problems by enacting general incorporation statutes, which created a simple administrative procedure by which firms could incorporate. Under the terms of these statutes, entrepreneurs simply filed a certificate with information about their firm with a government office, and when their certificate was recorded their firm was

Eric Hilt is associate professor of economics at Wellesley College and a research associate of the National Bureau of Economic Research.

I would like to thank Naomi Lamoreaux, Tim Guinnane, Richard Brooks, and John Wallis, along with participants at the NBER Civil Society conference held at Yale University, for helpful comments. For acknowledgments, sources of research support, and disclosure of the author's or authors' material financial relationships, if any, please see http://www.nber.org /chapters/c13508.ack.

1. The historical origins of the doctrine that incorporation was possible only through a special law are explored in Hurst (1970). At the time, legal barriers made it necessary for corporations to be incorporated in the state in which they operated. See the discussion below.

2. On the corruption associated with special chartering, see Wallis (2006).

incorporated. Incorporation became a routine, inexpensive matter outside the realm of political influence.

General incorporation statutes thus democratized access to an important organizational technology. They have been highlighted as momentous reforms that created open-access orders (North, Wallis, and Weingast 2009), changed the legal conception of the corporation to one that is fundamentally private in nature (Horwitz 1977), and weakened the role of the state in regulating corporations (Berle and Means 1933). Yet owing to the difficulty of identifying and analyzing the different states' and territories' early general statutes, little systematic information has been collected about them, and there is considerable uncertainly in the literature about the contents, or even the dates, of most states' early general acts. Most of the scholarship on these statutes resorts to making broad generalizations on the basis of relatively little evidence.[3] Given the importance that is generally ascribed to these statutes, this lack of systematic analysis is surprising. It is not possible to assess the impact or significance of the transition to general incorporation without first understanding when and where it occurred, and the content of the laws that were actually enacted.

This chapter analyzes the general incorporation statutes for manufacturing enterprises enacted by the American states in the years up to 1860. It presents new, comprehensive data on the adoption of general statutes and on the content of those statutes. These data are then used to analyze the political and economic forces that shaped the decision to adopt a general act, and to document the variation in the substance of general acts across regions and over time. A number of hypotheses related to assertions made in the literature about early general statutes are then investigated.

The analysis proceeds in three steps. First, I present a new chronology of the earliest general incorporation acts for manufacturing firms of each state or territory prior to 1860, obtained from a careful search of state session laws, legal codes, and statute revisions. The resulting list improves upon the widely used tabulations of Hamill (1999), and in particular includes eight general incorporation acts omitted from that list. The new chronology indicates that a number of states enacted general laws for manufacturing corporations several decades earlier than had been previously reported.

In the second step, I use the new list of general acts to analyze the political and economic determinants of states' transitions to general incorporation. Using newly available data on the total number of special charters for business corporations in each state from Sylla and Wright (2013), and census data on the social and economic structure of the states and territories, I estimate a simple linear probability model of the decision to adopt a general

---

3. The most prominent example is Berle and Means (1933, 126–27), who argue on the basis of a wholly incomplete chronology of general acts. An important exception is Hamill (1999), who presents a chronology of the dates of adoption of these statutes.

act prior to 1860. The results indicate that states with higher proportions of their population engaged in agriculture or commerce were less likely to adopt a general act, which may be a reflection of interest-group politics, if those sectors were opposed to the proliferation of limited liability corporations. The results also indicate that smaller states were less likely to adopt a general act. In a small state, the costs of petitioning the state government for a charter may have been lower, and the willingness of a state government to accommodate such petitions may have been higher—both of which would have reduced the benefits of adopting a general act. Evidence consistent with this latter point is found in the data on special-act charters, which indicate that the states that did not adopt general statutes typically offered extraordinarily liberal access to special charters. This suggests that broad access to the corporate form was sometimes achieved without general statutes, and that the enactment of a general statute may not always have created a substantial, discrete increase in the accessibility of incorporation.

Early general acts did not grant entrepreneurs the freedom to configure their enterprises however they wished, but instead created an organizational template that corporations were required to adopt. This template sometimes imposed strict conditions on the size, industry, operations, capital structure, and internal governance of the corporations created. But the rigidity and restrictiveness of the organizational template varied considerably across states. In the third step, I present a detailed analysis of the terms of the states' general incorporation acts as amended in 1860. The statutes often contained detailed provisions intended to protect the interests of creditors, such as limits on indebtedness, regulations of capital contributions, disclosure requirements regarding paid-in capital, and punitive measures that stripped directors or stockholders of their limited liability in response to actions that imperiled the firms' capital. Many of the other regulations written into the statutes were intended to give the state leverage over the firms, for example, by limiting the duration of their incorporation.

The analysis of the terms of the statutes also reveals that there was considerable variation in the degree of their restrictiveness across states. Southern states' general laws in particular tended to be more permissive than those of other states. On the other hand, Southern states frequently imposed rules that either explicitly forbade certain segments of society from making use of their general statutes, or granted discretion over the use of the law to a government official, who could choose to exclude anyone from using the law for any reason. The early general laws of Southern states were thus at once more permissive and more restrictive than those of other states, and perhaps can only be termed "general" laws in a qualified sense. General statutes did not always create truly open access to the corporate form.

The data and analysis presented in this chapter contribute to a large and prominent literature on the evolution of American corporation law over the nineteenth century, and the resulting changes in the relationship between the state and the corporation. A number of works in this literature have focused on the role of general statutes in this evolution, with some arguing that they circumscribed the state's role in constituting or regulating corporations (e.g., Berle and Means 1933; Horwitz 1977), whereas others have emphasized the strict regulations imposed in many early general acts (Millon 1990; Hurst 1970). What is missing from this literature is a systematic analysis of the terms of these statutes—the regulations they imposed, and the matters they left unregulated. These statutes also created some of the earliest regulations of dividend payouts, financial reporting, director elections, capital contributions, and the rights of creditors. The analysis of this chapter therefore complements the literatures on the historical origins of such regulations in the United States.

A smaller literature has analyzed the history of general statutes in particular states (e.g., Seligman 1976), the rates at which the statutes of individual states were utilized (e.g., Kessler 1940; Bodenhorn 2008), and the forces influencing states' decisions to implement general statutes (Butler 1985). This chapter complements those earlier works by presenting comprehensive data that can be used to understand the extent to which individual states' experiences are representative, and to evaluate hypotheses regarding the determinants of the adoption of general laws.

This chapter also contributes to the literature on the suitability of the corporate form in general, and American corporation laws in particular, for the needs of small- and medium-sized enterprises (SMEs). Recent contributions to this literature have argued that the corporate form was inflexible in important respects, and the alternative forms that became available in the twentieth century, such as the limited liability company (LLC), were superior for the needs of SMEs (Guinnane et al. 2007). This chapter contributes to that literature by providing detailed documentation of the ways in which the states' corporation laws were restrictive or permissive.

5.2   Early General Acts: Their Adoption and Their Terms

In order to collect a comprehensive list of early general incorporation statutes, a careful search of each state's session laws, legal codes, and statute revisions up to 1860 was undertaken.[4] The results of this search are presented in table 5.1, which lists the date of each state or territory's first general incorporation statute—or in cases where a statute was repealed, the date of their second statute—along with the citation of the statute

---

4. The names by which these statutes refer to the corporations they create vary widely, and include "joint stock companies," "corporations," "companies," "associations," and even "private associations and partnerships," which makes identifying these acts within a state's laws difficult. The names given in previously documented general statutes were used to create search terms, and as new statutes were identified, any new terms that arose were used to conduct further searches.

Table 5.1   American states' and territories' first general incorporation acts for manufacturing firms, 1811–1860

Year	State	Citation; major amendments or additional legislation up to 1860
1811	New York	Laws, Ch. 67; Laws, 1848, Ch. 40, 1853, Ch. 333, 1855, Ch. 301, 1857, Ch. 29, Ch. 262
1812	Ohio* (repealed 1824)	Laws, Ch. 15
1816	New Jersey* (repealed 1819)	Laws, Feb 9, 1816
1824	Illinois* (repealed 1833)	Laws, December 16, 1824
1836	Pennsylvania	Laws, No. 194; Laws, 1849, No. 368, 1851, No. 295, 1852, No. 371, 1853, No. 186, 1860, No. 341
1837	Connecticut	Laws, Ch. 63; Revised Statutes (1854), Title III
1837	Michigan*	Laws, No. 121; Laws, 1853, No. 41, 1855, No. 19, 1857, No. 76
1846	Ohio (first after repeal of 1812 act)	Laws, Feb. 9, 1846; Laws, May 1, 1852, April 17, 1854, May 1, 1854, March 30, 1857, April 12, 1858
1846	New Jersey (first after repeal of 1816 act)	Laws, Feb. 25, 1846; Laws, March 2, 1849, March 7, 1850, February 25, 1852, March 10, 1853, March 15, 1860, March 22, 1860
1847	Georgia*	Laws, December 22, 1847
1847	Iowa	Laws, Ch. 81; Revised Statutes (1860), Title X
1848	Louisiana	Laws, No. 100; Revised Statutes (1856)
1849	Wisconsin	Laws, Ch. 51; Revised Statutes (1858), Ch. 73
1849	Illinois* (first after repeal of 1824 act)	Laws, Feb. 10, 1849; Laws, February 18, 1857, April 26, 1859
1849	Missouri*	Laws, March 12, 1849; Revised Statutes (1855), Ch. 37, Laws, 1855, Ch. 34
1850	California	Laws, Ch. 128; Compiled Laws of California (1853), Ch. 77, Ch. 78, Laws, 1858, Ch. 181
1850	Tennessee	Laws, Ch. 179; Code of Tennessee (1858), Title 9, Ch. 2
1851	Arkansas*	Laws, Jan 2, 1851
1851	Vermont	Laws, No. 60; Compiled Statutes (1851), Ch. 83
1851	Massachusetts	Laws, Ch. 133; General Statutes (1859), Chs. 60 and 61
1852	Alabama	Code of Alabama, Part 2, Title 2, Ch. 3
1852	Florida	Laws, Ch. 490
1852	Indiana	Revised Statutes, Ch. 66
1852	Maryland	Laws, Ch. 322; Maryland Code (1860), Art 26
1852	North Carolina	Laws, Ch. 81; Revised Code (1854), Ch. 26, Laws, 1855, Ch. 31
1854	Kentucky	Laws, Ch. 1012
1854	Virginia	Laws, Ch. 47; Code of Virginia (1860), Ch. 57
1857	Mississippi	Revised Code, Ch. 35
1858	Minnesota	Laws, Ch. 78
1859	Kansas Territory	Laws, Ch. 490; Revised Statutes (1855), Ch. 28

*Denotes statutes not included in the Hamill (1999) tabulation.

itself and any important amendments or supplemental legislation. General statutes not included in the Hamill (1999) tabulation are identified with an asterisk.

The list presented in the table suggests that the transition to general incorporation began with halting experimentation. In the first four decades of the nineteenth century, just seven states enacted general laws, and three ultimately repealed them and reverted to regimes of special incorporation. Beginning in the mid-1840s, however, growing numbers of states began to enact—and retain—general statutes, and by 1860 the vast majority of the states and organized territories had one in place.

The adoptions of general statutes began in two small waves, the first occurring in 1811–24 and the second in 1836–37. The first wave commenced around the time of the War of 1812, and the statutes enacted during that period were likely intended to encourage the development of domestic manufacturing. Trade restrictions enacted prior to the war, such as the Embargo Act of 1807, blocked American access to imports and created opportunities for domestic firms to replace foreign sources of manufactured goods.[5] In the years 1808–1811, incorporations of manufacturing firms via special-act charters rose significantly, reflecting a substantial increase in demand for charters, as well as an apparent willingness of state governments to accommodate that demand.[6] Finally, in 1811 the State of New York took the radical step of enacting a general incorporation statute for manufacturing firms.[7] Laws similar to New York's were passed in Ohio in 1812, in New Jersey in 1816, and in Illinois in 1824.[8]

New York's 1811 act imposed a relatively rigid template on the firms it created, but the template itself was quite similar to the terms of special-act charters of manufacturing companies granted by the state during the preceding years. Some elements of the law were also likely influenced by the state's 1784 general incorporation act for religious congregations. The statute precisely enumerated the industries in which the firms could operate; limited the size of the board of directors to nine persons, who were required to be stockholders; limited the capital stock to a maximum of $100,000 and limited the duration of the firms' existence to twenty years; and required that each stockholder be granted "as many votes as he owns share of the stock"

5. The effects of these disruptions on domestic manufacturing are assessed in Irwin and Davis (2003).

6. For example, in 1909 and 1910, the state of New York granted charters to twenty-five manufacturing corporations; for all years prior to 1909, the state had only chartered three (*Laws of New York* 1784–1810).

7. In the discussion that follows, citations of individual states' statutes are omitted, as they are provided in table 5.1.

8. These laws are not noted in much of the previous scholarship on general incorporation statutes (e.g., Hamill 1999). No comprehensive data on their use seems to survive. McCormick and McCormick (1998) include a detailed description of one firm that incorporated through Ohio's first general act.

of the company in director elections.[9] Other parts of the act empowered the directors to write the firms' bylaws, limited the liability of the stockholders to "the extent of their respective shares in the company, and no further," and enumerated the powers of the corporations created.[10] The statute also made company stock personal estate, and transferable "in such manner as shall be prescribed by the laws of the company." Finally, it required that all directors be residents of the state in its stipulation that their "removal out of the state" would create a vacancy on the board.

The statutes of Ohio, New Jersey, and Illinois all followed the structure and language of New York's 1811 statute, but modified particular terms. For example, the statutes of New Jersey and Illinois followed New York in imposing a rule of one vote per share, whereas Ohio mandated a graduated voting-rights scheme in which the number of votes per share each shareholder was entitled to was a decreasing function of the number of shares held.[11] And whereas Ohio and New Jersey followed New York in granting shareholders limited liability (with New Jersey imposing the rule that stockholders were responsible for the amount of their shares plus all the accumulated dividends they received), the statute of Illinois made shareholders personally liable for their firms' debts. But with the exception of New York's, these acts were all repealed: New Jersey's in 1819, Ohio's in 1824, and that of Illinois in 1833—at which point New York was once again the only state or territory with a general statute for manufacturing enterprises.

A second brief wave of adoption of general statutes began in 1836, when Pennsylvania enacted a general incorporation law for iron manufacturers. Pennsylvania's law was similar in some respects to those that preceded it, but it applied only to firms in a narrowly defined industry, and required a *minimum* of $100,000 in capital.[12] Pennsylvania's law is noteworthy because it introduced the innovation of requiring the attorney general and the governor to scrutinize all certificates of incorporation, and empowered the governor to withhold approval of incorporations if there were any doubt regarding the "lawfulness" of the proposed enterprise or the amount of

9. Following the state's general act for religious congregations, the statute refers to the directors as "trustees." The general act for religious congregations required those organizations to have boards of trustees of three to nine persons as well (*Laws of New York* 1784, ch. 18).

10. This language with respect to shareholder liability was interpreted by the courts to mean what would be termed today "double liability" (see Howard 1938). Most of the subsequent statutes that granted limited liability to shareholders did so with similar language.

11. Ohio's statute stated that "each stockholder shall be entitled to one vote for each share he may own below ten; for all above ten and not exceeding twenty, one vote for every two shares; and for every five shares above twenty, one vote." On graduated voting rights, see Hilt (2008; 2013).

12. Pennsylvania's law applied only to firms "manufacturing iron from the raw material, with coke or mineral coal" and specifically excluded firms producing iron "which has not been manufactured from the ore, with coke or mineral coal." Pennsylvania's 1836 act was also unusual in that it imposed graduated voting rights, and included several special charters for specific corporations, including a coal company and turnpike road company.

the capital stock "actually paid in." In contrast, in the other states' laws, incorporation was automatic once a certificate was filed. Although the language of Pennsylvania's statute could be interpreted as merely enforcing compliance with its terms, the discretion granted to the government officials scrutinizing certificates may have been broad enough to enable them to reject proposed incorporations for other reasons.[13]

In 1837 Michigan, having just become a state, enacted a general incorporation law quite similar to those of the 1811–24 period, but like Illinois it imposed unlimited liability for all shareholders.[14] Also in 1837, Connecticut passed a general incorporation act that was the first to not specifically enumerate the industries that could be pursued, or to limit the duration of the existence of the corporations it created. The Pennsylvania and Connecticut laws from this period were also the first to require corporations to make an annual report to the state.

No subsequent general acts were passed until the second half of the 1840s. The beginning of this third period of activity in enacting general laws coincides with episodes of fiscal distress among many American states, some of which responded with significant constitutional reforms, particularly regarding provisions relating to corporations (Wallis 2005).[15] The first states to enact general laws in this period were Ohio and New Jersey, which passed new laws in 1846. Georgia and Iowa followed in 1847, Louisiana in 1848, and in 1849, Wisconsin and Missouri enacted general laws for the first time, while Illinois enacted its first since the repeal of its 1824 law. Whereas most of these statutes were similar to those of earlier decades, Iowa's 1847 law was radically innovative. It imposed *no restrictions whatsoever* on the internal governance of the firms it created, and in fact did not even mention directors or a procedure for voting or decision making. It simply said that any number of persons—even just one—may incorporate a firm, make its shares transferable, and "exempt [their] private property from corporate debts." With regard to governance institutions and procedures, it stated that the incorporators "may make such regulations as they please in relation to the management of their business." Iowa's statute also did not impose any restrictions on the size of the capital stock, although it did limit the duration of the corporations' existence to twenty years.

In contrast, Iowa's neighbor to the northeast, Wisconsin, adopted a statute that was as restrictive as Iowa's was permissive. Wisconsin's statute not only regulated the structure and governance of corporations, but it imposed unlimited liability on stockholders and also required them to employ a rule

13. Pennsylvania substantially revised its law in 1849, making it applicable to firms in a broad range of industries, and removing the provision granting the governor authority over access to the act.

14. Michigan substantially revised its law in 1846, with new terms that granted shareholders limited liability.

15. As Wallis notes, beginning in this period many states amended their constitutions to prohibit incorporation through special act. The dates of these constitutional prohibitions are tabulated in Hamill (1999).

of one vote per *shareholder* in director elections. Wisconsin was the only state ever to impose such a rule in its corporation law in the period under study. The legislatures of both Iowa and Wisconsin were controlled by Jacksonian Democrats at the time their general statutes were enacted (Dubin 2007). In one, concerns about corporate privilege led to the adoption of an extraordinarily flexible law, likely intended to produce a rapid proliferation of new corporations that would undermine the exclusivity of corporate privileges.[16] In the other, those same concerns produced a law with terms so restrictive they bordered on the punitive, which was intended to restrain corporations and their controlling shareholders.

In the 1850s, another fifteen states and territories adopted general acts, including a substantial number of Southern states (among all those that would secede from the United States in the Civil War, only South Carolina and Texas failed to adopt a general incorporation act for manufacturing firms prior to 1860). Many of the statutes adopted during this period, particularly those of western states, incorporated passages from New York's statute, which was revised in 1848 to include a number of provisions intended to protect the interests of creditors.[17] The laws of Southern states, however, were not as influenced by the New York statute, and were in fact quite different from those of the mid-Atlantic states or the New England states in many respects. Relative to the laws implemented in other regions, Southern states' general acts tended to impose fewer restrictions on the internal governance of corporations.[18] In addition, some of the Southern statutes included provisions that gave discretion over access to incorporation to a government official. This official, sometimes a judge, the attorney general, or the governor, was given the power to exclude individuals seeking to incorporate a business from doing so, in language that was often much more explicit than that of Pennsylvania's 1836 law. Mississippi's statute, for example, states that "the governor may require amendments to or alterations to be made [to proposed corporations' certificates] . . . or if deemed expedient by him, he may withhold his approval entirely."[19] Some Southern states even took this a step further by completely excluding particular groups, usually nonwhite persons, from access to their laws. For example, the statute of Georgia applied only to "free white citizens of the State" and the border state of

16. Horack (1904) notes that previous experience with corporate charters in Iowa demonstrated the "evils of special incorporation."

17. These provisions included a limit on firm indebtedness, prohibitions against paying dividends out of the firm's capital or in insolvency, a requirement that the list of shareholders be kept publicly accessible "every day except Sunday and the Fourth of July," and detailed provisions governing procedures by which shareholders could increase or decrease their firms' capital stock.

18. For example, the statutes of both Mississippi and Alabama make no mention of a board of directors or president—incorporators were permitted to choose whether or not to have a board, and if so, to structure it however they wished. Alabama's statute did, however, impose a rule of one vote per share, whereas Mississippi's granted incorporators discretion over the allocation of voting rights.

19. The statutes of Louisiana and Virginia granted similar discretionary powers to judges.

Maryland's statute prohibited "free negroes and mulattoes" from forming corporations.[20]

Also during the 1850s, a number of states that adopted general acts in the 1840s and early 1850s amended their laws, perhaps motivated by experience with their own statutes, or by legislation enacted in other states. Many of these amendments were focused on limits on capitalization; Tennessee and Illinois imposed such limits for the first time, whereas Connecticut and Massachusetts raised theirs. But there were much more significant changes as well. In 1858, Wisconsin substantially rewrote its corporation laws, removing its unusual provisions of unlimited liability for shareholders and the rule of one vote for each shareholder. And in 1852 Ohio radically revised its corporation laws, with new provisions that eliminated all restrictions on capitalization and board structure, while imposing unlimited liability on shareholders. This revision may have had unintended consequences, as the law was revised again in 1854, with provisions that restored limited liability to shareholders.

By 1860, twenty-seven of thirty-two states and organized territories had adopted general incorporation acts. The proliferation of general acts is illustrated in figure 5.1. Although the number of states with a general law remained quite small until the mid-1840s, New York's population was such a large share of the nation's that the fraction of the population living within a state with a general law was around 20 percent after 1811. The figure clearly illustrates the rapid adoption of these acts after 1845, which caused the fraction of the population living in a state or territory with a general law to increase from about 30 percent to more than 90 percent by 1860.

There was nonetheless considerable variation across regions in the rate at which general acts were adopted. Figure 5.2 presents the diffusion of general acts within the different regions of the country, with each panel depicting the share of the population of the region residing in states with general acts. Led by New York, the mid-Atlantic states adopted general incorporation much earlier than the other regions. Ohio and Illinois's adoption and repeal of general acts produced early volatility in the pattern for the Midwest, which eventually adopted general acts at high rates beginning in the late 1840s. By 1860, nearly 100 percent of the population of both the mid-Atlantic and Midwestern states had access to general incorporation. In contrast, New England stands out as being considerably more resistant to general incorporation than all the other regions. By 1860 only 60 percent of the region's population resided in states with general acts.

The South stands out as adopting general incorporation statutes later than the other regions. There were no early adopters in the South, and the

---

20. The Georgia statute did, however, authorize the free whites of the state to form corporations with "such others as they may associate with them," which was likely intended to enable them to form corporations with investors from out of the state.

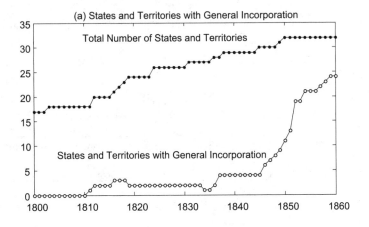

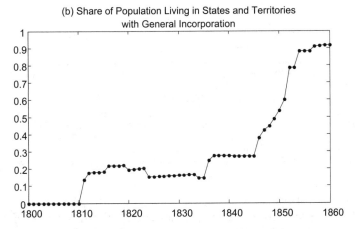

Fig. 5.1   Adoption of general incorporation acts by states and territories

Note: The upper figure presents total states and organized territories included in the most recent decennial census. The lower figure presents the share of total population in states and territories with general incorporation acts for manufacturing enterprises in place. Population levels for individual states linearly interpolated between census years.

first general act there was Georgia's of 1847. As with the Midwest, most of the South's general acts were introduced in the 1850s, and ultimately general incorporation became the norm in the region. By 1860 all but one of the Southern states had made the transition.

5.3   Political Economy of the Adoption of General Incorporation Acts

The adoption of a general statute created a significant political transition in which access to incorporation (with important conditions and exceptions) was opened to all entrepreneurs. The state legislature could no longer

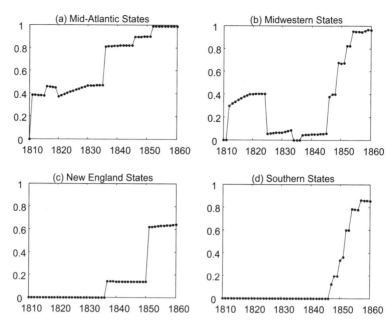

Fig. 5.2   Proliferation of general acts among different regions

Note: The figure presents the share of total population in states and territories with general incorporation acts for manufacturing enterprises in place for each region. The mid-Atlantic states are defined as New York, New Jersey, Pennsylvania, Maryland, and Delaware. Virginia is included among the Southern states, which are defined as those that seceded during the Civil War. Population levels for individual states linearly interpolated between census years.

exercise control over access to the form, except in cases where entrepreneurs sought to create firms that did not conform to the terms of the general statute. In some cases incumbent interests resisted the adoption of general acts for some time, and it took economic and political crises to weaken those interests sufficiently for a general act to be adopted.

The political party most often associated with the adoption of general acts was the Democrats. The Jacksonian anticorruption impulse, which sought to undermine special privileges and vested rights, animated the efforts of the Democrats to push for their adoption. And indeed, at the time when the states finally did implement a general statute, 67 percent of the upper houses of their governments, and 57 percent of their lower houses, had Democratic majorities. Both houses had Democratic majorities 48 percent of the time.[21]

But the ultimate cause of the adoption of a general act, or the failure to adopt one, was not the relative influence of a political party, but the deeper

21. These calculations were made from data presented in Dubin (2007). The calculations were made for the period of the Second Party System (late 1820s until early 1850s). Legislators identified with parties allied with the Democrats, such as the Free Soil Party, were counted as Democrats in the calculations.

Fig. 5.3   Adoption of general incorporation among the eastern states, 1860

Note: The shaded states are those that had adopted general incorporation for manufacturing enterprises by 1860. Those that had not adopted general incorporation included Maine, New Hampshire, Rhode Island, Delaware, and South Carolina. States and territories that had adopted general incorporation but are not included in the figure include California and the Kansas Territory.

economic and political forces that led to that political party's ascendance. In order to understand the adoption of general acts, we must therefore analyze the characteristics of the states' social and economic structure that may have contributed to the emergence of political factions friendly to general acts.

Some preliminary insights into the forces influencing the decision to adopt a general act can be obtained by simply looking at a map. Figure 5.3 presents the eastern United States, with the states that had adopted general incorporation by 1860 shaded gray. The near ubiquity of the gray shading in every region of the map illustrates the prevalence of general acts at that time. But there are some states that failed to adopt general incorporation—Maine, New Hampshire, Rhode Island, Delaware, and South Carolina—and they were all located along the coast. Since the structure of economic activity within coastal states was likely somewhat different from that of inland states, this may be an indication that the composition of economic activity influenced whether a state adopted general incorporation. In particular, shipping, trade, and commerce were likely to be more important to coastal economies than inland economies, and these activities may have been particularly reliant on commercial credit networks in which personal liability for debts was the norm. If general incorporation was expected to facilitate the creation of large numbers of businesses with limited liability that would seek to attract credit from banks and other lenders, then existing commercial borrowers may have feared that their access to credit would deteriorate as a result.[22] The adoption of a general incorporation law may therefore have been perceived to risk disrupting the credit networks that were so essential to the operations of commerce.

With the exception of South Carolina, the states that failed to adopt general incorporation were also relatively small. Perhaps in a small state, the costs associated with obtaining special charters, and therefore the benefits of the transition to general incorporation, were somewhat lower. Certainly the expenses associated with traveling to the state capital to petition the legislature would have been lower; perhaps businesspeople were also more likely to have regular personal contact with legislators as well, which might also have made special charters more accessible.

The small size of a state may also have influenced its behavior toward granting corporate charters through the forces of jurisdictional competition. The small states that failed to adopt general incorporation were located near large, economically important states such as Massachusetts, New York, or Pennsylvania. At the time, corporations could not easily operate in states that had not granted them charters,[23] but entrepreneurs and investors could relocate their firms to nearby states or invest in firms located in other states. Small states, whose markets were of limited size, would have felt this threat most acutely, and may therefore have been inclined to be quite liberal in their grants of corporate charters. And if these pressures induced small states to offer generous access to corporate charters, the benefits of a transition to general incorporation would have been smaller. This also suggests that general incorporation statutes were not the only available response to jurisdictional competition; liberal access to special charters might also address this issue.[24]

22. At a minimum, the emergence of large numbers of new borrowers would have driven up the cost of borrowing for incumbents. But if the new entrants were expected to be of lower "quality" or higher risks, and if lenders were potentially unable to clearly distinguish among the quality of various borrowers, perhaps because of their large incorporated capitals, then incumbent borrowers might have suffered the consequences of increased adverse selection in credit markets.

23. At the time, states' laws discriminated against "foreign" corporations in various ways (see, e.g., Henderson 1918); corporations that operated in multiple states, such as large canals or railroads, typically were incorporated in all the states in which they operated. The modern form of jurisdictional competition, which results from businesses' freedom to incorporate in any state, irrespective the location of their operations, did not exist in the antebellum United States.

24. Butler (1985) argues that jurisdictional competition in the era when businesses could incorporate in any state led to the adoption of liberal general incorporation statutes. The analysis of this chapter suggests that the mobility of capital in the early nineteenth century may have influenced states' willingness to grant special charters, and thereby slowed the adoption of general statutes.

Another mechanism by which the size of a state may have influenced its propensity to adopt a general act is modeled by Mulligan and Shleifer (2005), which formalizes an idea due to Demsetz (1967). If imposing new regulations has fixed costs, then the supply of regulation is limited by the extent of the market or the size of the state. If there was a fixed cost associated with implementing and administering a general statute, this could explain the small states' reluctance to adopt such legislation. Note, however, that this hypothesis should be related more closely to population size rather than geographical area, an implication that can be tested empirically.

Other elements of a state's economic and social structure may also have influenced its propensity to adopt general laws. For example, agrarian interests, while not necessarily hostile to manufacturing, may have regarded limited liability corporations as potentially disruptive financially and opposed a transition to open access to the corporate form. States with a larger share of their population engaged in agriculture may therefore have been more likely to resist the adoption of a general statute. In addition, some states may have developed stronger associational cultures or institutions that encouraged participation in political or economic organizations, or reform movements. Those states would have been more likely to adopt statutes that facilitated access to the corporate form. Finally, the importance of slavery in a state's economy may have influenced the openness of its institutions (Engerman and Sokoloff 2002), and perhaps its political system's willingness to make the corporate form openly accessible to the population.

We can begin to investigate these hypotheses more carefully by comparing various characteristics of states that did and did not adopt general incorporation by 1860. In order to avoid the potential for general incorporation acts to influence the measures of economic and social structures under analysis, these data will be taken from the year 1840, before most states had adopted general acts. It should be noted that this will restrict the sample of states to those for which census data is available in 1840.[25]

Simple comparisons of means are presented in table 5.2. The data in the first three rows of the table offer statistical confirmation that small states, both in terms of geographical area and population, were less likely to adopt general incorporation acts, and that states located along the Atlantic seaboard were also less likely to adopt such laws. The data in the fourth row, which presents the total number of special charters granted to businesses up to 1840, scaled by 1840 population, indicate that the states that did not adopt general incorporation acts were far more liberal in granting charters to businesses. The mean among those that did not adopt general acts, 0.117 charters per 100 persons, was more than twice as high as that of the states that did adopt general acts (0.052 charter per 100 persons), and the differ-

---

25. This results in the exclusion of Texas, California, Minnesota, and Kansas from the analysis. Of these, only Texas failed to adopt a general act prior to 1860.

Table 5.2   Characteristics of states that did and did not adopt general laws prior to 1860

	States that did not adopt general statutes by 1860 (1)	States that did adopt general statutes by 1860 (2)	Difference (3)
Area (square miles)	16,156	45,246	−29,089***
	(7,307)	(4,559)	(8,202)
Population, 1840	313,536	643,833	−330,297**
	(103,078)	(118,226)	(153,353)
Location: Atlantic	1.000	0.417	0.449**
seaboard	(0)	(0.103)	(0.186)
Charters granted per	0.117	0.052	0.065**
100 persons, 1840	(0.030)	(0.008)	(0.029)
Share population in	0.235	0.230	0.004
agriculture, 1840	(0.031)	(0.012)	(0.031)
Enslaved people per	11.672	16.661	−4.989
capita, 1840	(10.856)	(3.916)	(10.819)

Sources: Total charters allocated to businesses are from Sylla and Wright (2013). Data for the total population, the share of the population in agriculture, and the number of enslaved people are from the federal census of 1840. States and territories that were not organized in 1840 or were not included in the 1840 census are not included in the table.

Note: A total of twenty-nine states are included in the table. Standard errors are reported in parentheses. The standard errors in column (3) are calculated from a regression with robust standard errors.
***Significant at the 1 percent level.
**Significant at the 5 percent level.
*Significant at the 10 percent level.

ence is highly statistically significant. Apparently, the legislatures of these states retained discretion over access to the corporate form only in a very limited sense, as entrepreneurs seeking charters were generously accommodated. In such states, the need for fundamental reform of the chartering process through a general act would have been perceived as less acute, as the scope for corrupt influence was likely quite narrow in an environment in which charters were granted to the vast majority of petitioners.[26]

The remaining rows of table 5.2 present data on economic structure. These data indicate that states that failed to adopt general incorporation were not statistically different from those that did, in the shares of their populations engaged in agriculture, and in the importance of slavery in their econo-

26. An alternative interpretation of the correlation between high numbers of charters and the lower propensity to adopt general incorporation is that the large numbers of businesses operating under those charters constituted a powerful interest group that resisted the transition to general incorporation and the new competition it would have created. However, the high rate at which the legislatures of those states apparently granted charters casts some doubt on this interpretation: incumbent corporations seeking to block access to the corporate form should have blocked access to charters, as well as general acts.

mies (measured as enslaved persons as a fraction of the total population in 1840). The variation in these characteristics of states, however, had a strong regional component, and in order to investigate their influence on states' propensity to adopt general statutes one should focus on the variation within regions. Moreover, outcomes such as the volume of charters granted may be interrelated with states' economic structure, or with other state characteristics such as the number of years they have been organized as states, which may have independently influenced the adoption of general incorporation acts.

In order to isolate the relative importance of these and other potential influences on states' adoption of general acts, I therefore estimate simple linear probability models. An indicator for whether or not the state adopted a general incorporation act prior to 1860 is used as the dependent variable.[27] Summary statistics of the data are presented in table 5.3, panel A. In addition to the variables examined above, the data include several other state characteristics, such as an indicator for statehood prior to 1800; a measure of the number of newspapers per capita, which might have helped facilitate the flow of political information; and the percentage of the population engaged in commerce, which as stated above was likely negatively correlated with the propensity to adopt general incorporation.

The results of this analysis are presented in table 5.3, panel B. All of the estimated specifications include region fixed effects. Column (1) presents regressions that include only measures of the size, location, and age of the states. These results indicate that the measure of the size of a state that influenced the adoption of a general act was its geographical size, and not the size of its population.[28] This may be an indication that in states that encompassed smaller areas, the costs of obtaining a special charter, and therefore the benefits of a general corporation statute, were indeed lower. States whose populations were small (conditional on the size of their geographical area, and on their location and age) were no less likely to adopt general acts. This contradicts the hypothesis regarding the role of fixed costs of regulations. The results also indicate that states located on the Atlantic

27. The fact that a few states had already adopted general incorporation prior to 1840 would present a problem for this analysis, if their acts resulted in substantial changes in some of the variables included in the regression. Among the states that had previously adopted general incorporation, two repealed their statutes, and another three adopted them only a few years before 1840. Only New York, with its long history of operation under general laws, presents a serious problem, and excluding New York from the analysis does not change the results significantly.

28. It is worth noting that one of these small states, Delaware, is the leading choice for firms incorporated away from the states in which they are located. The small size of the state has been proposed as a form of a hostage that the state can offer to corporations, to make a commitment to continually maintain favorable statutes credible (Romano 1985; Grandy 1989). It is possible that a similar mechanism may have operated in the nineteenth century—small states such as Rhode Island and Delaware may have been able to commit to a more favorable special chartering regime.

Table 5.3   **States' adoptions of general incorporation acts prior to 1860**

	Mean	SD	Min.	Max
A. Summary statistics				
General incorporation act adopted prior to 1860	0.82	0.39	0	1
Log area (square miles)	10.259	1.053	7.343	11.48•
Log population, 1840	12.825	1.095	10.339	14.70:
Location: Atlantic seaboard	0.517	0.509	0	1
Statehood prior to 1800	0.552	0.506	0	1
Charters per 100 persons, 1840	0.06	0.05	0.01	0.19
Newspapers per 100 persons, 1840	0.01	0.00	0.00	0.02
Share of population employed in agriculture, 1840	23.09	6.10	11.91	37.20
Share of population employed in commerce, 1840	0.69	0.47	0.22	2.43
Share of population enslaved, 1840	15.80	19.75	0	55.02

	(1)	(2)	(3)
B. Regression analysis of whether a state adopted a general incorporation act prior to 1860			
Log area (square miles)	0.206**		0.186*
	(0.095)		(0.107)
Log population, 1840	0.008		0.0186
	(0.042)		(0.061)
Location: Atlantic seaboard	−0.379*		−0.484**
	(0.189)		(0.199)
Statehood prior to 1800	0.224		0.380**
	(0.190)		(0.169)
Charters granted per 100 persons, 1840		−6.178**	−3.878
		(2.265)	(2.410)
Newspapers per capita, 1840		39.610**	47.640*
		(17.790)	(22.590)
Share of population in agriculture, 1840		−0.041**	−0.050***
		(0.018)	(0.016)
Share of population in commerce, 1840		−0.158*	−0.218***
		(0.080)	(0.069)
Enslaved people per capita, 1840		0.002	0.006
		(0.007)	(0.006)
Constant	−1.130	1.670***	−0.339
	(1.180)	(0.303)	(0.875)
Observations	29	29	29
R-squared	0.435	0.494	0.706
Region FE	YES	YES	YES

Note: Robust standard errors in parentheses.

***Significant at the 1 percent level.

**Significant at the 5 percent level.

*Significant at the 10 percent level.

seaboard were indeed less likely to adopt general acts, even controlling for their age, size, and region.

The second column in the panel presents the results of regressions that include only variables measuring the states' social and economic structure. As expected, the number of charters per capita previously granted to business corporations in a state was negatively associated with the adoption of a general act, and the number of newspapers per 100 persons was positively associated with adoption of an act. Also as expected, the fraction of the population engaged in agriculture was negatively associated with the adoption of a general act, as was the fraction of the population engaged in commerce—the only available measure of the importance of trade and distribution in a state's economy. The fact that these latter estimates are statistically significant, whereas the raw comparisons of means were not, is a reflection of the effect of controlling for states' prior grants of corporate charters. Only conditional on chartering behavior does economic structure matter. Finally, the regression in column (2) also includes the number of slaves as a percentage of the states' total population. The estimated effect is positive but small and insignificant, indicating that slavery and the adoption of general statutes were not strongly related.

Finally, in column (3) of the panel, the variables from the specifications of both columns (1) and (2) are included together, in order to determine whether the influence of the variables in column (1), which measured states' size, location and age, was due to their relationship to states' economic performance, or whether they exerted some independent influence. For the most part, the inclusion of both sets of variables does not radically alter the size and significance of the estimated effects; most of the parameters are of similar size and levels of significance. This suggests that these different categories of variables exerted at least partially independent influences on states' adoption of general acts. That is, even though small states were older and more likely to have a particular economic structure, the effect of state size on the propensity to adopt a general act is important even conditional on its economic structure. The major exception is states' previous grants of charters. Conditional on states' size and location, the effect of this variable on states' adoption of general acts is diminished significantly. Apparently the estimated effect in column (2) was mainly due to the fact that small states located along the Atlantic seaboard granted larger numbers of charters. Another estimate that changes in magnitude to an important extent is the indicator for the age of a state, which increases significantly.

These results clearly indicate that a state's economic structure influenced its probability of adopting general incorporation, but other forces related to geography, and perhaps politics, mattered as well. States with large commercial and agricultural sectors were less likely to make the transition, whereas those with large numbers of newspapers were more likely to make the transition. In addition, smaller states, states located along the Atlantic seaboard, and younger states were all less likely to adopt general incorporation. The effect of a state's size may have influenced the costs of acquiring a special charter, and, through the forces of jurisdictional competition, the willingness of a state to accommodate requests for special charters.

Among those small states that failed to adopt general incorporation, grants of special charters were quite generous. This suggests that in practical terms access to incorporation may not have been dramatically greater in states that adopted general incorporation relative to those that did not. Although general acts almost certainly did improve access to the corporate form, the states that failed to adopt those acts were a highly selected group that granted corporate charters quite liberally. Researchers seeking to analyze the effect of general acts or to use general acts as indications of liberal access to the corporate form must take care to account for the selected nature of the states adopting such laws.[29]

5.4   The Choice of Terms of General Incorporation Acts

As the discussion of the history of general incorporation statutes in section 5.2 made clear, there was substantial variation in the terms of the laws enacted by different states. Some were generally quite prescriptive, whereas others granted entrepreneurs greater freedom to configure their enterprises as they wished. Some imposed regulations intended to protect the rights of creditors or give the state a measure of control over the enterprise, whereas others included fewer such terms. And some states restricted access to their laws in various ways, sometimes to such an extent that their laws cannot truly be said to have facilitated open access to the corporate form. The transition to general incorporation was not a simple binary choice, but rather a complex array of choices made by legislators. In order to understand the impact and significance of these statutes, it is necessary to understand what was in them and how and why their terms varied across states.

Without much more detailed and specific knowledge of nineteenth-century enterprise management and legal practice, it is not possible to conclusively identify which of the terms of these laws were the most important or onerous to contemporary entrepreneurs. In addition, the language of the statutes was subject to judicial interpretations, which may have magnified or minimized their practical importance.[30] What follows is a descriptive char-

---

29. In particular, any simple cross-sectional comparison will likely understate the effects of a general act, since the states that failed to adopt general incorporation—and therefore constitute the comparison or "control" group of any study—offered liberal access to the corporate form, whereas those that adopted general acts in some cases were much more restrictive in their corporate chartering.

30. An important example is the issue of stockholder liability. New York's 1811 act stated that "the persons . . . composing such company shall be individually responsible to the extent of their respective shares of stock in the said company, and no further." This slightly ambiguous language was interpreted in different ways by contemporaries, but New York's courts eventually held that the shareholders faced double liability (Howard 1938).

acterization of the text of the states' general incorporation acts, as amended in 1860. Simple tabulations of important terms are used to document the variation in the substance of general acts across states, as well as to analyze the determinants of the states' choices of the terms of their laws.

Most states' general acts included at least some restrictions on the governance institutions of firms. These were likely intended to ensure that the interests of investors were adequately represented in the management of the corporations, but they may have had the effect of constraining the corporations in other ways as well.[31] Table 5.4, panel A, presents summary statistics for a series of simple indicator variables summarizing common restrictions imposed on firms' internal governance in general acts. In 67 percent of these laws, the corporations were specifically required to have a president, and 59 percent of the time, the statutes specified a particular configuration of voting rights for shareholders. Also 59 percent of the time, the size of the board of directors was restricted, either with a minimum number of members, a maximum, or both. The table panel also includes summary statistics for these variables by region; with each, there is relatively little variation across regions, except in the South, whose statutes look quite different from those of the rest of the country. In particular, the general acts of Southern states were far less likely to impose these restrictions, and for two of the three variables the difference is highly significant.

Most general acts also included provisions intended to protect the creditors of corporations, and table 5.4, panel B, presents summary data for several important examples of these. Limits on leverage—usually expressed as a rule that the total debts of a corporation could not exceed its capital, or some multiple of its capital—were imposed 48 percent of the time. Annual reports, whose content varied substantially across states but typically stated the firms' paid-in capital and total debts, were required 55 percent of the time.[32] Around a third of the statutes prohibited loans to stockholders, which could be used by unscrupulous insiders to withdraw their investment in the firm and weaken its capitalization. And 20 percent of the statutes required shareholders' contributions to the firms' capital to be in cash. Only two of the twenty-seven states imposed some form of unlimited liability on stockholders in 1860—California and Minnesota.[33] Thirty-seven percent of

---

31. For example, a substantial literature has developed that analyzes the purpose and effects of rules dictating particular configurations of stockholder voting rights within early corporations. On their political significance, see Dunlavy (2004); see Hansmann and Pargendler (2010) on their effects on consumers. Hilt (2013) presents a synthesis.

32. Often these reports were required to be published in a local newspaper or submitted to the state government. Many states also required that the board of directors "make a report" to the stockholders at the corporations' annual meetings.

33. Two states, Wisconsin and Ohio, imposed unlimited liability in earlier statutes, but then amended them prior to 1860. In addition, thirteen states imposed unlimited liability on shareholders for debts to employees, and most states stripped directors of their limited liability in cases of fraud or violation of other prohibitions such as those against loans to stockholders or debts in excess of their capital.

Table 5.4   Variation in the terms of states' general acts, 1860

A. Regulations of internal governance

	Must have president	Specific stockholder voting rights system imposed	Board size restricted
New England	1.00	0.67	1.00
Mid-Atlantic	1.00	0.75	1.00
Midwest or West	0.82	0.64	0.73
South	0.22	0.44	0.11
All	0.67	0.59	0.59
p-value, South versus other	0.0001	0.22	0.0001

B. Creditor protections

	Limit on leverage	Annual report required	Loans to stockholders prohibited	Unlimited liability	Capital contributions required to be in cash	Minimum capital
New England	0.67	0.67	0.33	0.00	0.00	0.67
Mid-Atlantic	0.75	0.75	0.75	0.00	0.25	0.50
Midwest or West	0.45	0.73	0.27	0.18	0.18	0.36
South	0.33	0.22	0.22	0.00	0.22	0.22
All	0.48	0.55	0.33	0.07	0.19	0.37
p-value, South versus other	0.29	0.012	0.40	0.31	0.73	0.27

C. State control of enterprise

	Duration of incorporation limited	Maximum capital	Exact industries specified	Director residency requirement	Incorporation terminated after two years nonuse
New England	0.00	0.67	0.00	0.33	0.00
Mid-Atlantic	1.00	0.00	0.25	1.00	0.50
Midwest or West	0.91	0.27	0.00	0.64	0.36
South	0.67	0.67	0.22	0.11	0.33
All	0.24	0.41	0.11	0.48	0.33
p-value, South versus other	0.55	0.055	0.21	0.005	1.00

Table 5.5   **Terms of states' general acts, 1860**

	Governance restrictions (1)	Creditor protections (2)	State control (3)	Exclusions (4)	Total restrictions (5)
	A. Summary measures				
New England	2.67	2.33	1.00	0.00	6.00
Mid-Atlantic	2.75	3.00	2.75	0.25	8.75
Midwest or West	2.18	2.18	2.18	0.00	6.54
South	0.78	1.22	2.00	0.56	4.55
All: Mean	1.85	2.00	2.07	0.22	6.14
Standard deviation	(1.17)	(1.33)	(0.95)	(0.42)	(2.58)
p-value, South versus other	0.002	0.029	0.78	0.002	0.020
	B. Correlations				
Governance restrictions	1.000				
Creditor protections	0.545	1.000			
State control measures	0.423	0.271	1.000		
Exclusions	–0.476	–0.205	–0.232	1.000	

the statutes imposed some minimum capitalization on firms. There is some regional variation in the frequency with which these rules were imposed, and in general, Southern states were somewhat less likely to impose them. But the differences between the South and the North are not nearly as strong as with the governance provisions.

A third category of provisions of general acts circumscribed the powers of corporations in various ways, and are perhaps best characterized as measures intended to ensure some degree of control by the state over the corporation. These are presented in table 5.4, panel C. For example, 24 percent of the laws limited the duration of the incorporation. The average value of this limit was 39.5 years. In 41 percent of the laws, a maximum capitalization was imposed, which in most cases ensured that firms wishing to reach a very large scale had to seek a charter from the state. Only 11 percent of the statutes specifically listed the industries that could be pursued by firms incorporated under the act, and 48 percent of the statutes required some fraction of the corporations' directors to be residents of the state. Finally, a third of the laws included a condition that if the firm failed to commence operations within two years, its status as a corporation would be terminated. Among these state control provisions, there is far less of a discernible regional pattern. Southern states were less likely to impose some of these provisions, but with most there is no meaningful difference.

Table 5.5, panels A and B, present statistics for aggregations of these variables. That is, each summary variable is defined as the sum of the components within its corresponding panel of table 5.4, but it includes two additional summary variables as well. The first is termed "exclusions." Two of the states, Georgia and Maryland, specifically restricted access to their statutes to free white persons. These exclusions may have been motivated by a desire to preserve the social and economic order, and ensure that nonwhites were not able to form business corporations that could potentially elevate their economic and social status. However, they may also have been motivated by a desire to prevent nonwhites from creating organizations that would enable them to associate and that enjoyed legal protections from state interference.[34] Another four states imposed a rule that the certificates of entrepreneurs wishing to incorporate their firms were not automatically recorded, but were instead scrutinized by some public official. Although these measures could in principle be used to simply ensure compliance with the terms of the statute, they also gave the state the authority to exclude groups, such as nonwhites, from access to the corporate form. As table 5.5, panel A, makes clear, the South was quite different from the rest of the country in the degree to which it included these exclusionary terms in its laws.

In addition, column (5) of table 5.5, panel A, includes summary data for a variable called total restrictions in act, which is defined as the sum of the entries in columns (1) through (4). This is an ad hoc measure of the overall degree of restrictiveness of a state's corporation law. It should not be interpreted as a true measure of the restrictiveness of a state's law, since it imposes equal weights on all of the provisions, whereas some were undoubtedly much more important than others. Even though the Southern states were more likely to impose exclusions in their laws, their overall level of total restrictions was lower than that of any other region, and the difference is statistically significant. Southern states' laws generally offered incorporators more freedom in the design and operation of their enterprises.

Table 5.6 displays the value of this measure for each of the twenty-seven states with general acts in 1860, organized by region. Although the small numbers of individual states make comparisons difficult, the New England and mid-Atlantic states are much more uniform in the degree of stringency of their laws, as indicated by the total number of restrictions in their acts. In contrast, there is considerable variation within the states grouped as the "Midwest and West," with Kentucky, Michigan, and Illinois's laws being quite different from those of Iowa, Kansas, and Ohio. In the South, with the exception of the outlier Tennessee, the statutes were quite unrestrictive.

Some of the different categories of restrictions may have served as substitutes for one another. One might imagine, for example, that a statute that imposed a strong degree of creditor protections might have been perceived as needing fewer measures to ensure that the state had adequate control over the enterprise. But table 5.5, panel B, presents the simple correlations among these provisions, and shows that they are almost always positive. That is, states with a higher level of governance restrictions tended to also have a

---

34. Southern states, in fact, restricted blacks from associating in numbers in the absence of white observers. See the discussion in Brooks and Guinnane (2014).

Table 5.6   **Index of restrictiveness of states' general acts, 1860**

State	Total restrictions in general act
New England	
Connecticut	6
Massachusetts	6
Vermont	6
Mid-Atlantic	
Maryland	9
New Jersey	8
New York	8
Pennsylvania	10
South	
Alabama	4
Arkansas	4
Florida	4
Georgia	5
Louisiana	3
Mississippi	4
North Carolina	2
Tennessee	10
Virginia	5
West	
California	8
Illinois	10
Indiana	6
Iowa	2
Kansas	3
Kentucky	8
Michigan	8
Minnesota	6
Missouri	10
Ohio	3
Wisconsin	8

higher degree of creditor protections and also a greater number of state control measures. This could be a sign that some state governments took a consistently more restrictive stance toward corporations than others. However, it could also be a sign that with experience, some states produced more detailed corporation statutes that covered a broader range of contingencies and included more detailed regulations. The one exception to this pattern of positive correlations is with the exclusions, which are negatively correlated with all of the other measures. Perhaps the Southern states were willing to grant broad freedoms to entrepreneurs, so long as they could ensure that those entrepreneurs did not include free blacks or other elements of their society who could potentially threaten the stability of their social order if they were empowered to create corporations.

Table 5.7   **Determinants of states' general act terms**

	Governance restrictions		Creditor protections	
	(1)	(2)	(3)	(4)
Charters per 100 persons	9.266*	3.495	7.622	3.497
	(5.126)	(5.866)	(5.888)	(6.431)
Years since first general act	0.0466**	0.0175	0.0252	0.00448
	(0.0171)	(0.0117)	(0.0229)	(0.0197)
South		−1.472***		−1.052
		(0.499)		(0.679)
Constant	0.749	1.977***	1.235**	2.113**
	(0.514)	(0.661)	(0.572)	(0.799)
Observations	24	24	24	24
R-squared	0.229	0.506	0.082	0.192
	State control measures		Exclusions	
	(1)	(2)	(3)	(4)
Charters per 100 persons	−6.800**	−8.490**	−2.080	−0.318
	(3.110)	(3.287)	(1.425)	(1.420)
Years since first general act	0.0177	0.00917	−0.0133*	−0.00442
	(0.0130)	(0.0154)	(0.00693)	(0.00520)
South		−0.431		0.449**
		(0.460)		(0.209)
Constant	2.293***	2.652***	0.530**	0.155
	(0.391)	(0.487)	(0.198)	(0.160)
Observations	24	24	24	24
R-squared	0.116	0.153	0.115	0.306

Note: Robust standard errors in parentheses.
***Significant at the 1 percent level.
**Significant at the 5 percent level.
*Significant at the 10 percent level.

On the other hand, the distinctive pattern of less restrictive corporation laws among the Southern states could simply reflect the fact that those states had far less experience with the corporate form since they had chartered relatively small amounts of corporations prior to 1840 (see table 5.2). They also adopted general acts at later times than states in other regions (see figure 5.2), so in addition to having less experience with administering and refining their law, they may have been influenced by any trend toward more permissive statutes that could have been present in the late 1850s.

In order to disentangle these two potential explanations for the permissive nature of the Southern statutes, table 5.7 presents a series of simple regressions in which the relationships between the statutes' characteristics and the states' level of corporate charters in 1840 and years of experience with its general act are estimated. These regressions are then repeated with the inclusion of a regional fixed effect for the South. If the differences between the South and the North are simply due to the timing of the South's acts or their infrequent grants of charters prior to 1840, then the patterns within the South and within the North of states with similar levels of charters in 1840 and years of experience with general laws should be the same—the inclusion of the South fixed effect should not reduce the estimated effect of those variables. If, however, the South is different for other reasons, then the South fixed effect should dominate.

The results in table 5.7 indicate that with respect to governance provisions, the South was genuinely unique. The estimated relationship between the level of charters in 1840 and years of experience with a general act is completely transformed with the inclusion of the Southern fixed effect, which is estimated to be negative and large. With creditor protections the estimated relationships are similar, but the coefficients are smaller and less precisely estimated. Southern states were unique in this respect as well, but the difference was not so sharp.

On the other hand, the estimated relationship between 1840 charters and years of experience with the state control measures included in general acts is quite robust to the inclusion of the South fixed effect. Those regressions clearly indicate that the states that had previously granted large numbers of charters were considerably less likely to include as many state control measures in their laws, and that relationship holds within the North and South. The states that already had large numbers of corporations felt it less necessary to circumscribe the powers of new corporations' in their general acts.

Finally, with regard to the exclusions, unsurprisingly the South was quite unique. Relative to other states that adopted their general acts relatively late, Southern states were far more likely to impose such measures.

With regard to many of the terms of general acts, then, there were significant differences between Northern and Southern states, and these appear not to be driven simply by the different timing of Southern states' adoption of their laws, or the lack of experience with chartered corporations in the South. The general acts of Southern states were less restrictive than those of Northern states, perhaps because they were much more likely to exclude access to their terms to elements of society over which they wished to retain control.

5.5   Conclusion: General Incorporation Acts and the Transition to Open Access

Over the course of the nineteenth century, business corporations became increasingly important within the American economy, and ultimately transformed economic life. The states' general incorporation acts facilitated the creation of the majority of these corporations and regulated their governance, capital structure, and operations. This chapter has documented the earliest general acts for manufacturing corporations in the United States and the terms they contained. It also analyzed the political, economic, and social forces that influenced the decision to adopt or resist general acts. Several distinct insights follow from the analysis.

First, many states adopted general acts far earlier than has previously been documented. Following New York's 1811 act, the states of New Jersey, Ohio, and Illinois adopted similar acts, although all three of the latter statutes were eventually repealed. Other states, including Georgia and Missouri, first adopted general incorporation acts somewhat later, in the 1840s, but this was several decades earlier than previous scholarship has indicated. Ascertaining the extent to which any of these statutes were actually utilized, and the reasons for the repeal of many of the early acts, will require further research. But these laws may have opened access to the corporate form, at least in a formal legal sense, much earlier than previously believed.

On the other hand, a second insight that follows from the analysis of this chapter is that the transition to general incorporation did not always represent a discrete change in the degree to which entrepreneurs enjoyed access to the corporate form. Rather than moving from limited access to truly open access, early general acts often represented more of an intermediate step. Many imposed restrictive terms such as limits on capitalization, or limits on the industries that could be pursued, which forced entrepreneurs to continue to seek special charters for enterprises that did not conform to those terms. Effectively, these states offered open access only to a somewhat limited set of enterprises, and retained discretion over access to the corporate form for all others. More significantly, some Southern and border states specifically excluded nonwhites from access to their statutes, or gave a state official broad authority to deny access to their statute. These were not yet truly impersonal rules in the sense of Wallis (2011).

Moreover, many states that did not adopt general acts offered liberal access to incorporation. Relative to their populations, several of those states granted charters to extraordinary numbers of businesses. Although a general act would have lowered the cost of incorporating and broadened access to the form at least somewhat, it seems likely that at least in the first half of the nineteenth century, states could offer relatively open access to incorporation through chartering, if they wished. This implies that researchers seeking to analyze the effect of general acts or to use general acts as indications of liberal access to the corporate form must take care to account for the selected nature of the states adopting (or failing to adopt) such laws.

Another insight from the analysis of this chapter is that the terms of general acts varied substantially across states. Although most states' laws included passages borrowed from those of other states, and many terms were copied whole cloth from influential acts such as New York's 1848 statute, there was significant variation across different regions, with Southern states generally adopting statutes that were less restrictive in many respects than those of other regions. This difference was not simply due to the fact that Southern states had less experience with corporations—even compared to other states with similarly low numbers of existing corporations, Southern states' laws were less restrictive. One might speculate that this was due in part to the extremely restrictive terms governing access to the laws in Southern states. Given that they could ensure that only the "right" elements of the population could use the laws, they may have felt that detailed restrictions on the enterprises they created were unnecessary.

But in addition to this regional variation, some states adopted laws that were quite idiosyncratic. Especially within the West and Midwest, there was substantial variation across states in the structure and degree of restrictiveness of general acts. Iowa's 1847 law—the most permissive of all statutes examined for this study—imposed almost no restrictions on the businesses it incorporated. In contrast, the statutes of the nearby states of Wisconsin, Illinois, and Missouri were substantially more restrictive, with Wisconsin even briefly imposing a rule of one vote per shareholder and unlimited liability. Whereas New England seems to have had its own legal culture and fairly uniform corporation statutes, and the same was true to a somewhat lesser extent of the mid-Atlantic states, there was considerably more variation among the states of the Midwest.

Finally, this chapter has focused on the political significance of the transition to general incorporation. Yet these acts may also have had important economic impacts, and the variation across states in the timing and content of general statutes suggest some fascinating questions that could be pursued in future research. For example, by lowering the cost of gaining access to the corporate form, general acts may have facilitated the formation of smaller corporations that could not have existed in their absence. This would have increased the number of manufacturing enterprises, and may also have changed the size distribution of manufacturing firms. In addition, some states' general acts were quite prescriptive, and included terms that strictly regulated the governance institutions of the businesses they created. The effect of these terms on the rate at which the statutes were utilized is another important question, with relevance to modern policy debates about the wisdom of imposing regulations on the governance institutions of public companies.

References

Berle, Adolf, and Gardiner Means. 1933. *The Modern Corporation and Private Property*. New York: Macmillan.

Bodenhorn, Howard. 2008. "Free Banking and Bank Entry in Nineteenth-Century New York." *Financial History Review* 15 (2): 175–201.

Brooks, Richard, and Timothy Guinnane. 2014. "The Right to Associate and the Rights of Associations: Civil-Society Organizations in Prussia, 1794–1908." Working Paper, Columbia University and Yale University.

Butler, Henry N. 1985. "Nineteenth-Century Jurisdictional Competition in the Granting of Corporate Privileges." *Journal of Legal Studies* 14 (1): 129–66.

Demsetz, Harold. 1967. "Toward a Theory of Property Rights." *American Economic Review* 57:347–59.

Dubin, Michael J. 2007. *Party Affiliations in the State Legislatures: A Year by Year Summary, 1796–2006.* Jefferson, NC: McFarland & Co.

Dunlavy, Colleen A. 2004. "From Citizens to Plutocrats: Nineteenth-Century Shareholder Voting Rights and Theories of the Corporation." In *Constructing Corporate America: History, Politics, Culture,* edited by Kenneth Lipartito and David B. Sicilia. New York: Oxford University Press.

Engerman, Stanley L., and Kenneth L. Sokoloff. 2002. "Factor Endowments, Inequality, and Paths of Development among New World Economies." NBER Working Paper no. 9259, Cambridge, MA.

Grandy, Christopher. 1989. "New Jersey Corporate Chartermongering, 1875–1929." *Journal of Economic History* 49 (3): 677–92.

Guinnane, Timothy, Ron Harris, Naomi Lamoreaux, and Jean-Laurent Rosenthal. 2007. "Putting the Corporation in Its Place." *Enterprise & Society* 8 (3): 687–729.

Hamill, Susan Pace. 1999. "From Special Privilege to General Utility: A Continuation of Willard Hurst's Study of Corporations." *American University Law Review* 49:81–177.

Hansmann, Henry, and Mariana Pargendler. 2010. "Voting Restrictions in 19th Century Corporations: Investor Protection or Consumer Protection?" Working Paper, Yale Law School, Yale University.

Henderson, Gerard C. 1918. *The Position of Foreign Corporations in American Constitutional Law.* Cambridge, MA: Harvard University Press.

Hilt, Eric. 2008. "When Did Ownership Separate from Control? Corporate Governance in the Early Nineteenth Century." *Journal of Economic History* 68 (3): 645–85.

———. 2013. "Shareholder Voting Rights in Early American Corporations." *Business History* 55 (4): 620–35.

Horack, Frank E. 1904. "Some Phases of Corporate Regulation in the Territory." *Iowa Journal of History and Politics* II (3): 381–93.

Horwitz, Morton. 1977. *The Transformation of American Law, 1780–1860.* Cambridge, MA: Harvard University Press.

Howard, Stanley E. 1938. "Stockholders' Liability under the New York Act of March 22, 1811." *Journal of Political Economy* 46 (4): 499–514.

Hurst, James W. 1970. *The Legitimacy of the Business Corporation in the Law of the United States, 1780–1970.* Charlottesville: University of Virginia Press.

Irwin, Douglas A., and Joseph H. Davis. 2003. "Trade Disruptions and America's Early Industrialization." NBER Working Paper no. 9944, Cambridge, MA.

Kessler, William C. 1940. "A Statistical Study of the New York General Incorporation Act of 1811." *Journal of Political Economy* 48:877–82.

McCormick, Virginia E., and Robert W. McCormick. 1998. *New Englanders on the Ohio Frontier: Migration and Settlement of Worthington Ohio.* Kent, OH: Kent State University Press.

Millon, David. 1990. "Theories of the Corporation." *Duke Law Journal* 1990:201–62.

Mulligan, Casey, and Andrei Shleifer. 2005. "The Extent of the Market and the Supply of Regulation." *Quarterly Journal of Economics* 120 (4): 1445–73.

North, Douglass, John Wallis, and Barry Weingast. 2009. *Violence and Social Orders: A Conceptual Framework for Interpreting Recorded Human History.* New York: Cambridge University Press.

Romano, Roberta. 1985. "Law as a Product: Some Pieces of the Incorporation Puzzle." *Journal of Law, Economics and Organization* 1 (2): 225–83.

Seligman, Joel. 1976. "A Brief History of Delaware's General Incorporation Law of 1899." *Delaware Journal of Corporate Law* 1 (2): 249–87.

Sylla, Richard, and Robert E. Wright. 2013. "Corporation Formation in the Antebellum United States in Comparative Context." *Business History* 55 (4): 653–69.

Wallis, John. 2005. "Constitutions, Corporations and Corruption: American States and Constitutional Change, 1842–1852." *Journal of Economic History* 65 (1): 211–56.

———. 2006. "The Concept of Systematic Corruption in American History." In *Corruption and Reform: Lessons from America's Economic History,* edited by Edward Glaeser and Claudia Goldin. Chicago: University of Chicago Press.

———. 2011. "Institutions, Organizations, Impersonality, and Interests: The Dynamics of Institutions." *Journal of Economic Behavior and Organization* 79:48–64.

Organizational Poisedness and the Transformation of Civic Order in Nineteenth-Century New York City

Victoria Johnson and Walter W. Powell

6.1 Introduction

When and why do new kinds of organizations emerge, persist, and spread? Some settings are more hospitable to novelty or exogenous perturbations than are others. We think explaining this relative social "poisedness" is essential to understanding when and why new organizational forms appear and take root. By poisedness, we mean the availability or vulnerability of a social and historical context to the reception of an innovation and subsequent reconfiguration by it (Padgett and Powell 2012, 26–28).[1] Poisedness thus refers to circumstances that

Victoria Johnson is associate professor of urban policy and planning at Hunter College in New York City. Walter W. Powell is professor of education (and) sociology, business, and engineering, and co-director of the Center on Philanthropy and Civil Society at Stanford University.

We are very grateful to Rebecca Sunde for exceptional research assistance. We have benefited from comments from the participants in seminars at the University of Mannheim, the Wirtschaftsuniversität Wien, the University of Cambridge, NYU, Cornell, Uppsala University, the National Bureau of Economic Research's Economic History Workshop, and the Economic Sociology and Networks and Organizations workshops at Stanford, as well as from Howard Aldrich, Tim Bartley, Julie Battilana, Christof Brandtner, Patricia Bromley, Joon Nak Choi, Nitsan Chorev, Jeannette Colyvas, Avinash Dixit, Mark Granovetter, Mauro Guillén, Ira Katznelson, Naomi Lamoreaux, Margaret Levi, Jonathan Levy, Mark Mizruchi, Chandra Mukerji, Wanda Orlikowski, Jason Owen-Smith, Charles Perrow, and John Wallis. For acknowledgments, sources of research support, and disclosure of the authors' material financial relationships, if any, please see http://www.nber.org/chapters/c13505.ack.

1. Our use of the term "poisedness" has provoked mixed reactions among readers, with several recoiling from it as unfamiliar jargon and others appreciating its dynamism. Several colleagues have suggested more familiar terms, such as "receptivity" or "amenable to." But we find these lacking. Poisedness conveys potential readiness for action, be it availability or vulnerability. The concept is a familiar one in mathematics and optimization research, where it refers to the geometry of an underlying interpolation set, and whether such estimates are easy or difficult constraints (Conn, Scheinberg, and Vicente 2005). It has also been used in philosophy in reference to changes in states of consciousness (Tye 2000). In contemporary evolutionary biology (Wagner 2005), a kindred term is evolvability, describing an environmental setting that is ripe for transformation.

are rich with potential, in which relations and trends at one level are available to be coupled with innovations at a different one. When such coupling occurs, the second level becomes a self-sustaining pool for these innovations. In turn, the fates of the two become intertwined and have cascading effects. The changes that ensue alter the nature of what is accessible, introducing new possibilities. The resulting interrelated pathways through social and economic structures afford the opportunity for novelty through unanticipated feedbacks across multiple contexts.

How do we analyze the architecture of social structures to understand which ones are more fertile for new forms of organization? Because "organizational genesis does not mean virgin birth" (Padgett and Powell 2012, 2), studying social poisedness requires situating innovators and their organizational projects with regard to the structural features of the social world into which they are introduced. Our approach emphasizes that historical development is an evolving, multilevel process in which new interests and new persons are catalyzed, and the criteria for accomplishment emerge out of this open-ended process.

The emergence of novelty, especially of new categories of people and organizations, is undertheorized in the social sciences. To be sure, there are hints at answers to these puzzles in a variety of subfields. Exogenous shocks are a familiar explanation: social upheavals, technological disruptions, and regulatory change can disturb the status quo and signal opportunities for new practices and new organizations. In such circumstances we often find differential selection, as new entrants replace established ones (Hannan and Freeman 1977; Arthur 1994). But selection by itself is limiting, not generative. A similar line of explanation unfolding at a different level of analysis argues that people on the periphery of a field, and thus less beholden to its practices, are more likely to initiate change (Leblebici et al. 1991). Other explanations stress complexity, conflict, and plurality, suggesting that those in contradictory positions are most able to initiate change (Thelen 2004). And another productive line of work calls attention to "critical junctures," or periods of contingency when the usual constraints on action are lifted or eased (Katznelson 2003).

Thus, whether the focus is on exogenous shocks, periphery-core dynamics, contradictory locations, or critical junctures, most explanations do not take into account the interlocking of individual human lives with large-scale social, cultural, political, and material changes. Historical sociologists have argued that time is lumpy, unpredictable, and discontinuous (Abbott 2001). Such a view alerts us, as Sewell (2005, 10) notes, "that the consequences of a given act are not intrinsic in the act but rather will depend on the nature of the social world within which it takes place." Temporal heterogeneity renders some actions incomprehensible or illegitimate at certain historical moments, yet easily comprehensible and legitimate at others.

In recent years, historically minded social scientists have demonstrated that comparative and longitudinal approaches throw into relief the shared, as well as distinct, characteristics of the social structures under investigation, thereby aiding in more accurate causal explanations and in the specification of scope conditions (Mahoney and Thelen 2010). We believe these methods offer powerful tools for explaining why some social contexts appear poised to support the emergence of particular organizational forms and others do not. To this end, we compare two moments from nineteenth-century urban history that might at first glance seem small and local, but are in fact deeply connected to important processes, events, and figures of their day. We chose our cases, each of which concerns an effort to introduce a research-focused botanical garden in New York City, for their similar beginnings and divergent outcomes. We use these rich examples, set against the backdrop of New York's transformation from a port town of 60,000 into a world city of nearly two million, to build arguments about how the success with which skillful individuals shepherd new organizational forms into their social worlds, and subsequently transform them, is powerfully shaped by the structural potentials present in those milieux.

We demonstrate the availability of a specific time and place (New York City near the end of the nineteenth century) to a novel organizational form (a research-intensive botanical garden) proposed by an engaged, entrepreneurial man of science, whose very presence was rendered possible by developments in the profession of American science. Our claim is that organizational models have resonance depending on their ability to couple with identifiable material, intellectual, and political-economic circumstances and connect with changes in the larger organizational landscape. Social poisedness, we argue, affords opportunities for new organizational forms to arise.

Our choice of cases emerged out of a broader inquiry into the history and organization of botany and botanical gardens in the United States. One of the most important botanical gardens in the world today, the New York Botanical Garden (NYBG), was founded in the Gilded Age through a collaboration of leading American industrialists with politicians and academic botanists. However, this institution was preceded by a similar garden founded ninety years earlier, when much of Manhattan was covered with farms and country estates. As we studied these cases side by side, we found striking parallels in the two founders' efforts and visions, coupled with a stark divergence in the respective outcomes.[2]

2. Primary research on these two organizational cases was conducted over two years, partly in the context of research for a book by Victoria Johnson on David Hosack and the Elgin Botanic Garden (Johnson, forthcoming). We consulted materials in the following archives: the American Philosophical Society; Columbia University (Manuscripts and Rare Books Division; the Special Collections of the College of Physicians & Surgeons); the Historical Society of Pennsylvania; the Library of Congress; the Mertz Library of the New York Botanical Garden; the New York Academy of Medicine; the New-York Historical Society; the New York Public Library (Lionel Pincus and Princess Firyal Map Division; Irma and Paul Milstein Division of United States History, Local History and Genealogy); and the Office of the Borough President, Manhattan. The main digitized collections we consulted were America's Historical Imprints and America's Historical Newspapers.

Our founders, David Hosack (1769–1835) and Nathaniel Britton (1859–1934), each recognized an opportunity to transform American botany. Separated by nearly a century, their projects show remarkable similarities that make them a rich pairing through which to explore the emergence of a new organizational form. Hosack was a Columbia professor of botany recently returned from Great Britain when he began, in the 1790s, to dream of establishing a botanical garden on Manhattan Island that would advance American botany, medicine, and agriculture. Winning the support of such eminent figures as Hamilton and Jefferson, he spent the next decade establishing the nation's most extensive botanical garden. Using private funds, he amassed more than 2,000 plant specimens and began to teach botany and medicine. Hosack's garden collapsed fifteen years later because he could not muster state or private funding, and the model he introduced—a research- and teaching-based botanical garden, spawned no imitators. Today, his garden is buried under Rockefeller Center.

In the late 1880s, Nathaniel Britton, also a Columbia professor of botany who had recently returned from travels to England, began to imagine creating a botanical garden that would advance American botany, medicine, and agriculture. Supported by contemporary colossi such as Carnegie and Rockefeller, he spent the next decade establishing a garden in New York City on a physical and scientific scale unrivaled in the United States. Today, the NYBG still thrives on 250 acres in the Bronx. What is more, soon after its creation in the 1890s, it spawned imitators in cities across the country. Thus Britton found enormous success in introducing the kind of research- and teaching-based, public/private botanical garden that Hosack strove in vain to root in New York soil. Why did one man's efforts lead to the introduction and diffusion of a new organizational form where the other failed?

The origins of botanical gardens lie in the medicinal gardens attached to European monasteries. During the Renaissance, the study of plants and their properties gradually shifted from monasteries to universities, and botanical gardens were established in the sixteenth and seventeenth centuries in towns such as Pisa, Padua, Leiden, and Oxford. An early focus of university-affiliated gardens was the training of medical students in plant-based pharmacology, as well as the discovery and classification of new plants (Drayton 2000). In the age of European colonial expansion, botanical gardens became increasingly important to national governments interested in the discovery, collection, and diffusion of medically and commercially useful plants, such as Peruvian bark (containing quinine), cacao, coffee, and nutmeg.

Although botanical gardens share certain features with ornamental gardens and public parks, they differ from these cultivated spaces in their central commitment to the scientific use, study, and organization of plants.[3] The

---

3. As an example, consider the case of three Paris institutions: the Jardin des Plantes, the gardens of Versailles, and the Bois de Boulogne. The Jardin des Plantes, originally known as

European botanical gardens familiar to Hosack and Britton were first and foremost sites of collection, classification, experimentation, and instruction. Each man incorporated these aspects of specific British botanical gardens as they founded their own gardens in nineteenth-century New York City. Cognizant, however, of the differences between imperial Britain and the United States, each carefully fashioned a new organizational form suited to the time and place in which he was working.

A meaningful definition of novelty emphasizes the unfamiliarity of a new form to the relevant audiences in the historically specific social context into which it is being introduced. Determining which audiences are relevant and where the boundaries of that social context fall depends on detailed empirical inquiry. As we show, these are not cases of mere diffusion. Both Hosack and Britton built organizations unlike any seen in New York City or, for that matter, in the United States of their day. Thus, although botanical gardens of varying types and missions had long since taken root in Europe, each of our founders sought to introduce what was a new organizational form in his social setting, with widely varying outcomes. These two comparable efforts in the same city at moments marked by different social, economic, and political structures afford an analytic window into the relationship between organizational forms and the social contexts in which they are born.

We begin with a discussion of our two founders and their efforts to introduce a novel organizational form. Attention to the similarities between their projects and biographies throws into relief the differences between their respective historical times. We note that while we find useful analytic purchase in the comparative case method, we diverge from traditional Mill-inspired case comparisons in our central concern to map and take account of the shifting causal relationships between the temporally distant contexts in which our two cases unfold. Instead of comparing the two cases for variables that are absent or present, our examination underscores how, in each case, relations at one level reinforce or hinder relations at another, rendering efforts at agency either viable and widely consequential or local with limited impact. Building on our empirical analysis, we turn to a theoretical elaboration of the concept of poisedness. The conclusion follows with methodological considerations for researchers interested in analyzing the poisedness of other times and places for other kinds of organizational forms.

Sociology is replete with attempts to theorize relations across levels, from

---

the Jardin du Roi, is a botanical garden that was founded in 1626 by Louis XIII for scientific inquiry into the medicinal uses of plants. The gardens at the Palace of Versailles, constructed for Louis XIV over several decades beginning in the 1660s, were primarily dedicated to the aesthetic display of plants; and the Bois de Boulogne, opened to the public in the 1850s, was primarily intended as an outdoor recreational space. Although the Jardin du Roi contained some "display" gardens and the gardens of Versailles contained some "applied" gardens (such as the *jardin potager* or kitchen garden), the core functions of these gardens differed from each other as well as from the later Bois de Boulogne. On the complex relations among French botany, horticulture, and political power, see Mukerji (1997).

individual interactions to groups, communities, and fields, and on to large political and social structures. In general, the conceptual language emphasizes aggregation across levels. Such views are a bit too tidy for our purposes. We consider cross-level concatenations in terms of new potentials that did not previously exist but that, once exploited, transform the landscape of what is available. Instead of alignment, in which there is always opportunity for behavior consistent with the past, we show the emergence of the possibility of building something that was not previously in view. To this end, we show that microlevel interactions can generate consequences that are independent of their local origins. Nathaniel Britton labored tirelessly to create the New York Botanical Garden; little did he know how much his efforts would shape other American cities or alter the kinds of roles that successful faculty members could play in public life. These reverberations into urban landscapes and policy circles reflect the amplifying effects of social changes, and reinforce an older point by Stinchcombe (1968) that the forces that create a new entity and those that sustain it are fundamentally different.

In his 1965 work on "Social Structure and Organizations," Stinchcombe reflected on the emergence, persistence, and diffusion of new organizational forms. New forms, he observed, are subject to social liabilities not faced by existing organizations, such as a lack of legitimacy and the unfamiliarity of new organizational roles. Building on Weber's sociology of organizations as well as midcentury interest in political revolutions and the organization of industrial societies, Stinchcombe hypothesized that new forms are most likely to emerge when a prospective founder discovers or invents a new, better way of organizing to accomplish a social or commercial goal. Settings rich in contacts between distinct social groups, he argued, are the most hospitable to the emergence of new forms, which persist and diffuse when founders effectively mobilize material and cultural resources and the form is institutionalized. Our ultimate aim is to explicate when larger structural forces are amenable to, and supportive of, individual-level efforts at innovation. To do so, we need to specify how tools for and models of organizing are made available as a consequence of changes in the material, social, and economic environments. Once such scaffolding is available, it alters the options available to entrepreneurially minded people. We take up this challenge by situating individual efforts at organizational innovation in historically specific configurations of material, social, and economic processes. First, however, we turn to a comparative examination of our founders and their efforts.

6.2   "An Almost Untrodden Field": Projects and Entrepreneurs

In September 1794, David Hosack, a young New Yorker recently returned from medical studies in Great Britain, wrote to his mentor about the urgent need he saw for scientific progress and instruction in botany in the new republic. In Edinburgh and London, Hosack had found the medical establishment deeply engaged in studying plants to prevent and treat illness. Upon arrival in New York he wrote to his former professor Benjamin Rush, a signer of the Declaration of Independence and the most famous doctor in the United States, to describe the access he had been given to British botanical gardens by eminent scientists and doctors. He also exulted in the opportunities for advancing American botany: "I have also, as I may call it, an almost untrodden field in this country for those pursuits."[4]

Organization scholars have developed numerous insightful accounts of how people find traction with novel projects. Although these accounts vary in their particulars, there is some consensus on the elements that are common to successful institutional projects. At the individual level, scholars have emphasized that the opportunity recognition that leads to an innovator's new *project* is facilitated by her or his *biographical trajectory* (McAdam 1989; Burton, Sørensen, and Beckman 2002). Biographical trajectories foster the *social skill* needed to persuade others (Fligstein 1997). They are also important in generating access to sponsors and representatives who connect these people to diverse contacts, resources, and sources of knowledge (Greve and Rao 2012). Culturally available organizational *templates* represent collective resources on which they may draw to articulate a new arrangement and acquire needed legitimacy and resources (Ruef 2000; Haveman and Rao 2006). We synthesize these common elements to offer an initial comparison of the two gardens under investigation here. In what follows, we situate the projects of David Hosack and his Gilded Age counterpart, Nathaniel Britton, with respect to these four elements—project, biography, template, and social skill—critical to organizational foundings. (For portraits of Hosack and Britton, see figures 6.1 and 6.2.)

Hosack's Project. In November 1797, Hosack, by this point a Columbia medical professor, addressed an appeal to the trustees of the College asking for an annual stipend to help establish a botanical garden. Although both European and American doctors believed an understanding of botany to be of critical importance in formulating and prescribing medicines, Hosack found himself teaching New York City's medical students without the aid of a botanical garden. Such a garden would permit Hosack to instruct his students not merely from books, but from plant specimens. The primary goal of medical instruction from specimens, both living and dried, was to help students understand how to identify, cultivate, and use known therapeutic plants for the prevention and treatment of illness. Students who developed facility in these areas might also one day identify new plant species and plant-based medicines.

In a young nation whose growing cities were regularly ravaged by yellow fever, scarlatina, and typhus epidemics, the development of new medicines and of doctors knowledgeable about their applications was critical. Indeed,

---

4. David Hosack to Benjamin Rush, Sept. 8, 1794, Historical Society of Pennsylvania.

Fig. 6.1   David Hosack

Source: Charles Heath. *David Hosack, M.D., F.R.S.*, n.d. Engraving after painting by Thomas Sully. US National Library of Medicine, Images from the History of Medicine. http://resource.nlm.nih.gov/101433834.

just two months before Hosack applied to the Columbia College trustees for funds, he had used a botanical remedy to save the life of Alexander Hamilton's son Philip, who was deathly ill with typhus (Chernow 2004, 544–45). Columbia agreed, and a committee convened by the trustees recommended that Hosack be allocated 300 pounds annually for the project: "The establishment of a botanical garden appears to be essentially necessary for the purposes of medical instruction" (quoted in D. Hosack 1811, 8). In 1800, Hosack submitted a memo to the state legislature appealing for additional funds; the state's committee was as supportive of the project as Columbia had been, reporting that "in their opinion the prayer of the memorialist ought to be granted" (ibid., 9–10).

Buoyed by this support, Hosack purchased twenty acres of land three-and-a-half miles north of New York City. Surrounded by farms and reached by a country lane, the hilly site afforded a view of both the East and Hudson Rivers. Hosack named his new establishment after his father's birthplace in Scotland, calling it the Elgin Botanic Garden. By 1806, he reported that the botanical garden boasted a conservatory nearly 200 feet long and that the "grounds are also arranged and planted agreeably to the most approved stile [*sic*] of ornamental gardening" with more than 1,500 American and foreign plants (D. Hosack 1806). He was soon offering regular courses to

Fig. 6.2   Nathaniel Britton
Source: The LuEsther T. Mertz Library of the New York Botanical Garden. http://sciweb
.nybg.org/science2/libr/finding_guide/britwb2.asp.html.

medical students there in the spring and summer and bringing specimens to
his winter classes at Columbia. In addition, Hosack was also growing and
collecting native and "exotic" ornamental plants and experimenting with
grains, cotton, and other commercial crops.

The Elgin Botanic Garden drew the praise of many prominent contemporaries for its contributions to the scientific life of the city, the state, and
the young nation. In 1806, Governor Morgan Lewis opened the legislative
term with a speech to the joint session of the New York State Assembly and
Senate that singled out Hosack's establishment (D. Hosack 1811, 12):

> I, in the course of last summer, paid it two visits, and am so satisfied with
> the plan and arrangement, that I cannot but believe, if not permitted to
> languish, it will be productive of great general utility.

In the same year, President Thomas Jefferson wrote to Hosack to say that
"should he have it in his power to be useful to his institution at any time
he shall embrace the occasion with that pleasure which attends every aid
given to the promotion of science."[5] The Elgin Botanic Garden achieved

---

5. Thomas Jefferson to David Hosack, Sept. 18, 1806, Thomas Jefferson Papers, Series 1:
General Correspondence, Library of Congress.

renown in foreign capitals, as well. Eminent botanists in London and Paris—including Napoleon's own chief botanist—exchanged plant specimens with Hosack throughout the early decades of the nineteenth century (A. Hosack 1861, 326). Before Hosack left London in 1794, he had been elected a fellow of the Linnean Society, repository of the most famous botanical collection in the world; after the founding of Elgin, he was also elected to the American Philosophical Society and the Royal Society of London.

Britton's Project. Ninety years later, in 1891, Professor Nathaniel Britton founded a 250-acre botanical garden in New York City that was second in size and organizational complexity only to the Royal Botanic Gardens at Kew, England. Two years earlier, in 1889, Britton and his wife had visited Kew on their honeymoon; when they returned, they spoke to their fellow members at the Torrey Botanical Club, a Columbia-based association, about the possibility of founding such an ambitious garden in New York. That year, under Britton's leadership, the club published a statement arguing that "a botanic garden of the highest class, established in New York City or its immediate neighborhood, would be placed at the best imaginable point to win a lasting reputation for itself and its founder, both in this country and abroad" (Torrey Botanical Club 1889, 4).

Armed with this proposal, Britton set about enlisting the support of New York's political and social elites. In 1891, he saw his efforts come to fruition. That April, Governor Roswell Flower signed an "Act . . . to Incorporate the New York Botanical Garden" that set aside a large parcel of city-owned land to be given to the garden if, by 1898, its founder had raised $250,000 in private funds. Britton did so by 1895, with the help of Columbia University and individual donors including Carnegie and Rockefeller. With these considerable resources secured, Britton oversaw the construction of the facilities needed to establish a botanical garden on a grand scale. In 1901, work was completed on a massive Italianate building that housed the herbarium, the library, laboratories, classrooms, and exhibits on systematic and economic botany. In 1902, Britton announced the opening of the biggest conservatory in the United States, enclosing 45,000 square feet under glass. Over the next decades of Britton's tenure as director in chief, he supervised the cultivation of the grounds and expansion of the living and preserved specimen collections. When he retired in 1929, the NYBG held more than 1.5 million specimens (Mickulas 2007).

From their respective vantage points at either end of the nineteenth century, Hosack and Britton each recognized an opportunity and worked doggedly to realize their visions. Clearly, opportunity recognition is a necessary, if not sufficient, element in such innovation. Why, then, were these men able to recognize these particular opportunities? The course of personal lives is bound to historical times, as differences in birth year expose people to quite distinct social worlds.

Hosack's Biography. Hosack was born in 1769 in Manhattan. After a childhood spent largely under the British occupation (1776–1783), he enrolled in 1786 at Columbia, then located at Park Place in lower Manhattan. There Hosack began a lifelong friendship with DeWitt Clinton, who would become a US senator, New York City mayor, and governor of New York. In 1788, Hosack transferred to the College of New Jersey at Princeton, graduating in 1789 (Robbins 1964, 20). His growing interest in medicine took him next to the University of Pennsylvania, where he enrolled in autumn 1790.

On completion of his medical studies in Philadelphia, Hosack moved with his new wife to Alexandria, Virginia, to begin practicing medicine near the future US capital. Within a year, however, he decided to further his studies in Edinburgh and London, where he learned firsthand of the importance of botany and botanical gardens to European medical education and practice. He resolved "whenever an opportunity might offer, to acquire a knowledge of that department of science" (A. Hosack 1861, 297). In late eighteenth-century London, a hotbed of botanical research, he found his opportunity. There, in the summer of 1793, Hosack studied daily at the Brompton Botanic Garden, and in 1794 he attended lectures given by the most eminent English botanist of the era, James Edward Smith, who invited him to study in the collections of the renowned Linnaean Herbarium.

On his return to New York, Hosack joined the medical practice of Samuel Bard, whose patients included Washington, Hamilton, and Burr. In 1795, Hosack was appointed Professor of Botany at Columbia, and in 1796 he became Professor of Materia Medica. Over the next decades, he became a pillar of the city's scientific and cultural life, helping to found the New-York Historical Society, the New-York Horticultural Society, the Academy of Fine Arts, and the Literary and Philosophical Society. He counted some of the most famous New Yorkers, and indeed Americans, among his patients and friends. Burr and Hamilton were both longstanding clients of his medical practice, but it was his close friend Hamilton whom Hosack attended at the fatal 1804 duel (Chernow 2004, 706). Among his many correspondents on scientific, cultural, and political matters were Sir Joseph Banks (president of the Royal Society), James Madison, and Thomas Jefferson. Hosack became the leading doctor in New York City, known for his innovative treatments of a wide range of medical conditions, from scarlet fever to infertility. He ministered to the most prominent New York citizens and was the medical expert chosen to testify at the most famous murder trial of the era.

Hosack's trajectory thus took him from the top medical school in the young republic to immersion in Britain's much older medical establishment, with its reverential attitudes to botanical study and application. Returning to his native terrain, he turned fresh eyes on American medical training and practices and immediately saw opportunities that others had not.

Britton's Biography. Nathaniel Britton, born in New York ninety years after Hosack, began his trajectory at a very different moment in the history of his country and his city, but just as for Hosack, it was a trip through the world of British botany that helped him see an opportunity for institutional innovation in the United States. He was born in 1859 on Staten Island. After demonstrating a strong interest in botany as a child, he studied botany and geology at Columbia, located since 1857 at 49th Street and Madison Avenue. In 1879, Britton received an Engineer of Mines degree from Columbia's School of Mines and joined the New Jersey Geological Survey as its botany specialist (Howe 1934, 171). Two years later, he earned his PhD with a dissertation titled "A Preliminary Catalogue of the Flora of New Jersey" (Mickulas 2007, 54–55). Over the next five decades, he published hundreds of articles and many books on botany (Howe 1934, 172). Britton's accomplishments as a student and with the New Jersey Geological Survey led to his appointment in 1890 as an adjunct assistant professor of botany at Columbia. In 1891, he was promoted to professor of botany (Sloan 1980, 57).

Britton was an active member of New York's intellectual life and an instrumental figure in local scientific societies. As an undergraduate, he joined the Torrey Botanical Club, New York's main organization for professional and amateur botanists. Named for John Torrey, a Columbia chemistry professor who first convened the gatherings in the 1860s, the club offered its members a forum for the discussion of plant specimens and the presentation of scientific papers (Mickulas 2007, 37). Under Britton's editorship (1889–1897), the monthly *Bulletin of the Torrey Botanical Club* became a significant outlet for advances in botany (Merrill 1938, 149). In 1880, before Britton had even completed his PhD, he was elected a member of the New York Academy of Sciences (NYAS); he rose to its presidency in 1906. He was instrumental in proposing and founding the Scientific Alliance of New York, created in 1890 to gather together the many scientific societies in the city (NYAS 1935, 88). As his prominence in New York scientific circles rose, Britton began to gain national recognition. He had attended the annual meetings of the American Association for the Advancement of Science (AAAS) since 1884 (Gleason 1960, 208). By 1892, the botanists of the AAAS formalized their section into an independent organization, which was constituted in 1893 as the Botanical Society of America. Britton was elected one of ten charter members; he was elected vice president in 1894 and president in 1898.

When Britton returned from his honeymoon visit to the Royal Botanic Gardens at Kew in 1888, he was inspired as both a scientist and a citizen to mount a campaign for a similar establishment in New York City. His reputation as a leading American botanist was complemented by his institutional ties to Columbia. When Britton was a Columbia student, his mentor had been John Strong Newberry, a professor of geology and paleontology who galvanized New York's scientific life as president of the New York Academy of Sciences and who was a charter member of the National Academy of Sciences (Sloan 1980, 39). As a Columbia professor, Britton enjoyed unusually close ties to Seth Low, the college's well-connected president (and a future mayor), who had already begun to figure in the city-wide movement to harness New York's financial and social resources in the service of cultural and educational institution-building. Like Hosack, Britton enjoyed a personal and professional trajectory that allowed him to recognize the possibilities for institutional innovation in American botany.

Personal experiences predispose certain people to observe opportunities more readily than others. Such recognition is not, however, sufficient; otherwise, the world would have many more successful new ventures. The challenge also lies in creating a model and fashioning an accompanying narrative that enrolls others. The ability to "connect the dots" between one's knowledge of a market or field and the recognition of an opportunity depends, in part, on constructing a template that enables one to perceive connections between seemingly unrelated changes or events. A template provides narrative materials that help innovators convey their vision to others who can help them realize it. Whether in the form of a prototype that signals an emergent pattern or an exemplar that builds on past experiences, the people who attempt to build new organizations need to construct a suitable and persuasive template for their projects. Precisely which practices and forms appear appropriate or desirable to these innovators depends in large part on their biographical trajectories through specific social and professional milieux.

Hosack's Template. When Hosack proposed the founding of a botanical garden in the late eighteenth century, the United States offered no organization that conformed to his vision. There was, simply put, no US model available to him. The handful of gardens in operation in the late eighteenth century were run by private citizens, not institutions, and none were used for formal medical training. The most famous of these was the nursery established outside Philadelphia in the 1720s by John Bartram and carried on by his son William. The Bartrams collected plants and seeds from around the world and also sent thousands of specimens from the American colonies to European correspondents, who used them both for scientific research and to adorn private gardens (Wulf 2008). Neither this garden nor the few others dotted along the Eastern seaboard was anything like the scientific and educational enterprise Hosack envisioned.

For his template, Hosack turned primarily to the British garden tradition, which he had imbibed through scientific excursions in London's Brompton Botanic Garden and study in the Linnean Society collections. Thanks in no small measure to the participation of the botanist Joseph Banks in the South Sea voyages of Captain Cook, England in the late eighteenth century was filled with botanists. The Brompton Botanic Garden was a private enterprise established soon before Hosack's arrival in London by a botanist named William Curtis, who supported his garden via subscriptions to his wildly popular botanical magazine. At the Linnean Society, a private organization comprising a museum, herbarium, and library, Hosack studied the plant classification system of the eminent Swedish botanist Carl Linnaeus (1707–

1778). While in London, he also learned about a rival classification system established by the French botanist Antoine Laurent de Jussieu (1748–1836), which was espoused at the (formerly royal and then republican) Jardin des Plantes in Paris. Hosack also learned about the Royal Botanic Gardens at Kew, outside London and not yet open to the public, where Sir Joseph Banks was chief botanist to George III and the Linnaean system prevailed.

As he worked to found the Elgin Botanic Garden, Hosack strategically recombined central elements of these gardens to fashion a new kind of garden suited to the context of the early republic. He had brought a number of dried specimens back from London, including some from Linnaeus's own collection, and to these he added indigenous and nonnative plants cultivated from seeds sent to him by friends and correspondents. Inspired by Kew, Brompton, and the Jardin des Plantes, he drew on the systems of both Linnaeus and Jussieu to organize his garden in a manner calculated to best teach medical students about the science of botany and its pharmacological applications.

At the same time, Hosack jettisoned many elements of the European models that would not be useful in America. Although botany was of interest to many gentlemen in Hosack's social milieu, the broader public was not sufficiently engaged to permit him to raise funds via a magazine subscription, as had been done at Brompton. In the absence of a monarchy, Hosack could not appeal for royal patronage to bankroll scientists, donate land, and buy specimens, as had been done at Kew and Paris. Instead, in addition to putting his own money into the enterprise, Hosack sought funding from Columbia College and the state legislature. He knew that Columbia's efforts to establish itself as a college rivaling the University of Pennsylvania and Harvard would be boosted by its affiliation with the first botanical garden in the new republic. The state legislature, for its part, was deeply interested in the medical, agricultural, and commercial progress of New York, and Hosack tailored his garden to meet these needs.

Britton's Template. Late in the century, Nathaniel Britton also turned to London, and Kew in particular, for his template, but he too recombined elements from the British tradition with newly fashioned elements suitable to his time and place. Kew, founded in 1759 as a private royal garden and made public in the 1840s, had become increasingly important to the British colonial economy in the second half of the nineteenth century. When Britton first visited in 1888, the garden already boasted nearly seventy acres of display gardens, but its primary activities were research and publication. Its first appointed director, William Jackson Hooker, who took up his post in 1841, was a British professor of botany who was instrumental in building the garden's collections of living and dried specimens and developing its research activities (Brockway [1979] 2002, 80). Hooker also set up a Museum of Economic Botany at Kew, which displayed—and made available for medical and industrial research—specimens collected from around the world on British colonial expeditions (Drayton 2000, 194). Botanical training and research on the specimens were conducted in laboratories built for that purpose.

As Britton began to organize his new garden, he turned to Kew for ideas:

> To serve adequately the various uses here indicated a botanic garden requires a somewhat spacious site. The Royal Botanic Gardens at Kew comprises sixty-seven acres, an area ample for its purposes. Fifty acres might be considered a reasonable amount of land for a New York botanic garden; half as much could be made to answer a good purpose; seventy-five acres would be none too much for its ultimate highest development. (Torrey Botanical Club 1889, 4)

In December 1890, Britton wrote to the director of Kew requesting information about its annual budget. He received a reply the following month: "Kew costs the Government in round figures £20,000 a year. I enclose herewith a printed list of our staff which will give you an idea of our organization."[6]

Britton's plan for an "American Kew," as the newspapers called it, represented a major innovation for botany in the United States. Although several small botanical gardens had emerged in the United States between the founding of Elgin and Britton's return from England, none approached Kew's organizational and scientific scale. If New York's new botanical garden were to attain the stature of Kew, Britton would need to establish laboratories, libraries, an herbarium, and a museum, in addition to laying out extensive grounds and building a collection of living specimens. Britton's correspondence from the 1890s shows this is what he set about doing. In October 1896, he wrote to an associate, "I have been occupied continuously for the past three months in endeavoring to get the Garden plans completed in every detail that seems desirable to incorporate in them . . . I am receiving a flood of material from all kinds of sources, living plants, museum and herbarium material, books and pamphlets and have a really enormous lot of stuff promised as soon as the buildings are ready for it."[7]

With neither land nor financial support, however, Britton would not be able to house his growing collections. Just as Hosack had before him, Britton reworked the British model to suit an American context in which no royal funds were available to donate land, purchase specimens, and support a scientific staff. In order to mobilize these crucial resources, Britton had to frame his project in a way that would appeal to the most powerful New Yorkers. As we show next, both David Hosack and Nathaniel Britton were highly capable in their articulation of frames that resonated with the most powerful members of their respective scientific, cultural, and political com-

---

6. William Thiselton-Dyer to Nathaniel Britton, Jan. 4, 1891, Britton Papers, Mertz Library, NYBG.

7. Nathaniel Britton to W. A. Stiles, Oct. 29, 1896, Britton Papers, Mertz Library, NYBG.

munities. They accomplished this in three ways: lecturing and writing about their projects; enrolling the press; and harnessing their visions to extant organizations, especially Columbia.

Hosack's Social Skill. In the first decade of the nineteenth century, David Hosack produced a series of pamphlets, letters, and speeches as he sought legitimacy and finances for his new enterprise. His central argument concerned the importance of a botanical garden to improving medical education in the United States; American doctors, he asserted, should have the level of training and expertise long since standard in Europe. In the preface to his 1806 Elgin catalogue, he sounded this theme forcefully:

> Hitherto the botanical gardens of *Edinburgh, Oxford, Cambridge, London, Paris, Copenhagen, Leyden, Upsal, Goettingen, &c.* have instructed the American youth in this department of medical education; and it is in some degree owing to those establishments that the universities and colleges of those places have become so celebrated, and have been resorted to by students of medicine from all parts of the world. (D. Hosack 1806, vii)

This framing was meant to appeal to Hosack's medical colleagues and other men of scientific learning in the young republic (not least President Jefferson) who were familiar with those eminent institutions.

To his medical arguments Hosack frequently added references to Elgin's potential contributions to the progress of American agriculture. In an 1803 lecture at Columbia, he noted:

> The student of agriculture will also here have an opportunity of observing, at a single view, the various grasses which compose our pastures and those which are injurious as weeds, or poisonous to cattle. For this purpose, a quarter will be applied to cultivation of this description of plants: in which not only the native grasses of this country will be exhibited, but those likewise which are esteemed most useful in different parts of the world. (D. Hosack 1803, 2)

The progress of agricultural production was a concern that cut across social classes. In 1792, a group of prominent New Yorkers—many of whom were to become friends and associates of Hosack—had founded the New-York State Society for the Promotion of Agriculture, Arts, and Manufactures (NYSSPAAM). Hosack himself joined in 1794. The Society's members sought to collect and disseminate knowledge about "the different modes of agriculture that are in practice; to suggest such improvements as may be found to be beneficial; [and] to excite among their fellow citizens, a spirit of making experiments for the amelioration of lands which have been exhausted, or in their natural state are unproductive or unfit for cultivation" (NYSSPAAM 1801, vi).

Even though elite New Yorkers generally prized scientific learning as well as the increasing self-sufficiency and prosperity of the United States, the Society reached further to recognize the critical contributions made to these goals by farmers themselves. They took "into fellowship a number of respectable characters throughout the state, from whose talents and diligence they have much to expect," circulating to these farmers a questionnaire that included queries such as "What kinds of grains or grass are found by experience to thrive best in any particular soil?" (NYSSPAAM 1801, x–xi). Thus when David Hosack described the agricultural benefits to be had from the Elgin Botanic Garden, he sought to appeal to the largest possible group of supporters, especially among the state's legislators, whose backing he needed for long-term funding.

Hosack's efforts to publicize the medical and agricultural benefits of his botanical garden bore fruit in newspapers and magazines from one end of the country to the other. Numerous periodicals published lengthy paeans that drew almost verbatim on Hosack's language. In 1810, for example, shortly after he distributed a pamphlet titled "Description of the Elgin Garden" (D. Hosack 1810), the *Georgia Journal* published an equally enthusiastic account that closely echoed Hosack's own turns of phrase: "The interior is divided into various compartments well calculated to instruct the student in the science of Botany by exhibiting to his view not only the plants which are used in medicine, but those that are cultivated by the agriculturalist, and which are employed in the arts and in manufactures" (*Georgia Journal*, May 1, 1810, 4).

Hosack also linked his nascent enterprise to the agendas of other organizations including NYSSPAAM, the Medical Society of the City and County of New-York, the New-York Hospital, and Columbia College. His proposed garden was greeted with marked enthusiasm by fellow New York physicians, medical professors, and students, who delivered a series of written statements in Hosack's support to the New York State Legislature.[8] For Hosack, as later for Britton, Columbia's enrollment in his project was critical. As he worked to build Elgin's greenhouses and collections, Hosack was also integrating his new organization into the routines of Columbia's medical school by offering botany courses at the garden in the summer and in the cooler months using garden specimens in the classroom.

Britton's Social Skill. The close of the nineteenth century saw Nathaniel Britton building alliances equal to Hosack's at the century's opening. Like Hosack, Britton emphasized both the scientific and practical contributions of his new enterprise and its potential elevation of the American profile in these areas vis-à-vis Europe. Also like Hosack, he tailored his accounts to the concerns of various contemporary constituencies. Describing the purposes of botanical gardens, he and his fellow Torrey Botanical Club mem-

---

8. For example, an 1810 statement from the Medical Society of the City and County of New-York reads, in part, "a botanic garden is absolutely necessary to complete the means required, for attaining a finished medical education. . . . On this subject there is no difference of opinion among your medical brethren in New-York" (D. Hosack 1811, 24).

bers noted that "first and foremost is the purely scientific and educational use. Subsidiary to this, but still of a marked degree of importance, are the pharmaceutical and horticultural uses, and lastly, the general use as a place of agreeable resort for the public at large" (Torrey Botanical Club 1889, 2). Britton was also adept at communicating his organizational template via the press. In March 1891, the *New York Times* published an editorial titled, "An American Kew Proposed," that drew nearly verbatim on language supplied by Britton himself:

> It is desired to give this city not merely a beautiful pleasure garden for pop-ular recreation and instruction, but a great scientific institution of high permanent value . . . Every city of any importance in Europe has a botanic garden. There are more than three hundred of them. The most important are the Kew Gardens, six miles from London, the Jardin des Plantes at Paris, the Royal Botanic Gardens and Museum at Berlin, and important gardens at Geneva, Rome, Florence, Padua, Vienna, and St. Petersburg. (*New York Times*, March 8, 1891, 13)

As fundraising and planning for the garden went into high gear, Britton reminded the press of the importance of rivaling Kew's scientific and practi-cal contributions. In a circular letter he sent to many newspapers and maga-zines in the summer of 1895, he called upon the public to be mindful of the great sums needed if this goal was to be accomplished. Just a few weeks later, an editorial in *Harper's Weekly* (*Harper's Weekly*, July 27, 1895, vol. 39, 697) adopted his framing:

> A botanical garden, it must be remembered, is not a mere pleasure-ground. It ought to be a centre of scientific research, and a fountain-head of that knowledge of plant life which is so essential to the development, protec-tion, and preservation of animal life. . . . Why should not New York's Botanical Garden aim to be in time to North America what Kew is to Europe?

Britton also made sure that his lectures in support of the garden reached a broader audience. An August 1896 address to the botanical section of the American Association for the Advancement of Science at the annual meet-ing in Buffalo was reprinted in *Science* magazine just ten days later (Brit-ton 1896), and Britton also sent copies of the text to popular periodicals, explaining to an associate:

> I thought when I wrote the document that this might be a good thing to do with it, and worded it somewhat for the purpose. The only thing that I hesitate about is that it may be too much published. It is in Science, in Garden & Forest, and in Bulletin Torrey Club [*sic*], and abstracts of it in the Newspapers.[9]

9. Nathaniel Britton to Charles F. Cox, Sept. 21, 1896, Britton Papers, Mertz Library, NYBG.

Like Hosack, Britton recognized the importance of anchoring his new project to Columbia College at both the administrative and the instructional levels. Here again Britton introduced a variation on the Royal Botanic Gardens, which were not attached to a university. As early as 1891, Britton engaged President Seth Low in conversations about the possible relationship between the college and the planned garden. Working with Low, Britton secured the transfer of Columbia's herbarium and botanical library to the new garden. The two drew up a legal agreement that institutionalized the interorganizational ties by stipulating that Columbia faculty and students would be allowed unfettered access to the herbarium and library, and that the college would be permitted to offer free classes at the garden to its students in botany, pharmacology, and any other "kindred subjects" (New York Botanical Garden 1896, 19–20). Britton, like Hosack before him, displayed great savviness as he articulated his institutional project and bound it to the routines of Columbia College.

6.2.1 Common Elements, Divergent Outcomes

Both Hosack and Britton were talented men who innovated in the context of their time. Yet despite the striking parallels between these men and their visions, the outcomes of their efforts differed dramatically. The Elgin Botanic Garden collapsed, physically and organizationally, within fifteen years of its founding. Hosack's organizational innovation flourished briefly, but failed to take root, nor did it inspire the founding of other similar organizations. Hosack had argued passionately that such an important and ambitious scientific undertaking was worthy of, and indeed required, government support. Yet despite the vocal support of his fellow physicians and many politicians in the state legislature, bills introduced in support of Elgin repeatedly failed to win full legislative backing.

In February 1800, a state legislative committee recommended that Hosack be paid 300 pounds, but no actual bill was introduced (D. Hosack 1811, 9–10). In March 1805, Hosack submitted another petition to the legislature and a second committee recommended support, but again no bill was taken up in the larger body (ibid., 11). In January 1806, Governor Lewis recommended in his opening address to the legislative session that the legislators offer ongoing support to Elgin (ibid., 14). This time a bill was introduced, receiving a "yes" vote in the state senate and a referral to the state assembly, only to be subsequently dropped from consideration by the lower house (ibid., 12–14). In 1808, Hosack submitted another appeal to the legislature; he was given strong written encouragement but was simultaneously informed that the session was too far advanced to introduce a new bill.

He renewed his efforts at the beginning of the 1809 session, with support from many New York doctors and medical students (ibid., 15–17). These supporting statements bolstered his case, and after protracted deliberations, the state of New York passed an "act for promoting medical science in the state of New-York" that pledged to purchase the Elgin Botanic Garden. The state's patronage fell short, however, of allocating funds for the garden's maintenance, and it soon fell into disrepair.[10] In 1814, the state donated the garden to Columbia College, which had been appealing to Albany for financial help. Instead of funds, the college found itself saddled with a plot of land that successive administrations considered a poor substitute for liquid assets. The garden thus continued to decline under Columbia's ownership, triggering frantic and frequent letters from Hosack to the administration about the death and theft of plant specimens.

Hosack had hoped that Elgin would eventually rank alongside the great botanical gardens of Europe. He had also envisioned that it would train many generations of American doctors and botanists and lead to the creation of a network of botanical gardens in the United States. It fell prey, instead, to the pressures and opportunities of expanding urbanization. At the time of Hosack's death in 1835, streets were being opened through the old garden land, and by the 1860s, Columbia had begun to sell off small parcels. In 1928, Columbia leased the remaining land to John D. Rockefeller Jr. for his new Rockefeller Center project; in 1985, Columbia sold the land to the Rockefeller Group for $400 million (*New York Times*, June 3, 1993, B3). Today, visitors to the site of David Hosack's Elgin Botanic Garden will find themselves walking through Rockefeller Center. At the corner of Hosack's land, on the spot where his conservatory once stood, is Radio City Music Hall.

Visitors to the NYBG, by contrast, can still tour Britton's original museum building and conservatory and stroll through nearly 250 acres of forested and cultivated grounds. Generations of botanists and biologists have trained

---

10. A proposed botanical garden at the University of Pennsylvania ran into similar difficulties. On March 19, 1807, the Pennsylvania State Assembly passed an act granting "to the University of Pennsylvania the sum of $3000—out of the monies they owe the State—for the purpose of enabling them to establish a Garden for the improvement of the Science of Botany, and for instituting a series of experiments to ascertain the cheapest and best food for Plants, and their medical Properties & Virtues" (Ewan and Ewan 2007, 553). Because the funds thus "allotted" were not actually in the possession of the university, the garden was never established (ibid., 554). A garden established in Cambridge, Massachusetts, in 1807 had better luck initially thanks to its early funding by a group of private subscribers, although it was outfitted with neither an herbarium nor a botanical library (Harvard University 1846). This garden soon began to languish from lack of funds, barely surviving until the galvanizing appointment in 1842 of Professor Asa Gray, a rising botanical star then teaching at the University of Michigan. In the early 1870s, Gray lobbied unsuccessfully to acquire for the botanical garden the bequest of merchant James Arnold, whose money went instead to the creation of an arboretum in Jamaica Plain. The most successful American botanical garden before the founding of the NYBG was Shaw's Garden in St. Louis. Founded as a private garden by the philanthropist Henry Shaw in the 1850s, it was opened to the public in 1859 and renamed the Missouri Botanical Garden. This garden, however, had very limited research and teaching components until after the founding of the NYBG (Grove 2005, xv).

at the organization Britton founded in the 1890s, and as we discuss below, soon after the garden's successful creation, civic leaders across the United States were inspired to launch similar campaigns to establish botanical gardens in their own cities. Within one generation, botanists trained at the NYBG began to advance the discipline in gardens, universities, and associations across the country. Britton also helped usher in a new era in American philanthropy by successfully mobilizing private fortunes and state funding in support of a public-serving organization managed by academic experts. In short, where Hosack failed to gain longstanding traction for his novel organizational form, Britton's innovative effort took root and spread, transforming American cities, science, and philanthropy in the process.

In the foregoing analysis, we have made use of a cluster of concepts—projects, biographies, templates, and social skill—that organization scholars have identified as instrumental in explaining the successful creation of a new organizational form (Clemens 1993; Fligstein 1997; McAdam, McCarthy, and Zald 1996; Burton, Sørensen, and Beckman 2002). With the aid of this conceptual toolkit, we have seen that both Hosack and Britton were gifted, well-connected men who articulated innovative projects that powerful contemporaries praised for their great scientific and cultural significance. These concepts have been valuable in helping explain these two innovators' ability to garner support from the most influential people of their eras. Nevertheless, the toolkit does not account for why only one of the projects led to the emergence and spread of an American model for botanical gardens. We show below that the decisive differences between Hosack and Britton lie not in the individual men, nor even solely in the field of botany, but in pronounced changes in American material, organizational, and professional life, as well as in the reverberations of those transformations for university careers and individual opportunities.

In the next section, we take up the question of why these strikingly similar organizational projects met with such divergent fates, showing that the answer lies in the dramatic differences between the worlds into which Hosack and Britton were born and between the kinds of individuals those worlds produced. We do so with three goals in mind: first, to make clear how material and cultural factors allow particular models to be viewed as either appropriate or welcome; second, to illustrate how the organizational character of the wider era, viewed here as models of both how tasks should be organized and how expertise is distributed, shaped the topology of the possible (Fontana 2006; Padgett and Powell 2012, ch. 1); and third, to demonstrate how social structures produce actors poised to recognize and act on possible opportunities. Examining poisedness—matching the character of innovative models with the structural features of the society into which they are introduced—is essential to explaining why new forms persist and propagate, as in Britton's case, or fall by the wayside, as in Hosack's.

6.3   "Chief City of the New World": Macrohistorical Change and New York City in the Nineteenth Century

In the first decade of the nineteenth century, David Hosack was unable to persuade his fellow citizens that a botanical garden was central to the scientific and cultural stature of New York City. In the last decade of the century, *Garden and Forest* magazine (Garden and Forest, July 3, 1895, vol. 8, 261) published an article in support of Nathaniel Britton's campaign for a botanical garden celebrating the fact that "New York is to have a garden worthy of its rank as chief city of the New World." The historical shifts that had unfolded over the course of the century rendered the organizational form of a botanical garden not only reasonable to New Yorkers, but in fact deeply desired.

First, the urbanization of Manhattan triggered dramatic changes in the way New Yorkers viewed the natural world. Second, the accumulation of industrial fortunes during the nineteenth century gave rise to a new class of moneyed New Yorkers whose travels on the "Grand Tour" exposed them to the cultural and scientific institutions that were the pride of European cities—museums, libraries, opera houses, orchestras, and botanical gardens—and also made them aware of the scale of private patronage that would be needed to maintain such institutions in the absence of a monarchy. Third, transformations in the organization of expert knowledge replaced the polymaths of the early republic—men who were at one and the same time politicians, doctors, and writers, or lawyers, painters, and philanthropists—with disciplinary specialists and professional managers, to whose expertise Gilded Age industrialist-philanthropists deferred.

The changes in Manhattan Island over the course of the century, the new organizational landscape, and the professionalization of science made the prospect of a public-private partnership for a research garden considerably more plausible and fundable. These processes not only reinforced and amplified one other but also contributed to the production of Nathaniel Britton as the very type of person—an academic expert in an organizational world that rewarded professional expertise—who was poised to capitalize on and expand these processes as he introduced his new form. In this section, we discuss central elements of these three processes in order to show how Britton, but not Hosack, operated in a historical context that was poised for the introduction of a world-class botanical garden.

6.3.1   The Material Environment

Human interactions with the material world profoundly condition both the ends to which organizations are put and the technologies designed to accomplish them. "Social life," as Mukerji (2009, 13) has argued, "is always dependent on the material possibilities of places and gives rise to forms of intellect that make sense there." We suggest that organizational forms should be counted among the "forms of intellect" made possible by historically and geographically specific dispositions of the material world. As we show, the organizational form of a botanical garden could not be rendered meaningful to the required constituents of Hosack's New York. The material disposition of Manhattan Island and the ways of thinking about the built and natural environments embodied in that disposition precluded full acceptance, and thus full support, of a botanical garden. By the end of the century, however, the transformation of Manhattan Island and its environs would render the organizational form of a botanical garden not only sensible but desirable.

In 1800, New York City occupied only the southern tip of Manhattan Island and had a population of about 60,000. Although the city itself was densely built, with busy shipping, commercial, and residential districts, most of the island remained bucolic. North of Bleecker Street (today's Greenwich Village) lay a sparsely populated landscape dotted by woods, streams, country estates, and farms. The famous New York City grid, which would give structure to the spread of buildings and streets on Manhattan, would not be mapped on paper for another decade, and it would take many more decades to unfold up and across the island. Concerns about the loss of green space that would lead to the creation of Central Park in the 1850s had not yet been voiced.

In this specific natural-environmental context, Hosack—unlike Britton nearly a century later—could hardly appeal to the importance of protecting Manhattan farmland from development by enclosing it behind the walls of a botanical garden. The difficulties Hosack faced in making his case are evident in an 1811 speech by a prominent professor of medicine in the city, Dr. Nicholas Romayne, who argued that it would be foolish for the state to purchase Elgin, for "in a country where every farm and forest affords a variety of plants sufficient to illustrate the principles of Botany, public animosity may be aroused" (Romayne 1811, 123). Unlike the urban botanical gardens of London and Edinburgh, a botanical garden on Manhattan Island in the first decade of the nineteenth century was too easily camouflaged by its rural surroundings. For the uninitiated, its institutional significance as a site for the production of locally and nationally valuable medical and agricultural knowledge was not evident from its physical appearance. Furthermore, by pasturing cows on part of the land, Hosack generated earned income for his organization, but inadvertently contributed to misunderstandings about its nature. "These animals, to the number of 20 or 30, attend the Botanical Garden and excite the ridicule of travellers passing there" (College of Physicians and Surgeons 1812, 18). Thus opponents who recognized the organizational form Hosack was attempting to establish but wished to thwart him for academic and social reasons found this identity problem could be handily deployed as a weapon in the struggle over the allocation of prestige and funds.

On the national scale, as in New York City, the early republic was characterized by a sense of natural abundance. At the outset of the nineteenth century, President Thomas Jefferson had doubled the size of the United States with the Louisiana Purchase and sent Lewis and Clark on an expedition to map the geography, flora, and fauna of the unknown continent. In 1825, the inventor John Stevens built and tested the first American steam locomotive across the Hudson from New York City in Hoboken. Over the next decades, as men like Cornelius Vanderbilt replaced canal and river shipping with railroad lines, American writers and painters began to celebrate a natural world they perceived to be under threat. In 1836, Ralph Waldo Emerson published his essay "Nature"; his friend Henry David Thoreau moved to Walden Pond in 1845, publishing *Walden* in 1854. Just fifteen years later, in 1869, the first transcontinental railroad was completed.

Westward expansion fundamentally transformed the way Americans experienced the natural world and also altered the very shape and texture of that world. The possibilities for industrial and agricultural progress seemed limitless to some, but others worried that hunters, railroads, and new human settlements were threatening whole species and landscapes with destruction. Senator Justin Morrill of Vermont, concerned that "the very cheapness of our public lands, and the facility of purchase and transfer, tended to a system of bad farming, [and] strip and waste of soil" (quoted in James 1910, 29), sponsored an 1862 act that donated public lands to the states for the establishment of agricultural colleges. In 1872, the first of the National Parks, Yellowstone, was created by President Grant. By the late 1870s, wide swaths of the social and political elite of the post–Civil War United States had become committed to the protection of nature (Taylor 2009).

In New York City, too, the expansion of human settlement had transformed the natural world of Manhattan Island over the course of the century. In 1800, the average population per square mile in New York City (then located entirely in lower Manhattan) was 3,000. By 1900 it was 90,400. Street by street, the grid plan laid out by city commissioners on paper in 1811 had been etched with dynamite and pavement into the face of the island. By the 1840s, prominent public voices, most notably poet and editor William Cullen Bryant, were voicing concerns about the steady disappearance of green space in the city (Bryant 1844). In the 1850s, wealthy and powerful citizens successfully mobilized for the creation of an enormous park at the heart of the island. As Central Park's vistas filled in, wealthy families built their Fifth Avenue palaces further and further uptown, and other neighborhoods began to fill with the waves of immigrants arriving through Castle Garden at the foot of Manhattan (Scobey 2002, 118). By the close of the century, the population of New York City was nearing two million, and almost all of Manhattan Island had been built up or paved over, except where land had been requisitioned for cemeteries (*Demographia* 2001). The city grew vertically, too; 300 buildings over nine stories tall were constructed between 1875 and 1900 (Domosh 1987, 233; Beckert 2001, 253). By 1880, city leaders had begun to worry that even Central Park and Brooklyn's 585-acre Prospect Park, opened in 1867, were inadequate to the needs of the growing populace, and a new effort was launched to establish parks in the less densely populated 23rd and 24th wards of the city, beyond Manhattan Island in the Bronx. The New York Park Association, founded in 1881 by *Herald* editor John Mullaly, lobbied hard and successfully for the creation of (in the words of the *New York Times*) "great breathing places beyond the Harlem River."[11] As Mullaly later recounted, the successful campaign owed much to the influence of New York's Gilded Age elite:

> Whenever the influence of a public man who believed in it could be obtained his co-operation was solicited. In this way men representing large interests in real estate, the Astors, the Belmonts, the Tiffanys, the Claflins, etc., appreciating the effect of the New Parks in the enhancement of values and profiting by the experience in the case of the Central [Park], gave their approval to the movement and united in an earnest appeal to the Mayor, the Legislature and the Governor in favor of the bill. (Mullaly 1887, 134)

Under pressure of population growth and new theories on public health, a striking shift had taken place in attitudes toward New York's "natural" spaces between the days of Hosack and the rise of the parks movement in the 1880s. The *Herald* lamented, with the ease of hindsight, the fact that these attitudes had not changed sooner: "It is to-day a cause of regret that the authorities of New York of a half a century ago, did not, while land was cheap, make proper provision for this important and attractive feature of the city." By the end of the nineteenth century, New York City had a high concentration of people who were unequal in both means and identities, a dramatic transformation from the early republic. Images of the island from 1798 and 1902, presented in figures 6.3 and 6.4, display the striking contrasts to which the nineteenth century's demographic and material changes in Manhattan gave rise. (For a timeline of pivotal moments in the national and civic shift from environmental expansiveness to concern, see figure 6.5.)

It was at precisely this moment of burgeoning national alarm about the loss of wild spaces and growing municipal worry about the loss of therapeutic landscapes that Nathaniel Britton chose to launch his campaign, which soon captured the imaginations of citizens concerned about both sorts of natural spaces. For preservationists and conservationists alike, the scientific expeditions and research programs of the great European botanical gardens offered a model for cataloguing and studying plants and developing

---

11. "London has 15 acres and Paris 8 acres to every 1 acre embraced within New York's park limits. New York, according to the views of the association, requires a park area of at least 5,000 acres, for she needs to provide not merely for her present population, but for the two millions of persons which she will contain a quarter of a century hence" (*New York Times*, Nov. 27, 1881, 14).

Fig. 6.3   Town of Haerlem (Harlem), northern Manhattan, in 1798
Source: Plate 60b in I. N. Phelps Stokes, *The iconography of Manhattan Island, 1498–1909*,
v. 1. New York: Robert H. Dodd, 1915–1928.

plans to protect the threatened flora of the North American continent. For
New Yorkers concerned about urban order and health, a beautiful research
landscape in the Bronx offered a partial answer to the dilemma of expanding populations and shrinking green spaces. Some of the city's wealthiest
citizens drew on their good reputations and considerable finances to support
Britton's botanical project. Their wealth, of course, had been derived in large
part from the very exploitation of nature that had given rise to the preservationist and conservationist movements. At the same time, their interest in
the industrial, medicinal, and agricultural advances promised by research at
the new garden emerged out of their own success with earlier such advances.

The state of the material world in which first Hosack and then Britton
worked integrally shaped the outcomes of their projects. Active in an environment lush with plant life, Hosack struggled to mobilize support for a
plant-focused organization whose scientific goals—advancing American
botany and medicine—remained abstract and unfamiliar to potential
funders. By contrast, Britton moved through a densely built environment
in which he recognized and harnessed rising concerns about the impover-
ishment of the natural world. When Britton introduced the organizational

Fig. 6.4. Manhattan skyline in 1902

Source: Irving Underhill, *1902 M, New York skyline*, Library of Congress Prints and Photographs Online Catalog. Lot 12475, no. 13 (OSF) [P&P]. http://www.loc.gov/pictures/item /2007662377/.

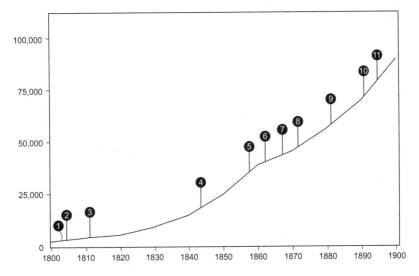

Population per square mile (density)[1]

❶ 1803—The Louisiana Purchase adds nearly 530,000,000 acres to the U.S.
❷ 1804—Lewis and Clark's Corps of Discovery departs from St. Louis for the Pacific Ocean
❸ 1811—Plan for a Manhattan street grid is published by the city of New York
❹ 1844—Poet and editor William Cullen Bryant issues public call for a major New York City park
❺ 1858—Central Park opens to the public
❻ 1862—Morrill Act sets aside government land for agricultural schools
❼ 1867—Prospect Park opens to the public
❽ 1872—Yellowstone National Park established by act of Congress
❾ 1881—New York Park Association founded
❿ 1891—Act creating institutional framework of the New York Botanical Garden passed by New York Assembly
⓫ 1895—New York City gives 250-acre parcel in the Bronx to the New York Botanical Garden

Fig. 6.5   Transformation of material environment in nineteenth-century New York City and United States

[1] "New York (Manhattan) Wards: Population & Density 1800–1910" *Demographia* (2001). http://www.demographia.com/db-nyc-ward1800.htm.

form of a research-intensive botanical garden, the materiality of that form had an allure for his contemporaries that was absent in Hosack's time. In sum, it mattered deeply to Hosack's ultimate failure and Britton's success how their contemporaries experienced the natural and built environments in which they lived.

6.3.2   Civic Organization in the Early Republic and the Gilded Age

Human lives are embedded within social relations with kith and kin, as well as with colleagues and rivals. The array of friendships and affiliations that one has provides both opportunities and resources to pursue various projects. We draw from Stinchcombe (1965) the insight that specific historical moments offer particular arrays of organizational forms. Both Hosack and Britton lived in eras marked by numerous membership organizations in which like-minded people routinely came together, yet the character of these associations was stamped by the circumstances of the early republic and the Gilded Age. As a number of chapters in the volume argue, the organizational forms available to citizens of the early republic were limited by politically motivated controls over the right to incorporate and to enjoy legal protections of incorporation. We extend these arguments by attending to the culturally available models of organizing in the early republic as opposed to the late nineteenth century. To Hosack's fellow New Yorkers, the organizational form of the botanical garden was neither fish nor fowl. It was neither a member-serving sanctuary for elite citizens, nor a charitable house for the needy. By the late nineteenth century, changes in the way elite New Yorkers understood and organized their philanthropic undertakings had rendered the botanical garden form far more plausible. Hence the options afforded to Hosack and Britton were dictated by the associational structure of their eras.

In the years following the British occupation, New Yorkers worked to rebuild the commercial and cultural life of their city. Voluntary organizations, both old and new, were central to this process. A handful of organizations that had been founded in the Colonial era were refashioned to serve the citizens of the new republic. This was the case, for example, with King's College, founded in 1754 and reopened in 1784 as Columbia. But it was via a wave of organizational foundings that elite New Yorkers sought most decisively to define the place of their city in the world's youngest democracy. These new enterprises were either member-serving organizations intended to educate and polish their constituents or charitable organizations intended to serve those in need. Both kinds of organizations received charters from the state government in increasing numbers in the post-Revolutionary era. And as Bloch and Lamoreaux argue in chapter 7 of this volume, New York was among the most active state governments in the early republic when it came to granting charters for charitable organizations in particular.

We contend that the prevalence and widespread acceptance of these two associational forms hindered Hosack's ability to raise funds for his own novel form, a research-intensive botanical garden. Typical of the member-serving organizations founded in early republic New York were the Calliopean Society (1788), the New York Academy of Fine Arts (1802), and the New-York Historical Society (1804); Hosack would eventually belong to all three. The Calliopean Society was organized "for the express purpose of improving education" (Scott 1933, 13). Members, limited to sixty in number, were drawn from New York's educated, professional elite. Early members included William Irving, a fur merchant and future US representative; Benjamin Moore, an Anglican minister and future president of Columbia College; and Samuel Latham Mitchill, a Columbia medical professor. The library was for members only, supported by quarterly dues. At the club's weekly meetings, members gathered to hear one another read an original composition, recite poetry, give a speech, or engage in a formal debate.

The Academy of Fine Arts was similarly oriented toward the refinement of its members. First suggested by Robert R. Livingston, President Jefferson's minister to France, it was devoted to the appreciation of art, especially classical art. Members' subscriptions went toward the purchase of sculptures and paintings that were displayed in the private meeting-space, discussed, and used for art instruction. Hard on the heels of the Academy of Fine Arts, the New-York Historical Society was founded by some of the same men. The Historical Society's primary purpose was to "discover, procure, and preserve" documents and artifacts relating to the history of the state of New York (Vail 1954, 451). Members paid dues in support of the purchase and maintenance of historical materials and in return received permission to peruse the fast-growing collections. It was hoped that such clubs and societies would contribute to the refinement both of their elite members and of the city.

The other primary type of voluntary organization of the era served a different purpose and clientele, although once again, we find some of the same men—and also a number of women—involved in their founding and operations. The Society for the Relief of Distressed Debtors was founded just a few years after the Revolution by a group of businessmen to help residents of the debtors' prison fulfill basic needs for food and clothing (Burrows and Wallace 1999, 381–82). Within a decade, the mission of this charity had expanded to include the distribution of meal tickets to the poor and the establishment of a soup kitchen on land donated by the city council. Its leaders included David Hosack and DeWitt Clinton (Bender 1987, 50). Hosack would also soon be involved with the New-York Free School Society, founded in 1805 to provide educational opportunities to indigent children.

Our primary and secondary research shows that New York City in the early republic was home to several dozen of these two types of organizations, the member-serving cultural society and the other-serving charity. David Hosack, who was a founder or member of a half-dozen such societies and charities by the time he launched Elgin, was intimately familiar with these successful models of civic organization. Elgin, however, conformed to neither. Hosack's vision was, instead, of a research and practice-based organization that would advance medicine, botany, and agriculture. Given the unfamiliarity of this model to local audiences, Hosack used his own money to create the garden while seeking funds from Columbia and the state legislature. The challenge he faced, and to which Elgin ultimately succumbed, was that the botanical garden as an organizational form fell between the two available stools. As an organization dedicated to the ancillary training of a small group of impecunious specialists—medical students—a botanical garden had no natural constituency of well-heeled potential members who would pay subscription fees in order to glean personal and civic benefits. And because medical students did not have the moral claim on the wealthy that impoverished widows, debtors, and street children had, the botanical garden form bore no resemblance to the other-serving charity. Hosack thus envisioned the garden as a specialist organization serving, above all, Columbia, an institution he reasonably believed would have an interest in educating its medical students at a level comparable to London and Edinburgh and exceeding Boston and Philadelphia. Even here, however, he ran into opposition. Some leaders of the academic medical community argued that a botanical garden was not the best use of institutional funds:

> The Censors are impressed with the advantages to be derived from the Botanical Garden but from its remote situation and the expenses which must follow, a donation to keep it up would be necessary. The Censors believe the advantages to be derived from the Botanical Garden would be far inferior to that derived from [a] chemical apparatus, an anatomical museum, a medical library. (quoted in Robbins 1964, 81)

Hosack also believed the garden would serve the large farming community of the state of New York, but here again the constituency was not a natural one for a member-serving, subscription-based society. Farmers were too scattered across the state to visit Elgin in person, and those who were likely to join agricultural associations were already members of local chapters of the New-York State Society for the Promotion of Agriculture, Arts, and Manufactures. Seen in the light of the organizational challenges Hosack faced, the brief life of the Elgin Botanic Garden was a notable accomplishment.

An additional challenge to Hosack's efforts was the shifting political terrain in which these organizations had been grounded (Neem 2008). In 1800, Jefferson's populist Democratic-Republicans wrested control of the state legislature from the pro-British Federalists; in 1804, after a significant change in its electoral laws, the New York City government also went to the Democratic-Republicans, who preferred to fund charities for the poor over elite educational projects. On December 22, 1807, in what turned out to be a major step on the path to the War of 1812, Congress passed an embargo act outlawing commerce with Great Britain that quickly crippled the economy of New York City and New York State (Taylor 2012, 117–18). Hosack, in short, was addressing his appeals to the city government and state legislature at a time when political developments were running counter to his project. Thus the organizational world into which Hosack brought the unfamiliar form of the botanical garden was not a fertile one. The organizational world of the late nineteenth century, in contrast, offered tillable soil for Britton's similar effort ninety years after Hosack's.

These propitious changes had begun to take shape decades before Britton launched his campaign for a botanical garden. Eric Hilt argues in this volume that the passage of general acts of incorporation beginning in the Northeast in the second decade of the nineteenth century led to a gradual loosening of state control over both commercial and charitable initiatives; Lu and Wallis demonstrate a similar process at work in banking. By the middle of the century, as Bloch and Lamoreaux argue, New York legislators in particular had substantially eased restrictions on the creation of charitable organizations. In the 1860s, the Civil War catalyzed the organization of large-scale philanthropic efforts across the United States, offering a testing ground for ideas about the best way to deliver charitable services while also opening new career paths to philanthropically minded men and women (Crocker 2003). Most notably, the US Sanitary Commission, signed into existence by President Lincoln in 1861 and yoking government support to private philanthropy, coordinated an enormous network of volunteers and professionals to provide nursing and other services for the wounded and displaced. Voluntary organizations that survived the Civil War grew in scale and complexity, and many ambitious new philanthropic efforts were launched during Reconstruction (Scott 1993). As DiMaggio (1982) has demonstrated for Boston, some of this postwar philanthropic activity was directed toward securing the boundaries between social classes. By the 1870s, wealthy industrialists, merchants, lawyers, and bankers had joined forces politically and culturally to respond to challenges from an increasingly restive and organized labor force (Beckert 2001). In New York City, an important outcome of this class struggle was the creation in the 1870s and 1880s of a set of cultural institutions that, as Beckert (2001, 267) has argued, "were financially dependent on bourgeois New Yorkers, derived their programmatic ideas from them, and principally catered to the city's economic elite. In turn, they became the focus of bourgeois philanthropy." In an era when upper-class New Yorkers were increasingly interested in marrying their daughters to titled Europeans, these institutions were modeled on those created and patronized by the aristocracy across the Atlantic.

By the time Britton founded the NYBG, New York's *haute bourgeoisie* had been working hard to catch up culturally with their European counterparts for more than a decade, starting with the incorporation in 1870 of the

Metropolitan Museum of Art. In 1874, the American Museum of Natural History laid its cornerstone, and in 1880, the Metropolitan Museum inaugurated its sumptuous new home on Fifth Avenue, thanks to the patronage of New Yorkers such as William H. Astor, Theodore Roosevelt, J. P. Morgan, and Cornelius Vanderbilt II. In 1883, the Metropolitan Opera was opened to accommodate newly wealthy New Yorkers who could not secure boxes at the existing opera house (the Academy of Music), controlled by the elite of Old New York (Kolodin 1966, 4). Although New York boasted all of these cultural institutions, it lacked a botanical garden.[12]

Britton skillfully positioned the new garden among this emerging cluster of Gilded Age institutions. An 1891 typescript in his papers makes such a reference explicitly:

> The necessary buildings for the purpose should obviously be erected by the city by means of a comparatively small annual interest charge, as was done for the Metropolitan Museum of Art, and for the Museum of Natural History, institutions which are yearly proving themselves to be of vastly greater value to the people than the cost. The buildings for the Botanic Garden should likewise be provided by the city, because private individuals could not be expected to raise money for buildings that would immediately become the property of the city itself. (Britton 1891)

The organizational form Britton proposed—a research-based botanical garden funded by a combination of private money and city and state support—was ideally suited to the industrialists whose patronage he needed. Vilified by the press for their labor and environmental practices, these men wholeheartedly embraced the opportunity to support an organization dedicated to serving the public good through research, teaching, and recreation. Britton thus benefited from, and actively capitalized on, the transformation of the civic order under way in Gilded Age New York, showing a capacity for fundraising that would be the envy of any university president or nonprofit director today. Britton inspired in his patrons a deep confidence in his talents—so much so, in fact, that Carnegie himself eventually tried to hire him away from the botanical garden (Rusby 1934, 110). Carnegie, Morgan, Rockefeller, and Vanderbilt each pledged $25,000 of their own money toward the requisite

---

12. In 1856, as Central Park was initially being planned, the financier Augustus Belmont sought to establish a privately run botanical garden there, noting that "a great many much smaller places than New York, such as Brussels, Antwerp, etc. have similar establishments without any aid of Government" (quoted in Rosenzweig and Blackmar 1992, 340). In 1857, the chief engineer for Central Park, Egbert Viele, was optimistic about including a botanical garden (*New York Times*, Jan. 20, 1857, 3). A number of the plans submitted for the 1858 park design competition contained botanical gardens, but the winning plan by Frederick Law Olmsted and Calvert Vaux did not, and none was built. In 1875, the president of the city's College of Pharmacy submitted a petition on behalf of various medical and pharmacological colleges and societies for the "establishment of a botanical garden in one of the parks of this city" (*New York Times*, Apr. 15, 1875, 8). The report was forwarded to Olmsted, superintendent and architect-in-chief of Central Park since 1858, but the campaign for a botanical garden still bore no fruit.

$250,000. Britton also set up an administrative structure for the garden that would keep these men involved. It included a board of managers, six scientific directors, and two ex-officio members (the mayor of New York and the city's Commissioner of Parks). Carnegie, Morgan, and Vanderbilt each accepted a formal position in the new garden's managerial ranks: Vanderbilt served as the garden's first president, Carnegie as its first vice president, and Morgan as its first treasurer (Mickulas 2007, 63). An 1893 letter to Britton from one of the garden managers, Charles Cox, conveys the extent to which Vanderbilt and Morgan engaged themselves in fundraising:

> My Dear Dr. Britton: . . . Mr. C Vanderbilt has started to get on paper the subscriptions to the Botanical Garden that have been promised in sums less than $25,000. His idea is not to have it generally known that these small subscriptions are being taken, but yet to get them down in black and white as fast as he hears of them, and to quietly obtain new ones without prejudicing Mr. Morgan's scheme for completing the larger list. He has also undertaken to poke Mr. Morgan up a little.[13]

The vast fortunes by which the United States had become a much more unequal society thus opened the door for a scale of support unimaginable from private citizens in the early republic (Zunz 2011). It might be tempting to see the Gilded Age fortunes as apples ripe for the picking, but this is not a story of mere availability of great wealth. These fortunes had to be diverted away from conspicuous consumption to public purposes. Britton showed great aptitude for this repurposing, inserting a significant, sustained research component into his plan for the garden and tying it to doctoral studies at Columbia University, two aims quite distant from the interests of his industrialist supporters.

To realize their vision of New York as the "chief city of the New World," Carnegie, Morgan, Vanderbilt, Rockefeller, and their fellow elites needed cultural and scientific institutions on a par with those sustained by royal patronage in Europe. These elites also needed talented experts such as Britton to organize and administer their complex philanthropic organizations. Here, too, a seismic shift had taken place between Hosack's time and Britton's, which we summarize in table 6.1. During the early years of the republic, a typical New York civic organization in the arts and sciences was organized, funded, and given its mission and content by the selfsame individuals. By the Gilded Age, this knot of roles had been pulled apart into separate strands: Carnegie was the philanthropist, but Britton was the expert. Philanthropic patronage enabled nonprofit organizations, and a new class of professional experts became their managers (DiMaggio 1991). Beginning in the 1880s, a sharp rise in the number of learned societies founded in the United States signaled the advent of that new class of experts, a process we analyze in

13. Charles F. Cox to Nathaniel Britton, Mar. 8, 1893, Addison Brown Papers, Mertz Library, NYBG.

Table 6.1   Changes in civic organization in nineteenth-century New York City

	Early Republic	Gilded Age
Primary organizational type in arts and sciences	Member-serving societies, funded by participants	Public-serving institutions, funded by patronage
Organizational goals	Education and refinement of members; general elevation of New York City and the young United States	Education and refinement of New York City citizens; general elevation of New York City
Organizational structure	Subscription based (managers, funders, and beneficiaries same people)	Expert managers (managers distinct from funders; beneficiaries include both but also broader public)
Examples	Society for the Promotion of Agriculture, Arts, and Manufactures (1792), New-York Historical Society (1804), Literary and Philosophical Society (1814)	Metropolitan Museum of Art (1870), American Museum of Natural History (1874), Metropolitan Opera (1883), New York Public Library (1895)

the next section. Figure 6.6 provides an overview of the transformation of associational life from small member- and other-serving organizations to expert-managed, large-scale institutions. This growth process was supported by the increase in access over the course of the nineteenth century to the rights of incorporation and legal protections, as documented by Bloch and Lamoreaux in this volume (chapter 7).

6.3.3   From Polymaths to Professionals: Changes in the Organization of Nineteenth-Century Knowledge

The status and power of experts in the late nineteenth century contrast sharply with the organization of knowledge in Hosack's era. The pursuit of knowledge in early New York—botanical or otherwise—was largely the domain of polymaths such as Hosack who pursued a calling while exploring many fields in a variety of formal and informal settings. Hosack himself was involved not only with the study of medicine, his official profession, but also botany, history, literature, manufacturing, agriculture, the visual arts, and natural history. This range of interests was the rule in his circles, rather than the exception; indeed, some of his contemporaries outstripped him in the breadth of their pursuits.[14]

14. As but one illustration, Samuel Latham Mitchill, a prominent New York doctor who went on to co-found the Rutgers Medical School, held professorships in natural history, chemistry, agriculture, botany, and medicine—and was an expert in ichthyology (Baatz 1990, 10). He was also a founder of both the NYSSPAAM and the Lyceum of Natural History of New York. He was a member of the New-York Historical Society, the Free School Society, the Literary and Philosophical Society, the New-York Horticultural Society, the New-York Hospital, the Calliopean Society, and the Friendly Club (Aberbach 1988). He also served as a president of the abolitionist Manumission Society and as a US senator from New York.

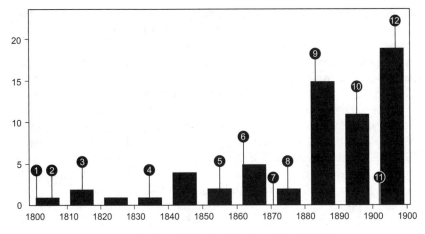

Number of learned societies founded in the U.S.[1]

❶ 1802—New York Academy of the Fine Arts founded
❷ 1805—New York Free School Society founded
❸ 1814—Literary and Philosophical Society founded
❹ 1834—New York Female Moral Reform Society founded
❺ 1854—Astor Library opened
❻ 1861—U.S. Sanitary Commission created by President Lincoln
❼ 1870—Metropolitan Museum of Art incorporated
❽ 1874—American Museum of Natural History founded
❾ 1883—Metropolitan Opera opened
❿ 1895—New York Public Library created out of a merger of the Astor and Lenox Libraries
⓫ 1902—General Education Board created by John D. Rockefeller
⓬ 1907—Russell Sage Foundation created by Margaret Olivia Slocum Sage

Fig. 6.6   Transformation of associational life in nineteenth-century New York City and United States

[1] Joseph Kiger, ed., *Research Institutions and Learned Societies*, Westport, Conn.: Greenwood Press, 1992.

In New York City in the early republic, botany was a rare pursuit. At best, it was among the most neglected of the many artistic and scientific topics that a cultivated "gentleman" might study; few colleges anywhere in the United States had dedicated professorships in botany (Rudolph 1996, 661). American botany was almost entirely an amateur endeavor. By the time Britton was working to found the NYBG, the conditions in which scientific knowledge was pursued had changed dramatically. In the early nineteenth century, the fields of law and medicine had seen an increase in expertise via the introduction of educational reforms, the establishment of board exams and licenses, and the diffusion of local, state, and national professional associations (Abbott 1988). The expansion of access by the mid-nineteenth century to organizational settings in which such work could be coordinated and pursued helped accelerate these developments. In the arts and sciences, the social production of the disciplinary "expert" took place more slowly, but by the 1870s, polymaths such as Britton's teacher John Strong Newberry—physician, geologist, botanist, and president of the multidisciplinary Lyceum of Natural History—were on the verge of extinction. Increasingly, academic scientists were professionalizing extant organizations such as the Lyceum or founding new ones that distanced themselves from the applied emphasis of amateur scientific societies and instead embraced the pursuit of science for its own sake. Scientists in many different fields also founded increasing numbers of specialized journals for the publication of discipline-based research. In New York botanical circles, this process began in 1870, with the Torrey Botanical Club's launch at Columbia of an academic journal dedicated to botany. In this setting, the first students, including Nathaniel Britton, were formed as professional botanists—rather than in the prior, broader category of natural historian. In the process, these scientists were effectively "restricting the rank of specialist to academics" (Sloan 1980, 48).

The trend toward specialization in the sciences can be read in Britton's own organizational affiliations. Unlike Hosack, who practiced his chosen profession of medicine while engaging with many other fields, Britton focused exclusively on academic science in general and botany in particular. As his career progressed, the organizations with which he was involved grew in scope and complexity. Britton was either a founder or an early member of the Torrey Botanical Club, the New York Academy of Sciences, the Natural Science Association of Staten Island, the Scientific Alliance of New York, the Botanical Society of America, and the American Association for the Advancement of Science, which became the preeminent scientific association in the United States. Through these organizations, he played a central role in forging the profession of scientific botany. His engagement with the production of botanical expertise gave him a platform from which to assert the scientific importance of botany for its own sake and thus an additional argument for the importance of a world-class botanical garden.[15]

At the same time, the transformation of Columbia from the struggling, indebted college of the early republic into the wealthy university of the late

15. One might be tempted to conclude that Hosack had trouble establishing New York's first botanical garden because he was a gentleman dabbler, whereas Britton, who succeeded, was an expert and a professional. We have shown that Hosack was indeed active in many fields and organizations, whereas Britton focused intensively on botany throughout his career. Did this intense specialization give Britton an advantage over Hosack that could explain the former's success and the latter's difficulty? Such an explanation would depend on the retrospective projection of contemporary values onto a historically distant social context. From the vantage point of the present, the expert Britton resembles our picture of organizational success rather more closely than the experimenting Hosack. In the early republic, however, men such as Hosack, along with his contemporaries Jefferson, Clinton, and Livingston, were politically and organizationally effective precisely because of—not in spite of—their wide-ranging interests and accomplishments, which were the source not only of knowledge and skills but also of great social prestige and many contacts. In the cultural and scientific milieu of the early nineteenth century, breadth and variety of pursuits were assets, not liabilities.

nineteenth century gave Britton access to resources that were simply nonexistent in Hosack's day. This expansion was, of course, spurred by New York City's population growth, but it was also tightly coupled with a national rise in specialization modeled on European academic systems. In the early republic, Columbia occupied a single building at Park Place, comprised an "arts" faculty and a medical faculty, and graduated just sixteen students in 1800. The college was often in the red and asked for repeated loans from the state legislature (McCaughey 2003). After the Civil War, however, national trends toward credentialing in the arts, sciences, and professions increased the demand for advanced degrees, driving up enrollments and tuition income. The first American PhD was granted by Yale University in 1861. Between 1861 and 1869, twelve PhDs were granted; between 1870 and 1880, the number jumped to 281.[16] This increased demand dovetailed with trends toward specialization among academics, and by 1893, Columbia was composed of not only its original college and school of medicine but also half a dozen graduate schools.[17] Its endowment had skyrocketed as well, thanks in part to rent from its Manhattan real estate—including the former site of the Elgin Botanic Garden, donated to Columbia by the state in 1814. In the 1890s, Seth Low presided over the construction of an expansive new campus in northern Manhattan.

Columbia's wealth in Britton's era contrasted sharply with the impoverished college of Hosack's day. Hosack's Columbia did not manage to make even the first of the annual payments of 300 pounds they had promised him for the new botanical garden in 1797 (Robbins 1964). Yet it was not at all inevitable that the Gilded Age administrators of Columbia would use their funds to support a botanical garden. Thanks to Britton's deep involvement in professional botany and his authority as a scientific expert, he occupied a position from which he both drove the process of specialization and reaped its academic and organizational rewards. For Britton, the primary reward was Columbia's financial, administrative, and reputational support in the creation of the NYBG.[18] Columbia's growth was mirrored nationally, as the

16. Pierson (1983, 22) and Gartner et al. (2006).

17. http://beatl.barnard.columbia.edu/stand_columbia/TimelineECU.htm. Accessed Jan. 3, 2013.

18. We noted earlier that our case comparison differs from traditional Mill-inspired methods. To throw into relief the differences between distinct macrohistorical conditions, we have chosen two efforts to introduce the same form to the same geographic region. This means that we face a version of an analytical challenge familiar to comparative-historical researchers: the possibility of actors' learning from one case to another, in a manner that muddies the causal relations. For many comparative-historical researchers, this concern takes the form of possible diffusion across national boundaries; for our two cases, diffusion is temporal rather than geographical. Did Britton succeed because he learned from Hosack's mistakes? Britton, as a member of the Torrey Botanical Club, founded by John Torrey, who had studied with Hosack, would likely have learned that Hosack had tried and failed to establish a botanical garden in New York ninety years earlier. Nonetheless, the historical context had changed so dramatically that Hosack's limitations, even if they had been clear to Britton, would have been irrelevant. Politically, culturally, and organizationally, Britton's world was fundamentally different. The

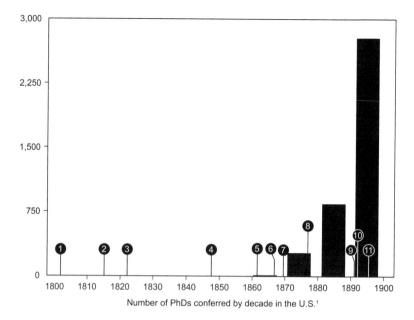

Number of PhDs conferred by decade in the U.S.[1]

❶ 1801—Elgin Botanic Garden founded
❷ 1815—Elgin dismantled by Columbia College
❸ 1822—New York Horticultural Society incorporated
❹ 1848—American Association for the Advancement of Science (AAAS) founded
❺ 1863—National Academy of Sciences founded
❻ 1867—Torrey Botanical Club founded
❼ 1870—Columbia's Torrey Botanical Club begins publishing academic botany journal
❽ 1877—Lyceum of Natural History of New York renamed the New York Academy of Sciences
❾ 1891—Columbia's Department of Botany founded
❿ 1893—Botanists of the AAAS formalize their section into the independent Botanical Society of America
⓫ 1896–97—Columbia College becomes Columbia University and moves to new Morningside Heights
        campus

Fig. 6.7   Transformation of science and botany in nineteenth-century New York City and United States

[1] Scott Sigmund Gartner, Michael R. Haines, Alan L. Olmstead, Richard Sutch, and Gavin Wright. "Degrees Conferred by Institutions of Higher Education, by Degree and Sex." Table Bc568–587. *Historical Statistics of the United States.* Edited by Susan B. Carter. New York: Cambridge University Press, 2006.

academy, and with it doctoral education, expanded markedly. (Figure 6.7 highlights the professionalization of science and botany and documents the sharp increase in academic credentialing that began in the 1870s.)

steps Britton took were skilled in his context and taken toward that context, rather than oriented away from Hosack's project. Moreover, we find no archival evidence that Britton was a beneficiary of a "second mover" advantage, in which he capitalized on Hosack's earlier failure to gain traction for the Elgin Botanic Garden.

6.3.4   The Propagation of an Organizational Form

Britton's success in establishing the New York Botanical Garden is evident in its 125 years of scientific and aesthetic achievements. For a new form to transform the organizational landscape, however, it must take on a life of its own, propagating beyond the original into new geographical and cultural domains. In creating the NYBG, Britton touched many cities far beyond the boundaries of New York, as his organization inspired a wave of garden foundings across the country. This new form also had ramifications outside the world of botany. The NYBG, the American Museum of Natural History, and the Metropolitan Museum of Art became exemplars of expert-led, privately financed organizations committed to cultivating knowledge and offering public enrichment.

The celebration of New York's world-class botanical garden in the national press as well as via social networks of wealthy citizens and professional networks of botanists and horticulturists led to a proliferation of botanical gardens across the United States.[19] In 1895, covering the founding of the NYBG from the other end of the continent, the Portland *Oregonian* ambitiously predicted that "the New World will show in 10 years from now as many botanical gardens as the Old" (*Oregonian*, December 27, 1895, 6). The prestige of the New York project and its leaders helped forge an association between botanical gardens and strong civic cultures. Wealthy civic leaders in other communities took their cue from the Manhattan elites who had successfully advanced the idea that an important city—whether American or European—included a botanical garden among its major institutions. Soon after Britton launched his campaign in New York, Pittsburgh's Henry Phipps—Andrew Carnegie's boyhood friend and longtime business partner—made a gift to his fellow citizens of a small botanical garden, hiring the same firm as Britton (Lord & Burnham Co.) to design the conservatory. In 1895, civic leaders in Buffalo established a botanical garden that also included a Lord & Burnham conservatory; the same year saw a similar establishment in Columbus. In 1896, a movement was begun for a garden in Baltimore (*Sun*, May 14, 1896, 1). In 1904, Detroit opened a botanical garden on Belle Isle, an island in the Detroit River that had been landscaped in the 1880s by Frederick Law Olmsted. In 1910, Brooklyn, which had been an independent city until 1898 and whose elites long sought to establish an array of cultural and scientific institutions to rival Manhattan, opened its

19. For national coverage of the first years of the NYBG, see, for example, "Botanical Garden Proposed," *Oregonian*, Feb. 22, 1891; "Topics in New York: A Great Display of Fine Orchids," *Sun* (Baltimore), Mar. 3, 1891; "New York," *Duluth News-Tribune*, May 2, 1891; "Topics in New York: How Public Spirit Increases and the City Is Improving," *Sun*, July 21, 1893; "A Botanical Garden: New Enterprise Full of Promise for New York City's Welfare," *Oregonian*, Aug. 15, 1895; "New York's Botanical Garden," *Kansas City Star*, Sept. 1, 1895.

own botanical garden (Brooklyn Institute of Arts and Sciences 1909). As the Brooklyn Botanic Garden was being organized during the first decade of the twentieth century, its creators turned repeatedly to Nathaniel Britton for plant specimens to help build their new collections as well as for administrative and botanical advice. More distant cities, too, soon saw the creation of gardens through partnerships between wealthy citizens and botanical experts, with San Francisco opening one in 1926 and Miami in 1938. In short, the NYBG helped define a major early twentieth-century American city as a place where it was de rigueur to maintain not only an art museum, a theater, a symphony, and an opera house, but also a botanical garden.

The establishment of the NYBG also affected the contours of associational and professional life closer to home. If Britton and his wealthy backers benefited from the legitimacy of partnerships between elite funders and semiprofessional directors that emerged in the 1870s and 1880s with the founding of the American Museum of Natural History, the Metropolitan Museum of Art, and the Metropolitan Opera, the highly public success of the NYBG added strength and visibility to this professional model. The earliest of these Gilded Age institutions were directed by polymaths, whereas many of the civic organizations founded after the NYBG were led by specialists trained in academic settings.[20] The business leaders who founded the Brooklyn Botanic Garden in 1910 recruited Dr. Charles Stuart Gager, a professor of botany at the University of Missouri, as its first director (Svenson 1944, 1–2). Under two decades later, the Museum of Modern Art was established with financial backing from Mrs. John D. Rockefeller Jr. and two other arts patrons; they chose as its founding director a Wellesley art history professor, Alfred H. Barr Jr. (Chernow 1999, 647). In 1907, Margaret Olivia Slocum Sage created the Russell Sage Foundation to improve living conditions for the poor, appointing lawyer John M. Glenn as its first director (*American Sociological Review* 1950, 680). The rise in status and power of professional experts in the late nineteenth and early twentieth century was perhaps most fully embodied by the Social Science Research Council, founded in New York City in 1923. Funded by the Rockefellers and organized by Charles E. Merriam, a Chicago professor who was president of the American Political Science Association, the SSRC brought together representatives from the leading social scientific professional associations—the American Economic Association, the American Historical Association, the American Psychological Association, the American Sociological Society, and the American Statistical Association—to foster expert knowledge for the improvement of public policy.

20. The first director of the American Museum of Natural History, John David Wolfe, was a retired businessman who dedicated his later years to philanthropic activities (Duyckinck 1872). The first director of the Metropolitan Museum of Art, Luigi Palma di Cesnola, was a soldier and diplomat who brought antiquities back to New York from a posting to Cyprus (Peterson 1986, 162).

These organizations represented a new era in American philanthropy, one in which academically trained experts became the mediators between public service and private trust. Before the Civil War, philanthropic activity in the United States had been overseen by men whose true careers lay in other domains. By century's end, the accumulation of enormous fortunes by men such as Carnegie, Morgan, Rockefeller, and Vanderbilt—whose religious leanings and reputational anxieties inclined them toward public largesse—had opened the floodgates for giving on a scale previously unseen in the States (Zunz 2011; Horvath and Powell 2016). As these tycoons sought advice on the disbursement of their money, men of learning and vision stepped forward to help them create the organizational vehicles. City and state officials offered financial and regulatory support for such philanthropic efforts when they saw in them opportunities to tackle problems attendant on urban growth and inequality.

Nathaniel Britton's success in fusing these disparate sources of support to create the NYBG, with himself as academic expert at the helm, gave force and substance to the spillover of a research-based garden into related professional domains. As further illustration of this reshaping of civic life, two organizations founded by Andrew Carnegie in the years following his involvement with the NYBG—the Carnegie Foundation (1906) and the Carnegie Corporation (1911)—took as their mission the production of expert knowledge in education, economics, the law, and a range of other disciplines (Lagemann 1989). Thus Britton's success with his botanical garden reverberated not only across the country, but also back into the academic world from which he had come and out into the wider world of professional philanthropy. Professional expertise was now sought not only inside the walls of the academy; professional renown became attached to the exercise of that specialized knowledge in the wider public sphere. A new cadre of elite academics was born, men who could cross among the privileged worlds of the university, foundations, and influential nonprofit organizations (DiMaggio 1991).

6.4   Discussion

In this section, we show that the concept of poisedness offers analytic purchase for identifying those moments when the political and economic context and the efforts of enterprising individuals combine to create possibilities for new forms. Our first point concerns the shift from project- and population-level analysis to multidomain, macrohistorical analysis. We began our case comparison with concepts that have often been used in isolation from a specific place and time. We set our analysis of the emergence of a new organizational form squarely in the midst of historical processes unfolding in nineteenth-century America. This approach leads us to think rather differently about the concepts of project, biography, template, and skill.

Given their considerable abilities, Hosack and Britton might well have had equal chances at success. But rather than seeing the founding of two botanical gardens through the eyes of two gifted men, we examine their efforts in the context of the rise of environmental and preservation movements and the almost complete urbanization of Manhattan Island over the course of the nineteenth century. We have shown that a botanical garden—an organization that would physically protect a piece of land from urban development and make it available for scientific research and aesthetic enjoyment—made sense by the century's end in ways that were unthinkable at its beginning.

But it is not only the organizational template of a garden that had different meanings; the skills of David Hosack and Nathaniel Britton were perceived differently as well. Hosack was the preeminent doctor of New York City, concerned with matters of public health and the training of the new cadre of young physicians, worried about how a young republic would survive without colonial resources and access to knowledge. Britton was a university professor, adept at research, marshaling evidence, organizing meetings, and building professional societies. His professional skills would have found little traction in 1801; indeed, a man of university science did not exist then. The early nineteenth century was an era in which breadth and variety of pursuits were the order of the day.

Thus the impact of macrolevel structures on the success of organizational projects does not depend solely on the knowledge or mobilization of those processes by individuals. To be sure, savvy innovators often recognize the way historical winds are blowing. Britton clearly saw the power of invoking the language of scientific expertise, yet he held the status of expert in botany not because he had sought it in order to see his project through, but because he matured in an intellectual era in which academic specialization in a branch of the natural sciences brought this esteem. Hosack had no such options. His notable biography included being the attending doctor at the duel of two of the most famous men in America. He could correspond with President Jefferson and converse with New York's most influential citizens, but he could not fashion a compelling case for a research-based garden at a time when land was plentiful. Transformations unfolded over the nineteenth century to produce new categories of persons (the expert, the preservationist, and the philanthropist) and different ways of thinking about the uses of a botanical garden (scientific progress, education of the public, enjoyment of a natural world that was disappearing). Britton and his botanical garden were the beneficiaries of these new categories of actor and thought.

To make the concept of poisedness empirically tractable, one needs to consider not only the presence of structural availability for an organizational innovation, but also its degree and duration. Different social settings will display greater or lesser poisedness for the emergence of particular organizational forms; at the same time, the availability of a given setting is temporally bounded and can be thought of as a window that opens for a time and then closes again. In our case comparison, an initial examination using the concepts of project, biography, template, and skill drew our attention to three decisive macrolevel processes with mesolevel reverberations: changes in the material environment, the character of civil society, and the organization of expert knowledge and intellectual life. Individually, as we have shown, each of these processes supported Britton's efforts to establish a botanical garden. These three processes also intertwined supportively with one another, thus affording Britton an exceptionally strong platform for the kind of organization he envisioned.

The transformation of the natural world during the nineteenth century at the hands of industrialists and real estate tycoons, many of whom chose to reside in New York, produced fortunes on a scale unimaginable in Hosack's day and at the disposal of private citizens. The concomitantly increasing complexity of private industrial, commercial, and financial operations fostered the emergence of a managerial class (Chandler 1977). At the same time, specialization and professionalization in the arts and sciences were giving rise to a cadre of experts via graduate training and credentialing. "[C]apital-owning New Yorkers admitted experts and managers to their social networks and cultural institutions because these networks and institutions themselves were central to their economic projects and could not exclude those who played important roles in running factories, merchant houses, and banks" (Beckert 2001, 254). The Gilded Age was not only the era in which high culture became a resource for the elite, it was also a period of emergence for a new professional, managerial, and intellectual class who did not share the ancestry of the elite but gained access to New York's institutions of cultural capital (Accominotti, Khan, and Storer 2017).

These experts would be critical to the creation and management of Gilded Age scientific and cultural institutions. Exposed through extensive travel to European history and habits, wealthy New Yorkers sought to create not only private surroundings but also public institutions on a par with those bankrolled by royalty in Europe. Some of these institutions responded to meet concerns about wholesome and edifying relaxation opportunities for the leisured and working classes alike. And in a related process, the heavy build-up of Manhattan triggered worries about hygiene and aesthetics; the New York Park Association was populated by many of the same industrialists who had joined together to create the American Museum of Natural History, the Metropolitan Museum of Art, Carnegie Hall, and other Gilded Age institutions. Finally, the development of Manhattan had also been the source of some of Columbia's good financial fortune, via its many property leases, in the second half of the nineteenth century. The expansion of Columbia from a small college into a complex university, in turn, supported Britton in his project both reputationally and financially.

The concatenation of these three lines of development, illustrated in table 6.2, meant that by approximately 1880, the previously separate domains

Table 6.2   **Impact of macrolevel shifts on meso- and microlevel processes**

Macro level (regional, national) shifts	Early Republic		Gilded Age	
	Impact on meso level (organizational)	Impact on micro level (individual)	Impact on meso level (organizational)	Impact on micro level (individual)
Material environment	Availability of land means no urgency re: preservation and beautification.	Hosack does not appeal to (or think of) preservation or beautification.	High urbanization gives rise to parks movement, mobilizing network of concerned elites.	Preservation and beautification of green space are salient arguments to which Britton can appeal.
Civic organization	Two organizational models: member serving and serving the needy; a botanical garden fit neither model.	Hosack has no natural constituency to mobilize; elites who praise garden are not direct beneficiaries and do not fund it; the most direct beneficiaries (medical students and farmers) are not in a position to fund it.	Rise in private fortunes, social climbing, social problems, and social gospel give life by 1880s to models of private-public collaboration, such as the Metropolitan Museum of Art and the American Museum of Natural History.	Britton profits from the familiarity of NYC citizens with these organizational templates and past civic successes.
Organization of expert knowledge	Elites are polymaths, but botany is not part of requisite education of a gentleman, as is learning in history and visual arts; hence the founding of the Historical Society and the Academy of Fine Arts, but not an Academy of Botany, and no private-elite funding for a botanical garden.	Hosack cannot mobilize private support for a specialist-training organization.	Rise in trust of experts in business, culture, and science meant familiarity of potential private funders with managerial model; establishment of department of botany at Columbia both signified and reinforced new status of botany as a science.	Britton can argue that botany *as a science* merits its own organization; he can also mobilize support for himself as expert.

of environmental consciousness, public-private initiatives, and academic science could be drawn together to fashion a vision for the NYBG. The ramifications of these cross-field effects opened new possibilities, unanticipated in any one domain alone. Thus the interlocking changes in the material environment, in modes of civic organization and philanthropy, and in the organization of expert knowledge coalesced in ways that strengthened the odds of Britton's success and, in turn, influenced ambitious civic elites across the country to establish botanical gardens in their own cities. Put sharply, Britton's project benefited from a very high degree of poisedness in his social and material context. It is for this reason above all that Britton was successful compared to Hosack, who did not have the winds of historical change at his back.

The poisedness of social structures profoundly shapes the chances of entrepreneurial projects, regardless how skilled the individual innovator. The structural characteristics we have analyzed are essential to explaining the divergent outcomes of these two efforts to create a botanical garden because they reveal two starkly different moments. Conceptually, poisedness captures the strength of concatenation among macro- and mesolevel processes, both laterally and vertically, vis-à-vis microlevel efforts at organizational innovation. The concept of poisedness also emphasizes how "evolvable" these relations are. By this we mean whether lateral and vertical spillovers to other geographic locales and related lines of work offer amplification for individual efforts at entrepreneurship.

A significant advantage of our approach is that it avoids the pitfalls of conflating instances of individual success with the structural availability that enabled their realization. Organization scholars have long recognized the challenges of studying failure and absence (Hannan and Freeman 1986; Powell, Packalen, and Whittington 2012). Organizational failures provide critical information for scholars seeking to understand the sources of success, yet failed efforts to found a new organization often yield limited records and therefore hinder data collection. Even more challenging is the study of organizational absence. When and why are specific kinds of organizations not being founded—or even conceived of at all? Answering these difficult questions is critical to the project of explaining how skilled actors do, on occasion, produce profound and wide-ranging organizational innovation.

Our analysis of nineteenth-century New York demonstrates that conditions were not receptive for the establishment and spread of a research- and teaching-intensive botanical garden in the United States until approximately 1880. Our overarching argument is not purely a structural one, however. Poisedness does not produce innovation absent individual effort. Britton's ultimate and resounding success in introducing a new organizational form was by no means inevitable. He worked tirelessly for many years as he developed and framed his organizational template; met with wealthy, public-spirited citizens such as Carnegie, Morgan, and Vanderbilt; pushed Columbia to partner with the garden; wrote opinion pieces and gave speeches about the need for a garden at clubs and associations; lobbied the city and state governments for land, subsidies, and building permits; announced requests for proposals; allocated contracts; and oversaw the landscaping and planting of the grounds. In short, Britton capitalized on the poisedness of his social setting with dogged persistence and consummate skill, in a manner akin to the entrepreneurs and activists documented by the literature on institutional entrepreneurship and social movements. We find these literatures lacking, however, with respect to the *origins* of those actors who are able to realize the potential inherent in particular social settings.

Scholars of institutional entrepreneurship and social movements have pointed out that individuals positioned at the intersection between organizational fields are most likely to recognize opportunities for organizational innovation. We agree there is ample evidence that positioning is important. Yet although attempts at organizational innovation are undertaken all the time, such efforts rarely succeed, and even more infrequently do they alter activities outside of their local context. We can see as much in David Hosack's valiant efforts to introduce a new organizational form, where in spite of his efforts he ended up reinforcing the organizational world he wished to change. One might say that the window of opportunity was closed to him; indeed, the archival evidence strongly suggests that no one could have realized his vision for New York City at that point in its history. By the last quarter of the nineteenth century, however, Manhattan was no longer bucolic; it was crowded and congested, as the data on population density illustrate. New kinds of public-private initiatives were being created, and abundant resources were available for creating these organizations. The window of opportunity was open.

Could anyone have recognized and realized this opportunity? We think not. To be sure, the linkages between material, organizational, and professional conditions afforded a scaffolding that supported the emergence of new organizational models. But for these new organizations to grow in scale and influence they needed people at their helm who could fuse private wealth with public-serving goals. The key to combining private money with public interests was the ability to harness the impartiality of professional expertise. Professional learned societies were one such domain of judgment, and they were populated by a growing number of experts in the form of newly minted PhDs. And in the years after the Civil War, the organization of social services and of educational and cultural activities passed from churches and almshouses to formal, bureaucratically structured public and nonprofit organizations. Philanthropy as a large-scale activity rose to unprecedented heights in the last two decades of the century when men such as Carnegie, Rockefeller, and others began dispersing their vast fortunes.

In crossing the domains of wealth, culture, and science, innovations were not simply carried from one realm to another as a form of export. New opportunities were created and amplified by such crossings. This transformed context made possible novel forms of organizing, but it also produced a new kind of actor: the scientific expert and manager. Nathaniel Britton was among those at the forefront of the growth of university-based science, and as a professor of botany at Columbia, he was a leader in a new field that was beginning to coalesce in academic departments and professional associations by the 1880s. Thus the very same structural processes that produced the strong poisedness of late nineteenth-century New York for the botanical garden form also produced the managerial and botanical expert Nathaniel Britton, who was by disposition and knowledge highly equipped to realize that potential.

6.5 Conclusion

In his classic essay, Stinchcombe (1965, 150) suggested a host of factors—"(a) general literacy and specialized advanced schooling; (b) urbanization; (c) a money economy; (d) political revolution; (e) a dense social life, including an already rich organizational life"—that catalyze organization building. In our two cases, David Hosack toiled in a young democracy formed by political revolution, with a mercantile economy and general literacy, but Nathaniel Britton worked a different soil, rich with a diverse organizational life and a growing specialization of knowledge, in a dense urban setting. The dominant associational form of the late nineteenth century was one in which funders, managers, and beneficiaries were separate; the expert professor, Britton, was a welcome intermediary who could cross these milieux. The donor-funded, expert-managed garden meshed closely with other Gilded Age scientific and cultural institutions bankrolled by private donors, managed by experts, and open to the New York City public. The organizational landscape was sloped in Britton's favor. His expertise was a sought-after commodity, which immunized him from the social and economic cleavages of his day. In contrast, Hosack's Elgin Botanic Garden was a victim of cultural and geopolitical struggles.

These two cases demonstrate that novelty arises from feedback among multiple social networks across material, organizational, and intellectual domains (Padgett and Powell 2012). Poisedness concerns not just enabling conditions or opportunity structures of the sort that Stinchcombe so usefully identified, but the concatenation of social, political, and economic forces that make new forms possible. The emergence of new categories of people and organization in our historical analysis was the result of new possibilities at the micro-, meso-, and macrolevels, which expanded the opportunities available at the end of the nineteenth century. This poisedness had fundamentally different ramifications not only for David Hosack and Nathaniel Britton, but for New York City in the nineteenth century as well.

We urge caution in how the idea of poisedness is used. It should not be thought of crudely as implying fitness or timely alignment. Social structures indeed both constrain and generate options, but there are always spaces in which struggles and oppositional framings can occur. Nor are we claiming simply that history and context matter. To be analytically meaningful, research must specify the contours and limitations of context. Without the discipline of a deductive framework, multi-level historical analyses can become ad hoc. Our contextual refinement, which enabled us to argue that Britton's world was more poised than Hosack's, is twofold. First, within the context of New York City in the nineteenth century, attitudes about the material world, appropriate beneficiaries of services, and the uses of expertise were critical in shaping responses to proposals for new types of organizations. Second, in the first decades of the nineteenth century, these elements all worked against David Hosack, but by century's end, these elements began to buttress one another, creating self-reinforcing linkages that enabled the emergence of new types of actors, social relationships, and organizations. When we see such overlays of the social-structural landscape, we find cascading moments of poisedness of the type we have analyzed here, in which circumstances are receptive to new forms of organization.

References

Abbott, Andrew. 1988. *The System of Professions: An Essay on the Division of Expert Labor*. Chicago: University of Chicago Press.

———. 2001. *Time Matters: On Theory and Method*. Chicago: University of Chicago Press.

Aberbach, Alan David. 1988. *In Search of an American Identity: Samuel Latham Mitchill, Jeffersonian Nationalist*. New York: Peter Lang.

Accominotti, Fabien, Shamus Khan, and Adam Storer. 2017. "How Cultural Capital Emerged in Gilded Age America: Musical Purification and Cross-Class Inclusion at the New York Philharmonic." Working Paper, Department of Sociology, London School of Economics.

Arthur, Brian. 1994. *Increasing Returns and Path Dependence in the Economy*. Ann Arbor: University of Michigan Press.

Baatz, Simon. 1990. *Knowledge, Culture, and Science in the Metropolis: The New York Academy of Sciences, 1817–1970*. New York: New York Academy of Sciences.

Beckert, Sven. 2001. *The Moneyed Metropolis: New York City and the Consolidation of the American Bourgeoisie, 1850–1896*. Cambridge: Cambridge University Press.

Bender, Thomas. 1987. *New York Intellect: A History of Intellectual Life in New York City from 1750 to the Beginnings of Our Own Time*. Baltimore: Johns Hopkins University Press.

Britton, Nathaniel Lord. 1891. (Typescript, No Title.) Mertz Library, New York Botanical Garden.

———. 1896. "Botanical Gardens: Origin and Development." *Science* 4 (88): 284–93.

Brockway, Lucile H. (1979) 2002. *Science and Colonial Expansion: The Role of the British Royal Botanic Gardens*. New Haven, CT: Yale University Press.

Brooklyn Institute of Arts and Sciences. 1909. *Prospectus.* New York: Brooklyn Institute of Arts and Sciences.

Bryant, William Cullen. 1844. "A New Public Park." *New-York Evening Post*, July 3.

Burrows, Edwin G., and Mike Wallace. 1999. *Gotham.* New York: Oxford University Press.

Burton, M. Diane, Jesper B. Sørensen, and Christine M. Beckman. 2002. "Coming from Good Stock: Career Histories and New Venture Formation." *Research in the Sociology of Organizations* 19:229–62.

Chandler, Alfred D., Jr. 1977. *The Visible Hand: The Managerial Revolution in American Business.* Cambridge, MA: Harvard University Press.

Chernow, Ron. 1999. *Titan: The Life of John D. Rockefeller, Sr.* New York: Vintage.

———. 2004. *Alexander Hamilton.* New York: Penguin.

Clemens, Elisabeth S. 1993. "Organizational Repertoires and Institutional Change: Women's Groups and the Transformation of US Politics, 1890–1920." *American Journal of Sociology* 98 (4): 755–98.

College of Physicians and Surgeons. 1812. *The Exposition of the Transactions of the College of Physicians and Surgeons.* New York: College of Physicians and Surgeons.

Conn, Andrew R., Katya Scheinberg, and Luis N. Vicente. 2005. "Geometry of Sample Sets in Derivative Free Optimization." *IMA Journal of Numerical Analysis* 28 (4): 721–48.

Crocker, Ruth. 2003. "From Gift to Foundation: The Philanthropic Lives of Mrs. Russell Sage." In *Charity, Philanthropy, and Civility in American History*, edited by Lawrence J. Friedman and Mark D. McGarvie, 199–215. Cambridge: Cambridge University Press.

Demographia. 2001. "New York (Manhattan) Wards: Population & Density 1800–1910." Accessed Jan. 3, 2013. http://www.demographia.com/db-nyc-ward1800.htm.

DiMaggio, Paul J. 1982. "Cultural Entrepreneurship in Nineteenth-Century Boston: The Creation of an Organizational Base for High Culture in America." *Media, Culture and Society* 4 (4): 33–50.

———. 1991. "Constructing an Organizational Field as a Professional Project: US Art Museums, 1920–1940." In *The New Institutionalism in Organizational Analysis*, edited by Walter W. Powell and Paul J. DiMaggio, 267–92. Chicago: University of Chicago Press.

Domosh, Mona. 1987. "Imagining New York's First Skyscrapers, 1875–1910." *Journal of Historical Geography* 13:233–48.

Drayton, Richard. 2000. *Nature's Government: Science, Imperial Britain, and the "Improvement" of the World.* New Haven, CT: Yale University Press.

Duyckinck, Evert A. 1872. *A Memorial of John David Wolfe.* New York: New-York Historical Society.

Ewan, Joseph, and Nesta Dunn Ewan. 2007. *Benjamin Smith Barton: Naturalist and Physician in Jeffersonian America.* St. Louis: Missouri Botanical Garden Press.

Fligstein, Neil. 1997. "Social Skill and Institutional Theory." *American Behavioral Scientist* 40 (4): 397–405.

Fontana, Walter. 2006. "The Topology of the Possible." In *Understanding Change: Models, Methodologies, and Metaphors*, edited by Andreas Wimmer and Reinhart Kössler, 67–84. New York: Palgrave Macmillan.

Gartner, Scott Sigmund, Michael R. Haines, Alan L. Olmstead, Richard Sutch, and Gavin Wright. 2006. "Table Bc568–87: Degrees Conferred by Institutions of Higher Education, by Degree and Sex." In *Historical Statistics of the United States*, edited by Susan B. Carter. New York: Cambridge University Press.

Gleason, Henry A. 1960. "The Scientific Work of Nathaniel Lord Britton." *Proceedings of the American Philosophical Society* 104 (2): 205–26.

Greve, Henrich R., and Hayagreeva Rao. 2012. "Echoes of the Past: Organizational Foundings as Sources of an Institutional Legacy of Mutualism." *American Journal of Sociology* 118 (3): 635–75.

Grove, Carol. 2005. *Henry Shaw's Victorian Landscapes: The Missouri Botanical Garden and Tower Grove Park*. Amherst, MA: Library of American Landscape History.

Hannan, Michael T., and John Freeman. 1977. "The Population Ecology of Organizations." *American Journal of Sociology* 82 (5): 929–64.

———. 1986. "Where Do Organizational Forms Come From?" *Sociological Forum* 1 (1): 50–72.

Harvard University. 1846. *Rules and Statutes of the Professorships in the University at Cambridge*. Cambridge, MA: Metcalf and Company.

Haveman, Heather A., and Hayagreeva Rao. 2006. "Hybrid Forms and the Organization of Thrifts." *American Behavioral Scientist* 49 (7): 974–86.

Horvath, Aaron, and Walter W. Powell. 2016. "Contributory or Disruptive: Do New Forms of Philanthropy Erode Democracy?" In *Philanthropy in Democratic Societies*, edited by R. Reich, L. Bernholz, and C. Cordelli, 87–122. Chicago: University of Chicago Press.

Hosack, Alexander Eddy. 1861. "A Memoir of the Late David Hosack, M.D." In *Lives of Eminent American Physicians and Surgeons of the 19th Century*, edited by Samuel D. Gross, 289–337. Philadelphia: Lindsay & Blakiston.

Hosack, David. 1803. "Botanic Garden." *The Evening Post*, June 29, 2.

———. 1806. *Hortus Elginensis*. New York: T. & J. Swords.

———. 1810. "Description of Elgin Garden." *Portfolio and Boston Anthology*, Jan.

———. 1811. *A Statement of Facts Relative to the Establishment and Progress of the Elgin Botanic Garden, and the Subsequent Disposal of the Same to the State of New-York*. New York: C. S. Van Winkle.

Howe, Marshall A. 1934. "Nathaniel Lord Britton, 1859–1934." *Journal of the New York Botanical Garden* 35 (416): 169–80.

James, Edward J. 1910. "The Origin of the Land-Grant Act." *University of Illinois University Studies* 4 (1): 7–32.

Johnson, Victoria. Forthcoming. *David Hosack in the Garden of the Early Republic*.

Katznelson, Ira. 2003. "Periodization and Preferences." In *Comparative Historical Analysis in the Social Sciences*, edited by James Mahoney and Dietrich Rueschemeyer, 270–301. Cambridge: Cambridge University Press.

Kolodin, Irving. 1966. *The Metropolitan Opera, 1883–1966*. New York: Knopf.

Lagemann, Ellen Condliffe. 1989. *The Politics of Knowledge: The Carnegie Corporation, Philanthropy, and Public Policy*. Chicago: University of Chicago Press.

Leblebici, Huseyin, Gerald R. Salancik, Anne Copay, and Tom King. 1991. "Institutional Change and the Transformation of Interorganizational Fields: An Organizational History of the US Radio Broadcasting Industry." *Administrative Science Quarterly* 36 (3): 333–63.

Mahoney, James, and Kathleen Thelen, eds. 2010. *Explaining Institutional Change: Ambiguity, Agency, and Power*. New York: Cambridge University Press.

McAdam, Doug. 1989. "The Biographical Consequences of Activism." *American Sociological Review* 54 (5): 744–60.

McAdam, Doug, John D. McCarthy, and Mayer N. Zald. 1996. "Introduction: Opportunities, Mobilizing Structures, and Framing Processes." In *Comparative Perspectives on Social Movements*, edited by Doug McAdam, John D. McCarthy, and Mayer N. Zald, 1–22. Cambridge: Cambridge University Press.

McCaughey, Robert A. 2003. *Stand, Columbia: A History of Columbia University in the City of New York, 1754–2004*. New York: Columbia University Press.

Merrill, Elmer D. 1938. "Biographical Memoir of Nathaniel Lord Britton, 1859–1934." *National Academy of Sciences Biographical Memoirs* 19:147–202.

Mickulas, Peter. 2007. *Britton's Botanical Empire: The New York Botanical Garden and American Botany, 1888–1929*. New York: The New York Botanical Garden Press.

Mukerji, Chandra. 1997. *Territorial Ambitions and the Gardens of Versailles*. Cambridge: Cambridge University Press.

———. 2009. *Impossible Engineering: Technology and Territoriality on the Canal du Midi*. Princeton, NJ: Princeton University Press.

Mullaly, John. 1887. *The New Parks beyond the Harlem*. New York: Record & Guide.

Neem, Johann N. 2008. *Creating a Nation of Joiners: Democracy and Civil Society in Early National Massachusetts*. Cambridge, MA: Harvard University Press.

New York Academy of Sciences. 1935. "Nathaniel Lord Britton." *Science* 81 (2091): 87–88.

New York Botanical Garden. 1896. "Agreement with Columbia University." *Bulletin of the New York Botanical Garden* 1 (1): 19–20.

New York State. 1891. "An Act to Provide for the Establishment of a Botanic Garden and Museum and Arboretum, in Bronx Park in the City of New York." In *Laws of the State of New York*, 523–25. Albany, NY: Banks & Brothers.

New-York State Society for the Promotion of Agriculture, Arts, and Manufactures. 1801. *Transactions*, vol. 1, 2nd ed. Albany, NY: Charles R. and George Webster.

Padgett, John F., and Walter W. Powell. 2012. *The Emergence of Organizations and Markets*. Princeton, NJ: Princeton University Press.

Peterson, Richard A. 1986. "From Impresario to Arts Administrator: Formal Accountability in Nonprofit Arts Organizations." In *Nonprofit Enterprise in the Arts: Studies in Mission and Constraint*, edited by Paul J. DiMaggio, 161–83. Oxford: Oxford University Press.

Pierson, George W. 1983. *Yale Book of Numbers: Historical Statistics of the College and University, 1701–1976*. New Haven, CT: Yale University Press.

Powell, Walter W., Kelley Packalen, and Kjersten Whittington. 2012. "Organizational and Institutional Genesis: The Emergence of High-Tech Clusters in the Life Sciences." In *The Emergence of Organizations and Markets*, edited by John F. Padgett and Walter W. Powell, 434–65. Princeton, NJ: Princeton University Press.

Robbins, Christine Chapman. 1964. *David Hosack: Citizen of New York*. Philadelphia: American Philosophical Society.

Romayne, Nicholas. 1811. "Anniversary Address to the Medical Society of the State of New York by the President Nicholas Romayne." *New York Medical & Surgical Journal* 2:123.

Rosenzweig, Roy, and Elizabeth Blackmar. 1992. *The Park and the People*. Ithaca, NY: Cornell University Press.

Rudolph, Emanuel D. 1996. "History of the Botanical Teaching Laboratory in the United States." *American Journal of Botany* 83 (5): 661–71.

Ruef, Martin. 2000. "The Emergence of Organizational Forms: A Community Ecology Approach." *American Journal of Sociology* 106 (3): 658–714.

Rusby, Henry Hurd. 1934. "Nathaniel Lord Britton." *Science* 80 (2066): 108–11.

Scobey, David M. 2002. *Empire City: The Making and Meaning of the New York City Landscape*. Philadelphia: Temple University Press.

Scott, Anne Firor. 1993. *Natural Allies: Women's Associations in American History*. Champaign: University of Illinois Press.

Scott, Eleanor Bryce. 1933. "Early Literary Clubs in New York City." *American Literature* 5 (1): 3–16.

Sewell, William H., Jr. 2005. "Theory, History, and Social Science." In *Logics of History: Social Theory and Social Transformation*, William H. Sewell Jr., 1–21. Chicago: University of Chicago Press.

Sloan, Douglas. 1980. "Science in New York City, 1867–1907." *Isis* 71 (256): 35–76.

Stinchcombe, Arthur L. 1965. "Social Structure and Organizations." In *Handbook of Organizations*, edited by James G. March, 142–93. New York: Rand McNally.

———. 1968. *Constructing Social Theories*. New York: Harcourt Brace.

Svenson, Henry K. 1944. "C. Stuart Gager (1873–1943)." *Ecology* 25 (1): 1–2.

Taylor, Alan. 2012. *The Civil War of 1812*. New York: Vintage.

Taylor, Dorceta E. 2009. *The Environment and the People in American Cities, 1600s–1900s: Disorder, Inequality, and Social Change*. Durham, NC: Duke University Press.

Thelen, Kathleen. 2004. *How Institutions Evolve*. New York: Cambridge University Press.

Torrey Botanical Club. 1889. "Appeal for a Public Botanic Garden in New York City." Mertz Library, New York Botanical Garden.

Tye, Michael. 2000. *Consciousness, Color, and Content*. Cambridge, MA: MIT Press.

Vail, Robert W. G. 1954. *Knickerbocker Birthday: A Sesqui-Centennial History of the New-York Historical Society, 1804–1954*. New York: New-York Historical Society.

Wagner, Andreas. 2005. *Robustness and Evolvability in Living Systems*. Princeton, NJ: Princeton University Press.

Wulf, Andrea. 2008. *The Brother Gardeners*. New York: Vintage.

Zunz, Olivier. 2011. *Philanthropy in America: A History*. Princeton, NJ: Princeton University Press.

7

Voluntary Associations, Corporate Rights, and the State
Legal Constraints on the Development of American Civil Society, 1750–1900

Ruth H. Bloch and Naomi R. Lamoreaux

New Jersey farmer George Hutchins catalyzed a major legal dispute in the late 1880s by bequeathing part of his modest estate to support the propagation of political radicalism. Hutchins's will set up a trust fund dedicated to the free distribution of the writings of Henry George, the popular critic of private property and leader of New York's United Labor Party, naming George and his "heirs, executors and administrators" as the trustees managing the fund.[1] Legally, this bequest fell into the realm of charitable trust law, a contested branch of (originally British) equity law that allowed testators to give property to groups without corporate charters as long as courts deemed their purposes to be sufficiently "charitable."[2] At the urging

Ruth H. Bloch is professor emerita of history at the University of California, Los Angeles. Naomi R. Lamoreaux is the Stanley B. Resor Professor of Economics and History at Yale University and a research associate of the National Bureau of Economic Research.

We would especially like to thank John Wallis, Jonathan Levy, Sally Clarke, Johann Neem, and Jonathan Sassi, who wrote comments on an earlier draft of this chapter, and Guillaume Frencia, Brittany Adams, and Ben Nelson, who assisted us with research. In addition, we benefited from valuable feedback from the anonymous referees for the University of Chicago Press and from the participants at preparatory conferences sponsored by NBER and the Yale Program in Economic History in 2012, 2013, and 2014. For acknowledgments, sources of research support, and disclosure of the authors' material financial relationships, if any, please see http://www.nber.org/chapters/c13511.ack.

1. *Hutchins' Ex'r v. George*, 44 N.J. Eq. 124 (NJ 1888), quote at 125.
2. In England, charitable trust law had since the sixteenth century allowed specific kinds of unincorporated groups to receive legacies. In the wake of the American Revolution several states, most notably Virginia, passed statutes rejecting British practice, though most other states (including New Jersey) did not. The courts' willingness to enforce charitable trusts varied widely from state to state until the US Supreme Court, in the 1844 case *Vidal v. Girard's Executors*, 43 U.S. 127 (also known as the *Girard's Will Case*), reversed a contrary decision of 1819 by recognizing charitable trusts as an embedded feature of American common law. Soon almost all American states either tacitly or actively came to accept that unincorporated groups pursuing religious, educational, or conventionally charitable purposes could receive bequeathed property. Useful surveys of this history include Jones (1969) and Miller (1961).

of Hutchins's widow and son, the will's executor asked the state's Chancery Court to invalidate the bequest. Since the American Revolution, state courts and statutes had overturned dozens of similar wills leaving legacies to unincorporated associations.[3] The outcome of this case proved no different. New Jersey's Chancery Court rejected Hutchins's bequests on what were in effect political grounds.

The legal question at the heart of the case, according to Vice Chancellor John Taylor Bird, was "What is a charity?"[4] Reviewing the precedents, Bird conceded that some types of voluntary associations, such as evangelical missionary societies, were routinely regarded as charitable even though they aimed to destroy "existing laws, customs, institutions, and religions."[5] He also acknowledged two recent path-breaking decisions by the Massachusetts and Pennsylvania supreme courts that defined charity widely enough to encompass bequests for the dissemination of abolitionist and atheist ideas (albeit only on the condition that the trustees accept their primary goal to be education and not opposition to the law or Christianity).[6] In Bird's view, however, the purposes of the book fund were more fundamentally subversive. George's vilification of private landholding posed too great a threat to the law for the trust to stand. "Whatever might be the rights of the individual author in the discussion of such questions in the abstract, it certainly would not become the court to aid in the distribution of literature which denounces as robbery—as a crime—an immense proportion of the judicial determinations of the higher courts. This would not be legally charitable."[7]

George successfully appealed to New Jersey's high court the following year, but the damage was done. Reversing the Chancery Court's verdict, Chief Justice Mercer Beazley ruled the key issue was not George's radicalism but Hutchins's intentions. The will itself, which benignly described George's works as "spreading the light" of "liberty and justice in these United States of America," disclosed no inclination to violate the law. Rather the book fund, Beazley concluded, was best understood as akin to a library and, therefore, stood squarely within the "charitable" domain of education.[8] Nonetheless, George's hard-won victory brought little satisfaction to him and his followers. According to a biography written later by his son, legal fees devoured a sizable portion of the bequest, and the public fallout from

3. For the key cases, see Miller (1961, 21–50). Well into the twentieth century, appellate decisions about the disposition of charitable trusts for political causes continued to vary according to judges' assessments of the threats posed by the recipient groups. See Note, "Charitable Trusts for Political Purposes," *Virginia Law Review* 37 (1951): esp. 988–94.

4. *Hutchins' Ex'r v. George*, quote at 126.

5. *Hutchins' v. George*, quote at 137.

6. *Jackson v. Phillips*, 96 Mass. 539 (1867); *Manners v. Philadelphia Library Company*, 93 Pa. 165 (1880).

7. *Hutchins' v. George*, quote at 139.

8. *George v. Braddock*, 45 N.J. Eq. 757 (1889).

the case damaged George's pride and reputation.[9] He was not only injured by the vice chancellor's hostile description of his work, but was also plagued by rumors that he personally profited from the legacy.

Without question, George and his fellow trustees would have been better off had they been able to organize as a nonprofit corporation. The wills of benefactors leaving property to incorporated groups stood on firmer legal ground because corporations had a standard right to "take" or "receive" property.[10] Not only would George's organization almost certainly have avoided going to court to get this legacy, but it also would likely have acquired several other valuable rights that came with corporate status: the right to acquire property by means other than bequests, the right to buy and sell property (as well as receive it), the right to sue and be sued as a party in court, the right to offer their members limited liability for debts, and the right to legally enforceable self-governance. This impressive menu of rights remained out of reach to virtually all nineteenth-century voluntary associations that advocated social and political change because they failed to meet the judicial and statutory requirements to incorporate. The only legal recourse available to them if they were bequeathed an endowment was to claim that they qualified as a charitable trust.

Being deprived of corporate rights did not mean that such associations could not exist or, in some cases, even thrive. American citizens were remarkably free as individuals to create or join organizations of most types without having to hide from the government. As Richard Brooks and Timothy Guinnane explain in their chapter for this volume, however, there is an important distinction between the right of individuals to associate and the right of associations to a collective legal identity. To use their terminology, the early United States offered extensive rights to individuals *to associate* in loosely defined groups and even *to aggregate* in ones with mutually understood rules.[11]

---

9. George (1900, 509–10). This loyal account also claims that the legacy of around $5,000 was too small to be worth the bother, and that George initially chose not to accept the legacy out of compassion for Hutchins's widow until other "collateral kin" who stood to benefit from the defeat of the will stood in his way. A degree of skepticism is in order. First of all, many charitable trust cases involved smaller amounts. Second, Hutchins's widow herself, along with their son, were the parties opposing the bequest; the biography itself depicts George as so offended by the Chancery Court's negative decision that he fought to appeal it. Third, New Jersey gave no rights to "collateral kin" in intestate cases except in the absence of widows or children. Shammas, Salmon, and Dahlin (1987, 240–41).

10. A partial exception was the state of New York, which in 1830 passed a statute denying corporations the automatic right to receive bequests. The state legislature, however, continued routinely to grant the privilege in special charters, and New York's general incorporation act of 1848 included it for "benevolent, charitable, scientific and missionary societies." There were no suits in New York that challenged bequests to corporations in the nineteenth century, whereas there were many such cases involving unincorporated groups (which from 1846 to 1893 were uniformly blocked from receiving them by the New York Constitution and courts). See Katz, Sullivan, and Beach (1985).

11. Brooks and Guinnane (chapter 8, this volume).

At the same time, however, the government significantly restricted associations' access to the benefits that came from being *legal entities* and *legal persons*. These associational rights depended primarily on access to the state-conferred right to incorporate (and, secondarily, in the special case of bequests, on judicial definitions of charity). Nineteenth-century legislators and judges in most parts of the country routinely extended such rights to large numbers of voluntary associations they regarded as politically neutral or benign, including churches and other religious societies, educational institutions like schools and libraries, and traditional charities providing aid to the poor. By contrast, organizations that were viewed by officials as socially or politically disruptive found themselves at a significant legal disadvantage—especially when their members wished to acquire or protect property in order to advance their cause.

Our argument that the government systematically withheld valuable associational rights from politically controversial groups raises fundamental questions about the Tocquevillian portrait of the early United States as an "open access" civil society.[12] Tocqueville famously marveled at the effervescence of American voluntary associations and relished their wide-ranging purposes. In his view, the state had no hand in their success. Unlike governments "established by law," these associations were "formed and maintained by the agency of private individuals" exercising a "natural" "right of association . . . almost as inalienable in its nature as the right of personal liberty."[13] For Tocqueville, this freedom from the state enabled voluntary associations to provide a crucial check on the despotism he regarded as inherent in democratic government.

The basic Tocquevillian perspective continues to dominate scholarship on the role of voluntary societies in democratic polities. Modern theorists of civil society not surprisingly take a more positive view of democracy than Tocqueville—often, for example, highlighting the constructive role played by egalitarian groups that challenge the government—but they, too, locate voluntary associations "outside the state."[14] American historians of social and political movements similarly reinforce Tocqueville's view of an unfettered civil society by focusing on the agency of dissident activists and limiting their descriptions of government intervention to instances of criminalization or forcible repression.[15] Historians of philanthropy and religion

12. Tocqueville (1945, vol. 1, 198–205; vol. 2, 114–28); see also Habermas (1989). On the United States, in addition to Tocqueville, the now classic articulation of this view is Schlesinger (1944).

13. Tocqueville (1945, vol. 1, 198, 203).

14. See Levy (chapter 3, this volume). Levy's useful typology distinguishes between the integrative, competitive, and oppositional roles that democratic theorists commonly attribute to voluntary associations. This chapter concentrates on their oppositional role, but it might be possible to argue that their competitive and integrative roles were similarly compromised by the selective allocation of associational rights.

15. This literature, encompassing much of the subfield of social history, is far too vast to summarize in a footnote. Efforts to "bring the state back in" have simulated legal histories

acknowledge the benefit of early incorporation in the United States, but they rarely depict it as a privilege denied to disfavored groups.[16] A few recent histories of voluntary associations highlight a degree of government intervention, but they, too, either overlook the discriminatory dispensation of charters or maintain that the discrimination had largely ended by the time Tocqueville arrived.[17] Historical sociologists and political scientists vary widely in their value judgments about the social impact of voluntary associations.[18] Whether they view them as beneficial or destructive to American democracy, however, these researchers still join Tocqueville in regarding nineteenth-century voluntary associations as private, civil society organizations separate from the state.

In contrast to this scholarship, we contend that the voluntary associations so admired by Tocqueville never really operated independently of the state.[19] Instead, nineteenth-century lawmakers systematically discriminated against certain groups by constraining their access to valuable entity and personhood rights. The net effect of this process was that the political judgments of government officials skewed the development of American civil society toward conservative and acquiescent groups at the expense of oppositional ones.

Our account of this history draws on the hundreds of legislative acts and court rulings between 1750 and 1900 that shaped this lopsided allocation of rights.[20] We divide the chapter into chronological sections that highlight major changes and continuities over time: (a) the American Revolution's opening of access to corporate rights to churches, evangelical societies, conventional charities, private schools, educational institutions like libraries and museums, and fraternal lodges; (b) the restriction of these rights, none-

---

documenting the government's treatment of subjugated and oppositional groups, but these almost never focus on voluntary associations as organizations. Our work builds on a few recent exceptions that, however, offer interpretations that differ in important respects from our own, including Novak (2001), Tomlins (1993), and North, Wallis, and Weingast (2009).

16. For example, Wright (1992), Hall (1992), McCarthy (2003), and Gordon (2014).

17. For example, Brooke (2010), Neem (2008), Koschnik (2007), and Butterfield (2015).

18. For example, Putnam (2000), Skocpol, Ganz, and Munson (2000), and Kaufman (2002).

19. In this chapter we use the term "voluntary association" synonymously with "nonprofit group," with both terms referring to any association organized by private citizens for nonbusiness purposes whether incorporated or not. This use seems to us most consistent with today's ordinary speech. In the nineteenth century, however, both terms possessed much narrower legal meanings: "voluntary association," which appeared frequently in case law and treatises, usually referred to an unincorporated group (whether for business or nonbusiness purposes); "nonprofit," "not for profit," and "not-pecuniary" were adjectives coined in late nineteenth-century statutes to distinguish nonbusiness corporations from business corporations. The word "philanthropy" rarely appears in our study because "charity," as a legal term, is more pertinent to our argument, and because its positive valence obscures the distinctions we make between favored and disfavored organizations.

20. One reason scholars have largely missed the importance of the government's role in dispensing these rights is that the national picture was virtually impossible to investigate until the advent of large electronic databases, because the process took place by means of piecemeal statutes and scattered judicial decisions on the state level.

theless, to essentially the same kinds of noncontroversial organizations that had already enjoyed privileges in the colonial period; (c) the manner in which postrevolutionary state legislatures and courts used their powers to grant and interpret charters to curb the rights of potentially dissident organizations composed of artisans and ethnic minority groups; (d) the transition in the mid-nineteenth century from special charters to general incorporation laws that increased access to new categories of politically acceptable organizations like social clubs and recreational groups; (e) the simultaneous mid-century expansion of the range of rights held by associations that received charters, including greater autonomy from judicial supervision; and (f) the state's persistent denial of access to corporate rights to voluntary associations with politically controversial goals, like radical reform societies, trade unions, and political parties. This denial is especially noteworthy in light of the increased opening of access to politically favored ones. It is the goal of this chapter to tell both sides of this history.

7.1   Expanding Access to Traditionally Favored Groups, 1750–1820

The impact of the American Revolution on the legal rights of voluntary associations was much more mixed than scholars generally recognize. On the positive side, American citizens largely won a de facto right to associate despite its absence from the Constitution. Ordinary people could immediately create numerous types of voluntary associations, including oppositional political parties as early as the 1790s. A significant subset of these associations also began to acquire the more explicit rights belonging to corporations—rights to entity and personhood status that went beyond the individual right of their members to associate. On the negative side, access to these corporate rights remained highly restricted for political reasons. The power to issue and enforce charters, previously held by Parliament and the king, shifted to state legislators and judges, who tended to favor the same types of associations as those previously favored under colonial law. This significant degree of continuity with British rule has gone largely unnoticed by celebrants of American voluntarism.

It is well known that political associations that challenged the state during the colonial era were considered illegal, and authorities often used force to repress them. Elites with connections in Parliament or the colonial provincial governments could usually make their criticisms heard, but inasmuch as they coalesced into associations, they were, in the parlance of the day, factions shrouded in secrecy rather than legitimate organizations. On the popular level, traditionally limited protests like bread riots enjoyed a partial legitimacy, but officials treated most public demonstrations of antagonism to government policies as criminal.[21] A few of the most prominent examples

---

21. On the tradition of extralegal crowd actions, see Maier (1970) and Countryman (1976).

of political repression during the late colonial period include the jailing of Baptists who refused to defer to the Church of England in Virginia, the mobilization of militias against the North Carolina Regulators and the Paxton Boys in Pennsylvania, and, of course, the use of royal troops to suppress the Sons of Liberty in Boston.[22]

What has been less often perceived is the extent to which British law recognized other kinds of privately organized voluntary associations as legitimate. The Elizabethan law of charitable uses endorsed the creation and support of parish churches, schools, workhouses for the poor, and other local organizations serving the indigent or disabled. These types of organizations were founded in the colonies as well as in Great Britain, supported both by the 1601 statute and, in some colonies, by extra laws passed by provincial legislatures.[23] The Glorious Revolution in the late seventeenth century extended legal toleration, if not equal rights, to dissenting Protestant churches. In addition, the king and Parliament granted corporate charters to especially favored organizations, such as the Church of England's missionary wing, the Society for the Propagation of the Gospel, and a similar Presbyterian Scottish evangelical group, both of which operated in America but were seated in Britain.[24]

These types of legally recognized groups had an important characteristic in common: they performed functions regarded by authorities as useful. No clear line divided public and private: some of these state-sanctioned enterprises were founded or funded by donors who freely contributed their own property; some were administered with minimal oversight by the government. Ultimately, however, what justified the privileged legal status of all of them was that they were seen as instruments, or extensions, of the state.[25] The Elizabethan statute and royal charters in effect functioned as official licenses that allowed groups organized by private persons to acquire property and have standing in courts as long as their goals were specifically endorsed by the government. By contrast, other kinds of voluntary associations, like elite social clubs and fraternal groups, possessed no legal status at all.[26]

22. On these instances of repression, see Isaac (1982, 146–77), Whittenburg (1977), Hindle (1946), and Morgan and Morgan (1953).

23. Shurtleff (1854, vol. 4, pt. 2, 488); *Acts and Laws of the State of Connecticut in America* (1796, 252–53, Hartford: Hudson and Goodwin). In the 1820s, the Pennsylvania jurist Henry Baldwin unearthed many examples of the British law of charities being used in colonial America, an argument that helped to persuade the United States Supreme Court in 1844 to change its earlier negative position of 1819. On Baldwin's scholarship and its impact, see Wyllie (1959).

24. Davis (1917, vol. 1, 38).

25. See Jones (1969), Jordan (1959), and Owen (1964). On the spread of private charities and private schools in mid-eighteenth-century America, see Bridenbaugh (1938, 392–98, 448–51).

26. Craft-based fraternities had traditionally been considered corporations with monopoly rights, but guilds had lost virtually all their medieval legal privileges by the late seventeenth century. For examples of early American crafts groups, social clubs, and fraternal societies, see Bridenbaugh's *Cities in the Wilderness* (1938, 36–37, 295, 303, 394–97, 436, 437–40, 457–64), Shields (1997, 175–208), and Bullock (1996, chs. 1–2).

In comparison to England, the legal standing of early American voluntary associations suffered in one important respect: the imperial government was loath to charter organizations created by colonists, largely for fear of their becoming independent of British control. The few exceptions tended either to be related to the Church of England, like William and Mary College, or to receive strong support from royal and proprietary governors whose authority derived from the king. Otherwise, legal protection for property held by colonial groups came from charitable uses law or from charters issued by provincial legislatures without royal approval. The reluctance of the Crown to incorporate organizations based in America produced friction already in the seventeenth century when defiant Puritan legislators issued acts of incorporation for Harvard College, and later Yale, without sending them to England for review.[27] Tensions over the issue of incorporation resurfaced in the late colonial period with several unsuccessful attempts by colonists to gain official approval. The College of New Jersey (later Princeton) and Eleazar Wheelock's missionary school (later Dartmouth) failed to secure charters, forcing their founders to postpone the projects until more sympathetic royal governors agreed to them.[28] In 1763, the imperial Board of Trade rejected the incorporation of a Congregationalist missionary society because the Massachusetts charter required too little government supervision and the group threatened to interfere with British policy toward Native Americans.[29]

The American Revolution gave rise to new rights of association. First and most importantly, the fight against British repression paved the way for the recognition of a de facto right to associate. As Arthur Schlesinger Sr. long ago emphasized, the political organizations formed by the revolutionaries themselves had the practical effect of enhancing the legitimacy of oppositional political groups.[30] Similarly, the upheaval of the Revolution emboldened dissident churches and radical sects that had been previously suppressed by officials supporting the colonial ecclesiastical establishments.[31] This revolutionary context shaped the interpretation of the fundamental rights declared in the First Amendment of the US Constitution: the rights of free worship and a free press, also proclaimed by virtually all state constitutions, and the rights of free speech and assembly, proclaimed by over half of them.[32] Although none of these documents explicitly provided for

27. Davis (1917, vol. 1, 19–22).
28. Davis (1917, vol. 1, 25, 46, 85–86).
29. Davis (1917, vol. 1, 80–81). For the purposes of this chapter we are not including instances of colonial governments chartering public corporations like townships (or the churches of the ecclesiastical establishment). For an emphasis on the importance of such colonial precedents on the prevalence of the corporate form after the Revolution, see Kaufman (2008).
30. Schlesinger (1944).
31. Isaac (1982, 243–95) and Marini (1982).
32. Of the state constitutions ratified before 1820, six lacked the right of speech (Massachusetts, New Jersey, Delaware, Maryland, Virginia, and South Carolina) and five lacked assembly (New York, New Jersey, Maryland, Virginia, and South Carolina). See NBER State Constitutions Project, http://www.stateconstitutions.umd.edu/texts/.

a right of association, they nonetheless provided legal grounding for the idea that Americans were free to form associations whose purposes did not otherwise break the law.

This background did not, however, immediately or completely secure the right of citizens to associate for political purposes. In the 1790s a decisive setback occurred when leaders of the Federalist Party tried to suppress Democratic-Republican clubs and the Jeffersonian oppositional press. Seventy Democratic-Republicans were jailed and fined under the notorious Alien and Sedition Acts of 1798, and after the Jeffersonians gained power, they briefly attempted to retaliate by prosecuting a few prominent Federalists under the common law of seditious libel.[33] Nonetheless, the expiration of the Alien and Sedition Acts in the early 1800s opened up a new era of increasingly accepted partisanship, and by the 1820s, organized political conflict had become widely recognized as an inevitable feature of popular rule.[34] Even so, the extent of the de facto American right to associate in the early republic should not be exaggerated. Laws passed in the South routinely denied free blacks and slaves the right to congregate for virtually any purpose, and Northern courts soon re-introduced the common-law doctrine of criminal conspiracy in order to curtail strikes by labor unions.[35]

Second, the American Revolution gave rise to new associational rights by widening access to incorporation. State legislatures assumed the power to issue charters that previously had been reserved to the king and Parliament, and in many states elected representatives reacted against the former stinginess of the British by passing acts of incorporation in large numbers. Whereas the right to associate was at best a de facto right possessed by individual citizens, the entity and personhood rights of corporations were at once formal and possessed by organizations. They were particularly important for organizations that aspired to last indefinitely, consisted of many members, and experienced high turnover in membership. At a time when the small size of most businesses enabled them to manage their property as partnerships and single proprietorships, voluntary organizations had more need for the form and therefore became corporations more often than businesses.[36] To be sure, not all eligible associations bothered to apply for

33. Only two of the nine known libel prosecutions against Federalists yielded convictions: Lipset (1963, 40–43) and Levy (1960, 296–309).

34. Hofstadter (1969). On the conflicts of the 1790s and the moderate Jeffersonian endorsement of free association, see Neem (2003) and Butterfield (2015, 31–54).

35. As is also noted in this volume by Brooks and Guinnane (chapter 8), "The Right to Associate." Other examples from later in US history include: Southern laws against abolitionists in the 1830s, the Congressional ban on polygamy against Utah Mormons in the 1880s, and the anticonspiracy and antiespionage acts used against Communists in the twentieth century. Laws against nineteenth-century trade unions are discussed later in this chapter; also see Levi et al. (chapter 9, this volume).

36. Maier (1993) and Kaufman (2008, 415, 417). This contrasts sharply with Prussia and France, where businesses received legal entity and personhood rights before nonprofit groups. See Brooks and Guinnane (chapter 8, this volume).

charters; those that were small, ephemeral, or propertyless had little incentive to do so.[37] Once postrevolutionary legislatures increased the availability of charters, however, voluntary associations that had common property to safeguard frequently took advantage of the greater opportunity to use the corporate form.

Another reason that numerous voluntary associations became corporations was that American revolutionary ideology undermined the British law of charitable uses that had previously protected private donations to churches, schools, and local charities. Republican sensibilities were offended by traditional charitable law for two reasons: first, it left jurisdiction over bequests to the juryless, inefficient, and often corrupt chancery courts (think *Bleak House*); and second, it gave perpetual control over donated property to trusts with inflexible mandates that potentially tied up wealth for generations without serving a useful purpose. Although some states continued to recognize British charitable law, others rejected it, which made incorporation by state legislatures the only viable route to legal status.[38]

The sorts of organizations that followed this route were generally the same sorts that the British had previously permitted to hold legal rights either as recipients of royal charters or as beneficiaries of charitable trusts.[39] Although the years between 1780 and 1840 witnessed a veritable explosion of voluntary groups ranging from unorthodox churches to fraternal orders and from political parties to utopian communities, the states mostly limited charters to those whose purposes were religious, educational, or conventionally charitable (either in the sense of aiding or uplifting the poor or, like hospitals, tending to the sick or disabled).[40] Churches and other

37. Historians have tended to overestimate the proportion of voluntary groups that procured charters because the kinds of well-established, propertied groups that became corporations are so heavily represented in printed sources (including charters). We found that only four (less than 5 percent) of 219 Massachusetts groups founded between 1807 and 1815 identified as broadly "charitable" (including evangelical, fraternal, mutual aid, poor relief, medical, and educational organizations) had received charters by 1816. This figure was produced by cross-checking the Massachusetts subset of the groups listed in the exhaustive appendix of Wright (1992, 244–60) with the acts of incorporation reported in *The Public and General Laws of the Commonwealth of Massachusetts, from Feb 28, 1807 to Feb 16, 1816*, vol. 4 (Commonwealth of Massachusetts 1816).

38. Fishman (1985). In Britain, popular hostility to charitable use law culminated with the passage of reform legislation in the 1820s that eliminated the worst abuses and enabled the basic law to persist (Jones 1969, 160–68). On the initial American rejection, see Miller (1961).

39. We thank Jason Kaufman for giving us access to his database of corporate acts collected from the 1780–1800 session laws of Massachusetts, Vermont, Connecticut, Pennsylvania, Ohio, Virginia, North Carolina, Kentucky, and Tennessee for the period (with variations by state). Many of our generalizations about the numbers and types of corporate acts before 1825 are based on searches within recently digitized compilations of state laws contained in Readex, "Archive of Americana": *Early American Imprints, Series I: Evans, 1639–1800*; *Early American Imprints, Series II: Shaw and Shoemaker (1801–1825)*, and in HeinOnline, *Session Laws Library*.

40. This conclusion is derived both from searches in annual sessions and from later lists of corporations published by Pennsylvania, Massachusetts, South Carolina, and Ohio, as follows: Commonwealth of Pennsylvania (1837–39, vol. 3, 213–368); Commonwealth of Massachusetts (1816, 1837, 1860); State of South Carolina (1840, 1–484); and Ohio, Secretary of State (1885, 147–225), containing a list for 1803–1851.

Protestant religious organizations, which often owned property acquired before the Revolution and comprised the majority of first applicants for charters, became the first beneficiaries of the general incorporation laws passed in the 1780s and 1790s.[41] General laws facilitating the incorporation of other traditionally privileged groups were not far behind. Indeed, Pennsylvania and the US Congress, acting for the Northwest Territory, passed general incorporation acts not just for churches but also for charitable and literary societies already in the 1790s.[42] By the 1830s several other states had passed one or more general incorporation acts for specific types of voluntary groups, ranging from fire companies to social libraries to medical societies.[43] Even without general legislation, legislatures in most states incorporated great numbers of such organizations by individual acts. Massachusetts had already issued so many special charters to "charitable" societies that in 1817 the state's weary legislators resorted to a barebones template conferring, in one short phrase, "all the privileges usually given."[44] In addition, when conventionally acceptable voluntary groups applied for charters, most states in most parts of the country took a pluralistic approach to incorporating them. Even elite institutions with colonial charters that established monop-

---

41. Fishman (1985, 632). The Revolution's support for ecclesiastical disestablishment led states to issue charters to churches as a sign of official religious toleration. Even in Massachusetts, where the Congregationalists continued to receive state support, the government offered to liberally incorporate dissenting churches and bristled when uncooperative Baptists and Universalists refused to take advantage of the opportunity. The state's strategy of attaching corporate rights to ecclesiastical rights (most importantly the rights to tax exemption and licensed marriage ceremonies) ironically backfired as a gesture of religious inclusion. See Cushing (1969).

42. Commonwealth of Pennsylvania 1810), and United States (1798). In Pennsylvania, a judicial opinion of the 1830s insisted on a narrow construction of the 1791 general law, claiming that "literary" never included institutions of higher learning and that "charitable" had always applied only to organizations "affording relief to the indigent and unfortunate." *Case of Medical College of Philadelphia*, 3 Whart. 454 (1838), quote at 18.

43. We found twelve additional general incorporation laws for specific types of voluntary associations passed between 1780 and 1830 (in addition to the many others for religious groups): Virginia Session Laws, October Session, 1787, Ch. 35, p. 25 (fire companies); New York Session Laws, 10th Legislature, 1787, Ch. 82, pp. 524–31 (colleges and academies), 19th Legislature, 1796, Ch. 43, pp. 695–99 (public libraries), and 36th Legislature, 1813, Ch. 40. Vol. 2, pp. 219–24 (medical societies); New Jersey Session Laws, 19th General Assembly, 1794, Ch. 499, pp. 950–52 (societies for the promotion of learning), 24th General Assembly, 1799, Ch. 827, pp. 644–45 (library companies), and 54th General Assembly, 2nd Sitting, 1829, pp. 19–25 (medical societies); Massachusetts Session Laws, January 1798, Ch. 65, pp. 200–201 (social libraries); January 1819, Ch. 114, pp. 181–83 (agricultural societies) and January 1829, pp. 219–20 (lyceums); Kentucky Session Laws, 6th General Assembly, 2nd Session, 1798, Ch. 42, pp. 78–79 (fire companies); Vermont Session Laws, October 1800, pp. 11–15 (social libraries). Here and throughout, the references to "Session Laws" are to HeinOnline's *Session Laws Library*, noted above.

44. For example, "An Act to Incorporate the Master, Wardens and Members of the Grand Lodge of Massachusetts," Massachusetts Session Laws, 1817, p. 408; and "An Act to Incorporate the British Charitable Society," Massachusetts Session Laws, January 1818, pp. 547. These barebones charters were a sharp contrast to the detailed 1786 and 1790 charters reprinted in *The Act of Incorporation, Regulations, and Members of the Massachusetts Congregational Charitable Society* (Boston: John Eliot, 1815, pp. 3–6) and *Rules and Articles of the Massachusetts Charitable Society* (Boston: Adams and Rhoades, 1803, pp. 3–7).

oly privileges, like Harvard College, fought losing battles in state legislatures to prevent rival organizations from becoming incorporated.[45]

Because the power to incorporate resided within state governments, however, local political considerations inevitably affected the distribution of charters in different regions. In general, the South incorporated fewer organizations than the North, both for nonprofit and for business purposes. The rural spread of the population and the slave-based economy discouraged the formation of the kinds of charitable organizations that, in Northern cities, served lower-class groups. Added to this was an especially virulent anticorporatism among Jeffersonians that stemmed from the revolutionary struggle to disestablish the Church of England and later legal battles to invalidate the colonial charters of institutions tied to the former religious establishment.[46] So extreme was Virginia's hostility to ecclesiastical corporations that the state forbade the incorporation of all churches, an example that was later followed by West Virginia, Arkansas, and Missouri.[47] South Carolina, by contrast, issued many charters to local churches but otherwise chartered few voluntary groups that ordinary people joined. Even as the Bible Belt stretched over the South during the Second Great Awakening, the large national evangelical organizations that elsewhere enlisted numerous Protestant ministers and lay activists incorporated few Southern state chapters or auxiliary societies (exceptions were the Virginia and North Carolina Bible Societies and the American Colonization Society chartered in Maryland).[48]

45. On the debates in the early 1820s over the Republican-sponsored charters for Berkshire Medical College and Amherst College, both of which threatened Harvard's monopoly, see Neem (2008, 75–77). Similarly, the University of Virginia corporation was founded by Democratic-Republicans to compete with the older Anglican monopoly, William and Mary College (whose charter the Jeffersonians first tried to destroy).

46. Key cases are *The Rev. John Bracken v. The Visitors of Wm. & Mary College*, 7 Va. 573 (VA 1790) (John Marshall defended the college) and *Terrett v. Taylor*, 13 U.S. 43 (1815) (a precedent for *Dartmouth*). James Madison blasted "the excessive wealth of ecclesiastical Corporations" and used his power as president in 1811 to veto a congressional bill incorporating the Protestant Episcopal Church in Washington, DC. See Campbell (1990, 154).

47. A Virginia law of 1799 declared the incorporation of religious groups to be "inconsistent" with religious freedom (a position written into the state's constitution of 1851). See Buckley (1995, esp. 449–51). Also see Campbell (1990, 154) and Note, "Permissible Purposes for Nonprofit Corporations," *Columbia Law Review* 51 (1951): 889–98. In 2002 a case brought by Jerry Falwell on First and Fourteenth Amendment grounds finally forced Virginia to change its constitution. *Falwell v. Miller*, 203 F. Supp. 2d 624 (US Western District of Virginia 2002). On anticorporatism in Virginia (and among Republicans more generally), see Hall (1992, 22–23), and Hall (1982, 85).

48. For an introduction to the so-called Benevolent Empire, see Griffen (1960). On the Virginia Bible Society, chartered in 1814, and its auxiliary organizations, see Bell (1930, 244–45). North Carolina Session Laws, 1813, p. 26. Three local chapters of the Bible Society were incorporated in Maryland (Baltimore, 1813) and South Carolina (Union, 1825; Charleston, 1826). Maryland incorporated the American Colonization Society, discussed further below, in 1831. Maryland Session Laws, General Assembly, December Session, 1830, pp. 201–2. Our searches for interdenominational bible and missionary societies prior to 1830 produced one result in Maryland (the Female Domestic Missionary and Education Society in Hagerstown, 1831) and no results in the Session Laws of Georgia, West Virginia, Kentucky, Tennessee, Alabama, Mississippi, and Louisiana.

Apart from local churches, the Southern voluntary associations that received the most charters either catered to the elite, like Masonic lodges, literary societies, and private academies, or existed primarily to protect property, like fire companies.[49] This narrow granting of charters, especially when taken together with Virginia's and Maryland's repudiation of British charitable law (which traditionally enabled religious, educational, and charitable groups to receive bequests without needing to be incorporated) may help to explain why so few Southern charitable and religious voluntary associations amassed resources and perpetuated themselves over time.[50] Within the terms of Jeffersonian ideology, political hostility to corporations was justified on high-minded egalitarian principles. But the reluctance of the South to grant extra associational rights to churches and charities probably served the interests of the elite more than those of ordinary citizens. By retaining state control over poor relief and curbing the rights of evangelical groups, the planter class effectively reduced the potential of organized opposition to its social and political dominance.

In the North, the chartering of colleges, academies, and cultural institutions founded by wealthy Federalists bred popular resentment just like the Federalist control of banks.[51] Jeffersonian anticorporate ideology lost much of its force, however, once the Democratic-Republicans gained power and were able to incorporate voluntary associations of their own. In New York, the Democratic-Republican ascendency in the early 1800s shifted the pattern of incorporation more toward fraternal groups of recent immigrants and artisans largely populated by their partisans.[52] These groups satisfied the

49. The cities of Baltimore and Charleston conformed more to a Northern pattern in having several incorporated charitable organizations. On the early general law incorporating Virginia fire companies, also see Davis (1917, vol. 2, 17). On Virginia incorporated academies, see Bell (1930, 168). South Carolina passed almost 450 acts of incorporation for voluntary groups between 1775 and 1835, of which 50 percent were churches and denominational organizations; 14.5 percent academies, seminaries, and colleges; 11 percent library, literary, and other cultural societies; 7 percent Masonic and other fraternal mutual aid associations; 5.5 percent militia and fire companies; 4 percent free schools and charities for the poor; 3 percent professional, agricultural, and commerce societies; and 5 percent other or unknown (State of South Carolina 1840). Our sampling of Georgia's Session Laws between 1789–1810 and 1820–1830 reveals much the same pattern. On Masonic lodges, our surveys found that seven of the thirteen states to incorporate Grand Lodges by 1825 were Southern: South Carolina (1791, 1814, 1818), Georgia (1796, 1822), North Carolina (1797), Louisiana (1816), Mississippi (1819), Maryland (1821), and Alabama (1821). The Northern states were Massachusetts (1817), New York (1818), New Hampshire (1819, 1821), Maine (1820, 1822), Connecticut (1821), and Vermont (1823).

50. Among historians of philanthropy, the term "Virginia Doctrine" refers to the reluctance of several states, especially in the South, to encourage private charities (especially by invalidating charitable bequests). See McCarthy (2003, 87), Miller (1961, xii, 50), and Hirschler (1938, 110).

51. Neem (2008) and Brooke (2010). On the politics of banking, see Qian Lu and John Wallis (chapter 4, this volume), and on New York, Hilt (2017).

52. In addition to the mechanics societies discussed below, the Caledonian Society (Scottish) and the Hibernian Provident Society (Irish), both incorporated in 1807, were particularly known for their history of partisanship (Young 1967, 401–2). Our sample of New York Session Laws indicates that most of the European ethnic societies incorporated prior to 1820 received their charters in 1804–7, during the early years of Democratic-Republican rule.

standard expectation that corporations be socially useful by pledging themselves to the "charitable" assistance of fellow members and their families in
need. Even the notoriously partisan Tammany Society of New York received
a charter in 1805 shortly after the Democratic-Republicans won control of
both houses of the state legislature.[53] Incorporated under terms that granted
more freedom of self-governance than usual for the period, the Tammany
Society easily withstood an 1809 challenge to its charter by a former member
who accused the organization of betraying its official "charitable purpose"
by becoming "perverted to the worst purposes of faction."[54] Tammany's
leadership in turn indignantly denounced this effort "to cancel its long list
of good actions and wrest from it its charter of incorporation, the basis
of its stability and existence."[55] Far from consistently opposing corporations, powerful Democratic-Republicans regarded a thin veneer of charity
as sufficient to qualify an organization for a charter if enough lawmakers
supported it on political grounds. Revolutionary-era hostility toward corporations never entirely disappeared, but as Democratic-Republicans in the
North jumped on the corporate bandwagon, the partisan quality of their
objections to incorporation started to lose traction. In response to chronic
demand, legislators issued more and more charters to nonprofit groups, as
well as to businesses, regardless of which party or faction was in power.[56]

Few organizations as blatantly partisan as the Tammany Society managed

53. New York Session Laws, 28th Legislature, 1804, p. 277–79. The distinction between
the "fraternal" Tammany Society and the partisan Tammany Hall (the General Democratic
Republican Committee of New York, which met in the building owned by the Society) enabled
the political machine in its heyday to dispense "charity" and raise private funds without government oversight (see Mushkat 1971, 10, 366). The Tammany charter was unusual in this period
in three important ways: in giving carte blanche to the group's own constitution and bylaws to
determine the mode of elections, types of officers, and admissions requirements; in containing
no term limit; and in allowing the corporation to "take" and "receive" property as well as to
purchase and hold it. The only significant restriction was a $5,000 property limit, which was
an average amount for fraternal benefit societies of the period. According to a 1807 New York
almanac, the society had a two-part constitution, one "public," relating to external matters, the
other "private," relating to "all transactions which do not meet the public eye, and on which its
code of laws are founded." Quoted from Longworth (1807, 78), as cited by Myers (1901, 24).
54. "Another Denunciation! From the Nuisance of Last Night," *The American Citizen* 10
(Mar. 1, 1809), p. 2. Myers (1901, 31–32) and Mushkat (1971, 37–38). An 1872 petition to the
New York legislature to revoke Tammany's charter similarly died in committee (State of New
York 1872, 175).
55. As quoted in Myers (1901, 32).
56. A comparison of the numbers of special charters issued by New York and Massachusetts
in the two years before and after the state first had both a Democratic-Republican governor
and legislative majority shows that that no overall cutback occurred. In New York, where the
Federalists lost power in 1802, the number remained constant for businesses and rose by 400
percent for nonprofits (from one to four: the small total number of nonprofit special charters
is due to New York's general incorporation acts for churches, libraries, and academies); and
in Massachusetts, where the Democratic-Republicans seized control temporarily in 1810–11,
chartering rose by 28.5 percent for businesses and 81 percent for nonprofits (from twenty-one to
thirty-eight). Averaging the numbers of special charters per year for 1800–1805 and 1834–1835,
the overall increase in incorporated voluntary associations between the two periods was 120
percent in Massachusetts (from twelve per year to twenty-six), 800 percent in New York (from
two to eighteen), and 100 percent in South Carolina (from four to eight).

to secure charters.[57] Throughout the first half of the nineteenth century, most incorporated voluntary groups fit into the conventionally privileged categories of religious, educational, and charitable groups.[58] To be sure, the stretched definition of "charity" now included fraternal associations whose charitableness mainly consisted of offering financial benefits to their own members, but even they could be regarded as contributing to the wider society by easing pressure on public poor relief. The traditional view that chartered groups benefited the general welfare continued to safeguard the legitimacy of the chartering process despite the political twists and turns of state legislators. Indeed, suspicions that corrupt officials rewarded their partisan allies only reinforced the widespread conviction that socially and politically divisive groups should be ineligible for corporate grants from the government. The Tammany Society, the glaring exception, received its charter early enough in the political battle between Federalists and Democratic-Republicans to slip under the wire, and even it professed a charitable purpose when its charter came under fire. In theory, if not always in practice, corporations were from the outset supposed to stay out of politics.

7.2   Legislative Constraints on the Corporate Rights of Disfavored Groups, 1790–1820

The notion that religious, educational, and charitable associations served the public good also justified a measure of governmental control over them. Even in the case of Protestant churches and other highly favored organizations, acts of incorporation often included limits on the amount of property they could own or the number of years their charters remained valid.[59]

57. Other political groups in the early republic built on Tammany's fraternal model, including the dozens of Washington Benevolent Societies organized by young Federalists starting in 1808, but our searches in the HeinOnline database of state session laws and in published lists of Massachusetts and New York corporations produced no evidence of their incorporation (contrary to Butterfield [2015, 50]). As we show below, partisan organizations became corporations in a few states at the end of the century.

58. Fire companies and mutual aid associations (both loosely considered "charitable") were the only sizable exceptions to these traditional categories. There was minimal change in the percentages of special charters for groups whose purposes were not either religious, educational, traditionally charitable (in the sense of aiding the poor or disabled), mutual aid, or fire protection. In Massachusetts, these exceptional types—the most common of which were agricultural and medical societies—constituted only 3 percent in 1800–1805 (out of a sample totaling seventy-three) and 2 percent in 1834–35 (out of fifty-three); in New York, 11 percent in 1800–1805 (out of eighteen) and none in 1834–1835 (out of thirty-seven); and in South Carolina, 4 percent in 1800–1805 (out of twenty-four) and 6.5 percent in 1830–1835 (out of forty-six).

59. On the limits typically placed on early corporations, see Maier (1993, 76–77). On property limits for church corporations, see Gordon (2014). A few of many other types of examples include: Beaufort Library Society (income limited to $5,000 and a term limit of fourteen years), South Carolina Session Laws, 1807, pp. 244–45; American Antiquarian Society (income limited to $1,500 and personal property to $7,000), Massachusetts Session Laws, 1812, Ch. 69, pp. 142–42; Baltimore Bible Society (income limited to $3,000), Maryland Session Laws, 1813, p. 15; Humane Society in New York (income limited to $3,000), New York Session Laws, 37th Session, 1814, Ch. 9, pp. 12–14; Handel and Hayden Society (personal property and real estate each limited to $50,000), Massachusetts Session Laws, 1816, Ch. 78, pp. 85–86.

New York's 1784 general act of incorporation for churches contained such detailed prescriptions about ecclesiastical governance—including procedures for democratically deciding which church members could vote, how corporate trustees would be elected, and how to determine the salaries of clergymen—that leaders of Episcopal and Dutch Reformed churches mounted a thirty-year campaign for changes that would accommodate their more hierarchical church polities.[60] Charitable and educational corporations serving the general public were typically subject to additional governmental constraints. Massachusetts General Hospital, for example, was required to offer free admission to the indigent, and many private colleges including Harvard and Yale needed to reserve seats on their boards for public officials until the 1860s and 1870s.[61]

Legislatures subjected the charter applications of associations run by socially and politically marginal people to far more discriminatory treatment. Regardless of which party dominated the state government, lawmakers often saw such organizations as raising the specter of social disorder and were reluctant to extend the same entity and personhood rights that they routinely granted to mainstream associations with similar goals. Catholic churches, for example, were routinely compromised by the Protestant bias toward lay ecclesiastical control that prevented high-ranking clergy from organizing as "corporations sole"—a corporate form that in Europe had long made it possible for bishops to rule over their dioceses.[62] Instead, Catholic parishes in the United States that incorporated were forced to entrust church property to local groups of trustees who lacked official religious authority.[63] More direct forms of discrimination undercut the efforts of laborers, blacks, ethnic minorities, and women who formed organizations to pursue otherwise acceptable educational and charitable purposes. For several decades beginning in the 1790s, members of socially subordinate groups submitted a growing number of petitions for charters. The Northeastern state legislatures ruling on these petitions often either rejected them outright or attached special provisions to reduce the corporate rights that charters ordinarily conferred.

---

60. The initial act is contained in New York Session Laws, 7th Session (1784), Ch. 18, pp. 613–18. Churches that did not conform to the law in the meantime received special charters. For the successive revisions, see New York Session Laws, 16th Session (1793), Ch. 40, p. 433; New York Session Laws, 36th Session, 1813, Ch. 60, Vol. 2, pp. 212–19.

61. Commonwealth of Massachusetts (1814) and Whitehead (1973, 191–240).

62. Maitland (1900).

63. Campbell (1990, 155–56). In one Pennsylvania case of 1822, this situation even gave rebellious lay members of St. Mary's Church an opening to try, albeit unsuccessfully, to revise the corporate charter to altogether exclude priests. *Case of the Corporation of St. Mary's Church (Roman Catholic) in the City of Philadelphia*, 7 Serg. & Rawle 517 (PA 1822). In antebellum Massachusetts, where Irish immigration inflamed Protestant nativism in the 1840s and 1850s, a legislative investigation also led to the rejection of a Jesuit college's bid for incorporation in 1849. For a scathing contemporary attack on the negative report, see *Brownson's Quarterly Review*, n.s., vol. 3, no. 3 (1849) pp. 372–97.

From the time of the Revolution, for example, labor groups experienced exceptional difficulties procuring charters because of longstanding worries by public officials about their potential to control wages. Two organizations of artisans formed in the late eighteenth century, one in Boston to prevent apprentices from quitting before their contracts expired and the other in New York to regulate the members' "affairs and business," were repeatedly denied charters on the grounds that they were "combinations" aiming to set "extravagant prices for labor."[64] A newspaper article written in 1792 by "A Friend to Equal Rights" bemoaned the fact that banks received "every attention" whereas the mechanics' "wish to be incorporated [has] been treated with contempt and neglect."[65] It soon became clear that corporate status for these and other labor organizations, as well as many associations of ethnic minorities, depended on persuading state lawmakers, regardless of the party in power, that they were exclusively "charitable" mutual benefit societies dedicated to providing aid to sick or impoverished members (or, when deceased, their widows and children), and, occasionally, to offering instruction in their trades.[66] In 1816, when the New York Typographical Society attempted to deviate from this formula by adding to its list of objectives the goal of improving conditions of labor, the legislature rejected the bill, passing it only two years later when this provision had been removed.[67]

When labor groups managed to secure charters, the acts of incorporation often contained threats of dire consequences should they stray from their declared purposes of mutual aid and education. In New York, where

64. Street (1859, 261–64; quotes on 261, 263) and Buckingham (1853, esp. 8–9, 50, 57–58, 95–96). The quote is from a later edition, Massachusetts Charitable Mechanic Association (1892, 2). Charters of these two organizations were finally granted in 1792 (New York) and 1806 (Boston). Alfred F. Young (1967, 201–2); New York Session Laws, 15th Legislative Session, 1792, Ch. 26, pp. 300–303; Buckingham (1853, 57, 95–96); Massachusetts Session Laws, February, March Session, 1806, p. 91.

65. Young (1967, 201), quoting from the *New York Journal*, Mar. 30, 1791.

66. For citations to other New York labor charters granted between 1790 and 1820, see below. Our systematic analysis focuses on New York since that state granted labor groups the most charters, but other states also periodically passed restrictive charters for them in this period, for example: The Newburyport Mechanick Association, in Massachusetts Session Laws, January Session, 1810, pp. 139–40 ("for charitable purposes; but . . . for no other purpose whatsoever"); The Stanton Benevolent Mechanic Society, in Virginia Session Laws, 1818, December Session, Ch. 93, pp. 138–39 (forbidden to pass bylaws "for regulating trade, or the wages of labor"). In Pennsylvania, where the Bricklayers' Company was incorporated in 1797 under the general law as a "charitable society," the group's unpublished bylaws deviated from its charter by including "some general rules for measuring, and standard prices for valuation," suggesting a surreptitious purpose concealed from official view. See Wrenn (1971, 73–75).

67. Stevens (1913, 78). Stevens states that the initial bill contained a "provision permitting the association to regulate trade matters." The official records of New York's Assembly, which contain few specifics, report that the problem lay in the "first enacting clause" and that the revised petition contained a "modification" as to the corporation's "intention" (State of New York 1817, 260; State of New York 1818, 195). In the Senate, the 1818 vote to accept the revised bill was still close (12 to 10) (State of New York 1818, 87–88). In 1816, the Senate also rejected another labor group's petition for incorporation, for reasons that are not clear (State of New York 1816, 235).

the largest number of "mechanics" and journeymen groups were incorporated before 1820 (largely owing to the power of Democratic-Republicans), the three earliest acts up to 1805 included the unusual requirement that the groups report to the chancellor to prove that funds were not being diverted to other purposes.[68] A little later this reporting requirement was dropped, but six of the thirteen New York charters issued between 1807 and 1818 contained extra provisions that specifically forbade the enactment of bylaws or rules "respecting the rate of wages, or relative to [their] business."[69] In addition, virtually every corporate grant made by the state to a labor group before 1820 imposed extreme punishments for the pursuit of unapproved objectives. Whereas it was normal for states to reserve the right to dissolve corporations that exceeded their mandates, the charters given to labor groups stipulated that the state could, in addition, confiscate all corporate property.[70]

These unusually restrictive conditions imposed on corporations of artisans reflected the pervasive hostility toward organized labor within early nineteenth-century law. In response to several strikes by journeymen, American courts drew on repressive features of the British common law to indict members of unincorporated labor groups on charges of "criminal conspiracy" to fix wages.[71] Although no state legislature outlawed "combinations" of workmen by statute, as Parliament did in the 1790s, the acceptance of criminal conspiracy law by the judiciary amounted to the denial of the basic right to associate. The inability of labor groups to incorporate unless they denied the intention to raise wages made them more vulnerable to prosecution. When a lawyer for striking Philadelphia cordwainers during the first conspiracy trial of 1806 claimed that workers' organizations had the same collective rights to make rules for their members as a corporation, the argument went nowhere, nipped in the bud by the prosecutor's rejoinder that "this body of journeymen are not an *incorporated society* [italics in original] whatever may have been represented," because corporate status depended upon having "benevolent purposes."[72]

---

68. Society of Mechanics and Tradesmen of New York City (1792); New York Session Laws, 15th Legislative Session, 1792, Ch. 26, pp. 300–303; Albany Mechanics Society (1801), *General Index of the Laws of the State of New York, 1777–1857*, ed. T. S. Gillett (Albany: Weed, Parsons & Company, 1859), p. 171; Society of Mechanics and Tradesmen of Kings County (1805), New York Session Laws, 1804, 28th Legislative Session, Ch. 86, pp. 208–11.

69. New-York Masons' Society (1807), New York Session Laws, 30th Legislature, 1807, Ch. 9, pp. 8–10; New-York Society of Journeymen Shipwrights (1807), New York Session Laws, 30th Legislature, 1807, Ch. 116, p. 130–32; Mutual Benefit Society of Cordwainers of New York (1808), New York Session Laws, 31st Legislature, 1808, Ch. 20, pp. 10–15; General Society of Mechanics in Poughkeepsie (1808), New York Session Laws, 31st Legislature, 1808, Ch. 235, pp. 254–57; Butchers' Benevolent Society of New-York (1815), New York Session Laws, 38th Legislature, 1815, pp. 59–60; New York Typographical Society (1818), New York Session Laws, 41st Session, 1818, Ch. 17, pp. 13–15.

70. This language was written into the charters of 85 percent (eleven out of a total of thirteen) laborers' fraternal benefit groups incorporated between 1790 and 1819.

71. Tomlins (1993, 107–79).

72. *The Trial of the Boot & Shoemakers of Philadelphia on an Indictment for a Combination and Conspiracy to Raise their Wages* (Philadelphia: B. Graves, 1806, 8).

Charitable and educational associations organized in the Northeast by European ethnic groups, African Americans, and women also encountered resistance when they attempted to incorporate, albeit to a lesser extent, and often received charters specifying similarly restrictive conditions. Most of the New York charters granted to mutual benefit groups formed by recent immigrant groups and free blacks in the first decades of the nineteenth century contained the same threat of property confiscation commonly directed at labor groups. If the group were to pursue any "purposes other than those intended and contemplated by this act," the bills stipulated, the corporation would "cease" and its "estate real and personal" would "vest in the people of this state."[73] The 1808 act that incorporated the New York Society for Promoting the Manumission of Slaves for the purpose of facilitating the funding of its charity school for black children and other "benevolent purposes" contained this provision as well.[74] A report issued by the New York's Council of Revision was unusually explicit in expressing anxiety about chartering immigrant groups. Explaining the veto of an act of incorporation for a German mutual aid society, the councilors proclaimed that "it will be productive of the most fatal evils to the State" to encourage "foreigners differing from the old citizens in language and manners, ignorant of our Constitution and totally unacquainted with the principles of civil liberty" and would "establish a precedent under which the emigrants from every nation in Europe, Asia, and Africa, who incline to seek an asylum in this State . . . [will] claim similar establishments."[75]

An analogous fear of social disorder underlay the initial hesitation to charter charities run by middle-class women. The Boston Female Asylum, founded in 1800, at first met frustration when seeking to incorporate in 1803. In the vitriolic words of a newspaper critic, "the consequences, which will naturally result from it, must be hostile to the peace of society, and to the regularity and harmony of families."[76] When the charter was finally secured, it contained a passage compensating for the fact that married women could not be sued, requiring that wives who handled organizational funds procure

---

73. Seventy-seven percent (seven out of nine) of European ethnic and all (two out of two) of free black fraternal benefit groups incorporated prior to 1820 contained this language. A comparison to other types of New York "religious and charitable" corporations, 1780–1848, based on a random sample of seventy-one organizations from the *General Index*, pp. 171–74, found this provision in 60 percent of other (nonlabor, nonethnic) fraternal groups; 60 percent of nonfraternal charities; and in none of the religious or educational societies. A word search in HeinOnline session laws found this language in many state franchises like turnpikes, which operated on public land. Otherwise, the provision was virtually nonexistent in charters of business corporations. At least one early charter of an ethnic benefit association, the German Society in New York City, incorporated in 1804, included in addition a reporting requirement like those in the first charters granted to labor benefit groups. New York Session Laws, 27th Legislature, 1804, Ch. 64, p. 609.

74. "Act to incorporate the Society, formed in the State of New-York, for promotion the Manumission of Slaves, and protecting such of them as have been or may be liberated," New York Session Laws, 31st Legislature, 1808, Ch. 19, pp. 256–58.

75. Street (1859, 273).

76. As quoted in Wright (1992, 114).

their husbands' consent and that their husbands take responsibility for any property of the organization they handled. Another section held that the treasurer always be a single woman with enough personal resources to "give bond, with sufficient surety or sureties" to cover "all money and property of said society coming to her hands."[77] Charters of women's charitable groups in Massachusetts contained this language routinely for decades.[78] Pennsylvania charters of the period similarly stipulated that only single women could serve as treasurers, a provision that protected husbands from suits but also prevented wives from assuming positions of fiscal leadership.[79] But the corporate rights of women depended on the specific language of charters, and states did not always so readily defer to the law of *coverture*. In New York, the acts that incorporated women's organizations between 1800 and 1840 typically exempted the husbands of members from financial responsibility, an approach that contrasted with Massachusetts and Pennsylvania and presumably meant to encourage men to allow wives to participate.[80] Either way, lawmakers remained convinced for decades that husbands required an extra layer of protection from the distinctive risks posed by incorporated associations of women.[81]

Despite the legal disadvantages of marriage, middle-class women in most places quickly overcame the initial resistance to their organizing. Aided by emergent cultural assumptions about the superiority of female virtue,

77. Massachusetts Session Laws, January Session, 1803, Ch. 64, pp. 122–24 (relevant sections on p. 123).

78. As stressed by Ginzburg (1990, 51–53) and McCarthy (2003, 41). All five of the Massachusetts charters we identified between 1803 and 1816 contained this provision. See also: Massachusetts Session Laws, May Session, 1804, Ch. 23, pp. 517–18; January Session, 1805, Ch. 62, pp. 619–20; January Session, 1811, Ch. 70, pp. 229–300; November Session, 1816, Ch. 63, pp. 294–97.

79. McCarthy (2003, 41).

80. See, for example, the charters of the following New York organizations issued between 1802 and 1838: The Society for the Relief of Poor Widows with Small Children, New York Session Laws, 25th Session, 1802, Ch. 99, p. 158; The Association for the Relief of Respectable, Aged, Indigent Females in the City of New-York, New York Session Laws, 38th Session, 1814, Ch. 69, pp. 74–76; The Female Assistance Society, New York Session Laws, 40th Session, 1816, Ch. 207, p. 245; and The Association for the Benefit of Colored Orphans in the city of New York, New York Session Laws, 61st Session, 1838, Ch. 232, p. 213).

81. It is puzzling why states included these various provisions at all. The rule of limited liability for members of corporations was gradually becoming an established feature of American law during this period and presumably would have offered husbands automatic protection against suits by corporate creditors. Many charters for business corporations specified the liability of members, thereby overriding the rule, but none of these charters did so. One possible explanation for the provisions is that *coverture* raised extra doubts about the sufficiency of the rule to protect husbands, particularly since American courts did not fully establish it until the mid-1820s. The phrasing of some of the charters also suggests another concern not covered by limited liability: that a wife's possible mishandling of funds risked a suit by the corporation itself (rather than a suit by a creditor against the corporation). Charters addressing a wife's possible "neglect or malfeasance" include the New York charters, cited above, and in a charter for the Savannah Female Asylum, in Georgia Session Laws, 1809, Annual Session, Section 6, p. 60. On the rise of limited liability in the early United States, see Handlin and Handlin (1945) and Perkins (1994, 373–76).

women's groups that stuck to activities like the distribution of Bibles and the care and moral uplift of indigent mothers and children secured charters in large numbers during the first half of the nineteenth century.[82] By the 1830s, the provisions designed to protect husbands from suits had, moreover, largely been dropped.[83] State legislatures concerned about the inadequacy of public poor relief not only welcomed the help of respectable women but also became more likely to give charters to working-class and immigrant mutual aid societies without attaching special restrictions.[84] The socially stabilizing effects of charitable and self-help organizations largely overrode the initial fears of lawmakers that artisans, ethnic minorities, and women would use corporate rights to subvert the social order. This is not to say that government officials had altogether lost their distaste for chartering organizations that professed beneficial purposes and yet stirred public controversies.[85] But the barriers to incorporation that previously stood in the way of otherwise acceptable organizations composed of low-status members largely, if not fully, came down.

7.3   Judicial Constraints on the Corporate Right of Self-Governance, 1800–1850

In the early nineteenth century, courts as well as legislatures had power over corporations that constrained the rights of politically suspicious voluntary associations. Virtually all the suits involving incorporated groups that rose to the appellate level originated in internal conflicts over matters of governance. The parties instigating the suits were members (or ex-members) of the organizations, not creditors or outside purveyors, and their complaints were about organizational rules, not debts or damages. States routinely gave corporations the right to enact bylaws that were legally binding on mem-

---

82. Ginzburg (1990, 48–53) and Cott (1977, 52–53). On the rise in perceptions of female virtue, see Bloch (2003).

83. The Massachusetts provisions, which appeared consistently in at least five charters between 1803 and 1816, were eliminated for seemingly the first time in a charter of 1821 (Massachusetts Session Laws, May Session, 1821, Ch. 11, pp. 577–78). They thereafter appeared intermittently, apparently ceasing altogether in 1838. Massachusetts Session Laws, January Session, 1829, Ch. 115, pp. 188–89; January Session, 1834, Chs. 30 and 163, pp. 30–31 and 228; and January Session, 1836, Ch. 133, p. 814–15.

84. The last highly restrictive charter we found was New York's 1818 charter for the Typographical Society (New York Session Laws, 41st Session, 1818, Ch. 17, pp. 13–15).

85. Our discussion of the late nineteenth century will return to the subject of ethnic discrimination. In the 1830s and 1840s, the best examples of states' political use of their chartering powers are decisions by Vermont, Rhode Island, and Massachusetts to revoke or revise charters previously given to Masonic lodges at the peak of the anti-Masonic crusade, and Massachusetts' shelving of a petition for incorporation by a Jesuit college in the midst of Protestant nativist reactions against the Irish immigration of the 1840s. On the Masonic charters, see Neem (2008, 112–13); Vermont Session Laws, 1830, Ch. 42, p. 54; and Rhode Island Session Laws, January, 1834, pp. 54–56. On the Jesuit college, see *Brownson's Quarterly Review*, n.s., vol. 3, no. 3 (1849), pp. 372–97.

bers, but charters rarely offered explicit guidance on governance apart from mandating the election of officers. Judges therefore had room to interpret whether an organization's right to self-governance permitted the enactment of a particular regulation or procedure. As virtually all of these cases reveal, courts proved particularly inclined to take an aggrieved member seriously when the complaint touched on issues of wider political significance or the organization's activities threatened to disturb the status quo.[86] Whereas voluntary associations without charters were usually free to govern themselves unless they advocated breaking the law, suspect voluntary groups that became incorporated traded the upside of other corporate benefits, like property ownership, for the downside of potential judicial interference.

Despite the constitutional guarantee of freedom of worship, the conviction that corporations were accountable to the government even threatened the autonomy of churches. In New England, where the colonial ecclesiastical establishments hung on for decades, the idea that the state should oversee the governance of church corporations died especially hard. The Massachusetts Supreme Court in 1807 went so far as to overturn the people of Tyringham's decision to fire the minister of their incorporated church because they no longer adhered to his orthodox beliefs. The bench forbade the removal of a minister without proof that he had grossly violated his office, despite the state's 1780 constitutional provision giving "all societies incorporated for religious purposes" the right to elect clergymen.[87] In Connecticut, court decisions in 1793 and 1816 similarly sought to protect the Congregational Standing Order by restricting the corporate right of parish majorities to run their own churches.[88]

Ecclesiastical disestablishment in New England soon eliminated the official privileges of Congregationalists, but corporate status nonetheless continued to offer a justification for judges who favored Congregationalism

86. Of the eight early appellate cases we found in which judges overturned the internal governance procedures of voluntary associations (most of them in the first and second decades of the nineteenth century), seven involved either New England church-state controversies or disputes within politically controversial Pennsylvania and South Carolina religious and fraternal corporations. The only case we found with no evident political significance was *Commonwealth v. Pennsylvania Beneficial Institution*, 2 Serg. & Rawle 141 (1815). A contrasting interpretation of judicial intent is offered in Kevin Butterfield's *Making of Tocqueville's America*, in which *Binns* and several Philadelphia mutual aids cases of the 1810s are described as examples of courts protecting the individual rights of members (see Butterfield 2015, 68–76, 151–62). Apart from *Binns*, however, only two of the cases resulted in actual verdicts, with notably mixed results: *Commonwealth v. Pennsylvania Beneficial Institution*, noted above, favored the individual, but the decision in *The Commonwealth vs. The Philanthropic Society*, 5 Binn. 486 (1813), favored the corporation. This chapter not only underscores the political nature of the early judicial interventions but also argues, contrary to Butterfield, that American courts in later decades increasingly deferred to the governance rights of associations, not individuals.

87. *Avery v. Inhabitants of Tyringham*, 3 Mass. 160 (MA 1807). In a slightly later case the Massachusetts Court similarly held that a town could not fire its established minister without the consent of a customary "council" consisting of ministers from other towns. See *Cochran v. Inhabitants of Camden*, 15 Mass. 296 (MA 1818).

88. *Howard v. Waldo*, 1 Root 538 (CT 1793); *Chapman v. Gillet*, 2 Conn. 40 (CT 1816).

to intervene in religious disputes. The best example is the well-known case *Smith v. Nelson* of 1846, in which Vermont's Supreme Court refused to enforce the Presbyterian synod's dismissal of a minister chosen by a local Presbyterian church.[89] Reversing a contrary lower court ruling, the justices defended the preferences of the church against the decision of the higher ecclesiastical body on the grounds that the church was a "corporate body" in which members were entitled to elect their own leaders. In the eyes of the court, the synod possessed no legal governance power despite the denomination's own rules. The description of the local church as a corporation apparently derived from New England custom rather than from any concrete evidence of registration. Technically, the battles over disestablishment were over, but behind the justices' distaste for the Presbyterian organizational hierarchy, and its reflexive support for local church autonomy, clearly lurked a lingering Congregationalist bias.

Even in Pennsylvania, where religious freedom had prevailed since the colony's founding, the corporate status of churches provided an opening for state intervention. Two church cases decided in 1815 and 1817 stand out as particularly egregious examples of judicial meddling in the internal governance of nonprofit corporations. Whereas the examples from New York and New England reflected longstanding rivalries between denominations over matters of church polity, these Pennsylvania cases reflected conflicts over race and ethnicity that extended well beyond ecclesiastical disputes. The growth of Philadelphia's population of free blacks and the arrival of Irish and German immigrants exacerbated deep-seated social tensions that played out in the religious organizations formed by minority groups. In 1794 the African American members of Philadelphia's Methodist Church formed their own house of worship, the Bethel Church of African Methodists, in response to acts of discrimination such as being forced to sit in the back. White leaders in the original church corporation continued, however, to control the church's property and the selection and pay of its visiting preachers.[90] Under the leadership of its minister, Richard Allen, Bethel tried in 1807 to amend its loosely worded charter of 1796, but when an expelled member, Robert Green, petitioned for a writ of mandamus to restore him to membership (a legal action specific to corporations), the Pennsylvania Supreme Court treated the church as subject to the corporate bylaws of the original Methodist Church "by which the African society is governed."[91] Green had been thrown out of the church by Allen and Bethel's deacons for

---

89. *Smith v. Nelson*, 18 Vt. 511 (VT 1846). For a similar ruling against a higher unincorporated body of the Methodist Church, see *Methodist Church v. Remington*, 1 Watts 218 (PA 1832).

90. A short first-person account is in *The Doctrines and Discipline of the African Methodist Episcopal Church* (Philadelphia: Richard Allen and Jacob Tapsico, 1817), pp. 4–9. See Nash (1988) and Gordon (2015).

91. *Green v. African Meth. Society*, 1 Serg. & Rawle 254 (PA 1815), at 254. See Newman (2008, 159–60). A year after this negative ruling Bethel Church finally received a special charter, and a later ruling in a similar case endorsed the church's own disciplinary procedures.

breaking a standard Methodist rule against suing another member. Since Pennsylvania gave basic corporate rights to all churches, including the power "to make rules, bylaws, and ordinances and to do everything needful for the good government and affairs of the said corporations," the legality of the rule was not itself in doubt.[92] Rather, Green and his white allies maintained that Bethel's officers lacked the authority to enforce the church's rules. Only if the majority of the parent corporation's membership had explicitly transferred the power of expulsion "by the fundamental articles, or some by-law founded on these articles," the court agreed, would the decision by "a select number" be legal.[93]

In 1817, the Pennsylvania court went to similarly remarkable lengths to sort out the irregularities in a disputed election within Philadelphia's German Lutheran church that caused an eruption of "tumult and violence."[94] Once again, the church was split between bitterly opposed factions and the conflict reflected deep social divisions within the city. German immigrant members who wanted church services conducted in their native language had won the election, and the more assimilated, English-speaking members enlisted a state prosecutor to challenge the legality of the vote. The lower court issued a blatantly anti-immigrant ruling, contending that unnaturalized foreign residents had no more right to vote in church corporations than they did in the wider polity. Upon appeal, the justices in the supreme court rejected that argument by noting the essential difference between "religious and political incorporations," but they, too, ruled against the immigrants. Rather than rely on any specific provision of the church's charter, which called for elections but said nothing about voting procedures, the court ruled that the election had in principle violated the terms of incorporation. The justices, deriving their notion of a fair election from other corporations as well as political life, especially objected to the fact that the immigrant faction had distributed marked ballots to their constituency (a practice that, ironically, American political parties would make standard within two decades). Had the church not been incorporated, it is clear that the case would never have found its way into court. The same bench dismissed a similar case brought by a faction of Methodists because their church had not become a corporation sufficiently in advance of the suit.[95]

The use of corporate status to justify intervention can also be seen in early nineteenth-century cases involving controversial fraternal associations. Like

---

92. For the general law, see Commonwealth of Pennsylvania (1810, vol. 3, 21).

93. *Green v. African Meth. Society*, quote at 255. In a reference to English corporate law, the concurring opinion stressed failure of the Bethel leadership to "set forth the particular facts precisely upon an amotion out of a corporation" (at 255).

94. *Commonwealth v. Woelper*, 3 Serg. & Rawle 29 (PA 1817).

95. *Commonwealth v. Murray*, 11 Serg. & Rawle 73 (PA 1824). This opinion cites *Woelper* and another Pennsylvania case of 1820, *Commonwealth v. Cain*, 5 Serg. & Rawle 510, in which the court intervened within a church corporation to settle a dispute over pews.

churches, fraternal societies were more fully private than most other types of nonprofit corporations in this period. Not only were their benefits directed primarily to their own members rather than a wider public, but, unlike churches, their selective admissions policies and secret practices meant that their internal affairs were almost entirely removed from outside scrutiny. Both their exclusiveness and their visible displays of high-minded patriotism upon civic occasions conferred social status to those who belonged, and, in most parts of the country, Masonic lodges and numerous smaller fraternities attracted growing numbers of elite and upwardly mobile middle-class men. Their pledges of mutual assistance gave a charitable dimension to their purposes that frequently enabled them, like groups of artisans, to secure charters. But along with corporate status came the ability of disgruntled members who disagreed with the leadership to bring their grievances into courts.[96]

Oaths of secrecy kept such suits to a minimum, but at least two cases about the internal governance rights of fraternal associations rose to the level of state supreme courts, one in Pennsylvania in 1810 and one in South Carolina in 1813. As in the cases involving church corporations, the courts conceived of their role as enforcing corporate charters. The involvement of the legal system was, once again, socially and politically charged because the trials jeopardized the reputations and relationships of prominent citizens.

In *Commonwealth v. St. Patrick's Society*, John Binns, a member of an Irish fraternal group in Philadelphia who had been thrown out in 1807 for "vilifying" another member, went to court to challenge his expulsion.[97] The man whom Binns had insulted was no less than the society's president, William Duane.[98] As the editor of Philadelphia's leading Jeffersonian newspaper, *The Aurora*, Duane had long been a leader of Philadelphia's Irish radicals and frequently spoke out against the Federalist judiciary and the English common law. Binns, a recent Irish immigrant, was allied with rural Republicans and had recently challenged Duane's authority by moving to Philadelphia and founding a rival newspaper supporting the aspiring "country" candidate for governor, Simon Snyder. As tensions mounted, Duane and his allies successfully ousted Binns from several other Irish associations without charters, but since St. Patrick's was a corporation, Binns possessed legal leverage to retaliate. By 1810, when the case finally came before the Pennsylvania Supreme Court, Binns's political fortunes had risen with Sny-

96. On the early American Masons, see Bullock (1996). By 1825, at least thirteen states had incorporated either state or local Masonic lodges. At the height of the anti-Masonic movement in the early 1830s, three New England states temporarily revoked or revised their charters, but had by the 1860s reinstated them.

97. *Commonwealth v. St. Patrick's Society*, 5 Binn. 486 (PA 1810).

98. Phillips (1977), Wilson (1998, 72–76), and Butterfield (2015, 68–76). Butterfield's view of the case as a prime example of courts granting members of associations increased individual rights is at odds with our stress on the politics of legal intervention and the growing rights of uncontroversial associations (often at the expense of individual rights), as we elaborate below.

der's election in 1808, and Duane's campaign against the court system had petered out after the government enacted a few minor reforms.[99] Technically, the justices' decision to adjudicate the dispute stemmed from St. Patrick Society's limited rights as a corporation, not from Duane's hostile stance toward the bench or Binns's increased influence. Even though St. Patrick's members had approved a bylaw forbidding rude behavior long before the expulsion of Binns, the justices adhered to a narrow, literal reading of the corporation's right to self-governance and reinstated Binns's membership.[100] Any expulsion was invalid, the court held, unless the offending member broke the law of the state, violated a rule that explicitly appeared in the charter, or interfered directly with the objects of the society. Rejecting the corporation's argument that cooperation among members was essential to the group's mission, the opinion declared that "vilifying a member, or a private quarrel, is totally unconnected with the affairs of the society, and therefore its punishment cannot be necessary for the good government of the corporation."[101]

For decades, the *Binns* precedent carried considerable weight in court decisions about expulsions from incorporated voluntary associations. The same Pennsylvania court upheld an expulsion for fraud in 1813, distinguishing the facts from the *Binns* precedent in part because the group's charter—rather than merely its bylaws—explicitly forbade "scandalous and improper" behavior.[102] Perhaps in response to *Binns*, New York's General Society of Mechanics and Tradesmen also added such a provision when renewing its 1792 charter in 1811, declaring that "notorious, scandalous, wicked practice" was subject to expulsion.[103] In Connecticut, an expulsion case of 1827 similarly hinged on the precise terms of incorporation. The court reinstated an ousted trustee of a private school corporation because its charter had not authorized expulsion for "disrespectful and contemptuous language towards his associates."[104]

In a South Carolina case, which, like *Binns*, involved a prominent fraternal association whose members were closely tied to the political world, the Chancery Court enforced a charter belonging to the Grand Lodge of South-Carolina Ancient York Masons in a manner that similarly overrode its internally chosen leadership.[105] South Carolina at the time contained two

99. Wilson (1998, 74) and Henderson (1937).
100. Anonymous (1804, 5–6).
101. *Commonwealth v. St. Patrick's Society*, at 450.
102. *The Commonwealth vs. The Philanthropic Society*, 5 Binn. 486 (PA 1813). The last case to directly follow the precedent of Binns seems to have been *Evans v. Philadelphia Club*, 50 Pa. 107 (PA 1865). Many other case reports erroneously described the 1810 decision as chiefly involving financial issues. As noted below, courts increasingly refused to reverse expulsions from fraternal associations unless the former member had lost promised death or sick benefits and the organization had violated its own governance rules.
103. New York Session Laws, 34th Session, 1811, Ch. 113, p. 195.
104. *Fuller v. Trustees School Plainfield*, 6 Conn. 532 (CT 1827), quote at p. 546.
105. *Smith v. Smith* (SC 1813) in DeSaussure (1817, vol. 3, 557–84).

competing Grand Lodges, the consequence of a mid-eighteenth-century split within international Masonry. Both lodges incorporated shortly after the Revolution. At the root of the case was an agreement by the rival Grand Masters to mend the schism by merging the two organizations under the name the Grand Lodge of South Carolina. The leaders polled all the subordinate lodges, which unanimously approved the merger, and then petitioned the state to repeal both the earlier acts of incorporation and issue a new one. In the meantime, however, a group of lodges affiliated with the Ancient York Masons bristled at the top-down enactment of "inauthentic" practices and defected from the consolidated body. The dissidents reorganized themselves into a separate body and appropriated the name of their former Grand Lodge, the South-Carolina Ancient York Masons. With the controversy intensifying, the state legislature voted against dissolving the old corporations and incorporating the new Grand Lodge, but since the continuing existence of the umbrella group did not require a new charter, each of the two groups claimed to be the legitimate successor of one or both of the original corporations.

The conflict came to a head when a debt originally owed to the Ancient York Masons was ordered by a lower court to be paid to the new Grand Lodge of South Carolina. The dissident Ancient Yorks launched a suit contesting this decision, and the Chancery Court saw this occasion as a chance to test the legitimacy of the merger. Going far beyond the matter of the debt, the chancellor evaluated the contested rules and rituals within the terms of Masonry itself, taking care to refer to arcane texts like the *Ahiman Rezons* in his written decision.[106] His attention to such minutia suggests the seriousness with which he took the Masonic split (it is reasonable to suspect that he, like others in the South Carolina elite, had a personal stake in the controversy). The opinion, whose logic is largely incomprehensible to an outsider, landed firmly on the side of the Ancient Yorks, concluding that the referendum organized by the Grand Masters had been based on deception. The original corporation of the Ancient York Masons had never been legally dissolved, and the new Grand Lodge had no right to collect the debt because it was "not a corporate body known to the law."[107]

As these examples indicate, the incorporation of voluntary associations during the early decades of the republic could be both a blessing and a curse. Incorporation gave organizations valuable entity and personhood rights, but it also required them to submit to the state's definition and enforcement of charter rights. Justices adjudicating suits could take issue with the decisions of internally chosen leaders on matters ranging from personal behavior to electoral procedures to institutional tradition. Voluntary associations that

---

106. Ibid., 566–71.
107. Ibid., 576–82 (quote on 581). The Grand Lodge of South Carolina was incorporated in 1815.

were not incorporated were rarely, if ever, subjected to this kind of judicial scrutiny, unless, like labor groups, their members could be accused of committing crimes. At a time when individual citizens enjoyed an increasing right to associate and officials generally lacked the administrative capacity to monitor groups on a routine basis, the government wielded little power over associations. It was the entity right of corporations to legal standing that brought them into the courts and gave justices an opportunity to discipline them.

These cases of judicial intervention also underscore the special vulnerability of voluntary associations regarded as socially or politically controversial.[108] Courts were most inclined to interfere with the self-governance rights of groups posing threats to the status quo because of the traditional view of corporations as creatures of the state. Especially when a dispute between members of an organization reflected broader social divisions, a judicial decision to curb the power of corporate leaders could be justified as a defense of the general welfare. This was true even in the case of corporations that authorities ordinarily viewed as publicly beneficial, like the South Carolina Masonic Lodges or the German Lutheran Church, when complaints against internal procedures bore on larger conflicts that authorities wished to contain.

Controversial voluntary associations thus needed to overcome three sets of state-imposed obstacles before they could exercise the entity and personhood rights ordinarily received by conventionally acceptable voluntary associations that became corporations. First, they needed to surmount the legislative barriers blocking access to incorporation; second, they needed to secure charters without unusually restrictive provisions; and third, they needed to avoid judicial decisions that curbed their right to self-governance. These obstacles prevented the very groups that were the most likely to challenge the government from competing on an equal basis with groups that enjoyed unreserved legislative and judicial approval.

7.4   Widening of Access Combined with Persistent Constraints, 1830–1900

Over the course of several decades around the middle of the nineteenth century, American lawmakers significantly widened access to the entity and personhood rights of corporations. Most states in the Northeast, Midwest, and West ended their nearly exclusive reliance on special charters by enacting more general incorporation laws making it easier for designated categories of businesses and voluntary associations to become incorporated

---

108. Controversial business corporations like banks were, of course, also widely perceived as violating the public good, but for a variety of reasons too complex to pursue here, business corporations were not as vulnerable to judicial scrutiny as nonprofit ones. On New York courts' tendency to ignore business violations of charter terms, see Hilt (2017, 20, 32). Our own research for a book in progress suggests that courts entertained complaints by minority stockholders against corporate managers only in cases of egregious financial fraud.

and removing the taint of favoritism by giving the same set of rights to organizations within each category.[109] The general laws of this period also moved beyond the earlier focus on narrow types of associations such as churches and libraries to pull together broader categories like "religious," "educational," "benevolent," and "charitable" into single pieces of legislation. Despite this general easing of access, however, the types of groups included within these privileged categories still conformed to the earlier pattern. Oppositional groups pursuing social and political change generally experienced the same difficulties acquiring corporate rights as they had in the era of special charters.

In 1848, New York set the new standards for incorporation by enacting the most sweeping general act to date. Passed in response to a provision in the Jacksonian-inspired Constitution of 1846 that mandated general laws for all corporations, it allowed for the incorporation of "benevolent, charitable, scientific and missionary societies."[110] Before this, the state's general incorporation laws covered only a few specific types of voluntary organizations other than churches—most notably, colleges and academies, libraries, Bible societies, and medical societies. The state had required special charters for all charities, mutual aid societies, and fraternal orders, as well as most kinds of religious associations, educational and cultural groups, and scientific and professional organizations. The loosely defined categories covered by the general law of 1848 therefore made incorporation much easier for an enormous range and number of voluntary associations. Nonetheless, because New York's Constitution still permitted the legislature to issue special charters if "the objects of the corporation cannot be attained under general laws," the state continued to reward politically favored groups by granting them permission to exceed the property limits written into the 1848 law.[111] Despite this loophole, the sheer comprehensiveness of the New York law became an

109. The South, which had always incorporated fewer voluntary associations, for the most part stuck to special charters. Of the seventeen states we have identified that passed multipurpose general acts for nonprofit groups between 1840 and 1860, twelve were in the Northeast or Midwest and one in the West (California, one of only two western states at that time). Alabama and North Carolina were the only states to join the eleven-state Confederacy that had passed such an act before 1860; the non-Confederate border states of Maryland and Kentucky did so as well. References to the acts, listed in chronological order, are included in the following footnotes. There was less regional variation in the case of businesses: for example, general laws for manufacturing firms had been passed throughout the country by 1860. See Eric Hilt's chapter 8 in this volume.
110. New York Session Laws, 1848, 71st Legislature, Ch. 319, pp. 447–449. For the context, see Katz, Sullivan, and Beach (1985). Other states that also passed general acts in the 1840s were Pennsylvania (amending its earlier act), Indiana, and Maine: "An Act Relating to Orphans' Court and Other Purposes," Pennsylvania, 1840, Act No. 258, Sections 13–16, pp. 5–7; "An Act to Authorize the Formation of Voluntary Associations," Indiana, 1846, 31st Session, Ch. 45, pp. 97–99; "An Act to Authorize the Incorporation of Charitable and Benevolent Societies," Maine, 1847, 4th Session, Ch. 1, pp. 27–28.
111. New York, Constitution of 1846, Article 8, Section 1. On the continuance of special charters, see Katz, Sullivan, and Beach (1985, 71, 81–82).

important model for other states to follow. Between 1850 and 1860, California, Ohio, Maryland, North Carolina, New Jersey, Kentucky, Massachusetts, Iowa, Kansas, Illinois, and Wisconsin passed similarly multipronged incorporation laws encompassing a vast number of acceptable nonprofit groups.[112]

A handful of these states for the first time even used the generic term "voluntary associations" in the titles of acts to signal their wide breadth.[113] In 1874, Pennsylvania moved still farther in this direction, dividing its law of corporations into two sections: those "for profit" and those "not for profit."[114] The not-for-profit category consolidated under one heading a uniform set of rules for ten different types of organizations ranging from charities to yacht clubs.[115] Only a glimmer of the earlier notion that corporations should contribute to the public good still survived. Now it was permissible to form corporations for purely private purposes, and judges needed merely to verify that a corporation's purpose was legal and "not injurious to the community." This trend toward greater generality and greater permissiveness continued in most states well into the twentieth century, facilitating the registration of more and more kinds of American voluntary associations as nonprofit corporations.[116]

112. "Act Concerning Corporations," California Session Laws, 1st Session, passed April 22, 1850; "To Provide for the Incorporation of Religious and Other Societies" (including "any religious sect, denomination, or association, fire company, or any literary, scientific, or benevolent association"), Ohio Session Laws, 1852, pp. 293–94; "An Act to Provide for the Formation of Corporations for Moral, Scientific, Literary, Dramatic, Agricultural or Charitable purposes," Maryland Session Laws, January 1852, Ch. 231 (no page number); "An Act to Incorporate Literary Institutions and Benevolent and Charitable Societies," North Carolina Session Laws, 1852, Ch. 58, pp. 128–29; "An Act to Incorporate Benevolent and Charitable Associations," New Jersey Session Laws, 77th Legislature, 1853, Ch. 84, pp. 355–58. "An Act for the incorporation of voluntary associations [approved 1854]," Kentucky, 1853, vol. 1, Ch. 879, pp. 164–65; "An Act to authorize the incorporation of Benevolent and Charitable Associations," Alabama Session Laws, 4th Biennial Session, 1854, pp. 282–83; "An Act Relating to the Organization of Corporations for Educational, Charitable and Religious Purposes," Massachusetts Session Laws, Acts and Resolves, January Session, 1856, Ch. 215, pp. 126–27; "An Act for the Incorporation of Benevolent, Charitable, Scientific or Missionary Societies," Iowa Session Laws, 7th General Assembly, 1858, Ch. 131, pp. 253–55; "An Act to Authorize the Formation of Voluntary Associations," Kansas Session Laws, 1858; 4th Session, Ch. 1, pp. 27–28; "An Act to Provide for the Incorporation of Benevolent, Charitable, Scientific, and Literary Societies," Wisconsin Session Laws, 1860, 13th Session, Ch. 47, pp. 131–33. "An Act for the Incorporation of Benevolent, Educational, Literary, Musical, Scientific and Missionary Societies" Illinois Session Laws, 1859, pp. 20–22; "An Act to Incorporate Benevolent and Charitable Associations," New Jersey Session Laws, 77th Legislature, Ch. 84, pp. 355–58.

113. Indiana (1846), Kentucky (1853), and Kansas (1858).

114. Illinois already in 1872 used the term "not for pecuniary profit" to designate corporations that were neither businesses nor religious organizations. Illinois Session Laws, 27th General Assembly, 1871, pp. 303–5.

115. "An Act to Provide for the Incorporation and Regulation of Certain Corporations" Pennsylvania Session Laws, General Assembly, 1874, pp. 73–74. An amendment in 1876 expanded the list to include both commercial and trade organizations and militia companies. Pennsylvania Session Laws, General Assembly, 1876, p. 30.

116. Another early example was Ohio's revised statutes of 1879 making incorporation possible "for any purpose for which individuals may lawfully associate themselves, except for dealing in real estate, or carrying on professional business" (State of Ohio 1879, § 3235, 837). On the mid-twentieth-century culmination of these trends, see Note, "Permissible Purposes for Nonprofit Corporations," Columbia Law Review 51 (1951): 889–98 and Fishman (1985).

But it is still crucial to recognize that this wider access to corporate rights never benefited all types of voluntary associations equally. The seemingly inclusive terms that the general laws used to define eligibility, like "charitable," still embraced only a subset of voluntary associations, and because the laws never stipulated which types they disqualified, the excluded groups remained largely hidden from view. The anti-Catholic bias against "corporations sole" silently remained a part of American corporate law for decades.[117] States also persisted in denying corporate rights to a great number of activist voluntary associations outside the social and political mainstream, including labor unions and radical reform organizations. Laws like New York's of 1848 that offered easy incorporation to seemingly broad categories of "charitable," "benevolent," and "educational" groups implicitly left out oppositional ones. This tacit exclusion meant that such groups still needed to submit to the political judgments of elected officials by petitioning for special charters when they sought corporate rights.

The exclusion of antislavery groups provides an especially telling example of persistent political discrimination. In addition to being excluded from the categories covered in general incorporation laws, they also had difficulty acquiring and utilizing special charters. Several antislavery societies in the North successfully petitioned for acts of incorporation shortly after the Revolution, but, as we have seen, legislators made sure that their main goals of assisting newly freed blacks fell squarely under the rubrics of education and charity.[118] The first national antislavery organization, the American Colonization Society founded in 1816 and incorporated by Maryland in 1831, never espoused a program of legal change but instead sought to send voluntarily manumitted slaves to Africa.[119] Despite the Society's conservative, evangelical purposes, Southern states in the 1830s began to challenge its corporate status as part of the backlash to the Nat Turner Rebellion. In 1837, following a spirited debate, the US Congress refused to incorporate the group within Washington, DC, and Virginia similarly denied its bid for incorporation the same year.[120] Although Maryland reaffirmed its support in 1837 by reissuing a charter significantly raising the group's property limit, the standing of the Maryland charter in other slave states continued to come

---

117. Campbell (1990, 55–56). Not until 1879 did the Massachusetts general law for religious organizations finally provide for the indefinite service of high-ranking Catholic clergymen on the incorporated boards of trustees of Catholic churches and guarantee that their successors in ecclesiastical office would automatically replace them (Commonwealth of Massachusetts 1882, Part I, Title IX, Ch. 38, § 48, 287). As late as 1899, a Wisconsin ruling held that the Catholic diocese in Milwaukee was subject to taxes because the archbishop held the land as an individual rather than as a corporation. *Katzer v. City of Milwaukee*, 104 Wis. 16 (WI 1899).

118. For example, the Pennsylvania Society for Promoting the Abolition of Slavery, incorporated in 1789; the Providence Society for the Abolition of Slavery, incorporated in 1790; and the New-York Manumission Society, incorporated in 1808.

119. "An Act to Incorporate the American Colonization Society, passed Feb 24, 1831." Maryland Session Laws, General Assembly, December Session, 1830. Ch. 189, pp. 201–2.

120. *The African Repository and Colonial Journal* (published by the American Colonization Society June 13, 1837, 41–48).

under assault in a series of court cases questioning the validity of wills in which masters bequeathed their slaves to the Society rather than passing them onto their heirs.[121] Until the 1850s, Southern appellate courts generally upheld the organization's corporate right to receive the slave property, but the grounds of these decisions became progressively narrow as the Northern antislavery movement gained ground and Southern states resorted to enacting statutes that specifically outlawed the bequest of slaves for the purposes of emancipating them.[122] In a ruling of 1857, the Georgia court argued definitively that a corporation could not inherit slaves like a natural person and that a state was not obligated to honor the rights of a "foreign" corporation whose aims were "repugnant to its policy [and] prejudicial to its interests."[123] This string of proslavery decisions is particularly notable for occurring after the Supreme Court's 1844 *Girard Will* decision establishing the validity of charitable bequests even if the recipient was not a corporation.

At the same time as slave-holding states were thwarting the corporate rights of the American Colonization Society, the Northern antislavery groups advocating immediate emancipation almost never received charters. The only two abolitionist groups to surface in our searches of session laws in Massachusetts, New York, Pennsylvania, and Ohio fell squarely under the rubric of education and religion: the Infant School Association in Boston "for the education of colored youth," incorporated by Massachusetts in 1836 (an effort planned but never executed by Garrisonian abolitionists); and an avowedly antislavery Baptist Church in Columbus, Ohio, chartered in 1851 under the state's general law for the incorporation of churches.[124] Other churches with abolitionist leanings undoubtedly incorporated as well, of course, without broadcasting their antislavery views in their names. How often other kinds of abolitionist associations tried to incorporate and failed is virtually impossible to determine, since few examples of failed applica-

---

121. "An Act to Incorporation the American Colonization Society, passed March 14, 1837." Maryland Session Laws, General Assembly, December Session, Ch. 274, pp. cccv–cccvii in HeinOnline (not paginated in original).

122. *Maund's Adm'r v. M'Phail*, 37 Va. 199 (VA 1839) (the ACS allowed to receive the legacy); *Ross v. Vertner*, 6 Miss. 305 (MS 1840) (same); *Cox v. Williams*, 39 N.C. 15 (NC 1845) (same); *Wade v. American Colonization Society*, 15 Miss. 663 (MS 1846) (same, but on narrow grounds, noting that the testator died before the passage of the 1842 statute); *Lusk v. Lewis*, 32 Miss. 297 (1856) (the ASC may not receive bequest because it violated the statute); *Lusk v. Lewis*, 35 Miss. 696 (1858) (reversing the 1856 decision because it was not an explicit condition in the will that the Society emancipate the slaves).

123. *American Colonization Society v. Gartrell*, 23 Ga. 448 (GA 1857), at 449 (citing Justice Taney's opinion in *Bank of Augusta vs. Earle*, 13 Peters 519, which defended the rights of a foreign corporation "unless" they were repugnant to a state's policy and interests).

124. Massachusetts Session Laws, 1836, Ch. 9, p. 653; Ohio Session Laws, 49th General Assembly, Local Acts, p. 70. In addition to employing word searches in annual session laws contained in HeinOnline, we examined these compilations of corporate charters covering the first half of the century: Commonwealth of Pennsylvania (1837–1839, vol. 3, pp. 213–368); Commonwealth of Massachusetts (1816, vol. 4); Commonwealth of Massachusetts (1837, vol. 7); Commonwealth of Massachusetts (1860, vol. 9); Ohio, Secretary of State (1885, 147–225, containing a list for 1803–1851).

tions surface in documents. When they do, however, the extent of legislative opposition becomes apparent. For example, the diary of an agent employed by the Free Will Baptists reveals that in 1833 the New Hampshire legislature denied a petition to incorporate the denominational publishers who produced a highly successful newspaper (subscriptions had rapidly grown to nearly 5,000) because a majority of the state's legislators regarded the paper as "a vehicle of abolitionism." That the group running the press was a religious denomination, whose church and evangelical associations received charters without difficulty, was not enough to convince hostile lawmakers.[125] The Free Will Baptist Printing Establishment's trustees "regularly presented their petition every year" and met "the same repulse, for the same reason" until 1846, when the balance of political power in New Hampshire shifted toward the antislavery cause.[126]

Ordinarily, abolitionists and other radical activists may have had little reason to incorporate their associations. They amassed only small amounts of property from contributors and hardly ever received legacies.[127] Nor did they have much occasion to benefit from the corporate right to legal standing since their organizations rarely, if ever, had occasion to be parties in civil suits, and corporate status was irrelevant in criminal prosecutions since the charges were against individuals.[128] Yet the few exceptional charters granted to antislavery groups between the 1830s and 1850s indicate that incorporation was occasionally valuable. More striking, the protracted failure of the Free Will Baptist publishers to receive a charter demonstrates that lawmakers, even in relatively liberal New England, deliberately refused to incorporate politically controversial groups. That states passed only a small number of acts of incorporation for abolitionists and other radicals needs to be attributed to resistance as much as to apathy.

Instances of failed attempts to incorporate become even harder to trace after state legislatures ceased having control of the process. Under general incorporation laws, the review of applications usually fell to administrative officials at the level of counties rather than states. In New York and Pennsylvania, however, where general incorporation laws required judicial approval, unsuccessful groups at times appealed their rejections in the states' highest

---

125. For example, New Hampshire Session Laws, 1825, November Session, Ch. 80, p. 335 (Free Will Baptist Church); 1835, June Session, Ch. 15, pp. 230–31 (Free Baptist Meeting House Society); 1838, June Session, Ch. 3, pp. 382–82 (Free Will Baptist Home Missionary Society).

126. Marks (1846, 352–53); for the act itself, see New Hampshire Session Laws, June Session 1846, Ch. 407, p. 409.

127. "No abolitionist society had a permanent fund or endowment" Quarles (1945, 63). The American Anti-Slavery Society, which had over a thousand auxiliaries by the late 1830s, raised more than $150,000 over a six-year period but still struggled to meet operating expenses. Its one sizable bequest was depleted in five years. The only bequest to be legally challenged was litigated after the Civil War, and, as in the Henry George case, the Massachusetts court directed the money away from William Lloyd Garrison's paper and women's rights advocates because their purposes were not deemed to be charitable. *Jackson v. Phillips*, 96 Mass. 539 (1867).

128. For example, Virginia Session Laws, 1835–36, Ch. 66, p. 44.

courts.[129] Scholars have uncovered a significant number of these cases in the late nineteenth and early twentieth centuries, and their outcomes indicate an ongoing pattern of discrimination, particularly against immigrant and religious minority groups. In Pennsylvania, for example, where the general law still contained a long list of eligible categories, courts in 1891 rejected the bid for incorporation of one social club on the grounds that its all-Chinese board of directors might not adhere to its declared purposes and of another because "the law has not provided for corporate capacity" to assist in "the cultivation and improvement of German manners and customs."[130] By 1897, a series of such rulings had established the precedent that all groups incorporated in the state had to conduct their affairs in English.[131] A judge in Pennsylvania also rejected the application of Christian Scientists on the grounds that their church's opposition to medical treatment posed a hazard to public health.[132] In New York, after the 1895 Membership Corporations Law repealed nearly a hundred state laws passed between 1796 and 1894 and generously covered virtually any nonprofit group, judges typically resorted to seemingly technical reasons for denying the applications of disfavored groups.[133] A panel ruling in 1896, for example, refused to incorporate a Jewish organization because it proposed meeting on Sundays, despite the fact that other corporations in the city already did so with impunity.[134]

The denial of applications for incorporation submitted by controversial groups remained a remarkably persistent (if poorly documented) practice in many parts of the country into the mid-twentieth century. As late as 1957, nine states with broadly written laws still made applications subject to the review of judges or administrative officials who could withhold certification at their discretion.[135] According to Norman Silber's history of nonprofit corporations, which concentrates on the twentieth century, rejected applications were rarely appealed except in Pennsylvania and New York, but cases "were reported occasionally in many states, including Alabama, Arkansas, Cali-

---

129. Close to 200 appellate cases in New York and Pennsylvania between 1890 and 1955 are included in the Note, "Judicial Approval as a Prerequisite to Incorporation of Non-Profit Organizations in New York and Pennsylvania," *Columbia Law Review* 55 (Mar. 1955): esp. 388–89.

130. As discussed in "Judicial Approval," pp. 388–99. For another such case of 1893 involving Russians, see Wood (1939–1940, 266).

131. A case of 1900, *Societa Italiana di Mutui Socoerso de Benefieinza*, 24 Pa. C.C. 84 (C.P. 1900), cited as precedent on this point the 1897 case *In re Society Principesso Montenegro Savoya*, 6 Pa. Dist. 486 (C.P. 1897).

132. *First Church of Christ Scientist*, 205 Pa. 543 (PA 1903).

133. New York Session Laws, 1895, Vol. 1, Ch. 559, pp. 329–67.

134. *Matter of Agudath Hakehiloth*, 18 Misc. 717, 42 N.Y. Supp. 985 (NY 1896). For a detailed analysis of several of the New York appellate cases stressing the social and political biases of judges into the middle of the twentieth century, see Silber (2001, 31–82).

135. Judges had the power to review applications in six states (New York, Pennsylvania, Virginia, Missouri, Georgia, and Maine) and state administrators in three states (Massachusetts, Iowa, and Mississippi). Note, "State Control over Political Organizations: First Amendment Checks on Powers of Regulation," *Yale Law Journal* 66 (February 1957): 551, fn. 41.

fornia, Colorado, Delaware, Florida, Indiana, Iowa, Michigan, Minnesota, Mississippi, Missouri, Nebraska, Louisiana, New Jersey, Tennessee, Texas, Washington, and Wisconsin, and more numerously in Illinois [and] Ohio."[136]

In addition to the evidence provided by sporadic court rulings, documentation of the persistently selective granting of corporate rights in the late nineteenth century can be found in the long lists of nonprofit corporations published by the states of Pennsylvania, New Jersey, New York, and Ohio.[137] Compared to the lists produced in the era of special charters prior to the Civil War, the only significant change was a greater number of incorporated recreational and social clubs. Otherwise, despite the progressive liberalization of general laws and the granting of more and more charters, the overwhelming majority of nonprofit corporations continued to fit into the same limited categories as before: Protestant religious organizations; charities assisting the poor and disabled; educational, cultural, and medical institutions; civic organizations like fire companies; and the major fraternal orders.

Even though it is well known that many social and political reform groups were active in the second half of the century, temperance organizations were the only ones to attain corporate status with any frequency. Their disproportionate success reflects both their close ties to Protestant churches and the weakness of their largely Catholic and immigrant opponents. Ethnic divisions over the consumption of alcohol were at play in an 1880 Michigan case, for example, in which a man who had borrowed money from a German society successfully argued that its suit to recover the debt was invalid because any organization that opposed the state's temperance law had no right to corporate legal standing.[138] In several states, general laws of incorporation added extra regulations to ensure that social clubs would not slip through the cracks of laws restricting the sale of alcohol.[139] The size, respectability, and political clout of the temperance movement, qualities that made it virtually unique among the many activist groups seeking social and political change, go a long way toward explaining its success at achieving corporate rights.

Because states could differ in their assessment of which reform groups were dangerous, organizations seeking incorporation at times succeeded in one state and then attempted to operate in more hostile territory. Despite the

---

136. Silber (2001, 67; ch. 3, endnote 2). His evidence comes from his investigation of the legal reference book *American Legal Reports*. However, he provides no other details on these cases, many of which may be from the twentieth century. Our own effort to dig into the nineteenth-century records of Missouri, one of the states that mandated review by county court judges, produced documents from St. Louis County with lists of successful applications but not failed ones.

137. These and the following generalizations about types of charters in these four states are based on the following sources, which contain lists of groups incorporated both by special acts and by general laws: Beitel (1874); New Jersey Session Laws, every five years, 1820–1870; New Jersey, Secretary of State (1892); Ohio Session Laws, every five years, 1820–1870.

138. *Detroit Schuetzen Bund v. Detroit Agitations Verein*, 44 Mich. 313 (MI 1880).

139. For example, Massachusetts Session Laws, 1890, Ch. 439, Secs. 1, 2, pp. 481–82.

negligible representation of politically controversial groups on state rosters, we know that some received charters from cases in state supreme courts where the opponents of a "foreign corporation" sought to block its local activities.[140] The American Colonization Society's legal battles in Southern states in the antebellum period, discussed earlier, partly revolved around disagreements about whether, as a Maryland corporation, the organization could wield corporate rights elsewhere. The best-known instances of this kind of repressive use of state corporate law occurred in the next century, in the context of escalating racial conflict in the 1920s and 1950s. State courts in Kansas and Virginia in the mid-1920s denied the right of the Ku Klux Klan to operate in their states because it was a foreign corporation incorporated in Georgia. In Virginia, the court determined that the Klan's sale of its paraphernalia constituted commercial transactions, forcing the corporation to pay a fine and relinquish the nonprofit status it had acquired in Georgia.[141] The Kansas attorney general attempted to prevent the organization from organizing local chapters by refusing to register it as a Kansas corporation, an effort that cost him his reelection (his successor gave it permission).[142] Southern states fighting desegregation in the 1950s similarly sought to oust the NAACP and CORE, both chartered in New York.[143] By then, the Supreme Court had come to view arguments about foreign corporations as antiquated. But for over a century, despite the passage of seemingly liberal general incorporation laws, the strategic refusal by legislatures, courts, and government officials to incorporate voluntary associations supplied a weapon to repress politically polarizing activist groups—even when other states had already incorporated them.

In the case of these kinds of activist reform groups, the political motivations behind state restrictions of their entity and personhood rights seem quite clear. Less obvious, perhaps, are the political assumptions behind the thousands of legislative decisions to charter groups that could be unequivocally viewed as "religious, educational, and charitable." As Justice Bird knew when he defended the 1888 decision to impede the advocacy of Henry

---

140. Most foreign corporation cases involving voluntary associations did not reflect serious objections to the purpose of the organization as much as territorial competition between it and a rival organization or conflicts over resources between parts of the same organization. When in 1882, for example, a member of a Michigan chapter of a national fraternal organization refused to pay an assessment levied by its "supreme lodge" incorporated in Kentucky, the 1882 Michigan Court overturned his expulsion and warned the Michigan Grand Lodge not to "subject itself, or its members to a foreign authority in this way." See *Lamphere v. Grand Lodge*, 47 Mich. 429 (1882), quote at p. 430. Also see *National Council, Junior Order American Mechanics, and Others v. State Council, Junior Order United American Mechanics*, 104 Va. 197 (1905).

141. *Ku Klux Klan v. Virginia*, 138 Va. 500 (1924).

142. *Kansas ex rel. Griffith v. Ku Klux Klan*, 117 Kan. 564 (KS 1925). Sloan (1974).

143. *NAACP v. Alabama*, 357 U.S. 449 (US Supreme Court, 1958); *NAACP v. Alabama*, 377 U.S. 288 (US Supreme Court, 1964); *CORE v. Douglas*, 318 F.2d 95 (Fifth Circuit Court, 1963). See Bloch and Lamoreaux (2017, 316–19).

George's ideas, much hinged on the question, "What is a charity?" For him and other authorities at the time, groups promoting social equality fell on one side of this dividing line, whereas groups viewing the sale of alcohol as a sin fell on the other. That the line itself was politically drawn must have been evident to the losing parties in isolated court cases. The dominant conservative consensus, however, was that "charity" was politically neutral (as were religion and education) and that corporations should be so as well, an assumption that conveniently buried the political judgments behind the use of these categories.[144]

7.5   Stronger Rights for Favored Groups, 1840–1900

The politically acceptable groups that typically benefited from greater access to incorporation also benefited from another midcentury development: the growth of corporate independence from governmental control. States not only facilitated the formation of nonprofit corporations by passing general laws, but also loosened the strings previously attached to the corporate form. Whereas legislatures and courts in the first decades of the century often disciplined suspect organizations by setting limits on the rights that charters conferred, states in the late nineteenth century relied more exclusively on denying access to incorporation altogether. The growing numbers of voluntary associations that acquired entity and personhood rights under the general laws enjoyed these rights more fully and more freely than before. This change is particularly apparent in relation to the associational right of self-governance, which, as we saw earlier, judges routinely overrode when thwarting the leaders of controversial groups. Starting around the middle of the century, judges almost always left matters of internal governance to the corporations themselves.

The shift away from government oversight of incorporated voluntary associations can partly be seen in the altered language of legislative acts. Previously, in the era of special charters, states mandated a number of governance rules. For example, they often required voluntary associations, like businesses, to hold annual elections of officers. At times, charters also set the month of elections, demanded that members be notified, and stipulated the specific titles and responsibilities of the officers. These electoral requirements remained standard throughout the century for business corporations but gradually faded away for nonprofit groups. Already in the 1820s New Jersey's and New York's general laws specifically exempted religious and library corporations from following the standard rules about the election

---

144. By contrast, property tax exemptions, which benefited the same kinds of groups and directly cost taxpayers, elicited outspoken criticism at various times in the nineteenth century. The fact that these critics repeatedly failed to sway lawmakers is another example of the political intransigence of these categories. On these efforts, see Diamond (2002).

of boards and officers that applied to business corporations.[145] Ohio in 1852 similarly exempted religious, fire, literary, and benevolent corporations from requirements to issue public reports.[146] By the 1870s, Massachusetts had lifted the requirement that nonprofit corporations, like business corporations, annually elect a board of directors. A long list of nonprofit groups, ranging from temperance associations to sports clubs, were permitted to shift what had earlier been "the power of directors" to "a board of trustees, managers, executive committee, prudential committee, wardens and vestry, or other officers."[147] Even the pioneering regulatory board created in 1867 by New York to oversee the state's charities left the vast majority of private religious and secular charitable enterprises free of supervision, restricting its oversight to groups that received government funding.[148] Ceilings on income and property remained the only common constraints on the rights of incorporated voluntary associations, and by the end of the nineteenth century some states had eliminated even those.[149] Significantly, at a time when states and the federal government were beginning to impose industry-wide regulations on railroads and other types of businesses, the vast majority of nonprofit groups, whether incorporated or not, entered what was virtually a laissez-faire zone.[150]

The stronger governance rights that legislatures granted to incorporated voluntary associations were steadily reinforced by a series of nineteenth-

---

145. "Act to Prevent Fraudulent Election by Incorporated Companies," New Jersey Session Laws, 50th Session, 1825, p. 83. Subsequent revisions of this New Jersey law retained the proviso excluding literary and religious societies until at least 1877. New York's *Revised Statutes* (1829), Vol. 1, Ch. 18, Title 4, stated that many specific rules about elections and other matters did not apply to incorporated libraries and religious societies (Sec. 11, 605). Of the four Titles within this chapter on the regulation of New York corporations, only the most general one, Title 3, applied to all incorporated voluntary associations. It was notably looser in all its requirements than Title 1 (on turnpikes), Title 2 (on banks and insurance companies), and Title 4 (which focused mostly on stock companies). Religious societies and schools were similarly exempted from another set of New York rules guiding corporations in equity suits and dissolutions (*Revised Statutes* 1829, Vol. 2, Ch. 8, Title 4, Articles 1–3).

146. Ohio Session Laws, 50th Assembly, General Acts, 1852, §72, p. 294.

147. Commonwealth of Massachusetts (1882, Ch. 115, § 6, 655). The more restrictive requirements for businesses are contained in Ch. 106, pp. 574–76.

148. Katz, Sullivan, and Beach (1985, 83).

149. For example, with the exception of cemeteries and agricultural societies, New York's 1895 "Act Relating to Membership Corporations" contained no property limits. See New York Laws of 1895, Vol. 1, Ch. 559, pp. 329–67. Between the 1850s and the 1880s, Massachusetts raised its property limit for virtually all incorporated nonprofit groups from $100,000 to $500,000. Commonwealth of Massachusetts (1860, Ch. 32, 207); Commonwealth of Massachusetts (1882, Ch. 115, § 7, 656).

150. In this respect, the United States presents a striking contrast with Germany, where the rights of voluntary associations continued to be far more restrictive than the rights of businesses. See Brooks and Guinnane (chapter 8, this volume). General incorporation acts for American businesses often contained governance rules and other prescriptions that were missing from acts for nonprofit groups. See Lamoreaux (2015) and chapter 8 in this volume (2, 17–18) by Erik Hilt. On the late nineteenth-century shift toward regulating businesses by passing general laws applying to each industry (in contrast to the earlier reliance on incorporation acts), see Crane (2017).

century judicial decisions. In 1826 the eminent jurist James Kent wrote that the *Dartmouth* decision had already thrown "an impregnable barrier" around the rights of "literary, charitable, religious, and commercial institutions" by guaranteeing their charters' "solidity and inviolability."[151] Despite the frequent insertion of reservation clauses meant to enable legislatures to alter charters (thereby getting around *Dartmouth*), legislatures almost never tried to change the charters of private nonprofit corporations, and courts in the 1830s and 1840s defeated their few attempts to do so.[152] As time went on, moreover, judges came to regard the self-governance rules made by associations as inviolable as the language of their charters. The Pennsylvania Court in 1837 swung decisively away from the 1810 *Binns* decision when it upheld the right of a mutual benefit society to oust a member for violating its bylaw against intoxication on the simple grounds that, as "a private corporation," it was authorized to follow its own rules.[153] The application of the *Binns* precedent contracted to a narrow defense of individual contractual rights. Only when membership came with promised insurance benefits that were lost upon expulsion did judges became concerned about the rights of members whose group had expelled them for offensive conduct, and they ruled on behalf of an expelled member only when they could prove that the disciplinary procedure that took away his benefits deviated from the common practice of the group.[154] Otherwise, American courts recognized camaraderie as a justifiable condition of continued participation and supported decisions to terminate membership for misbehavior even when valuable benefits were lost. In a notable case of 1896, an Illinois court upheld the expulsion of a disagreeable member of the Women's Catholic

151. Kent (1826, vol. 4, 392).

152. Campbell (1990, 158–63).

153. *Black and White Smiths' Society v. Vandyke*, 2 Whart. 309 (PA 1837).

154. Kevin Butterfield identifies a similar shift toward contractualism as early as the 1830s (Butterfield 2015, 81–84, 151, 173–80, 219–20). This process was gradual. As late as the 1860s at least two cases still awarded reinstatement to expelled members: *Evans v. Philadelphia Club*, 50 Pa. 107 (PA 1865) (a late use of the *Binns* precedent, stating that expulsion was not necessitated by the purpose of the corporation); *The State ex rel. of James J. Waring v. The Georgia Medical Society*, 38 Ga. 608 (GA 1869) (a Reconstruction case overturning the Georgia Medical Society's expulsion of a doctor whose activities on behalf of blacks had been deemed "ungentlemanly"). For a few selected cases from across the country that exemplify the shift toward contractualism, see the citations here and in the following notes: *Anacosta Tribe v. Murbach*, 13 Md. 91 (MD 1859) (refusing the right of a member to sue his incorporated tribe since it had conformed to its own rules); *Gregg v. Massachusetts Medical Society*, 111 Mass. 185 (MA 1872) (upholding the expulsion of homeopathic doctors because the internal tribunal of the medical society was itself recognized to be a "court"); *State ex. re. Shaeffer v. Aurora Relief Society*, 1877 Ohio Misc. (no number in original; LEXIS 120) (OH 1877) (district court upholding an expulsion based on implicitly understood rules); *Bauer v. Samson*, 102 Ind. 262 (IN 1885) (defending the contractual right of a member to sue a fraternal organization on a matter of money as opposed to discipline); *Commonwealth ex rel. Burt. v. Union League of Philadelphia*, 135 Pa. 301 (PA 1890) (upholding an expulsion, with *Binns* cited only by the losing counsel); *Beesley v. Chicago Journeymen*, 44 Ill. App. 278 (IL 1892) (expulsion upheld on the grounds that, unlike *Binns*, the corporation had incurred injury).

Order of Foresters despite her potential loss of financial benefits, reasoning that property interests were not sufficient justification for suits by expelled members because many mutual benefit organizations were also "social and fraternal in their nature."[155] In 1897, the US Circuit Court in Washington, DC, declared that social and benevolent clubs had the right to expel members for "conduct unbecoming a gentleman" as long as the provision appeared in their bylaws.[156]

These late nineteenth-century expulsion cases almost always concerned corporations, but corporate status became notably less central to the decisions of American courts once judges backed away from supporting abused members and took the same hands-off approach to the governance of corporations that had always been taken with respect to unincorporated groups. Justices also began to insist that the equity action of mandamus, traditionally available to a member of a corporation wishing to overturn an expulsion, could no longer be used as a way to regain benefits.[157] A former member of the Chicago Board of Trade was denied the right to contest his ouster because the organization was not a business but a "voluntary association." "It is true," the court conceded, that the board was a corporation like "churches, Masonic bodies, and odd fellow and temperance lodges; but we presume no one would imagine that a court could take cognizance of a case arising in either of those organizations, to compel them to restore to membership a person suspended or expelled from the privileges of the organization."[158] Nonprofit corporations could now discipline their members for violating internal rules with little fear of state scrutiny (as had always been the case for unincorporated groups). Contrary to the experience of socially and politically suspect groups in the first half of the century, corporate status no longer meant accepting a potential loss of control over internal governance in return for the advantages of other associational rights, like property ownership, that charters routinely secured.

As a corollary to this growing right of self-governance, incorporated voluntary associations gained several additional rights in the nineteenth century that further enhanced their autonomy. A few of these rights, moreover, including the right of limited liability, extended beyond the ones granted to business corporations. By 1830, the default common law rule that members of corporations enjoyed protection from liability for corporate debts had become well established in American courts, but states could override this

---

155. *People ex rel. Keefe v. Women's Catholic O. of F.*, 162 Ill. 78 (IL 1896).

156. *United States ex rel. De Yturbide v. Metropolitan Club of Washington*, 11 App. D.C. 180 (DC 1897). The same principle was confirmed in later cases, for example: *Commonwealth ex rel. v. Union League*, 135 Pa. 301 (PA 1890); *Brandenburger v. Jefferson, Club Association*, 88 Mo. App. 148 (MO 1901).

157. Instead, "the property remedy" for a cheated member became an ordinary common law suit. *Lamphere v. Grand Lodge*, 47 Mich. 429, at 431 (MI 1882). Many later cases cited this decision to affirm this point.

158. *People ex. rel. Rice v. Board of Trade*, 80 Ill. 134 (IL 1875), quote at 136.

common law rule by passing statutes to the contrary.[159] In the case of business corporations, special charters and general incorporation laws often imposed significantly higher levels of shareholder liability (e.g., double or triple the par value of their shares).[160] In the case of nonprofit corporations, however, special charters generally overlooked the issue of liability entirely, implicitly defaulting to the common law rule. General incorporation laws that covered both businesses and nonprofit groups similarly left the common law rule intact by stating that their sections on liability applied only to businesses. The laws of Missouri and Kansas made it clear, for example, that "none of the provisions of this article, imposing liabilities on the stockholders and directors of corporations, shall extend to literary or benevolent institutions."[161] In our survey of the general acts passed in the middle of the century for nonprofit corporations, we found only four states (less than a quarter of the total) that imposed liability on members or directors. Two of them (New Hampshire and Florida) had reversed themselves by 1870, and the other two, Ohio and New York, made only trustees or directors, not ordinary members, liable.[162]

In 1876, the right of nonprofit corporations to shield themselves from damaging suits was reinforced by the introduction of the doctrine of "charitable immunity" into American law. In the landmark case *McDonald v. Massachusetts General Hospital,* the Massachusetts Supreme Court invalidated the suit of a patient who had been injured during surgery performed by an unauthorized hospital employee. In the words of the opinion, "A corporation, established for the maintenance of a public charitable hospital, which has exercised due care in the selection of its agents, is not liable for injury to a patient caused by their negligence."[163] The English precedents for this ruling

159. See Livermore (1935), Handlin and Handlin (1945, 8–11) and Perkins (1994, 373–76). An 1844 Connecticut case, involving a bank's attempt to recover a debt owed by a church, clarifies the lack of liability of its members by comparing them to the members of "incorporated academies, colleges, and other literary institutions." *Jewett v. The Thames Bank,* 16 Conn. 511 (1844), at 515.

160. See Horwitz (1992, 94) and Blumberg ([1986]; on liability, especially 587–604).

161. Missouri Session Laws, 1845, 12th General Assembly, Revised Statutes, Ch. 34, p. 235; Kansas Session Laws, 1855 (Territory), 1st Session, Ch. 28, Section 21, p. 190.

162. State of New Hampshire (1867, Ch. 137, 286) (changes a provision of *Revised Statutes* of 1842 to apply only to shareholders); Florida Session Laws, 1868, Ch. 1641, pp. 131–32 (eliminates a provision contained in Florida Session Laws, 1850, 5th Session, Ch. 316, p. 36, making trustees, if not members, "jointly and severally liable for all debts due"); Ohio Session Laws, 50th Assembly, General Acts, 1852, §79, p. 295; New York Session Laws, 71st Legislature, 1848, pp. 448–49. New York's 1848 law was slightly revised in 1853 but otherwise persisted through the state's 1895 Membership Corporation Law. New York Session Laws, 76th Legislature, 1853, Ch. 847, p. 949 (modifies the rule so that trustees were liable only if they personally acquiesced to the loan); New York Session Laws, 1895, 188th Legislature, Vol. 1, Ch. 559, p. 336 (directors are "jointly and severally liable for any debt of the corporation"). Since New York is the focus of so many studies, its importance has been magnified. For the 1926 elimination of this law, see Fishman (1985, 649).

163. *McDonald v. M.G. Hospital,* 120 Mass. 432 (MA 1876). Also see *Haas v. Missionary Society of the Most Holy Redeemer,* 6 Misc. 281 (NY 1893).

dated back to the 1840s, but whereas in England these decisions had already begun to lose traction by the 1870s, the doctrine of charitable immunity began to spread rapidly across the United States. In cases that for the most part concerned hospitals, courts repeatedly ruled that shielding charities from tort suits at once served the public interest and prevented charitable funds from being diverted from their intended use. According to the scholars Bradley C. Canon and Dean Jaros, "seven state high courts had accepted it by 1900, 25 had by 1920, and 40 had by 1938."[164] Only in 1942 did the tide of legal opinion begin to shift the other way.[165]

Another example of the wide latitude given to nonprofit corporations was their exceptional right to hold stock of other corporations. This form of investment was usually denied to business corporations (the major exception being insurance companies) until New Jersey radically broke from precedent and permitted it for all corporations in 1889–90. Nonprofits had, however, routinely bought stock of other corporations since the middle of the century. By 1855, this development had become significant enough for Joseph Angell and Samuel Ames to observe in the fifth edition of their classic treatise, "There are large classes of corporations which may and do rightfully invest their capital or funds in the stock of other corporations, for the purpose of secure and profitable investment." These classes, the passage went on, consisted primarily of "religious and charitable corporations, and corporations for literary and scientific purposes."[166]

Certain nonprofit corporations, unlike business corporations, also gained the right to control subsidiary corporations. Grand lodges of fraternal orders routinely exercised power over their lower affiliate lodges, a practice that dated back to the supremacy of the Masonic Grand Lodge of London in the eighteenth century. The early acts of incorporation for Masons passed by South Carolina, Georgia, Louisiana, and Alabama explicitly authorized Grand Lodges to assume jurisdiction over their affiliated local lodges.[167] Even the states that did not mandate the subordination of local lodges tacitly deferred to the order's top-down governance structure by allowing corporations to establish their own rules. Although the eruption of the anti-Masonic movement in the late 1820s led to the temporary revocation of Masonic charters in Vermont, Massachusetts, and Rhode Island, all three states reincorporated them by 1860, and general incorporation acts passed between 1846 and 1858 by many Midwestern and Southern states—including Illi-

164. Canon and Jaros (1979, quote at 971).
165. Ibid.; also see Note, "The Quality of Mercy: 'Charitable Torts' and Their Continuing Immunity," *Harvard Law Review* 100 (Apr. 1987): 1382–99.
166. Angell and Ames (1855, § 158, 143).
167. South Carolina Session Laws, 1814, pp. 34–36; Georgia Session Laws, January Session, 1796, p. 16 (no pagination in original); Louisiana Session Laws, 2nd Legislature, 2nd Session, 1816, pp. 98 and 100 (confirmed in Louisiana Session Laws, 4th Legislature, 1st Session, 1819, pp. 16 and 18); and Alabama Session Laws, 3rd Session, 1821, pp. 22–23.

nois, Indiana, Kansas, Missouri, Kentucky, and Georgia—contained specific provisions for the incorporation of Masons, Odd Fellows, and Sons of Temperance that implicitly sanctioned the rule of the state-level bodies over local ones.[168] In a Massachusetts case of 1880 involving two rival lodges of the Royal Arch Masons, the state supreme court firmly upheld the right of Grand Lodge corporations to exercise power over their lesser chartered affiliates.[169] Grand Lodges that lacked corporate status, by contrast, could not count on legal recognition of their right to rule subordinate lodges. Important rulings in New York in 1857 and Indiana in 1885 prohibited unincorporated Grand Lodges of the Odd Fellows and the Knights of Pythias from appropriating property owned by local lodges that had split off or been kicked out of the order by their superiors.[170]

Over time, some organizations without charters gained a few of the entity and personhood rights ordinarily held only by corporations. Unincorporated local churches had long exercised the right to receive and hold at least limited amounts of property in perpetuity, and landmark court cases in the 1870s established that higher church bodies did not need to be corporations to secure their governance powers over lower ones.[171] In the middle of the nineteenth century, a growing number of states further extended the property rights not only of churches but also of other conventional religious, educational, and charitable groups even if they lacked corporate charters. The main catalyst for this development was the 1844 decision by the United States Supreme Court in the *Girard's Will Case* that recognized British charitable trust law as part of American common law, thereby according these kinds of groups the right to receive bequests and build permanent endowments in states without statutes to the contrary.[172] Several states after 1850

168. Indiana Session Laws, 31st Session (1846 [approved 1847]), Ch. 45, pp. 97–99; Illinois Session Laws, 1855, 19th General Assembly, pp. 182–84; Kansas Session Laws, 4th Session (1858), Ch. 1, pp. 27–28; Missouri Session Laws, 1851, 16th General Assembly (1850 [approved 1851]), 1st Session, pp. 56–57; Kentucky Session Laws (1853 [approved 1854]), Vol. 1, Ch. 879, pp. 164–65; Georgia Session Law, "Public Laws" (1855–1856), Title 34 "Charitable Societies," p. 272.
169. *Chamberlain v. Lincoln*, 129 Mass. 70 (MA 1880).
170. *Austin v. Searing*, 16 N.Y. 112 (NY 1857); *Bauer v. Samson Lodge, Knights of Pythias*, 102 Ind. 262 (IN 1885).
171. By the 1840s, states often gave churches corporate rights whether they were incorporated or not. See, for example, *Christian Society in Plymouth v. Macomber*, 46 Mass. 155 (1842) (confirming a longstanding statutory rule in Massachusetts); *Cahill v. Bigger*, 47 Ky. 211 (1847) (confirming that in Kentucky an unincorporated church had equity rights to property deeded originally to individual deacons). For church cases affirming the authority of denominational rules (and thereby narrowing or disputing the decision in the 1846 case *Smith v. Nelson* discussed above), see especially: *Watson v. Jones*, 80 U.S. 679 (US Supreme Court 1871); and *Connitt v. Reformed Protestant Dutch Church*, 54 N.Y. 551 (NY 1873). Even Virginia, which passed statutes in the postrevolutionary period disallowing charitable bequests, passed laws in the 1840s designating churches and fraternal lodges as property-holding trusts (Commonwealth of Virginia 1849, Title 22, Chs. 76–77, 357–69).
172. *Vidal v. Girard's Executors*, 43 U.S. 127 (also known as the *Girard's Will Case*). On the history of charitable trust law in nineteenth-century America, see Miller (1961).

in addition gave all voluntary associations, whether or not they were incorporated, an associational right to stand as parties in suits.[173]

Despite these late nineteenth-century developments, voluntary associations without corporate status continued to suffer important comparative disadvantages under American law. Most states at the end of the century still did not give unincorporated groups the right to sue and be sued, and in places that did, legal standing could prove a double-edged sword to controversial groups, such as labor unions, by making them more vulnerable to judicial repression. Nor did the great access to charitable bequests automatically benefit unincorporated associations, as we saw in the case of Henry George's book fund. Other important rights acquired by nonprofit corporations during this period never extended to unincorporated groups, including the right to charitable immunity and the right to control subsidiary organizations. On balance, the legal changes of the late nineteenth century compounded the advantages of corporations while only partly increasing the advantages of other associations. Not only did corporations gain new rights, but they also shed previous constraints on their rights, such as low property limits and judicial threats to self-governance. The extraordinarily wide latitude the government now gave to nonprofit corporations therefore made the inability of disfavored groups to qualify for corporate status all the more discriminatory.

7.6   Constraints on the Associational Rights of Labor Unions and Political Parties, 1860–1900

For the most part, the politics behind the unequal dispensation of associational rights in the late nineteenth century remained hidden from public view. Decisions by officials to deny corporate rights were buried inside of hundreds of obscure state statutes and court rulings, and the groups damaged by them tended to be small and marginal. In the case of two exceptionally visible and contentious groups, however, the politics behind these decisions became glaringly evident around the turn of the century. For a brief period of time, both labor unions and political parties straddled the political fence dividing voluntary associations that received corporate rights from those that did not.

With rare exceptions, political parties and labor unions did not become corporations in the nineteenth century, and they still do not today. Indeed, since 1900 several ways that the government treats them differently from nonprofit corporations have been written into federal laws dealing with tax

173. Connecticut Session Laws, 1867, p. 77; Wyoming Session Laws, 1890–1891, Ch. 76, § 2, p. 328; Maine Session Laws, 1897, Ch. 191, p. 224; Michigan Session Laws, 1897, No. 15, p. 25; Rhode Island Session Laws, 1906, Ch. 1348, pp. 66–67. In 1851, New York passed a similar law extending to any unincorporated "company or association" the right to sue and be sued in the name of its treasurer or president (New York Session Laws, 1851, Ch. 455, p. 654).

exemptions, campaign regulations, and collective bargaining. But what is clear today was not so clear in the late nineteenth century. As states became more permissive in granting corporate status to voluntary groups, the long-standing prohibition on incorporating political parties and labor unions was, for a few decades, thrown into doubt.

For labor organizations, like other voluntary associations, increases in membership and financial resources enhanced the appeal of corporate legal and property rights. When unions began to confront interstate railroads and other national business corporations after the Civil War, they rapidly expanded beyond specific trades and localities, amassed substantial strike funds, and branched out to run cooperative shops and stores. Between the 1860s and 1880s several of the largest labor unions made political demands to incorporate alongside their other (now far better-known) legislative goals like the eight-hour day and the exclusion of Chinese workers.[174] Longstanding resistance finally gave way to pressure from prominent elected officials who threw their weight behind the unions' position. At the instigation of the legislative committee of the Federation of Organized Trades and Labor Unions, which had in 1883 elected Samuel Gompers its president, Congressman Thompson Murch, a prounion politician from Maine, shepherded an 1886 bill through Congress enabling the incorporation of national trade unions in the District of Columbia.[175] Among the allowable corporate purposes listed in the statute was "the regulation of [members'] wages and their hours and conditions of labor" and any "other object or objects for which working people may lawfully combine."[176] Within a few years, several states enabled the incorporation of unions by enacting similar general laws: Maryland (1884), Michigan (1885), Iowa (1886), Massachusetts (1888), Pennsylvania (1889), and Louisiana (1890).[177] Massachusetts still imposed more stringent conditions on unions than on other nonprofit corporations, but most of these states allowed unions to incorporate on the same terms as

174. Commons et al. (1918–1935, Vol. 2, 24, 66–67, 140, 165, 314, 325–26). On the repeated demands for incorporation between 1865 and 1885 by the New York Workingmen's Assembly, the Federation of Organized Trades and Labor Unions, and, in 1884, the Knights of Labor, see Hattam (1993, 131–34).

175. Commons et al. (1918–1935, Vol. 2, 329–30).

176. "An Act to Legalize the Incorporation of National Trade Unions." U.S. Statutes at Large, 49th Congress, 1886, Session 1, Ch. 567, p. 86.

177. Maryland Session Laws, January Session, 1884, Ch. 267, p. 367 (adding unions to the 1868 list "of educational, moral, scientific, literary, dramatic, musical, social, benevolent [etc.] societies"); Michigan Session Laws, Public Acts, Regular Session, 1885, Act No. 145, pp. 163–65 (supplementing an 1869 law allowing labor unions to incorporate only for "charitable" purposes); Iowa Session Laws, 21st General Assembly, 1886, Ch. 71, p. 89 (adding unions to the 1873 general law of incorporation for nonpecuniary purposes); Massachusetts Session Laws, 1888, Ch. 134, secs. 1–5, pp. 99–100 (a self-contained law with unusual special provisions); Pennsylvania Session Laws, Regular Session, 1889, No. 215, pp. 194–96 (a self-contained law declaring that employees ought to have the same privileges as "associations of capital"); Louisiana Session Laws, 1890, p. 42 (adding unions, along with Knights and Farmers Alliances, to its 1886 general law for "literary, scientific, religious and charitable" corporations).

other nonprofit groups (as did New York, the following decade, in its sweeping Membership Corporation Law).[178]

No sooner had they gained permission to incorporate, however, than most unions changed their position and declined to do so. The main reason for this change of heart was the series of antiunion decisions by American courts that occurred between 1885 and 1900. These rulings effectively gutted the influential 1842 decision in *Commonwealth v. Hunt* that had repudiated the British law of conspiracy and regarded labor unions as similar to other kinds of voluntary associations.[179] Emboldened by the Interstate Commerce Act of 1887 and the Sherman Act of 1890, conservative judges devised a new version of conspiracy doctrine that applied, if not to organizing per se, to basic union strategies like picketing, boycotting, and even, most broadly, the calling of strikes leading to "restraint of trade."[180] Corporate status did not help in these cases. Justices used their equity power of injunction to order the arrest and imprisonment of labor activists, whether their unions were incorporated or not. Moreover, several court decisions of the 1890s showed how the legal standing of corporations could backfire by making unions more vulnerable to crippling lawsuits.[181]

It soon became clear that unincorporated unions had distinct advantages in states that stuck to the old common law rule that groups needed corporate status to stand as parties in court. In Massachusetts, for example, the state supreme court in 1906 invalidated a conspiracy suit against unions of bricklayers and masons because "there is no such entity known to the law as an unincorporated association, and consequently it cannot be made a party defendant." For a suit against an unincorporated voluntary association to have standing, the court went on, every member "must be joined as a party defendant" or, following equity rules, several members could be named as the party as long as the plaintiff could show that these individuals were representatives of the entire group.[182] The requirement to identify everyone in

178. Massachusetts Session Laws, 1888, Ch. 134, § 2, p. 99 (requiring the state commissioner of corporations to verify the lawfulness of a union's purposes).

179. Tomlins (1993, 209–16).

180. Tomlins (1985, 46–51) and Hovenkamp (1988). Victoria Hattam stresses the resurgence of conspiracy prosecutions against labor already in the late 1860s, and the use of these indictments in combination with antilabor injunctions in the 1880s and 1890s (see Hattam 1993, 112–79).

181. For example: *Lucke v. Clothing Cutters & T. Assembly*, No. 7507, K. of L., 77 Md. 396 (MD 1893); *Meurer v. Detroit Musicians' Benevolent & Protective Ass'n*, 95 Mich. 451 (MI 1893); *Lysagt v. St. Louis operative Stonemasons' Association*, 55 Mo. App. 538 (MO 1893); *People v. Musical Mutual Union*, 118 N.Y. 101 (NY 1899); *Weiss v. Musical Mutual Protective Union*, 189 Pa. 446 (PA 1899).

182. *Picket v. Walsh*, 192 Mass. 572 (MA 1906), quotes at 589–90. Also see *Reynolds v. Davis*, 198 Mass. 294 (MA 1908). For similar examples elsewhere, see: *Union Pacific Railroad v. Ruef et al.*, 120 F. 120 (US Circuit Court 1902); *St. Paul Typothetae and Another v. St. Paul Bookbinders' Union No. 27 and Others*, 94 Minn. 351 (MN 1905); *Indiana Karges Furniture Co v Amalgamated Woodworkers Union*, 165 Ind. 421 (IN 1905).

a union who supported a strike or else demonstrate that a group of leaders had the consensual support of every member was, from a practical point of view, nearly impossible.

Even though several other states had by then passed laws granting unincorporated voluntary associations the legal personhood rights to sue and be sued, cases involving the illegal actions of only a subset of individual members still foundered if the suit was against the organization. A stream of decisions by the New York Supreme Court beginning in 1892 held that the state's 1880 statute enabling unincorporated associations to be parties in suits did not supersede the requirement that every member be equally liable as an individual—a condition requiring such detailed knowledge about specific actions and identities that large unions in New York were effectively immune from lawsuits for over a century.[183] Other states, however, such as New Jersey, Connecticut, Ohio, and Michigan, decided this question differently, either by court rulings or by passing more explicit laws imposing corporate-like liability on unincorporated groups.[184] Whether or not they incorporated, unions in the late nineteenth century apparently lost more than they gained when they acquired an associational right to legal standing. In this respect, they experienced the same disadvantages as the controversial nonprofit corporations in the first half of the nineteenth century whose rights to self-governance were subverted by conservative courts. Moving further in the same direction, Congress in 1898 added to the judicial damage by mandating that unions incorporating under the federal law of 1886 expel workers who used "violence, threats, or intimidation" to prevent others from working during strikes, boycotts, or lockouts.[185] Not surprisingly, when Louis Brandeis sought to persuade Samuel Gompers that the labor move-

---

183. Rubinstein (2006). The case that initiated this line of interpretation did not involve a union but another type of nonprofit group: *McCabe v. Goodfellow*, 133 N.Y. 89 (NY 1892).

184. For example, New Jersey Session Laws, General Public Acts, 1885, pp. 26–27 (applied to labor unions in *Michael Mayer et al. v. The Journeymen Stonecutters' Association et al.* [NJ 1890]; *Barr vs. Essex Trades Council* [NJ 1894]); Ohio Session Laws, 50th General Assembly, 1852, Vol. 51, § 37, p. 62 (applied to labor unions in *Hillenbrand v. Building Trades Council et al.*, 14 Ohio Dec. 628 [OH 1904]); "An Act Relating to Voluntary Associations," Connecticut Session Laws, January Session, 1893, Ch. 32, p. 216; Michigan Session Laws, 1897, No. 15, p. 25 (applied to labor union in *United States Heater Co. v. Iron Molders' Union of North America* [Mich. 1902]). Similar rulings were, in Nevada, *L. C. Branson v. The Industrial Workers of the World* (NV 1908) (citing "Section 14 of the Civil Practice Act of Nevada [Comp. Laws, 3109]"); and, in a federal circuit court, *American Steel & Wire Co. v. Wire Drawers' & Die Makers' Union Nos. 1 and 3 et al.* (US District Court 1898 [citing US Rev. St., § 954]). The key case establishing that unions were suable under federal law was *United Mine Workers v. Coronado Coal Co.*, 259 U.S. 344 (1922). By 1980 only four states—Massachusetts, Illinois, Mississippi, and West Virginia—still followed the common law rule that unincorporated associations could not sue or be sued (as reported in the case in which Massachusetts finally abandoned the rule, *DiLuzio v. United Electrical, Radio and Machine Workers*, 435 N.E. 2d 1027 [MA 1982]).

185. "An Act Concerning Carriers Engaged in Interstate Commerce and Their Employees," US Statutes at Large, 55th Congress, Session 2, pp. 424–28, § 8, p. 427.

ment should seize the opportunity of acquiring corporate rights, Gompers responded without hesitation, "No, thank you!"[186]

For political parties, like unions, the widening access to incorporation during the second half of the nineteenth century briefly opened up an opportunity to expand their associational rights that ended up being decisively closed. During the period of expansion, New York, long the home of the Tammany Society corporation, unsurprisingly went the farthest in granting corporate rights to politically partisan groups. Tammany's leaders, by then at the heart of the Democratic political machine, were able in the 1850s and 1870s to brush off renewed questions about the legitimacy of the Society's 1805 special charter as a charitable group, and in 1867 they even successfully petitioned the legislature to increase the corporation's property limit.[187] Around the same time, New York extended similar rights to other groups. In 1875 it revised its general incorporation law in 1875 to include "political, economic, patriot" societies and clubs along with athletic, social, musical, and other recreational ones.[188] Then it followed with a separate act in 1886 allowing for the incorporation of "political clubs" that omitted an earlier provision for visitorial powers by the Supreme Court that applied to other nonprofit groups.[189] The New York Membership Corporations Law of 1895 revoked these earlier laws and abandoned the long string of adjectives that previously defined corporate eligibility, but its inclusive language still left open the possibility of parties or partisan organizations incorporating.[190] As we will see, the courts soon cut off that possibility.

No state other than New York seems to have explicitly included political groups in a general incorporation law. Nonetheless, scattered evidence suggests that "Democratic" and "Republican" clubs received special acts of incorporation in several states during the late nineteenth century, including New Jersey, Maryland, South Carolina, Tennessee, and Kentucky.[191] It is not possible to know simply from the names of these groups whether they

186. "The Incorporation of Trade Unions," 1 Green Bag 2d 306 (Spring 1998), quote at 306. Gompers's reply originally appeared in the *Boston Globe*, Dec. 5, 1902.

187. On the 1850s challenge to the charter, see Mushkat (1971, 273, 283). In the 1870s, there were two similarly failed challenges, a legislative petition to revoke the charter and a law suit: State of New York (1872, 175) and *Thompson v. Society of Tammany*, in Hun (1879, vol. 24, 305–16). The 1867 charter revision can be found in New York Session Laws, 90th Legislature, 1867, Vol. 2, Ch. 593, p. 1615.

188. "An Act for the Incorporation of Societies or Clubs for Certain Lawful Purposes," New York Session Laws, 97th and 98th Legislatures, 1875, Ch. 267, pp. 264–66.

189. "An Act of the Incorporation of Political Clubs," New York Session Laws, 109th Legislature, 1886, Ch. 236, pp. 409–11.

190. "An Act Relating to Membership Corporations," New York Session Laws, 118th Legislature, 1895, Vol. 1, Ch. 559, pp. 329–67.

191. This evidence is based on searches in the HeinOnline Session Laws database, which yielded acts of incorporation for groups with titles that contained "Democrat," "Democratic," and "Republican." For example, in addition to those cited below, New Jersey Session Laws, 1870, Ch. 196, pp. 459–60; Maryland Session Laws, 1868, pp. 821–23; Tennessee Session Laws, 1867–68, p. 385; Connecticut Session Laws, Special Acts and Resolutions, January 1897, p. 1243.

were affiliated with political parties—they could have been educational or civic groups upholding broader "democratic" and "republican" principles. At least one of them, however, the Republican State League of Kentucky, stated on its petition for incorporation in 1886 that its objects were "to advocate, promote and maintain the principles of the Republican Party."[192]

This fledgling development of political corporations quickly fell victim to an onslaught of electoral reforms that changed the legal status of political parties.[193] Previously, states had left parties essentially free of regulatory control. Partisan electoral practices had since the Jacksonian era regularly included the nomination of candidates at closed party conventions and the distribution of premarked ballots at polling places. At the end of the nineteenth century, Progressive politicians asserted state regulatory authority over elections, passing laws that mandated direct primaries and secret ballots in an effort to clip the power of party machines. At least thirty states had by 1900 specified procedures for the conduct of conventions and primary elections.[194] At the same time, states moved against partisan corporations, either categorically denying the incorporation of political clubs or tightening their control over nonprofit corporations with partisan purposes.

In Pennsylvania, courts seized on the legal rationale that the 1874 general act had not explicitly included political groups in its list of qualified organizations. A precedent-setting lower court opinion of 1889 held that clubs of Democrats and Republicans could incorporate only if they described themselves purely as social organizations and not political ones.[195] The suspicion that a purportedly social and educational club was truly a partisan group similarly thwarted the bid by a Republican club for a charter in 1897, with the judge declaring emphatically that "the law does not authorize the incorporation of political clubs, and in all reported cases the courts have refused charters where the articles of association disclosed a political purpose."[196]

In 1900, New York took much the same step. Despite the legislature's recent passage of incorporation laws suggesting the contrary, the New York Supreme Court's interpretation of the state's Primary Election Law of 1899 held that parties were no longer to be regarded as private associations but as parts of the state. Writing for the majority, Chief Justice Parker refused

192. "An Act to Incorporate the Republican State League of Kentucky," Kentucky Session Laws, 1886, Vol. 3, Ch. 1638, p. 1128. By contrast, the "Planter's Republican Society" of South Carolina was listed in the index as a "benevolent" organization. South Carolina Session Laws, 1873–74, p. 6.

193. Epperson (1986, 46–151).

194. Epperson (1986, 51).

195. *In re. Charters of the Central Democratic Association, and Young Republican Club of the Thirtieth Ward*, 8 Pa. C.C. R. 392 (1889). Pennsylvania justices cited this case well into the twentieth century. For example: *In re Forty-Seventh Ward Republican Club*, 17 Dist. R. 509 (C. P. Phila., 1908); *Fourth Ward Democratic Club* (1911) 20 Dist. R. 841 (Northhampton, 1911); *Republican League Incorporation*, 63 Pa. D. & C. 643 (1948).

196. *In re Monroe Republican Club*, 6 Dist. R. 515 (Allegheny, 1897), quote at 516. This case was also cited in the 1908 and 1911 cases noted above.

to allow the Democratic General Committee of Kings County to expel an elected delegate because he was disloyal to the principles of the party.[197] The opinion differentiated the case from another one tried by the same court in 1890, in which the justices decided that a party committee, as a voluntary association, was free to conduct itself however it wished.[198] The intervening passage of the election reform law, however, had rendered that decision irrelevant. As Parker put it, "the voluntary character of the county general committee has been destroyed."[199] Justice Cullin, who argued that the Kings County Democratic Committee had the same rights as a corporation, stood alone in dissent.[200] In other states where political party groups retained access to incorporation, moreover, corporate status lost its characteristic ability to confer autonomy from the state. In Missouri, political groups still sought corporate status in the early years of the twentieth century, but the legislature passed a statute in 1907 mandating the strict scrutiny of all "leagues, committees, associations, or societies" that published material about candidates for public office. Whether "incorporated or unincorporated," the law made clear, such political groups had to fully disclose all their sources of information, submit detailed reports on the amount of money they raised, and provide the names and addresses of their contributors.[201]

By the turn of the century, political parties no longer could operate with minimal interference from the state. They had moved from being unregulated voluntary associations, typically without corporate status, to being, much like earlier corporations, closely regulated extensions of the state. Of course, political parties had never been privately organized in the same way as most other voluntary groups. Politicians stood at their helms, and partisan positions structured the work of public officials inside the government as well as informing the views of private citizens within the electorate. Because parties were so deeply intertwined with the government, meaningful constraints on their freedom were necessary to lower the high risks of political

197. *People v. Democratic General Committee of Kings County*, 164 N.Y. 335 (NY 1900). Also see Epperson (1986, 75–77).

198. *McKane v. Democratic General Committee*, 123 N.Y. 609 (NY 1890).

199. *People v. Democratic General Committee of Kings County*, 164 N.Y. 335 (NY 1900) at 342.

200. *People v. Democratic General Committee of Kings County*, 164 N.Y. 335 (NY 1900), at 347–48.

201. "An Act to Regulate Civic Leagues and Like Associations," Missouri Session Laws, 44th General Assembly, 1907, pp. 261–62. Special thanks to Michael Everman of the Missouri State Archives, who provided the names of organizations that filed pro forma papers with the St. Louis county court as part of the process of applying for incorporation (Missouri, like New York and Pennsylvania, was unusual for requiring judicial approval under its general act of incorporation for voluntary groups). These applications date back to the mid-nineteenth century, but explicitly partisan organizations did not request incorporation until 1901. Although the state's general law of incorporation of 1879 specifically excluded groups with political purposes, this language was dropped in the 1889 version. Missouri *Revised Statutes*, 1879, § 978, p. 280, and 1889 *Revised Statutes*, Article 10, § 2829, p. 721. The Missouri regulatory law of 1907 coincided with congressional passage of the Tillman Act forbidding corporate involvement in political campaigns.

corruption (Tammany Society, again, being a case in point). Theoretically, states or the federal government could have regulated parties as corporations by adding provisions to incorporation laws, but the state of Missouri proved to be unusual in taking this route. In Pennsylvania and New York, where the general laws for nonprofit corporations were ambiguous about the eligibility of partisan groups, justices chose to invalidate political corporations outright.

It was in this context that Congress passed the Tillman Act of 1907 forbidding corporate involvement in political campaigns.[202] The act was a reaction against corrupt political activities of business corporations, specifically the insurance industry, not voluntary associations. Understandably, the political influence of for-profit corporations was perceived as especially dangerous, both because they commanded greater wealth than nonprofits and because the government more actively regulated them. But it would be a mistake to think that the resurgence of anticorporate feeling that underlay the act was entirely directed toward business. The Tillman Act expressed the same normative logic as the denial of corporate status to political parties: corporations and politics should not mix.

In the case of both political parties and labor unions, access to corporate rights widened at roughly the same time as governments took other legal steps to curb their associational rights. In some ways, the outcome by the turn of the twentieth century was very different for these two types of groups. Unions remained unrecognized as legal entities, preferring to negotiate with businesses without the backing of the state because of the dangers of judicial intervention. Political parties, by contrast, assumed the legal status of entities through the government's enactment of campaign legislation, thereby losing their earlier freedom from state control. At the same time, however, the common failure of both types of groups to gain the extensive associational rights ordinarily held by corporations reveals an underlying similarity between them. Both unions and political parties were socially and politically polarizing. They came closer to incorporating than many other contentious groups of the period, in large part because of their wide public acceptance and official support, but each of them ended the period besieged by politically powerful foes. Their stories illustrate how difficult it was for polarizing groups to acquire strong associational rights even after the great expansion of access to corporate status. In the end, both groups acquired a set of associational rights via government regulation—parties during the Progressive era, and unions during the New Deal—albeit they both still lacked, for better and worse, the extraordinary degree of autonomy that nonprofit corporations had already achieved by the end of the nineteenth century.[203]

---

202. See Winkler (2000) drawing a comparison between parties and business corporations, but not nonprofit ones.
203. On unions, see Levi et al. (chapter 9, this volume).

7.7 Conclusion

From the Revolution to the turn of the twentieth century, public officials generally agreed that corporations should stay out of politics at the same as they made essentially political decisions about which voluntary associations could incorporate and what rights corporations would receive. During the first decades of the nineteenth century, when politicians routinely rewarded their partisan allies with charters, the nonprofit organizations that succeeded in becoming corporations needed to appear, at least on the surface, to be nonpartisan. Churches, colleges, mutual benefit societies, and other "educational or charitable" groups were ostensibly worthy of charters because they served the common welfare, whereas groups that fostered social and political change served only a dissident faction. Later in the century, the allocation of charters generally ceased to be determined either by partisan loyalty or by the requirement that corporations serve the common welfare. Yet fundamentally political decisions still defined which groups had access to incorporation, and on what terms.

As we have seen, the largest categories of groups chronically deprived of corporate rights consisted of political parties, labor unions, and social reform societies. Organizations formed by (or on behalf of) religious and ethnic minorities also experienced difficulty becoming incorporated, more frequently at the beginning of the century than at the end. Meanwhile, the overwhelming majority of voluntary associations that become corporations throughout the century were uncontroversial, mainstream groups whose access to corporate rights frequently depended on their acquiescence to the social and political status quo. This distinction between politically acceptable and politically unacceptable persisted despite the widening of access to the corporate form. Although some organizations without corporate status became able by the late nineteenth century to claim limited entity and personhood rights, particularly the right to property, they, too, needed to conform to recognized definitions of religion or "charity" (like the ones used for and against the Henry George book fund).

At the same time as this pattern of exclusion persisted, moreover, the rights of acceptable nonprofit corporations grew even stronger, a development that made corporate status all the more valuable. By the end of the century, the multiple benefits of incorporation included not only the legal protections needed to accumulate large amounts of property and avoid membership liability, but the ability to own stocks and control subsidiary corporations. In addition, the reduced risk of judicial intervention in internal disputes bolstered the standard corporate right of self-governance. As courts and legislatures paved the way to this enlarged field of potential advantages, the state's discriminatory role as gatekeeper still functioned much as it did in the earlier era of special charters. Tocqueville to the contrary, the widespread freedom of individuals to associate in American civil society never meant that the associations they formed were equally free.

This nineteenth-century history might lead one to think that removing the barriers to corporate status would reduce the politicization of associational rights. Developments since then, however, suggest otherwise.[204] States in the mid-twentieth century eliminated almost all of the restrictive categories and veto powers built into earlier general incorporation laws. Today, nonprofit corporations can be organized by virtually anyone for virtually any purpose. The opening of nearly complete access to incorporation has not, however, completely equalized access to associational rights. Important vestiges of the nineteenth-century distinctions between favored and disfavored groups survive, most notably in the federal tax code.[205] The same types of elite and religiously and culturally conservative nonprofit organizations that have always found it easy to incorporate have disproportionately benefited from the right of their donors to make tax-deductible contributions—a right that remains out of reach to "political" organizations as well as to otherwise eligible "charitable" organizations without the resources to comply with IRS requirements.[206] Despite the fact that most nonprofit groups are permitted to claim exemptions on all or part of the organization's own income, the qualifications for this benefit still varies substantially among different types of organizations. A labor union officially recognized by the National Labor Relations Board (NLRB), for example, may take a deduction for its aid to striking workers whereas another labor organization distributing aid to union members for the same authorized strike cannot.[207] More well known is

---

204. Valuable surveys of twentieth-century developments include Silber (2001), Hall (1992), and Hansmann (1989).

205. On this shift, see especially Silber (2001). Already in the colonial period many churches and other privileged categories of voluntary associations (and businesses) benefited from tax exempt status, benefits that persisted through the nineteenth century. Until the inauguration of the federal income tax at the beginning of the twentieth century, tax exemptions typically pertained only to property taxes on a group's land and did not confer any benefits to donors.

206. The most relevant sections of the Internal Revenue Code are sections 501(c)(3) ("Religious and Charitable"), 501(c)(4) ("Social Welfare"), and 527 ("Political"). For an overview of these rules, see http://www.irs.gov/Charities-&-Non-Profits. For more detailed information, see chapters 2–4 in http://www.irs.gov/publications/p557/.

207. This rule emerged from a 1976 IRS decision to deny a deduction to a group of workers belonging to "various" unions who started a strike fund. The disqualification was based on the fact that it was composed of "private persons" without the "authority" to represent its members in collective bargaining. IRS Publications, "IRC 501(c)(5) Organizations," p. J-16, at http://www.irs.gov/pub/irs-tege/eotopicj03.pdf. Presumably meant to discourage union members from forming nonunion support organizations, this rule seems to contradict the IRS definition of a qualified "labor organization" as not restricted to unions (J-4), as well as other rulings in 1959 and 1974 that enabled nonunion groups to qualify for deductions (J-5–J-6). For a current treatise confirming that, in practice, "labor organization" refers only to unions and union-controlled organizations (without explicitly stating that NLRB certification is necessary), see Hopkins (2016, § 16.1, 445–48). On the history behind the NLRB's official recognition of unions, including its costs to classes of excluded workers, see Levi et al. (chapter 9, this volume).

the right of nonprofit groups with political leanings, including organizations registering in the "social welfare" category that permits legislative lobbying and limited election spending, to conceal the identities of their donors in their tax filings. Political parties and political action committees (PACs) classified as "political" (because their activities are "primarily" electoral), however, must publicly disclose the names of their contributors.[208] With these "extra" associational rights of tax deductibility and donor anonymity hanging in the balance, it is not surprising that IRS employees, much like Judge Bird in 1888, struggle to distinguish between "charitable," "social welfare," and "political" purposes. Henry George and his followers could today easily become a nonprofit corporation with an entity right to receive property, but their association would most likely still lack the full range of associational rights conferred by the law.

In the century following the American Revolution, access to basic corporate rights clearly provided advantages to the typically mainstream voluntary associations that most often acquired them. A corollary of the systematic denial of such rights to politically dissident and socially marginal groups was to keep their associations relatively small and ephemeral. Tocqueville himself may be forgiven for celebrating the liberty of United States citizens to associate. His failure to perceive the unequal rights granted by the state to the voluntary associations they formed, however, need no longer obscure our historical understanding of American civil society.

References

Angell, Joseph Kinnicut, and Samuel Ames. 1855. *A Treatise on the Law of Private Corporations Aggregate*, 5th ed., rev., corr., and enl. Boston: Little Brown.

Anonymous. 1804. *The Constitution of the St. Patrick Benevolent Society*. Philadelphia: No Publisher.

Beitel, Calvin G. 1874. *A Digest of Titles of Corporations Chartered by the Legislature of Pennsylvania . . . 1700 [to] 1873*, 2nd rev. and enl. ed. Philadelphia: John Campbell & Son.

Bell, Sadie. 1930. *The Church, The State, and Education in Virginia*. Philadelphia: Science Press.

208. IRS Publications, 4221-PC, p. 24, at http://www.irs.gov/pub/irs-pdf/p4221pc.pdf. Also see http://www.irs.gov/Charities-&-Non-Profits/Political-Organizations/Political-Organization -Filing-and-Disclosure. Since the US Supreme Court's *Citizen's United* decision in 2011 opened the doors to corporate campaign spending, groups have extra incentives to file as "social welfare" organizations because they can report donations to SuperPACs using the names of the organization rather than the names of the original donors. On these currently controversial issues, see "Left and Right Object to I.R.S. Plan to Restrict Nonprofits' Political Activity," *New York Times*, Feb. 13, 2014, p. A15; "A Campaign Inquiry in Utah Is the Watchdogs' Worst Case," *New York Times*, Mar. 18, 2014, p. A1; "Democrats Lean Heavily on PACs in Coordinated Push to Counter G.O.P.," *New York Times*, Oct. 5, 2014, p. A1.

Bloch, Ruth H. 2003. *Gender and Morality in Anglo-American Culture, 1650–1800*. Berkeley: University of California Press.

Bloch, Ruth H., and Naomi R. Lamoreaux. 2017. "Corporations and the Fourteenth Amendment." In *Corporations and American Democracy*, edited by Naomi R. Lamoreaux and William J. Novak, 286–325. Cambridge, MA: Harvard University Press.

Blumberg, Phillip I. 1986. "Limited Liability and Corporate Groups." *Journal of Corporation Law* 11 (Summer): 573–631.

Bridenbaugh, Carl. 1938. *Cities in the Wilderness: The First Century of Urban Life in America, 1625–1742*. New York: Oxford University Press.

Brooke, John L. 2010. *Columbia Rising: Civil Life on the Upper Hudson from the Revolution to the Age of Jackson*. Chapel Hill: University of North Carolina Press.

Buckingham, Joseph T. 1853. *Annals of the Massachusetts Charitable Mechanic Association*. Boston: Crocker and Brewster.

Buckley, S. J., Thomas E. 1995. "After Disestablishment: Thomas Jefferson's Wall of Separation in Antebellum Virginia." *Journal of Southern History* 61 (3): 445–80.

Bullock, Steven C. 1996. *Revolutionary Brotherhood: Freemasonry and the Transformation of the American Social Order, 1730–1840*. Chapel Hill: University of North Carolina Press.

Butterfield, Kevin. 2015. *The Making of Tocqueville's America: Law and Association in the Early United States*. Chicago: University of Chicago Press.

Campbell, Bruce A. 1990. "Social Federalism: The Constitutional Position of Nonprofit Corporations in Nineteenth-Century America." *Law and History Review* 8 (2): 149–88.

Canon, Bradley C., and Dean Jaros. 1979. "The Impact of Changes in Judicial Doctrine: The Abrogation of Charitable Immunity." *Law and Society* 13 (Summer): 969–86.

Commons, John R., et al. 1918–1935. *History of Labor in the United States*, vols. 1–4. New York: MacMillan.

Commonwealth of Massachusetts. 1814. "An Act to Incorporate Certain Persons by the Name of the Massachusetts General Hospital." In *Laws of the Commonwealth, from February 28, 1807 to . . . 1814*. Boston: Thomas and Andrews.

———. 1816. *The Public and General Laws of the Commonwealth of Massachusetts, from Feb 28, 1807 to Feb 16, 1816*, vol. 4. Boston: Wells and Lilly.

———. 1837. *Private and Special Statutes of the Commonwealth of Massachusetts, for the Years 1830–1837*, vol. 7. Boston: Dutton and Wentworth.

———. 1860. *Private and Special Statutes of the Commonwealth of Massachusetts, for the Years 1849–1853*, vol. 9. Boston: William White.

———. 1882. *The Public Statutes of the Commonwealth of Massachusetts*. Boston: Rand, Aberg, and Company.

Commonwealth of Pennsylvania. 1810. "Laws, Statutes . . . 1700–1800." In *Laws of the Commonwealth*, 4 vols. Philadelphia: Bioren, 3:20.

———. 1837–1839. *Proceedings and Debates of the Convention of the Commonwealth of Pennsylvania to Propose Amendments of the Constitution, Commenced and Held at Harrisburg on the Second Day of May, 1837*, vol. 3. Harrisburg: No Publisher.

Commonwealth of Virginia. 1849. *The Code of Virginia*. Richmond: Ritchie.

Cott, Nancy F. 1977. *Bonds of Womanhood: "Woman's Sphere" in New England, 1780–1835*. New Haven, CT: Yale University Press.

Countryman, Edward F. 1976. "'Out of the Bounds of the Law': Northern Land Rioters in the Eighteenth Century." In *The American Revolution: Explorations in the History of American Radicalism*, edited by Alfred F. Young, 37–69. DeKalb, IL: Northern Illinois University Press.

Crane, Daniel A. 2017. "The Dissociation of Incorporation and Regulation in the Progressive Era and the New Deal." In *Corporations and American Democracy*, edited by Naomi R. Lamoreaux and William Novak. Cambridge, MA: Harvard University Press.

Cushing, John D. 1969. "Notes on Disestablishment in Massachusetts, 1780–1833." *William and Mary Quarterly* 26 (Apr.): 172–85.

Davis, Joseph Stancliffe. 1917. *Essays in the Earlier History of American Corporations*, vols. 1–2. Cambridge, MA: Harvard University Press.

DeSaussure, Henry William. 1817. *Reports of Cases Argued and Determined in the Court of Chancery of the State of South-Carolina*, vol. 3. Columbia, SC: Cline & Hones.

Diamond, Stephen. 2002. "Efficiency and Benevolence: Philanthropic Tax Exemptions in 19th-Century America." In *Property-Tax Exemption for Charities*, ed. Evelyn Brody, 115–44. Washington, DC: Urban Institute Press.

Epperson, John W. 1986. *The Changing Status of Political Parties in the United States*. New York: Garland.

Fishman, James J. 1985. "The Development of Nonprofit Corporation Law and an Agenda for Reform." *Emory Law Journal* 34 (Summer): 617–83.

George, Jr., Henry. 1900. *The Life of Henry George, by His Son*. London: William Reeves.

Ginzburg, Lori D. 1990. *Women and the Work of Benevolence*. New Haven, CT: Yale University Press.

Gordon, Sarah Barringer. 2014. "The First Disestablishment: Limits on Church Power and Property before the Civil War." *University of Pennsylvania Law Review* 162 (2): 307–72.

———. 2015. "The African Supplement: Religion, Race, and Corporate Law in Early National America." *William and Mary Quarterly* 72 (3): 385–422.

Griffen, Clifford S. 1960. *Their Brothers' Keepers: Moral Stewardship in the United States, 1800–1865*. New Brunswick, NJ: Rutgers University Press.

Habermas, Jürgen. 1989. *The Structural Transformation of the Public Sphere: An Inquiry into a Category of Bourgeois Society*, trans. Thomas Burger. Cambridge, MA: MIT Press.

Hall, Peter Dobkin. 1982. *The Organization of American Culture, 1700–1900: Private Institution, Elites and the Origins of American Nationality*. New York: New York University Press.

———. 1992. *Inventing the Nonprofit Sector and Other Essays on Philanthropy, Voluntarism, and Nonprofit Organizations*. Baltimore: Johns Hopkins University Press.

Handlin, Oscar, and Mary F. Handlin. 1945. "Origins of the American Business Corporation." *Journal of Economic History* 5 (1): 8–17.

Hansmann, Henry B. 1989. "The Evolving Law of Nonprofit Organizations: Do Current Trends Make Good Policy?" *Case Western Reserve Law Review* 39 (3): 807–29.

Hattam, Victoria C. 1993. *Labor Visions and State Power: The Origins of Business Unionism in the United States*. Princeton, NJ: Princeton University Press.

Henderson, Elizabeth K. 1937. "The Attack on the Judiciary in Pennsylvania, 1800–1810." *Pennsylvania Magazine of History and Biography* 61 (Apr.): 113–36.

Hilt, Eric. 2017. "Early American Corporations and the State." In *Corporations and American Democracy*, edited by Naomi R. Lamoreaux and William Novak. Cambridge, MA: Harvard University Press.

Hindle, Brooke. 1946. "The March of the Paxton Boys." *William and Mary Quarterly* 3 (Oct.): 461–86.

Hirschler, Edward S. 1938. "Note: A Survey of Charitable Trusts in Virginia." *Virginia Law Review* 25 (Nov.): 109–15.

Hofstadter, Richard. 1969. *The Idea of a Party System: The Rise of Legitimate Opposition in the United States, 1780–1840*. Berkeley: University of California Press.

Hopkins, Bruce R. 2016. *The Law of Tax-Exempt Organizations*, 11th ed. Hoboken, NJ: Wiley & Sons.

Horwitz, Morton J. 1992. *The Transformation of American Law: 1870–1960*. New York: Oxford University Press.

Hovenkamp, Herbert. 1988. "Labor Conspiracies in American Law, 1880–1930." *Texas Law Review* 66 (Apr.): 949–57.

Hun, Marcus Tullius, ed. 1879. *Reports of Cases Heard and Determined by the Supreme Court of the State of New York*, vol. 24. New York: Banks and Brothers.

Isaac, Rhys. 1982. *The Transformation of Virginia, 1749–1790*. Chapel Hill: North Carolina University Press.

Jones, Gareth. 1969. *History of the Law of Charity, 1532–1827*. Cambridge, UK: Cambridge University Press.

Jordan, W. K. 1959. *Philanthropy in England, 1480–1660*. London: George Allen and Unwin.

Katz, Stanley N., Barry Sullivan, and C. Paul Beach. 1985. "Legal Change and Legal Autonomy: Charitable Trusts in New York, 1777–1893." *Law and History Review* 3 (1): 51–89.

Kaufman, Jason. 2002. *For the Common Good? American Civic Life and the Golden Age of Fraternity*. New York: Oxford University Press.

———. 2008. "Corporate Law and the Sovereignty of States." *American Sociological Review* 73 (June): 402–25.

Kent, James. 1826. *Commentaries on American Law*. New York: O. Halsted.

Koschnik, Albrecht. 2007. *"Let a Common Interest Bind Us Together": Associations, Partisanship, and Culture in Philadelphia, 1775–1840*. Charlottesville: University of Virginia Press.

Lamoreaux, Naomi R. 2015. "Revisiting American Exceptionalism: Democracy and the Regulation of Corporate Governance in Nineteenth-Century Pennsylvania." In *Enterprising America: Businesses, Banks, and Credit Markets in Historical Perspective*, edited by William J. Collins and Robert A. Margo, 25–72. Chicago: University of Chicago Press.

Levy, Leonard W. 1960. *Freedom of Speech and Press in Early American History: Legacy of Suppression*. Cambridge, MA: Harvard University Press.

Lipset, Seymour Martin. 1963. *The First Nation: The United States in Historical and Comparative Perspective*. New York: W. W. Norton.

Livermore, Shaw. 1935. "Unlimited Liability in Early American Corporations." *Journal of Political Economy* 43 (Oct.): 674–87.

Longworth, David. 1807. *Longworth's American Almanac, New York Register and City Directory for the Thirty-Second Year of American Independence*. New York: David Longworth.

Maier, Pauline. 1970. "Popular Uprisings and Civil Authority." *William and Mary Quarterly* 27 (Jan.): 3–35.

———. 1993. "The Revolutionary Origins of the American Corporation." *William and Mary Quarterly* 50 (Jan.): 53–55.

Maitland, F. W. 1900. "The Corporation Sole." *Law Quarterly Review* 16 (Oct.): 335–54.

Marini, Stephen A. 1982. *Radical Sects of Revolutionary New England*. Cambridge, MA: Harvard University Press.

Marks, David. 1846. *Memoirs of the Life of David Marks, Minister of the Gospel*, edited by Marilla Marks. Dover, NH: William Burr.

Massachusetts Charitable Mechanic Association. 1892. *Annals of the Massachusetts Charitable Mechanic Association, 1795–1892*. Boston: Rockwell and Churchill.

McCarthy, Kathleen D. 2003. *American Creed: Philanthropy and the Rise of Civil Society, 1700–1865*. Chicago: University of Chicago Press.

Miller, Howard S. 1961. *The Legal Foundations of American Philanthropy, 1776–1844*. Madison: State Historical Society of Wisconsin.

Morgan, Edmund M., and Helen M. Morgan. 1953. *The Stamp Act Crisis: A Prologue to Revolution*. Chapel Hill: North Carolina University Press.

Mushkat, Jerome. 1971. *Tammany: The Evolution of a Political Machine, 1789–1865*. Syracuse, NY: Syracuse University Press.

Myers, Gustavus. 1901. *The History of Tammany Hall*. New York: Published by the Author.

Nash, Gary B. 1988. *Forging Freedom: The Formation of Philadelphia's Black Community, 1720–1840*. Cambridge, MA: Harvard University Press.

Neem, Johann N. 2003. "Freedom of Association in the Early Republic: The Republican Party, the Whiskey Rebellion, and the Philadelphia and New York Cordwainers' Cases." *Pennsylvania Magazine of History and Biography* 127 (July): 259–90.

———. 2008. *Creating a Nation of Joiners: Democracy and Civil Society in Early National Massachusetts*. Cambridge, MA: Harvard University Press.

New Jersey, Secretary of State. 1892. *Corporations of New Jersey: List of Certificates Filed in the Department of State from 1846 to 1891, Inclusive*. Trenton: Naar, Day & Naar.

Newman, Richard S. 2008. *Freedom's Prophet: Bishop Richard Allen, the AME Church, and the Black Founding Fathers*. New York: NYU Press.

North, Douglass C., John Joseph Wallis, and Barry R. Weingast. 2009. *Violence and Social Orders: A Conceptual Framework for Interpreting Recorded Human History*. New York: Cambridge University Press.

Novak, William J. 2001. "The American Law of Association: The Legal-Political Construction of Civil Society." *Studies in American Political Development* 15 (Oct.): 163–88.

Ohio, Secretary of State. 1885. *Annual Report of the Secretary of State, to the Governor of the State of Ohio, For the Year 1885*. Columbus: Westbote Co.

Owen, David. 1964. *English Philanthropy, 1660–1960*. Cambridge, MA: Harvard University Press.

Perkins, Edwin J. 1994. *American Public Finance and Financial Services, 1700–1815*. Columbus: Ohio State University Press.

Phillips, Kim T. 1977. "William Duane, Philadelphia's Democratic Republicans, and the Origins of Modern Politics." *Pennsylvania Magazine of History and Biography* 101 (July): 365–87.

Putnam, Robert D. 2000. *Bowling Alone: The Collapse and Revival of American Community*. New York: Simon and Schuster.

Quarles, Benjamin. 1945. "Sources of Abolitionist Income." *Mississippi Valley Historical Review* 32 (June): 63–76.

Rubinstein, Mitchell H. 2006. "Union Immunity from Suit in New York." *New York University Journal of Law & Business* 2 (Summer): 641–82.

Schlesinger, Arthur M. 1944. "Biography of a Nation of Joiners." *American Historical Review* 50 (Oct.): 1–25.

Shammas, Carole, Marylynn Salmon, and Michel Dahlin. 1987. *Inheritance in America: From Colonial Times to the Present*. New Brunswick, NJ: Rutgers University Press.

Shields, David. 1997. *Civil Tongues and Polite Letters in British America*. Chapel Hill: University of North Carolina Press.

Shurtleff, Nathaniel B., ed. 1854. *The Records of the Governor and the Company of the Massachusetts Bay in New England, 1661–1674*, vols. 1–5, 1853–54. Boston: William White.

Silber, Norman I. 2001. *A Corporate Form of Freedom: The Emergences of the Modern Nonprofit Sector*. Boulder, CO: Westview.

Skocpol, Theda, Marshall Ganz, and Ziad Munson. 2000. "A Nation of Organizers: The Institutional Origins of Civic Voluntarism in the United States." *American Political Science Review* 94 (Sept.): 527–46.

Sloan, Jr., Charles William. 1974. "Kansas Battles the Invisible Empire: The Legal Ouster of the KKK from Kansas, 1922–1927." *Kansas Historical Quarterly* 40 (Fall): 393–409.

State of New Hampshire. 1867. *The General Statutes of the State of New Hampshire*. Manchester: John B. Clarke, State Printer.

State of New York. 1816. *Journal of the Senate of the State of New-York, at Their Thirty-Ninth Session*. Albany: J. Buel.

———. 1817. *Journal of the Assembly of the State of New York, at Their Fortieth Session*. Albany: J. Buel.

———. 1818. *Journal of the Assembly of the State of New York, at Their Forty-First Session*. Albany: J. Buel.

———. 1872. *Journal of the Senate of the State of New York at Their Ninety-Fifth Session*. Albany: Argus Company.

State of Ohio. 1879. *The Revised Statutes and Other Acts . . . of the State of Ohio, in Force January 1, 1880*, vol. 1. Columbus: H. W. Derby and Company.

State of South Carolina. 1840. *Statutes at Large of South Carolina*, vol. 8, edited by David J. McCord. Columbia: A. S. Johnston.

Stevens, George A. 1913. *History of New York Typographical Union No. 6*. Albany, NY: J. B. Lyon.

Street, Alfred B., ed. 1859. *The Council of Revision of the State of New York*. Albany, NY: William Gould.

Tocqueville, Alexis de. 1945. *Democracy in America*, vols. 1 and 2, trans. Henry Reeve and Francis Bowen. New York: A. A. Knopf.

Tomlins, Christopher L. 1985. *The State and the Unions: Labor Relations, Law, and the Organized Labor Movement in America, 1880–1960*. New York: Cambridge University Press.

———. 1993. *Law, Labor, and Ideology in the Early American Republic*. New York: Cambridge University Press.

United States. 1798. *Laws of the Territory of the United States North West of the River Ohio*. Cincinnati: Edmund Freeman.

Whitehead, John S. 1973. *The Separation of College and State: Columbia, Dartmouth, Harvard and Yale, 1776–1876*. New Haven, CT: Yale University Press.

Whittenburg, James P. 1977. "Planters, Merchants, and Lawyers: Social Change and the Origins of the North Carolina Regulation." *William and Mary Quarterly* 34 (Apr.): 215–38.

Wilson, David A. 1998. *United Irishmen, United States: Immigrant Radicals in the Early Republic*. Ithaca, NY: Cornell University Press.

Winkler, Adam. 2000. "Law and Political Parties: Voters' Rights and Parties' Wrongs: Early Political Party Regulation in the State Courts, 1886–1915." *Columbia Law Review* 100 (Apr.): 873–900.

Wood, William. 1939–1940. "What are Improper Corporate Purposes for Nonprofit Corporations?" *Dickinson Law Review* 44 (Oct.–May): 266.

Wrenn III, George L. 1971. "The Bricklayers Company of the City and County of Philadelphia." *Bulletin of the Association for Preservation Technology* 3 (4): 73–75.

Wright, Conrad Edick. 1992. *The Transformation of Charity in Postrevolutionary New England.* Boston: Northeastern University Press.

Wyllie, Irwin G. 1959. "The Search for an American Law of Charity, 1776–1844." *Mississippi Valley Historical Review* 46 (Sept.): 203–21.

Young, Alfred F. 1967. *The Democratic Republicans of New York: The Origins 1763–1797.* Chapel Hill: University of North Carolina Press, for the Institute of Early American History and Culture, Williamsburg, VA.

8

The Right to Associate and the Rights of Associations
Civil-Society Organizations in Prussia, 1794–1908

Richard Brooks and Timothy W. Guinnane

Was der Mensch ist, verdankt er der Vereinigung von Mensch und Mensch.[1]

In many countries today, the freedom to associate is seen as a fundamental right. A comprehensive survey of the world's written constitutions reveals that as of 2012, 93 percent include a right to assembly and 94 percent a right of association.[2] That these rights are provided as de jure entitlements in constitutional documents does not, to be sure, guarantee they are respected by officials in practice. In most modern democracies, however, entitlements of assembly and association are well-established bedrock features of democratic order and practice. Civil-society groups in these countries often enjoy additional civil and political rights that make it easier for these groups to cohere and to advance an agenda. Such has not always been the case. Freedom of association has not been the historic norm throughout the world. Even in liberal European regimes, such as revolutionary France, which

Richard Brooks is the Charles Keller Beekman Professor of Law at Columbia University Law School. Timothy W. Guinnane is the Philip Golden Bartlett Professor of Economic History in the Department of Economics at Yale University.

This chapter has been prepared for the NBER Conference "Organizations, Civil Society, and the Roots of Development." For comments we thank Carolyn Dean, Naomi Lamoreaux, John Wallis, and other conference participants. We appreciate the able research assistance of Mathilde Laporte, Rachel Jones, and Kelli Reagan. For acknowledgments, sources of research support, and disclosure of the authors' material financial relationships, if any, please see http://www.nber.org/chapters/c13512.ack.

1. "Man is what he is thanks to his association with his fellow man." This is the first line of Gierke's (1868) famous history of associations in German law.

2. See Chilton and Versteeg's (2016) survey of contemporary written constitutions, which included 186 countries. Surveys of older constitutions, undertaken by the Comparative Constitutions Project, found that for constitutions promulgated before 1900, 36 percent included freedom of assembly, and 46 percent had freedom of association. For 1900–1945, the comparable numbers are 77 percent and 83 percent. (Comparative Constitutions Project, Characteristics of National Constitutions, V.2.0: available at http://comparativeconstitutionsproject.org/download-data/.)

viewed themselves as leading the charge for human liberty and the democratization of political rights, entitlements to associate and entitlements of associations were largely restricted and not at all assured.

In this chapter we focus on Prussia, to examine the logic of limitations on the right of civil association and how these limitations evolved and weakened in the latter part of the nineteenth century. The Prussian example highlights a connection to the rights of business associations: in general, business organizations enjoyed associational rights prior to the liberalization of the analogous rules for civil-society organizations. Close study of particular cases is an ideal way to make progress on a question such as this, but we acknowledge the danger of implicitly generalizing from a single country's experience. To add context we offer a general framework of associational rights, illustrated by reference to American associational expansion over a similar period as our Prussian study. We also briefly reference France, both its internal experience and the influence it exerted over the other German states, that in some cases prodded Prussian developments.[3] We conclude by drawing out the connections between business law and the development of associational rights.

To start we distinguish two basic kinds of association rights. First is the right *to* associate, that is, the right of persons to come together or create relations with each other. Second is the rights *of* associations: rights granted directly to associations rather than indirectly through their members, agents, promoters, or other proxies. While it is commonly agreed that the right of association is fundamental to a well-functioning civil society, the term "association" invites competing interpretations. As an initial matter, association is distinct from assembly, itself a highly variable entitlement, as we illustrate below by reference to state and federal constitutions at the founding of the United States. To be associated with another person is not the same as assembling with that person. The right to associate is separate and superior to the right of assembly. Assembly is but a single means, albeit an important one, through which persons may associate. Moreover, the right to associate, properly understood, is often incidental to other higher-order constitutional guarantees. In contemporary US constitutional jurisprudence, for instance, courts have granted persons a derivative right to associate in order to secure primary rights of political and religious expression as well as rights of privacy. That these "primary" rights, at times, have been bolstered by privileges of association reveals the historically contingent character of the right *to*

3. Prussia was the core and dominant state in the German empire formed in 1871. Prior to 1871, the individual German states regulated associations, although the confederation formed in 1815 also weighed in on the question. The federal constitution adopted in 1871 allocated responsibility for different spheres between the states and the national government. Some areas of law remained at the state level for some years after the empire's formation. We focus on Prussian law until 1908, when the empire adopted a common statute on association. We use "Prussia" as opposed to "Germany" advisedly. For a different German state, see Meyer (1970), who studies associational life in the city of Nürnberg, which became part of Bavaria in 1806.

associate. A right to associate as a legal basis of interracial and same-sex marriage among other unions would have been unthinkable in 1776. Modern rights *of* associations, granted to groups currently engaged in civil and political (as opposed to commercial) activities, would be even harder for eighteenth-century observers to envision.[4]

We attempt to unbundle the loose package of "associational rights" by characterizing a typology of these rights, illustrated with examples taken from US history. We consider two further examples, Prussia and France. In all three countries today (Germany substituting for Prussia), the right to associate and rights of associations are so clear as to be taken for granted. But in all three countries, the right to associate and the rights of associations were initially less universal than one might think. This was even true in the United States and France, two countries founded after revolutions fought in the name of liberty. Prussia, however, is our primary historical focus: it provides the principal context where we demonstrate the contingency of associational rights as they evolved from the eighteenth century to the second half of the nineteenth century. Conveniently, German sources tend to distinguish the right to associate (*Versammlungsrecht*) from the rights that attach to associations (*Vereinsrecht*). Thus the distinction we draw is embedded in the main historical context that we study.

Although our primary concern is civil-society associations, these associations cannot be considered in isolation from commercial associations. To be sure, associating to earn a return on labor or invested capital is different, in important ways, from associating to discuss philosophical ideas or political trends, but the two gatherings raise similar issues in the eyes of the law. As we will elaborate, early restrictions on civil-society associations in Prussia presumed that all such meetings could be forbidden and police presence was mandated, if not actually carried out, in any tolerated meeting. Commercial associations were in practice spared these burdensome prohibitions and mandated surveillance, as that undoubtedly would have discouraged the formation of multiowner enterprises and generally undermined business activity. Hence business organizations were regarded as distinct from civil-society groups in many, if not most, contexts. Sometimes the distinctions between civil-society associations and business organization were less clear; German

---

4. Even today, it is difficult for lay and expert observers, as well as legal officials, to imagine, characterize, and reconcile how associational fictions come to possess constitutional rights directly. As evidence of this difficulty, Blair and Pollman (2015), for instance, point to the confounded US Supreme Court's jurisprudence on corporate constitutional rights. Notwithstanding contrary judicial rhetoric, Blair and Pollman advance an interpretation that the US Supreme Court has not, in actuality, granted constitutional rights to corporations directly, that is, "to corporations in their own right," but rather only derivatively and instrumentally in order to protect the interests and entitlements of natural persons represented by corporations. Taking the court at its word, however, it is impossible to deny the court's recognition of rights resting directly in corporate bodies themselves. Whether the court was motivated to recognize constitutional *rights* of corporations in order to protect the *interests* of natural persons is a question separate from the fact that the court has granted such rights to corporations.

cooperatives, to take one example, were ostensibly business organizations but strongly associated with political ideas inimical to the state. In seeking to improve their legal situation qua business organization, the cooperatives helped advance the cause of civil society. In both Prussia and France, the first civil-society groups given expanded privileges were cooperatives, no doubt due to their economic character. In still other contexts, civil-society groups pursued a strategy of legal innovation by assimilating rights first granted to business organizations. Businessmen, familiar with and accustomed to the privileges and conveniences of their business forms, were particularly effective agents of their civil-society groups.

Acquisition of *corporate* rights was key to the growth and success of civil-society associations. We use "corporate" here to refer to rights belonging to the "body" of a group or society, as opposed to its members or other associates. The right simply to meet or to privately assemble is the prerequisite for any civil society. But even granting that, a government could effectively hinder civil-society development by denying such groups additional legal rights, from restricting their public assembly to withholding a variety of conventional legal means that allow citizens to operate large, long-lived organizations. These additional rights have been fundamental to the expansion of associations that characterize American civil society.[5] Imagine the American Civil Liberties Union (ACLU) if it could not sue in its own right, or own property, or contract with staff or others.[6] This ACLU would be little more than a debating society. We stress the developments of these additional "corporate" rights because they are crucial to development of associations and their ability to play a meaningful role in civil society.[7]

Prussia's historical context is particularly instructive here. Until the early twentieth century, Prussian law explicitly restricted its citizens' right to associate. The rules changed several times during the nineteenth century, but the common thread was that authorities who deemed an assembly or association threatening could forbid it, and possibly apply criminal sanctions against those responsible for organizing it. Governments today, of course, continue to outlaw associations deemed dangerous to the public good or the constitutional order.[8] The difference with the Prussian regime in the nineteenth

5. See Bloch and Lamoreaux (chapter 7, this volume).

6. By "could not" we mean that the ACLU could not exercise these rights and privileges without adopting cumbersome and expensive devices that are unnecessary to a business firm. Section 8.4 provides detailed examples.

7. The collective rights that organizations can exercise are central to the creation of civil-society organizations that can play their "third-sector" role. See discussion in the volume contributions by Bloch and Lamoreaux (chapter 7) and Johnson and Powell (chapter 6).

8. The German government today has the explicit power to outlaw organizations that it views as threats to the constitutional order. The government has only used it against groups that *declare their goal* to be the government's overthrow. In the nineteenth century a group did not have to declare itself hostile to the constitutional order to be unable to meet.

century was its usage of law to prevent a wide range of associations that did not so much threaten the government as annoy it.[9] Like Prussia, most European states restricted associations in the nineteenth century, which is not to suggest that associations were in and of themselves disagreeable to the state.

Every political order relies on associations. Prussia, in fact, compelled participation in certain associations. Prussian political order rested on differences among the king's subjects, differences that were often expressed through status-based organizations. Some, but not all, of these groups were based on birth, such as the nobility. Membership was determined and mandated by the state, not chosen voluntarily by individuals. The law sought to limit *voluntary* organizations, groups that were not themselves directly or indirectly creations of the state. As Nipperdey (1976, 174) puts it, a person could join or leave these voluntary associations, and the association's members could decide to dissolve it. These groups were independent of their membership; participation was not limited to a particular class, nor could one's membership in a class be threatened by participation in an association. They existed only to meet the ends decided on by their members.

Again, most European states took a similar approach. An important and informative comparison is France. Prior to the French Revolution, France looked much like Prussia (in this respect). After, France restricted the right to associate at least as strictly as Prussia. This apparent similarity seems puzzling at first, since even after the Bourbon restoration France remained a political order very different from that which continued in Prussia. The ideals underlying the French discomfort with societies were different from those expressed in Prussia; the divergence, as we describe later, turns largely on differing conceptions of the state and the citizen's role in that state.[10] Nonetheless, despite important differences in political structures and political cultures, we observe similar restrictions on associations in these two places.

9. Prussia was in good company in restricting corporate rights to most bodies (including business firms) until the 1870s; France, for example, did not introduce general incorporation until 1867, and in Russia this step came even later (Guinnane et al. 2007; Gregg 2014). The few business corporations the Prussian government did charter had to agree both to oversight (which could amount to micromanaging) and often to transfer some of the benefits of association to the government.

10. We elaborate on this comparison below, briefly, with the following caveat: we will not engage deeper questions of political formation and its interpretation. For both Prussia and France, the question of association carries considerable ideological freight. A key referent for Germany is Gierke and his conception of the "*Genossenschaft.*" It is also worth noting that few of the nineteenth- and early twentieth-century business- or cooperative-law discussions most relevant here mention Gierke. The French context is even more complicated, because the right of association invokes central themes from the revolution and the restoration, and also draws on Tocqueville and his enthusiasm for his vision of American society. We cannot do justice to the deeper roots of these debates in this chapter. Our central aim is to describe the legal and economic character of civil associations, according to an organizing framework to which we develop in the next section.

8.1   Associating and Association: A Framework with Reference to the US Context

To be precise in our treatment of associations, we briefly lay out a typology based on four terms, labeled R1 through R4 for future reference:

R1. *Associate* (a verb). Two or more persons engaged in some joint activity or relation (e.g., they might assemble for a rally, or meet to have coffee, discuss a book, undertake some longer-term activity, or they may be associated by virtue of a marital relation, a fraternal organization, or a political affiliation). A mere coincidence of physical presence is not sufficient. Two strangers squeezed together on a crowded bus are simply in "serial" association, as Sartre (1960) wrote, not associated, as we define it. We use the abbreviation *R1* or associate hereafter.

R2. *Associational aggregate* (a noun): An aggregate or group consisting of two or more associated persons (e.g., an unincorporated church or school or a group of persons running a going concern while sharing profits and losses, which may create an association called "partnership"). An associational aggregate, which we also call a mere association, can have its own internal organization and rules, to which its members consent, and that *may* be legally enforceable by and against members, but the association itself can neither legally bind or be bound by others. We use the abbreviation *R2* or "aggregate" hereafter.

R3. *Associational entity*: an association recognized by law as a distinct legal entity, separate from the persons, legal or natural, who comprise it (e.g., a partnership having entity status, a club or concern that can own property, sue and be sued in its own name). We use the abbreviation *R3* or "entity" hereafter.

R4. *A legal person*: a legal entity, associational or otherwise, that is treated as a person in law, possessing a legal personality, which may be determinative for particular entitlements unavailable to mere entities. For most purposes legal personality (entailed in R4) and entity status (present in R3) are equivalent, but occasional differences in treatment may result when an association is considered a "person" as opposed to an "entity." We use the abbreviation *R4* or "legal person" hereafter.

We do not claim any general, one-to-one mapping between these four definitions and any particular organization or application of legal rules. That is to say, although R1 through R4 may be characterized in terms of specific rights, powers, privileges, and immunities along with their jural correlatives, we do not mean to suggest that states grant or recognize these entitlements in a consistent manner across our four categories. Controls deployed by the state are highly variable. States could and did restrict associational entitlements according to the number of people involved, and whether meetings took place indoors or outdoors. Restrictions sometimes turned on the identity of those involved. Specific prerequisites, such as mandating use of the German language, were required of certain associations. Though today the law often requires that formal associations hold annual meetings and maintain minutes of meetings and such, one must resist casual ascription of familiar mandates and entitlements to associations in different times and places. American business partnerships, for example, possess or lack entity status depending on the time and the state in which those associations were formed or considered. Relatedly, today we think of limited liability as a cornerstone of business associations, but in the nineteenth century it was an uncommon aspect of firms. Even an association taking R3 and R4 may not have limited liability extended to its members and managers depending on the time, place, and other considerations. These and other qualifications threaten to leave our simple framework without any traction. But when applied to a specific time and place, the typology above may usefully clarify certain aspects of the civil-society landscape.

We illustrate the typology above by briefly considering the American associational context from the late eighteenth century through the early twentieth century. The American context is useful because of its fecund associational character during this period, as famously observed by Tocqueville. It is important to emphasize, however, that our aim is not to present a full historical account of associational custom and regulation in America. For that, turn to the comprehensive account (chapter 7, this volume) by Bloch and Lamoreaux on the law and development of voluntary organizations in the United States from 1780 to 1900. Our aim here is rather to refine and add content to the suggested framework before turning to (and applying the typology to) the less familiar account of associations in nineteenth-century Prussia.

While the American historical context is offered primarily to clarify our typology, it is also the case that the typology allows for a more nuanced appreciation of associational entitlements in the United States. Casual observers are often surprised to learn that the US Supreme Court did not recognize a distinct right of association until 1958.[11] A common myth asserts that associational rights largely existed since the founding, but in fact, as Bloch and Lamoreaux show, at the state level most of the key developments occurred during the nineteenth century. At the national level, key features of US associational law were forged during the twentieth century around the Civil Rights movement. Moreover, in the very recent past, doctrines concerning rights of associations have experienced extraordinary shifts, not to mention the practical innovations in the media, forms and memberships of associations.[12] From "virtual" associations on the Internet to newly inte-

---

11. NAACP v. Alabama, 357 U.S. 449 (1958).
12. Striking a shaky balance between expression norms in the First Amendment and anti-discrimination norms of the Fourteenth Amendment and other laws, such as Title IX of the

grated membership rolls (by ethnicity, race, gender, sexuality, and so on), the American associational landscape today is quite different than it was at the birth of the nation.

What the first citizens of the United States understood of their rights and limits of associations may be gleaned from the nation's founding documents. These inaugural citizens belonged to various associations that predated the United States of America, of course, and numerous other associations grew out of its battle for independence from England.[13] From the beginning, the framers of the US Constitution looked askance on some of these associations and sought to regulate, discourage, or prohibit them. For example, participants in the original constitutional debates critically scrutinized the Society of the Cincinnati, a hereditary association of Revolutionary War officers and their male descendants. George Washington was the association's first president. Its membership included numerous other war heroes and founding fathers of the country. Yet notwithstanding the high regard in which the framers held Washington and other officers of the Continental Army, they passed Article I, sections 9 and 10 of the 1787 federal constitution (along with comparable restraints in many state constitutions) to express their disapproval of hereditary associations and to explicitly ban the state's participation in sponsoring and recognizing such groups.

But while the federal constitution discouraged some associations, it also encouraged and enabled others. In 1791 associations in the United States received their chief enabling statute. The First Amendment of the federal Constitution (1791) implicitly recognized a right to gather for the purpose of political and religious expression and expressly provided a right of assembly.[14] Some state constitutions, such as Massachusetts's (1780) and New Hampshire's (1784), preceded the federal guaranties of political and religious expression and also assured their citizens a right to assembly "in

---

Civil Rights Act of 1964, US federal courts have significantly revised associational law based on *inter alia* sex, gender, and sexuality over the past forty years and will no doubt continue the adjustments into the twenty-first century. See, for example, Roberts v. United States Jaycees, 468 U.S. 609 (1984); Rotary Int'l v. Rotary Club of Duarte, 481 U.S. 537 (1987); Boy Scouts of America et al. v. Dale, 530 U.S. 640 (2000); Gloucester County School Board v. G.G., 579 U.S. ___ (2016).

13. From the earliest colonial settlements, churches and religious groups formed the basis of civil society in America, but they were not the only associations; take, for example, the Ancient and Accepted Free Masons, founded in Boston in 1733. Skocpol (2003, 22) observes, "In colonial America, [Arthur Schlesinger] asserts, voluntarily established associations were few and far between and typically tied to local church congregations. But the struggles of the colonists for independence from Britain taught 'men from different sections valuable lessons in practical cooperation,' and 'the adoption of the Constitution stimulated still further application of the collective principle.'"

14. The First Amendment to the United States Constitution states that "Congress shall make no law respecting an establishment of religion, or prohibiting the free exercise thereof; or abridging the freedom of speech, or of the press; or the right of the people peaceably to assemble, and to petition the Government for a redress of grievances" (emphasis added).

an orderly and peaceable manner" for "the common good."[15] Other state constitutions granted more liberal associational rights. Delaware's 1792 Constitution, for example, simply conferred upon its citizens a right "to meet," without the restriction for "the common good,"[16] while still other states explicitly allowed their citizens to assemble for *their* own good, which apparently was the intended (but not included) language of the federal assembly clause.[17]

Permissive constitutional language aside, the practice of assembly and association did not proceed unfettered in the country's first years. As early as 1792, the primordial national Congress and president began a campaign against the so-called democratic-republican societies, local political associations that convened regular meetings critical of the federal administration.[18] Their growing numbers and criticisms throughout 1793 inspired George Washington's charge, in the annual presidential address to Congress in 1794, "that 'associations of men' and 'certain self-created societies' had fostered violent rebellion."[19] By linking the democratic-republic societies to

15. Massachusetts's 1780 Constitution (sec. XIX) states, "The people have a right, in an orderly and peaceable manner, to assemble to consult upon the common good; give instruction to their representatives, and to request of the legislative body, by way of addresses, petitions or remonstrances, redress of the wrongs done them, and the grievances they suffer." New Hampshire's 1784 Constitution (Part I, Bill of Rights Art. XXXII) similarly observes that "The people have a right, in an orderly and peaceable manner, to assemble and consult upon the common good, give instruction to their representatives, and to request of the legislative body, by way of petition or remonstrance, redress of the wrong done them and the grievances they suffer."

16. "Although disobedience to laws by a part of the people, upon suggestions of impolicy or injustice in them, tends by immediate effect and the influence of example, not only to engender the public welfare and safety, but also in governments of a republican form, contravenes the social principles of such governments founded on common consent for common good, yet the citizens have a right, in an orderly manner, to meet together, and to apply to persons intrusted with the powers of government for redress of grievances or other proper purposes, by remonstrance or address" (Constitution of Delaware [1792], Article I, Sec. 16).

17. See, for example, Constitution of Kentucky (1792), Article XII, Sec. 22: "That the citizens have a right in a peaceable manner to assemble together for *their* common good, and to apply to those invested with the powers of government for redress of grievances, or other proper purposes, by petition, address, or remonstrance." (emphasis added); Constitution of Mississippi (1817), Article I, Sec. 22: "That the citizens have a right, in a peaceable manner, to assemble together, for *their* common good, and to apply to those invested with the powers of government for redress of grievances or other proper purposes, by petition, address, or remonstrance." (emphasis added); Constitution of Alabama (1819), Article I, Sec. 22: "The citizens have a right, in a peaceable manner, to assemble together for *their* common good, and to apply to those invested with the powers of government for redress of grievances, or other proper purposes, by petition, address, or remonstrance." (emphasis added); Constitution of Arkansas (1836), Article II, Sec. 20: "That the citizens have a right in a peaceable manner to assemble together for *their* common good, to instruct their representatives, and to apply to those invested with the powers of government for redress of grievances, or other proper purposes, by address or remonstrance." (emphasis added). See Inazu (2010), regarding the intended but omitted language in the federal assembly clause.

18. See Bloch and Lamoreaux (chapter 7, this volume) and associated references.

19. Inazu (2010, 580). "Robert Chesney suggests that '[t]he speech was widely understood at the time not as ordinary political criticism, but instead as a denial of the legality of organized and sustained political dissent'" (ibid.).

the widely unpopular Whiskey Rebellion, Washington, with support from the Congress, expanded the disfavor with which these "self-created societies" were held. A few years later, in 1798, Congress would pass the Sedition Act, allowing it to sanction citizens and associations it deemed too critical of the federal government. All told, American political associations faced significant state scrutiny in the last ten years of the eighteenth century.

Nineteenth-century associational entitlements were progressively liberalized for white men, while remaining restrictive for women and disfavored racial and social groups, as described by Bloch and Lamoreaux. By focusing on these restrictions we may better observe distinctions among types of associational entitlements. Restrictions on race-based groupings marked the most prominent prohibitions on voluntary associations in the United States, particularly in the South. Southern states restricted the number of blacks who could gather outside of the company of white observers. Free blacks associating with slaves were strictly prohibited by statute, especially in the wake of the Denmark Vesey slave insurrection controversy in 1822 when South Carolina, followed by a number of other Southern states, passed so-called Negro Seamen Acts, to quarantine black sailors and thereby prevent the "moral contagion" of their presence on slaves.[20] Intimate association between blacks and whites was also de jure proscribed, even if de facto prevalent. These restrictions on intraracial and interracial associations fall under the associating (R1) category and were applicable to public ("outdoor") and private ("behind doors") gatherings of natural persons, especially at nighttime. Restrictions on mere aggregations, R2 in our typology, included labor-based associations of white and nonwhite workers. Through the early nineteenth century state courts invoked the English common law doctrine of criminal conspiracy to prevent laborers from associating for common purposes. By the 1840s the presumption of criminal conspiracy was largely relaxed, but states still maintained a robust managerial position over these associations.[21]

Southern states also outlawed, limited, or maintained surveillance of church-based gatherings of blacks, particularly following the 1831 Nat Turner slave rebellion. These (R2) black churches maintained a continuity beyond the one-shot assembly of multiple individuals, but they generally did

20. South Carolina's Negro-Seamen Act required black sailors stay on vessels docked at local ports or else face arrest and possible enslavement. The law passed in significant part out of fear that free black sailors would stir unrest among slaves if the two groups associated. Alabama, Georgia, Louisiana, Maryland, North Carolina, and Tennessee also restricted the association of free blacks and slaves (see Lightner 2006; Schoeppner 2010).

21. Chief Justice (of Massachusetts) Lemuel Shaw's opinion in Commonwealth v. Hunt, 45 Mass. 111 (1842), held that it was not per se illegal for workingmen to associate for common purposes. As a matter of practice a number of American jurisdictions had already taken this position, but Shaw was the first really explicit departure from the English common law of criminal conspiracy. This departure did not, of course, mean that everything that workers agreed together to do was thought to be legal—as the robust later history of labor injunctions shows (see Tomlins 1993). See also Bloch and Lamoreaux (chapter 7) and Margaret Levi et al. (chapter 9), both in this volume.

not acquire legal entity status. Exceptions to this pattern include an African Methodist Episcopal (AME) Church, incorporated in Louisiana by free persons of color in 1848. Berea College, a private college incorporated in Kentucky in 1855 for the purposes of interracial educational association, also represents an uncommon case. As legal entities (R3), both the AME Church and Berea College appreciated advantages of the corporate form. But, viewed as creatures of the state, they were also subject to heightened regulation by the state. Both associational entities were effectively banned by subsequent legislative amendments.[22]

Beyond having entity status, some associations are recognized as distinct persons, possessing legal personality (R4).[23] As persons in law, associations established as corporations possess entitlements distinct from its individual members, as well as from any aggregation of them. For example, under the so-called intracorporate conspiracy doctrine, recognized in some US courts, a corporation, as a single distinct person, cannot be subject to conspiracy charges (even if several of its officers or other agents engage in conspiratorial acts on its behalf).[24] Legal persons (R4) are not simply entities (R3). They may possess characteristics and rights as persons, which are not legally cognizable in entities.

We close this section by returning to the animating purpose of this brief overview of American associations and their regulation: namely, to illustrate our typology of associating and associational forms. While this short review cannot possibly capture the rich and complex character of associational life in nineteenth- and early twentieth-century America, recall that was not our aim. Rather, it was to use the complex character and history of American associational order, captured in statutes and cases, to observe operational variance in our typology. Take, for example, the case of *People's Pleasure Park Co. v. Rohleder*, which involved an association of "negroes" led by a former slave, who formed a corporation, the People's Pleasure Park Company, to purchase land they could not acquire themselves due to their race.

22. Berea College presents an especially interesting case. Fifty years after its founding, Kentucky passed a segregation law (the Day Law) aimed specifically at the college, disallowing "any [public or private] college, school or institution where persons of the white and Negro races are both received as pupils." The US Supreme Court denied Berea's claimed right to continue its integrationist policy by invoking the state's reserved discretion, which allowed it to amend charters through legislation. The court suggested a different conclusion may have been reached if Berea College was not incorporated, but it limited its inquiry to "the power of a State over its own corporate creatures." Perhaps if Berea was not incorporated, the natural persons associated with the college would have had a stronger constitutional claim to voluntary interracial association. On the other hand, Kentucky prevented voluntary association through its antimiscegenation laws, and the state would certainly have argued that application of the Day Law to natural persons "was a reasonable exercise of its police power . . . to prevent miscegenation." On the AME Church, see *African Methodist Episcopal Church v. City of New Orleans* and discussion by Inazu (2010, 32).

23. They have been recognized as such by the US Supreme Court since its ruling in Trustees of Dartmouth College v. Woodward, 17 U.S. (4 Wheat.) 518, 636 (1819).

24. See McAndrew v. Lockheed Martin Corp., 206 F.3d 1031, 1036 (11th Cir. 2000).

The court recognized the corporate transaction as valid, notwithstanding the fact that it was "a corporation composed exclusively of negroes," chartered (R3) to "develop a pleasure park for the amusement of colored people" for play (R1). In that case, the court concluded that People's Pleasure Park Company was, by law, simply a corporate entity, and "in law, there can be no such thing as a colored corporation."

A striking feature of this case is that even though the organizers of the People's Pleasure Park Company faced racial restraints in acquiring property, they appeared to have full access to form a business corporation. This illustrates the later liberalization of commercial incorporation for business associations as compared to the continuing restrictions on civil associations for disfavored groups. The case also illustrates practical implications among distinct associational types, that is, R2, R3, and R4. The extent to which natural persons, legally defined as black or nonwhite, acting as individuals or as a group were constrained in their legal capacity to sue, to contract or to acquire property for their associational ends in nonentity partnerships or associations (R2), associational entities offered advantages so long as the court recognized the entity (R3) as legally distinct from the natural persons.[25] Yet, even if distinct from its members, as legal persons corporations (R4) are sometimes treated as possessing entitlements and features common to natural persons, such as race, ethnicity, and gender. The court could have attributed a racial identity to the corporate person, as a number of courts have since done, transferring the legal disabilities or advantages of race to the corporation itself (Brooks 2006).

Bearing in mind these distinctions between natural persons and legal persons (R4), entities (R3), aggregates (R2), and associating (R1), we now consider the rights and restraints on civil associations in nineteenth-century Prussia.

8.2   Associations in Prussian History

From at least the last decades of the eighteenth century, Germany witnessed the rise and spread of associations of many types: patriotic associations, gymnastic associations, associations to advocate literacy and education, other types of "social welfare" associations, and associations simply for fellowship. At the end of the eighteenth century there were some 270 "reading societies" alone, this in a poor country with low literacy. This may puzzle, given this chapter's focus on the limits placed on associations. Prussian law never forbade association; rather, it allowed the authorities to deny R1 and R2 rights to groups thought dangerous to the state. The authorities explicitly focused on certain types of associations (secret, or clearly politi-

---

25. Married women, burdened by legal disabilities under the common law doctrine of coverture, may have similarly exploited the corporate form.

cal) and certain practices (such as using the wrong language). The groups that flourished under this regime either avoided political issues, or carefully disguised the political content of their activities. As we stress in the examples to follow, enforcement depended considerably on time and place, with particular groups receiving official favor at first and then facing banishment. The overarching theme here is not universal prohibition, but the development of association only at the sufferance of the government.

Why would Prussia or any other state view civil-society organizations as a threat? The reasons shifted over time, but we can see two strands in the arguments against civil-society groups. Sometimes, especially during and just after the struggle with revolutionary France, Prussian authorities viewed civil-society organizations as direct conspiracies against the state. More generally in the early nineteenth century, this kind of organization threatened the *theory* of the Prussian polity. Civil-society organizations crossed status boundaries, and implicitly threatened the idea of organizing citizens into separate status-based or "ascriptive" groups. They also created a life outside the control of state and thus "challenged the State and Church's monopoly on interpretation, questioning matters that previously could not be questioned" (Nipperdey 1976, 195; see also Sheehan 1995).

Hueber (1984, 132) usefully divides the years 1794–1908 into four periods. First, the period 1794–1819 was characterized by a relatively permissive general code undermined by more repressive edicts. Second, that legal environment did not change much in the second period (1819–1847), but a broad flowering of associational life reflected the complicated relationship between law and social outcomes. Many political thinkers stressed free expression as a fundamental right, and included association as part of expression. In the more liberal German states (such as Baden, where French ideas enjoyed more influence than in other areas), these ideas led to brief periods of relaxed rules on association. Third, the right to associate played an important role in the struggles of the revolutionary period (1848–49). Had the revolutionary Frankfurt constitution survived, Germans would have enjoyed freedom to associate rivaling the United States or the United Kingdom at the time. Fourth, the postrevolutionary period began with a severe reaction that ignored some of the constitutional guarantees agreed upon during the 1848–49 period, but for the rest of the nineteenth century the legal framework slowly liberalized. The 1908 Reich Act on association extended Prussia's by-then relatively permissive treatment of association to the entire country.

Throughout the period we discuss, the Prussian Crown could always extend R3 or R4 rights to a specific, favored organization. The organization could be a scientific or cultural group, or a business corporation. Such charters, even to a business organization, carried the sense of a favor, one that could be withdrawn (or at least not extended beyond the original date). This created an opening for the state to pry into and even micromanage the organization. In our terms, then, until the end of the nineteenth century, Prussians had almost no R1 or R2 rights, and anything related to R3 or R4 required a grant of privilege to a specific organization. At the end of the nineteenth century, the legal situation changed considerably. Germans (as Prussians were by then) had some R1 and R2 rights, and could establish organizations with some of the R3 and R4 rights afforded to the most sophisticated business firms. Changes in the right to associate took place throughout the nineteenth century, and the final major legislation of our period (in 1908) was still fairly restrictive. Extension of R3 and R4 rights, on the other hand, did not come until the end of the nineteenth century. Only with the Weimar Constitution (1919) did Germans acquire as fundamental rights the ability to associate and to create associations.

8.2.1   Before 1819

Until the late eighteenth century, most German states (like most "old regime" states) severely restricted both R1 and R2 rights. Tillmann (1976, 5) refers to these regimes as "police states." The first important change came with Fredrick the Great's 1794 law code for Prussia (*Das Allgemeine Landrecht für die Preußischen Staaten*, hereafter ALR).[26] The ALR explicitly granted R1 and R2 rights, although the code still allowed the authorities to suspend or restrict these rights if they thought order demanded it. Thus the ALR represented in principle a great liberalization in the right to association. The ALR also provided a basic framework for associations. The code defined an association (*Gesellschaft*) as the combination of several members of the state for a common end (II(6), §1). Such associations were either "permitted" (*erlaubt*) or "not permitted." An association was permitted so long as its purpose was consistent with the common good (*gemeine Wohl*) (II(6), §2). The code did not precisely define the common good or its opposite; it just said that groups whose purpose or activities violated the "calm, security, and order" were not tolerated. The government also had the right to forbid associations that were in principle allowed, if such groups disguised their intentions or took a form that was dangerous.

The ALR (II(6) §11–21) also defined the rights of permitted associations (*erlaubte Privatgesellschaften*). Permitted associations could write rules binding the members of the association (they had R2 rights), but these agreements had no effect on third parties (the associations had no R3 or R4 rights). Thus a permitted association could adopt rules that functioned as enforceable agreements among its members, but it could not contract as

---

26. Fredrick died in 1786, but the Code was his project. The ALR deals with matters that were later treated separately in civil, commercial, and criminal codes. Parts of Prussia used French civil law in the period 1815–1900. While different in important respects, the French code was similar to the ALR for the issues discussed here, and in any case, the relevant Prussian law was increasingly outside the code.

an entity with third parties. In our terms, permitted associations had only R1 and R2 rights.

The ALR's liberality did not long survive in practice. Prussia's involvement in war with revolutionary and Napoleonic France led to occupation of considerable Prussian territory, and even before occupation, Prussian authorities had good reason to fear French influence, especially in its western territories. A Prussian royal edict issued October 20, 1798, in principle, forbade all secret and political organizations that aimed to change either the constitutional order or the administration. This edict reflected fear of disloyalty and French influence. Changes to the constitutional order or administration potentially covered most aspects of public life, so the edict could be used to suppress a wide range of organizations, even those who viewed themselves as enthusiastic supporters of the Prussian Crown. The underlying idea was that subjects had no right to play any role in the state's affairs, whether alone or in groups. Nipperdey (1976, 199) quotes Nassau's minister Ibell as expressing the idea, somewhat later, in brutal form: "It is both unreasonable and illegal to convince or persuade private persons that they, alone or in combination with others, can participate in Germany's great national affairs."[27] But this fear of association competed with a more pragmatic instinct: that toleration of some types of associations might foster German patriotism and a stronger allegiance to the state. This more tolerant view reached as high as the upper reaches of the Prussian ministry, where Freiherr von Stein and others promoted greater participation in public affairs as a way of cementing the relationship between the king's subjects and his state.[28] Stein succeeded in establishing representative bodies in cities. The influence of Stein and people who shared his outlook probably accounted for the uneven enforcement of the October 1798 edict.

Prussia's resurgence and ultimate victory over French forces in the "War of Liberation" (1813) rested in some measure on widespread patriotic feelings, fostered in part by the type of associations that had been the target of the 1798 edict. For a while, Prussian reformers held sway, and they thought freedom of association could help them achieve the political reforms they wanted. Hueber (1984, 117) notes that Prussian officials learned not to apply their restrictive law, particularly against patriotic associations that held out the Prussian king as their ideal monarch. Another edict issued January 6, 1816, repealed the 1798 edicts' provisions (Tillmann 1976, 5–6), in effect restoring the conditional right to associate found in the ALR. In lifting

---

27. "Es ist eine ebenso unvernünftige als gesetzwidrige Idee, wenn Privatpersonen glauben mögen berufen oder ermächtigt zu sein, einzeln oder auch in Verbindung mit anderen selbständig oder unmittelbar so jetzt als künftig zu den großen Nationalangelegenheiten Deutschlands mitzuwirken."

28. This is the "Stein" of the Stein-Hardenberg reforms, a series of political and economic reforms initiated in Prussia during the first decades of the nineteenth century (see Duchhardt 2007).

earlier restrictions, the edict referred explicitly to the role such associations had played in liberating Prussia from Napoleon.

8.2.2   1819–1848

This liberality did not last. Most German states, Prussia included, renewed or strengthened their limits on association starting in 1819. The German *Bund's* 1819 Carlsbad Decrees also renewed press censorship and efforts to suppress voluntary associations. The new stance reflected the defeat of Prussia's most important reformers, along with continued fear that revolutionary ideas would spread from France. "The participatory energies which had once been seen as a necessary source of state power were now condemned as the source of unrest and revolution" (Sheehan 1995, 9). The Prussian state's urgency in repressing many of these groups illustrates the threat it perceived in such organizations; many of them were patriotic, anti-French associations that viewed themselves as bulwarks of the state. A notable example is the *Burschenschaften* first formed in 1815. Composed entirely of male university students, many of whom were veterans of the military campaign against Napoleon, the *Burschenschaften* saw themselves as enthusiastic German patriots. Their meetings and festivals honored key moments in German history in general, and the struggle against Napoleon in particular, but the Carlsbad Decrees outlawed them. Various permutations of the group continued to work in secret, but they were ruthlessly suppressed as part of the reaction following the 1848–49 revolution. This history seems a little odd for a group whose motto was "honor, freedom, and fatherland" (*Ehre, Freiheit, Vaterland*). Some parts of the *Burschenschaft* agenda caused discomfort to the Prussian Crown. One example would be calls for Germany to be a single constitutional monarchy. Even though the selected monarch would most likely be a Hohenzollern, the Prussian royal house rejected any idea of national unification based on popular movements.[29] But the *Burschenschaft* example reflects more importantly the fundamental discomfort with voluntary associations: the Prussians suppressed organizations that held among their central tenets patriotism and enthusiasm for the Prussian royal house.

Even ostensibly apolitical groups could run afoul of the restrictions. The "circle" (*Kreis*) was a type of informal group of like-minded people who would meet to discuss politics and related issues. Sperber (1991, 94) emphasizes the *Kreis's* limitations as a source of political transformation; inherently local, these groups recruited based on prior connections, and so had little capacity to become the basis of anything important. One well-known circle consisted of Prussian Army officers, for example. The first gymnastic societies (*Turnvereine*) were patriotic, paramilitary groups that arose as part

---

29. *Burschenschaften* exist today as student groups whose political leanings are, if anything, conservative. The connection between the modern organization and the associations discussed in the text is tenuous.

of the movement opposed to Napoleon. Although loudly committed to the Prussian monarchy, they were suppressed at the time of the Carlsbad Decrees as being "too active and threatening," as Sperber (1991, 94) puts it. The gymnasts reemerged in the 1840s, adopting a more explicitly political coloring, with both left- and right-wing associations of gymnasts. When the revolution broke out, gymnasts were to be found on both sides of the conflict. This later history might validate the Prussian authorities' suspicion that the gymnasts were more interested in politics than exercise, but it also illustrates that the nature of a group's views was not the problem.

The offense ascribed to the *Burschenschaften*, some "circles," and some gymnasts was simply presuming to discuss affair of state, even if only to support the king. Not all agreed; Baden legalized political associations in 1829, only to be overruled on July 5 of 1832, when the German *Bund* issued wide-reaching rules concerning censorship and associations. This decree (§2) forbade all organizations with political goals and organizations whose goals could be used for political purposes, and also (§3) regulated festivals and, in particular, forbade political addresses at festivals.[30]

Sperber (1984, 30–35) discusses two associations with wide appeal: lay brotherhoods and "sharpshooters" clubs (*Schützenvereine*). The brotherhoods, usually named for a saint, had a variety of roles, including praying for the deceased and some mutual aid. These organizations were very old by the early nineteenth century. A variant had emerged during the late eighteenth century, one that served similar goals but was more secular, sometimes even mixing Catholics and Protestants in the same group. The sharpshooters also claimed a venerable lineage, but many such clubs that existed in the early nineteenth century reflected the transformation of older, confessional organizations into a secular body that existed primarily to organize festivals and, as the name suggests, shooting contests.

Government opposition to such organizations seems hard to fathom; what is the harm in praying for the dead or, for the sharpshooters, marching around in odd uniforms? (Today one could imagine a government fearing groups organized around guns and marksmanship, but this was not, at least overtly, the concern about the sharpshooters.) Part of the answer lies in the danger that even these harmless-sounding groups could erupt into political discussion or expression. Sperber notes that two lay brotherhoods took the

30. These "ten articles" (formally, "Zweiter Bundesbeschluß über Maßregeln zur Aufrechterhaltung der gesetzlichen Ruhe und Ordnung im Deutschen Bunde") followed an earlier "six articles" that limited popular representation in the German states. Section 2 "Alle Vereine, welche politische Zwecke haben, oder unter anderm Namen zu politischen Zwecken benutzt werden, sind in sämmtlichen Bundesstaaten zu verbieten und ist gegen deren Urheber und die Theilnehmer an denselben mit angemessener Strafe vorzuschreiten." Section 3 requires that irregular festivals ("Außerordentliche Volksversammlungen und Volksfeste"), that is, those not associated with particular days of the year, receive prior approval from the authorities. Reprinted in Hardtwig and Hinze (1997, 99–102). Zweiter Bundesbeschluß "über Maßregeln zur Aufrechterhaltung der gesetzlichen Ruhe und Ordnung im Deutschen Bunde."

name of local Masonic lodges, suggesting openness to sinister ideological influences. In 1847, the invitation to a Düsseldorf sharpshooters contest contained veiled political commentary that most contemporaries would understand. More generally, a wide variety of ostensibly apolitical groups increasingly took on a political coloring. Organizations such as singing clubs and other recreational associations sometimes concealed what was really a political association. Robert Blum (later executed for his role in the 1848–49 revolution) used the Leipzig *Schillerfest* of 1841 as cover for a liberal agenda. Even the Chambers of Commerce (*Handelskammern*) (which in Germany have a quasi-official status) could become forums for political discussion.

Concern about a different type of association may be easier to understand, and often formed a pretext for harassing the harmless groups. The most overtly revolutionary individuals in prerevolutionary Germany had largely emigrated, and if they continued their activities they did so from abroad. The groups they formed in exile became famous after Marx and Engels transformed one of them into the Communist league, but there were many such groups operating secret cells all over Prussia. On more than one occasion the police would infiltrate and break up a cell operating in Prussia, using the group's (forbidden) existence to suggest broader international conspiracies. France's 1830 July Revolution gave those claims some credibility; the violent introduction of a constitutional monarchy in France terrified more than one German ruling house. Sperber and others, however, doubt the claim of conspiracies involving ties between German Liberals and radicals, and the 1848–49 revolution in Germany provides little evidence of radical influence on those leading the opposition to the current order.

8.2.3   Revolution

The 1840s began with an economic upswing. At the same time, a sharpening of social problems and a relatively lax enforcement of laws on association also led to a boom in new associations: some were new versions of old groups, like the gymnasts, while others reflected the variety of concerns the developing economy provoked. There were associations to promote education for poor children, to build hospitals, and for a broad array of efforts to help the working classes. It was a "period of associations" (Nipperdey 1976, 176).

The decade ended, however, with a combination of economic crisis and political opposition culminating in the revolution of 1848–49. Freedom from censorship and the right to associate were high on the list of goals for many at the Frankfurt Parliament. The Constituent National Assembly's constitution drafted in 1849 (the so-called "Paul's Church" constitution) never came into force because it was rejected by the Prussian and other governments. But its "Bill of Rights" (Section VI) indicates what Liberals of the era wanted. Article VIII (§161–§163) gave all Germans the right to assemble without permission of the authorities, and decreed that public meetings could only be forbidden if a cause of immediate danger (*dringender Gefahr*) to public order and security. It goes on to say that all Germans had the right to create associations. Both provisions even applied to members of the military, so long as the associations did not interfere with military discipline.[31]

8.2.4   Reaction and Slow Liberalization

The Prussian constitution promulgated on January 31, 1850, promised a return to the associational freedom guaranteed by the ALR.[32] Prussians now had the right to meet without permission of the authorities, declared §29, so long as such meetings were indoors and the participants were unarmed. Outdoor meetings still required prior permission. This amounts to a partial R1 right. The constitution further granted Prussians the right to create associations (*Verein*) (§30), so long as these groups' purposes were not forbidden by the criminal law. In our terminology, these organizations possessed entitlements characterized, at best, as R2, but even these R2 privileges were not absolute; the same clause gave the government the right to forbid or limit political organizations. The government also reserved the right to regulate, via legislation, how these privileges were exercised. Furthermore, the government fully retained the power to withhold or extend R3 and R4 rights (§31).

In any case, even these provisions meant little in the reaction that followed the revolutions. The 1850 Prussian constitution came about under considerable pressure. Royal edicts and legislation (passed by an assembly elected with a reactionary three-class voting system) quickly backtracked, however, on the relatively liberal guarantees of freedom of expression and association. Legislation enacted on March 11, 1850, so restricted the rights of association as to make the constitutional guarantee meaningless. The law described a class of rules that applied only to groups that intended to discuss public affairs (*öffentliche Angelegenheiten*). Such groups were required to inform the police at least twenty-four hours in advance of any meeting. The group's leaders had to provide its articles of association and a list of members to the police at least three days before coming into being. The police had the right to send to these meetings up to two police officers or other persons (§4).[33] And the authorities could immediately end any meeting that had not been properly registered, where speakers called for illegal actions, or where attendees were armed. Groups that deal with public affairs could not have as members women, school-age children, or apprentices. The restrictions on public meetings were even more detailed and punitive (see Koch 1862, 521–40).

---

31. Reichs-Gesetz-Blatt 1849.
32. Hardtwig and Hinze (1997, 347–57) reprints the relevant clauses.
33. Such observers had to wear their uniforms if police officers, or other identifying signs if not police. So the intention was not to send spies.

The 1850 law also forbade "associations of associations." This provision sought to restrict association to those who could physically meet, which meant, given incomes and the transportation technology of the day, that associations would be small and necessarily parochial. If an association could become part of a larger, umbrella organization, then the regime risked the possibility of mass movements. Even worse, if a Prussian association could be part of a larger, international association, then radical émigrés might find a back door into Prussian life. Later these restrictions would be used against the labor movement, but in the 1850s the fear was far more a resurgence of the pan-German, liberal ideas that informed the Frankfurt Parliament.

To appreciate how much these laws could limit the right to associate, we need to consider their broad language. Some topics clearly do not qualify as "public affairs," and these would presumably include the affairs of a business firm. But it is easy to see why Prussian authorities thought the 1850 law gave them the right to interfere with virtually any other organization. The ALR's references to "common good" and the like opened even more doors, as we shall see.

The statutes gave the authorities the right to suppress a wide range of associations. We do not know how often this actually happened, and, in fact, many associations thrived in the period of greatest repression. Notions of order and common good left room for officials to suppress bodies they found simply inconvenient. On the other hand, arbitrary application of the law conflicted with a long Prussian tradition of the rule of law and a professional administrative bureaucracy. For us to know just how much trouble the limits on association posed for most civil-society groups would require the fruits of research not yet undertaken.

The Reich's 1871 constitution gave it the right to regulate associations, but for the first few decades of its existence the Reich left the matter to the states. The conflict with the Liberals largely ended by 1871, but Bismarck's political repertoire included attacks on associational rights for other disfavored groups. Bismarck's conflict with the Catholic Church (the "*Kulturkampf*") that intensified starting in 1871 relied heavily on the association laws. In 1872 a group of leading Catholics had formed what they hoped would become a national organization capable of defending the freedom to practice their religion. Formally called the "Association of German Catholics" (*Verein der deutschen Katholiken*), the group came to be called the Mainz Association because it was founded in that Hessian city, in part to avoid Prussian laws on association (Sperber 1984, 211). The Association organized itself on the basis of a legal fiction: even individuals who resided outside Hesse (e.g., in Prussia) were enrolled with the Hessian organization, meaning, the Association hoped, that the Prussia restrictions on association would not apply. In practice, most members lived in the Prussian provinces of Rheinland and Westphalia. Soon after its creation the Mainz Association came under attack from the state, and in 1876 the Prussian Supreme Court ruled it had violated the association laws, rejecting the ploy that there were no actual organizations on Prussian soil (214). Bismarck's later "anti-Socialist" laws (1878–1890) also worked partly by denying R1 and R2 rights to groups associated with the Social Democratic Party. Efforts to combat Polish national aspirations in Prussia's eastern provinces drew on the same tactics.

Conflict with the labor movement illustrates another way associational rights remained problematic. The majority of German trade unionists belonged to unions affiliated with the Social Democratic Party (according to Prager [1904, 287], about two-thirds of the 1.3 million union members counted in 1903). Restrictions on unions and strikes in Prussia had been lifted in 1869 (the liberalization extended to the Reich in 1871), but unions as associations remained potentially subject to the laws of association in the various German states until the 1908 act discussed below. Lujo Brentano quipped that the result was a situation where workers had the right to form unions, but were punished for doing so.[34] There were two general problems. First, although Germany had one law on unions, it had twenty-six different state-level laws governing associations. Second, while strict application of those state laws might leave unions in the clear, some of the unions' activities were plausibly "political" and so gave conservative officials a pretext for treating the unions as an association subject to their limitations. For unions to operate successfully in a large country, they had to undertake activities that might bring them afoul of the law. For example, unions had good reason to try to combine in regional and national groupings. Yet the association law could be construed to forbid one association to belong to another.

The formal end to restrictions on R1 and R2 rights came with a Reich Act (April 19, 1908) on the right to meet and to form associations. This act overrode both earlier edicts and all state laws, thus creating a single, uniform set of rules for the entire country. Romen (1916, 11–12) stress this uniformity and the end of conflicts between Reich and state-level law as the new measure's great achievement. The 1908 act marked a significant liberalization in some ways. Most notably, women could now participate in meetings and associations devoted to public affairs. The government's justification for this innovation stressed changes in the economic and social role of women; many women held positions formerly held only by men, the government stressed, and many women were economically independent and so had a right to participate in the affairs that affected their lives. Women could still not vote, but the government's defense of the law did not make that connection.[35] More generally, Prussia's law of association, although conservative by later

---

34. Brentano's remark appears in several sources, but none cite an original. Wiberg (1906, 1) begins his text with it. Wiberg is a brief account of the way the law of association constrained the German union movement at the time he wrote.

35. Entwurf eines Vereinsgesetzes (1908), "Begründung," especially pp. 22–23.

standards, allowed more freedoms than found in other states, such as the two Mecklenburgs. By extending the relatively liberal Prussian approach to some more conservative states, the 1908 act also brought new associational freedom to some areas. The 1908 act retains many features of the 1850 legislation discussed above, including the requirement to notify the police of meetings. These limitations would not pass from German law until the Weimar Republic. Even the 1908 act (§7) required that public meetings be conducted in German. The authorities could issue a waiver if they wanted, but the law gave the authorities the right to force Poles, for example, to hold meetings in a language many could not understand.

8.2.5   Corporate Rights for Civil-Society Organizations

The 1908 act concerned R1 and R2 rights only. By removing or limiting most restrictions on gatherings, the new law made associations possible, but did not extend so far as to include R3 and R4 rights. Developments in the R3 and R4 rights of associations came relatively late, and cannot be discussed separately from developments in company law. The 1861 *Allgemeine Deutsche Handelsgesetzbuch* (hereafter ADHGB) created a distinct business code that extended to (nearly) all the German states. While it did not require general incorporation, the ADHGB allowed states to choose that option (although only a handful of states did so). Most German states retained the concession system for establishing business corporations. The ALR treated business firms (*Handlungsgesellschaften*) differently from the permitted associations discussed above. But they had something in common with the permitted association: in II(6) §22–24, the code reserved the right for the government to extend additional rights to associations, whether business or "privileged association."

The "privilege" in this phrase referred to additional rights beyond R2, and reflected the state's desire to advance particular goals or to reward favored individuals. The Prussian State could and did charter special business corporations, for example, and extend them R3 and R4 rights. The practice of granting corporate charters had become so common, after the coming of the railroad and some earlier projects to build toll roads, that in 1843 Prussia adopted a statute to standardize the corporations formed under this concession system. But distrust of the corporate form meant that prior to the adoption of general incorporation, few new firms were created with these rights. Similarly, the Crown sometimes chartered a body for a specific charitable or cultural end, endowing it with R3 and R4 rights. For our purpose, the important feature of this aspect of the legal regime was the idiosyncratic nature of such charters. Clearly the organizations involved, whether business or civil-society, had to be advancing the government's goals and had to share some of the benefits of their organization with the government. Corporate grants for business firms, for example, usually involved implicit or explicit transfers to the state. It is hard to imagine business people on bad terms with the government being granted a special charter.

An important liberalization in company law took place in 1870, when Germany as a whole allowed general incorporation for business firms for the first time. The earlier ADHGB included another provision that was more immediately important. After providing basic information to a public business registry, a partnership acquired important R3 rights. According to the ADHGB's partnership rules, "The firm can, under its own name, acquire rights and contract responsibilities, acquire ownership and other rights in land, sue and be sued in court."[36] Similar provisions had been part of the business law of some German states earlier. A next, important step came with the creation of the *Gesellschaft mit beschränkter Haftung* (GmbH) in 1892. The government intended the GmbH as a business form. The vast majority of GmbHs were in fact for-profit ventures. But the law explicitly stated that the GmbH could be used for any legal purpose, and from the start, a small number of civil-society organizations took advantage of the GmbH form. The GmbH (§13) could sue and be sued, contract and own property, and so forth, and it its owners all had limited liability. This new legal form afforded groups all the R4 rights of a corporation.[37]

The final development in our period came with the introduction of the first all-German civil code (*Bürgerliches Gesetzbuch* [BGB]) in 1900. The BGB (§21–§79) created a new "registered association" that came into being by entry in a new association registry and adhering to certain norms. The registered association gave to any civil-society group organized in that way full R3 rights; such organizations could sue and be sued, contract in their own name, and were subject to bankruptcy proceedings.[38] The system worked similarly to the registration system for business firms or cooperatives, and in fact, the new registered association had the same minimum membership,

36. The ADHGB implicitly created two types of business organizations: those covered by the ADHGB, which are the firms discussed in the text, and those that remain under the ALR or other civil law in regions that did not use the ALR. The ADHGB rules applied to both ordinary and limited partnerships. The implicit contrast is to the situation obtaining before 1861 in Germany, or in the United States or Britain at the time. The ADHGB did not make partnerships full legal persons; for example, a partnership's existence was tied to specific individual members.

37. The GmbH differs from a corporation in important ways; see Guinnane et al. (2007) for discussion. For civil-society groups, an important feature of the GmbH is the rule that requires a notarial act for transfer of ownership shares. If the group made ownership in the GmbH synonymous with membership in the organization, a changing membership could be quite expensive. The 1884 Corporations Act also allows the corporation for any legal purpose. Few civil-society organizations took advantage of the 1884 act for this purpose, presumably because the 1884 act also required large minimum shareholdings and expensive governance and oversight provisions.

38. The entity is called *eingetragener Verein* in German and abbreviated e.V. Some English texts refer to it as an "incorporated association," which conveys the impression that it is more like a US not-for-profit corporation than it really is. We use the clumsy "registered association" because it seems more accurate.

seven, as cooperatives. An *eingetragener Verein* registered in a special public registry of such bodies, listing its officers and some other information. Most civil-society groups today take the form of registered associations. But the form is elastic, and some professional and even industry groups organize this way. For-profit firms can also organize an association to represent their interests politically, and so long as that lobbying group does not earn profits, it can be organized as an *eingetragener Verein*.[39]

The civil code dealt with private-law matters only. In the period 1900–1908, that is, after the new BGB but before the new Reich Act of 1908, permitted associations could acquire considerable R3 and R4 rights, but the remaining public-law limitations on associations meant that some associations remained forbidden. The BGB's §61 explicitly allowed local authorities to object to registration of an association that was forbidden under the public-law restrictions on associations. After 1908, however, such objections could only reflect the Reich's more liberal association law, which established a general right of association.

8.3   Germany's Cooperatives

We now turn to a single, important example that illustrates the issues we have discussed here. The first modern German cooperatives were formed starting in the 1840s, with a second, more rural branch taking off in the 1860s. By 1914 there were some twenty thousand cooperatives across Germany. Estimates put cooperative membership in the millions, and since many nonmembers dealt with cooperatives, the cooperatives featured as important enterprises in the lives of many more. Most cooperatives were eventually organized under the Reich law of 1889, which we discuss below. This law allowed a cooperative to take form for any purpose related to advancing member economic interests. The most numerous cooperatives were credit cooperatives, but there were also consumer cooperatives, cooperatives for purchasing inputs and marketing products (especially in rural areas), and a few production cooperatives. The (itself often ideological) historiography has often focused on the political motivations of the consumer cooperatives, which often had strong ties to Social Democratic and other labor organizations. This focus understates the size and diversity of German cooperation. Fairbairn (1994) has stressed that German cooperatives had far more members than did the Social Democratic Party; as mass movements go, cooperation might have been less revolutionary in intent but it involved far more Germans.

The most famous early cooperative leader, Hermann Schulze-Delitzsch, was also a leading Liberal figure. As a member of the first elected Prussian

---

39. Section 22 allows the German state where the association is located to grant this status to for-profit groups, as well.

Parliament, he was among those prosecuted for voting to refuse the taxes the government wished (the literature calls this incident the 1849 *Steuerverweigerungsprozess*). Prussian officials at first viewed his cooperatives as extensions of his political agenda, and used the association law to frustrate their development. By the time the rural cooperatives started to develop in the 1860s, the state was less hostile. Friedrich Raiffeisen, the man most associated with the rural cooperatives, received modest government support for his organizational activities. By the end of the nineteenth century the Prussian government had set up a new banking institution intended to foster further growth in the cooperative movement.[40] In the early years, however, officials used the association laws to harass the cooperatives. Under the ALR, a cooperative was at best a permitted association, which left the groups vulnerable to officials who might construe the cooperative's leaders, or goals, as a threat to order. A cooperative, like any other group, could always apply for special corporate rights, but Schulze-Delitzsch rejected this approach. He recognized that corporate rights would give the government legal grounds for extensive "oversight and interference."[41] He usually stressed such oversight as contrary to the cooperative's purpose, which was to develop a class of experienced, self-reliant small businesspeople, farmers, and others. But in other statements he noted that corporative rights, even if granted, would open the door to interference from the cooperative's political enemies.

Several cooperative histories recount the problems Schulze-Delitzsch and his colleagues faced because of the association laws. The two original credit cooperatives, in Delitzsch and Eilenburg, both in Prussian Saxony, at first enjoyed the good fortune to have as the local county commissioner (*Landrat*) the sympathetic von Pfannenberg. But Pfannenberg was soon replaced by von Rauchhaupt, whom Ruhmer (1937, 227) calls "a fanatical opponent of German credit cooperatives." The cooperative leaders thought that von Rauchhaupt's opposition to the credit cooperatives was really just opposition to Schulze-Delitzsch and other Liberals.[42] Other officials used their power and the cooperatives' legal status to undermine these bodies as well as their Liberal backers, although we know less of those incidents.

40. The *Preußische Central Genossenschaftskasse* formed in 1895. For more than you ever wanted to know about German cooperatives, see Guinnane's publications listed in the reference list (2001, 2012, 2013; Guinnane and Martínez-Rodríguez 2011).

41. "Sodann ist aber auch die Aufsicht und Einmischung eines Regierungsbeamten in die Vereinsgeschäfte überaus hemmend und lästig, wie sie von Erteilung der Korporationsrechte untrennbar ist" (from Schulze-Delitzsch's address to the Congress of Economists, quoted in Thorwart 1909, 369). In the period prior to the adoption of general incorporation in 1870, Prussia and other German states used a variety of means to regulate and control the corporations they chartered. One approach was to insist that a state official act as a corporation's commissioner (*Kommissar*).

42. Ruhmer (1937, 227–28) quotes von Rauchhaupt as claiming that the two cooperatives were led by the politically most dangerous persons (*"politisch gefährlichsten Persönlichkeiten"*). He also claimed the cooperatives were just a vehicle for the two political leaders to assemble funds for their political activities.

Von Rauchhaupt attacked the cooperatives as both illegal and dangerous to the public. His legal argument relied on two different features of the ALR and later legislation on association. He denied the cooperatives' status as "permitted associations." The cooperatives had been approved as associations of artisans, he argued, but they also included wage-laborers, farmers, and others. Thus the cooperatives had violated the terms on which they were formed (*ultra vires*) and approved as "permitted." When one cooperative leader attempted to remedy this problem by applying for corporate status for his group, the county commission denied the request. That denial gave von Rauchhaupt a pretext for demanding that the regional government in Merseburg dissolve the cooperative entirely.

The regional government rejected von Rauchhaupt's demand as without legal basis. Von Rauchhaupt then appealed to the governor (*Oberpräsident*) of the Prussian province of Saxony. This time Rauchhaupt stressed the ALR's criterion for tolerating private bodies: he argued that because the cooperative harmed the public good, the government could forbid it. In March 1857 the provincial government rejected that claim, which in effect restored to the Eilenburg cooperative the status of a permitted association.

Von Rauchhaupt's argument that the cooperatives did actual harm might have been a pretext, but it illustrates the fragility of groups that could be suppressed on the grounds that they harmed the public good. His claim rested on two undeniable facts. The credit cooperatives charged interest rates that Rauchhaupt estimated as 11–12 percent per annum. The local *Sparkasse* (a state-backed savings bank) was charging 5 percent. The "harm" the cooperatives were doing was charging apparently exorbitant interest rates. These rates were typical of the early days of the Schulze-Delitzsch credit cooperatives, and apparently much lower than the costs of credit from moneylenders. (We do not know enough about *Sparkassen* lending practices, but the literature suggests that most cooperative borrowers would be turned away from the *Sparkasse*.) Von Rauchhaupt's second argument concerned the unlimited liability then required for cooperative members, which was a consequence of the ALR's rules and the lack of a corporate charter. He noted that this set-up meant very poor people risked losing all of their assets should the cooperative be unable to satisfy its debts. He also seemed to think unlimited liability was a form of communism, an odd claim given that most businesses at the time had unlimited liability.[43]

Von Rauchhaupt's complaints that the organization had tricked the government about its membership might have been easy to overcome by restating cooperative membership. But the claim about harm raises a different issue; the ALR allowed the government to ban any organizations that were

---

43. This account of von Rauchhaupt and his opposition to the Delitzsch and Eilenburg cooperatives is based on Ruhmer's account (1937, 227–39). The basic outlines here agree with references in the writings of Schulze-Delitzsch and his allies, and Ruhmer bases much of his version on von Rauchhaupt's own reports from the official archives.

harmful. Close attention to subsequent history might convince us that an 11 percent interest rate was better than the only alternative, which was a money-lender charging a much greater percentage, and that unlimited liability posed little risk for poor people with nothing to lose and little hope of economic improvement without the cooperative. But von Rauchhaupt's stated position was not ludicrous. Consider the following thought experiment: if we described a lender charging 12 percent to academics today, how many would sympathize with von Rauchhaupt's view that they are dangerous?

The authorities' power to use the police power to forbid, harass, or control cooperatives was a constant theme in the cooperative accounts of the 1850s. Some German states were worse than Prussia, with Saxony apparently winning the dubious distinction of being most hostile to cooperatives. In some cases the authorities did not try to shut down the cooperative, they just wanted to micromanage it. Schulze-Delitzsch complained that in another case of protracted conflict (involving the Eisleben cooperative), the authorities asserted the right to approve every single loan![44]

This government harassment ceased only when a changing political environment made the Liberals part of the government's coalition. The change in the political atmosphere meant that by the early 1860s, the cooperatives had effective R1 and R2 rights. But Schulze-Delitzsch and his colleagues had long thought that cooperatives suffered as well from a lack of R3 rights. They began to use their new political positions (as members of the Prussian *Landtag*) to push for a special enabling law for cooperatives. The effort yielded fruit in 1867. The historiography of cooperative law has stressed the issue of limited liability, which was indeed contentious at a later point. But in the 1860s, Schulze-Delitzsch stressed the cooperative's lack of entity status. Under the ALR, a group like a cooperative was just a collection of individuals in some agreement, R2. As the ALR puts it, "Such associations do not constitute legal persons in relation to others, and as such cannot contract in the society's name for land or capital."[45] This status forced the cooperative to use expensive and imperfect workarounds to achieve what would be easy for a group with R3 rights. Consider the specific example of a member taking a loan from a credit cooperative. After 1867, the cooperative could (through its officers) contract with the borrower *as the cooperative*. Before 1867, the cooperative lacked any status with respect to third parties (including a borrower). Cooperatives operating before 1867 had to adopt one or

---

44. This is part of his defense of his first draft of a cooperative law (quoted in Thorwart 1909, 369–70).

45. Quoting more extensively: "§12 Bei Handlungen, woraus Rechte und Verbindlichkeiten gegen Andere entstehen, werden sie nur als Theilnehmer eines gemeinsamen Rechts, oder einer gemeinsamen Verbindlichkeit betrachtet. §13 Dergleichen Gesellschaften stellen im Verhältnisse gegen Andere, außer ihnen, keine moralische Person vor, und können daher auch, als solche, weder Grundstücke, noch Capitalien auf den Namen der Gesellschaft erwerben. § Unter sich aber haben dergleichen Gesellschaften, so lange sie bestehen, die inneren Rechte der Corporationen und Gemeinen" (Band III, Titel 6).

more stratagems to deal with this impediment. All entailed significant costs. A cooperative could have all members sign a particular contract. Contracts set up this way were really between the third party and each member (signatory) and not with the cooperative per se. This cumbersome mechanism was apparently rarely used. The sources stress other methods. Sometimes the cooperative's treasurer contracted in his own name (Crüger 1894, 395). The approach worked well if the treasurer's position did not turn over frequently, but clearly put a burden on the treasurer and required trust in his probity. More commonly, it appears that cooperative members gave their power of attorney (*Bevollmächtigung*) for relevant business to the cooperative's leadership (Crüger 1894, 394). Establishing the power of attorney required either a notarized document or personal appearance in front of an official, both of which could be costly.[46]

These legal and practical disabilities were not limited to cooperatives; they attached to any association or enterprise that did not acquire a special charter. Many small businesses were viewed by the ALR in the same way as the cooperatives. But two features of the cooperatives made this legal problem more serious than for most businesses. Business partnerships rarely had more than three or four members. Cooperatives, on the other hand, often had more than 100 members, and some had several hundred as early as the mid-1860s. With these numbers it was easy for a single power of attorney to be invalid, and a single invalid power of attorney could force a cooperative to reinitiate a legal action to, for example, recover a debt. In addition, by their nature cooperatives had a constantly changing membership. Every time someone joined or left a cooperative, the institution had to incur the legal costs mentioned above, and every change in membership raised the possibility of defective documents.

The ADHGB introduced a new principle into German law, recognizing the legal rights of entities such as partnerships that were not full legal persons (Joël 1890, 420). Because these partnerships had limited but important rights to act collectively, they were clearly R3 groups in our terms. Schulze-Delitzsch's contribution to the new cooperative law was to apply this principle to cooperatives. The 1867 cooperatives act gave cooperatives R3 rights the same way the ADHGB gave R3 rights to business partnerships. The act created a public registry of cooperatives (*Genossenschaftsregister*) that paralleled the register of firms used to track partnerships and corporations. Cooperatives that took advantage of the 1867 law had to register and to keep their membership lists up to date. In return, they acquired the R3 rights that applied to business partnerships under the ADHGB.

The 1867 act initially applied only to Prussia, but was extended to the

---

46. The distinction we make warrants stress. The cooperatives found ways to operate without R3 rights, but this does not amount to saying those methods did not entail significant costs.

North German Confederation in 1868. Most other federal states also accepted the Prussia law after 1871, with Bavaria delaying acceptance to 1873 and Saxony to 1874 (Joël 1890, 421). The 1867 act gave cooperatives most of the R3 rights they had sought. The act also settled the question of whether cooperatives could be harassed under the law related to association: bodies that had their own special act were doubtless "permitted." The interesting feature of the 1867 act was its connection to the business code. Schulze-Delitzsch never raised the idea of making cooperatives part of the business code. This would not have been absurd; while cooperatives in some countries (such as the United Kingdom) have their own distinctive enabling statutes, in most countries the law treats cooperatives as a special kind of business corporation. Such had been the case in Saxony and Bavaria. Rather, his approach to cooperative law simply borrowed an important feature of the then-new ADHGB: a partnership could have R3 rights simply by registering.

Schulze-Delitzsch's use of the principles underlying the ADHGB's provisions on partnerships illustrates two important points. First, the R3 and R4 rights civil-society groups need are virtually the same as those business firms need. Second, while Schulze-Delitzsch did not want the corporate status that could bring state oversight, he saw the value of tying his cooperatives to the business law, making them more secure from ideological enemies.

Within a few years efforts were under way to pass a new law at the Reich level. Much of the debate over new proposals took place *within* the cooperative movement; even those seeking to introduce features most resisted by cooperatives did so in the spirit of what they thought would enhance the movement's viability. The 1889 Reich Cooperatives Act introduced three changes. First, it allowed cooperatives to be members of each other, thus legalizing the practices of regional cooperative "centrals." Cooperative centrals were larger, regional entities that provided services to local cooperatives. Most centrals were banking institutions, but others served wholesale functions. Note how similar this organization is to what is common in the business world, where business firms own other firms. Second, the act required external auditing for all cooperatives. This requirement preceded mandatory external auditing for banks or business firms, and thus is striking on its own for going beyond any such provision for business firms. Finally, and most notably, the 1889 act allowed cooperatives to organize with either unlimited or limited liability. Subsequent discussions of the 1889 act have focused heavily on this feature, probably exaggerating its immediate impact. Few cooperatives took advantage of the limited liability form at first. But it meant that cooperatives could acquire one common corporate entitlement, limited liability, that was at the time strictly limited for business firms.

This sketch of the cooperatives and their encounters with the several aspects of association law illustrates an important and general feature of the entire issue. The law never sought to repress all associations. When the cooperatives did not fit with the prevailing political trends, some officials used the law of association to harass them. With a changing political environment that harassment ceased, and by the end of the nineteenth century many German governments offered (modest) direct and indirect subsidies to cooperatives. This pattern can be found throughout the nineteenth century, as Nipperdey (1994, 267–68) observes: at the same time as the law allowed governments to restrict or outlay associations, the same governments supported a range of educational and mutual-assistance organizations. The nineteenth century was the century of associations, as Nipperdey puts it; most Germans belonged to at least one, and many Germans belonged to several. But Germans only belonged to associations the government thought conducive to its own ends.[47]

8.4   France: A Brief Comparison

Were the restrictions we discuss a Prussian, or German, peculiarity? They were not, and to make this point concrete we turn to a brief comparison with France. This comparison does not carry with it the suggestion that France and Prussia were alike in any simple sense. Rather, we use it to indicate the common themes in associational rights present even in quite different societies. Even though democratic ideas and institutions appeared earlier and had more force in France than in Prussia, the limits on the right to associate were similar.

The French Revolution introduced basic democratic precepts and institutional forms that subsequent regimes at first severely limited, but never fully abolished. The restored Bourbon monarchy (1814/15–1830) tolerated an advisory parliament, and its successor, the so-called July monarchy (1830–1848) limited the Crown's power while expanding the franchise. By the third Republic (1870–1940), France enjoyed core democratic institutions that have endured: universal (at first, manhood) suffrage, ministerial responsibility, and so forth. Prussia, on the other hand, retained a three-class parliamentary voting system until the Weimar Republic (1918). The Reich introduced universal manhood suffrage with its foundation in 1871, but both Prussia and the Reich retained a parliamentary system in which the ministers were responsible to the king/emperor, rather than to the Parliament. Political historians debate how "democratic" this system was, but Germany clearly did not enjoy the same political culture and institutions as France until 1918. For all the political differences between France and Prussia in the nineteenth century, both regimes share a common skepticism about civil associations

---

47. "Das Jahrhundert wird das Jahrhundert der Vereine, jeder steht—oft mehrfach—in ihrem Netzwerk" (Nipperdey 1994, 267).

and repressed them with equal vigor. The final removal of the most severe restrictions in France took place not long before the Reich's 1908 act.

The French historical experience demonstrates that comparable restrictions on civil-society institutions existed in regimes other than absolute monarchies, as Prussia was until the 1850s. This account focuses on the law rather than the ideational underpinnings. One source of the restrictions on associations stems from Rousseau's notion of the "general will," which informed much French thought on democracy and democratic rights. France under the *ancien régime* was at once an absolutist state and a society riven with groups that claimed special privileges: by virtue of birth, or occupation, or the king's favor (see, e.g., Jacob Levy's thoughtful discussion of Montesquieu and the *corps intermédiaires* in chapter 3 of this volume). Democracy existed to overcome the expression of these particular interests in favor of the general will. Rousseau argued that associations that existed in the space between the citizen and the state (which he called "*sociétés partielles*") could only frustrate the development of the general will; they could advance their member's interests, but not assist their members in shaping the general will.[48] The French restrictions on association reflected, in part, this conception of the general will.

Unease with associations had a more pragmatic basis, as well. The various French governments saw in political associations a sort of counter to the state that menaced the state's functioning and even legitimacy.[49] Clubs were a useful tool in the struggle to overthrow a regime, but dangerous to the new constitutional order established in its place (Jaume 2001, 77). Even those who had been members of such associations prior to the Revolution opposed them once in power. The nuances are different, but the core of the pragmatic opposition to associations is identical to the Carlsbad Decrees and other efforts to suppress opposition in Germany.

Under the *ancien régime*, the French authorities limited association in ways similar to those we described above for Prussia in the early nineteenth century. These limitations were part of a broad strategy of controlling speech and potential political opposition, just as in Prussia. France's revolutionary government enacted strong, systematic restrictions on association. The *loi Le Chapelier* of June 14, 1791, declared "n'est permis à personne d'inspirer aux citoyens un intérêt intermédiaire, de les séparer de la chose publique par un esprit de coopération." This act followed soon after the "Allarde Decree" of March 1791. Together the two decrees outlawed a broad group of bodies that had played important roles in prerevolutionary society, or

---

48. See Rousseau (1865, 45). Also see Levy (chapter 3) in this volume.

49. Jaume (2001, 75): "les divers gouvernements redoutent dans l'association à caractère politique une forme de pouvoir (ou de contre-pouvoir), d'organisation, et d'unité d'opinion, qui menacerait le fontionnement et même la *légitimité* de l'Etat."

that threatened the democracy the revolutionaries wanted to develop. The decrees forbade combinations for the benefit of economic interests ("corporations"): no guilds, no other worker combinations, no organizations to benefit particular business or professional interests. These bodies and the benefits they enjoyed had constituted a primary target during the first days of challenges to the *ancien régime*, as they reflected a political economy that privileged groups of insiders against everyone else. The Allard Decree in particular aimed to create an entirely free market in labor, one that would depart radically from earlier French experience, as well as from much of the rest of Continental Europe. The decrees also forbade other associations, especially those with political intent or overtones. These associations (many, but not all, were called "clubs") violated the core idea in Rousseau's conception of liberty: a body intended to discuss ideas and then present a common front to the rest of society can only frustrate expression of the general will.

Thus both Prussia and France ended up with similar legislation on associations, but for dramatically different reasons. Postrevolutionary France distrusted all associations; with some exceptions, the post-1815 regimes did not allow re-creation of the bodies suppressed by the Revolution, and at the same time the French forbade new voluntary groups. Prussian society in the period after 1815 was still largely *based* on the older associations that revolutionary France had outlawed, but, as we have seen, Prussia (and the rest of the German *Bund*) asserted the right to forbid voluntary associations. The motives for these restrictions differed considerably, however. The particular critique that drove much French opposition to associations, the feeling that they were part of a system of conferring benefits on specific people, had little resonance in Prussia. Much discussion, of course, concerned which people should receive which benefits, but with the exception of the Liberals, few Prussians in the early nineteenth century saw much wrong with giving special privileges to those of a particular background or connection to the Crown.

One more difference warrants stress. The early nineteenth-century French effort to control associations focused on workers' groups, "syndicats," and related bodies similar to trade-unions. Some of this concern reflected placing the interests of employers over employees, but the focus on workers also betrays some unease with the "mob." Prussia and most other German states did not abolish guilds until the 1840s and later, and one would have to squint hard to detect anywhere in Germany an urban proletariat or labor movement until the 1850s, at least. Prussian conflict over associations did not shift to workers until later, as noted above.

The French monarchy's restoration in 1814–15 did not lead to change in the association law. Even the more liberal regime brought in by the 1830 revolution made no difference. The relevant provisions from the 1810 penal code appeared in the 1832 version:

No association of more than twenty persons, whose object is to meet every day, or on certain set days, to deal with religious, literary, political, or other matters, may form without the agreement of the Government, and under the conditions the public authority chooses to impose on the society.[50]

Section 292 stated that any group that met in defiance of this restriction, or that failed to adhere to the conditions imposed on it by the authorities, would be dissolved and its leaders fined. Section 294 required that individuals not host a meeting of such an association without permission of the municipal authorities, *even if the group in question was authorized*. And §293 held the leaders responsible for the groups' actions: "If by addresses, exhortations, invocations or prayers, in any language, or by reading, signs, publication or distribution of any writings" there are crimes or offenses,[51] then the leaders of this group would be punished both for the crimes of the groups' members and face additional punishment as leaders. The members would also be punished for their individual conduct.

These provisions limited R1 and R2 rights, and they were remarkably similar to the Prussian law quoted above. The July monarchy (1830) was France's first constitutional government and usually considered liberal by the standards of earlier governments as well as the day. But it still made it a crime to meet in groups of any size.

France relaxed these restrictions in several steps. The 1848 constitution guaranteed freedom of association, but this was withdrawn a year later. The *loi Ollivier* (May 25, 1864) made it possible for workers to organize and to strike under certain conditions. The more important *loi Waldeck-Rousseau* (March 21, 1884) abrogated *le Chapelier* and permitted the creation of groups that existed to advance the economic conditions of people following similar occupations (syndicats). This change led to both labor unions and cooperatives. The only government role for these groups was a publicity requirement (they had to deposit their articles of association with the local authority and keep the authorities apprised of their leadership). The reference to "more than 20 persons" in §2 overrides §291–94 of the penal code. Section 3 stressed that the 1884 act only applied to groups whose purpose was to "defend the economic interests" of individuals in a narrowly defined occupational group. The point was to enable the creation of economic organizations such as cooperatives and not to relax restrictions on groups of a possibly political nature. Rosanvallon (2004, 280–92) stresses this implication of the 1884 law: it privileged *one* kind of association, *one*

---

50. Section 291, "Nulle association de plus de vingt personnes, dont le but sera de se réunir tous les jours, ou á certains jours marqués, pour s'occuper d'objets religieux, littéraires, politiques ou autres, ne pourra se former qu'avec l'agrément du Gouvernement, et sous les conditions qu'il plaira à l'autorité publique d'imposer à la société."

51. The French text refers to both crimes and "délits," less serious offenses.

reason for combining with other citizens. Some contemporary opposition to the 1884 measure focused on just this fact; participants in the parliamentary debate noted that the partial relaxation amounted to a departure from the principle of equality before the law and a reintroduction of the privileges for specific groups that the revolutionary decrees had sought to erase. The 1884 law's supporters carved out this exception by limiting the scope of syndicats recognized in this way to defending their members' economic interests: that is, no politics.[52]

Successive French governments relaxed restrictions on association in the last decades of the nineteenth century. The association law of 1901 introduced both R1 and R2 rights, and some R3 rights for associations that adhered to certain norms such as registration. French associations under the law of 1901 had to have two members, and could not have as their aim anything contrary to "good morals" or France's republican form of government. If the association provided basic information on its leaders and aims to the local prefecture, then it enjoyed the R3 rights of acting in its own name for legal purposes. Thus the 1901 French law's effect was similar to the combination of the German BGB's registered association provisions and the Reich 1908 act on associations.[53]

Even before the 1901 associations law, France no more suppressed all associations than did the Prussians. Sometimes the French state explicitly tolerated or even encouraged associations. Rosanvallon notes that the chambers of commerce were one of the "corporations" that affronted the Revolution. Yet Napoleon reintroduced them in 1802. The chambers of commerce show that not all civil-society organizations had to be autonomous; the chambers were as much organs of the state as entities that represented member interests (Rosanvallon 2004, 389). Especially under Louis Napoleon, France saw the flowering of voluntary, mutual insurance associations. Rosanvallon notes that as the French government became more and more concerned with hygiene over the nineteenth century, it began to draw upon bodies of experts constituted as associations to advise and help shape policy (391). Associations that served the state's goals were welcome.

8.5   Conclusion: Business Firms as an Exception?

We propose a classification for the rights to associate and the rights of association. They correspond, if not always neatly, to the rights afforded citizens and their associations since the late eighteenth century. Some governments sought to limit or forbid individuals from associating or simply assembling, R1, in our typology. Denying R1 rights reflects a fear that asso-

---

52. "Les syndicats professionnels ont exclusivement pour object l'étude et la defense des intérêts économiques, industriels, commerciaux et agricoles" (§3).
53. Andrieu, Béguec, and Tartakowsky (2001, 701–5) reprints the text of the law of 1901.

ciating will lead to associations, at least certain types of associations, that threaten established order. To function as an organization many, if not most, associations need rights to construct rules that bind their members to certain actions. The entitlement of associations to bind their members cannot be taken for granted, as Bloch and Lamoreaux demonstrate in their discussion concerning the challenges faced by civil associations attempting to expel and sanction members who violated internal rules. We label associations possessing this entitlement as "associational aggregates," R2, which operate essentially by agreements or contracts among the association's members. Entitlements derived from these agreements, however, do not reach beyond the association's membership, unlike "associational entities," R3, which have legal capacity to hold themselves out to third parties as distinct entities and, most concretely, to hold and acquire property, to sue and be sued, and to enter into contracts directly. Associational entities exercise their entitlements independently, not through pairwise agreements with all its members, but in the name of the collectivity. Finally, associations are sometimes treated as more than entities, as persons, legal persons and, whether by legal formalism or expediency, are afforded entitlements unique to persons "in law," R4.

Regimes seeking to suppress civil society can do so by discouraging or denying citizens the privilege of assembling or otherwise associating, R1 rights. As we have stressed, however, suppression of civil society may be most effectively pursued by curtailing the ability of associations themselves to conduct their affairs through the forms we label R2 through R4. These forms matter a great deal for civil-society organizations to achieve their goals.

We have documented the ways denial of, or restrictions on, rights beyond R1 were at the core of debates over associations in Prussia, as well as in France and the United States. Our choice of countries was deliberate and intended to challenge superficial views contrasting nineteenth-century Germany, on the one hand, with France and the United States of the same period, on the other hand: Prussia was, to many nineteenth-century Germans, synonymous with political repression and a monarchy opposed to constitutional government, while nineteenth-century France and the United States were each born out of revolutions that stressed individual liberty. Yet all three governments limited association and the rights of association when they saw fit. They did so differently, to different degrees and with their own peculiar concerns, to be sure, but they also restricted associations in a number of surprisingly similar ways. From the number of individuals permitted to meet to the language spoken at meetings as well as distinctions regarding daytime versus nighttime gatherings and indoor versus outdoor meetings, nineteenth-century officials relied on a familiar set of tools to restrict associations. Their greatest common restrictions on civil-society associations, however, would be on those entitlements we characterized as R2, R3, and R4.

Finally, we conclude by drawing out a theme running through our accounts, particularly in Prussia and in France. This theme concerns both the exceptional treatment of businesses and commercial associations during the most restrictive periods, and the way developments of R3 and R4 rights first extended to cooperatives and other civil-society groups with economic purposes. There is something puzzling in this disparate treatment between civil and commercial associations. Seven people meeting to discuss business were seven people meeting. Why would anxious government authorities automatically assume the seven conveners were not a threat? Why not insist they provide prior notice of their meetings and enforce other provisions of the laws discussed above? The exceptions granted to business associations are all the more surprising when we consider that some of the leading opposition figures were businesspeople: a standard "Manchester" liberal in the 1840s might be as offensive to official thought as a radical bent on workers' rights. Government officials showed no reservations about regulating or restricting broad areas of economic life, and they were unapologetic about limiting the right to form business enterprises of specific types, most notably corporations. Granting business firms automatic waivers on the laws of association seems like offering a license to some committed opponents of the regime. Why did privileges for associational business interest develop in this way?

We can think of several reasons. First, even in a state like Prussia in 1800, which was bolstered by elites whose economic interests were threatened by free enterprise and the development of modern industry, officials still recognized the importance of tax revenue and employment for citizens. To the extent economic development required multiowner business enterprises, tolerating association for this purpose was a necessary evil. Second, as worrisome as business-oriented Liberals may have been to the regime, they were less of a threat than the real or imagined revolutionaries seeking to overthrow the government. Take, for example, David Hansemann (1790–1864), a leading Rhineland businessman and Liberal politician. On occasion Hansemann deeply annoyed Prussian officials, but he had little interest in the state's undoing. Official attention was better focused on those more radical.[54] Third, in many ways the interests of the state and businesses were largely aligned. Following the postrevolutionary reactions of the early 1850s, the business community (and the Liberals) had been brought into a larger consensus about the future of the Prussian and then German state, and there was little danger of conflict in which the business community would oppose

54. While an explicit focus on left-wing and labor groups did not develop until after the 1848–49 revolutions, a subtext in much concern about groups earlier in the nineteenth century centered on the allegedly wild character of large public gatherings of working-class people. This fear can be seen in the distinction between indoor and outdoor meetings, and has something to do with the suppression of the gymnasts. Even the *Burschenschaften*, whose members hardly counted as working class, promoted displays with an enthusiasm that could seem excessive, even if just expressions of respect for the king.

the state. The cooperatives benefited indirectly from this political realignment. More generally, by the 1860s many Germans were turning their focus to the effects of industrialization in creating a class of people uprooted from rural life and suffering from poverty, illness, and lack of education. Focus on this "social question" in Germany was to some extent driven by genuine sympathy for those left behind by economic development. Official focus on the social question, however, also reflected a concern that various working-class movements would coalesce to challenge the existing order if Germany's leaders did not find some way to reform the harshest features of the new society. Here cooperatives and other economic bodies could be seen (and quite clearly *were* seen) as part of a bulwark against revolution. It may be that German governments worried about association per se, because free association threatened the state's assignment of persons to classes and ranks. The exception for business association suggests a willingness to overlook the deeper threat if the association helped to advance the state's goals.

References

Allgemeines Landrecht für die Preußischen Staaten. 1825. (Unveränderter Abdruck der Ausgabe von 1821). Berlin: Nauck.

Allgemeines Deutsches Handelsgesetzbuch von 1861 (reprinted 1973). Darmstardt, Germany: Scientia Verlag Aalen.

Andrieu, Claire, Gilles Le Béguec, and Danielle Tartakowsky, eds. 2001. *Associations et Champ Politique: La Loi de 1901 à l'épreuve du Siècle.* Paris: Publications de la Sorbonne.

Blair, Margaret M., and Elizabeth Pollman. 2015. "The Derivative Nature of Corporate Constitutional Rights." *William & Mary Law Review* 56:1673–743.

Brooks, Richard R. W. 2006. "Incorporating Race." *Columbia Law Review* 104:2023–94.

Bürgerliches Gesetzbuch nebst Einführungsgesetz. 1909. (From Aug. 18, 1896.) Berlin: Guttentag.

Chilton, Adam S., and Mila Versteeg. 2016. "Do Constitutional Rights Make a Difference?" *American Journal of Political Science* 60 (3): 575–89.

Crüger, Hans. 1894. "Die Zulassung von Genossenschaften mit beschränkter Haftpflicht durch das Genossenschaftsgesetz vom 1. Mai 1889." *Archiv für öffentliches Recht* Band 9:389–455.

Duchhardt, Heinz. 2007. *Stein: Eine Biographie.* Münster, Germany: Aschendorff.

Entwurf eines Vereinsgesetzes. 1908. *Verhandlungen des Reichstages* XII. Legislaturperiode, I. Session. Anlagen zu den Stenographischen Berichten Nr. 471, bis. 526, bd. 243, no. 482. Berlin: Sittenfeld.

Fairbairn, Brett. 1994. "History from the Ecological Perspective: Gaia Theory and the Problem of Cooperatives in Turn-of-the-Century Germany." *American Historical Review* 99 (4): 1203–39.

Gierke, Otto. 1868. *Rechtsgeschichte der Deutschen Genossenschaft.* Berlin: Weidmann.

Gregg, Amanda. 2014. "Factory Productivity and the Concession System of Incorporation in Late Imperial Russia, 1894–1908." Working Paper, Yale University.

Guinnane, Timothy W. 2001. "Cooperatives as Information Machines: German Rural Credit Cooperatives, 1883–1914." *Journal of Economic History* 61 (2): 366–89.

———. 2012. "State Support for the German Cooperative Movement, 1860–1914." *Central European History* 45 (2): 208–32.

———. 2013. "Creating a New Legal Form: the GmbH." Working Paper, Yale University.

Guinnane, Timothy W., Ron Harris, Naomi Lamoreaux, and Jean-Laurent Rosenthal. 2007. "Putting the Corporation in Its Place." *Enterprise and Society* 8 (3): 687–729.

Guinnane, Timothy W., and Susana Martínez-Rodríguez. 2011. "Cooperatives before Cooperative Law: Business Law and Cooperatives in Spain, 1869–1931." *Revista de Historia Económica-Journal of Iberian and Latin American Economic History* 29 (1): 67–93.

Hardtwig, Wolfgang, and Helmut Hinze. 1997. *Deutsche Geschichte in Quellen und Darstellung. Band 7: Vom Deutschen Bund zum Kaiserreich 1815–1871.* Stuttgart: Reclam.

Hueber, Anton. 1984. "Das Vereinsrecht im Deutschland des 19. Jahrhunderts." *Historische Zeitschrift (Beiheft)* 9:115–32.

Inazu, John D. 2010. "The Forgotten Freedom of Assembly." *Tulane Law Review* 84:565–612.

Jaume, Lucien. 2001. "Une liberté en souffrance: l'association au XIXᵉ siècle." In *Associations et Champ Politique: La Loi de 1901 à l'épreuve du Siècle*, edited by Andrieu, Le Béguec, and Tartakowsky, 75–100. Paris: Publications de la Sorbonne.

Joël, Max. 1890. "Erläuterung" für "Das Gesetz Betreffend die Erwerbs- und Wirthschaftsgenossenschaften vom 1. Mai 1889." *Annalen des Deutschen Reichs für Gesetzgebung, Verwaltung und Statistik.*

Koch, Christian Friedrich. 1862. *Allgemeines Landrecht für die Preußischen Staaten*, 3rd ed., vol. II. Berlin: Trautwein. Accessed from: http://dlib-pr.mpier.mpg.de/m/kleioc/0010/exec/bigpage/%22129324_00000531.gif.

Lightner, David L. 2006. *Slavery and the Commerce Power: How the Struggle Against the Interstate Slave Trade Led to the Civil War.* New Haven: Yale University Press.

Loi Relative à la Création des Syndicats Professionnels. 1884. Mar. 21.

Meyer, Wolfgang. 1970. *Das Vereinswesen der Stadt Nürnberg im 19. Jahrhundert.* Nürnberg: Stadtarchiv Nürnberg.

Nipperdey, Thomas. 1976. "Verein als Soziale Struktur in Deutschland: Im Späten 18. und Frühen 19. Jahrhundert. Eine Fallstudie zur Moderisierung I." In *Gesellschaft, Kultur, Theorie: Gesammelte Aufsätze zur neueren Geschichte.* Göttingen, Germany: Vandenhoeck & Ruprecht.

———. 1994. *Deutsche Geschichte 1800–1866: Bürgerwelt und starker Staat.* Munich: Beck.

Nouveau Code Pénal. 1832. Dijon: Victor Lagier.

Prager, Max. 1904. "Grenzen der Gewerkschaftsbewegung." *Archiv für Sozialwissenschaft und Sozialpolitik* 20:229–300.

Romen, Antonius. 1916. *Das Vereinsgesetz vom 19. April 1908.* Berlin: Guttentag.

Rosanvallon, Pierre. 2004. *Le Modéle Politique Français: La Société Civile Contre le Jacobinisme de 1789 à nos Jours.* Paris: Éditions du Seuil.

Rousseau, Jean-Jacques. 1865. *Du Contrat Social ou Principes du Droit Politique*, 2nd ed. Paris: Bureaux de la Publication.

Ruhmer, Otto. 1937. *Entstehungsgeschichte des Deutschen Genossenschaftswesens: Die Ersten Deutschen Genossenschaften.* Hamburg: Krögers Buchdruckerei und Verlag.

Sartre, Jean-Paul. 1960. *Critique of Dialectical Reason: Theory of Practical Ensembles,* translated by Alan Sheridan-Smith. London: Verso.

Schoeppner, Michael A. 2010. "Navigating the Dangerous Atlantic: Racial Quarantines, Black Sailors and the United States Constitutionalism." PhD diss., University of Florida.

Sheehan, James J. 1995. *German Liberalism in the Nineteenth Century.* Amherst, NY: Humanities Press.

Skocpol, Theda. 2003. *Diminished Democracy: From Membership to Management in American Civic Life.* Norman: University of Oklahoma Press.

Sperber, Jonathan. 1984. *Popular Catholicism in Nineteenth-Century Germany.* Princeton, NJ: Princeton University Press.

———. 1991. *Rhineland Radicals: The Democratic Movement and the Revolution of 1848–1849.* Princeton, NJ: Princeton University Press.

Thorwart, F., ed. 1909. *Hermann Schulze-Delitzsch's Schriften und Reden,* vol. I. Berlin: Guttentag.

Tillmann, Hans. 1976. "Staat und Vereinigungsfreiheit im 19. Jahrhundert—Von der Paulskirche zum Reichsvereingesetz 1908." PhD diss., University of Gießen.

Tomlins, Christopher L. 1993. *Law, Labor, and Ideology in the Early American Republic.* Cambridge: Cambridge University Press.

Verfassung des Deutschen Reichs. 1849. Reichs-Gesetz-Blatt 16. Apr. 28.

Verhandlungen des Reichstages. 1908. XII. Legislaturperiode. I. Session. Band 243: Anlagen zu den Stenographischen Berichten. Berlin.

Wiberg, Alfred. 1906. *Das öffentliche Vereinsrecht und die Gewerkschaftsbewegung.* Leipzig: Noske.

Opening Access, Ending the Violence Trap
Labor, Business, Government, and the National Labor Relations Act

Margaret Levi, Tania Melo, Barry R. Weingast, and Frances Zlotnick

9.1 Introduction

Throughout American history, open access has been contested. Those in power used violence to deny various groups the right to organize effectively or to otherwise make political claims. In their attempt to date open access in the United States, North, Wallis, and Weingast (hereafter NWW; 2009) focused on general incorporation. This criterion dates open access in the United States in the 1840s following a series of general incorporation laws that opened access to business organizations.

We raise two problems with the NWW account of the emergence of open access in the United States. First, widespread open access in the United States was more fraught and contested than NWW suggest, and it certainly took longer to achieve than they originally realized. Open access to labor organization, for example, would take a century longer than open access for business. The claims of African Americans for full citizenship were ignored or repressed for a century after emancipation, and the explicitly racial violence against them was too long tolerated. This aspect of open access remains a struggle to this day. Second, demands for open access by excluded groups evoked violence by government, private actors, and claimants.

Margaret Levi is director of the Center for Advanced Study in the Behavioral Sciences (CASBS) and professor of political science at Stanford University, and Jere L. Bacharach Professor Emerita of International Studies at the University of Washington. Tania Melo is a PhD candidate in the Department of Political Science at the University of Washington. Barry R. Weingast is the Ward C. Krebs Family Professor in the Department of Political Science at Stanford University and a senior fellow of the Hoover Institution. Frances Zlotnick is senior data scientist at GitHub.

For acknowledgments, sources of research support, and disclosure of the authors' material financial relationships, if any, please see http://www.nber.org/chapters/c13504.ack.

In this chapter, we extend the NWW argument about the emergence of open access where that access was violently contested. In particular, we follow North and Weingast (1989) to argue that the solution of the violence problem required inventing a new set of credible commitments. This chapter extends the understanding of how difficult credible commitments are to achieve and sustain even in seemingly democratic civil societies.

Some excluded groups made insistent claims for open access, most notably labor organizations. Yet for the century prior to the New Deal of the 1930s, labor was denied organizational rights and privileges.[1] During the century previous to the New Deal, firms and governments actively suppressed labor organization, firing workers who struck, blacklisting and arresting labor leaders, and deporting those who were immigrants.

The United States during this 100-year-long period failed two critical conditions articulated by NWW as requisite for open access: first, and most obviously, the denial of open access to labor; and second, the use of violence to suppress labor. At least until the end of the turmoil of the 1930s, many firms employed private armies to protect them from strikes and unionization. Ford's "Service Department," composed of underworld thugs and mercenaries, was infamous for its violence and intimidation tactics (Bernstein 1971, 735–51). Governments used the police, National Guard, and the US Army at times to crush nascent labor organization, leading frequently to killings and mass beatings.

Labor peace emerged only with the invention of new administrative structure and process; that is, a set of new regulatory institutions that solved a series of commitment problems that plagued the emergence of nonviolent resolution of disputes. These new institutional solutions to the commitment problem arose in the New Deal with the passage of the National Labor Relations Act (NLRA) and the creation of the National Labor Relations Board (NLRB) in 1935. Since the late 1930s, labor violence has been far lower and labor-firm cooperation far higher. In the words of Taft and Ross (1969, 292), "The sharp decline in the level of industrial violence is one of the greatest achievements of the National Labor Relations Board."

This short sketch of labor history raises several questions that remain unanswered in the literature. Why was the labor violence so intractable? What exactly did the NLRA/NLRB do that—somehow—solved the problem of violence? And, if this legislation solved the problem, why didn't Congress do so earlier, thereby saving the deadweight losses associated with years

---

1. Other excluded groups seemingly acquiesced in the face of violent repression, notably African Americans. Robert Dahl, one of the great champions of pluralist democracy, effectively argued that where there was no noise, there was no claim (Dahl 1961). The civil rights movement convinced him that sometimes, as his critics Bachrach and Baratz (1962, 1963; Lukes [1974] 2005) argued, smoldering anger and frustration lay behind quiescence.

of violence, strikes, and a considerably lower level of cooperation between firms and their workers?

Although substantial gains from cooperation existed among the three major groups, all three faced commitment problems. Business—fearful of labor's threat to its control over business management, the labor force, and to corporate profits—could not commit to eschew violence. Nor could government commit to being an impersonal arbiter instead of being an agent of firms against labor. Too often, government officials associated labor organization with anarchy and revolution, and it considered business a source of stability and economic growth. Further, the law of property and contracts favored business, providing an important legal basis for government to collaborate with firms. Labor could not commit to eschewing political demands for foundational changes in the economy, nor could it commit extremists to forgo violence at moments when the great majority would prefer not to.

The stakes were therefore high. Legalization of unions would foster the growth of powerful actors in opposition to business, making labor demands more pressing. Without solving labor's commitment problems, business was rationally reluctant to support legislation that would authorize unions. The result was ongoing violent suppression of labor with considerable forgone gains from cooperation between labor and business.

The 1930s legislation channeled labor-business conflict to focus on wages and working conditions, an outcome that was not preordained. Much of the literature implicitly accepts these bounds by ignoring the central problem of violence. So why and how was solution institutionalized in the NLRA? Motivating the change was labor's existential threat to business during this period when unions and labor organizations were perceived as potential collaborators in a growing radical, even revolutionary, movement in the United States (Katznelson 2013). We further argue that the acceptance and sustaining of the legislation also required transformations in the substance and implementation of administrative law.

The NLRA had several well-known accomplishments. It legalized unions, and required collective bargaining; it defined a number of common antiunion tactics as "unfair labor practices" and hence illegal; and it created an enforcement mechanism to make it work.

In addition, however, the legislation accomplished several ends largely unrecognized in the literature. We list three. First, the NLRA dramatically lowered the stakes for firms. It narrowed considerably the legitimate range of bargaining between labor and business, focusing on wages and conditions; the legislation removed labor's threat to business management and firm capital; it also prevented unauthorized strikes, helping unions control their more radical and extreme elements who favored goals beyond wages and benefits.

Second, the legislation transformed government from an advocate of business using violence against labor into an impersonal arbiter, impersonal in the sense that regulators had incentives to punish either side for failing to abide by the rules.[2] Equally important, the legislation provided obvious advantages for labor. It legitimized unions, allowing labor organization to form, grow, and advance workers' interests. As union ranks grew considerably, labor became an important political force, able to support its position in a manner not previously possible. By counterbalancing business, labor provided new and substantive support for the NLRA, an impersonal arbiter.

Third, to accomplish these ends, organizational and legal innovations were necessary to create a new form of regulatory delegation that sat comfortably within the constitutional framework. Put simply, for the new system to work, political officials and the courts had to solve the principal agency problem that we now take for granted: creating a regulatory agency that implements the intentions of Congress, while not transgressing the due process rights of citizens and firms.

Our framework affords answers to each of the questions we asked at the outset. Labor violence proved long lived and intractable because of commitment problems. None of the three parties—labor, business, and government—were willing or capable of unilaterally eschewing violence. The NLRA ended a century of violence because it solved the various commitment problems facing the three sets of players. Finally, this legislation could not have been implemented earlier because it required significant innovation in public law and organization that occurred only in the context of the multipronged regulatory framework of the New Deal.

Labor unions, more than most other civil-society organizations, were perceived as threatening; and given the various the problem of violence reflecting difficult commitment problems, this perception was rational.

This chapter proceeds as follows. Section 9.2 provides a brief history of the labor movement up to the early 1930s, including the legal context that, prior to 1930, favored business over labor, leading the government to protect property and hence to side with business. Section 9.3 provides a simple game theoretic analysis showing why, prior to the mid-1930s, violence remained a central component of the equilibrium. Section 9.4 considers the historical and institutional shifts that ultimately produced a relatively nonviolent equilibrium under the NLRA and NLRB. In section 9.5, we adapt the game presented in section 9.3 to incorporate the new institutions created by the NLRA; this analysis reveals how the NLRA solved the various commitment problems facing the three major actors, business, government, and labor. Section 9.6 develops a new interpretation of the constitutional controversies of the 1930s that led to solving the commitment problems. In section 9.7, we present our implications and conclusions.

---

2. Although the NLRB became an impersonal arbiter, the legislation was nonetheless biased in favor of organized labor.

9.2   A Brief History of the Labor Movement

The barriers to organizing were high and remained insurmountable for most workers in the United States until the 1930s.[3] The most important obstacles were the unremitting hostility of the managers, the alliance of the government with the corporations, and the diversity of interests, demands, and organizational strategies within the labor movement itself. None of the parties could credibly commit to refrain from violence. Management believed it was their right to defend their prerogatives and profit with private armies and physical intimidation. Government believed corporate interests trumped those of labor and regularly brought in the National Guard to settle strikes on behalf of industry owners. Labor had no means to control those in their ranks who chose violent confrontation.

Numerous accounts contrast the business ideology in the United States with other countries from at least the nineteenth century on. American business had a longstanding opposition to unionization that distinguished it—well into the twentieth century—from many European countries (Friedman 1988; Swenson 2002; Mares 2003). The federal government generally shared that opposition except for particular moments in time, such as World War I, when government depended on the unions sufficiently to overcome its antagonism and act as a mediator between business and labor. Strikes over time in the United States reveal that periods in which government engaged in mediation or impersonal intervention in strikes helped resolve the violence problem while also facilitating effective bargains and unions, those that were able to compromise and promote productivity (Geraghty and Wiseman 2011).

The particular history of the relations among business, government, and labor affected union organizing and legislative strategies with consequences for the timing of the achievement of open access. The rise in labor militancy in the mid- to late nineteenth century set the stage for the practices and laws that would influence access until the 1930s. Currie and Ferrie (2000), for example, explore heterogeneous state-level legal frameworks that emerged as workers engaged in disputes to win collective bargaining and how those laws affected subsequent strike activity. Using data from 1881 to 1894, they document the relationship between a higher incidence of labor disputes when legislation, most notably injunctions, reduced worker certainty about strike outcomes; they report a lower incidence of disputes where legislation, most notably protective laws such as maximum hours, increased worker certainty.

3. For accounts of the history of American labor unions in the nineteenth and early twentieth centuries, see Montgomery (1989), Hattam (1993), Perlman (1928), Voss (1993), and Foner ([1947] 1988). For accounts that extend into the early 1940s, see Bernstein (1969, 1971, 1985) and Lichtenstein (2002). Also, see Brecher (1997) for a provocative history of strikes in the United States.

Other research focuses on the organization strategies of unions. Friedman (1988), for example, compares France with the United States and argues that the more hostile government attitude in the United States led unions to avoid or prevented them from relying on the state. The American Federation of Labor (AFL), the first successful long-lived union confederation, embodied the approach to disputes that Friedman outlines. It was built on craft workers, rather than industrial workers. The crafts unions were the first to succeed at legal organization through their control of jobs and accreditation, achieving the acceptance of employers and government by the end of the nineteenth century. These unions monopolized the supply of craft labor through an apprenticeship system and hiring halls, effectively requiring employers to come to the unions and pay the union-set rates. The founding of the American Federation of Labor (AFL) in 1886 further consolidated the craft workers' legal and political position, but at the expense of the unskilled workers and the newer immigrants (Perlman 1928).

The AFL victories derived largely from agreements with employers in a given industry; the Federation seldom appealed to government to set minimum wages or maximum hours. Its self-stated mantra was "voluntarism"— that is, "relying on their own voluntary organizations . . . defended the autonomy of the craft union against the coercive intervention of the state" (Rogin 1962, 521–22). The Federation lobbied, but most determinedly to reduce job competition; among its major campaigns was immigration restriction. During the 1930s, for example, the AFL expressed cautious support of social security and considerable nervousness about all legislation, including the National Labor Relations Act and other legislation that might interfere with its internal affairs (Eidlin 2009, 253).

By contrast, industrial unions had a far more difficult time establishing themselves. Employers and governments often met large-scale strike waves, generally coinciding with the cycle of depressions that began in the mid-nineteenth century, with violence. Industrial unions also experienced numerous stops and starts. The Knights of Labor was the first large-scale labor American organization; it experienced a period of rapid growth after its founding in 1869, but was dead by the 1890s (see Voss 1993; Foner [1947] 1988). Labor activism intensified at the end of the nineteenth century and again in the second decade of the twentieth century, but the same pattern prevailed: worker mobilization followed by repression.

The rise of the Industrial Workers of the World (IWW) or "Wobblies" created a new kind of political threat. The IWW professed revolutionary goals, and it believed in direct action over political action (cf. Adler 2011; Kimeldorf 1999). It used strikes to disrupt the economy, not just to improve working conditions. A militant union that organized all workers, craft and industrial, IWW's presence was particularly strong among miners, lumberjacks, and dockworkers. Its name became associated with violence in the public mind when its leadership, most notably "Big Bill" Haywood, who was also on the executive committee of the US Socialist Party, was accused of masterminding the assassination of Governor Frank Steunenberg of Idaho in 1905, presumably in retaliation for putting down an 1899 miners' strike the governor had labeled an "insurrection." The prosecution was secretly bankrolled by the mine owners, but Clarence Darrow's defense led to the acquittal of the accused (Lukas 1997). Haywood was also among the hundred or so IWW members convicted in 1918 under the Espionage Act of 1917, but he escaped prison by fleeing to the Soviet Union where he lived his remaining years.

The "Red Scare" of 1919 closed a chapter in American labor history. While "the Great War" raged in Europe, but also in its immediate aftermath, the United States experienced multiple major strikes, considerable labor organizing, violent confrontations between police and unions, terrorist acts (including bombings and assassinations) by revolutionary anarchists, and Socialist electoral victories. Some of these actions were illegal and violent; others, such as the Seattle General Strike of 1919 (Johnson 2008) and the Boston Police Strike of the same year (Levi 1977), were peaceful but illegal; and some, such as the electoral strategy of Eugene V. Debs and the Socialist Party, were non-violent and legal. But all ultimately got tarred with the same brush, as fear of mayhem and revolution became widespread among the public.

Although President Woodrow Wilson proclaimed his support of labor during the Versailles discussions (Lichtenstein 2002, 4), the United States simultaneously attempted to rid the labor movement of its militant leadership. The Espionage Act of 1917 and the Immigration Act of 1918 increased the power of the federal government to deport any persons it deemed dangerous to the national interest. The "Palmer Raids" of 1919 that bear the name of the attorney general Wilson appointed, permitted jailing of leaders and members of radical organizations and the closing down of their offices. Newspapers, business leaders, and government officials fueled "the rationality of fear" (De Figueiredo and Weingast 1999), and Americans, as a rule, feared the violent revolution they had come to believe was possible if its perpetrators were not repressed.

Fear of a revolutionary labor movement resurfaced in the 1930s, but with significant differences. The Great Depression created a large pool of dispossessed, unemployed, and disgruntled citizens. The Communist Party offered an alternative vision of the future with promises of economic security and equity that the present United States did not seem capable of delivering— economically or politically. Although committed in principle to the violent overthrow of the United States, the Communist Party did not use violence, was legal until the 1940s, and worked with and through numerous other organizations, including unions. Deportation was no longer an effective weapon given that almost all the workers—militant social reformers, and Communists—were American-born citizens. However, employers and governments still used repression. The Minneapolis Teamster strike of 1934 exemplifies the times: a more radical local was put down by a combination of the international union and the federal government, which jailed some of the strike leaders in part for being Trotskyists (Ahlquist and Levi 2013).

Large-scale industry, which had begun in the late nineteenth century, was steadily expanding and automobile manufacture had become one of the biggest. The assembly line that began with the Ford Motor Company put workers side by side in huge factories. The assembly lines were dehumanizing, but they also gave workers new power to disrupt production.

The new industrial unions, too, differed from those that had preceded them. John L. Lewis, head of the mineworkers, first proposed in 1928 what was to become the Congress of Industrial Organizations (CIO). Although not actually established until 1935, the strategies and ideologies of the CIO's leaders were the dominant influence on the big strikes of the 1930s. The leaders were, as a rule, committed social democrats; even those affiliated with the Communist Party lacked the revolutionary fervor of earlier radical leadership; and some, such as Lewis himself, were relatively conservative politically and strongly anticommunist (Bernstein 1969, 126). Leaders focused on organizing all the workers within their factories and industries, be they skilled or unskilled, but also on forming effective alliances across industries. And they were willing to engage in large-scale strikes.

9.2.1   The Legal Context

Although some unions gained the right to exist in some states and for some occupations in the early nineteenth century, industrial unions did not gain full associational rights until the 1930s.[4] If one follows the fourfold distinction in Brooks and Guinnane (chapter 8, this volume), both the rights to assemble (R1) and to form a "mere association" (R2) were legally problematic and often physically repressed throughout the nineteenth century (see Bloch and Lamoreaux, chapter 7, this volume). Obtaining legal recognition as an "associational entity" (R3) was granted unevenly, with some craft unions firmly winning that right by the end of the nineteenth century, industrial unions only in the 1930s, and public employees and farmworkers not until the last part of the twentieth century. Full incorporation (R4) as a legal person or entity was increasingly permitted but often rejected by unions, which resisted state intervention in their internal affairs and attempted to evade the possibilities of suits against the labor organization itself.[5] More-

4. Even with the passage the National Labor Relations Act (NLRA) in 1935, many unions, most notably those among agricultural or domestic workers, did not receive full associational rights. Moreover, within a decade of the passage of the NLRA, concerted opposition to open access by unions began to succeed.

5. Although unincorporated, unions could still be subject to suit, however. In *United Mine Workers of America v. Coronado Coal Co.*, 42 S.Ct. 570 (1922), at (576) the court found "In this state of federal legislation, we think that such organizations are suable in the federal courts for their acts, and that funds accumulated to be expended in conducting strikes are subject to execution in suits for torts committed by such unions in strikes."

over, the early bases for incorporation depended on qualifying as a mutual aid society or charity. Legal incorporation has little to do with and often inhibited the essential characteristics of unions: collective bargaining and the right to strike. For labor organizations, open access means the combination of legal recognition of their right to exist, bargain, and strike.

Prior to the New Deal, the law systematically favored employers against labor. The police powers were designed to protect life and property. In general, "Even where the police were not directly suborned by employers, their primary duty was the defense of the employer's property, and in this sense they participated in industrial disputes as partisans. The very presence of the police or troops at a struck plant carried with it the implication that the strikers were lawbreakers. It signified that strikers were the enemies of public order, for quite obviously the police had not been summoned to protect them, but company property from them" (Gitelman 1973, 17).

General incorporation laws worked positively to support business organization and to further a range of legitimate business purposes, such as their right to use the courts to protect their interests. The same did not hold for labor. In the late nineteenth and early twentieth centuries, "The common law legality of unionism, however, did not confer a right to organize. It merely left workingmen free to form unions when and if they could" (Gitelman 1973, 6). The absence of a legitimate way to organize meant that striking workers were often seen as a mob potentially threatening employer property, which the law was designed to protect.

The absence of legislation legitimizing labor and, especially, labor organization, had a series of implications. While labor sought to interpret strikes and walkouts as temporary absences, many firms interpreted strikes as a permanent disruption of employment, making it legal for them to hire new employees (seen by workers as strikebreakers). As Gitelman explains (1973, 9), "The expectation of returning to work at the conclusion of a strike was jeopardized by the legal and popularly sanctioned right of employers to hire and fire at will."

Moreover, the legal system in the late nineteenth and early twentieth centuries tolerated what we would today think of as "unorthodox"—indeed, illegitimate—means of resisting labor's attempts to organize and bargain with firms. Firms used armed men against strikers, fired labor organizers, and dismissed workers for joining unions; firms also refused to listen to workers' complaints or grievances, suppressed worker free speech, and widely used spies and agent *provocateurs* who, for example, sought to incite workers to use violence and even initiated violence.

The government and employers also used legal tools against labor. These included antitrust laws used against labor organizations, as discussed in section 9.5. Injunctions became a staple used to prevent strikes and reduce labor's leverage (Frankfurter and Greene [1930] 1963). Forbath (1991) presents a table of estimated labor injunctions over time (see table 9.1). The table

Table 9.1   Labor injunctions by decade, 1880–1929

Decade	Injunctions
1880s	105
1890s	410
1900s	850
1910s	835
1920s	2,130

Source: Forbath (1991, appendix B).

provides evidence of the frequency with which employers and governments used this legal tool to suppress labor activity and organization.

During the late nineteenth and early twentieth centuries, the AFL led a battle against the use of injunctions and other judicial devices for restraining labor's associational power (Tomlins 1985, 61–68). Increasingly, an argument emerged over the legal personhood of the union. Without it, there was a judicial and legislative question of whether the unions could be held accountable for their members' actions and could, therefore, contract on their behalf. Indeed, "as early as 1895, arguments were held in Congress advocating the treatment of unions in law as organizations possessed of the capacity to bind their members. By doing so, it was held, unions could be enlisted as disciplinary agents in the service of labor-management peace" (Tomlins 1985, 84).

The debate about the appropriate legal status of unions was at the heart of the discussion of the Erdman Railway Arbitration Act in the 1890s, a bill that represented an effort to give labor organizations legal personality (Tomlins 1985, 84–86). The Railway Brotherhood supported the bill, but the AFL opposed it on the grounds that it was against the interest of unions to be held accountable for members.

In the years immediately preceding World War I and during the war years themselves, the law became more tolerant of unions, although far from recognizing full associational rights. Since the passage of the Sherman Anti-Trust Act in 1890, the courts had defined labor organizations as monopolies; this act was the basis of most of the injunction activity. The Clayton Act of 1914 exempted labor organizations from the monopoly and cartel provisions of the Sherman Act and, in principle, limited the used of injunctions to circumstances where property was threatened. During World War I, the dependence of business on its increasingly scarce labor led to an enhancement of union rights and benefits in practice, if not always in law.

With the end of WWI and the rise of antiradicalism embodied in Attorney General Palmer's raids, antiunionism again became the norm. The law continued to favor employers, placing a large number of varied constraints against labor organization. The passage of the Railway Act of 1926 was the first significant sign of thaw, but it was not until the New Deal that labor organizations more generally gained open access.

9.3   The Labor Organization Game, 1880–1930

From the late nineteenth century through the early 1930s, the United States faced a "violence trap" (Cox, North, and Weingast 2017) with respect to labor. None of the key players—the government, labor, and business—had the ability to commit not to use violence. Although we assume that each player preferred legalization, negotiation, and no violence to violence, commitment problems prevented the three players from obtaining this outcome.

To understand the commitment problems, we model the union (U), business (B), and government (G) interaction as a three-player game.[6] We use variants on a game to represent three different periods: between roughly 1880–1930, 1933–1936, and 1937 forward. In focusing on these three players, we abstract from differences among unions, among businesses, and within the government. In doing so, we gain greater analytic power to derive important implications about labor violence and some of the major mechanisms that helped solve the problem of violence.

Here we outline the initial game. We shall discuss each of the subsequent games following the periods of history that affected them.

9.3.1   Labor Organization Game, Period 1: 1880–1930

The sequence of play in the first game (1880–1930) is as follows: U has the initial move and must choose from three choices (see figure 9.1). First, U can strike within limits, meaning that U avoids violence and that U limits its demands to wages and working conditions. Second, U can strike without limits, possibly using violence and possibly demanding more from employers than just wages and better conditions (such as representation in management or a seat on the corporate board). Finally, U can choose to revolt, possibly leading to a better political compromise for labor but, more likely, to disorder, repression, and large-scale violence. Specifically, if U chooses this option, nature (N), a nonstrategic player, chooses between two outcomes: with probability p_1, N chooses A, in which U wins an attractive political compromise; and with probability $(1 - p_1)$, N chooses outcome C, an unattractive outcome. The subscript on p indicates the period. We define L_{31} as the implied lottery following U choice of revolt, where the first subscript indicates the lottery number (in this case, 3) and the second subscript indicates the time period (1 for 1880–1930, 2 for 1933–36, and 3 for 1937 forward); thus, $L_{31} = p_1A + (1 - p_1)C$.

---

6. This game follows in the tradition established by Golden's (1997) analysis of labor institutions that explains why strikes in some countries are far more severe than in others.

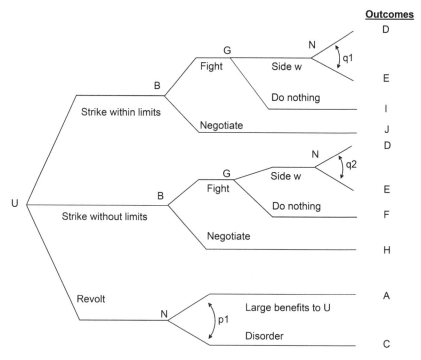

Outcomes

Fig. 9.1   1880–1930

If U chooses to strike (either within or without limits), B has the next move and must choose between responding with violence or by negotiating with U.

Finally, consider G's decisions between siding with business and doing nothing. If U strikes (with or without limits) and G sides with B to fight U, N chooses an outcome. If U has chosen to strike within limits, then with probability q_1, N chooses outcome D representing attractive concessions from B to U; and with probability $(1 - q_1)$, N chooses outcome E, resulting in violence against workers, destruction of the union organization, and no concessions. These three choices by U, B, and G yield lottery $L_1 = q_1 D + (1 - q_1)E$. If, in contrast, U chooses to strike without limits, then N chooses between D and E, but the probability of D (concessions from B) is q_2 while the probability of E is $(1 - q_2)$. The implied lottery of N's choice is $L_2 = q_1 D + (1 - q_1)E$. We assume that $q_2 > q_1$; that is, U has greater leverage when it ignores limits on its actions and hence U is more likely to prevail if it does not adhere to limits on its demands.

Based on the history presented above, the players' preferences are as follows: First, U prefers D (concessions) to E (destruction of the union). Second, it prefers L_2 to L_1. To see this, notice that if U chooses to strike within limits, the lottery L_1 ensues; if strike without limits, the lottery L_2 ensues. The only difference between the two lotteries is the probability of the concessions to labor. Because $q_2 > q_1$, U prefers L_2 over L_1; technically, we have $L_2 = q_2 D + (1 - q_2)E > q_1 D + (1 - q_1)E = L_1$. Third, given the relatively low likelihood (p_1) of a successful revolt during this period, U prefers L_2 to L_{31}.

Next consider B's preferences: If U strikes (with or without limits), B is best off fighting. The reason is that B prefers L_1 to I and L_2 to F. Because U cannot commit to refrain from violence, negotiation means that B gives concessions, while U cannot commit to honoring the concessions it makes.

Finally, consider G's preferences. The period under consideration, 1880–1930, is a largely Republican era in which that party typically held the presidency and a majority in both houses. Republicans favored business generally and, particularly, the protection of property rights and freedom of contract. Both union organization and labor violence threatened business through restriction of property rights and freedom of contract. Hence, during this era, G prefers to support business and use violence to suppress labor. Specifically, G preferred L_1 to outcome I; and L_2 to outcome F.

We can now solve for the equilibrium of the game using backward induction. Consider the first terminal node in the upper right; U has chosen to strike within limits and B has chosen to fight. Because G prefers L_1 to I, G chooses to side with B. Next, consider the second terminal node. If U chooses to strike without limits and B chooses to fight, then G also chooses to side with B (G prefers L_2 to F). Working backward one node to B's decisions. If U has chosen to strike (with or without limits), B chooses to fight since it prefers L_1 to J and L_2 to H. Finally, consider U's choice at the initial node of the game. We have established that U prefers L_2 to L_1; and because p_1 is low, it prefers L_2 to L_{31}. Hence U will choose to strike without limits. Along the equilibrium path, then, U chooses to strike without limits; B chooses to fight; and G sides with B against U.

The equilibrium of this game represents an ongoing and sometimes violent conflict between business and labor, with the government siding with business against labor. Labor strikes without limits, and hence violent confrontations between business and labor are ongoing, and the government actively attempts to suppress labor organization and bargaining with firms.

The passage of the Wagner Act changed the incentives of the players and, therefore, the equilibrium of the game.

9.4   NLRA and NLRB

Congress passed the National Labor Relations Act (NLRA), also known as the Wagner Act, in 1935 in part to stem a rising tide of industrial violence in the 1930s. The National Industrial Recovery Act (NIRA) of 1933, intended to foster economic recovery, inadvertently spurred unrest by providing symbolic support for worker organization, but without the institutional machinery necessary to implement and protect that right. The NIRA encouraged a major organizing drive by labor unions, but a lack of enforcement encouraged employers to resist. Increasing disparity between labor's de jure and de facto rights led to unprecedented levels of industrial conflict, which impeded the already fragile economic recovery.

The NIRA suspended antitrust law and permitted industry and trade associations to formulate codes of competition that would regulate production within industries. Recognizing that allowing economic combination of firms would greatly advantage business relative to workers in the labor market, language was added to strengthen the position of labor. Section 7(a) required all industry codes to meet three conditions: provide a right for employees to organize and bargain collectively through representatives selected without interference from their employer, prohibit compulsory membership in company unions, and require employers to comply with minimum wage rates, maximum hour limitations, and other regulations on working conditions as approved by the president.

Labor interpreted section 7(a) as a call to organize, and launched an unprecedented organizing drive in 1933. Strike activity, which had declined to historic lows in the 1920s, surged. As both economic activity and organizational drives increased, man-days lost to work stoppages jumped, from fewer than 603,000 monthly in the first half of 1933 to 1,375,000 in July and 2,378,000 in August, threatening the fragile economic recovery (Bernstein 1950, 58).

9.4.1   Empowering an Impersonal Arbiter

Perhaps the most important accomplishment of the NLRA was its provision of the board with the structure and powers necessary to enforce the constraints on both sides. The explosion in industrial unrest after the passage of NIRA stemmed largely from the disconnect between the rights promised to labor under section 7(a) and those actually realized. This disconnect resulted from a virtually complete lack of enforcement (Gross 1974, 129).

Section 3 of the NLRA empowered the NLRB, a quasi-judicial, independent agency of the federal government, to oversee union elections, certify representatives, and investigate and prevent unfair labor practices. The design of an effective NLRB involved two different processes. First, a process of learning, in part through trial and error; and second, a more careful study of the regulatory and administrative structure and process previously sanctioned by the Supreme Court, such as the Federal Trade Commission (1914) and the Interstate Commerce Commission (1887), as Irons (1982) emphasizes.

Between 1933 and 1935, the Roosevelt administration, officials from the NRA and the Department of Labor, and interested parties from Congress experimented with the agency structure. The first National Labor Board (NLB) was established in August 1933, to adjudicate, mediate, and conciliate disputes arising under section 7(a) of NIRA. But the board had limited investigatory powers, and relied upon other agencies, often with conflicting interests, for enforcement. At the request of NLB chairman and senator Robert Wagner, Roosevelt issued a series of executive orders to strengthen the board by reducing the level of review that other agencies had over NLB decisions and giving the board authority to oversee representation elections. Yet the board still had no enforcement power, and overlapping jurisdictions between the NLB and the NRA led to contradictory statements of policy and encouraged employers to ignore the board's orders. Reliance on the Department of Justice for access to the courts caused further bureaucratic and administrative problems (see Tomlins 1985, 109–19).

Following an unsuccessful attempt to pass a precursor to the NLRA, Congress instead passed Public Resolution 44, which replaced the NLB with a new board called the National Labor Relations Board (hereafter the *old* NLRB). This board had a nonpartisan structure, greater investigatory powers, and more independence through nonreviewable findings of fact. Yet, the old board's election orders were reviewable by circuit courts, which allowed employers to delay elections through court challenges, and the board still relied upon other agencies for enforcement of its decisions.

The final structure and process of the NLRB under the NLRA solved a number of the problems that had plagued prior agencies and that had undermined their effectiveness. The most important innovations concerned three aspects of the board's power: (a) strengthening investigatory powers, allowing the board to amass sufficient evidence; (b) providing the board with exclusive jurisdiction so that other agencies with conflicting goals could not block the board; and (c) removing barriers to enforcement of board decisions. Like the definition of unfair labor practices and the election and bargaining unit provisions, these aspects of the board's structure were in part the product of prior boards' members' experiences in battling with employers to enforce section 7(a) of the NIRA.

Section 11 of the NLRA outlined the board's investigatory powers, providing it with the authority to subpoena witnesses and evidence, the ability to appeal to district courts for enforcement of subpoenas, and requiring that other government agencies provide information upon request. Section 12 provided for substantial penalties, including up to one year of jail time, for interference with or resistance to board investigations. Prior boards' lack of subpoena power had two adverse effects: it allowed employers to impede investigations by simply ignoring board requests to testify; and it impeded enforcement, as the pre-NLRA boards had to rely on either the National Recovery Administration or the Department of Justice (DOJ) for enforcement. The DOJ required cases referred by the board to be complete in all legal details before it would accept them, and since the board had no subpoena powers, it could not meet this requirement. Sections 11 and 12 of the NLRA solved these problems.

Section 10(e) allowed the board to bypass these middlemen entirely and petition the circuit courts for enforcement of orders directly; it also made the board's findings of fact conclusive. Enforcement through the DOJ and NRA had been ineffective for reasons greater than the board's lack of evidence-gathering powers. The NRA's only enforcement tool was to rescind businesses' Blue Eagles, the license allowing them to operate under NIRA industry codes. In practice, removal of Blue Eagles had little effect, and the agency was disinclined to do so, since its own mandate was to promote economic activity rather than inhibit it. Similarly, the DOJ was unenthusiastic about enforcing board orders, and initiated all proceedings de novo, due to the weakness of the boards' own investigatory powers. Board members thought the DOJ staff to be "unsympathetic, lax, and in many cases incompetent" (Gross 1974, 129), and the duplicative investigations slowed down enforcement to the point of total nullification: between July 1934 and March 1935, for example, no judgments were obtained in any of the thirty-three NIRA noncompliance cases referred to the DOJ by the board (Bernstein 1950, 87).

Direct appeal to the courts increased the autonomy of the board by removing the effective, if informal, veto power that the NRA and the DOJ exercised over the board's judgments. Section 10(a) gave the NLRB an exclusive right to prevent unfair labor practices. The law's authors sought to make the NLRB the "supreme court" of labor, to prevent the confused jurisdiction over labor disputes that had arisen under NIRA as the board, the NRA, and Roosevelt himself all sought independently to solve labor disputes arising under section 7(a). Without exclusive jurisdiction, the board's decisions were frequently undermined by contradictory statements of policy from the NRA. Roosevelt often got involved in negotiations to try to bring major work stoppages to an end, and to that end carved whole industries out of the early boards' jurisdiction in order to give them dispensations from board principles.

To summarize our argument, the NIRA asserted various labor rights to organize, but failed to create effective administrative structure and process to enforce them:

- The NIRA provided no clear mandate, command structure, or process to create rules and precedents with which to regulate union activity and labor-firm bargaining. For example, it failed to define adequately the type of acceptable organizations designed to represent union members, and it created no process, structures, or substance by which a firm could be found not in compliance with the law.
- Unclear lines of authority created a range of bureaucratic and administrative problems: The law required that the NLB rely on the NRA and DOJ for enforcement, each of which had their own priorities that conflicted with those of the NLB.
- President Roosevelt intervened in ad hoc ways inconsistent with the NRA.

- The constitutional status of the law and hence NLB regulations remained uncertain, affording employers the ability to delay and resist NLB authority.

In the face of this confusion, the absence of clear constitutionality, and the inability of the government to enforce the rules, employers resisted at every turn. The disparity between promise and actuality in the context of the Depression generated unprecedented labor unrest.

9.4.2 What Did the NLRA Do?

The NLRA resolved each of these problems. It granted the NLRB a clear mandate with a substantially more effective mandate and effective structure and process. The act clarified lines of authority. It also gave the board the direct ability to enforce its rulings without relying on other organizations, including subpoena powers. By making the NLRB the sole legal authority in its area, the act also removed the ability of the president to intervene within the agency's jurisdiction. In stark contrast to the 1933 legislation, the act was consciously designed to maximize the likelihood that the Supreme Court would find it constitutional. Finally, the Supreme Court's acceptance of the NLRA's constitutionality led to enforcement of the act, employer compliance, and an end to violence associated with labor.

Broadly, the NLRA accomplished two ends. First, it asserted a federal right for workers to organize and bargain collectively, via a representative of their own choosing. Second, section 3 established the National Labor Relations Board (NLRB), an independent, quasi-judicial agency to adjudicate disputes arising under the law. Yet neither of these institutions originated in the NLRA. As noted, the right to organize was first asserted in NIRA (the language of section 7 of the NLRA was drawn directly from section 7[a] of the NIRA), and precursors to the NLRB had existed since August 1933. These earlier measures failed, however, to stem the violence problem that pervaded labor relations in the 1930s and earlier. How, then, did the NLRA differ?

The NLRA succeeded where prior attempts had failed because it went beyond earlier legislation in five ways: (a) It defined a number of unfair labor practices that by nature interfered with the meaningful enjoyment of the organizing and bargaining rights created in the law, imposing clear and uncontestable constraints on employers; (b) it provided a board-controlled process for election of representatives, effectively constraining labor as well; (c) it provided the NLRB with the power and independence necessary for effective enforcement of those constraints upon both workers and their employers; (d) it cleared up lines of authority so that, first, the president could not intervene on an ad hoc basis, and second, the NLRB did not depend, as did its predecessors, on other organizations for enforcement; and (e) it created a regulatory process that the Supreme Court held constitutional and hence legally binding on employers.

The last two accomplishments are the basis for the development of administrative law that transforms the right of open access into a reality.

9.4.3   Constraints on Employers

The unfair labor practices defined in section 8 of the NLRA provided explicit statutory support for NLRB prosecution of one general and four specific employer practices that undermined workers' right to organize, hold recognition elections, and bargain collectively. To provide the board with the flexibility to address practices not anticipated during the writing of the legislation, section 8(1) included a blanket prohibition on "interference with, restrain[t], or coerc[ion]" of employees in their exercise of rights guaranteed in section 7. Sections 8(2) through 8(4) banned employer dominated (company) unions, discrimination of any sort to encourage or discourage membership in unions, and discrimination or retaliation against workers who testified or filed charges under the NLRA. Section 8(5) addressed the most common and disruptive reason for labor conflict during this period, by making the refusal to bargain collectively with elected representatives an unfair labor practice.

The definition of unfair labor practices provided, for the first time, a statutory basis for NLRB intervention in a set of employer practices that undermined workers' stated right to organize. The NLRB's predecessor boards had established precedents for such intervention, but the lack of a clear legislative mandate and contradictory statements by the National Recovery Administration (NRA) and Roosevelt had encouraged employers to challenge or ignore these decisions.

9.4.4   Constraints on Workers

The 1935 NLRA defined only employer-side unfair labor practices; prohibitions on union-side activities would be added more than a decade later in the 1947 Taft-Hartley amendments. On its face, New Deal labor policy thus appears to impose limits on employers without constraining the behavior of unions. We argue, however, that the law provided meaningful limits on both employers *and* unions. The election process and rules defined in section 9 of the NLRA provided a standardized process for acquiring the benefits of NLRA-protected collective bargaining. This process, and the gatekeeping role of the NLRB in certifying the outcome, effectively constrained the behavior of workers and their unions as well as employers.

Section 9 of the NLRA established the rules and procedures for the election of bargaining representatives, and the role of the NLRB in this process. First, section 9(a) codified two important principles that had been the source of many legal challenges to bargaining: majority-rule elections and an exclusive right to representation for the winner of such an election. Under NIRA, employers had challenged the results of union elections by arguing that majority-rule elections deprived the minority of the right to be represented by an organization of their choice. Both employers and unions, when they lost an election, asserted that representatives preferred by minority groups should have standing to bargain as well.

The authors of the NLRA, many of whom were members of the NLRB's predecessor boards, feared that the fracturing of bargaining authority would undermine the goal of collective bargaining and exacerbate the problem of interlabor disputes. Bernstein writes: "The experience of the Auto Board [an industry-specific labor board that had allowed for multiple representatives] convinced the draftsmen that pluralism provoked confusion and strife, defeating collective bargaining" (1950, 96). Section 9(a) of the act therefore declared that "[r]epresentatives designated or selected for the purposes of collective bargaining by the majority of the employees in a unit appropriate for such purposes, shall be the exclusive representatives of all the employees in such unit for the purposes of collective bargaining[.]"

Second, section 9(b) gave the NLRB the right to define the scope of the bargaining unit. This issue was the source of significant opposition from the AFL, since it moved decision-making power on a critical strategic problem to regulators. Elections take place within the bargaining unit; therefore, the definition of the unit has the potential to make or break unions. These decisions are highly strategic—unions want the unit to be big enough to have leverage against the employer, but election campaigns are easier to manage within a smaller unit. Because the selection of the bargaining unit size and composition has important implications for the relative strength of employer versus union, the drafters placed this power in an impersonal party: the NLRB. Bernstein writes, "[T]hey sought to avoid placing the authority in the employer, which might invite violations of the act, and to employees, who might use it to defeat the majority principle, and, by the creation of small units, impede the employer in running his plant" (1950, 96).

This authority meaningfully limited union activity, as is evident by the growing hostility of the AFL to the board after the passage of the act. The authority to determine bargaining units had the unintended effect of putting the NLRB in the center of the quickly growing intralabor fight between craft and industrial organizing. By all accounts, the decision to give this power to the board was made before anyone anticipated the split between the AFL and the CIO in 1937. Yet by the AFL convention in that year, the AFL was so incensed by the board's perceived favoring of industrial organizing that it unanimously adopted a resolution to "assemble evidence in proof of the maladministration of the [Wagner] act," to authorize the AFL president and executive council to petition the president of the United States "for prompt and adequate relief" and amendment of the Wagner Act (Gross 1974, 251). The AFL would later join forces with opponents of the NLRA to support the Taft-Hartley amendments. Section 9(c) gave the board the right to oversee and certify the election of representatives, while section 10(a) provided it with the right to prevent the unfair labor practices defined in section 8.

The board was thus empowered to issue legally enforceable orders for employers to bargain with unions. The obverse is that this also empowered the board to *withhold* certification and bargaining orders when unions engaged in unacceptable behavior, violence in particular. And indeed, the board has on multiple occasions withheld bargaining orders from otherwise entitled unions when they have been found to have engaged in severe violence (Gitto 1982).[7]

On the labor side, the NLRA provided a set of benefits to unions and an institutional structure to protect those benefits. But it also created a gatekeeper with the right and ability to withhold those benefits for misbehavior. Unions that wanted access to the protections and bargaining status provided by the NLRA thus had to take care not to antagonize the referee by engaging in the type of violent unrest the act was designed to prevent.

The industrial unions began to develop new tactics to shield them from accusations of being perpetrators of violence. The most famous instance was the Flint sit-down strike in 1936–37 at General Motors. The workers locked themselves in and simply sat down, engaging in no work while eschewing violence. The Flint Strike proved a pivotal moment (Bernstein 1969, 519–51). The United Auto Workers (UAW) found a way to ensure that strikers could not be accused of initiating violence against persons during a labor struggle; any violence would be initiated by the employers or government. Moreover, the negotiations, led by John L. Lewis as president of the new CIO, were not only with the company but involved, as well, the governor of Michigan and, most importantly, Frances Perkins, the secretary of labor, who was throughout in close touch with President Roosevelt. When the governor of Michigan did consider enforcing an injunction by calling in the National Guard, the Roosevelt administration prevented that move. This action signaled the beginning of a new era, with the federal government intervening to enforce the rules in employer-union conflict instead of siding with employers.

9.4.5 How Did the NLRA Come About?

The passage of the National Labor Relations Act of 1935 resulted from a remarkable coalition that had not previously existed. Several factors made it possible.

The first was the growth of the labor movement. The numbers mobilizing in unions and as voters started growing in the early 1930s. By 1939, in the aftermath of labor legislation, there were more than nine million union members (Katznelson 2006, 56). Union members were largely democratic voters with union leadership deeply engaged in mobilizing their votes. Increasingly

---

7. The board has only rarely withheld bargaining orders, and the first time they did so appears to be in 1963, in the *Laura Modes Co.* case, well after the union-side unfair labor practices were added. It is not clear whether the board could have done this prior to Taft-Hartley.

the unions, especially those affiliated with the CIO, made demands of government to recognize unions and their representation of workers, regulate labor conflict, and provide social insurance. The CIO was key to a new coalition of Northern Democrats; they mobilized voters on their behalf and persistently pressured for liberalizing legislation (Schickler 2016). Lichtenstein documents labor demands for "industrial democracy"; for the workers "the new unionism represented not just a higher standard of living but a doorway that opened onto the democratic promise of American life" (Lichtenstein 2002, 30).

The second factor stimulating change was fear and anxiety. The 1930s was "an anguish-filled environment . . . the most constant features of American political life continually threatened to become unstable, if not unhinged" (Katznelson 2013, 10). There was fear of communism and revolution, and some federal officials and legislators came to feel the labor unions and recognition of labor rights was a good bulwark against that threat (Bernstein 1950, 102; Goldfield 1989, 1268–69).

The other key to success of the legislation, well documented by Katznelson (2006, 53–67; Katznelson 2013, 228–32) was the support of the Southern Democrats. A critical part of the New Deal coalition, this faction of the Democratic Party went along with important labor legislation. Unions were largely unheard of in the South, so this was a fairly easy trade of votes, but it came at the price of the NLRA's exclusion from the right to organize and bargain of occupations that might attract African Americans: the act explicitly exempted two of the biggest sources of southern labor, agriculture, and housework.

The changes in unions, the government, and business, during and partially as a consequence of the Depression, combined to set the stage for a new equilibrium among labor, employers, and government. The resulting compromise at once provided gains for each while solving the problem of violence. The unions were willing to play by the rules and eschew revolutionary aspirations and violence, but in return they expected union recognition, collective bargaining, improved working conditions, and social benefits from both employers and government. Business management—fearful of the disruptive effects of large-scale strikes and worried that disorder and revolution were possible—became willing to accept terms with the unions they previously rejected as the price of labor peace and productivity. The government under the leadership of the Democratic Party came to recognize that it could gain electoral support through union growth if it came to play a more impersonal, if still interventionist, role by establishing a regulatory framework for labor-employer strife and enforcing the rules.

The NLRA was the final step in a series of efforts made in the wake of NIRA-inspired unrest to improve and make permanent a set of institutions to encourage the peaceful resolution of labor disputes. Section 1 of the NLRA makes clear the underlying assumption that legal protection of the right to organize and bargain would increase safeguards on business by increasing the capacity for "the friendly adjustment of disputes."

9.5   Labor Organization Game Redux

9.5.1   Period 2: 1933–36

The Great Depression represented a massive change in circumstances, particularly for workers who were unemployed or who feared losing their jobs. A surprisingly large portion of workers were out of jobs for years, and the prolabor movement grew. Moreover, as we explained in section 9.3, sympathy for more radical change has grown among workers and within organized labor. In addition, Democrats held a dominant party, whose support drew from labor as well as business. These changes affect the preferences of the players, so that those in period 2 differ from those in period 1.

We model this change in circumstances by assuming that the probability of a successful revolt has risen. During the Depression, violent aggression and revolt were more appealing than prior (Katznelson 2013, 10, 449). In terms of the model, the danger of a revolt exceeded the danger in the previous period. If the country failed to address labor problems, labor may well choose radical action and defect from the Democratic Party. Thus we have that $p_2 > p_1$, where p_2 is the probability of a successful revolt in period 2.

We do not analyze period 2 in detail. Instead, we focus on a particular comparative static result reflecting the rise in probability of success if U chooses to revolt. We observe that there exists a critical probability threshold, p^*, such that if $p_2 > p^*$, U will choose revolt over striking. We assume for this period that p_2 is less than p^*, but approaching it. Hence, revolt and disorder have become a real threat. In the absence of appropriate commitment technologies, cooperation is not feasible. Outcome J, as discussed in the game in period 1, allows unions to take advantage of firms.

The model also implies that, with the rise of p_2 toward p^*, the value of the outcome of cooperation and negotiation between U and B has risen for all the players. During periods 1 and 2, commitment problems mean that this outcome cannot be implemented. Specifically, because the Supreme Court has failed to give constitutional sanction to G's labor regulation, G has no way to enforce a set of impersonal rules governing union-business negotiation.

9.5.2   Period 3: The NLRB Comes on Line

The final period we study begins in early 1937 with the Supreme Court's ruling that the NLRA and its progeny, the NLRB, were constitutional, allowing the NLRB to enforce its rules. Circumstances in period 3 differ from period 2 in several ways. Because of the threat of disorder, many businesses came to favor compromise, as represented in the NLRA, which gained far more than majority support in Congress.

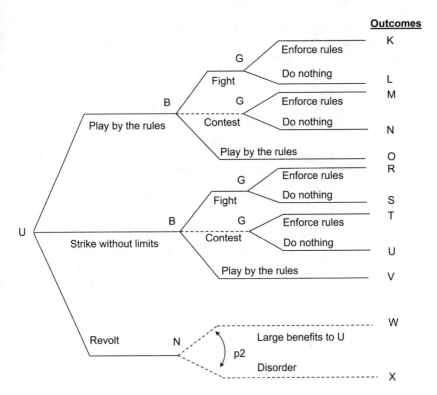

Outcomes

K

Fight — G — Enforce rules

Do nothing — L

M

B — Contest — G — Enforce rules

Do nothing — N

Play by the rules

Play by the rules — O

R

Fight — G — Enforce rules

Do nothing — S

T

B — Contest — G — Enforce rules

Do nothing — U

Strike without limits

Play by the rules — V

W

Revolt — N — Large benefits to U — p2

Disorder — X

Fig. 9.2   1937 forward

For our purposes, the main implication of this ruling is that the government gained the ability to sanction both labor and business if they fail to play by the (NLRA/NLRB) rules. As we show, the ability of G to sanction both business and labor for failing to play by the rules allows the three players to implement cooperation between U and B that involves mutual respect for the rules and hence an absence on violence.

To see how this cooperative equilibrium works, we modify the game to reflect G's enforcing the NLRB rules. As before, U has three choices at the first node of the game, though they differ somewhat from U's choices in period 1. First, U may choose to play by the rules; second, it can continue striking without limits, hence retaining violence potential; and third, it can choose to revolt. We assume that the probability of a successful revolt (from U's standpoint) is p_2, close to p^*, but not quite; as before, we assume that if the Depression continues and labor sees too few concessions, p_2 may rise above p^* (see figure 9.2). As in game 1, if U chooses to revolt, then nature chooses whether labor is successful (outcome W) or if disorder results (outcome X). The implied lottery is $L_{33} = p_2 W + (1 - p_2)X$.

If U chooses to play by the rules or to continue striking without limits, then B has the next move and may choose from among three options: fight (continue to use violence against U), contest U within the system, or to play by the rules, here meaning recognize the union and negotiate with it in good faith. Finally, if B chooses to fight or contest U, then G, now in the form of the NLRB, must choose whether to enforce the rules.

We make the following assumptions about the players' preferences. U prefers the result when it plays by the rules given that B chooses to also play by the rules (outcome O) to two other outcomes: (a) the outcome of revolting ($L_{33} = p_2 W + (1 - p_2)X$), and (b) the outcome when it chooses continuation of the status quo (striking without limits, B contests U's actions, and then suffer punishment by G).

For B, we assume that if U chooses to play by the rules, B prefers to play by the rules. If U chooses to continue striking without limits, it prefers to contest U's actions. For G, reflecting its expectation of electoral gain by having solved the problem of labor violence, we assume that it prefers enforcing the rules over doing nothing. In terms of the model, this means that G will punish either party if it fails to play by the rules. As with the failed NIRA, if G fails to implement the rules, it will gain no electoral support from the new labor legislation as the violence between labor and business continues, possibly allowing p_2 to rise above p^*, leading U to choose revolt instead of cooperation.

As before, we solve the game using backward induction. At each decision node involving G, G will choose to enforce the rules. Doing so gains it electoral support and forestalls potential revolution. Working back a node, B has three choices: if U has chosen to play by the rules, fighting risks punitive actions by G so B is best off choosing to play by the rules. If, instead, U chooses to continue striking without limits, then B is best off contesting U's actions and G will impose sanctions on U. We now come to the first choice of the game, U's decision among playing by the rules, striking without limits, and revolting. If U chooses to play by the rules, outcome O occurs in which both U and B play by the rules and hence negotiate in good faith. In contrast, if U chooses to continue to strike without limits, then B will contest U's strikes and G will then rule against U. Whereas if U chooses to revolt, the outcome is that of the lottery $L_{33} = p_2 W + (1 - p_2)X$. Among these three options, U prefers to play by the rules. Hence the equilibrium path of this game is for U to choose to play by the rules and B to choose to play by the rules.

The main conclusion is that the new mechanisms created by the NLRA create G as an impersonal enforcer of the new rules. The act provides for meaningful sanctions on either B or U if they violate the rules; in particular, if either chooses violence. By creating the appropriate structure and process, the act created the appropriate commitment mechanisms, allowing the three parties to sustain a new, cooperative equilibrium.

9.6   A Dialogic Reinterpretation of the Constitutional Controversies over the New Deal

The NLRA was the culmination of several decades of legal innovation, innovation that is largely responsible for contemporary administrative law jurisprudence. Politics were an obvious component of the eventual finding of New Deal laws as constitutional beginning in 1937. But the traditional account of the New Deal constitutional controversies overemphasizes politics and underemphasizes the role of the development of doctrine and the mechanisms of administrative delegation. The standard wisdom is that after FDR threatened to "pack the court," Justice Roberts made his famous "switch in time," and the justices acquiesced to his New Deal legislation. Although a caricature, this brief summary of the standard wisdom in constitutional law books captures their essence.

We argue that a far more complex and interesting story hides in legal doctrine (Cushman [1998] makes a similar claim). The NLRA was a clear and direct attempt to respond to concerns about the New Deal's constitutionality as articulated by the court in the early New Deal cases. By doing so, Congress invented new structures and processes that the court would hold in *National Labor Relations Board v. Jones & Laughlin Steel Corporation* (301 U.S. 1, 1937) as satisfying constitutional restrictions.

We assert that Congress and the court engaged in a dialogue concerning issues of delegation, political control, oversight, and the means of ensuring rights of due process. By trying new structures and processes and having them, at times, struck down and, at times, upheld, Congress and the court jointly created a major expansion of administrative law. And, in the process, they were able to ensure enforcement of the law and the credibility of its commitments.

In the two precedents most relevant to the NLRA, *Panama Refining* and *Schechter*, the Supreme Court analyzed two constitutional issues with great care: (a) the structure and process of regulatory delegation, and (b) Congress's regulatory authority under the commerce clause. In these precedents, we see Congress, the president, and the court struggling to interpret the commerce clause and to define the bounds of proper regulatory delegation.

Both *Panama Refining* and *Schechter* were decided prior to the passing of the NLRA in Congress. While *Panama Refining* was decided on January 7, 1935, prior to Congress's consideration and passage of the Wagner Act, *Schechter* was decided on May 27, 1935, between the dates of the Senate and House debates of the act. And while they were not the only precedents that the drafters of the NLRA had to contend with, they were representative of the general issues plaguing the New Deal acts.

So as to better understand the dialogic nature of the relationship between the court and Congress in constitutional cases, we take a closer look at these cases and how Congress responded to them in the NLRA. Last, we will look at how the court responded to Congress's implementation of its guidelines through its decision in *Jones & Laughlin Steel*.

9.6.1   The Delegation Issue

Panama Refining Panama Refining Co. v. Ryan (293 U.S. 388, 1935) was the constitutional challenge to the regulation of petroleum goods under the National Industrial Recovery Act (NIRA). The court held this regulation an improper and hence unconstitutional delegation of legislative power (431). In *Panama Refining*, the Court sidestepped the commerce clause issue, as a majority of the justices agreed to the unconstitutionality of the regulation based on the delegation question.

Importantly, the court did not simply rule Congress's actions as outside the bounds of constitutionality. Through a careful analysis of previous instances of delegation, they determined why the delegation presented in this case failed to meet established criteria.

The NIRA incorporated many provisions now considered outlandish in their failure to assure due process and to prevent arbitrary and capricious public actions. As Irons (1982) and others suggest, the authors of this legislation paid little attention to constitutional issues; specifically, they made little effort to assure that the legislation would meet the standards set in recent cases approving regulatory delegations by the national government. For example, they (a) delegated authority without sufficient definition of terms or limits on authority; (b) delegated regulatory authority to private groups; (c) paid little attention to legal decisions about existing legislation with which the New Deal legislation interacted (such as the Federal Trade Act); and (d) did not ensure respect for rights of due process; for example, it did not require that the president make a finding prior to acting.

The court pointed to these delegation failures of the NIRA in *Panama Refining* (415). It then argued that, to approve this new set of regulations, Congress needed to set clear guidelines and procedures to the agency.

Schechter also raised the delegation issue. In *A.L.A. Schechter Poultry Corp. v. United States* (295 U.S. 495, 1935), a unanimous court ruled that the act was unconstitutional as it was both an invalid delegation of legislative power and an improper regulation of interstate transactions with only an indirect effect upon intrastate commerce.

In *Schechter*, as in *Panama Refining*, the court was critical of Congress's haphazard delegation of power (541–42). However, the court went further in *Schechter*, not only describing the failures on the NIRA delegation scheme, but also comparing it to a proper administrative delegation scheme, that of the Federal Trade Commission. In *Schechter*, the court compared the administrative delegation in the Federal Trade Commission Act (FTCA) and the NIRA and found that, while the FTCA contained adequate safeguards and limits, the NIRA lacked them (534–35).

If one of the main failures of the drafters of the NIRA was that they paid little attention to legal decisions about existing New Deal legislation, the drafters of the NLRA proved to be not only attentive to preceding legal decisions, but also directly responsive to them. From the very beginning the proponents of the Wagner Act, as the NLRA became known, were "[C]ommitted to the model of a full blown, full-fledged judicial agency like the Federal Trade Commission" (Bernstein 1950, 228). This is a model that had been previously accepted by the court (see *Federal Trade Commission v. Gratz*, 253 U.S. 421, 1920).

Further, unlike the drafters of the NIRA, drafters of the Wagner Act were meticulous in delineating the agency's power. For example, section 10 of the act provides that: "[T]he Board is empowered, as hereinafter provided, to prevent any person from engaging in any unfair labor affecting commerce." Every part of this declaration is defined and limited. The "board," "person," "unfair labor practice," "affecting commerce," and "commerce" are all defined in the act, thus delineating under which circumstances and over whom the administrative agency has authority. Furthermore, the NLRA delegated authority to an administrative agency, not private industry boards.

This attention to the New Deal precedent and concerted effort to address the court's concerns paid off. In *Jones & Laughlin Steel*, holding the Wagner Act constitutional, the court acknowledged that Congress had fixed the delegation issue under the NIRA. After declaring that the *Schechter* case is "not controlling here," (41) the Court goes on to outline the standards to which the board had to conform (47) and declare that the act properly defines and delineates the scope of the board's authority (30).

The NIRA had (a) delegated authority without sufficient definition of terms or limits on authority, (b) delegated regulatory authority to private groups, (c) paid little attention to legal decisions about existing legislation with which the New Deal legislation interacted, and (d) did little to ensure respect for rights of due process. Therefore, the court ruled it unconstitutional. The Wagner Act deliberately sought to remedy these defects; it (a) delegated authority with sufficient definitions of terms and limits on authority; (b) delegated authority to the National Labor Relations Board, a government administrative agency; (c) responded to concerns expressed by the court in previous New Deal cases and modeled the administrative schema on an existing and established agency; and (d) ensured due process rights through delineating the structure and processes through which the agency was to exercise its authority. It learned from the court's previous decisions, and when drafting the NLRA, Wagner and his writers placed the new agency comfortably within constitutional bounds.

9.6.2   Congress's Regulatory Authority under the Commerce Clause

In the delegation issue, the court communicated clear criteria to Congress. It explained in both *Schechter* and *Panama Refining* proper and improper delegation of power. The dialogue between the court and the president and

Congress on the issue of the commerce clause was less clear. For several decades, the court struggled with the nature of constitutionally proper bounds of federal power, and at times sending conflicting messages to Congress. However, as in the delegation cases, the court and Congress engaged in a bargaining process over the national government's commerce authority that ultimately determined the constitutional bounds.

The Dialogue between Court and Elected Branches, 1890–1932

The dialogue between the court and the elected branches over the commerce clause had always been present. With respect to the issue of labor and labor violence, it picked up in 1895. At that time, Congress sought to exercise its commerce clause power in the Sherman Act (15 U.S.C. §§ 1–7, 1890). In 1895, the court applied the Sherman Act to labor struggles. In *In re Debs* (158 U.S. 564, 1895), the court tested and upheld the validity, under the commerce clause, of the labor injunction to stop strikes in the railways. After the Pullman strike ended, Debs and six others were charged with contempt of court for violating a labor injunction. They perpetrated no violence, but were found guilty of communicating with strikers. For that, they were sentenced to six months in prison. The court upheld the prison sentence, holding that it was proper for the Sherman Act to apply to labor injunctions as railway labor struggles impeded the interstate movement of goods. Thus, these struggles were under Congress's commerce clause power. *In re Debs* was a broad reading of federal powers and expansion of the application of the Sherman Act.

This decision followed a narrow reading of the Sherman Act in *United States v. E. C. Knight Co* (156 U.S. 1, 1895). The Supreme Court decided this case just five months before *In re Debs*. In *E. C. Knight*, the court interpreted the Sherman Act narrowly, ruling that the Sherman Act did not cover manufacturing as it only indirectly affected interstate commerce. Thus, manufacturing was beyond Congress's commerce clause power, which covered only direct effects to interstate commerce.

The court's indecision on how broadly to define the commerce clause led to many years of inconsistent jurisprudence. Between *E. C. Knight* and the New Deal cases, the court tried several different tests to determine the bounds of the commerce clause. For example, the court's ruling on constitutionality in *E. C. Knight* hinged on the test of direct versus indirect effects on interstate commerce. However, in *Stafford v. Wallace* (258 U.S. 495, 1922), the court broadened the test and argued that the entire "stream of commerce among states" was under the regulatory power of the commerce clause. It explained that, "streams of commerce among the states are under the national protection and regulation, including subordinate activities and facilities which are essential to such movements, though not of interstate character when viewed apart from them (519)." The court's struggles about the narrowness of the commerce clause arose in response to

Congress's attempts to use the commerce clause to regulate different aspects of commerce. As Congress tried new regulatory structure and process in various regulatory legislation, the court upheld or struck down these new mechanisms, thus continually refining the complex definition of the commerce clause.

While *In re Debs* applied the Sherman Act to railway strikes, an inherently interstate venture, *Loewe v. Lawlor* (1908) broadened the act's application to labor. *Loewe* involved the United Hatters of North America's charges of restraint of trade under the Sherman Act due to their boycott activities. The workers were not involved in interstate commerce and did not obstruct the movement of goods, as had happened *In re Debs*. Even so, the court concluded that their acts must be considered as a whole and thus found that the purpose of their conspiracy was to prevent manufacture and inhibit interstate commerce. In yet another reading of the commerce clause after *E. C. Knight*, in *Loewe*, the court found that the Sherman Act does apply to manufacturing as it concerns labor. The loss in *Loewe* led labor unions to demand legislative changes. In particular, they wanted to be excluded from coverage under the Sherman Act. Labor unions obtained an attempt to create this exclusion with section 6 of the Clayton Act (15 U.S.C. § 12–27, 1914). However, in *Duplex Printing Press Co. v. Deering* (254 U.S. 443, 1921), the court reaffirmed its prior ruling in *Loewe* by rejecting a blanket exclusion of labor from antitrust laws.

The NLRA

The writers of the NLRA drafted the act in the shadow of this inconsistent commerce clause jurisprudence. In his legislative history of the Wagner Act, Bernstein explains that even as the drafters worked on perfecting "the bill's substantive and procedural provisions," they were aware of the "constitutional quicksand on which they rested" (1971, 229). Ultimately, regardless of the delegation issue, the drafters knew that "the Wagner Act was bottomed on the commerce clause" (1971, 229). In an effort to prompt the Supreme Court to give an expansive reading to the clause, the drafters heavily borrowed legal language from the court's decisions in favorable commerce clause cases.

In the bill's carefully crafted Declaration of Policy, the act's drafters made sure to argue that the denial of the rights to organize and bargain collectively necessarily led "to strikes and other forms of industrial strife and unrest," which in turn constricted the flow of goods into the "channels of commerce" and adversely affected level of employment and wages (229–30). The drafters took this language directly from *Gibbons v. Ogden* (22 U.S. 1, 1824) and *Stafford v. Wallace* (1922), two of the Supreme Court's broader readings of the commerce clause.

While drafts of the NLRA were being circulated in Congress, *Schechter* was decided. Although the court abstained from the commerce clause issue in *Panama Refining*, it engaged with it directly in *Schechter*, finding that Congress's power under the commerce clause did not reach into what the court held to be intrastate matters. It explained that, "the authority of the federal government may not be pushed to such an extreme as to destroy the distinction, which the commerce clause itself establishes, between commerce 'among the several States' and the internal concerns of a state . . . We are of the opinion that the attempt through the provisions of the code to fix the hours and wages of employees of defendants in their intrastate business was not a valid exercise of federal power" (549–50).

Concerned about the court's most recent narrow reading of the commerce clause, the drafters of the NLRA immediately changed the language of the act so as to accommodate the court's objections in *Schechter*. In response to *Schechter*, Wagner had the Declaration of Policy rewritten before the House debate. "It was revised, to emphasize the effect of labor disputes on interstate commerce and to de-emphasize the mere economic effects which had been rejected by the Court . . . For example, the bill's definition of the term 'affecting commerce' was changed from acts 'burdening or affecting commerce' to those 'burdening or obstructing commerce.'" (n. 16, internal citations omitted).

Their efforts of the act's drafters paid off. The NLRA was challenged in *National Labor Relations Board v. Jones & Laughlin Steel Corporation* (301 U.S. 1, 1937). In *Jones & Laughlin Steel*, the court held that the act's purpose was proper under the commerce clause (31).

Wagner's borrowing of favorable commerce clause cases and changes to the Declaration of Policy appeared to work. The language used—language that the court had previously found to be constitutional—increased the likelihood that the NLRA would be upheld. In *Jones & Laughlin Steel*, the court settled on the bounds of constitutionality as it related to the commerce clause. Following *Jones & Laughlin Steel*, the court made a concerted effort to clean up its inconsistent commerce clause jurisprudence.

The court's inconsistency and Congress's efforts to pass new and creative laws are different sides of a dynamic dialogue and bargaining process around constitutional issues. At the same time that the court struggled to determine the new bounds of federal power, Congress struggled to figure out what new forms of that power would survive constitutional muster.

Instead of seeing the court as stubbornly obtuse and only willing to change once threatened, it is more advantageous to see it as a conservative body trying to keep order in times of great uncertainty. Rather than interpret the 1937 "switch" as a strictly political move by a bullied court, we should view it as part of the dialogue over the content of new constitutional doctrines in which Congress and the president accommodated many of the court's concerns, especially with respect to the delegation of political authority to regulatory agencies. Reciprocally, the court accommodated the political branches' authority to address national crises through the delegation of regulatory authority. The court, the president, and Congress tried, rejected, and accepted various new configurations of political control and oversight. By the end of the 1930s and the early 1940s, they had worked out the new technology of delegation. This new technology of delegation is one solution to the commitment problems in the labor violence case.

9.7   Implications

The games modeling the interaction of labor, business, and government reveal important insights about labor history, violence, and, more generally, about open access. These games allow us to interrogate the history to answer all three major questions asked at the outset: why did labor violence persist for so long, how did the NLRA finally solve the problem of violence, and why did the government have incentives to design the NLRA and to become an impersonal player in the NLRB regulatory process?

The model shows why the violence associated with labor persisted for so long. We stipulate that both labor and business would be better off under a regulatory framework that fostered cooperation rather than confrontation. In the absence of an impersonal government, neither U nor B could commit to foreswear violence. Each side could take advantage of the other by continuing to use violence even if the other has stopped using violence. For this reason the political equilibrium involved a century of violence and a lack of cooperation.

The design of the NLRA, in combination with the Supreme Court's sanction of the law, altered both the set of moves available to the players and their incentives. This legislation gave the government the ability to behave as an impersonal party overseeing the rules involving recognition of unions and to punish both parties for violating the rules.

The key to the new, post-NLRA cooperative equilibrium is threefold. First, the ongoing and lengthening Depression increased the likelihood of success of a revolt by labor, making this action more plausible. This outcome would make both B and G much worse off. The potential attractiveness of revolt to U, in turn, raised the value of compromise to B and G; for this reason, they were willing to help design a new system. Third, the new equilibrium involved G inventing a new regulatory process, which included the ability to sanction both firms and labor unions for violating the rules. Democrats in control of the national government gained electorally from a law that at once solved the problem of violence and allowed it to become an impersonal player administering the rules, enforcing the rules against either party in the event that they break the rules.

This logic also explains why the NLRA solved the century-long problem of violence where previous administrations could not. The threat of revolt was not present. Further, the Republican Party dominated the national government from 1880 to 1930 and did not believe it could gain electorally by legalizing unions and creating an impersonal regulatory process governing the labor process. In the wake of the Great Depression, Democrats took control of the national government in 1933; over time, they came to see that they could benefit from helping labor to organize.

We realize that this chapter is just one step in the analysis of open access for labor. Major aspects of labor behavior, regulation, and open access would appear during World War II and the immediate years following the war, including the 1947 Taft-Hartley legislation that reduced the perceived bias of the system in favor of labor.

We conclude by discussing the larger issues in the construction of open access. Open access to labor organizations seemed impossible as long as the commitment problems remained unsolved and the violence problems continued. Our approach highlights problems with open access faced by other civil-society organizations, such as the civil rights groups and the women's movements. In these and similar cases, the demands for recognition threatened powerful interests who had the political and economic clout to inhibit open access. The American experience with open access to business corporations, therefore, occurred decades earlier than open access to labor organization.

Our approach has larger implications for political development and open access. By investigating the violence problem as an important factor in determining when certain kinds of organizations and groups attain open access, we are better able to address the uneven development of open access and its consequences for pluralist democracy. Open access to the corporate form of organization in the United States occurred in the 1840s. North, Wallis, Weingast (2009) note the importance of this access for economic and political development. Similarly, Brooks and Guinnane argue (chapter 8, this volume) "acquisition of *corporate* rights was key to the growth and success of civil society." The first set of authors miss the limited and fragile access of other organizations and voices that define a pluralist democracy. The second recognize that open access for some organizations is hard won, but they ignore the importance of the violence problem.

The perspective of this chapter has implications for several of the other papers studying open access to business organizations. Until recently, few worried about the timing or explanation of these, as if the value of the corporate form itself was sufficient explanation for its existence. The common view has no explanation for why new business forms emerged, the timing of that emergence, or the administrative apparatus designed to support open access to these business forms.

Many questions remain. Why do we observe so much experimentation and hesitation with the legislation proposing to open access for firms? This hesitancy and experimentation suggest that the proponents of the new legislation were trying to solve problems—what were these? Put another way, the opening of access to the corporate form seems to have been characterized by problems whose solution was not obvious in the beginning. Moreover, the general incorporation (see Lu and Wallis, chapter 4, this volume) that opened access for other organizations was not necessarily the best route to open access for labor organizations, whose essential associational rights comprise not only legal recognition but also collective bargaining and the right to strike.

Finally, our chapter has implications for the maintenance of democracy and open access over the long term. Even the strongest and most stable of democracies face episodic threats to their survival; the mystery is how they manage to survive these threats and whether they can continue to do so.[8] Democratic stability cannot be taken for granted. As the problem of labor violence illustrates, nothing made peaceful resolution inevitable; and, under other conditions (e.g., absent the Great Depression), the long-term violence equilibrium might have continued longer.

Open access, a presumed hallmark of democracy, is part of the solution to maintaining democratic stability, but it also creates part of the problem. Open access is an ideal type. In practice, those countries approximating open-access orders moved piecemeal toward greater openness, meaning that they allowed open access for some types of groups and organizations while suppressing others. The uneven spread of open access means the suppression of certain voices holds the risk of disruption into protest, violence, and disorder.

The century-long history of labor violence is not unique in American history. Southern suppression of African Americans and the US suppression of Native Americans represent other cases. Illegal, violent groups, such as the Molly Maguires or the Ku Klux Klan, also occur with some frequency. Maintaining democratic stability requires a constant process of balancing existing interests, accommodating new or previously excluded interests, and suppressing groups who use violence to accomplish their ends. This process of accommodation and change necessarily implies risk. Success at each stage is not assured, so democracy and open access remain fragile to a degree, even in the seemingly most stable of countries.

At issue in this chapter is how failures of American pluralist politics contribute to the fragility of US democracy. In Ira Katznelson's magisterial *Fear Itself* (2013), he demonstrates how the New Deal saved a floundering democratic state that the Depression had destabilized. The emergence of a procedural state might appear to offer favorable conditions for an open-access society, but in fact, it also produces the possibility for the blocking of organizations by powerful interests within Congress. The new institutional arrangements permitted the serious post–World War II violations of privacy

---

8. Mittal and Weingast (2012) study the process of adaptive efficiency in the face of changing circumstances; that is, the degree to which countries adapt peacefully to major shocks in their environment.

and liberty embodied in the practices of the House Un-American Activities Committee, Senator Joseph McCarthy, and the FBI as they sought out Communists and Communist sympathizers.

These observations raise the deeper questions: What are the requirements for a truly open-access society? When does government behavior violate open access and thus threaten the equilibrium open access helps bulwark?

References

Adler, William M. 2011. *The Man Who Never Died: The Life, Times, and Legacy of Joe Hill, American Labor Icon.* New York: Bloomsbury.
Ahlquist, John S., and Margaret Levi. 2013. *In the Interests of Others.* Princeton, NJ: Princeton University Press.
Bachrach, Peter, and Morton S. Baratz. 1962. "Two Faces of Power." *American Political Science Review* 56 (4): 947–52.
———. 1963. "Decisions and Nondecisions: An Analytical Framework." *American Political Science Review* 57 (3): 632–42.
Bernstein, Irving. 1950. *The New Deal Collective Bargaining Policy.* Berkeley: University of California.
———. 1969. *The Lean Years: A History of the American Worker, 1920–1933.* Boston: Houghton Mifflin.
———. 1971. *Turbulent Years: A History of the American Worker, 1933–1941.* Boston: Houghton Mifflin.
———. 1985. *A Caring Society: The New Deal, the Worker, and the Great Depression: A History of the American Worker, 1933–1941.* Boston: Houghton Mifflin.
Brecher, Jeremy. 1997. *Strike!* Cambridge, MA: South End Press.
Cox, Gary W., Douglas C. North, and Barry R. Weingast. 2017. "The Violence Trap: A Political-Economic Approach to the Problems of Development." Working Paper, Hoover Institution, Stanford University.
Currie, Janet, and Joseph Ferrie. 2000. "The Law and Labor Strife in the United States, 1881–1894." *Journal of Economic History* 60 (1): 42–66.
Cushman, Barry. 1998. *Rethinking the New Deal in Court.* New York: Oxford University Press.
Dahl, Robert A. 1961. *Who Governs? Democracy and Power in an American City.* New Haven, CT: Yale University Press.
De Figueiredo Jr., Rui J. P., and Barry R. Weingast. 1999. "The Rationality of Fear: Political Opportunism and Ethnic Conflict." In *Civil Wars, Insecurity, and Intervention,* edited by B. Walter and J. Snyder. New York: Columbia University Press.
Eidlin, Barry. 2009. "'Upon This (Foundering) Rock': Minneapolis Teamsters and the Transformation of US Business Unionism, 1934–1941." *Labor History* 50 (3): 249–67.
Foner, Philip S. (1947) 1988. *History of the Labor Movement in the United States, vol. 1: From Colonial Times to the Founding of the American Federation of Labor.* New York: International Publishers.
Forbath, William E. 1991. *Law and the Shaping of the American Labor Movement.* Cambridge, MA: Harvard University Press.
Frankfurter, Felix, and Nathan Greene. (1930) 1963. *The Labor Injunction.* Gloucester, MA: Peter Smith.

Friedman, Gerald. 1988. "Strike Success and Union Ideology: The United States and France, 1880–1914." *Journal of Economic History* 48 (1): 1–25.

Geraghty, Thomas M., and Thomas Wiseman. 2011. "Conflict and Compromise: Changes in US Strike Outcomes, 1880 to 1945." *YEXEH Explorations in Economic History* 48 (4): 519–37.

Gitelman, H. M. 1973. "Perspectives on American Industrial Violence." *Business History Review* 47 (1): 1–23.

Gitto, Donald R. 1982. "Strike Violence: The NLRB's Reluctance to Wield its Broad Remedial Power." *Fordham Law Review* 50 (6): 1371–98.

Golden, Miriam. 1997. *Heroic Defeats: The Problems of Job Loss*. Cambridge: Cambridge University Press.

Goldfield, Michael. 1989. "Worker Insurgency, Radical Organization, and New Deal Labor Legislation." *American Political Science Review* 83 (4): 1257–82.

Gross, James A. 1974. *The Making of the National Labor Relations Board: A Study in Economics, Politics, and the Law, Volume 1 (1933–1937)*. Albany, NY: State University of New York Press.

Hattam, Victoria C. 1993. *Labor Visions and State Power: The Origins of Business Unionism in the United States*. Princeton, NJ: Princeton University Press.

Irons, Peter. 1982. *The New Deal Lawyers*. Princeton, NJ: Princeton University Press.

Johnson, Victoria. 2008. *How Many Machine Guns Does it Take to Cook One Meal? The Seattle and San Francisco General Strikes*. Seattle: University of Washington Press.

Katznelson, Ira. 2006. *When Affirmative Action Was White*. New York: W. W. Norton.

———. 2013. *Fear Itself: The New Deal and the Origins of Our Time*. New York: Liveright.

Kimeldorf, Howard. 1999. *Battling for American Labor: Wobblies, Craft Workers, and the Making of the Union Movement*. Berkeley: University of California Press.

Levi, Margaret. 1977. *Bureaucratic Insurgency: The Case of Police Unions*. Lexington, MA: Lexington Books.

Lichtenstein, Nelson. 2002. *State of the Union*. Princeton, NJ: Princeton University Press.

Lukas, J. Anthony. 1997. *Big Trouble*. New York: Simon & Schuster.

Lukes, Steven. (1974) 2005. *Power: A Radical View*. New York: Palgrave Macmillan.

Mares, Isabela. 2003. *The Politics of Social Risk*. New York: Cambridge University Press.

Mittal, Sonia, and Barry R. Weingast. 2012. "Self-Enforcing Constitutions: With an Application to Democratic Stability in America's First Century." *Journal of Law, Economics, and Organization* 29 (2): 278–302.

Montgomery, David. 1989. *The Fall of the House of Labor: The Workplace, the State, and American Labor Activism, 1865–1925*. New York: Cambridge University Press.

North, Douglass C., John Wallis, and Barry Weingast. 2009. *Violence and Social Orders: A Conceptual Framework for Interpreting Recorded Human History*. New York: Cambridge University Press.

North, Douglass C., and Barry R. Weingast. 1989. "Constitutions and Commitment: The Evolution of Institutions Governing Public Choice in Seventeenth-Century England." *Journal of Economic History* 49 (4): 803–32.

Perlman, Selig. 1928. *A Theory of the Labor Movement*. New York: Augustus M. Kelley.

Rogin, Michael. 1962. "Voluntarism: The Political Functions of an Anti-Political Doctrine." *Industrial and Labor Relations Review* 15 (4): 521–35.

Schickler, Eric. 2016. *The Civil Rights Realignment*. Princeton, NJ: Princeton University Press.

Swenson, Peter. 2002. *Capitalists Against Markets*. New York: Oxford Paperbacks.

Taft, Philip, and Philip Ross. 1969. "American Labor Violence: Its Causes, Character, and Outcome." *Violence in America: Historical and Comparative Perspectives* 1:221–301.

Tomlins, Christopher L. 1985. *The State and the Unions: Labor Relations, Law and the Organized Labor Movement in America, 1880–1960*. New York: Cambridge University Press.

Voss, Kim. 1993. *The Making of American Exceptionalism: The Knights of Labor and Class Formation in the Nineteenth Century*. Ithaca, NY: Cornell University Press.

Cases Cited

Gibbons v. Ogden, 22 U.S. 1 (1824)

United States v. E. C. Knight Co, 156 U.S. 1 (1895)

In re Debs, 158 U.S. 564 (1895)

Loewe v. Lawlor (1908)

Federal Trade Commission v. Gratz, 253 U.S. 421 (1920)

Duplex Printing Press Co. v. Deering, 254 U.S. 443 (1921)

Stafford v. Wallace, 258 U.S. 495 (1922)

Panama Refining Panama Refining Co. v. Ryan, 293 U.S. 388 (1935)

A. L. A. Schechter Poultry Corp. v. United States, 295 U.S. 495 (1935)

National Labor Relations Board v. Jones & Laughlin Steel Corporation, 301 U.S. 1 (1937)

United States v. Darby Lumber Co., 312 U.S. 100 (1941)

Laws Cited

Sherman Act (15 U.S.C. §§ 1–7, 1890)

Federal Trade Commission Act (15 U.S.C. §§ 41–58, 1914)

Clayton Act (15 U.S.C. §§ 12–27, 1914)

Contributors

Ruth H. Bloch
Department of History
University of California, Los Angeles
6265 Bunche Hall
Box 951473
Los Angeles, CA 90095-1473

Dan Bogart
Department of Economics
3151 Social Science Plaza
University of California, Irvine
Irvine, CA 92697-5100

Richard Brooks
Columbia University Law School
Jerome Greene Hall, Room 919
435 West 116th Street
New York, NY 10027

Timothy W. Guinnane
Department of Economics
Yale University
PO Box 208269
New Haven, CT 06520-8269

Eric Hilt
Department of Economics
Wellesley College
106 Central Street
Wellesley, MA 02481

Victoria Johnson
Department of Urban Policy and
    Planning
Hunter College, City University of
    New York
695 Park Avenue
New York, NY 10065

Naomi R. Lamoreaux
Department of Economics
Yale University
Box 208269
New Haven, CT 06520-8269

Margaret Levi
Center for Advanced Study in the
    Behavioral Sciences
Stanford University
75 Alta Road
Stanford, CA 94305

Jacob T. Levy
Department of Political Science
McGill University
855 Sherbrooke West
Montreal, Quebec H3A 2T7
Canada

Qian Lu
Central University of Finance and
    Economics
39 South College Road, Haidian District
Beijing, P.R. China 100081

Tania Melo
Department of Political Science
University of Washington
Box 353530
Seattle, WA 98195

Walter W. Powell
Center on Philanthropy and Civil
    Society
Stanford University
431 Ceras Building
Stanford, CA 94305-3084

John Joseph Wallis
Department of Economics
University of Maryland
College Park, MD 20742

Barry R. Weingast
Hoover Institution and Department of
    Political Science
Stanford University
Stanford, CA 94305

Frances Zlotnick
Department of Political Science
Stanford University
616 Serra St., Encina Hall West, Room
    100
Stanford, CA 94305-6044

Author Index

Abbott, A., 180, 213
Aberbach, A. D., 212n14
Accominotti, F., 221
Acemoglu, D., 25n3, 77, 110n2
Adler, W. M., 336
Ahlquist, J. S., 338
Allen, R. C., 69
Ames, S., 272n166
Andrieu, C., 324n53
Angell, J. K., 272n166
Appiah, A., 90n19
Appleby, J. C., 29n12
Arthur, B., 180
Asch, R. G., 29n11
Aspromourgos, T., 51n2, 55n10, 57n12, 63n18, 71
Austin, J. T., 126n14, 127n19
Azariadis, C., 53n7

Baatz, S., 212n14
Bachrach, P., 332n1
Baratz, M. S., 332n1
Barzel, Y., 59n16, 63
Bates, R. H., 52, 59n16, 77
Beach, C. P., 233n10, 259n111, 268n148
Beckert, S., 202, 209, 221
Beckman, C. M., 185, 199
Béguec, G. Le, 324n53
Beitel, C. G., 265n137
Bell, J. A., 57n12, 242n48
Bender, T., 207

Benoit, J.-P., 6
Benson, L., 133n32
Berle, A., 148, 148n3, 150
Bernstein, I., 33n3, 338, 350, 357
Besley, T., 73n26, 74, 77
Billias, G. A., 126n13, 126n14
Blackmar, E., 210n12
Blair, M. M., 293n4
Blau, P. M., 5n3
Blaug, M., 52n4
Blumberg, P. I., 271n160
Bodenhorn, H., 140n40, 150
Bogart, D., 34, 37n23
Bonnot, É., 74n27
Bowen, H. V., 24n1, 39n25, 40
Bridenbaugh, C., 237n25
Britton, N. L., 182, 210
Brockway, L. H., 192
Brody, E., 267n144
Brooke, J. L., 235n17, 243n51
Brooks, R., 170n34
Broz, L., 25n3
Bruce, J., 28, 30
Brue, S. L., 52n4
Bryant, W. C., 202
Buckingham, J. T., 247n64
Buckley, S. J., 242n47
Bullock, S. C., 237n26, 255n96
Burkett, J., 8n5
Burrows, E. G., 207
Burton, M. D., 185, 199

Butler, H. N., 150, 160n24
Butterfield, K., 235n17, 239n34, 245n57,
    255n98, 269n154

Campbell, B. A., 246n63, 261n117, 269n152
Canon, B. C., 272n164, 272n165
Cantillon, R., 74n27
Carlos, A. M., 26n5
Carruthers, B. G., 25n3
Cassidy, I., 28n10
Chandler, A. D., Jr., 221
Chaudhuri, K. N., 24n1, 26n5, 28
Chernow, R., 186, 189, 218
Chilton, A. S., 291n2
Clark, G., 25n3
Clemens, E. S., 199
Coase, R. H., 5n3
Colley, L., 38
Conn, A. R., 179n1
Constant, B., 95n29, 95n30, 96n32, 96n33,
    96n34, 97n35, 97n36, 97n37, 98n41,
    99n42, 100n44, 100n45
Cott, N. F., 251n82
Countryman, E. F., 236n21
Cox, G. W., 13, 25n3, 38, 56, 59, 73, 341
Crane, D. A., 268n150
Crocker, R., 209
Crüger, H., 318
Cruickshanks, E., 33n19, 34
Currie, J., 335
Cushing, J. D., 241n41
Cushman, B., 355
Cyert, R., 5n3

Dahl, R. A., 332n1
Dahlin, M., 233n9
Davis, J. H., 152n5
Davis, J. S., 237n24, 238n27, 238n28, 238n29
Dean, J. W., 127n19
De Figueiredo, R. J. P., Jr., 337
Demsetz, H., 161
Dennis, A. W., 128n22, 140
Desai, T., 24n1, 36n21
DeSaussure, H. W., 256n105, 257n106,
    257n107
Destutt de Tracy, A. C., 99n43
DiMaggio, P. J., 5n3, 209, 211, 219
Dixit, A. K., 59
Dodd, E. M., 130n26, 130n27
Domosh, M., 202
Drayton, R., 182, 193

Dubin, M. J., 113, 114, 115, 155, 158n21
Duchhardt, H., 305n28
Duyckinck, E. A., 218n20

Eidlin, B., 336
Ekelund, R. B., Jr., 73n25
Eltis, W. A., 51n2
Engerman, S. L., 161
Epperson, J. W., 279n193, 279n194
Ewan, J., 198n10
Ewan, N. D., 198n10

Fairbairn, B., 314
Fearon, J. D., 60
Fears, J. R., 87n11
Ferrie, J., 335
Fishman, J. J., 240n38, 241n41, 260n116
Fligstein, N., 185, 199
Foner, P. S., 335n3, 336
Fontana, W., 199
Forbath, W. E., 339, 340
Forbes, D., 71
Foster, W., 29, 29n13, 30
Franke, S. G., 25n2
Frankfurter, F., 339
Freeman, J., 180, 223
Friedman, G., 335, 336
Fudenberg, D., 6

Ganz, M., 235n18
Gartner, S. S., 215n16
Gauci, P., 32n16, 33n18
Gellner, E., 85n5, 104n52, 105n53, 105n54
George, H., Jr., 233n9
Geraghty, T. M., 335
Gibbons, R., 5
Gierke, O., 291n1
Ginzburg, L. D., 250n78, 251n82
Gitelman, H. M., 339
Glaisek, C., 137n36
Golden, M., 341n6
Golemboski, D., 86n6
Goodman, P., 125n7, 125n8, 125n11,
    125n12, 126n14, 127n18
Gordon, S. B., 235n16, 245n59, 253n90
Grandy, C., 163n28
Grant, R. R., 52n4
Grassby, R., 31n15
Greene, N., 339
Gregg, A., 295n9
Griffen, C. S., 242n48

Griffith, E. C., 127n19
Griffiths, T., 25n3
Gross, J. A., 344, 349
Grossman, R., 25n3
Grossman, S. J., 5n3
Grove, C., 198n10
Guinnane, T. W., 150, 170n34, 295n9,
    313n37, 315n40

Haakonssen, K., 55n10, 57n12
Habermas, J., 234n12
Hall, P. D., 235n16, 242n47, 283n204
Hamill, S. P., 148, 148n3, 152, 154n15
Handley, S., 33n19, 34, 36n22
Handlin, M. F., 110, 130n26, 132n31, 140,
    140n41, 250n81, 271n159
Handlin, O., 110, 130n26, 132n31, 140,
    140n41, 250n81, 271n159
Hannan, M. T., 180, 223
Hansmann, H. B., 283n204
Hardtwig, W., 307n30, 309n32
Hart, O. D., 5n3
Hattam, V. C., 335n3
Hayton, D. W., 33n19, 34, 36n22
Hébert, R. F., 73n25
Hejeebu, S., 26n5
Henderson, E. K., 256n99
Henderson, G. C., 160n23
Henderson, W., 55n10, 57n12, 63n18
Hildreth, R., 140n39
Hilt, E., 137n36, 153n11, 167n31, 209,
    243n51, 258n108
Hindle, B., 237n22
Hinze, H., 307n30, 309n32
Hirschleifer, J., 59
Hirschler, E. S., 243n49
Hirschman, A. O., 74n27, 85n4
Hofstadter, R., 239n34
Hollander, S., 51n2, 57n12
Holt, M. F., 133n32
Hont, I., 57n12
Hopkins, B. R., 283n207
Horack, F. E., 155n16
Horvath, A., 219
Horwitz, H., 33, 33n19
Horwitz, M. J., 148, 150, 271n160
Hosack, A. E., 186, 188, 189
Hosack, D., 194, 195, 195n8, 197
Howard, S. E., 166n30
Howe, D. W., 110n2
Hueber, A., 303

Hume, D., 74n27
Hun, M. T., 278n187
Hunt, P., 25n33, 38
Hurst, J. W., 147n1

Inazu, J. D., 299n17, 299n19
Irons, P., 344
Irwin, D. A., 152n5
Isaac, R., 238n31

James, E. J., 202
Jaros, D., 272n164, 272n165
Jaume, L., 321n49
Jennings, J., 96n34
Jha, S., 26
Joël, M., 318, 319
Johnson, N. D., 26n4
Johnson, S., 25n3
Johnson, V., 337
Jones, G., 231n2, 237n25, 237n26

Kalyvas, A., 83n1
Katz, S. N., 233n10, 259n110, 259n111,
    268n148
Katznelson, I., 83n1, 180, 333, 350, 351, 352
Kaufman, J., 235n18, 238n29, 239n36
Kennedy, G., 55n10, 57n12, 74n28
Kent, J., 269n151
Kessler, W. C., 150
Khan, S., 221
Kimeldorf, H., 336
Klerman, D., 25n3
Koch, C. F., 309
Kolodin, I., 210
Koschnik, A., 235n17
Koyama, M., 26n4
Krause, S., 90n19
Krishna, V., 6

Lageman, E. C., 219
Lake, W. S., 125n6
Lamoreaux, N. R., 14, 137n36, 139, 142,
    268n150
Leblebici, H., 180
Legler, J. B., 116, 130, 140n40
Levi, M., 59n16, 337, 338
Levy, J. T., 83n1, 87n11, 105n55
Levy, L. W., 239n33
Lichtenstein, N., 337, 351
Lieberman, D., 71
Lightner, D. L., 300n20

Lipset, S. M., 239n33
Livermore, S., 271n159
Longworth, D., 244n53
Lovejoy, P. E., 6n4
Lukas, J. A., 337
Lukes, S., 332n1

Macfarlane, A., 54n9, 65
Mahoney, J., 181
Mahoney, P. G., 25n3
Maier, P., 110, 236n21, 239n36, 245n58
Maitland, F. W., 246n62
March, J. G., 5n3
Mares, I., 335
Marini, S. A., 238n31
Marks, D., 263n126
Martínez-Rodríguez, S., 315n40
Maskin, E., 6
McAdam, D., 185, 199
McCarthy, J. D., 199
McCarthy, K. D., 235n16, 243n49, 250n78, 250n79
McCaughey, R. A., 215
McCormick, R. P., 133n32
McCormick, R. W., 152n8
McCormick, V. E., 152n8
Means, G., 148, 148n3, 150
Merrill, E. D., 190
Meyer, W., 292n3
Mickulas, P., 190, 211
Miller, H. S., 231n2, 243n49
Millon, D., 150
Mitchell, B. R., 33
Mittal, S., 363n8
Moehling, C. M., 137
Mokyr, J., 25n3
Montesquieu, C. de, 74n27, 88n13, 89n15, 89n16, 89n17, 89n18, 90n20, 90n21, 90n22, 91n24, 91n25, 91n26
Montgomery, D., 335n3
Morgan, B., 27n6
Morgan, E. S., 237n22
Morgan, H. M., 237n22
Morison, S. E., 126n14
Moss, L. S., 55n10
Mukerji, C., 183n3, 200
Mullaly, J., 203
Mulligan, C., 161
Munson, Z., 235n18
Mushkat, J., 278n187
Muthoo, A., 60

Myers, G., 244n53, 244n55
Myint, H., 51n2

Nash, G. B., 253n90
Neal, L., 38, 44n29
Neem, J. N., 235n17, 239n34, 242n45, 243n51, 251n85
Newman, R. S., 253n91
Nicholas, S., 26n5
Nipperdey, T., 295, 303, 305, 308, 320, 320n47
North, D. C., 2, 7, 13, 23, 24, 25n2, 25n3, 27, 31, 52, 56, 57, 59, 59n16, 60, 62, 71, 73, 78, 84n2, 88n12, 111n3, 148, 235n15, 322, 341, 362
Novak, W. J., 235n15

Ober, J., 64n20
O'Brien, D. P., 51n2
O'Brien, P., 25n3, 38
Olson, M., 6, 59n16
Ostrom, V., 85n3
Ottewill, W. T., 31n14

Packalen, K., 223
Padgett, J. F., 5n3, 179, 180, 199, 225
Paterson, S., 126n14
Perkins, E. J., 250n81
Perlman, S., 335n3, 336
Persson, T., 73n26, 74, 77
Peterson, R. A., 218n20
Philips, C. H., 24n1, 40, 41, 42, 43n28
Phillips, K. T., 255n98
Pierson, G. W., 215n16
Pincus, S., 25n3
Pocock, J. G. A., 83n1
Pollman, E., 293n4
Posner, R., 63
Powell, R., 60
Powell, W. W., 5n3, 179, 180, 199, 219, 223, 225
Putnam, R. D., 87n9, 235n18

Quinn, S., 25n3, 26n4
Quintyn, M., 25n2

Richardson, D., 6n4
Robbins, C. C., 189, 208, 215
Robbins, L., 52n4
Robins, N., 24n1
Robinson, J. A., 25n3, 77, 110n2

Robinson, W. A., 125n9, 125n10
Rogin, M., 336
Romano, R., 163n28
Romayne, N., 201
Romen, A., 311
Rosanvallon, P., 324
Rosenblatt, H., 95n31
Rosenzweig, R., 210n12
Ross, P., 332
Rothschild, E., 51n2, 54n9, 65, 66, 71
Rousseau, J.-J., 321n48
Rubinstein, M. H., 277n183
Rudolph, E. D., 213
Ruef, M., 185
Ruhmer, O., 315n42, 316n43
Rusby, H. H., 210

Salmon, M., 233n9
Scheinberg, K., 179n1
Schickler, E., 351
Schlesinger, A. M., 238n30
Schmitter, P. C., 86n8
Schoeppner, M. A., 300n20
Schumpeter, J. A., 52n4
Schwartz, A., 140
Schweikart, L., 140
Scobey, D. M., 202
Scott, A. F., 207, 209
Scott, W. R., 5n3, 26, 27, 28, 29, 30, 31, 32,
    32n17, 33
Seaburg, C., 126n14
Sedgwick, R., 36n22
Seligman, J., 150
Sen, A., 51n2, 54n9, 65, 66, 71
Sewell, W. H., Jr., 180
Shammas, C., 233n9
Sheehan, J. J., 303
Shields, D., 237n26
Shleifer, A., 161
Shurtleff, N. B., 237n23
Silber, N. I., 265n136, 283n204, 283n205
Simon, H. A., 5n3
Skinner, A. S., 52n3, 52n4, 55n10, 57n12, 66
Skocpol, T., 235n18
Sloan, D., 190, 214
Smith, A., 92n27, 93n28
Sokoloff, K. L., 161
Sørensen, J. B., 185, 199
Sparks, E. S., 140
Sperber, J., 306, 307, 310
Stachurski, J., 53n7

Stasavage, D., 25n3
Steckel, R. H., 8n5, 137
Stern, P. J., 24n1, 39n25
Stetson, A. W., 129n24, 129n25
Stevens, G. A., 247n67
Stinchcombe, A. L., 184, 206, 225
Storer, A., 221
Street, A. B., 247n64, 249n75
Sullivan, B., 233n10, 259n110, 259n111,
    268n148
Sussman, N., 25n3
Sutherland, L., 37, 38, 39
Svenson, H. K., 218
Swenson, P., 335
Sylla, R. E., 116, 130, 140n40, 141, 148

Taft, P., 332
Tartakowsky, D., 324n53
Taylor, A., 209
Taylor, C., 86n7, 91n23
Taylor, D. E., 202
Thelen, K., 181
Thomas, R. P., 57
Thorwart, F., 315n41, 317n44
Tiebout, C. M., 85n3
Tillman, H., 304
Tilly, C., 59n16, 77
Tocqueville, A. de, 102n46, 103n47, 103n48,
    103n49, 103n50, 104n51, 234n12,
    234n13
Tollison, R. D., 73n25
Tomlins, C. L., 235n15, 248n71, 276n179,
    276n180, 300n21, 340
Trim, D. J. B., 27n7, 27n9
Tye, M., 179n1

Vail, R. W. G., 207
Valentine, J., 137n36
Versteeg, M., 291n2
Vicente, L. N., 179n1
Voss, K., 335n3, 336

Wagner, A., 179n1
Wallace, M., 207
Wallis, J. J., 2, 7, 8n5, 9, 14, 23, 24, 27, 52,
    59, 59n16, 62, 71, 78, 84n2, 88n12,
    111n3, 116, 130, 140, 140n40, 147n2,
    148, 154, 174, 235n15, 362
Ward, L., 90n21
Warren, R., 85n3
Watson, P., 33n18

Weber, M., 5n3
Weber, W. E., 140
Webster, T., 24n1, 42
Weingast, B. R., 2, 7, 13, 23, 24, 25n3, 27,
    31, 52, 56, 59, 59n16, 62, 62n17, 63,
    64n20, 71, 72, 73, 73n25, 78, 84n2,
    85n3, 88n12, 111n3, 148, 235n15, 322,
    337, 341, 362, 363n8
Wells, J., 25n3
Whitehead, J. S., 246n61
Whittenburg, J. P., 237n22
Whittington, K., 223
Wiberg, A., 311n34
Wilentz, S., 110n2
Williamson, O., 5n3
Wills, D., 25n3
Wilson, D. A., 255n98, 256n99
Winch, D., 55n10, 57n12, 75

Winkler, A., 281n202
Wiseman, T., 335
Wood, G. S., 83n1
Worley, T. R., 140
Wrenn, George L., III, 247n66
Wright, C. E., 235n16, 240n37, 249n76
Wright, R. E., 148
Wulf, A., 191
Wyllie, I. G., 237n23

Yafeh, Y., 25n3
Young, A. F., 243n52, 247n65

Zahedieh, N., 25n3
Zald, M. N., 199
Zim, R., 27n8
Zunz, O., 211, 219

Subject Index

Note: Page numbers followed by "f" or "t" refer to figures or tables, respectively.

abolitionist groups, denial of charters to, 262–63
Academy of Fine Arts, 207
adherent organizations, 6; coalitions as, 8
African American associations, challenges to incorporate, 249
A. L. A. Schechter Poultry Corp. v. United States, 355–56
American Colonization Society, 261–62, 266
American Federation of Labor (AFL), 336
American Revolution: effect of, on charitable trust law, 240; formation of associations and, 298; impact of, on voluntary associations, 236; new rights of associations and, 238–40
antislavery groups, incorporation laws and, 261–63
associate, defined, 296
associational aggregate, defined, 296
associational entity, defined, 296
association rights, kinds of, 292–93
associations: government restriction of, 234; in Prussian history, 292n3, 302–14; right *of* vs. right *to* and, 16–17; typology for, 296–302. *See also* fraternal associations, constraints on incorporation of; organizations; voluntary associations

banking: historical sources of, in Massachusetts, 112–21; Massachusetts as innovator in, 116, 116f, 117f; open access and, 13–14, 109–11
Bank of England, 35
banks, as rent-generating organizations, 13
Berea College, KY, 301, 301n22
Binns decision (*Commonwealth v. St. Patrick's Society*), 255–57, 269
Boston Female Asylum, 249–50
botanical gardens, 182n3; changes in organization of nineteenth-century knowledge and, 212–16; civic organization in early republic vs. in Gilded Age and, 206–12; effect of urbanization of Manhattan and, 200–206; as examples of open access, 16; impact of macro-level shifts on meso- and microlevel processes on, 221t; origins of, 182–83; spread of, 217–18. *See also* Britton, Nathaniel; Elgin Botanic Garden; Hosack, David; New York Botanical Garden (NYBG); poisedness
British East India Company. *See* English East India Company
Britton, Nathaniel, 182, 187f; biography of, 189–91; botanical garden of, 188; botanical garden template of, 192–94; cultural landscape of, 209–10; legacy

Britton, Nathaniel (*continued*)
of, 198–99; as organizational builders, 183–84; organizational vision of,
210–11; skill set of, 220; social skills
of, 195–97. *See also* botanical gardens;
New York Botanical Garden (NYBG)

Calliopean Society, 207
charitable immunity, doctrine of, 271–72
charitable trust law, 231–32; American
Revolution and, 240
charitable use law, 237–38, 240, 240n38
Charles I (king of Great Britain), 28–29
Charles II (king of Great Britain), 30–31
charters, special, regime of, 147
Child, Josiah, 31, 32
churches: court restraints on incorporation
of, 252–55; Hume's critique of establishment, 92–93; Smith's critique of
establishment, 92–95
civic organizations: in early republic vs.
in Gilded Age, 206–12; nineteenth-
century changes in New York City, 212t
civil society: eighteenth and early nineteenth
century use of phrase, 101; Gellner's
model of, 104–5; open-access order
and, 104–6
civil-society organizations, 2; in Prussia,
293–94
Clayton Act of 1914, 340
Clive, Robert, 38–39
coalitions, 7–8; as adherent organizations, 8
Columbia University, 214–215, 217
commerce clause, Congress's regulator
authority under, 357–59
commerce revolution, rise of towns and, 72
Commonwealth v. St. Patrick's Society
(*Binns* decision), 255–57, 269
Congress of Industrial Organizations (CIO),
338
Constant, Benjamin: associational pluralism
and, 95–100; republican government
and, 97–99
contractual organizations, 6
cooperatives, German, 314–20
corporate independence, growth of, 267–70
corporate laws, state, repressive use of, 266.
See also incorporation statutes, general
corporate rights, success of civil-society
organizations and, 294
corporations: economic vs. noneconomic,
3; in France and Germany, 18; open

access to, in US, 109–10; as technique
of elite control, 15
corporatism, 86–87
corps intermédiaires, 88–92; Tocqueville
and, 103–4
Courteen, William, 28–29
courts, constraints on incorporation by,
251–58
craft groups, 237n26
craft unions, 336. *See also* labor unions
Cromwell, Oliver, 29–30
Cunningham, James, 28

Democracy in America (Tocqueville), 101–2
Democratic-Republican Party (MA),
109–10
"doorstep" conditions, 10–11, 24

East India Company. *See* English East India
Company; Scottish East India Company; United East India Company
economic development, 12; rise of towns
and, 54
Elgin Botanic Garden, 186–88, 198, 208;
civic organization in early republic and,
206–12; urbanization of Manhattan
Island and, 200–206. *See also* Hosack,
David
elites, 3; corporations as technique of control by, 15; fear of social unrest and, 18;
historical sources on, in Massachusetts,
112–21
English East India Company, 11–12; in
aftermath of Glorious Revolution,
31–35; under Cromwell, 29–30; 1813
charter of, 25; monopoly of, 24–25; origins of, 26–27; restoration of monarchy
and, 30–31; under the Stuarts, 27–29.
See also United East India Company
establishment churches, Hume's critique of,
92–93
executive moral hazard, feudalism and, 73
experts, status and power of, and organization of nineteenth-century knowledge,
212–16

Federalist Party (MA), 109
feudal equilibrium: economic effects of, 58;
logic of natural state and, 62; as lowest
state of poverty and barbarism, 57–58;
Smith on, 55–56; as violence trap,
61–63

feudalism: executive moral hazard and, 73; military competition and, 61–62; predation and, 73; property rights and, 63–64; rise of towns and end of, 65–70; Smith on, 53; as "violence trap," 53–54

folk-theorem intuition theory, of organizations, 6–7

Fox, Charles James, 40

France: associations in, vs. Prussian associations, 320–24; corporations in, 18; incorporation laws in, 3; right to associate in, 295; role of state and civil-society, 17–18; Tocqueville's study of old regime of, 102–3

fraternal associations, constraints on incorporation of, 254–58

free trade, East India Company and, 42–44

gardens. *See* botanical gardens

Gellner, Ernest, 104–5

George, Henry, 231–33, 233n9, 266–67

Germany: cooperatives in, 314–20; corporations in, 18; incorporation laws in, 3. *See also* Prussia

Gerry, Elbridge, 112, 126–27

gerrymandering, 112, 127

Gilded Age, effect of, on civic organization, 206–12

Girard's Will Case, 273

Glorious Revolution, 11; English East India Company and, 31–35

government oversight, shift from, 267–74

governments: third parties and, 7–9; of towns, 71

Hosack, David, 182, 186f; biography of, 188–89; botanical garden of, 184–88; botanical garden template of, 191–92; legacy of, 197–98; as organizational builders, 183; organizational challenges of, 208; political challenges of, 208–9; skill set of, 220; social skills of, 194–95; society and charity memberships of, 207–8. *See also* botanical gardens; Elgin Botanic Garden

Hume, David, critique of establishment churches by, 92–93

incorporation failures, difficulty to trace, 263–64

incorporation statutes, general, 147–48; adoption and terms of early, 150–57,
151t; analysis of, 149; choice of terms for, 166–73; churches and religious organizations as beneficiaries of, 240–41; data collection for, 150–57; determinants of states' terms, 172t; early, 149; factors affecting adoption of, by states, 157–66; index of restrictiveness of states', 170–71, 171t; literature on, 149–50; North vs. South, 242; persistent constraints to, 1830–1900, 261–67; political economy of adoption of, 157–66; restrictiveness of by states, 1860, 170, 171t; terms of states', 169t; transition to open access and, 173–75; variation in terms of, 1860, 168t; Virginia's hostility to ecclesiastical, 242; for voluntary associations, 240–42; widening of access to, 1830–1900, 258–60

independence, corporate, growth of, 267–74

industrialization, open access and, 3

industrial unions, 336. *See also* labor unions

Industrial Workers of the World (IWW), 336–37

In re Debs, 358, 359

insider lending, 140

intraelite conflicts, 110–11

James I (king of Great Britain), 27–28

Jones & Laughlin Steel, 356, 357

Knights of Labor, 336

knowledge, changes in organization of nineteenth-century, 212–16

Ku Klux Klan, 266

labor, organized, hostility toward, 248

labor groups, difficulties of, to obtain charters, 247–48

labor movement, US, history of, 335–38

labor organization game: period 1, 1880–1930, 341–43; period 2, 1933–36, 352; period 3, NLRB comes on line, 352–54

labor unions, 18; constraints on associational rights of, 1860–1900, 274–81; craft vs. industrial, 336; legal context of, 338–41; procuring charters and, 247–48

land: as power, 63; primogeniture and, 64–65; property rights in, 63–65

Lectures on Jurisprudence (Smith), 55

legal person, defined, 296

liberty, rise of towns and, 71–72

liberty, Smith's use of term, 71–72
limited access social orders, 2, 23–24; open access social orders vs., 9–11
limited liability, right of, incorporated voluntary associations and, 270–72
limited markets, importance of, 23–24
Loewe v. Lawlor, 359

Manhattan Island, effect of urbanization of, on botanical gardens, 200–206, 204f, 205f
markets, limited, importance of, 23–24
Massachusetts: bankers in, 117–19, 118f, 119f, 120t, 121f; banking officers and state legislators in, 111; Bank War, 1811–1815, 126–29; Democratic-Republic Party in, 109–10, 124–25; Federalist Party in, 109, 111, 122–24; historical sources on elites, factions, and banks in, 112–21; insider lending in, 140; intraelite conflict in, 111; Merchant's Bank of Salem and, 127–29, 140; moving to open access, 1815–1829, 129–32; open access and banking in, 13–14; open access to corporations and banks in, 109–11; political parties after 1830, 132–33; politics, parties, and banks from 1784 to 1811 in, 121–25; reasons for moving toward open access in, 138–41; resolving complications with banking data for, 133–36; State Bank of, 127–30; wealth of bankers in, 136–37
McDonald v. Massachusetts General Hospital, 271–72
Merchant's Bank of Salem (MA), 127–29, 140
military competition, feudalism and, 61–62
Montesquieu, Baron de, 13; Constant and, 96–98; *corps intermédiaires* and, 88–92

National Industrial Recovery Act (NIRA) of 1933, 343–44; delegation issue of, 356–57; summary of, 346–47
National Labor Relations Act (NLRA) of 1935, 18, 332, 343; accomplishments of, 333–34, 347–48; constraints on employers, 348; constraints on workers, 348–50; development of, 350–52; drafting of, 359–61; empowering NLRB by, 344–45; precedents relevant to, 355;

solving labor violence and, 361–64; violence and, 334
National Labor Relations Board (NLRB), 332–33, 345–46; accomplishments of, 333–34
natural state, logic of, 13; feudal equilibrium and, 62
New Deal, reinterpretation of constitutional controversies over, 355–61
New York Botanical Garden (NYBG), 181, 198–99; changes in organization of nineteenth-century knowledge and, 212–16; civic organization in Gilded Age and, 206–12; effects of success of, 217–19; urbanization of Manhattan Island and, 200–206. *See also* botanical gardens; Britton, Nathaniel
New York City: changes in civic organizations in nineteenth-century, 212t; civic organization from early republic to Gilded Age, 206–12; in nineteenth century, 200–206; transformation of science and botany in nineteenth-century, 216f
New York Free School, 207
New York Historical Society, 207
nonprofit corporations, 235n19; damaging lawsuits and, 271–72; right of limited liability and, 270–72; right to control subsidiary corporations and, 272–73; right to hold stock and, 272. *See also* voluntary associations
North, Lord Frederick, 39

open access social orders, 3, 23–24; banking in Massachusetts and, 13–14, 109–11; botanical gardens as examples of, 16; civil society and, 104–6; competition and, 84–85; difficulty of transitioning to, 19; "doorstep" conditions to, 10–11, 24; eighteenth-century thinkers and, 13; general incorporation statutes and, 148; industrialization and, 3; as integrative phenomenon, 85–87; legal infrastructures of, 63; limited access social orders vs., 9–11; opposition and, 87–88; property rights and, 63; type of government and, 3
organizations: adherent, 6, 8; as bundles of relationships, 5–7; civil-society, 2; contractual, 6; folk-theorem intuition the-

ory of, 6–7; as preoccupation of social sciences, 5–6, 5n3; rise of, in nineteenth century, 1–2; role of state and civil-society, 17; rules and policies affecting citizens' ability to form, 16; as sources of rents, 2; study of, 1–2; transition of, from "limited access" to "open access," 2. *See also* associations; poisedness

Panama Refining Co. v. Ryan, 355–56
Papillion, Thomas, 32
Papillion syndicate, 32
Penkevell, Richard, 27–28
People's Pleasure Park Co. v. Rohleder, 301–2
pluralism, 12–13; Constant and, 95–100
pluralistic social orders: competition and, 84–85; integrative phenomenon of, 85–87; oppositional model of, 87
poisedness, 219–23; defined, 179–80. *See also* botanical gardens; organizations
political exchange: escape from violence trap and, 56; between kings and towns, 66–68
political parties, constraints on associational rights of, 1860–1900, 278–81
political practice, political theory and, 83–84
political theory, political practice and, 83–84
polymaths, decline of, and organization of nineteenth-century knowledge, 212–16
Porter, Endymion, 28
power, in land, 63
predation, feudalism and, 73
primogeniture, 64–65
property rights: feudal system of, 63–64; in land, 63; open access social orders and, 63; primogeniture and, 64–65; of religious, educational, and charitable groups, 273–74
Prussia: associations and, 292n3; associations before 1819, 304–6; associations during revolution of 1848–1849, 308–9; associations from 1819 to 1848, 306–8; associations in, vs. French association, 320–24; civil-society associations in, 293–94; commercial associations in, 293–94; cooperatives in, 314–20; corporate rights for civil-society organizations in, 312–14; history of associations in, overview of, 302–4; liberalization

of associations in, 309–12; right to associate in, 294–95; role of state and civil-society organizations in, 17–18. *See also* Germany

Railway Act of 1926, 340–41
relationships, organizations as bundles of, 5–7
religious freedom, constraints on self-governance and, 252–54
religious groups, treatment of, in *The Wealth of Nations*, 92–95
rents, organizations as sources of, 2, 4–5

Scottish East India Company, 28
security revolution, rise of towns and, 72–73
self-governance, growing right of, 267–74
Sherman Anti-Trust Act of 1890, 340
Smith, Adam, 12; central question posed by, 51–52; critique of establishment churches by, 92–95; feudal equilibrium and, 55–56; on feudalism, 53; implications of violence for arguments of, 59–65; on political exchange and escape from violence trap, 56; summary of his analysis on differences in wealth of nations, 53; use of "liberty" term by, 71–72; on violence, 55; violence as central impediment to economic growth, 52–53, 55
Smith v. Nelson, 253, 253n89
social unrest, fear of, 18
Society for the Relief of Distressed Debtors, 207
Stafford v. Wallace, 358
State Bank (MA), 127–29, 138–39
state corporate laws, repressive use of, 266. *See also* incorporation statutes, general

Tammany Society, 244–45, 244n53
third parties, governments and, 7–9
Three Percent Consol, 38
Tillman Act of 1907, 281
Tocqueville, Alexis de, 3, 234–35; art of association and, 101–4; *corps intermédiaires* and, 103; *parlements* and, 103–4
town organization, 71–73
towns, rise of, 68–70; commerce revolution and, 72; economic development and, 54; end of feudalism and, 65–70; and escape from violence trap, 54, 68; expansion of,

towns, rise of (*continued*)
68–70; liberty revolution and, 71–72; macroinstitutional analysis of, 73; microinstitutional analysis of, 70–73; political development and, 74–75; political exchange between king and, 66–68; security revolution and, 72–73

unions. *See* labor unions
United East India Company: Charter Act of 1813 and, 41–44; charter renewal in 1792 and, 40–41; customs revenues and, 44, 45t; from formation to battle of Plessy, 36–38; free trade and, 42–44; influence of, in Parliament, 40–41, 41t; loans to government and, 37–38; monopoly of, 37–38; survival of, in late eighteenth century, 38–41. *See also* English East India Company
United Joint Stock, 30
United States: associations in colonial era, 298, 298n13; formation of association law in, 297–99; history of labor movement in, 335–38; history of open access in, 331; nineteenth-century associational entitlements in, 300–301; open access to organizations, 1, 3; organizational rights of labor organizations in, 332–33
United States v. E. C. Knight, 358

violence: implications of, for political-economic development, 61; implications of, for Smith's arguments, 59–65; logic of, 59–60; National Labor Relations Act of 1935 and, 334; Smith on, 52–53, 55

violence trap: as characteristic of feudal society, 53–54; escape from, and rise of towns, 54, 68; feudal equilibrium as, 61–63; Smith on political exchange and escape from, 56
voluntary associations, 235n19, 260; of African Americans, difficulties to incorporate and, 249; British law and, 236–37; categories of incorporated, in first half of nineteenth century, 245; discrimination against, 235; of European ethnic groups, difficulties to incorporate and, 249; impact of American Revolution on, 236, 238–40, 241n41; incorporated, right of limited liability and, 270–72; judicial constraints on corporate right of self-governance and, 251–58; legal standing of early American, 238; legislative constraints on corporate rights of disfavored, 1790–1820, 245–51; Northern, 243–44; reasons for incorporation, 239–41, 240n37; repression of, during colonial era, 236–37; run by middle-class women, difficulties to incorporate and, 249–51; Southern, 242–43, 243n49. *See also* associations; nonprofit corporations

Wagner Act of 1935. *See* National Labor Relations Act (NLRA) of 1935
Walpole, Robert, 36, 37
wardship, 65
Washington, George, associations and, 299–300
Wealth of Nations, The (Smith), 51–52, 55; treatment of religious groups in, 92–95